THE RHETORIC OF
THE BOOK OF JUDGES

SUPPLEMENTS

TO

VETUS TESTAMENTUM

VOLUME LXIII

THE RHETORIC OF
THE BOOK OF JUDGES

BY

ROBERT H. O'CONNELL

E.J. BRILL
LEIDEN · NEW YORK · KÖLN
1996

The paper in this book meets the guidelines for permanence and durability of the Committee on Production Guidelines for Book Longevity of the Council on Library Resources.

Library of Congress Cataloging-in-Publication Data

The CIP-data has been applied for.

BS
1305.2
.026
1996

ISSN   0083-5889
ISBN   90 04 10104 7

PRINTED IN THE NETHERLANDS

TO
J. A. EMERTON

TABLE OF CONTENTS

PREFACE

This monograph represents the culmination of seven years of study in the book of Judges, nearly half of that period being spent in full-time research on the subject. The main research was carried out in Cambridge with the help of grants from The Committee of Vice-Chancellors and Principals of the Universities of the United Kingdom, London; The Lamb Foundation, Dallas; Interstate Battery System of America, Dallas; Lakeshore Bible Chapel, Waterloo, Ontario; Fitzwilliam College, Cambridge; and The University Registry, Cambridge. The present work would not have been possible without their generous support.

For many insights and suggestions given during the period of my research in Cambridge, I wish to thank Professor J. A. Emerton, now Regius Professor of Hebrew Emeritus at the University of Cambridge, and Professor R. P. Gordon, newly appointed the Regius Professor of Hebrew. For some further recommendations for improvement, I am indebted to Professor W. Horbury, University Lecturer in Divinity at the University of Cambridge, and to Professor E. W. Nicholson, Provost of Oriel College, Oxford. I am grateful also for the privilege of discussing some problems of the text of Judges with Professor B. Lindars, SSF, formerly Ryelands Professor of Biblical Criticism and Exegesis at the University of Manchester, in May of 1991, just five months before his death. Thanks to A. D. H. Mayes, the recent publication of Lindars's unfinished commentary on Judges has allowed scholars further opportunity to interact with his rich textual analysis of the first five chapters of the book. I would be remiss if I failed to acknowledge with thanks also the early but significant influence that one of my former professors, Dr W. R. Bodine, had upon my approach to the theory and practice of textual criticism, particularly in the book of Judges.

In recent years, while in Denver, I have had opportunity to explore further several issues related to the rhetoric, redaction and textual transmission of the book of Judges, and these insights have been incorporated into the work. For many revisions and suggestions for improvement, I am grateful to my colleagues, Robert G. Buller, who carefully edited the final draft, and Frank R. Ames, who checked the format of the proofs. I should also like to thank Dr Hans van der Meij of E. J. Brill for his patience and guidance in helping me to prepare the camera-ready copy. Special thanks belong to the members of the editorial board responsible for assessing and approving the work for publication as a Supplement to Vetus Testamentum.

Finally, I should like to acknowledge the debt of love and gratitude that I owe my wife, Mina, and my two sons, Nathan and Sean, for enduring the many hours that I was away from home labouring on this work and for the utopian hours between.

Denver, Autumn 1995   Robert H. O'Connell

ABBREVIATIONS

α´	Aquila
AASF	Acta/Annales Academiae Scientiarum Fennicae
AB	Anchor Bible
AbrN	*Abr-Nahrain* (Leiden)
abs.	absolute
acc.	accusative
ad loc.	*ad locum* (at the [appropriate] place)
AHw	*Akkadisches Handwörterbuch*, W. von Soden (ed.), (3 vols., Wiesbaden, 1965-1981)
AION	*Annali dell'Istituto Orientale di Napoli* (Naples)
Akk.	Akkadian
ALUOS	*Annual of the Leeds University Oriental Society* (Leeds)
AnBib	Analecta biblica
ANEP	*The Ancient Near East in Pictures Relating to the Old Testament*, J. B. Pritchard (ed.), (Princeton, 2d edn, 1969)
ANET	*Ancient Near Eastern Texts Relating to the Old Testament*, J. B. Pritchard (ed.), (Princeton, 3d edn, 1969)
Ant.	*Antiquities of the Jews* (Josephus)
AOAT	Alter Orient und Altes Testament
aor.	aorist
AOS	American Oriental Series
Arab	Arabic (version)
Arab.	Arabic (language)
Aram.	Aramaic
Arm	Armenian (version)
Arm-edn	variant(s) in the tradition of the Armenian (version)
ATANT	Abhandlungen zur Theologie des Alten und Neuen Testaments
ATD	Das Alte Testament Deutsch
AUUSSU	Acta Universitatis Upsaliensis, Studia Semitica Upsaliensia
AV	*The Holy Bible, Containing the Old and New Testaments* (London, 1611) ["Authorized Version"]
B.	Babylonian Talmud
BA	Biblical Aramaic
BA	*Biblical Archaeologist* (New Haven, Connecticut; later Ann Arbor, Michigan)
BAR	*Biblical Archaeology Review* (Washington, D.C.)
BASOR	*Bulletin of the American Schools of Oriental Research* (New Haven, Connecticut; later Ann Arbor, Michigan)
BBB	Bonner biblische Beiträge
BDB	*A Hebrew and English Lexicon of the Old Testament*, F. Brown, S. R. Driver, C. A. Briggs (eds.) (Oxford, 1906)
BFCT	Beiträge zur Förderung christlicher Theologie
BH	Biblical Hebrew

BH^{2,3}	*Biblia hebraica*, R. Kittel (ed.), (Stuttgart, 2d edn, 1913; 3d edn, 1929–1937) [R. Kittel on Judges]
BHS	*Biblia hebraica stuttgartensia*, K. Elliger, W. Rudolph (eds.), (Stuttgart, 1967–1977) [R. Meyer on Judges]
Bib	*Biblica* (Rome)
BibRev	*Bible Review* (Washington, D.C.)
BIOSCS	*Bulletin of the International Society for Septuagint and Cognate Studies*
BJRL	*Bulletin of the John Rylands Library* (Manchester)
BLS	Bible and Literature Series
BN	*Biblische Notizen* (Bamberg)
BO	*La Bible*, E. Osty (trans.), (Paris, 1973)
BSC	Bible Student's Commentary
BTB	*Biblical Theology Bulletin* (St. Bonaventure, N.Y.; later South Orange, N.J.)
BWANT	Beiträge zur Wissenschaft vom Alten und Neuen Testament
BZ	*Biblische Zeitschrift* (Paderborn)
BZAW	Beihefte zur *ZAW* (Giessen, later Berlin)
c.	common
C.	century
CAD	*The Assyrian Dictionary of the Oriental Institute of the University of Chicago* (Chicago, 1956–)
CAT	Commentaire de l'Ancien Testament
CBC	Cambridge Bible Commentary on the New English Bible
CBQ	*Catholic Biblical Quarterly* (Washington, D.C.)
CFTL	Clark's Foreign Theological Library
coh.	cohortative
conj.	conjunctive
cons.	consecutive
cstr	construct
CTA	*Corpus des tablettes en cunéiformes alphabétiques découvertes à Ras Shamra–Ugarit de 1929 à 1939*, A. Herdner (Paris, 1963)
Cyr.	Cyril of Alexandria
denom.	denominative
dir. obj.	direct object
disj.	disjunctive
DJD	Discoveries in the Judaean Desert (of Jordan), (Oxford, 1955–)
EB	*Die Heilige Schrift in deutscher Übersetzung* ["Echter-Bibel"]
Ebib	Etudes bibliques
Eg.	Egyptian
EHAT	Exegetisches Handbuch zum Alten Testament (Münster, i. W.)
EHO	*Early Hebrew Orthography*, F. M. Cross, Jr, D. N. Freedman (New Haven, Connecticut, 1952)
emph.	emphatic
ET	English translation
Eth	Ethiopic (version)
EvQ	*Evangelical Quarterly* (Exeter)

EVV	English versions
ex corr	*ex correctura* (by the corrector)
ExpTim	*Expository Times* (Edinburgh)
f.	feminine
fig.	figuratively
FRLANT	Forschungen zur Religion und Literatur des Alten und Neuen Testaments
gen.	genitive
GKC	*Gesenius' Hebrew Grammar*, W. Gesenius (E. Kautzsch [ed.], A. E. Cowley [trans. and ed.], Oxford, 2d edn, 1910)
GT	German translation
GTW	Grundriss der theologischen Wissenschaften
HAH	*Hebräisches und aramäisches Handwörterbuch über das Alte Testament*, W. Gesenius (R. Meyer, H. Donner, U. Rüterswörden [eds.], Berlin, 18th edn, 1987-)
HALAT	*Hebräisches und aramäisches Lexikon zum Alten Testament* (4 vols., Leiden, 3d edn, 1967-1990) [L. Koehler, W. Baumgartner, vols. 1-2; L. Koehler, W. Baumgartner, J. J. Stamm, vols. 3-4]
HAR	*Hebrew Annual Review* (Columbus, Ohio)
Hi.	Hiphil
HKAT	Handkommentar zum Alten Testament (Göttingen)
Ho.	Hophal
Holm–Pars	*Vetus Testamentum Græcum cum variis lectionibus*, R. Holmes, J. Parsons (eds.), (Oxford, 1798-1827)
*HSAT*²,³,⁴	*Die Heilige Schrift des Alten Testaments* ... (Bonn, 2d edn, 1896); E. Kautzsch (ed.), (3d edn, 1909-1910); A. Bertholet (ed.), (4th edn, 1922-1923) [R. Kittel on Judges in 3d and 4th eds]
HSM	Harvard Semitic Monographs
HUCA	*Hebrew Union College Annual* (Cincinnati, Ohio)
IB	*The Interpreter's Bible*, G. A. Buttrick et al. (eds.), (12 vols., Nashville, 1953)
ICC	International Critical Commentary (Edinburgh)
IEJ	*Israel Exploration Journal* (Jerusalem)
impf	imperfect
impv	imperative
indir. obj.	indirect object
inf(s).	infinitive(s)
Int	*Interpretation* (Richmond, Virginia)
ISBL	Indiana Studies in Biblical Literature
ITL	International Theological Library
JANES	*Journal of the Ancient Near Eastern Society* (New York)
JB	*The Jerusalem Bible* (Garden City, New York, 1966) [English revision of SBJ²]
JBL	*Journal of Biblical Literature* (Philadelphia; later Missoula, Montana; later Atlanta, Georgia)
JEA	*Journal of Egyptian Archaeology* (Oxford)
JETS	*Journal of the Evangelical Theological Society* (Wheaton)

JFI	*Journal of the Folklore Institute* (Bloomington, Indiana)
JJS	*Journal of Jewish Studies* (Oxford)
JNES	*Journal of Near Eastern Studies* (Chicago)
JNSL	*Journal of Northwest Semitic Languages* (Leiden)
JPOS	*Journal of the Palestine Oriental Society* (Jerusalem)
JPSV	*The Holy Scriptures according to the Masoretic Text* (Philadelphia, 1917; 2d edn, 1962–1982) ["Jewish Publication Society Version"]
JQR	*Jewish Quarterly Review* (Philadelphia)
JSOT	*Journal for the Study of the Old Testament* (Sheffield)
JSOTS	Journal for the Study of the Old Testament Supplement Series
JSS	*Journal of Semitic Studies* (Manchester)
JTS	*Journal of Theological Studies* (Oxford)
KAI	*Kanaanäische und aramäische Inschriften*, H. Donner, W. Röllig (3 vols., Wiesbaden, 1963)
KB	*Lexicon in Veteris Testamenti libros*, L. Koehler, W. Baumgartner (Leiden, 2d edn, 1953)
KEHAT	Kurzgefaßtes exegetisches Handbuch zum Alten Testament (Leipzig)
KHAT	Kurzer Hand-Commentar zum Alten Testament (Tübingen)
KVHS	Korte Verklaring der Heilige Schrift
L	Codex Leningradensis (B 19^A)
Lach.	Lachish letter
LBS	Library of Biblical Studies
loc.	locative
L–Sh	*A Latin Dictionary*, C. T. Lewis, C. Short (Oxford, 1879)
LSJ	*Greek–English Lexicon*, H. G. Liddell, R. Scott (H. S. Jones [rev.], Oxford, 9th edn, 1925–1940)
LXX	Septuagint
Malbim	Meir Loeb ben Yeḥiel Michael (1809–1879 CE)
m.	masculine
M.	millennium
mg	margin
MGWJ	*Monatsschrift für Geschichte und Wissenschaft des Judentums*
mid.	middle
Moab.	Moabite
MPIL	Monographs of the Peshiṭta Institute, Leiden
Mṣdt Dvd	*Meṣudat David* (Commentary by Yeḥiel Hillel Altschuler, 18th C. CE)
MS(S)	manuscript(s)
MT	Masoretic Text
Mur.	Murabbaʿât Hebrew inscription
N	number
NAB	New American Bible (New York, 1970)
NASB	New American Standard Bible (New York, 1963)
NCBC	New Century Bible Commentary
NEB	New English Bible (Cambridge and Oxford, 1970)
N Heb.	Northern Hebrew
Ni.	Niphal

NIV	New International Version (East Brunswick, New Jersey, 1973, 1978, 1984)
nom.	nominative
NRSV	New Revised Standard Version (New York, 1989)
NS	New Series
O´	Origen
obj.	object
OBO	Orbis biblicus et orientalis
OBT	Overtures to Biblical Theology
OG	Old Greek
OLat	Old Latin (version)
Or	*Orientalia* (Rome)
OTG	Old Testament Guides
OTL	Old Testament Library
OTS	*Oudtestamentische Studiën* (Leiden)
PEFQS	*Palestine Exploration Fund, Quarterly Statement* (London)
perf(s).	perfect(s)
Phoen.	Phoenician
Pi.	Piel
PIBS	Publications of the Israel Bible Society
pl.	plural
pluperf.	pluperfect
PN	proper noun/personal (or tribal) name
Po.	Poel
prep(s).	preposition(s)
pres.	present
pret.	preterite
pron(s).	pronoun(s)/pronominal
PS	*A Compendious Syriac Dictionary*, J. Payne Smith (ed.), (Oxford, 1903)
Psht	Peshiṭta
ptcp(s)	participle(s)
Qimḥi	Rabbi David Qimḥi (ca. 1160–1235 CE)
Ralbag	Rabbi Levi ben Gershon (ca. 1288–1344 CE)
Rashi	Rabbi Solomon Isaaki (ca. 1040–1105 CE)
RB	*Revue biblique* (Jerusalem and Paris)
REB	Revised English Bible (Cambridge and Oxford, 1989)
rell	*reliquae/us* (the remainder/rest [of the MSS])
RevQ	*Revue de Qumrân* (Paris)
RL	*Die Bibel oder Die Ganze Heilige Schrift des Alten und Neuen Testaments nach der Übersetzung M. Luthers* (1967) ["Revidierte Lutherbibel"]
RSV	Revised Standard Version (New York, 1952)
RTR	*Reformed Theological Review* (Hawthorn, Australia)
RV	Revised Version (Oxford, 1881)
σ´	Symmachus
Sah	Sahidic (version)

Sam. Ost.	Samaria Ostraca
SAT	Die Schriften des Alten Testaments in Auswahl (Göttingen)
SBB	Soncino Books of the Bible
SBC	*La Sainte Bible* (Paris, 4 vols., 1928–1947) ["La Bible du Centenaire"; A. Lods on Judges]
SBET	*Scottish Bulletin of Evangelical Theology* (Edinburgh)
SBJ [1,2,3]	*La Sainte Bible* (Paris and Jerusalem, 1948; 2d edn, 1957) [A. Vincent on Judges]; or *La Bible de Jérusalem* (Paris, 3d edn, 1973)
SBLDS	Society of Biblical Literature Dissertation Series
SBLMS	Society of Biblical Literature Monograph Series
SBLSCS	Society of Biblical Literature Septuagint and Cognate Studies
SBOT	*The Sacred Books of the Old Testament: A Critical Edition of the Hebrew Text Printed in Colours*, P. Haupt (ed.), (16 vols., Leipzig, 1894–1904) [G. F. Moore on Judges, vol. 7]
SBT	Studies in Biblical Theology
SCBS	Smaller Cambridge Bible for Schools
ScrHier	Scripta Hierosolymitana
sg	singular
S Heb.	Southern Hebrew
SOTSMS	Society for Old Testament Study Monograph Series
SSN	Studia semitica neerlandica
subj.	subject
suff(s).	suffix(es)
SVT	Supplements to Vetus Testamentum
Syh	Syro-Hexaplar
Syr.	Syriac (language)
TA	*Tel Aviv* (Tel Aviv)
TAPS	Transactions of the American Philosophical Society
TEV	Today's English Version (New York, 1976)
Tg	Targum
θ'	Theodotion (so-called)
Thdt	Theodoret
TICP	Travaux de l'institut catholique de Paris
TLZ	*Theologische Literaturzeitung* (Leipzig, later Berlin)
TOTC	Tyndale Old Testament Commentaries
TSK	*Theologische Studien und Kritiken* (Hamburg, Gotha)
TT	Tekst og Tolkning
TTL	Theological Translation Library
TynBul	*Tyndale Bulletin* (Cambridge)
TZ	*Theologische Zeitschrift* (Basel)
Ug.	Ugaritic
Vg	Vulgate
vid	*ut videtur* (as it appears)
VT	*Vetus Testamentum* (Leiden)
WBC	Word Biblical Commentary
WMANT	Wissenschaftliche Monographien zum Alten und Neuen Testament

WO	*Die Welt des Orients* (Göttingen)
YOSRes	Yale Oriental Series, Researches
ZAW	*Zeitschrift für die alttestamentliche Wissenschaft* (Giessen, later Berlin)
ZB	*Die Heilige Schrift des Alten und Neuen Testamentes* (Zürich, 1955) ["Zürcher Bibel"]
ZDMG	*Zeitschrift der deutschen morgenländischen Gesellschaft* (Wiesbaden)
ZDPV	*Zeitschrift des deutschen Palästina-Vereins* (Wiesbaden, later Tübingen, later Stuttgart)
ZTK	*Zeitschrift für Theologie und Kirche* (Tübingen)

TEXT-CRITICAL SIGLA

*	conjectured/proposed original form
<	derived from
>	transformed to
a	correction by the same/a contemporary hand
b	correction by a later hand
]	separates a word/phrase of the citation from its variants
|	separates variants of different words/phrases
:	separates variants of the same word/phrase
[ ]	encloses variants relating to the preceding citation
<> or < >	encloses a proposed emendation to the text
□	omitted from
−	minus/omits
+	plus/adds
※	hexaplaric asterisk (in Syh, Arm and LXX MS G)—alleged minus in the OG according to Origen
÷	hexaplaric obelus (in Syh, Arm and LXX MS G)—alleged plus in the OG according to Origen

INTRODUCTION

This work offers four lines of evidence leading to an understanding of the rhetoric of the book of Judges. Throughout the work, the term 'rhetoric' is understood to refer to the ideological purpose or agenda of the Judges compiler/redactor with respect to the implied readers of the book. Use of the designation, 'the Judges compiler/redactor', or the like, leaves open the possibility that there may be multiple layers of composition in the book (see excursus 1). The main aim of this work, however, is to present a coherent reading of the present form of the book. The rhetorical purpose of the Judges compiler/redactor is inferred from formal structures and motivic patterns that recur throughout the narrative framework of the book as well as from patterns of plot-structure and characterization that recur amongst the plot-based narratives of Judges' deliverer stories and its closing double dénouement.

Chapter 1 presents a rhetorical analysis of both the deuteronomic and tribal–political schemata that are superimposed upon the deliverer accounts of the book of Judges. Chapter 2, the main division of the study, is an analysis of formal structures in Judges that focuses upon the role that plot-structure plays in determining the rhetorical concerns of the book. Chapter 3 offers a rhetorical analysis of narrative strategies in Judges, among which predominate the strategies of entrapment, monarchical idealization and the use of narrative patterns analogous to some used in 1 Samuel. Finally, chapter 4 presents an assessment of the ostensible situation of Judges' composition as implied by its form. These considerations lead to the conclusion that the rhetorical purpose of the book of Judges is to enjoin its readers to endorse a divinely appointed Judahite king who, in contrast to either foreign kings or previous non-Judahite deliverers in Israel, upholds such deuteronomic ideals as the need to expel foreigners from the land and the need to maintain intertribal loyalty to YHWH's cult and regulations concerning social justice.

A. Rhetorical Concerns of Judges' Tribal-Political and Deuteronomic Schemata

Chapter 1 examines, in turn, the tribal–political and deuteronomic agendas that appear superimposed upon the following main sections of

Judges. It seems appropriate that redaction-critical and literary studies have stressed the role that the double prologue (1:1–2:5; 2:6–3:6) and double dénouement (17–18; 19–21) play in framing the deliverer accounts of the book. The south-to-north tribal–political schema of Prologue-A (1:1–2:5) provides the basic schema for the order of episodes in the body of the book and portrays the tribe of Judah as preeminent among the tribes of Israel.[1]

Elements of the twelve-part religious–historical cycle, introduced in Prologue-B (2:6–3:6; especially 2:11-15, 16-19), recur in each of the following accounts of Israel's tribal heroes. The analysis of Judges' twelve-part cycle-motif offered in this study presents new evidence that its aggregate schema was bifurcated so as to distinguish the portrayal of Israel's alienation (described using deuteronomic phraseology) from the portrayal of their restoration to blessing in the land (which refrains from using deuteronomic language even though it alludes to ideas present in Deut. 4:27-31; 30:1-10). When the elements that constitute this aggregate schema are presented in the order in which they generally recur among the accounts, there is an analogous complementarity between the elements of the alienation phase and those of the restoration phase. This evidence may further clarify the rhetorical function of the cycle-motif as an evaluative framework intended to present Israel's alienation from YHWH (expressed in covenant language) as distinct from their restoration to the blessing in the land (expressed only in terms of YHWH's grace).

I find inherent in the relationship between the tribal–political and deuteronomic concerns of the prologue, on the one hand, and those of the deliverer accounts, on the other, an implicit definition of the rhetorical purpose of Judges. This dual rhetorical concern becomes epitomized and clarified by Judges' two final narrative accounts (17–18; 19–21).

B. RHETORICAL CONCERNS OF JUDGES AS A LITERARY FORM

Chapter 2 treats the rhetoric of formal structures and characterization in Judges. The main contribution of chapter 2 is that it presents a new

---

[1] Z. Kallai noted the south-to-north order as a fixed pattern in the pre-exilic arrangements of tribal allotments ("The Southern Border of the Land of Israel—Pattern and Application", *VT* 37 [1987], pp. 439-40 and n. 5). He argued that, in pre-exilic writings, the north-to-south order is standard only when extreme boundaries are stated, e.g., the merismus "Dan to Beersheba" in Judg. 20:1 (p. 440 and n. 6).

approach to Judges' plot-based narratives in which plot-structure and characterization form the basis for observations about rhetorical concerns in the deliverer accounts (3:7–9:57; 10:6–12:7; 13–16) and the accounts of the double dénouement (17–18; 19–21). Since the double prologue (1:1–2:5; 2:6–3:6) and so-called 'minor' judge accounts (10:1-5; 12:8-15) offer only short reports, which lack either plot-structure or round characters, these accounts are described only insofar as their formal structure and function contribute to the patterns of arrangement that advance the main rhetorical point of the book.[2] Further, in chapter 2 I note the evaluative role that rhetorical devices such as satire and narrative analogy play in portraying characters (e.g., foreign kings, deliverers, tribes of Israel, YHWH). In the plot-based narratives of Judges, there is a regular pattern of parallel characterization between the main characters and the larger populace of which they are a part. The pervasiveness of this pattern among the deliverer accounts suggests that it was the Judges compiler/redactor who designed this scheme of escalated parallelism to demonstrate corresponding deficiencies in Israel and its deliverers.

The priority, arrangement and proportion of space given to the portrayal of the tribes in Prologue-A (1:1–2:5) corroborates the thesis that the tribal–political arrangement of Judges was designed to enjoin its readers to endorse Judah as the tribe divinely appointed to lead the other tribes of Israel. Prologue-B (2:6–3:6) sets forth the cyclical religious–historical paradigm by which the religious–historical events presented in the deliverer accounts of 3:7–16:31 are to be measured.

While it is obvious that the traditions constituting each deliverer account were selected and remodelled to serve the rhetorical concerns of the deuteronomic framework, what is newly presented in chapter 2 is a demonstration of the way in which the plot-structure of each deliverer account and the characterization of each deliverer have been crafted to suit Judges' overall rhetorical purpose.

---

[2] The decision to handle the 'minor' judge reports in this way does not stem from any assumed difference in the official role served by either a 'major' judge (here called a deliverer) or a 'minor' judge. That there was thought to be no essential difference of official role between them may be discerned both from the fact that the account of Jephthah closes with a pattern of formulae (Judg. 12:7) used elsewhere only in the 'minor' judge reports (cf. 10:2, 3-5; 12:8-10, 11-12, 13-15) and from the fact that Tola, a 'minor' judge, is said to have arisen "to deliver Israel" (10:1)—a description elsewhere limited to the 'major' judge accounts (cf. A. J. Hauser, "The 'Minor Judges'—A Re-evaluation", *JBL* 94 [1975], p. 200; E. T. Mullen, Jr, "The 'Minor Judges': Some Literary and Historical Considerations", *CBQ* 44 [1982], p. 201).

When Judges 17–21 are read in relation to the body of the book (3:7–16:31), one gains a sense that they were appended to epitomize the book's main themes and to clarify the rhetorical aims of the compiler/redactor. Yet, despite this, some features of this dual dénouement initially frustrate one's search for continuity with the preceding chapters. For instance, in the dénouement little remains of the mixed characterizations so prominent in the portrayals of most of the main characters in the hero stories (Ehud, Barak, Jael, Gideon, Jephthah, Samson). Indeed, while one may fairly designate the accounts of 3:7–16:31 as 'hero stories', that would not be a fitting designation for the accounts of Judges 17–18 and 19–21. Thus, while individual characters propel the action in the last two episodes, one gains the distinct impression that the main interest of the compiler/redactor was rather in the tribe-wide cultic apostasy and the social disintegration to which the consequences of individuals' actions escalate.[3] Hence, to the extent that the themes of cultic apostasy and social disintegration feature in the hero stories of Judges, the closing episodes of Judges epitomize the prevailing concerns of the compiler/redactor.

Perhaps one of the chief contributions of chapter 2 is its use of plot-structure in determining the rhetorical purpose of the stories in Judges. In this study, plot is defined as the "organization of incident to achieve a single purpose".[4] Indeed, this is the first study of Judges to understand that this notion of plot must control all decisions about the rhetorical strategy of the compiler/redactor. Most who have attempted to account for narrative plot-structures in Judges have followed a 'scenic principle', which does not sufficiently recognize that every ideological system—and biblical narrative is ideological literature— supports an ideal by which characters and circumstances in the story are implicitly measured. In order for a narrative analysis in Judges to

---

[3] The theme of religious apostasy, introduced in Prologue-A (especially 2:1-3) and Prologue-B (2:10-3:6), recurs throughout the accounts of 3:7–16:31 (cf. 3:7, 12, [19, 26]; 4:1a; 6:1a, 10b; 8:33-34; 10:6, 10b, 13a, 16a; 13:1a). This continuity should not be minimized (cf. L. R. Klein, *The Triumph of Irony in the Book of Judges* [JSOTS 68, BLS 14, Sheffield, 1988], pp. 142, 144). However, it is the discontinuity between chapters 17–21 and the rest of Judges that attracts attention (Klein mentions the abrupt disappearance of any central character such as those who dominated in previous chapters [pp. 14, 175], the imposition of a new refrain [p. 14]—though it, too, stresses religious apostasy—and the abrupt and disjointed narrative form [pp. 14-15, 146]).

[4] So T. A. Boogaart, "Stone for Stone: Retribution in the Story of Abimelech and Shechem", *JSOT* 32 (1985), p. 47. L. Ryken defines plot similarly as "a series of events arranged around a central conflict and possessing a unified development" (*The Literature of the Bible* [Grand Rapids, 1974], p. 26).

be truly rhetorical, it must attempt to discern those ideological criteria that may have controlled the compiler/redactor's decisions about the organization of events in the account. Thus, this study's approach to plot-structure analysis stands apart from those of previous treatments of Judges in that it defines plot-structure in terms of plot-levels rather than successive scenes. The designation 'plot-level' pertains to the purpose-driven exposition, development and resolution or dissolution of a theme related to some situational problem that prevents characters of the story from enjoying an ideal situation of equilibrium. Normally, the first plot element, the exposition, discloses both the situational problem that needs to be resolved within that plot-level and the main character or protagonist, whose identity as the one designated to solve the problem sometimes becomes clear only after reading the whole plot-level. The second basic element is the development, the beginning of which is marked by the main character's first attempt to take up the quest to solve the problem and which continues as long as attempts are made to resolve that problem. The third plot element is a resolution or dissolution, the beginning of which is marked, respectively, by the successful solving of the problem or by an irrevocable failure. Sometimes a resolution or dissolution comes about in separate, partial stages. Besides these basic elements of plot-structure, various additional aspects of plot should be considered. The climax, for example, refers to that timeless seam that marks the transition from the moment of highest tension in the development to either a partial or the final resolution or dissolution. There may be as many climaxes as there are full or partial resolutions or dissolutions within a plot-level or plot-levels within a story. A complication may occur if the narrative introduces a new or unforeseen problem that frustrates the protagonist's attempts to continue the original quest for a resolution. Indeed, many a complication is but the exposition of a new situational problem and marks the beginning of a new subplot that has its own exposition, development and resolution/dissolution. A prolongation that portrays various responses to the outcome may follow the resolution or dissolution of the plot. Additionally or alternatively, a dénouement may follow and unravel any as yet unexplained details or tangles in the plot-line.

Whereas the analysis of story narrative according to scenes has tended to demarcate successive blocks of narrative on the basis of changes of setting and/or character groupings, the analysis of story narrative according to plot-levels recognizes that certain themes undergo development and, like all themes, may be superimposed upon or follow patterns of interchange with other themes. The analysis of story narrative according to a purely scenic principle tends to run roughshod over multiple layers of exposition, development and resolution/dissolution that may proceed in parallel (but not always successive) lines through a complex story. The analysis of story narrative according to plot-levels requires more awareness of the agendas that control the arrangements of events—agendas that are almost always introduced in the exposition of each plot-level. Even so, it is primarily in the relationship between agendas and events that the rhetoric of a story is to be found.

C. The Rhetorical Strategy of Judges

In chapter 3 I discuss Judges' rhetorical strategy of entrapment and the function of the book to foreshadow evaluatively, through proleptic narrative analogy, the portrayals of Saul and David as figureheads of kingship in 1 Samuel. While the two episodes of Judges' dénouement structurally counterbalance the two parts of the book's prologue, they present a number of genre complications. First, how does the controlling purpose of the book, as discerned from the tribal–political and deuteronomic schemata presented separately in Judges' prologue and superimposed in its body, relate to the monarchist refrain repeated in the double dénouement (17:6; 18:1; 19:1; 21:25)? Second, why do both stories feature a Levite and finish with reference to Shiloh (18:31; 21:12-24) in spite of the fact that neither Levites nor Shiloh have been mentioned previously in Judges? Third, why is the ark of YHWH mentioned only in 20:27 and perhaps 18:30b[5] despite the many 'holy wars' of the book? This 'dénouement', rather than unravelling the complications of the book's intriguing design, only entangles the reader with the need to make a reassessment of first impressions and binds upon the reader the conviction that he or she has been subjected to a rhetorical strategy of entrapment. Thus, as for the book's characters so for its readers: things are not as right as they at first appear.

The introduction of these complications in chs. 17–21 invites the reader to reassess Judges' central section (3:7–16:31) to discern how it might cohere with a belated interest in both kingship and cult centre. This rhetorical strategy, by which the compiler/redactor withheld essential information until the dénouement, seems to have been designed to entrap the reader into a premature assessment of Judges' hero stories so as to invite a retroactive reassessment of the book's

---

[5] See the appendix.

characters (if not of the reader's perceptions of leadership in Israel). From a rhetorical perspective, it may be the 'incongruity' of Judges' thematic concerns that offers the best clue to its overall strategy.

This feature of Judges may be of particular interest to redaction criticism, since this literary theory proceeds on the assumption that redactional layers can be discerned precisely because such layers continue to bear vestiges of their original style, ideology and rhetorical aims even though such aspects may be at cross purposes with the organizing principle of the framework into which they have been embedded. If this were so in Judges, to what extent could the central episodes of Judges be said to cohere at all with the rhetorical aims of the prologue and epilogue sections except by the design of a compiler/redactor who was exploiting several exemplars of one genre (the traditional 'hero story') so as to misdirect the reader as to the framework's strategy of entrapment? Far from hindering the success of this compiler/redactor's rhetorical design, the recontextualization of Israel's tribal hero stories into a framework that inverts their heroic characterization actually enables this compiler/redactor to achieve his/her rhetorical aim.

From a consideration of the factors listed above, it would appear that the book of Judges was designed to achieve a reorientation of its readers toward higher standards of religious and intertribal leadership in Israel. Such standards resemble, for the most part, those of YHWH's covenant with Israel as set forth in the book of Deuteronomy. Although the present form of Deuteronomy addresses directly the matter of leadership (especially judgeship [Deut. 16:18-20] and kingship [Deut. 17:14-20]), Judges' interest in the deuteronomic tradition resides mainly with the matters of occupation of the land and national loyalty to the cult and covenant justice. However, in the tribal arrangement of materials in 1:1-2:5 and the body of the book (3:7-16:31), Judges shows concern to idealize Judah as the divinely appointed leader of the tribes of Israel.

The recognition by the compiler/redactor of the role that narrative analogy plays in characterization is already evident in the selection of the traditions incorporated into Judges. Indeed, the deliberate patterning of events and phraseology to furnish analogies to the narrative patterns and phraseology used to characterize Saul and David in 1 Samuel seems to be a deliberate stratagem of the Judges compiler/redactor. Most proleptic narrative analogies in Judges offer negative portrayals of the kinds of covenant compromise that later come to characterize Saul in 1 Samuel. In doing so, they imply that Judges was concerned not only to legitimize the Davidic monarchy through a portrayal of the preeminence of the Judah tribe but also to vilify the Saulide monarchy.

D. The Rhetorical Situation Implied by Judges

Chapter 4 focuses upon the relation between the rhetorical situation of Judges (i.e., the ostensible situation of compilation/redaction as implied by its surface strategy) and its real intention vis-à-vis its internal chronology and historical scope. Looking ahead to the portrayal of the emergence of the monarchy in 1 Samuel, it is a corollary of my thesis that the book of Judges, while preserving elements derived from originally separate stories of tribal heroes, is ostensibly the work of a compiler/redactor who selected and melded these stories into his/her own narrative framework in order to engender a deuteronomic idealization of Israelite kingship. The compiler/redactor did this to lead his/her readers to endorse the dynasty of David at the expense of that of Saul, whose kingship would be seen to resemble both the leadership of previous non-Judahite deliverers and the kingship of foreign nations. Since the Judges compiler/redactor used covenant ideals borrowed from traditions then preserved in Deuteronomy to construct a standard of kingship in Israel, it may be asserted that the rhetorical purpose of Judges includes the objective of evaluating, through deuteronomic foreshadowing, the portrayals of Saul and David in 1 Samuel 1– 2 Samuel 4.

Although there is a clear relationship between the two schemata introduced in Judges' double prologue and their recurrence among the accounts of Judges, this relationship alone yields little explicit information about essentials such as the circumstances of the compiler/redactor and the readers at the time of the book's compilation/redaction; their respective tribal, political and religious affiliations; or even the changes that the book was designed to effect in its readers. Such matters, which are needed to form a poetics that gives maximal significance to the interrelation of details in the book, must instead be inferred from the complex of details in the body of Judges and by comparison with what is known about Israelite history from other biblical sources. Only on the latter basis may it become apparent what is the significance of the superimposition of both schemata introduced in the prologue onto the deliverer accounts of the main body of Judges. For this reason and in order to avoid prejudicing judgements about the circumstances of the Judges compiler/redactor, I have avoided where possible characterizing material or ideals as 'deuteronomistic', since that term invites too many connections with inherited scholarly theories about the compilation/ redaction of Joshua–Kings and/or with various proposed schemes for dating the compilational strata in Judges. Instead, where connections with the book of Deuteronomy can be shown, the material or ideals are designated simply 'deuteronomic'.

E. THE EXCURSUSES AND APPENDIX OF THIS STUDY

It was not possible to discuss in detail the compilational stratigraphy of Judges or the history of scholarship regarding source criticism or redaction criticism in Judges. Instead, the Hebrew text of the appendix presents in outline the stratigraphy of the text of Judges that forms the basis of the rhetorical analysis in this study. Aspects of concern to the stratification of Judges that appears in the appendix are discussed in the first excursus, "Compilation, Redaction and the Rhetoric of Judges".

Likewise, while this study is not primarily a study of the textual transmission of Judges, it attempts to take account of the manuscript evidence where such is seen to bear upon one's understanding of Judges' rhetoric. Thus, although the relationship between the text of Judges and its rhetoric could not be discussed in detail, some textual problems have been described in the notes of the appendix. The principles used for restoring the text are summarized in the second excursus, "Scribal Developments and the Rhetoric of Judges".

CHAPTER ONE

RHETORICAL CONCERNS OF JUDGES' TRIBAL–POLITICAL AND DEUTERONOMIC SCHEMATA

The aim of this and the following chapters is to discern the primary rhetorical purpose of Judges from its formal structure and poetics. It is my main thesis that Judges was designed to enjoin its readers to endorse a divinely appointed Judahite king who, in contrast to foreign kings and previous non-Judahite deliverers, exemplified loyalty to the deuteronomic ideals of expelling foreigners from the land and maintaining intertribal loyalty to YHWH's covenant, cult and social order. Both the tribal–political agenda (with its concern for the endorsement of Judahite leadership/kingship) and the deuteronomic agenda (with its concern for occupation of the land, intertribal covenant loyalty, cultic order and social justice) feature in almost all the major sections of the book of Judges and reflect the concerns and ideals of its compiler/redactor with respect to his/her purposes for compiling/editing the book. Since my overall aim is to explain the rhetorical purpose of Judges from its formal structure and poetics, it should be emphasized that the present chapter contributes to that aim by attempting to discover and explain the controlling rhetorical concerns and ideals of Judges.

The deuteronomic concerns and ideals are most apparent in the second part of Judges' double prologue (2:6–3:6), in the double dénouement, where the issues of idolatry (17–18) and social injustice (19–21) loom large, and in the recurring cycle-motif that comprises the framework for the hero stories. However, to varying degrees, these concerns are evident also in the traditional hero stories, which suggests that the stories themselves may have been selected and/or remodelled to accord with Judges' deuteronomic ideals.

The tribal–political concerns and ideals of Judges are most apparent in the first part of Judges' double prologue (1:1–2:5), where Judah is portrayed as preeminent among the tribes and the tribe that YHWH favours (1:2), and in the double dénouement (17–18; 19–21), where YHWH again prefers Judah (20:18) and where kingship is implicitly endorsed as the means of attaining the covenant ideals of land occupation, intertribal covenant loyalty, social justice and adherence to the cult (17:6a; 18:1a; 19:1a; 21:25a). These tribal–political concerns and ideals frame and characterize those of the deliverer stories and double dénouement where Judges portrays the negative effects of the tribes' covenant compromises, which compromises include their general indolence in expelling foreigners from their land, their lapses into idolatry, their disregard for maintaining the Levites and the national cult, their intertribal fragmentation, and their failure to uphold covenant justice. The combination of the tribal–political portrayals in the framework and deliverer accounts seems to suggest that the ills of tribal Israel could be overcome only by a united endorsement of a divinely appointed Judahite king who, in contrast to foreign kings or previous non-Judahite leaders, modelled loyalty to the ideals of land occupation, intertribal covenant unity, cultic order and social justice as prescribed in YHWH's covenant.

As to Judges' idealization of a model of kingship distinct from that of foreigners, it may be averred that the deliverer accounts portray foreign kings in such a way as to make them objects of satire. Much of the satire seems already to have been evident or latent in the traditional stories, but the recontextualization of these stories into Judges' dual framework heightens their ridicule of foreign kings by their contrast with the framework's glorification of YHWH. As to Judges' idealization of a type of leader distinct from that modelled by non-Judahite deliverers of Israel, it may be inferred that the portrayal of premonarchial leadership among the deliverer accounts in Judges serves as a foil to the ideal of kingship to which it is implicitly contrasted in Judges' double dénouement (17:6a; 18:1a; 19:1a; 21:25a). Indeed, most of the deliverer accounts, but especially the two stories of the double dénouement, show how the foibles of flawed tribal leaders could escalate to tribal or even national levels.

The tribal–political and deuteronomic concerns and ideals just described are also reflected in two distinct patterns of arrangement, the schemata of which provide a dual framework for the book: one schema presents Israel's tribes (Judg. 1:1–2:5) and their heroic representatives (3:7–16:31) in the same general order; the other schema presents Judges' religious–historical cycle-motif (2:11–3:6) as a recurring feature in each of the deliverer accounts (3:7a–16:31). The two schemata, which are introduced separately in the two phases of Judges' double prologue, are superimposed on the body of Judges. Since it is my purpose to discern the rhetorical motive of the compiler/redactor for superimposing these schemata, I will analyse each separately in order to discern what role it plays in determining Judges' overall rhetorical strategy. Thus, the following analysis of Judges' superimposed schemata is divided into two segments. The first seeks to discover what rhetorical concerns are implicit in the tribal–political arrangement of Judg. 1:1–2:5, the deliverer accounts of 3:7–16:31 and in the tribal characterizations of chs. 17–18 and 19–21. The second segment aims to discern what concerns are implied by the form of Judges' deuteronomic cycle-motif.

A. CONCERNS OF JUDGES' TRIBAL-POLITICAL SCHEMA

When read together with their cycle-motif elements, the deliverer stories and 'minor' judge reports (3:31[?]; 10:1-5; 12:8-15) of Judges constitute narrative entities in their own right.[1] While it is probable that constituent elements of these accounts once existed among separate sources, their present arrangement in the book of Judges discloses something of the rhetorical purpose of the compiler/redactor. In an attempt to discern the rhetorical motivation underlying the selection and arrangement of these stories and reports, I shall examine their overall arrangement according to their tribal affiliations.

The overall arrangement of the book of Judges gives prominence to those tribes most important to the political and religious concerns of the compiler/redactor. Prologue-A (1:1–2:5) highlights the preeminent status of Judah (described first and at greatest length, 1:3-20) as compared with the other tribes of Israel, among which Benjamin and Dan (the southern- and northernmost tribes outside Judah) feature prominently in what at first appear to be the framing positions in the second half of Prologue-A (1:21, 34-36).[2] Nor does the double dénouement

---

[1] Judg. 5 is exceptional in that it is poetic and contains no cycle-motif elements. However, it is framed by a narrative that does bear the cycle-motif and should, therefore, be read within that context.

[2] The main subdivisions of Prologue-A (1:1–2:5) commence with the verb עלה used in a military sense. This furnishes thematic unity throughout the section. However, the content of each tribal subdivision shows contrast as well: first, between the second (1:3-20) and third (1:22-36) subdivisions; then, between the first (1:1-2) and final (2:1-5) subdivisions. Only two tribes are said to have "gone up" with (the help of) YHWH: Judah (ויעל יהודה ויתן יהוה, 1:4) and Joseph (ויעלו בית־אל ויהוה עמם, 1:22). Accordingly, the subdivisions containing accounts of the conquests of Judah (1:3-20) and of the 'Joseph' tribes (1:22-36) begin in complimentary terms. However, in the former (1:3-20) the focus remains upon the successes of Judah (minimizing or excusing their role in the implied loss of the plain cities Gaza, Ashkelon and Ekron [1:19b] and of Jerusalem [cf. 1:8, 21]), whereas in the latter (1:22-36) the description comes to focus upon failures, culminating in the failure of Dan. Significantly, Benjamin's failure is described in 1:21, which forms a fulcrum between and notably outside of the framing tribal subdivisions. The continuity between 2:1-5 and the foregoing subdivisions is evident from its introduction: ויעל מלאך־יהוה מן־הגלגל אל־הבכים (2:1). However, here too there is a contrast to

(17–18; 19–21) stray far from the order or concerns reflected in this tribal schema, since it features, in both its episodes, a similar present-ation of concern as appears in Prologue-A and body of the book with the successes and failures of Judah (showing interest in Jebus/ Jerusalem and Bethlehem), the Joseph tribes (i.e., regional Ephraim) and, in reverse order, Dan (17–18) and Benjamin (19–21). This straightforward south-to-north arrangement is represented in the following table:[3]

Prologue-A 1:1-36		*Double Dénouement:* *A* 17–18	*B* 19–21
Judah	1:3-20	Levite < Bethlehem (Leaving Judah)	Father-in-law < Bethlehem (Setting A: Judah)
Benjamin	1:21		Rapists < Gibeah (Setting B: Benjamin) Fugitives < Benjamin (Leaving/Returning)

Joseph:
  Manasseh
  Ephraim
Zebulun
Asher
Naphtali
	1:22-26
	1:27-28
	1:29
	1:30
	1:31-32
	1:33
		Micah < Ephraim
		(Main Setting)
			Levite < Ephraim
			(Leaving/Returning)

Dan	1:34-36	Migrants < Dan (Leaving Dan)	

what precedes, for YHWH is no longer 'with' his people but opposes them for their covenant waywardness. Judg. 2:1-5 essentially provides both a thematic and structural counterpart to 1:1-2, which began Prologue-A by asking YHWH מי יעלה־לנו (1:1b[i]), to which YHWH replied יהודה יעלה (1:2a[ii]). Judg. 2:1-5 confronts the same בני ישראל (1:1aβ; 2:4aγ) with a comparable claim, אעלה אתכם ממצרים (2:1bα), which implicitly rebukes the tribes for failing to dispossess the Canaanite nations and their idols by means of allusion to YHWH's covenant stipulations. Cf. Deut. 7:7-24 on the correlation between YHWH's conquest of Egypt and the assurance that Israel can conquer Canaan with YHWH's help (= Judg. 2:1b, 3a); cf. the stipulations in Deut. 7:1-5, 16, 25-26 to avoid treaties with the Canaanites and to destroy both the people and their idols (= Judg. 2:2a, 3b). See R. H. O'Connell, "Deuteronomy vii 1-26: Asymmetrical Concentricity and the Rhetoric of Conquest", *VT* 42 (1992), pp. 248-65.

[3] Locations in parentheses give details of the heritage/habitation of the judges/characters that are crucial to the tribal schematization of the book. On the south-to-north editorial schematization of Judges, see A. Malamat, "Charismatic Leadership in the Book of Judges", in *Études Sémitiques*, Paris, 1975, pp. 30-35; reprinted in *Magnalia Dei: The Mighty Acts of God: Essays on the Bible and Archaeology in Memory of G. Ernest Wright* (F. M. Cross et al. [eds.], New York, 1976), pp. 152-68; W. J.

According to the tribal correspondences between Prologue-A and the double dénouement, the Joseph tribes (among whom Ephraim was preeminent) represent the greater part of Israel's northern tribes. Indeed, Ephraim's reappearance throughout the body of the book emphasizes the prominent role that this tribe played in Judges as representing the 'middle' tribes of Israel (cf. 3:27; 5:14; 7:24–8:3; 10:1; 12:1-6, 15). The following table shows how the south-to-north geographical schema of Prologue-A serves as a model for the organization of the judges' narratives in the body of the book (3:7–16:31).[4]

Deliverer Accounts		'Minor' Judge Reports	
Othniel < Judah	3:7-11		
Ehud < Benjamin	3:12-30		
		Shamgar < ?	3:31
		([Beth-]Anath/Benjamin?)	
Deborah < ?	4:1–5:31		
(Ephraim)			
Barak < Naphtali			
Jael < Kenites/Judah			
(Naphtali)			
Gideon < W Manasseh	6:1–8:32		
	Abimelech < ?	8:33–9:57	
	(Shechem/Ephraim)		

Dumbrell, "'In Those Days There Was No King in Israel; Every Man Did What Was Right in His Own Eyes': The Purpose of the Book of Judges Reconsidered", *JSOT* 25 (1983), p. 25. Cf. A. Globe's discussion and schema of the geographical arrangement of Judges in "'Enemies Round About': Disintegrative Structure in the Book of Judges", in *Mappings of the Biblical Terrain: The Bible as Text* (V. L. Tollers and J. Maier [eds.], Bucknell Review 33/2, Lewisburg, Pa., 1990), pp. 236-45.

[4] In point of fact, the basic model for the order of tribes in Judges probably derives from the general order of tribes among the inheritance lists of Josh. 14–19, that order being Judah (14:6-15; 15:1-63), then the Joseph tribes (16–17; i.e., first Ephraim [16:5-10], then Manasseh [17:1-18]), and then 'the seven': Benjamin (18:11-28), Simeon (19:1-9), Zebulun (19:10-16), Issachar (19:17-23), Asher (19:24-31), Naphtali (19:32-39) and Dan (19:40-48). Among all the tribal lists of Hebrew Scripture, it is only in those of Josh. 14–19 and Judg. 1 that Judah heads a list of Cisjordan tribes in which the order Zebulun, Asher, Naphtali and Dan occurs (cf. L. G. Stone, "From Tribal Confederation to Monarchic State: The Editorial Perspective of the Book of Judges" [PhD diss., Yale University, 1988], pp. 219-22). Nevertheless, within the book of Judges, Prologue-A furnishes a cameo of the tribal arrangement for the book as a whole.

Deliverer Accounts (cont'd)		*'Minor' Judge Reports (cont'd)*	
		Tola < Issachar	10:1-2
		(Shamir/Ephraim)	
		Jair < ?	10:3-5
		(Kamon/Gilead)	
Jephthah < ?	10:6–12:7		
(?/Gilead)			
		Ibzan < ?	12:8-10
		(Bethlehem/Zebulun)[5]	
		Elon < Zebulun	12:11-12
		(Aijalon/Zebulun)	
		Abdon < ?	12:13-15
		(Pirathon/Ephraim)	

Samson < Dan	13:1–16:31

In the body, as in the prologue, Benjamin and Dan frame the presentation of the northern ('Joseph') tribes of Israel. Only Manasseh,
Ephraim, Zebulun and Naphtali are represented in both the prologue
and body.[6] In both prologue and body, Judah appears first and in juxtaposition with Benjamin, who functions as Judah's foil.[7] The basic

---

[5] On Bethlehem of Zebulun (cf. Josh. 19:15), see C. F. Keil and Franz Delitzsch,
Biblischer Commentar über das Alten Testament, vol. II/1, *Josua, Richter und Ruth*, by
C. F. Keil (Leipzig, 1863), ET: *Biblical Commentary on the Old Testament*, vol. 4,
Joshua, Judges, Ruth (J. Martin [trans.], CFTL 4/VIII, Edinburgh, 1868); repr. edn,
Commentary on the Old Testament, 10 vols., vol. 2, *Joshua, Judges, Ruth, I & II Samuel*
(Grand Rapids, 1976), p. 398; G. F. Moore, *A Critical and Exegetical Commentary on
Judges* (ICC, Edinburgh, 1895), p. 310; C. F. Burney, *The Book of Judges with Introduc-
tion and Notes* (London, 2d edn, 1920), pp. 290, 334; A. E. Cundall, *Judges*, in A. E.
Cundall and L. Morris, *Judges and Ruth: An Introduction and Commentary* (TOTC 7,
London, 1968), p. 152; R. G. Boling, *Judges: Introduction, Translation and Commentary*
(AB 6A, Garden City, N.Y., 1975), pp. 215-16; J. A. Soggin, *Judges: A Commentary*
(J. Bowden [trans.], OTL, London, 2d edn, 1987), p. 223; J. Gray, *Joshua, Judges, Ruth*
(NCBC, Basingstoke, 2d edn, 1986), p. 322. Those who prefer Bethlehem of Judah
include: Josephus (*Ant.* V.vii.13 §271), Rashi, Qimḥi, Ralbag and L. Wood, *Distressing
Days of the Judges* (Grand Rapids, 1975), p. 271. Both the focus on the northern tribes
in 3:12–16:31 and the proximity of Ibzan's account to that of Elon of Zebulun (12:11-12)
support the view that the reference is to Bethlehem of Zebulun.

[6] Asher is represented only in the prologue (1:31-32), Issachar (i.e., Deborah, Tola)
and Gad/Gilead (i.e., Jephthah) only in the body.

[7] In the prologue, Judah receives twenty verses, Benjamin only one. Judah's portrayal
is basically positive (but cf. C. J. Goslinga on 1:19b, in *Richteren–Ruth* [KVHS, Kampen,
The Netherlands, 3d edn, 1966], ET: *Joshua, Judges, Ruth* [R. Togtman (trans.), BSC,
Grand Rapids, 1986], p. 254), Benjamin's only negative. On the negative characterization
of Benjamin in 1:21 Goslinga remarked that, "Their neglect [to dispossess the Jebusites
from Jerusalem] was all the more serious because they really had to do nothing more than
reap the harvest that had been prepared by Judah and Simeon (see v. 8)" (p. 254). In the
body, the account of the Judahite Othniel takes on paradigmatic significance in that it

correspondence between the schematic arrangement of tribes in Judg. 1:1–2:5 and that of 3:7–16:31 confirms that concern with tribal–political preeminence controlled the arrangement of accounts in Judges. Although there is an inverted correlation between the order of Benjamin and Dan in both Prologue-A (between 1:21 and 34-36) and the body of Judges (between 3:12-30 and 13–16), on the one hand, and the reversal of that order in Dénouements A and B (between 17–18 and 19–21), on the other, it remains doubtful that the author was concerned to present the deliverer accounts of 3:7–16:31 according to a concentric arrangement or ring structure.[8]

Judah holds the preeminent position in this tribal arrangement. An implicit promotion of Judah through the structural arrangement of Judges would comport with an ideology, elsewhere evident in Israel's traditions, in which Judah was predestined, both through patriarchal blessing (Gen. 49:8-12) and divine election (Ps. 78:68 [cf. v. 70]), to rule among Israel's tribes.[9] Whether these particular literary traditions antedate the compilation/redaction of Judges may be difficult to establish, but that the emergent role of Judah was intended to be

---

contains all but one element of the cycle-motif introduced in Prologue-B; the account of Ehud of Benjamin lacks the second (idolatry/apostasy, but note references to "idols" in 3:19, 26), third (YHWH's anger) and eighth (YHWH's spirit) elements (see below).

[8] Contra D. W. Gooding, "The Composition of the Book of Judges", in *Eretz-Israel: Archaeological, Historical and Geographical Studies*, vol. 16, *Harry M. Orlinsky Volume* (Jerusalem, 1982), pp. 70*-79*; and Globe, "Enemies" (1990), pp. 245-48, 249. The motifs and themes adduced by Gooding as evidence of a concentric arrangement of accounts in Judg. 3:7–16:31 are often of little rhetorical consequence within at least one of the allegedly matching accounts. Contrariwise, the pattern of correspondences between juxtaposed accounts of themes, motifs and genres that are rhetorically significant seems to be the result of deliberate design (e.g., see below concerning [1] the collocation of key words at the climax of the accounts of Ehud and Deborah/Barak/Jael, [2] the corresponding portrayals of the villain's death at the hand of a woman in the climax of the accounts of Deborah/Barak/Jael and Gideon/Abimelech, [3] the formal similarity between portrayals of YHWH's reluctance to save Israel that preface the Gideon and Jephthah accounts, between the divine commission of Gideon [6:11-17] and the elders' call of Jephthah [11:5-11] and between the role of conflicts with Ephraim in the accounts of Gideon and Jephthah, and [4] the correspondence of site names between the account of Samson and that of the migration of the Danites). Another formal correspondence that disrupts the concentric scheme proposed by Gooding is that between the theophanic recognition type-scenes in the accounts of Gideon/Abimelech (6:11-12a, 18-24) and Samson (13:15-23). Cf. also the criticisms of Stone, "Tribal Confederation" (1988), pp. 61-64.

[9] That Judah (Gen. 49:8-12) and Joseph (49:22-26) are given the longest blessings in Gen. 49 agrees with the fact that they were to become the leading tribes of southern and northern Israel, respectively. However, in the context of Gen. 49, Judah's destiny to rule is unique among the tribes.

inferred from Judges' tribal arrangement is corroborated in the two places, ostensibly framing the book, where Judah is divinely appointed to lead the tribes (1:1-2; 20:18).[10] Therefore, both the present tribal structure and at least two explicit reports of divine election, positioned at the beginning and end of Judges, promote the ideology that Judah was predestined to lead the tribes of Israel.

The interest of the compiler/redactor in elevating Judah in relation to Benjamin may be discerned from comparing the characterizations of these tribes in the framing sections of the book, Prologue-A and Dénouement-B. The rhetorical concern in Prologue-A (1:1-2:5) to contrast the characterizations of Judah and Benjamin with respect to the conquest of Jebus/Jerusalem may be inferred from the pivotal role played by the two verses in which Jerusalem is mentioned, 1:21 (the structural axis of 1:1-2:5) and 1:8 (the axis of 1:3-18). It is the concern with Jerusalem that puts Benjamin into contrast with the other tribes of Israel and, more specifically, with Judah. This contrasting characterization in Prologue-A (1:1-2:5), where Judah is the divinely elected representative of "all Israel", finds analogy in Dénouement-B (19-21), where Judah is again elected to represent the interests of "all Israel" against Benjamin, a tribe whose covenantal failure is described in relation to their implicit toleration of foreigners at Jebus (19:10aγ-13).

Some have argued that, because the traditional hero stories and reports in the main body of Judges (3:7-16:31) show interest primarily in the northern tribes of Israel, this cycle originated before Judah's entry into the tribal league. The addition of the first part of the prologue (1:1-2:5), the Othniel story (3:7-11) and the double dénouement (17-21), in which Judah or specifically Bethlehem figures prominently, would thus constitute a later accretion to the book. However, while it may be right on redaction-critical grounds to infer that these passages were added to Judges at a later stage (see excursus 1), the second inference that Judah itself therefore came late into the tribal league proceeds under the assumption that what one has in Judges is compilation/redaction devoid of ideological preference.[11]

---

[10] In an originally independent version of 19:2-21:24, the aim of 20:18 may have been to show that YHWH appointed Judah to be the first tribe to execute justice only because it was a concubine from Judah who was victimized by the Gibeahites (cf. Deut. 13:10aβb; 17:7a).

[11] Even on redaction-critical grounds, one must be cautious about inferring relative dates of materials on the basis of observations related to form or subject matter. For example, upon observing that the tribal groupings in both the prologue and main body of the book are analogously segregated (i.e., Judah [1:1-20 = 3:7-11] followed by Benjamin [1:21 = 3:12-20], the Ephraimite league [1:22-33 = 4-12] and Dan [1:34-36 = 13-16]),

If, however, the present form of the book of Judges holds a predilection for the tribe of Judah that a previous form of the book did not (perhaps because of its northern origin), then one must ask whether the segregation of northern tribes in the main body of the work was not primarily the result of an earlier compiler's interest in only northern tribes. Their apparent segregation in the form of the book composed by a later redactor might therefore reflect a rhetorical penchant for viewing the northern tribes *en masse*, as comprising a single religious-political entity.

What needs to be proved is that at least two successive editions were necessary to account for the integration of the Judah materials into the pre-existing framework that bound together the accounts of Ehud, Deborah/Barak/Jael, Gideon, (possibly Jephthah and Samson) and the 'minor' judges. However, while it is probable that interest in Judah, introduced in Prologue-A (1:1–2:5) and subsequently resumed in the Samson account (15:9, 11), in Dénouement-A (17:7, 9; 18:12) and in Dénouement-B (19:2; 20:18), was an innovation of a later redactor of Judges, there is only marginal evidence that an earlier, self-standing anthology of hero stories was formed by means of some or all elements of the cycle-motif introduced in Prologue-B (e.g., two forms of the introductory cycle-motif element in 3:12a and 3:12bβ). A multistage process involving compilation and later redaction(s) of Judges is not necessary to account for the present tribal arrangement of the book, even though such a scenario seems quite probable.[12]

In any case, any hypothesis that assigns materials showing an interest in Judah to a redactional stratum (not part of the original compilation) will need to demonstrate both the use of redactional devices, such as editorial ('resumptive') repetition, and degrees of incompatibility between themes of the Judah sections and themes of the cycle-motif elements that made up the framework of Judges at any stage of its compilation/redaction.[13] Yet, if such thematic tensions as

---

an inference that the Judah sections must be secondary either because they are analogously segregated and, hence, represent a distinct redactional layer or because they evidence primary interest in Judah—an interest that varies from that inherent in the northern tribal arrangement—would seem to be inference drawn from assumption.

[12] Note the persuasive case that has been made for a three-stage process of compilation/redaction in Judges by Stone, "Tribal Confederation" (1988), especially in the first three chapters, though Stone's thesis focuses upon the role of the final redaction (pp. 113-29; cf. pp. 132-35, 186-87).

[13] Stone's work, "Tribal Confederation" (1988), offers a particularly cogent account of the peculiarities of an alleged pro-Judahite recension of the book of Judges. For examples of possible uses of editorial ('resumptive') repetition in Judges, see Stone, "Tribal

now appear in the book are indeed incompatibilities that resulted from redaction, they have now been so harnessed to serve the rhetorical interests of the final redaction that it may be tendentious to assume that they ever were incompatibilities.[14] Thus, while it is true that Judg. 3:7-11 features the same interest in Judah as does Prologue-A (1:1–2:5), the mere fact that it comprises an example story made up almost entirely of elements borrowed from the cycle-motif of Prologue-B (2:6–3:6) hardly precludes the possibility that 3:7-11 was created by a single compiler who designed Judges' cycle-motif in its entirety.[15]

B. CONCERNS OF JUDGES' DEUTERONOMIC SCHEMA

Specific references to pre-existing deuteronomic stipulations occur in Judg. 2:1-3, 11-15 [16-19]; 2:20–3:4; 3:7; 6:7-10 [25-26]; [8:27]; [9:56-57]; 10:6-16; [18:31].[16] Most of these passages contain explicit condemnation of Israel for failure to uphold YHWH's covenant stipulations. Thus, these passages reflect the rhetorical intention of a

---

Confederation" (1988), pp. 123, 170, 183, 319, 335. On possible editorial uses of the framing device of inclusio, see pp. 202, 209, 210, 215, 229, 231, 232, 234, 235, 236, 237, 239, 241, 327. However, one should also recognize—as Stone apparently does—that such devices are as readily used for purely aesthetic purposes as for editorial ones, so their presence is not always necessarily an indication of redactional activity.

[14] J. Barton labels this the problem of "the disappearing redactor" (*Reading the Old Testament: Method in Biblical Study* [Philadelphia, 1984], pp. 56-58). Cf. Stone, "Tribal Confederation" (1988), pp. 95, 121-29.

[15] From the similarity of the description of Othniel in relation to Caleb as הקטן ממנו (Judg. 3:9 and 1:13), Stone inferred that Judg. 3:7-11 derived from the same hand that prefixed Judg. 1 (as well as 2:1-5; 3:31; 6:7-10; 8:22-27, 30-35; 9; 10:1-5, 10-14; 12:8-15; 16; and 17-21) to the penultimate form of the book of Judges (cf. "Tribal Confederation" [1988], pp. 127-28, 202-7, 283, 285). Yet, even while I am persuaded of the sensibility of Stone's thesis, which distinguishes a tribal edition of Judges from a later monarchical recension of it, the indications that Judges actually existed in a premonarchical form remain rather subdued in a rhetorical reading of its present form.

[16] The form of an alleged deuteronomic covenant document at the time of Judges' compilation is not entirely evident, though it stands to reason that at least those stipulations to which the book of Judges refers must have pre-existed Judges' compilation. Concomitantly, it is unlikely that the royal stipulations of Deut. 17:14-20 were present in the deuteronomic document at the time of Judges' compilation, otherwise one might have expected a more direct reference to them in Judges' monarchical idealization. Rather, the composition of Deut. 17:14-20 probably postdates the present form of Judges, 1 Samuel and 1 Kings, since it seems to have been drawn from connections with 1 Sam. 8, 16 (cf. 1 Sam. 8:5, 20 with Deut. 17:14; 1 Sam. 16:1, 3 with Deut. 17:15a), Judg. 9 (cf. Deut. 17:15b) and 1 Kgs 10-11 (cf. 1 Kgs 10:14-25, 26-29; 11:1-13 with Deut. 17:16-17).

compiler/redactor to bring the hero stories of Judges into a framework in which actions and motives could be assessed by the standards of YHWH's covenant. It is understandable, then, that most redaction-critical studies of Judges have seen in these explicit references to covenant stipulations the hand of a 'deuteronomic' or 'deuteronomistic' compiler/redactor. Indeed, it is the aim of the following discussion to demonstrate the extent to which deuteronomic phraseology and ideological concerns have affected the rhetorical structure of Judges' cycle-motif.

In regard to Judges' cycle-motif (often called the "pragmatic formula"), R. G. Boling commented, "Actually the only clear lexical or stylistic parallel with Deuteronomy in this formula is the statement "they did evil" (cf. Deut. 17:2)—exceedingly slim support for the notion that the book of Deuteronomy guided the bulk of the internal organization of Judges".[17] However, although Deuteronomy had little effect on the tribal–political structure of Judges, deuteronomic phraseology and ideology have significantly influenced the rhetorical design of Judges' cycle-motif. Indeed, the phraseological parallels between Judges' cycle-motif and Deuteronomy comprise half of Judges' cycle-motif elements (i.e., elements A1a, A1b, A2a, A2b, B1, B2a, B3b^j[?] and C; see below). Therefore, one may infer that the Judges compiler/redactor deliberately used deuteronomic phraseology in the cycle-motif. Moreover, from a rhetorical standpoint, it appears that the compiler/redactor framed in deuteronomic language only the alienation phase of Judges' cycle-motif in order to characterize the Israelite tribes of this period as repeatedly rebelling against the terms of YHWH's covenant as it is expressed in Deuteronomy. Thus, YHWH's repeated initiation of the restoration phase—a phase for which deuteronomic parallels are lacking—would have to be perceived as the manifestation of YHWH's undeserved grace to a people of vacillating loyalty.

Superimposed upon the tribal arrangement of materials in the body of Judges (3:7–16:31) is a twelvefold repetition (with some gaps and variations) of a sequence of twelve or more elements. An artificial aggregate of Judges' cycle-motif might appear as follows:

---

[17] Boling, *Judges* (1975), pp. 35-36; endorsed by Gooding, "Composition" (1982), p. 72*.

ויעשׂו בני־ישׂראל את־הרע בעיני יהוה	A1a
איש הישר בעיניו יעשׂה	A1b
ויעבדו את־הבעלים ואת־העשׁתרות	A2a
וילכו אחרי אלהים אחרים וישׁתחוו להם	
ויעזבו את־יהוה אלהיהם	A2b
ויחר־אף יהוה בישׂראל	B1
ויתנם יהוה ביד־PN	B2a
וימכרם יהוה ביד PN	B2b
ויעבדו בני־ישׂראל את־PN N שׁנים	B3a
והוא לחץ את־בני ישׂראל N שׁנה	B3b
ויזעקו בני־ישׂראל אל־יהוה	C
ויקם יהוה מושׁיע לבני ישׂראל ויושׁיעם	D1
ותהי עליו רוח־יהוה	D2a
ויתקע בשׁופר	D2b(?)
ויכנע PN לפני בני ישׂראל	E1
ויתן יהוה את־PN ביד [ישׂראל]	E2a
וימכר יהוה את־PN ביד [ישׂראל]	E2b
וישׁפט PN את־ישׂראל N שׁנים	F1
ותשׁקט הארץ N שׁנה	F2
וימת PN	G1
ויקבר בקבר PN	G2

One should note that, after its introduction in Prologue-B (2:10–3:6), this cyclical framework recurs at least once (usually partially) in each of the twelve accounts of the judges. The following table, which presents all possible attestations of cycle-motif elements in Judges, is presented on four successive pages. The first two pages present a single table on which appear all attestations of elements A1a through C (i.e., the alienation phase of Judges' cycle-motif). The next two pages likewise present a single table on which appear all attestations of elements D1 through G2 (i.e., the restoration phase of Judges' cycle-motif).

	Prlg-A	Prlg-B	1st	2nd	3rd	4th	5th	6th
A1a "Israelites did evil before YHWH"	(2:2b[i])	2:11a (20bδ)	3:7aα	3:12a 12bβ	4:1a	6:1a (10b)		
A1b "right ... eyes"	(2:2b[ii])						(9:16) (19a)	
A2a "served the Baals ... followed other gods and worshipped them"		2:11b 12aγ-ε 13b 17aβ-δ 19aβ-ε 3:6b	3:7b				8:33aγ-b	
A2b "they forsook YHWH ..."		2:12aαβ 13a	3:7aβ				8:34	
B1 "YHWH's anger burned against Israel"		2:(12b) 14aα 20a	3:8aα					
B2a "YHWH gave them into hand of ..."		2:14aβ			(3:12bα)	6:1b[i-ii]		
B2b "YHWH sold them into hand of ..."		2:14bα	3:8aβγ		4:2a			
B3a "Israelites served ... N years"		(2:14bβ- 15a)	3:8b	3:14αβ		6:1b[iii] (2a)		
B3b "oppressed the Israelites ... N years"					4:3bβ		(9:22)	
B3b[i] "oppressed (לחץ)"	(1:34a?)	(2:18bβ)				(6:9aβ)		
B3b[ii] "distressed (צרר)"		2:15b						
C "Israelites cried to YHWH"	(1:1aβγ)		3:9aα	3:15aα	4:3a	6:6b 7a		

	7th	8th	9th	10th	11th	12th	Dnmt-A	Dnmt-B
A1a		$10{:}6a\alpha\beta$				$13{:}1a$		
A1b		$10{:}15a\beta\gamma$				$(14{:}3b\beta)$ $(7b)$ $(16{:}21a\beta)$ $(28b\beta)$	$17{:}6b$	$19{:}24a\gamma\delta$ $21{:}25b$
A2a		$10{:}6a\gamma\text{-}\varepsilon$ $(10b\gamma)$ $(13a\beta)$ $(16a\alpha)$						
A2b		$10{:}6b$ $(10b\alpha\beta)$ $(13a\alpha)$ $(16a\beta)$						
B1		$10{:}7a$				$(14{:}19b\alpha)$		
B2a						$13{:}1b^{\text{i-ii}}$ $(16{:}23b\beta\gamma)$ $(24b\beta)$		$(20{:}28b\beta)$
B2b		$10{:}7b\alpha^{\text{i}(\text{ii})}\beta$				$<\!10{:}7b\alpha(\beta)\!>$		
B3a						$13{:}1b^{\text{iii}}$		
B3b		$10{:}8ab\alpha$						
B3b^{i}		$(10{:}12a\beta)$						
B3b^{ii}		$10{:}9b$ $14b^{\text{ii}}$ $(16b?)$ $11{:}7b\beta$						
C		$10{:}10a$ $(12b\alpha)$ $(14a)$ $(12{:}1a\alpha)$ $(2b\alpha)$				$(15{:}18a\beta)$ $(16{:}28a)$		$(20{:}18a\alpha\beta)$

	Prlg-A	*Prlg-B*	*1st*	*2nd*	*3rd*	*4th*	*5th*	*6th*
D1 "YHWH raised up ... to save them"		2:16abα 18aα,γ	3:9aβ	3:15aβ		(6:15aβ) (36b^i) (37bδ^i)		10:1aα
D2a "YHWH's spirit ... upon ..."		(2:18aβ)	3:10aα^i			6:34a	(9:23a)	
D2b "sounded the ram's horn"(?)				3:27aβ		6:34bα		
E1 "[enemy] humbled ... before/by hand of [Israel]"				3:30a	4:23	8:28aαβ		
E2a "gave ... into hand of [Israel]"	(1:2b) (4aβ)	(2:23b)	3:10aγδ	3:28aβ	(4:14aβ)			
E2b "sold ... into hand of [Israel]"					(4:9aδε)			
F1 "... judged ... Israel (N years)"		(2:18aδ)	3:10aα^{ii}		4:4b (5b)			10:2a
F2 "land had peace N years"			3:11a	3:30b	5:31b	8:28b$^{i\text{-}ii}$		
G1 "and ... died"	(1:1aα)	2:(8) 19aα	3:11b	<4:1b>		8:32a^i <33aα(β)>	(9:54b^{ii}) (55a^{ii})	10:2b^i
G2 "was buried ... at"		(2:9a)				8:32bα		10:2b^{ii}

	7th	8th	9th	10th	11th	12th	Dnmt-A	Dnmt-B
D1	10:3aα	(10:11b*?) (12bβ) (14b[i]) (12:2bβ) (3aα)				(13:5b)		
D2a		11:29a				13:25aαβ[i] 14:6aα 19aα 15:14bα (19aγ) (16:19bβ) (20bγδ)		
D2b								
E1		11:33b						
E2a		11:21a 30b 32b 12:3aγ				(16:23bβγ) (24bβ)		20:28bβ
E2b								
F1	10:3b	12:7a	12:8α 9b	12:11aα 11b	12:13a 14b	15:20[i,iii] 16:31b		
F2								
G1	10:5α	12:7baβ	12:10α	12:12a	12:15a	16:30b		
G2	10:5β	12:7bγ	12:10β	12:12b	12:15b	16:31aβ-δ		

From the foregoing overview it should be apparent that there may be as many as twenty distinct and recurrent elements in Judges' cycle-motif. These twenty distinguishable elements may be segregated into twelve essential elements (eight of which are binary): (i) A1a A1b, (ii) A2a A2b, (iii) B1, (iv) B2a B2b, (v) B3a B3b/^{i}/^{ii}, (vi) C, (vii) D1, (viii) D2a D2b(?), (ix) E1 (x) E2a E2b, (xi) F1 F2, (xii) G1 G2. Many scholars affirm that only four to six of these twelve elements constitute Judges' framework since they aver that the recurrence of a motif must be pervasive throughout the book before it can be said to constitute an element of its interpretative framework.[18] However, a criterion of pervasive recurrence for each motif before it is allowed to constitute an essential element of Judges' framework is neither required nor implied as a controlling convention of Judges' rhetorical structure. It may be

---

[18] G. W. Trompf observed four elements in Judges' cycle-motif: (i) defection, (ii) oppression, (iii) prayer (the importance of which becomes obvious after ch. 2), (iv) deliverance ("Notions of Historical Recurrence in Classic Hebrew Historiography", in *Studies in the Historical Books of the Old Testament* (J. A. Emerton [ed.], SVT 30, Leiden, 1979], pp. 219-20). A. D. H. Mayes observed six elements (*The Story of Israel between Settlement and Exile: A Redactional Study of the Deuteronomistic History* [London, 1983], pp. 61-62):

(i) The statement that "Israel did what was evil" (2:11; 3:7, 12; 4:1; 6:1; 10:6; 13:1).

(ii) The statement, with variations, that Israel was handed over to an enemy ("YHWH sold them into the hand of", 2:14; 3:8; 4:2; 10:7; "YHWH strengthened ... against Israel", 3:12; "YHWH gave them into the hand of", 6:1; 13:1).

(iii) The statement that "Israel cried to Yahweh" from their oppression (3:9, 15; 4:3; 6:6; 10:10).

(iv) The statement that "Yahweh raised up a deliverer" (3:9, 15)—though, because infrequent, Mayes doubted its independence as an element of the framework and so made it subordinate to the third and fifth elements.

(v) The statement that the enemy was subjugated (3:30; 4:23; 8:28; 11:33).

(vi) The statement that "the land had rest" (3:11, 30; 5:31; 8:28).

This six-member framework was endorsed also by D. M. Gunn, "Joshua and Judges", in *The Literary Guide to the Bible* (R. Alter and F. Kermode [eds.], Cambridge, Mass., 1987), pp. 104-5.

F. E. Greenspahn deemed only five clauses to recur with sufficient regularity to be considered part of the presumably earliest, all-embracing framework of Judges ("The Theology of the Framework of Judges", *VT* 36 [1986], p. 388).

	Intro.	Oth.	Ehud	Deb.	Gid.	Jeph.	Samson
(i) ויעשׂו בני־ישׂראל את־הרע בעיני יהוה	x	x	x	x	x	x	x
(ii) וימכרם יהוה ביד	x	x	חזק	x	נתן	x	נתן
(iii) ויזעקו בני־ישׂראל אל־יהוה		x	x	x	x	x	
(iv) ויכנעו ... לפני/מפני	נתן						
בני ישׂראל	ביד	x	x	x	x		
(v) ותשׁקט הארץ X שׁנה		x	x	x	x		

argued that the cycle-motif framework of Judges includes every element that recurs among its various accounts. Hence, from a literary perspective, all motif elements that appear to be the result of an attempt to establish a pattern of historical recurrence among the hero stories should be taken to make up the book's cycle-motif. It may be that redaction-critical concerns have played an unnecessarily dominating role in the preference of scholars for judging that Judges' framework comprises only pervasive motif elements rather than all the elements that can be seen to recur among accounts. Special note should be taken of: (1) the allusion to the cycle's second (binary) element (A2a, A2b) in the transition to the Abimelech episode (8:33aγ-b, 34); (2) the recurrence of the cycle's seventh (D1), eleventh (F1 only) and final (binary) elements (G1 G2) in the Tola and Jair accounts (Tola: 10:1aα, 2a, 2b^i/2b^{ii}; Jair: 10:3aα, 3b, 5α/5β); and (3) the repetition of only the eleventh (F1 only) and final (binary) elements (G1 G2) in the accounts of Ibzan, Elon and Abdon (Ibzan: 12:8α, 9b; 12:10α/10β; Elon: 12:11aα, 11b; 12:12a/12b; Abdon: 12:13a, 14b; 12:15a/15b). All three of these examples of recurrence of elements from Judges' cycle-motif appear also elsewhere among the deliverer accounts of Judges. Thus, even though the Abimelech and 'minor' judge accounts may constitute distinct redactional strata in Judges, there was a demonstrable attempt on the part of a compiler/redactor to diffuse among the different accounts elements originally characteristic of a particular stratum and thus to network the individual hero stories into a coherent compilation/ redaction. Since the Abimelech account and 'minor' judge reports present only a few excerpts of the twelve-part cycle, they do not, within themselves, repeat the cycle, but it seems safe to suggest that the compiler/redactor of Judges intended that they should in each instance signal it.

The interpretative framework of Judges, which comprises the network of these recurring motifs, implies that each hero account is to some extent a manifestation of the same religious–historical phenomenon recurring cyclically in Israel's history.[19] Hence, as the text of Judges now stands, there may be little compelling evidence for identifying more than one compiler, the rhetorical strategist of the traditional materials contained within Judges (as M. Noth once inferred).[20] This does not preclude the possibility that there was indeed

---

[19] Greenspahn, "Theology" (1986), p. 385.

[20] See M. Noth, *Überlieferungsgeschichtliche Studien, I. Die sammelnden und bearbeitenden Geschichtswerke im Alten Testament* (Schriften der Königsberger Gelehrten Gesellschaft, 18. Jahr.; Geisteswissenschaftliche Klasse, Heft 2; Halle, 1943, pp. 43-266;

a multilayer compilation/redaction of the book, but, apart from possible scribal glosses (e.g., in Judg. 18:30b), a proposed double edition of Judges may not be empirically necessary to account for the varied literary phenomena of the book.[21] What seem to be traces of different editorial strata may be but ideological tensions resulting from the combination of varied sources that were melded together by a single compiler.

In support of the possibility that the components of Judges' cycle-motif were inserted into the hero traditions under a single rhetorical strategy one may adduce the remarkable similarity of their recurrences. More significant, however, are the differences that attest how these recurrences were nuanced to suit them to their individual contexts. For example, the A1a motif elements follow a similar form and placement, usually at nodal points between the narrative accounts:

A1a "Israelites did evil before YHWH"

את־הרע בעיני יהוה		ויעשׂו בני־ישׂראל		2:11a
את־הרע בעיני יהוה		ויעשׂו בני־ישׂראל		3:7aα
הרע בעיני יהוה	לעשׂות /	בני ישׂראל	ויספו	3:12a
את־הרע בעיני יהוה		על כי־עשׂו		3:12bβ
הרע בעיני יהוה	לעשׂות /	בני ישׂראל	ויספו	4:1a
הרע בעיני יהוה		ויעשׂו בני־ישׂראל		6:1a
הרע בעיני יהוה	לעשׂות /	בני ישׂראל	ויספו	10:6aαβ
הרע בעיני יהוה	לעשׂות /	בני ישׂראל	ויספו	13:1a

(cf.	ולא־שמעתם בקלי	2:2b[i])
(cf.	ולא שמעו לקולי	2:20bδ)
(cf.	ולא שמעתם בקולי	6:10b)[22]

Recurrences of this motif element appear in the prologue and at the opening of each of the six major hero accounts. There are two forms for this element: an initial form and a resumptive form. The appearance of both forms in combination in 3:12a and 3:12bβ may suggest that one of its forms—presumably that which is resumptive—was

Tübingen, 2d edn, 1957), ET of 2d edn, pp. 1-110: *The Deuteronomistic History* (JSOTS 15, Sheffield, 1981), especially pp. 42-53.

[21] *Pace*, for example, R. D. Nelson, *The Double Redaction of the Deuteronomistic History* (JSOTS 18, Sheffield, 1981), especially pp. 43-69, 119-28.

[22] In this and subsequent tables of Judges' cycle-motif elements, verse citations follow the Hebrew text and therefore appear to its right. In subsequent tables, where the Hebrew text may be broken into two or more horizontal lines, the verse citations appear to the right of the bottom line of Hebrew text. The cross-references (following 'cf.') cite clauses that express similar meanings, but with alternative phraseology.

secondary, added perhaps when 3:7-11 was prefixed to a series of hero accounts that began with *3:12-30. Thus, 3:12-30 may already have evidenced this motif element prior to the prefixing of 3:7-11 to the series of hero accounts. But if redaction were involved, why did the redactor not simply alter the existing statement of this motif in *3:12 to make it resumptive rather than add a second? The presence of an initial rather than resumptive form of the motif in 6:1a shows that, from the perspective of the compiler/redactor, there was no rhetorical reason to limit later recurrences of the motif to its resumptive form after its initial appearance in 3:7aα (though the absence of the direct object marker את is a further anomaly of this motif's recurrence in 6:1a). Indeed, a modified form of motif A1a recurs in 2:2bⁱ, 20bδ, and 6:10b in usages that suggest that these too had their source in the Judges compiler/redactor. Most scholars recognize this motif as constituting an essential element of Judges' interpretative framework. This is not the case, however, with the next motif, which varies in form and position among the narrative accounts of Judges:

A1b   "right ... eyes"

		עשה־אתה לנו /		
	בעיניך		ככל־הטוב	10:15aβγ
(	בעיני		כי־היא ישרה	14:3bβ)
(	בעיני שמשון		ותישר	14:7b)
	בעיניו		איש הישר	
		יעשה		17:6b
	להם /	ועשו /		
	בעיניכם		הטוב	19:24aγδ
	בעיניו		איש הישר	
		יעשה		21:25b

(cf.	את־עיניו	וינקרו		16:21aβ)
(cf.	משתי עיני מפלשתים	ואנקמה נקם־אחת		16:28bβ)

(cf.		עשיתם	מה־זאת	2:2bⁱⁱ)
(cf.	ותמליכו את־אבימלך //	אם־באמת ובתמים / עשיתם	ועתה /	
	עם־ירבעל ועם־ביתו /	עשיתם	ואם־טובה	
	לו	עשיתם	ואם־כגמול ידיו	9:16)
(cf.	עם־ירבעל ועם־ביתו היום הזה	אם־באמת ובתמים עשיתם	וא	9:19a)

This motif is not pervasive but appears to have been deliberately diffused among accounts in Judges in anticipation of its important role in the double dénouement. Except for the possibly reduced form of motif A1b in 2:2bⁱⁱ (contiguous with the modified form of A1a in 2:2bⁱ), this motif appears only in the latter half of the book and then after the introduction of its main theme, in reduced form (without בעיני) in 9:16; 9:19a; 16:21aβ and 16:28bβ. Among the hero accounts, this motif seems confined to the Samson story, where its usage does not appear to be formulaic—perhaps indicating its genuineness within that story. Its appearance in 10:15aβγ occurs within a section (10:6-16) commonly recognized as a compiler/redactor's insertion and may, therefore, represent a secondary diffusion of this motif. In 14:3bβ the 3 f. sg pronoun היא before the Qal perf. 3 f. sg ישרה seems super-fluous, since there is hardly cause for emphasis here. Perhaps the unusual syntax (where one might otherwise have expected the adjective טובה) may indicate an innovation of the compiler/redactor to diffuse the A1b motif throughout the Samson account.[23] The appearance of motif A1b in 17:6b, together with one of two appearances of the monarchical motif that occur at nodal points in chs. 17–18 (i.e., 17:6a, 18:1abα), may likewise be secondary to the account of chs. 17–18 that, in other respects, shows assimilation with the Samson story. The motif reap-pears in 21:25b, on analogy with 17:6b, and in 19:24aγδ, on analogy with 10:15aβγ.[24] The irregularity of expressions used in 9:16 and 9:19a shows that there was no deliberate attempt to conform them to the pattern of A1b even though they were similar in sense. It may be right to infer that the different form of this motif element in the Abimelech account attests its genuineness within that story as well, though, if these verses at all reflect the work of a compiler/redactor, this compiler/redactor may have intended only to draw attention to the irregularity of the Abimelech account.

This motif (A1b) is related to the preceding (A1a) by three of is con-stituents: (a) the regular use of עשה as the main verb—as in A1a; (b) the repeated reference to perspective using the metonymy (subject for mental adjunct) בעיני—though here the reference is usually to human perspective rather than, as in A1a, to that of YHWH; (c) the reference to that which is right/good, הישר/הטוב—the antithesis of that which is evil, הרע, given in A1a.

---

[23] Any poetic justice for Samson's having his eyes put out (16:21aβ, 28bβ) would only be enhanced by the reference to Samson's perspective in 14:3bβ, 7b (cf. the dénouement motif 17:6b; 21:25b).

[24] Motif A1b in 19:24aγδ seems intrinsic to its context and probably alludes to the same expression in Gen. 19:8, where Lot addresses the mob of Sodom regarding the rape of his daughters, or possibly to 1 Sam. 11:10, where the besieged citizens of Jabesh-Gilead address the Ammonites regarding the intention to blind the right eyes of all who surrender. Cf. S. Lasine, "Guest and Host in Judges 19: Lot's Hospitality in an Inverted World", *JSOT* 29 (1984), pp. 40-41, 43.

Because the following two motifs appear most often in juxtaposition with occurrences of A1a, they have been designated A2a and A2b, respectively. However, neither A2a nor A2b recurs pervasively throughout Judges, though each does appear in the loci of Judges where covenantal concerns predominate. The motif elements A2a and A2b serve to specify the moral aberrations described in A1a and A1b by limiting them to the religious–covenantal sphere.

A2a "served the Baals ... followed other gods and worshipped them"

2:11b	ויעבדו את־הבעלים
	וילכו אחרי אלהים אחרים /
	[מאלהי העמים אשר
	סביבותיהם /]
2:12aγ-ε	וישתחוו להם
2:13b	ויעבדו לבעל ולעשתרות
	כי זנו / אחרי אלהים אחרים /
2:17aβ-δ	וישתחוו להם
	[ישבו והשחיתו מאבותם /]
	ללכת / אחרי אלהים אחרים /
2:19aβ-ε	לעבדם ולהשתחות להם
3:6b	ויעבדו את־אלהיהם
3:7b	ויעבדו את־הבעלים ואת־האשרות
	ויזנו אחרי
	הבעלים //
8:33aγ-b	וישימו להם בעל ברית לאלהים
	ויעבדו את־הבעלים ואת־העשתרות
	ואת־אלהי ארם
	ואת־אלהי צידון
	ואת אלהי מואב /
	ואת אלהי בני־עמון /
10:6aγ-ε	ואת אלהי פלשתים
10:10bγ)	(ונעבד את־הבעלים
10:13aβ)	(ותעבדו אלהים אחרים
10:16aα)	(ויסירו את־אלהי הנכר מקרבם

There appear to be three (or possibly four) elements in the varied formulaic statements of A2a: (a) the verb עבד usually followed by some reference to הבעלים; (b) a verb equivalent to הלך followed by אחרי אלהים אחרים; (c) a reference to some religious–historical phenomenon (e.g., gods of the surrounding peoples, rebellion of the forefathers); and possibly (d) a reference to worship of other gods: וישתחוו להם, or the like, though this element may complement (b). Several occurrences of A2a may be found in Judg. 2:6–3:6. Judges 2:11b and 2:12aγ-ε complement each other to make up a complete statement of this motif. The alternative forms of 2:13b and 2:17aβ-δ also complement each other but are too remote from each other to constitute a single statement. Instead, 2:13b may simply parallel 2:11b/12aγ-ε, as do 2:17aβ-δ and 2:19aβ-ε. Judges 3:6b, which lacks reference to הבעלים, stands alone at the end of 2:6–3:6. Judges 3:7b presents only the first element. Judges 8:33aγ-b offers a unique combination of the first and second elements, though the verbs vary from the norm in each instance. The final statements, comprising 10:6aγ-ε (with [a] and [c]), 10:10bγ (with [a] alone), 10:13aβ (with [a] and [b]), and 10:16aα (with a reversal of the [c] in 10:6aγ-ε) occur within the insertion of 10:6-16 and lack only the fourth component. This motif bears a remarkable resemblance to the arrangement of elements in the following motif, designated A2b.

A2b "they forsook YHWH ..."

ויעזבו	את־יהוה אלהי אבותם /	המוציא אותם מארץ מצרים	2:12aαβ
ויעזבו	את־יהוה		2:13a
וישכחו	את־יהוה אלהיהם		3:7aβ
ולא זכרו בני ישראל / את־יהוה אלהיהם //	המציל אותם מיד כל־איביהם מסביב		8:34
ויעזבו	את־יהוה		
ולא עבדוהו			10:6b
חטאנו לך / <>כי		(	
עזבנו	את־	אלהינו	10:10bαβ)
ואתם עזבתם	אותי		10:13aα)
ויעבדו	את־יהוה		10:16aβ)

This motif comprises three elements: (a) a verb implying covenantal aberration, usually עזב—which corresponds antithetically and paronomastically to the verb עבד of element (a) in A2a; (b) a reference to YHWH their god—which corresponds antithetically to element (b) in A2a; (c) a reference to some religious–historical phenomenon (e.g., the Exodus from Egypt, deliverance from enemies)—which corresponds to element (c) in A2a. As in A2a, the clustered assemblage of 10:6b (with [a] alone), 10:10bαβ (with [a] and [b]), 10:13aα (with [a] alone) and 10:16aβ (with a reversal of [a] and [b]) occurs together in the insertion of 10:6-16. In two recurrences of element (a), its intended complementarity with element (a) of A2a is apparent for, in 10:6b and 10:16aβ, עבד is used in the (a) position—once negatively, once positively—in reference to YHWH. This may imply that, throughout the recurrences of motif element A2b, עזב was intended to function as the antithetical complement to עבד in motif element A2a.

For A2a and A2b, 8:33aγ-b and 8:34, respectively, diverge most
from the formulaic pattern of verbs. However, their themes and choice
of nouns show that both 8:33aγ-b (with elements [a] and [b]) and 8:34
(with [a], [b] and [c]) adhere to the general pattern of A2a and A2b,
respectively. Anomalous in 8:33aγ-b are the verbs ויזנו (in element [b])
and וישׂימו [להם] (in element [a]); anomalous in 8:34 are the verb and
subject ולא זכרו בני ישׂראל (in element [a]), though the verb is semantically merely the opposite of the anomalous verb וישׁכחו in element (a)
of 3:7aβ. The semantic relationship may illustrate an editorial relationship between 3:7aβ (within 3:7-11) and 8:34. Since 8:33aγ-b and 8:34
(within the Abimelech account) manifest the same irregularity in relation to the patterns of A2a and A2b that 9:16 and 9:19a (likewise in the
Abimelech account) manifested in relation to A1b, one might infer that
a compiler/redactor desired to direct attention to the abnormality of the
Abimelech account.

After the 'A' motifs, which describe Israel's covenant aberrations,
come a series of motifs (designated 'B') that describe the disasters that
resulted from YHWH's anger and retribution against Israel. The motif
of YHWH's anger (B1) is another example of an element in Judges'
cycle-motif that is not pervasive in its recurrences.

B1 "YHWH's anger burned against Israel"

(		יהוה	ויכעסו את־	2:12b)
	ויחר־אף	יהוה בישׂראל		2:14aα
	ויחר־אף	יהוה בישׂראל		2:20a
	ויחר־אף	יהוה בישׂראל		3:8aα
	ויחר־אף	יהוה בישׂראל		10:7a
(		ויחר אפו		14:19bα)

Five recurrences of this motif use the expression ויחר־אף or the like.
Four of these identify the anger as that of יהוה and have ישׂראל as
object (the exception being the final statement of the motif in 14:19bα,
where the subject is Samson). The reference to Israel's provocation in
2:12b, with YHWH as the object of ויכעסו, is unique and may not comprise a legitimate example of the B1 motif, but it seems fair to suggest
that, as the first indication of YHWH's provocation, it anticipates
2:14aα. YHWH's anger in motif B1 leads to YHWH's retribution
expressed in the B2a and B2b motif elements.

Elements B2a and B2b, which are often considered alternative forms
of the same motif element, are generally considered to be among the
pervasive elements of Judges' framework. However, one should

maintain the distinction between these related motif elements. The components that constitute element B2a appear as follows:

B2a "YHWH gave them into hand of ..."

ביד־שסים			ויתנם	2:14aβ
(	את־עגלון מלך־מואב על־ישראל		ויחזק יהוה	3:12bα)
ביד־מדין [שבע שנים]			ויתנם יהוה	6:1b^i-ii
ביד־פלשתים			ויתנם יהוה	13:1b^i-ii
(	בידנו		נתן אלהינו	
		את שמשון אויבינו		16:23bβγ)
(	בידנו		נתן אלהינו	
		את־ אויבנו		16:24bβ)
(	בידך		כי מחר אתגנו	20:28bβ)

Of the seven occurrences of motif element B2a, six employ some form of נתן linked with an indirect object introduced by the prepositional form ביד־. The form of 3:12bα is exceptional, since it alone uses the verb ויחזק and lacks an indirect object introduced by the prepositional form ביד־. As to the six examples with נתן and ביד־, it is noteworthy that only the last occurrence (20:28bβ) is presented as direct speech by YHWH (the remainder being narrated in the third person).

The recurrences of B2a present Israelites being given into foreigners' hands (2:14aβ; 6:1b^i-ii; 13:1b^i-ii)—Israel being the antecedent of the 3 m. pl. verbal suff. (dir. obj.) of ויתנם—or, worse, an Israelite deliverer being given into the hands of foreigners who ironically employ the B2a motif when they mock Samson (16:23bβγ, 24bβ; cf. the same verses under motif E2a). This negative development of motif B2a reaches the peak of ironic reversal when it is finally used as though synonymous with motif E2a in YHWH's speech (20:28bβ). Here YHWH gives an Israelite tribe (Benjamin) into the hands of the Israelite tribal league—an act that inverts the first statement of motif E2a (1:2b), where YHWH elected Judah to be first to conquer the land.

Although the form of motif B2a in 3:12bα is exceptional, its formulaic structure and thematic function seem sufficiently analogous to the theme and form of the B2a motif to warrant its inclusion as a variant. It is, perhaps, significant that this variant occurs in the account of the Benjaminite deliverer Ehud (3:12-30). Since the portrayal of Judah's deliverer in 3:7-11 was most likely a compiler/redactor's composition, it may be significant that only in the following Benjaminite hero's account (3:12-30) does it become explicit that YHWH was allied with Israel's enemies, strengthening them to overpower his rebellious people. The strategic position of this anomalous-form occurrence of B2a suggests that it may have been designed to heighten the reader's awareness of YHWH's especial opposition to Israel when Israel's deliverer was to emerge from the tribe of Benjamin.

The recurrences of the related B2b motif appear as follows:

B2b "YHWH sold them into hand of ..."[25]

	ביד אויביהם מסביב	וימכרם 2:14bα
(מלך ארם נהרים) /	ביד כושן רשעתים /	וימכרם / 3:8aβγ(δ)
מלך־כנען /	ביד יבין /	וימכרם יהוה
אשר מלך בחצור		4:2a
	(ביד־פלשתים) /	וימכרם
	וביד בני עמון	10:7bαⁱ⁽ⁱⁱ⁾β
<	ביד־פלשתים /	וימכרם
	(וביד בני עמון)	10:7bα(b)>

The verb in motif B2b is מכר and, as in the B2a motif, the verb is linked with an indirect object introduced by the prepositional form ביד־. Moreover, as in motif B2a, Israel is the antecedent of the 3 m. pl. verbal suff. (dir. obj.)—in this case, of וימכרם (2:14bα; 3:8aβγ; 4:2a; 10:7b). By mentioning the Philistines along with the Ammonites in 10:7b, the compiler/redactor anticipated the oppressors of the Samson account, for which there is otherwise no B2b element (cf. a similar displacement of element G1 in 4:1b and 8:33aα[β]), and perhaps intended thus to indicate that these periods of oppression had occurred simultaneously.

The relationship among the motif elements so far designated 'B' is evident from their contiguity in Judg. 2:14aα (B1), 2:14aβ (B2a) and 2:14bα (B2b). A restatement of this relation in the same context may appear between 2:20a (B1) and a negative statement of motif E2a in 2:23b (synonymous with B2a), though a cause–effect relation is not here apparent because of the reversed chronological sequence. The three 'B' elements never recur elsewhere within one episode, though sometimes two appear in contiguity: e.g., in 3:7-11, 3:8aα (B1) is followed by 3:8aβγ (B2b) and, in the Jephthah account, 10:7a (B1) is followed by 10:7b (B2b). Because these 'B' elements are contiguous within 2:14 (in the prologue) and because at least the B1 and B2b elements are contiguous in 3:8 (of the Othniel account) and in 10:7 (of the

---

[25] S. R. Driver noted that this figure is almost peculiar to the compiler of Judges (2:14; 3:8; 4:2; 10:7; differently in the older narrative 4:9) and to the kindred author of 1 Sam. 12 (cf. 12:9; *An Introduction to the Literature of the Old Testament* (ITL 1, Edinburgh, 9th edn, 1913], p. 164 n. *). He saw the phraseology as a point of contact with Deut. 32:30. On the standard formulaic order and its variation, see D. F. Murray, "Narrative Structure and Technique in the Deborah–Barak Story (Judges iv 4-22)", in *Studies in the Historical Books of the Old Testament* (J. A. Emerton [ed.], SVT 30, Leiden, 1979), p. 175 n. 38.

Jephthah account), it seems that they were intentionally related to each other within Judges' cycle-motif. Moreover, the formal and functional similarity of B2a and B2b suggests that they constitute alternative forms of one binary motif (B2).

Two further 'B' elements, which appear to make up yet another binary motif, are those designated B3a and B3b/ⁱ/ⁱⁱ. The 'B3' binary motif states the consequence of YHWH's retribution expressed in the 'B2' binary motif in those instances in which it pertains to YHWH's retribution against Israel (not foreigners). The recurrences of element B3a are as follows:

B3a "Israelites served ... N years"

3:8b	ויעבדו בני־ישראל	את־כושן רשעתים	שמנה	שנים
3:14αβ	ויעבדו בני־ישראל	את־עגלון מלך־מואב /	שמונה עשרה שנה	

ולא־יכלו עוד / לעמד לפני	אויביהם:		(cf.
בכל אשר יצאו / יד־	יהוה היתה־בם לרעה /		
כאשר דבר	יהוה /		
2:14bβ-15a)	וכאשר נשבע	יהוה להם	
6:1bⁱⁱⁱ	[ויתנם	יהוה	cf.
	ביד־מדין]	שבע	שנים
6:2a)	ותעז	יד־מדין	על־ישראל (cf.
	[ויתנם	יהוה	cf.
13:1bⁱⁱⁱ	ביד־פלשתים]	ארבעים	שנה

Only two clear examples of the subservience motif B3a appear in Judges, those of 3:8b and 3:14αβ. These feature: (a) the verb ויעבדו with (b) subject בני־ישראל, (c) the name of a foreign ruler as direct object (את־) and (d) a period expressed in a number of years. Two further references to periods of Israel's subjugation in a number of years, 6:1bⁱⁱⁱ and 13:1bⁱⁱⁱ, appear to coincide with occurrences of motif B2a so as to credit YHWH with the commencement of such periods. This interest in divine cause may justify reading the description of YHWH's recurrent subjugation of Israel to foreigners in 2:14bβ-15a as an anticipation of motif B3a.

Recurrences of the related motif B3b/ⁱ/ⁱⁱ, which, like B3a, state a consequence of YHWH's retribution, appear as follows:

B3b "oppressed the Israelites ... N years"

4:3bβ	והוא לחץ	את־בני ישראל	בחזקה	עשרים	שנה
10:8abα	וירעצו וירצצו	את־בני ישראל / בשנה ההיא //	שמנה עשרה שנה

9:22)	וישר אבימלך	על־ישראל	שלש	שנים

B3bⁱ "oppressed (לחץ)"

(		מפני לחציהם ודחקיהם	2:18bβ)
(		ומיד כל־לחציכם	6:9aβ)
(	אתכם	לחצו	10:12aβ)

(cf.	את־בני־דן ההרה	וילחצו האמרי	1:34a?)

B3bⁱⁱ "distressed (צרר)"

	מאד	להם	ויצר	2:15b
	לישראל מאד	ותצר	10:9b
	צרתכם	בעת	10:14bⁱⁱ
	לכם	צר	כאשר	11:7bβ

(cf.	ישראל	ותקצר נפשו בעמל	10:16b?)

The form of B3b comprises: (a) main verbs denoting oppression and whose subjects are foreigners; (b) the direct object אֶת־בְּנֵי יִשְׂרָאֵל (or עַל־יִשְׂרָאֵל in 9:22); (c) an adverbial clause (absent from 9:22) and (d), like B3a, a period expressed in a number of years. Thus, the only consistent formal feature among the recurrences of the B3a and B3b elements is the repetition of a period expressed in a number of years, but their rhetorical function and position within Judges' cycle-motif is virtually the same. Although the presentation of 4:3bβ after 4:3a (motif element C) seems out of normal sequence for the cycle-motif, the logical–causal sequence between 4:3a and 4:3bβ shows that the oppression described in 4:3bβ chronologically preceded Israel's cry of 4:3a.

The aggregate of recurrences of either B3a or B3b in the same position of the motif cycle, when either appears in contiguity with 'B2' elements, implies that B3a and B3b were designed to function as alternative elements of a single (binary) motif. Three times B2a and B3a elements appear in proximity or contiguity: 3:12bα (B2a) with 3:14αβ (B3a); 6:1bⁱ⁻ⁱⁱ (B2a) with 6:1bⁱⁱⁱ (B3a); and 13:1bⁱ⁻ⁱⁱ (B2a) with 13:1bⁱⁱⁱ (B3a). Analogously, twice B2b and B3b elements appear in proximity or contiguity: 4:2a (B2b) with 4:3bβ (B3b) and 10:7b (B2b) with 10:8abα (B3b). Only in Prologue-B and the Othniel account is there contiguity between B2b and B3a elements: namely, 2:14bα (B2b) with 2:14bβ-15a (B3a)—2:14aβ (B2a), though present, is not contiguous— and 3:8aβγ (B2b) with 3:8b (B3a). The B3b element at 9:22 is unique and serves as one more evidence of the anomalous nature of the Abimelech account within the sequence of Israel's judges. Indeed, the position of 9:22 (B3b) at a point in the narrative where it might be misconstrued thematically with element F1 only heightens the irony that Abimelech's rule, far from being a time under one of Israel's judges, was actually a period of foreign oppression. Outside Prologue-B (2:6–3:6) and the Othniel account, the correlation among the 'B2' and 'B3' motif elements generally conforms to an alternating pattern of presentation:

B2a	*B2b*	*B3a*	*B3b*
	2:14bα	(2:14bβ-15a)	
	3:8aβγ	3:8b	
3:12bα		3:14αβ	
	4:2a		4:3bβ
6:1b^i-ii		6:1b^iii	
		(2a)	
			(9:22)
	10:7b		10:8abα
13:1b^i-ii		13:1b^iii	

Given this phenomenon, it appears that the B3a and B3b elements were intended to function as alternative elements of a binary motif designed to complement the binary B2a and B2b elements, respectively, within Judges' cycle-motif framework. Like the A1a motif, all the 'B' motif elements so far discussed are positioned at nodal points in the deliverer stories, nowhere functioning as elements intrinsic to earlier narrative sources, so it appears that the 'B' elements were, like the A1a motif, a rhetorical innovation of the Judges compiler/redactor.

The B3b^i and B3b^ii variants of B3b form instances in which Israel's oppression or distress is described using either לחץ (B3b^i) or צרר (B3b^ii) but without the duration expressed in number of years that characterizes motif B3b. Apart from the number element, a distinction between the B3b^i/ii and B3b variants is difficult to establish because most recurrences of B3b^i/ii take place within the three short sections of Judges that explore the sincerity of Israel's repentance when they experience oppression (i.e., 2:11-19[20–3:6]; 6:7-10; 10:6-16). Indeed, most of Judges' cycle-motif elements cluster in 2:11-19[20–3:6] and 10:6-16.

The anomalous reference to oppression (לחץ) in 1:34a occurs in Prologue-A and, therefore, before Judges' cycle-motif has been established (in Prologue-B [2:10–3:6]). Hence, it probably does not constitute a recurrence of motif B3b^i—though it may present an anticipation of it. Since the reference to distress in 11:7bβ is intrinsic to its narrative context, it probably does not represent an innovation by the compiler/redactor (i.e., a recurrence of the B3b^ii motif). Although

Judg. 10:16b uses different vocabulary from recurrences of motif B3b[ii], its contiguity with and reference to the distress of Israel, as well as the paronomasia between קצר and צרר, suggests that it may be related to B3b[ii].

So far I have accounted for five of the twelve motif elements constituting Judges' cycle-motif: (i) A1a A1b, (ii) A2a A2b, (iii) B1, (iv) B2a B2b, (v) B3a B3b/[i]/[ii]. They show the downward trend in the cycle that leads from Israel's apostasy from YHWH, expressed in motif elements (i) A1a A1b and (ii) A2a A2b, to Israel's outcry to YHWH, expressed in element (vi) C. Indeed, the C element marks the turning point in the downward trend of the cycle-motif.

The recurrences of element C follow a fairly standard pattern, appear in all the major deliverer accounts and, like the A1a and 'B' motif elements, usually appear at nodal positions in the accounts of Judges:

C "Israelites cried to YHWH"

(לאמר	ביהוה /	בני ישראל /			וישאלו	1:1aβγ)
	אל־יהוה	בני־ישראל			ויזעקו	3:9aα
	אל־יהוה	בני־ישראל			ויזעקו	3:15aα
	אל־יהוה	בני־ישראל			ויצעקו	4:3a
	אל־יהוה	בני־ישראל			ויזעקו	6:6b
	אל־יהוה	בני־ישראל	זעקו	ויהי כי־		6:7a
לאמר	אל־יהוה	בני ישראל /			ויזעקו	10:10a
(	אלי				ותצעקו	10:12bα)
(	אל־האלהים /			לכו /	וזעקו	10:14a)
	אשר בחרתם בם					
(ויאמר	אל־יהוה				ויקרא	15:18aβ)
(ויאמר	אל־יהוה	שמשון			ויקרא	16:28a)
(	בית־אל]				[ויקמו ויעלו	
ויאמרו /	באלהים				וישאלו	
	בני ישראל					20:18aαβ)

(cf.	איש אפרים	ויצעק	12:1aα)
(cf.	אתכם	ואצעק	12:2bα)

Its predominant elements include the use of: (a) זעק or צעק as the main verb (in ten of fourteen possible cases); (b) בני־ישראל as the subject of the verb (in eight cases); (c) אל־יהוה as the indirect object (eight times אל־יהוה, once אלי [YHWH speaking]), though once אל־האלהים refers to foreign gods in the sardonic injunction of 10:14a. In both the first and final cases—the only recurrences that appear outside the main body of Judges—וישאלו is the main verb and, appropriately, the object has prefix ב: ביהוה in 1:1aβγ and באלהים in 20:18aαβ.

All fourteen cases listed above display at least one of the four elements of this motif. However, 12:1aα and 12:2bα, in which the verb צעק appears, are the only instances where a god is not being invoked. The fact that these juxtaposed instances are positioned out of normal sequence in the cycle-motif and do not occur at a nodal point in the Jephthah narrative tells against their inclusion in the cycle-motif.

In two exceptional cases, קרא is the main verb (15:18aβ; 16:28a) and שמשון, who substitutes (symbolically) for בני־ישראל, invokes YHWH to avenge him for his affliction—a variation of Israel's cry to YHWH for deliverance. In the Samson narrative, however, this call for vindication occurs out of normal sequence in the cycle-motif—in the finale of both the sequence of chs. 14–15 and that of ch. 16. In the latter case, the partial victory for Israel is a posthumous one for Samson, making it ostensibly a defeat (cf. 16:30b). Further, in five instances the C motif formulae are followed by some form of the verb אמר introducing a quotation of the request being made of YHWH. Three of the five are positioned in sections that are probably the work of the Judges compiler/redactor (1:1aβγ in Prologue-A [1:1–2:5]; 10:10a in 10:6-16; 20:18aαβ in Dénouement-B [19–21]). Only in the case of 15:18aβ and 16:28a is the material in the quotation intrinsic to the narrative, so, unless the compiler/redactor adapted this variation of motif C into the Samson narrative, it may be warranted to infer that 15:18aβ and 16:28a were neither innovations of the compiler/redactor nor intended to function as constituents of Judges' cycle-motif. Yet it is not impossible that the compiler/redactor adapted motif C into the Samson narrative, since another instance of one of Judges' motifs also seems intrinsic to the Samson narrative, namely, the development of motif D2a concerning YHWH's spirit (see below).

Although some form of the C motif appears in every major deliverer story—attesting, by its pervasiveness, that it is an innovation by the Judges compiler/redactor—it is absent from the paradigmatic exordium of Judg. 2:10–3:6. What appears in its place is the statement of 2:18b: כי־ינחם יהוה מנאקתם "for YHWH would have compassion because of their groaning". This statement may offer some clarification about the cause for Israel's subsequent invocations of YHWH (motif C). So far as the paradigm of 2:10–3:6 is concerned, each subsequent instance of Israel's 'cry of repentance' was motivated by the duress of oppression rather than by anything resembling a freely motivated change of religious ideology or devotion. This seems to present a perception that the compiler/redactor of Judges deemed significant, since on two further occasions (e.g., 6:7-10; 10:6-16; cf. 2:1-5) the sincerity of Israel's cry of repentance while they are being oppressed is called into question.

The six motif elements that follow—(vii) D1, (viii) D2a D2b(?), (ix) E1 (x) E2a E2b, (xi) F1 F2, (xii) G1 G2—make up the restoration phase of Judges' cycle-motif. Recurrences of the D1 motif, which most agree constitute part of Judges' framework, may include the following:

D1 "YHWH raised up ... to save them"

		ויושיעום	שפטים //	יהוה	ויקם	2:16abα
			שפטים /	וכי־הקים יהוה להם		
	והושיעם מיד איביהם		[והיה יהוה עם־השפט] /			2:18aα,γ
	ויושיעם	ישראל	לבני	מושיע	יהוה ויקם	3:9aβ
		מושיע	להם	יהוה	ויקם	3:15aβ
(	אושיע				במה	6:15aβ)
	את־ישראל					
(	מושיע				אם־ישך	6:36bⁱ)
[כאשר דברת]	בידי את־ישראל					
(	תושיע				כי־	6:37bδⁱ)
[כאשר דברת)]	בידי את־ישראל					
	להושיע	אבימלך	אחרי		ויקם	10:1aα
	את־ישראל					
		אחריו			ויקם	10:3aα
(הלא ממצרים						
ומן־האמרי						
ומן־בני עמון						
ומן־פלישתים						10:11b)
(ואושיעה						
מידם	אתכם					10:12bβ)
(יושיעו		המה				
[בעת צרתכם]	לכם					10:14bⁱ)
(ולא־הושעתם						
מידם	אותי					12:2bβ)
(	מושיע	ואראה כי־אינך				12:3aα)
(	יחל להושיע	והוא /				
מיד פלשתים	את־ישראל					13:5b)

The D1 motif comprises a compound formula whose verbal forms, when present, include both קום and ישׁ׳. There appear to be six elements in the aggregate of this motif (though not strictly in this order): (a) the main verb ויקם; (b) יהוה as subject (when ויקם is *waw* cons. + Hi. pret. 3 m. sg); (c) one of two nominal forms as object: שׁפט or מושׁיע; (d) some verbal form of ישׁע; (e) ישׁראל as direct or indirect object; (f) an enemy from whom (מיד) Israel was saved.

Among the most formulaic recurrences of motif D1 (2:16abα, 18aα,γ; 3:9aβ, 15aβ; 10:1aα), only the first two use the term שׁפטים

for element (c). These two uses seem to reflect the concern of the compiler/redactor to set up an analogy, in the exordium of the cycle-motif (Prologue-B), between the title 'judge' and the function of saving Israel. The analogy between judge and saviour derives from the correspondence between the positions of the title 'judge' in 2:16abα, 18aα,γ (D1) and the title 'saviour' in 3:9aβ, 15aβ (D1)—alternative titles that serve for element (c) of motif D1.[26] Further, the substantive form of שפט in D1 may be analogous to the use of its verbal form in motif F1 ("... judged ... Israel [N years]") in that, whereas characters referred to in F1 "judged Israel", such 'judges' were the ones who "saved them" in at least the first two instances of motif D1. The foregoing correlations are presented not to suggest that titles and functions related to שפט or ישע are philological synonyms, only that the Judges compiler/redactor may have intended them to indicate analogous roles and functions in the present form of the book.

In the retrospective evaluation of Israel's covenant sincerity in 10:6-16, a recurrence of motif D1 may appear in the rhetorical question posed in 10:11b (anacoluthon?) and in 10:12bβ, where it has an indefinite past reference that, with the mention of seven enemy nations (Egyptians, the Amorite, Ammonites, Philistines, Sidonians, Amalek and Midian [so OG; MT: ומעון]), may have been intended to recall all of YHWH's deliverances—not just those portrayed in Judges. The deliberation of 10:11-14 complicates Judges' cycle-motif by delaying the expected deliverer. The complication is furthered by the sardonic tone of motif D1 in 10:14bⁱ, in which YHWH incites Israel's gods to save them. This sardonic tone complements the mocking injunction of 10:14a noted above (C) and was probably intended to indicate a change in YHWH's disposition toward Israel's recurring repentance of convenience (contrast 2:18b with 6:7-10; 10:6-16).

It is interesting to note that, whereas the Gideon account lacks a recurrence of the D1 motif, the expanded 'call narrative' (6:11-17, [18-24]) that serves in its place makes reference to its saviour element in 6:15aβ.[27] Since the latter reference seems intrinsic to its narrative context, it may not constitute an innovation of the compiler/redactor.

---

[26] It may be a further argument in favour of the analogy between the roles of judge and saviour that, whereas the first 'minor' judge, Tola, "arose after Abimelech to save" (ויקם אחרי אבימלך להושיע, 10:1aα), in the analogous position of the 'minor' judge reports of 12:8a, 11aα, and 13a, each "judged after [his predecessor]" (וישפט אחריו).

[27] On the 'call narrative', see N. Habel, "The Form and Significance of the Call Narratives", ZAW 77 (1965), pp. 297-323. Exemplars cited include: Judg. 6:11b-17; Exod. 3:1-12; Jer. 1:4-10; Isa. 6:1-13; Ezek. 1:1-3:15; and Isa. 40:1-11.

However, if 6:15aβ were embedded into the call narrative by the compiler/redactor of Judges, it shows with what sensitivity the compiler/redactor melded cycle-motif elements into the narrative. These comments pertain also to 6:36b^i, 37bδ^i. The variation on motif D1 in 12:2bβ, 3aα seems likewise intrinsic to its narrative context, though, in the mouth of Jephthah, it ironically converts the normal concern of this motif for Israel's welfare to concern for the welfare of one person (i.e., אותי occurs in the position normally reserved for element [e] ישׂראל). A third example of motif D1 that seems intrinsic to its narrative context occurs in 13:5b, though, like 2:1-3, 6:7-10 and 10:6-16, it may have been introduced by the compiler/redactor. It is probably no coincidence that Samson is the only character of whom it is said that he would "begin (יחל) to save Israel" (13:5b). The anomalous verb יחל will reappear some twenty verses later in connection with motif D2a (see below on 13:25aαβ^i). Nevertheless, the fact that three of the recurrences of this motif are intrinsic to narrative development may support the view that the cycle-motif innovations of Judges' compiler/redactor were not always limited to the narrative framework that occurs between the deliverer accounts.

The arising of Tola and Jair (cf. וַיָּקָם, waw cons. + Qal pret. 3 m. sg) in 10:1, 3 should be distinguished from YHWH's raising up (וַיָּקֶם, waw cons. + Hi. pret. 3 m. sg) in 2:16a, 18aα; 3:9aβ, 15aβ.[28] In 10:1, unlike 10:3, the individual who arose is explicitly said to have done so "to deliver Israel" להושׁיע את־ישׂראל, an element of this motif that is otherwise limited to the accounts of the major deliverers. By virtue of the formulaic similarity and contiguity of 10:3 with 10:1 and the continuity implied by אחריו (10:3), one may infer that Jair too arose "to deliver" Israel. At least in the case of Tola, one is presented with a 'minor' judge report of one of Israel's deliverers who, by virtue of military success, became a ruling judge—as had, perhaps, Gideon and Jephthah. This seems significant to the extent that a distinction between the 'minor' judge reports and the 'major' accounts of Israel's deliverers should not be made with respect to the issue of the nature of their office—representatives from both groups act as deliverers and representatives from both groups become long-standing rulers in Israel.

In four of the deliverer stories, motif D2a ("YHWH's spirit ... upon ...") recurs seven times, suggesting that, although it is not a pervasive motif, it was deliberately diffused among these episodes by

---

[28] Cf. Noth, *Überlieferungsgeschichtliche Studien, I* (1943), ET: *Deuteronomistic History* (1981), p. 119 n. 19.

Judges' compiler/redactor—perhaps, even deliberately repeated seven times). Possible recurrences of motif D2a appear as follows:

D2a "YHWH's spirit ... upon ..."

(עם־השפט	יהוה		והיה	2:18aβ)
	רוח־יהוה	עליו	ותהי	3:10aαⁱ
לבשה את־גדעון /	ורוח יהוה		ותהי	6:34a
	על־יפתח רוח יהוה		ותהי	11:29aα
לפעמו [במחנה־דן] /	רוח יהוה		ותחל	13:25aαβⁱ
	רוח יהוה	עליו	ותצלח	14:6aα
	רוח יהוה	עליו	ותצלח	14:19aα
	רוח יהוה	עליו	ותצלח	15:14bα

(cf. בין אבימלך	רוח רעה		וישלח אלהים	
ובין בעלי שכם				9:23a)
(cf. ויחי	רוחו		ותשב	15:19aγ)
(cf.	כחו		ויסר	
		מעליו		16:19bβ)
(cf.	יהוה	והוא לא ידע / כי		
		מעליו	סר	16:20bγδ)

The key element of motif D2a is the expression רוח יהוה. Usually related is some verbal expression that the spirit of YHWH "came", "clothed" or "rushed" upon (על־) the deliverer.

Given that: (1) at least four recurrences of motif D2a occur in the Samson account (Judg. 13–16), (2) neither of the verbs used in the Samson account is repeated outside that account and (3) the deployment of this motif within the Samson account manifests concern for narrative development, it may be that motif D2a was original to the Samson traditions and that the compiler/redactor reused it when nuancing the accounts of Othniel, Gideon and Jephthah, where its occurrences are neither indispensable to narrative development nor as intricately networked as they are in the Samson account. In all cases, except perhaps that of Othniel (where a story line is virtually absent), recurrences of this motif are positioned outside the framework and function rhetorically within their respective narrative contexts.

The first occurrence of motif D2a in the Samson account (13:25aαβⁱ) is significant because: (1) it commences with the verb ותחל, which harks back to the use of the same verb in connection with motif D1 in 13:5b; (2) its connection with ותחל ... לפעמו ("began ... to pound him") may network motif D2a with the *Leitwort* פעם in the Samson account (i.e., 15:3; 16:18, 20 [cf. 20:30, 31], 28 [cf. 6:39]; cf. 5:28);[29]

---

[29] My thanks to Robert Alter for this insight in response to my question about the nuancing of narrative formulae on the occasion of his lecture, "Putting together Biblical

and (3) its connection with במחנה־דן furnishes a vital link with the temporally anterior but presentationally delayed portrayal of the departure of the Danite tribe from the same locale (cf. Judg. 18:12). The latter is an example of withholding information that is essential to understanding Samson's solitary role in Judges as the deliverer who never summoned his tribe to battle and who suffered a tragic demise both for his own foibles and for lack of his tribe's military backing.

The word order in 6:34a is emphatic—ורוח יהוה is introduced by *waw* disjunctive—which perhaps further illustrates the sensitivity with which this motif was adapted to the story line of the contexts into which it was diffused. Indeed, one possible form of motif D2a, that of 9:23a, shows how YHWH may issue a spirit of an entirely different nature to achieve his ends.

Twice in Judges a deliverer is said to have sounded the ram's horn, with the result that tribes were summoned to battle:

D2b "sounded the ram's horn"(?)
3:27aβ ויתקע בשופר בהר אפרים
6:34bα ויתקע בשופר

While the two occurrences of D2b scarcely constitute an independent motif in Judges, the close connection between the clothing of YHWH's spirit (motif D2a) in 6:34a and the sounding of the ram's horn in 6:34bα prompts one to see a link between the function of motif D2a, which always anticipates some heroic feat against an enemy of Israel, and that of the two occurrences of 'motif' D2b, both of which inaugurate battles leading to the Israelite tribes' deliverance.

Recurrences of the E1, E2a and E2b motifs describe the result of the efforts of judges equipped by YHWH's spirit, namely, the subjugation of

---

Narrative", at the Jewish Book Event, 5 March 1989, Pembroke College, Cambridge. The addition of לפעמו ... ותחל to the D2a motif describing Samson's first experience of the spirit of YHWH may be: (1) *ominously* related to Delilah's final instruction to the Philistines, עלו הפעם ("Come *once more*", 16:18a)—whereupon Samson's strength left him (16:19bβ), (2) *ironically* related to his presumption in 16:20, אצא כפעם בפעם ואנער והוא לא ידע כי יהוה סר מעליו ("I shall go out as on *previous occasions* and shall shake myself free—but he was unaware that YHWH had departed from him"), and/or (3) *poignantly* related to his final plea in 16:28 that YHWH restore his strength אך הפעם הזה ("only this *once*"). It is because of the networking of the D2a motif with the *Leitwort* פעם in the Samson account that I have included 16:19bβ, 20bγδ as tacit recurrences of motif D2a despite the absence of its key element רוח יהוה. Along the same line, 15:19aγ, which makes explicit Samson's preeminent concern with the resuscitation of his own human "spirit/strength" (15:18-19), was positioned to mark the transition to his relative lack of concern for respecting YHWH's spirit as the source of his superhuman strength (cf. 16:19bβ, 20bγδ that follow).

enemy oppressors. E1 consistently employs the verb כנע (3:30a; 4:23; 8:28aαβ; 11:33b), E2a uses נתן (1:2b, 4aβ; 2:23b; 3:10aγδ, 28aβ; 4:14aβ; 11:21a, 30b, 32b; 12:3aγ; [16:23bβγ, 24bβ]; 20:28bβ) and E2b uses מכר (4:9aδε). The latter motifs are clearly the antithetical counterparts to motifs B2a and B2b, respectively. Most scholars acknowledge that the 'E2' motifs, while perhaps not as pervasive as motifs A1a, B2a/B2b, C and D1, nevertheless constitute an essential element within Judges' cyclical framework. The four recurrences of E1 appear as follows:

E1   "[enemy] humbled ... before/by hand of [Israel]"

ותכנע מואב ביום ההוא / תחת יד ישראל			3:30a
ויכנע אלהים ביום ההוא /	את יבין מלך־כנען //		
לפני בני ישראל:			4:23
ויכנע מדין /	לפני בני ישראל /		8:28aαβ
ויכנעו בני עמון /	מפני בני ישראל		11:33b

All occurrences of E1 are positioned at nodal points in their respective narratives, though the occurrence in 11:33b is more melded with its context than are the others. The usual elements of this motif include: (a) the main verb כנע—three times Niphal, once Hiphil; (b) an enemy as subject of the Niphal or once as a direct object (with את) of the Hiphil; and (c) [בני] ישראל as the genitive of either [תחת] יד or מפני/לפני. A repeated phrase, ביום ההוא, links 3:30a and 4:23. Judges 4:23 is exceptional in that it alone employs the Hiphil verb.

Motif E1 in Judg. 4:23 is followed by two clauses in 4:24 that embellish it (i.e., // ותלך יד בני־ישראל הלוך וקשה / על יבין מלך־כנען עד אשר הכריתו / את יבין מלך־כנען:). Similarly, the E1 motif of 8:28aαβ is followed by one clause in 8:28aγ that embellishes it (i.e., ולא יספו לשאת ראשם). The presence of these 'embellishments' probably attests that the E1 motifs were the compiler/redactor's innovation at positions where alternative summaries of the subjugation of an enemy (which now appear as 'embellishments') had already existed. A similar redundancy is evident between 3:30a (E1) and 3:29 (i.e., ויכו את־מואב בעת ההיא / כעשרת אלפים איש / כל־שמן וכל־איש חיל // ולא נמלט איש:) and between 11:33b (E1) and 11:32b-33a (i.e., ויכם ויתנם יהוה בידו: מערוער ועד־בואך מנית עשרים עיר / ועד אבל כרמים / מכה גדולה מאד), though in these cases the summaries of the enemy's defeat precede, rather than follow, motif E1.[30]

---

[30] On Judg. 11:32b as an exemplar of motif element E2a, see below.

Recurrences of motif E2a include:

E2a "gave ... into hand of [Israel]"

(	בידו	את־הארץ	הנה נתתי 1:2b)
(		[את־הכנעני ו]הפרזי	ויתן יהוה
	בידם		1:4aβ)
(	ביד־יהושע		ולא נתנם 2:23b)
	בידו /		ויתן יהוה
	את־כושן רשעתים מלך ארם		3:10aγδ
	איביכם	את־	כי־נתן יהוה
	בידכם	את־מואב	3:28aβ
[כי זה היום אשר]			
	בידך	את־סיסרא	נתן יהוה 4:14aβ)
ישראל		ויתן יהוה אלהי־	
ואת־כל־עמו	את־סיחון		
ביד ישראל ויכום			11:21a
	את־בני עמון	אם־נתון תתן	
	בידי		11:30b
	בידו	ויתנם יהוה	11:32b
	בידי	ויתנם יהוה	12:3aγ
(	בידנו	אלהינו	נתן
אויבינו	את שמשון		16:23bβγ)
(	בידנו	אלהינו	נתן
אויבנו	את־		16:24bβ)
	בידך	כי מחר אתננו	20:28bβ

Motif E2a represents foreigners having been given into the hands of Israelites, though some occurrences represent Israelites having failed to conquer foreigners (2:23b). All thirteen examples of motif E2a use נתן and ביד־. The first and last occurrences (1:2b; 20:28bβ) are presented as the direct speech of YHWH, while those in 3:28aβ; 4:14aβ; 11:21a, 30b; 12:3aγ; 16:23bβγ, 24bβ are presented as the direct speech of Ehud, Deborah, Jephthah and the Philistines (the remainder being narrated in third person). Since 20:28bβ is related to the general context of ch. 20, where Judah is again elected to lead the Israelite tribal league (20:18), one may be justified in proposing that the development from thesis (1:2b) to antithesis (20:28bβ) was designed by the compiler/ redactor to relate Israel's failure to the issue of Judah's preeminence over Benjamin. It seems not by accident that three of the five recurrences of E2a that present foreigners being given into Israelite hands (i.e., 1:2b, 4aβ; 3:10aγδ) pertain either to Judah's success or to Israel's success under a Judahite deliverer. The occurrences in 16:23bβγ, 24bβ are unusual because they are ironic and because, like many instances of short quotations in Judges, they are presented in verse. Perhaps significantly, many occurrences pertain to the Israelites' success under anomalous or negatively characterized leaders: a left-handed Benjaminite, Ehud (3:28aβ); a reluctant warrior, Barak (4:14aβ), who may be partly discounted because Sisera himself is never delivered into his hand; and an opportunistic manipulator of YHWH (cf. 11:30b, 32b) and of intertribal rivalry (12:3aγ), Jephthah. As to Ehud, if one considers the correlation of motif B2a with the portrayal of Judah and left-handed Benjaminites elsewhere in Judges (cf. 20:16 with 20:28bβ), it may be that the account of Ehud was designed to heighten Judges' implicit foil of Judah against Benjamin.

One factor that may weigh against the view that the E2a motif is a compilational/redactional innovation is the fact that, while 11:32b is positioned so close to the E1 motif of 11:33b as to appear designed, the same pattern of proximity occurs between recurrences of E1 and other, variously worded statements of the subjugation of enemies (cf. E1 in 3:30a with 3:29 [but E2a in 3:28aβ], E1 in 4:23 with 4:24 [but E2a in 4:14aβ], E1 in 8:28aαβ with 8:28aγ [but no E2a in this account]). Nevertheless, the phraseological correspondence between motif E2a and B2a, which parallels that between E2b and B2b, supports the probability that motif E2a was diffused among the deliverer accounts and Dénouement-B by the compiler/redactor (possibly from its primary use in one of the accounts). It should be emphasized, as has just been implied, that motifs E2a/E2b furnish a thematically analogous complement to motifs B2a/B2b. This analogy may be further substantiated by the relative positions of the 'B2' and 'E2' elements in the aggregate order of elements in Judges' cycle-motif (see below).

Only once is there an example of an element that might constitute a E2b motif in which an enemy of Israel is the object of YHWH's retribution:

E2b "sold ... into hand of [Israel]"
(/ כי ביד־אשה

4:9aδε)   ימכר יהוה את־סיסרא

This clause predicts that an individual enemy will fall into the hands of (note the emphatic word order) a woman (4:9aδε)—yet not even she will prove to be a bona fide Israelite (cf. 1:16; 4:11, 17, 21).[31]

---

[31] The appearance of motif E2b in 4:9aδ may have been intrinsic to the narrative before the compiler's innovations. Cf. Murray's observation that, contrary to the formulaic nature of this so-called 'committal-formula', the present example is nonstereotypical: "the present usage is unique in Judges in syntactical form, in occurring in a narrative rather than in an editorial context, and in a normal 'Holy War' usage of the committal-formula, rather than the editorial 'anti-Holy War' usage" ("Narrative Structure" [1979], p. 178 n. 42).

Like motifs A1a, B2a/B2b, C, D1, E1 and E2a/E2b, motifs F1 and
F2 are often regarded among the essential motifs of Judges' framework. The succeeding motif (F1) is one of the most pervasive motif
elements in Judges, for it recurs in all the accounts of the 'minor'
judges as well as those of the 'major' judges:

F1   "... judged ... Israel (N years)"

(			כל ימי השופט	2:18aδ)
		את־ישראל	וישפט	3:10aαii
	בעת ההיא	את־ישראל	היא שפטה	4:4b
(		בני ישראל	ויעלו אליה	
			למשפט	4:5b)
שנה	עשרים ושלש /	את־ישראל	וישפט	10:2a
שנה	עשרים ושתים /	את־ישראל	וישפט	10:3b
שנים	שש	את־ישראל יפתח	וישפט	12:7a
		את־ישראל אחריו	וישפט	12:8a
שנים	שבע	את־ישראל	וישפט	12:9b
		את־ישראל אחריו	וישפט	12:11aα
שנים	עשר	את־ישראל	וישפט	12:11b
		את־ישראל אחריו	וישפט	12:13a
שנים	שמנה	את־ישראל	וישפט	12:14b
[בימי פלשתים]		את־ישראל	וישפט	
שנה	עשרים	עשרים		15:20i,iii
שנה	עשרים	את־ישראל עשרים	והוא שפט	16:31b

The components of the F1 formula usually include: (a) the verb שָׁפט,
(b) the direct object את־ישראל and (c) a period expressed in a number
of years. The formulaic regularity of this motif is so apparent that
almost all scholars acknowledge this as one of the pervasive motifs of
Judges' framework. Most recurrences of this motif within the deliverer
stories are positioned at nodal points in the narrative (3:10aαii; 12:7a;
15:20i,iii; 16:31b). Those at 4:4b, 5b are unusual in both form (4:4b
using the Qal active ptcp f. sg) and position (at the beginning of the
account) and thus may have been part of the traditional form of the
Deborah/Barak/Jael account, which the compiler/redactor later
nuanced (perhaps by adding 4:4b, in which the usual temporal
component of F1 [c] is contextualized to בעת היא).[32] Of the two occurrences in the Samson account (15:20i,iii and 16:31b), it is the former
that conforms most closely to the standard form of the motif. This suggests that the latter was either primary, if the difference was
unmotivated, or altered for rhetorical reasons—perhaps also to furnish
a masculine counterpart to the feminine form of 4:4b (i.e., היא שפטה
[Qal ptcp] of 4:4b resembles והוא שפט [Qal perf.] of 16:31b).

---

[32] Pace Moore, Judges (1895), p. 113.

It is probably the sparse detail of the 'minor' judge reports (10:1-5; 12:8-15) that prompted scholars to view motif F1 as a primary component of these reports. The strict alternating pattern and contiguity between the ending formula of 12:8a, 11aα and 13a (cf. 10:2a, 3b), on the one hand, and the beginning formula of 12:7a, 9b, 11b and 14b, on the other, may have prompted this perception. Some allege that the compiler/redactor borrowed the F1 'judge' motif from these 'minor' judge reports and diffused it among the deliverer accounts, positioning it at nodal points in their respective narratives to lend coherence to the book, which thus became a composite of judge and deliverer accounts. But the fact that the ending formula recurs in 15:20[i,iii] and, in modified form, in 16:31b (concluding the Samson account)—indeed, the very contiguity of 12:7a with the succeeding pattern of alternation—should caution one against surmising too hastily that its presence in 12:7a (at the end of the Jephthah account) proves that the name of Jephthah once also appeared in an alleged roster of 'minor' judges that the compiler/redactor incorporated into the book. It may be, rather, that motif F1 was inserted at 12:7a under the same editorial concern that prompted its insertion at 15:20[i,iii], 16:31b and (minus the number formula) 3:10aα[ii]. Hence, the interposition of the Jephthah deliverer account (10:6–12:7) between two rosters of 'minor' judges (10:1-5; 12:8-15) may have been prompted, not because this had been the position that the Jephthah-as-'minor'-judge report held within an original judge roster, but because the compiler/redactor intended to break the roster of 'minor' judges precisely where the deliverer account of "Jephthah the Gileadite" (11:1aα) would occur in contiguity with the account of a 'minor' judge of Gilead, namely, "Jair the Gileadite" (10:3-5). Judges 12:7a (F1), as well as the terminal elements of 12:7bαβ (G1) and 12:7bγ (G2) (see below), may only then have been appended to the Jephthah account to bring it into agreement with the succeeding 'minor' judge reports.

The four F2 motif recurrences are as follows:

F2 "land had peace N years"

ותשקט הארץ ארבעים שנה	3:11a
ותשקט הארץ שמונים שנה	3:30b
ותשקט הארץ ארבעים שנה	5:31b
ותשקט הארץ ארבעים שנה [בימי גדעון]	8:28b[i-ii]

The F2 formula includes: (a) the main verb ותשקט, (b) the subject הארץ and (c) a period expressed in a number of years. The fact that F1 and F2 find their closest analogy in their expression of a period in a number of years (element [c]) parallels the fact that motifs B3a and B3b share the expression of a period in a number of years (element [d]). When this is considered alongside the implicit antithesis between the themes of motif elements B3a/B3b (servitude/oppression) and F1/F2 (independence/peace), there is good reason to surmise that the compiler/redactor intended the 'F' motifs to provide an analogous complement to the 'B3' motifs within Judges' cycle-motif. This analogy becomes even more apparent when one considers the relative positions of the 'B3' and 'F' motifs in the order of the cycle-motif (see below).

Two out of four appearances of motif element F2 are linked with F1 in the same account. Yet, because of a general pattern of analogous complementarity elsewhere among accounts that contain either F1 or F2 but not both, it is probable that one of the two was diffused by the compiler/redactor who, by means of its insertion, may have intended to provide each judge account with a summary of the postdeliverance period expressed in a number of years. Only in the Othniel account (which admits to being an innovation of the compiler/redactor) and in the Deborah/Barak/Jael account (by the accident that 4:5b sufficiently resembled motif F1 to prompt the compiler/redactor to insert 4:4b [F1]) do F1 and F2 motifs appear together in the same account. But it is the contiguity of the F1 and F2 motifs in 3:7-11 that best attests the compiler/redactor's intention that they be seen to function analogously within Judges' recurring cycle-motif.

Unlike motifs F1 and F2, which seem to show an analogous complementarity in distribution among the accounts, motifs G1 and G2 appear juxtaposed in all but three accounts, and both are absent from only one (that of Deborah/Barak/Jael). It is surprising, therefore, that, unlike motifs A1a, B2a/B2b, C, D1, E1, E2a/E2b and F1/F2, motifs G1 and G2 are not always included among those elements generally considered to be essential to Judges' editorial framework.[33] The G1 motifs recur as follows:

---

[33] Cf. Trompf, "Notions" (1979), pp. 219-20; Mayes, *Story* (1983), pp. 61-62; Greenspahn, "Theology" (1986), p. 388.

G1   "and ... died"

(	מות יהושע		אחרי	ויהי	1:1aα)
(	יהושע בן־נון עבד יהוה //	וימת			
בן־מאה ועשר שנים					2:8)
	במות השופט			והיה	2:19aα
	עתניאל בן־קנז	וימת			3:11b
<	ואהוד				
		מת			4:1b>
[גדעון בן־יואש בשיבה טובה]		וימת			8:32aⁱ
<(/ וישובו בני ישראל)	גדעון	מת	כאשר	ויהי	8:33aα(β)>
(		וימת	[וידקרהו נערו]		9:54bⁱⁱ)
([איש־ישראל				[ויראו	
[ויקבר בשמיר]	אבימלך	מת	כי		9:55aⁱⁱ)
		וימת			10:2bⁱ
	יאיר	וימת			10:5α
הגלעדי	יפתח	וימת /			12:7bαβ
	אבצן	וימת			12:10α
הזבולני	אלון	וימת			12:12a
בן־הלל הפרעתוני	עבדון	וימת			12:15a
(		ויהיו המתים אשר המית במותו /			
		רבים מאשר המית בחייו			16:30b)

The usual components of motif G1 are: (a) the verb מות or היה in combination with a derivative of מות and (b) the personal name of a judge (sometimes with epithet). This motif element, like D1, F1, and G2 (see below), is one of the regular elements in the 'minor' judge reports (10:1-5, 12:8-15). Unlike G2, however, it occasionally appears in deliverer accounts in the first half of the book (3:11b; 4:1b; 8:32aⁱ, 33aα; 9:54bⁱⁱ, 55aⁱⁱ). Judges 4:1b, which would have been expected after 3:30, may have been displaced to interlock the Ehud and Deborah/Barak/Jael accounts by the insertion of both the Shamgar notice (3:31)—designed to anticipate the mention of Shamgar in 5:6a—and the A1a motif (4:1a). This displacement has the additional effect of showing a close, almost causal connection between the death of the judge and Israel's relapse into apostasy (cf. 2:19). One may note a similar rhetorical function for 8:33aα in 8:33-34.

The possible case of G1 in 1:1aα could be discounted as a cycle-motif element on the ground that it is modelled after the first clause of Josh. 1:1, ויהי אחרי מות משה, and thus is probably not an innovation of the compiler/redactor. The occurrence in 2:8 that, like its surrounding verses, is borrowed from Josh. 24:29aγb could also be discounted as a creation of the compiler/redactor. However, in the light of the recurring role that the mortality of leaders plays in Judges' cycle-motif, it remains possible that Judges' compiler/redactor intended even these

borrowings from the book of Joshua to function as recurrences of motif
G1. At the very least, its presence within Prologue-B (2:19aα) con-
tends for the view that the compiler/redactor may have intended motif
G1 to function as an essential element of Judges' cycle-motif. In the
account of the antideliverer Abimelech, the G1 motif (9:55a) does not
describe the point from which Israel resumes doing evil but at which
they return to their homes (9:55b; cf. 2:6b).

Recurrences of the related motif G2 include:

G2 "was buried ... at"

(	ויקברו אותו בגבול נחלתו /	
	בתמנת־חרס	
	בהר אפרים	2:9a)
ויקבר /	[בקבר יואש אביו /	
	בעפרה אבי העזרי]	8:32bα
[וימת] ויקבר	בשמיר	10:2bⁱⁱ
ויקבר	בקמון	10:5β
ויקבר	בע<י>ר<ו>	12:7bγ
	<ב[מ]צפה> גלעד	
ויקבר	בבית לחם	12:10β
ויקבר	באילון	
	בארץ זבולן	12:12b
ויקבר	בפרעתון	
	בארץ אפרים /	
	בהר העמלקי	12:15b
ויעלו ויקברו אותו בין צרעה ובין אשתאל /		
בקבר מנוח אביו		16:31aβ-δ

The two components of motif G2 are: (a) the main verb קבר (usually
Ni. pret. 3 m. sg, ויקבר; though twice Pi. pret. 3 m. pl., ויקברו) and
(b) a location prefixed with preposition ־ב. It is perhaps significant that
the majority of G2 recurrences are contained in the second half of the
book, which, also in other respects, presents an ever-darkening mood.

Like the possible occurrence of G1 in Judg. 2:8, which is borrowed
from Josh. 24:29aγb, the possible case of G2 in Judg. 2:9a, which
edits Josh. 24:30, could be discounted as a cycle-motif element.
However, the contiguity of Judg. 2:8 (G1) with 2:9a (G2) and their
analogy with the forms of the G1 and G2 motifs may indicate the
compiler/redactor's concern to link the mortality of Joshua as a leader
with the mortality of the succeeding judges. The similarity of form
between 2:9a and 16:31aβ-δ may weigh in favour of viewing the latter
as a cycle-motif element within the Samson account.

The consistent form of the recurrences of motifs G1 and G2 in the
'minor' judge reports (10:1-5; 12:8-15) has prompted scholars to infer

that these elements, like that of F1, were primary to an alleged roster that the compiler/redactor used as a source for these accounts.[34] Of course, it remains possibile that this regularity of form reflects nothing more than the compiler/redactor's consistent application of these death and burial formulae to the shorter reports of the 'minor' judges. Yet, the combination of these recurrences with the occurrence of G1 in 3:11b and the recurrences of G1 and G2 in combination (2:8, 9a; 8:32a^i, 32bα; and perhaps 16:30b, 31a$\beta\gamma$) seems to evidence the compiler/redactor's concern to diffuse these motifs among the deliverer stories. Further, the diffusion of the G1 and G2 motif elements among the deliverer accounts is a factor that weighs against the hypothesis that Jephthah's name necessarily appeared in the alleged judge roster because it retains vestiges of motif elements G1 and G2. Just as Judg. 12:7a (F1), which ends the Jephthah account, may have been appended to the account only to bring it into closer harmony with the succeeding 'minor' judge reports (see above), so also the terminal elements of 12:7b$\alpha\beta$ (G1) and 12:7bγ (G2), on analogy with their insertion at the end of other deliverer accounts (i.e., G1 at 3:11b, 8:32a^i, [16:30b]; G2 at 8:32bα, 16:31aβ-δ), may have been inserted only to bring this account into closer harmony with the 'minor' judge reports.

I shall now attempt to formulate a judgement about the rhetoric of Judges' cycle-motif. The aggregate structure of Judges' cycle-motif appears to have been ordered into two discernible phases. The aliena- tion phase, which comprises (i) A1a A1b, (ii) A2a A2b, (iii) B1, (iv) B2a B2b, (v) B3a B3b/$^{i/ii}$ and (vi) C, stems from Israel's ignorance of/apostasy from YHWH (i and ii) and leads to Israel's recognition of/cry to YHWH for deliverance (vi). The restoration phase, which comprises (vii) D1, (viii) D2a D2b, (ix) E1, (x) E2a E2b, (xi) F1 F2 and (xii) G1 G2, stems from YHWH's raising up of a saviour (vii) and leads to the eventual demise of that saviour (xii). The first and final ele- ments of both phases (i.e., i-ii, vi; and vii, xii, respectively) mark the turning points of the cycle—the final element, in each case, furnishing the necessary condition for the first element of the next phase in what may be deemed a 'ring pattern'. The function of the final element to prepare for the next phase seems patently obvious in the relation between motifs C and D1. It is less obvious in the case of G1/G2 and A1a, but such a preparatory connection would explain the displacement

---

[34] The preposition (וֹ)אחרי, which appears in each of and almost exclusively in the 'minor' judge reports (10:1aα, 3aα; 12:8a, 11aα, 13a; but cf. אחרי in 1:1aα), is also adduced as evidence of the report form used in the alleged judge roster.

of Judg. 4:1b (G1), which normally would follow 3:30, to follow both the Shamgar notice (3:31; cf. 5:6a) and, more significantly, the succeeding A1a motif (4:1a). The interlocking of motif elements G1 (4:1b) and A1a (4:1a) has the rhetorical effect of showing a close, almost causal connection between the death of the deliverer/judge and Israel's return to apostasy. Indeed, this is the connection explicitly drawn in 2:19 and 8:33-34.

The intermediary motif elements of each phase (i.e., iii, iv, v; and viii, ix, x, xi), while facilitating the transition from the first to the final elements of each phase, appear to follow an antithetical sequence— (viii) and (ix) reverse (iii), (x) reverses (iv), and (xi) reverses (v). Note the correspondences in the following schema:

ALIENATION PHASE: *RESTORATION PHASE:*

Problem Conceived:		*Solution Initiated:*
(i)	A1a A1b Israelites did evil before YHWH/ right ... eyes	
(ii)	A2a A2b served the Baals ... followed other gods and worshipped them/ forsook YHWH	(vii) D1 YHWH raised up [judge] to save

(iii)	B1 YHWH's anger burned against Israel	≠	(viii)	D2a [D2b] YHWH's spirit ... upon [judge]
		≠	(ix)	E1 [enemy] humbled ... before Israel
(iv)	B2a B2b YHWH gave/sold [Israel] into hand of ...	≠	(x)	E2a E2b gave/sold ... into hand of [Israel]
(v)	B3a B3b/ⁱ/ⁱⁱ Israelites served/ oppressed ... N years	≠	(xi)	F1 F2 judged ... Israel/ land had peace N years

Problem Acknowledged/ Solution Requested:		*Dissolution:*
(vi)	C Israelites cried to YHWH	(xii) G1 G2 [judge] died/ was buried ...

Whereas it could be argued that some elements of this twelve-part cycle-motif were diffused among the accounts at redactional stages later than the original compilation of Judges, it is evident that the selection, arrangement and nuancing of these accounts was such as to conform to the exigencies of the cycle-motif scheme outlined above. Indeed, it is difficult to find any substantial analogy or coherence among all the various accounts apart from that which is furnished by the recurring cycle-motif, which attests a coherent editorial aim.[35] There is no reason to deny the likelihood that the stories had distinct origins, traditions, forms and functions in separate tribal enclaves of Israel prior to their assemblage into the book of Judges, but neither do there seem to be compelling indications that the individual accounts and stories of Judges must have been combined into the present corpus through a minimum of two editorial stages just because there may be at least two different types (genres) of account (e.g., the 'minor' judge reports vs. the deliverer stories) so incorporated.[36] All elements of the cycle-motif, which any of the various accounts now have in common, cohere under the editorial scheme outlined above, so there seems little empirical evidence to support the view that there was more than one edition of Judges.[37] If there ever was a distinctive form of the cycle-motif used by an earlier compiler, a later redactor of Judges so subsumed it under the final aggregate form of the cycle-motif that whatever lines that may have distinguished the earlier form from the later have disappeared.

Support for the view that Judges' cycle-motif conforms to the concerns of a single rhetorical design may be adduced partly from the bifurcated, nearly symmetrical form of the cycle-motif. Almost all the

---

[35] However, it remains an unconfirmable possibility that certain aspects of the "heroic emplotment" of Judges' deliverers (e.g., all overcome some anomalous personal characteristic that made them unlikely candidates as heroes or heroines) were imposed by the compiler/redactor as a device for achieving historiographic coherence (cf. R. A. Wood, "The Major Judges and the Judgment of the Deuteronomist", unpublished paper presented at the SBL Annual Meeting, Anaheim, California, November 19, 1989, pp. 21-25).

[36] While it may be true that there are traces of different regional dialects between various longer accounts, unless the compiler/redactor deliberately employed dialectal verisimilitude, he/she made little attempt to suppress the impression that he/she borrowed his/her materials from the heroic lore of culturally diverging tribes whom he/she may thus have been upbraiding for disunity. It may further have been part of the rhetorical design of Judges that the compiler/redactor represented the tribal heroes according to their own traditional lore and regional dialects so as to reduce the suspicion that he/she was actually bent on a strategy to undercut (through a rhetoric of entrapment) the probable original design of these stories to exalt tribal representatives through heroic emplotment.

[37] Possible later glosses, such as that of 18:30b, do not constitute redactional strata.

motif elements contained in the alienation phase of the cycle-motif find phraseological parallels in the deuteronomic phraseology of Joshua 23–24 or the book of Deuteronomy:

A1a		Deut. 4:25bγ^i; 9:18bβ^i; 17:2bβ^i; 31:29bβ; ($\neq$ 6:18a; 12:25bβ, 28bβγ; 13:19b; 21:9b)
A1b		$\neq$ Deut. 12:8aα/b
A2a	Josh. 23:7bβγ, 16aβ-δ; 24:16b, 20aβ	Deut. 5:9a; 6:14; 7:16bα,γ; 8:19aγ-ε; 11:16bγ; 31:16bαβ, 18b, 20bα
A2b	Josh. 24:5b-6aα, 16aγ, 17aβ, 20aα	Deut. 4:20a, 37b; 5:6β; 6:12b, 21b; 8:14bβ; 9:26b; 31:16bγ, ($\neq$ 17aα), [cf. 20bβ]
B1	Josh. 23:16bα	Deut. 4:25bγ^{ii}; 31:29bγ Deut. 7:4bα; 11:17aα; 31:17aα
B2a	$\neq$ Josh. 24:8bα, 11b	$\neq$ Deut. 7:2a
B3b^i		Deut. 26:7bβ
C	Josh. 24:7aα	Deut. 26:7a

Since phraseological parallels can be found in Deuteronomy for Judges' motif elements A1a, A1b, A2a, A2b, B1, B2a, B3b^i and C—motif elements exclusively contained within the alienation phase of Judges' cycle-motif—one may justly disagree with Boling's assertion that the only clear lexical or stylistic parallel with Deuteronomy in the 'pragmatic formula' (i.e., Judges' cycle-motif) is the statement "they did evil" (cf. Deut. 17:2).[38] That no such conformity to deuteronomic phraseology can be found in the restoration phase of Judges' cycle-motif results in a bifurcated schema that reflects a strategy to portray, in the alienation phase, Israel's propensity to rebel against the covenant stipulations of YHWH attested in Deuteronomy and, in the restoration phase, YHWH's grace in repeatedly restoring Israel to the blessing of peace in the land.

---

[38] Boling, *Judges* (1975), pp. 35-36; so Gooding, "Composition" (1982), p. 72*.

CHAPTER TWO

RHETORICAL CONCERNS OF JUDGES AS A LITERARY FORM

In the present chapter, I shall examine the formal arrangement of the prose and poetic accounts of Judges so as to determine their rhetorical concerns. All the deliverer accounts and both of the accounts of the double dénouement (17–18; 19–21) are plot-based. Thus, in these sections, the rhetorical analysis will be controlled primarily by concerns made evident from analysis of the plot-structure, though characterization will also play a significant role. Judges' double prologue (1:1–2:5; 2:6–3:6) is not controlled by a plot-structure, so the rhetorical analysis of these sections must be determined on the basis of concerns made evident from matters such as change of subject, order of arrangement, relative proportion and, where relevant, characterization.

A. JUDGES' DOUBLE PROLOGUE

Covenantal concerns, implicit in the presentation of Israel's tribal heroes in Judges and in the content and arrangement of Judges' pervasive cycle-motif, are already evident in the two parts of Judges' double prologue (1:1–2:5; 2:6–3:6). Judges' double prologue introduces two successive exordia—one for its tribal schema, one for its cycle-motif schema—that are superimposed upon the body of Judges (3:7–16:31). In the first two sections of the present chapter, I shall examine what rhetorical role each part of the double prologue plays in orienting the reader to the subject of the book. It should be evident that, in both parts of the double prologue, the language and standards by which the tribes are measured resemble the language and standards of YHWH's covenant with Israel as set forth in the book of Deuteronomy. Thus, already in the double prologue it appears that Judges was concerned to show that the effects of Israel's covenant compromise—namely, their indolence in expelling Canaanites from their land, repeated lapses into idolatry, disregard for maintaining the national cult and the Levites, intertribal fragmentation and failure to uphold covenant justice—could be overcome only by their united endorsement of a leadership that would uphold the ideals of land occupation, intertribal unity, cultic order and social justice prescribed by YHWH's covenant with Israel. The rhetorical function of Judges' double prologue, therefore, is to expose the problematic character of Israel's indolence toward YHWH's commission to expel the Canaanites from the land and the problem of their propensity to relapse into idolatry.

As an exposition of the problems that prevent Israel from covenant loyalty, the double prologue contributes little toward the final resolution of those problems. However, the deuteronomic phraseology in Prologue-A (1:1–2:5) and Prologue-B (2:6–3:6) that alludes to Deuteronomy 4–11 (especially ch. 7), 20, 31 and to Joshua 23–24 discloses that the focus of the compiler/redactor's concern was on the problem of the tribes' covenant (cultic) disloyalty to YHWH in the land.[1] Concern about the interdependence of cultic loyalty to YHWH and the occupation of the land is evident in the prologues' emphasis upon either failure to occupy the land (Prologue-A) or cultic disloyalty (Prologue-B). The cycle-motif pattern of Prologue-B outlines problems that relate to Israel's undulating pattern of alienation from and restoration to YHWH, but it never furnishes a resolution to the problems introduced by Prologue-A, namely, Israel's toleration of foreigners in the land and consequent propensity toward idolatry. Indeed, the various deliverer episodes contained in the body of Judges (3:7–16:31), each of which has its own problem–resolution plot-structure (that follows the cycle-motif pattern of Prologue-B), only illustrate the problematic effects of the covenant (cultic) compromise introduced in Prologue-A.[2]

§1. *Prologue-A (1:1–2:5): The Dependence of Land Occupation upon Cultic Loyalty*

Conquest of neighbouring foreign peoples figures prominently in the characterization of Judah, Benjamin and the tribes associated with the "House of Joseph" in Prologue-A (1:1–2:5), but the main focus remains upon the more fundamental issue that the expulsion of foreigners was to be but an expression of Israel's national commitment to

---

[1] The extent to which these are also thematic concerns in Joshua has been brought out by D. M. Gunn, "Joshua and Judges", in *The Literary Guide to the Bible* (R. Alter and F. Kermode [eds.], Cambridge, Mass., 1987), pp. 107-12.

[2] Prologue-A may hint that a resolution may be expected to emerge from the tribe of Judah, since this tribe's characterization is the most favourable of the tribes depicted in 1:1–2:5. Prologue-A may further hint that Jerusalem, which features prominently in the structure of 1:1–2:5 and which plays a prominent role in the contrasting characterizations of Judah vs. Benjamin, may be a token of YHWH's divine favour. However, such hints are not obvious during one's first reading of Prologue-A and become apparent only after one reflects upon the significance of the monarchical idealization introduced in chs. 17–21.

YHWH and his covenant with them (1:1-2; 2:1-5). In the structure of
Judg. 1:1-2:5, it is not simply the tribes' partial success in conquering
Canaan (1:3-36) that offers the reason for YHWH's judgement that
Israel should thereafter have only partial success in conquering Canaan
(2:3abα) and suffer consequent seduction to the foreigners' idolatry
(2:3bβ). Rather, implicit in the allusions to Deut. 31:14-29 and Joshua
23-24 that are contained in YHWH's final denunciation (Judg. 2:2b-3) is
a rebuke that Israel's failure to conquer is but an expression of their
more fundamental failure of covenant loyalty to YHWH (cf. 2:1).

Following a short portrayal of Judah's election to be first among the
tribes to conquer the land after Joshua's death (1:1-2), Prologue-A
shows, in three subdivisions, how and why the conquest had failed
(1:3-20; 1:22-36; 2:1-5). Each subdivision commences with "and N
went up": that concerning Judah (1:4aα, ויעל יהודה), that concerning
the Joseph league (1:22a, ויעלו בית־יוסף גם־הם) and that showing how
YHWH's angel condemned "all Israel" for disregarding YHWH's
prohibition against forming treaties with the native inhabitants of the
land (2:1, ויעל מלאך־יהוה).[3]

The designation בית־יוסף (1:22a, 23a, 35b) serves as an inclusio to
frame 1:22-36.[4] Thus, the northern tribes are grouped together with
"the house of Joseph", whose mention frames the tribes listed in
1:22-36. Since the fifteen verses that these repetitions embrace propor-
tionally balance the eighteen verses that feature Judah–Simeon
(1:3-20), it was probably the compiler/redactor's intention to portray
Judah–Simeon as one entity to be compared with the Joseph league.[5]
This leaves the intervening portrayal of Benjamin (1:21) conspicuously

---

[3] Other uses of עלה do occur (1:1b, 2a, 3a, 16a; 2:1b), but they do not have the structural prominence that these uses attain by virtue of their sentence-initial position, each
time demarcating the beginning of a subdivision.

[4] So A. G. Auld, "Judges i and History: A Reconsideration", *VT* 25 (1975), p. 267;
B. G. Webb, *The Book of the Judges: An Integrated Reading* (JSOTS 46, Sheffield, 1987),
p. 92.

[5] That this was intended is made more apparent by the insertion of גם־הם in 1:22a after
the demarcating clause ויעלו בית־יוסף (cf. Webb, *Judges* [1987], p. 92). L. R. Klein
observed that, because Judah–Simeon are nowhere said actually to "take" a city but only
to "destroy" the city Zephath (1:17), Simeon is demonstrably excluded from the divine
promise to give the land only to Judah (1:2) (*The Triumph of Irony in the Book of Judges*
[JSOTS 68, BLS 14, Sheffield, 1988], pp. 23-24, 29). Nevertheless, the framing position
of references to the Judah–Simeon pact (1:3, 17) within the section that features these two
tribes (1:3-20) still suggests the compiler/redactor's intention to portray Judah–Simeon as
a single entity (even if Simeon was assimilated; Klein, *Triumph of Irony* [1988], pp. 24,
224 n. 26) and as distinct from the Joseph conglomerate.

isolated from both tribal entities—a phenomenon that rhetorically parallels Benjamin's portrayal in Judges 19–21, where this tribe is isolated as the object of "all Israel's" holy war.[6]

Framing this introduction (1:1–2:5) are two portrayals of בני ישראל (1:1a, בני ישראל; 2:4a, כל־בני ישראל; cf. ישראל alone in 1:28a) standing before YHWH in cultic submission: first, voluntarily (1:1-2), then, remorsefully (2:1-5). As contextualized between these divergent characterizations of the entire nation, the contrast between the minor failures of Judah–Simeon (1:3-20) versus the major failures of the Joseph group (1:22-36) furnishes yet another antithetical portrayal that, in turn, flanks the depiction of Benjamin's total failure (1:21). As viewed from the perspective of the outer flanking tiers (1:1-2; 2:1-5), the main cause of the failed conquest was Israel's failure to obey YHWH's covenant stipulation to shun peaceful relations with the natives of the land. Judah–Simeon, to some degree, and the Joseph tribes, to a greater degree, failed in this regard, but, with a focus upon the structural turning point (1:21), one might want to infer that the compiler/ redactor regarded Benjamin's failure to dislodge the Jebusites from Jerusalem as the greatest failure. Indeed, the centrality of the note on Benjamin's failure to expel the Jebusites from Jerusalem (1:21) may implicate this tribe in such a way as to suggest that Benjamin was at the centre of the compiler/redactor's concern with "all Israel"— particularly since 1:21 is strategically wedged between explicit statements that "YHWH was with" Judah and the Joseph league (1:19a, ויהי יהוה את־יהודה; 1:22, ויהוה עמם ... ויעלו בית־יוסף גם־הם) to grant them at least partial success in their occupation of the land. Might Benjamin's lack of even partial success be taken to imply that YHWH was not with Benjamin?[7] It is perhaps important for discerning the

---

[6] Note how the word order of 1:21a is reversed in relation to that which describes the sparing of foreign cities by other tribes (see the table on 1:27-36, below). As a historical parallel, note that, in the aftermath of Saul's death described in 2 Sam. 1–4, the Benjaminites (and the citizens of Jabesh-Gilead) were alone in maintaining strong support for the Saulide dynasty (cf. 2 Sam. 2:15; 3:19 vs. 3:17 [re: Jabesh-Gilead, cf. 1 Sam. 31:11-13; 2 Sam. 2:4b-7]). The other tribes, who had continued to follow the house of Saul out of old-order loyalty (and perhaps geopolitical proximity), were becoming less inclined to follow the Saulide dynasty than to follow David (cf. 2 Sam. 3:17 vs. 3:19; 5:1, 3).

[7] A. B. Ehrlich, however, considered Benjamin to have been linked solely with Judah: "Denn unser Verfasser denkt offenbar an die Zeit, wo Israel in zwei Reiche geteilt war, weshalb er den Stamm Benjamin zum Reiche Juda zählt. Demgemäss nennt er das andere Reich V. 22 und 23 בית יוסף und zählt dazu die in V. 27-34 genannten Stämme" (*Randglossen zur hebräischen Bibel: Textkritisches, sprachliches und sachliches* [7 vols., Leipzig, 1908–1914], vol. 3, *Josua, Richter, I und II Samuelis* [1910], repr. edn [Hildesheim, 1968], p. 69).

compiler/redactor's rhetorical motive for isolating Benjamin at 1:21 to notice there the single point of condemnation: they did not expel the Jebusites from Jerusalem. That the compiler/redactor's rhetorical concern in 1:1–2:5 focuses upon a contrast between Judah and Benjamin with respect to Jerusalem may be inferred from the pivotal role played by the two verses in which Jerusalem is mentioned, namely, 1:21 (the structural axis of 1:1–2:5) and 1:8 (the axis of 1:3-18; see below). It is the compiler/redactor's implicit concern with Jerusalem that puts Benjamin into contrast with Israel, in general, and with Judah, in particular.

The four main subdivisions of Prologue-A, each of which opens with a demarcating use of עלה, frame the pivotal description of Benjamin's failure (1:21) in the following way:

A   Cultic Assembly: YHWH's commission of *all Israel*   /מי יעלה־לנו

       to follow *Judah* and conquer the land 1:1-2   יהודה יעלה

B   Accounts attesting the general success of   ויעל יהודה

       Judah–Simeon in conquering their cities 1:3-18

    C a Concluding Summary: YHWH's presence and

         Judah's relative success (except plains) 1:19

         (1:19a) ויהי יהוה את־יהודה / וירש את־ההר

       b Parade Example: *Judah's* occupation and

         dispossession of Hebron's citizens (3 giants)

         1:20

    AXIS: Failure of *Benjamin* to conquer Jerusalem 1:21

    Cⁱ a Anticipatory Summary: YHWH's presence and   ויעלו בית־יוסף

         Joseph league's promise of success 1:22   גם־הם

         (1:22b) ויהוה עמם

       b Parade Example: *Joseph league's* conquest

         through concession with one of Bethel's

         citizens 1:23-26

   Bⁱ   Accounts attesting the general failure of the

       Joseph league in conquering their cities 1:27-36

Aⁱ   Cultic Assembly: YHWH's rebuke of *all Israel*   ויעל מלאך־יהוה

     for failure to alienate natives of the land 2:1-5

Within the subunit 1:3-20, the conquest accounts of Judah are arranged to accord with an ascent–descent strategy: ascent in Judg. 1:4-7/8, descent in 1:9-16/17/18 (cf. 1:9, ואחר ירדו בני יהודה). The first conquest account of the 'ascent' section, 1:4-7, begins ויעל יהודה (1:4aα) and continues ויכום (1:4bα). Note the parallel verbal arrangement in the 'descent' section between 1:10aα, which begins וילך יהודה and continues ויכו (1:10b), and 1:17aα, which begins וילך יהודה and continues ויכו (1:17aβ). Both verses rename the conquered city (1:10aγ and 1:17bβ). Thus, 1:10 and 1:17 frame the descent section with similarly structured accounts. The longer intervening account, 1:11-15, presents an anecdotal parallel to 1:4-7 and essentially parallels the other accounts: it begins וילך (1:11aα), resumes ויאמר כלב אשר־יכה (1:12aβ) and interposes a renaming of the conquered city (1:11b).[8]

For Judg. 1:1-20, Webb proposed the following structural schema:[9]

A	*Prospect*: Yahweh's promise to give Judah victory		v. 2
B	The Judah–Simeon alliance		v. 3
X	Judah's successful campaign	up	vv. 4-8
		down	vv. 9-16
Bⁱ	The Judah–Simeon alliance		v. 17
Cⁱ[*sic*]	*Retrospect*: Yahweh was with Judah		v. 19

Noticeable omissions from this schema are: 1:1 (of the couplet 1:1-2) and 1:18.

Webb's schema is helpful, insofar as it accents the ascent–descent scheme within 1:3-20, but the position of Jerusalem in 1:8 should probably be recognized as the structural axis, if not the summit of this ascent–descent portrayal of Judah's wars of occupation. The schema that follows presents an alternative rhetorical analysis of 1:3-18:

aa		Formation of Judah–Simeon coalition 1:3
bb	a	Ascent scheme summary 1:4
	b	Judah's ascending conquest of Bezek 1:5-7
Axis:		Judah's conquest of Jerusalem 1:8
bbⁱ	a	Descent scheme summary 1:9
	b	Judah's descending conquest of Hebron, Debir, negeb of Arad 1:10-16/[17]/18
aaⁱ		Conquest (descending) of Zephath by Judah–Simeon coalition 1:17
bbⁱⁱ	bⁱ	Judah's (descending) capture of Gaza, Ashkelon, Ekron 1:18

---

[8] Gunn's five-tiered panelled and concentric analysis of Josh. 23–Judg. 2:10 (i.e., A Josh. 23; B 24:1-27; C 24:28-31; D 24:32-33; E Judg. 1:1-8; F 1:16; Eⁱ 1:17-21; Aⁱ 1:22-36; Bⁱ 2:1-5; Cⁱ 2:6-9; Dⁱ 2:10) seems unconvincing for several reasons: it lacks corroboration from the canonical division of the books, requires more evidence than is offered to prove that its alleged structure was intended (though Judg. 2:6-9 is clearly dependent upon Josh. 24:28-31) and demands an explanation as to why it was thought necessary to leave Judg. 1:9-15 out of consideration ("Joshua and Judges" [1987], p. 111).

[9] Webb, *Judges* (1987), p. 90.

If the structure of 1:3-18 focuses upon Jerusalem as a city conquered by Judah (1:8), and if, in turn, 1:1–2:5 focuses upon Jerusalem as a city whose inhabitants were not expelled by Benjamin (1:21), then one might infer that this connection evidences the compiler/redactor's concern to make the conquest of Jerusalem the basis of contrast between Benjamin and Judah. At the very least, such a concern would be consistent with the compiler/redactor's desire, evident elsewhere in Judges, to depict Jerusalem as a Jebusite enclave so as to implicate Benjamin (cf. 19:10-14).

Judges 1:19-20 comprises a concluding summary (1:19) and parade example (1:20) of Judah's wars of occupation. Judges 1:20, which is redactionally and thematically related to 1:10, features the conquest of Caleb: ויורש משם את־שלשה בני הענק (1:20b). It may be no coincidence that 1:19b describes Judah's failure to meet a similar challenge in analogous language: כי לא להוריש את־ישבי העמק כי־רכב ברזל להם. Both 1:19b and 1:20b employ ירש (contrastively) and the objects, את־שלשה בני הענק and את־ישבי העמק, are paronomastically analogous. As for the legitimacy of Judah's excuse for limited success (i.e., כי־רכב ברזל להם), one eventually comes to see that chariots need not have proven to be an insurmountable obstacle (cf. 4:3, 13, 14-16). Thus, within the present form of Judges, Barak's triumph retroactively nullifies the legitimacy of Judah's excuse for failing to occupy its allotment, and the contrasting juxtaposition of 1:19b with the account of Caleb's expulsion of the giants of Hebron (1:20) might further implicate Judah were it not for the fact that Caleb is counted among the members of Judah. Thus, while the concluding summary of 1:19 is generally positive (in contrast to that of all other tribes), it is tempered by the realization that not even Judah was entirely without fault.

J. Gray noted in 1:21 the close association between Benjamin and Judah (1:1-20) as indicating the condition of these tribes since the time of David.[10] J. D. Martin (commenting on the NEB) contended that 1:21 rightly coheres with the "negative account of the conquest" in 1:21/22-36.[11] From the pivotal position of 1:21 within the foregoing

---

[10] J. Gray, *Joshua, Judges, Ruth* (NCBC, Basingstoke, 2d edn, 1986), p. 238. Webb assigned 1:21 to an appendix (1:18-21) that he linked with the "Judah section" (1:3-21) (*Judges* [1987], p. 92). Webb was following the suggestion of Auld that, "if 21 should be viewed as the final verse of the first part of the chapter, then it becomes increasingly likely that in 19-21 (or even 18-21 according to the LXX) we should recognize a series of 'corrections' of the record in 1-17(18)" ("Judges i" [1975], p. 274; cf. p. 276 on 1:21 and 1:22-26).

[11] J. D. Martin, *The Book of Judges* (CBC, Cambridge, 1975), p. 26.

structural analysis, however, it would appear that the Benjamin account serves an intermediary role in 1:1–2:5: it is a key transition between the Judah block (1:3-20) and the Joseph block (1:22-36). It is important to note the disjunctive syntax used in 1:21, which breaks the narrative sequence of verb forms in 1:3-19 (excepting the parenthesis of 1:16 and the concluding negative qualification of 1:19b).[12] Certainly from the standpoint of geographical mimesis, the structure of 1:3-36 mimics the geopolitical division of the land into the major regions of south and north, with Benjamin in an intervening position.

Recognition of the intervening role of Benjamin could be further developed if one were to assume, as underlying the writing of Judg. 1:1–2:5, a situation in which the southern and northern tribes were prevented by Benjamin from achieving the religious and political ideals implicitly endorsed by the framing sections (cf. 1:1-2, 2:1-5). That this interpretation of Benjamin's role in Judges' opening section (1:1–2:5) is plausible may be corroborated by the fact that this is precisely the role that Benjamin plays in the structurally complementary closing section of Judges' dénouement (19–21).

Within Judg. 1:22-36, the anticipatory summary of 1:22 and the conquest account of 1:23-26 present the Joseph tribes' structural and thematic counterpart to the concluding summary of Judah's overall success (1:19) and occupation of Hebron (1:20). R. G. Boling rightly noticed that the northern account of 1:22-36 begins with a conquest anecdote (1:22-26) in a fashion analogous to the southern account of 1:3-20 beginning with 1:4-7.[13] However, whereas the northern section begins with its only conquest anecdote, that of the south contains conquest anecdotes throughout. Other than the structural analogy between the summaries (1:19, 22) and parade examples (1:20, 23-26), the accounts of 1:3-20 and 1:22-36 are not internally parallel. Moreover, these southern and northern tribal sections were evidently intended to function in relation to one another not as internally parallel structures but as complementary concentric units centring about 1:21. However, although 1:22-36 cannot be said to parallel 1:3-20 on the basis of internal structural analogy, it may still be legitimate to suggest that 1:22-26 and 1:4-7 are analogous narrative accounts, since the expression גם־הם after ויעלו in 1:22a resumes ויעל used to report Judah's going up in

---

[12] Cf. Webb, *Judges* (1987), pp. 93, 236 n. 53.

[13] R. G. Boling, *Judges: Introduction, Translation and Commentary* (AB 6A, Garden City, N.Y., 1975), p. 65. So also Webb, *Judges* (1987), p. 93.

1:4a.[14] The latter factor, in addition to a similarity of form (a short account of a city's conquest and the fate of one of its citizens), may be sufficient to link 1:22-26 with 1:4-7.

In this connection, it is appropriate to take notice of Boling's observation that the treaty enacted in 1:22-26 is implicitly condemned by YHWH's statement of covenant violations in 2:2a, despite its parallel to the treaties with Rahab and the Gibeonites and despite the report that this former citizen of Luz (and his family) did not remain among the Joseph tribes.[15] Webb elaborated this thesis in his analysis of 1:22-26.[16]

---

[14] A similar use of גם־המה in Josh. 9:4, in an introductory comment referring to the Gibeonites' shrewd conduct (ויעשו ... בערמה) and the pact (Josh. 9:15) and protection that would result (Josh. 9:26; 10:6-7, 9-10), may have been intended to show the resumption of a pattern established by Rahab's shrewd conduct (Josh. 2:1-13, especially 2:12-13), which likewise resulted in a pact (Josh. 2:14, 17-21) and protection for a native otherwise destined for destruction (Josh. 6:22-23, 25).

It is no moot point, therefore, that Webb discovered in Judg. 1:22-26 an example of narrative analogy with the account of the conquest of Jericho (Josh. 2:1-21; 6:1-27) (Webb, *Judges* [1987], pp. 96-97). Webb's outline, with slight modification, is as follows:

Judg. 1:22-26	*Josh. 2:1-21; 6:1-27*
1. Anticipatory summary: YHWH was with the Josephites (22b)	1. (See #11)
2. Josephites set up a reconnaissance of Bethel (23a)	2. Joshua sends out spies (2:1a)
3. Sentries meet a man leaving the city (24a)	3. Spies meet a harlot in the city (2:1b)
4. —	4. Harlot helps the spies (2:3-6)
5. חסד made with the man (24b)	5. חסד made with harlot (2:8-14)
6. Man helps Joseph enter (25aα)	6. Harlot helps spies escape (2:15-21)
7. Bethel captured (25aβ)	7. Jericho captured (6:1-21)
8. Man and family spared (25b)	8. Harlot and family spared (6:22-25)
9. Man dissimilates from Israel/moves to "the land of the Hittites" (26a)	9. Harlot assimilates to Israel/resides "in the midst of Israel" (6:25)
10. Man rebuilds "Luz" (26b)	10. Curse on man who rebuilds Jericho (6:26)
11. (See #1)	11. Concluding summary: YHWH was with Joshua (6:27)

This narrative analogy proves to hold a much stronger resemblance than that between Judg. 1:22-26 and Josh. 7-8, which are critically regarded as analogous traditions (Webb, *Judges* [1987], p. 237 n. 61). The analogy with the account of the conquest of Jericho in the book of Joshua effects the same negative characterization of the Joseph tribes (portrayed as compromising the covenant). This negative portrayal of the Joseph tribes as covenant compromisers may be further corroborated by comparing the account of the conquest of Bethel in Judg. 1:22-26 with the traditions of Jacob and Bethel in Gen. 28 and 35 (cf. J. P. Fokkelman, *Narrative Art in Genesis: Specimens of Stylistic and Structural Analysis* [SSN 17, Assen, The Netherlands, 1975; Biblical Seminar 12, Sheffield, 2d edn, 1991], especially chapter 2 on Gen. 28:10-22; Webb, *Judges* [1987], pp. 95-96).

[15] Boling, *Judges* (1975), p. 65.

[16] Webb, *Judges* (1987), pp. 93-95, 99, 100-101.

According to Webb, the spies' promise to the man from Bethel, וְעָשִׂינוּ עִמְּךָ חֶסֶד (1:24bγ), illegitimately introduces an additional obligation to that of conquering Bethel—the spies become obligated to protect a Canaanite (so Webb; though, perhaps, a Hittite) and his family. The discharge of that obligation in 1:25b leads to the surprising 'reversal' that Luz is not irrevocably conquered. It is rebuilt at a distance (1:26).[17] In retrospect, one discovers the anticipatory function of "Luz" in 1:23b.[18] Within the context of 1:1–2:5, which coheres around the idea that Israel's military success was a direct reflection of their covenant loyalty to YHWH, one can discern that 1:22-26 "is a story about an agreement made with a Canaanite, and not only, or even essentially about the conquest of [a] Canaanite city".[19] That the focus of interest in 1:22-26 is on the illegitimate military strategy used to capture Bethel is evident from the compiler/redactor's rhetorical strategy. This explains why there is a reference to YHWH's presence in 1:22b (echoing 1:19aα), which generates the expectation that Joseph will succeed at Bethel as Judah had at Bezek.[20] However, this expectation is raised only to be frustrated when, as the negative consequence of the compromising covenant of 1:22-26, it is not merely a Canaanite [Hittite] family that survives Joseph's conquest of Bethel (1:25b) but Canaanite culture as well (1:26).

As a subunit of 1:22-36, Judg. 1:27-36 describes the failure of six tribes to evict the Canaanites or Amorites and to occupy their land. These six tribes are described according to three fields of information: (1) failure to evict banned foreigners (Canaanites) from allotted tribal cities; (2) increasing degrees of coresidence with such foreigners (Canaanites/Amorites); (3) eventual subjection of such foreigners (Canaanites/Amorites) to corvée.[21] This arrangement may be displayed schematically as follows:

---

[17] Webb, *Judges* (1987), pp. 96, 99.

[18] Webb, *Judges* (1987), p. 93.

[19] Webb, *Judges* (1987), p. 94.

[20] Webb, *Judges* (1987), pp. 94, 95.

[21] Cf. L. G. Stone, "From Tribal Confederation to Monarchic State: The Editorial Perspective of the Book of Judges" (PhD diss., Yale University, 1988), pp. 235-39.

	A Failure to evict from cities	B Degrees of foreign coresidence			C Foreigners subjected to corvée	A^i Summary: Failure to evict
		a	b	c		
		ויואל ההכנעני/ ההאמי לשבת ב...	וישב הכנעני בקרבו [ב...]	[...]וישב ברב הכנעני ישבי הארץ		
Manasseh	1:27a	1:27b			1:28a	1:28b
Ephraim	1:29a		1:29b			
Zebulun	1:30a		1:30bα		1:30bβ	
Asher	1:31			1:32a		1:32b
Naphtali	1:33aα-β			1:33aγ	1:33b	
Dan		1:(34-)35a			1:35b	

This arrangement evidences a pattern of organization that highlights the tribes' increasing degree of coresidence with banned foreigners (item B). Indeed, apart from the presence or absence of the other elements, item B is the only variable item in the repetition pattern, is the only item consistently present and is, thus, probably the focal point of interest in the rhetorical strategy of 1:27-36. Each of the three formulae that describe the tribes' coresidence with foreigners is stated twice: Bb, of Ephraim and Zebulun, is repeated in juxtaposed units (1:29b, 30bα); Bc, of Asher and Naphtali, is repeated in juxtaposed units (1:32a, 33aγ); Ba, of Manasseh and Dan, frames the subsection (1:27b, [34-]35a). Hence, controlling interest in item B may have been the deciding factor in limiting this account to only six tribes. References to the subjection of banned foreigners to corvée (item C) are positioned after each instance of Ba (1:28a, 35b) and once only after each pair of either Bb or Bc (1:30bβ, 33b, respectively). Lists of key cities from which each tribe failed to evict Canaanites (item A) introduce each tribal unit except the last, which concerns Amorites. Generalized summary statements (item A^i) conclude the first and third units only (1:28b, 32b). The order of succession (A through C, with A recapitulated) never varies throughout the subsection.[22]

---

[22] If the unit on Jebusite coresidence with Benjamin (1:21) is considered in this connection, it is seen to present a similar structure. Its statement of item B (1:21b), the phraseology of which is quite similar to that of Bb in 1:27-36, likewise follows a statement of item A, which alone uses emphatic word order (1:21a).

When Judg. 1:22-26 is viewed in combination with 1:27-36, it is evident that the point of coherence is the emphasis that both sections place on covenant compromise among the Joseph tribes.[23] The conquest of Bethel was achieved through a compromise to spare a family that was under YHWH's ban (1:23-26; cf. 2:2a, Deut. 7:1-2abα, 16a), and this precedent-setting compromise led to the increasing toleration of and coresidence with Canaanites (1:27-36; cf. Deut. 7:17-24) that would eventuate in the concession to idolatry (2:2b; cf. Deut. 7:3-5, 16b, 25-26).[24] Indeed, each recurrence of item C in the report of Judg. 1:27-36 allusively echoes the instruction of Deut. 20:11b, which permitted subjugation to corvée (יהיו לך למס) of only distant city-dwellers. In the

---

[23] Webb has outlined a complementary inverse progression between Israelite conquest and Canaanite residence, modified in the following schema of Judg. 1:22-36 (*Judges* [1987], p. 99):

	Joseph tribes' diminishing conquest of the land:	*Canaanites' increasing residence in the land:*
1:(22)23-26	Josephites defeat (נכה) Canaanites [Hittites]	Canaanites [Hittites] freed to live at a distance/city of Luz
	Tribes that did not dispossess (לא הוריש) Canaanites (27-33):	
1:27-28	Manasseh	Canaanites determined to live in the land
1:29-30	Ephraim/Zebulun	Canaanites live among (בקרב) tribes
1:31-33	Asher/Naphtali	Tribes live among (בקרב) Canaanites
1:34-35(36)	Canaanites [Amorites] constrain (לחץ) Danites	Tribe forced to live at a distance/Amorite determined to live in [Danite cities]

[24] As corroboration of the Joseph tribes' compromise, note the allusion in Judg. 1:27-28 to the broader context in Josh. 17. Whereas Judg. 1:27 edits *Josh. 17:11-12, and Judg. 1:28 edits *Josh. 17:13, Josh. 17:11-13 was followed by an account (i.e., 17:14-18) in which the Joseph tribes requested that Joshua allot them territory elsewhere than in the plains of Beth-shan and Jezreel, where the Canaanites used "iron chariots" (Josh. 17:16). Joshua there conceded to their request but retorted that the Joseph tribes should nevertheless dispossess these Canaanite cities despite their "iron chariots" and the fact that they were "strong" (כי חזק הוא; Josh. 17:18b). Thus, the denial that the Joseph tribes later dispossessed these cities, even once Israel "became strong" (כי־חזק ישראל), is a point of reproach in Judg. 1:28 (as in Josh. 17:13 in its context). The allusive relationship between Judg. 1:27-28 and Josh. 17:11-13 evokes Josh. 17:14-18, implicitly reproaches the Joseph tribes for compromising Joshua's injunction to dispossess these five Canaanite cities and brings this intertextual reinterpretation to bear upon the relation that Judg. 1:27-28 has with the Joseph tribes' compromise in Judg. 1:22-26.

same context (Deut. 20:16-18), more proximate city-dwellers—that is, the same as those identified in Judg. 1:3-36 (i.e., Canaanites, Perizzites, Jebusites, Hittites, Amorites)—were specifically precluded from being subject to corvée (cf. Deut. 7:1-2abα; Josh. 24:11a).

If one views 1:3-36 as a single section, the alternation of foreigners with whom each tribe is in conflict groups the Israelite tribes into four divisions:

Israelite Tribes	Foreigners
1) Judah–Simeon	Canaanites[/Perizzites/Anakites]
2) Benjamin	Jebusites
3) Manasseh-Ephraim-Zebulun-Asher-Naphtali	Canaanites [/Hittites?]
4) Dan	Amorites

According to this schematization, Benjamin and Dan figure as anomalies in the more general scheme of tribal compromise/competition with the Canaanites.[25] The distinction of Benjamin and Dan by this means harmonizes with the prominent positioning of the accounts of their representative deliverers at the outer limits of the body of Judges (3:12-30; 13–16) and with the dominant role that these two tribes play in the apostasies described in Judges' double dénouement (17–18; 19–21).[26]

---

[25] Several tribes are omitted from this list of nine tribes: i.e., all three Transjordan tribes (Reuben, Gad and half-Manasseh), the 'landless' tribe Levi and the Cisjordan tribe Issachar—the latter omitted without apparent reason (cf. also Deut. 33).

[26] Webb proposed a structural schema of Judg. 1:3-36 as follows (*Judges* [1987], p. 92):

	v. 3	The Judah/Simeon alliance Wars of 'Judah', including Calebites/Kenizzites		v. 22	The house of Joseph Wars of the house of Joseph, including (in addition to Manasseh and Ephraim) Zebulun, Asher, Naphtali, Dan
	v. 17	The Judah/Simeon alliance		v. 35	The house of Joseph
	vv. 18-21	Appendix		v. 36	Appendix

This schema of 1:3-36 follows the redactional structure proposed by Auld ("Judges i" [1975], pp. 275-76, 278 on 1:36), but it seems less than viable as a rhetorical schema of the section. On the rhetorical level, the 'appendices' of 1:18-21, 36 are not shown sufficiently to function as such; nor, by this schema, would 1:1-2:5 serve as a structural cameo of the tribal arrangements in the body of Judges. Indeed, by this schema, Benjamin (1:21), far from taking a central place in the rhetorical structure of 1:1-2:5, is given no prominence at all. As a further point, although the mention of "the House of Joseph" ostensibly frames the accounts of 1:22-36, it would probably be mistaken to infer that

Judges 2:1-5 contains several key phrases that allude to Joshua 23–24, Deuteronomy 7 and 31:

Judg. 2:1bα	Josh. 24:5b-6aα?, 17aβ?	Deut. 4:20a?, 37b?; 5:6β?; 6:12b?, 21b?; (7:9b?); 8:14bβ?; 9:26b?
Judg. 2:1bβ		Deut. 6:10aαβ^i?; 7:1aαβ; 8:7a?
Judg. 2:1bγ		Deut. 6:10aβ^{ii}?, 18bγ?; 7:8aβ, 12bγ?, 13bδ?; 8:1bγ, 18b?; 11:21aγ?
Judg. 2:1bδε		≠ Deut. 31:16bδε?, 20bγ?
Judg. 2:2aαβ	Josh. 23:12a?	Deut. 7:2bβ^i
Judg. 2:2aγ		Deut. 7:5aβ
Judg. 2:3a	Josh. 23:9aα?, 13a?; 24:18aα?	
Judg. 2:3b	Josh. 23:13bαβ?	Deut. 7:16bβ?

The allusion to Deuteronomy 7 recalls a passage that enjoins Israel's extermination of the Canaanite nations (including the Canaanites, Perizzites, Jebusites, Hittites, and Amorites mentioned in Judg. 1:3-36; cf. Deut. 7:1-2abα) as an evidence of covenant loyalty to YHWH. Since Deut. 31:14-29 and Joshua 23–24 focus upon Israel's problem with covenant loyalty, Judges' compiler/redactor was probably emphasizing, through allusion, the illegitimacy of Israel's residing with, making covenant with and assimilating to the religion of the occupants of the land. Indeed, the allusions to Deut. 31:14-29 and Joshua 23–24 evoke from these final speeches of Moses and Joshua a rebuking recollection of the warning that Israel would not be able to obey the terms of YHWH's covenant once they had entered the land (cf. Deut. 31:16-18, 20-21, 27, 29; Josh. 23:12-13, 16; 24:14-27).

Some of the elements of Judg. 2:1-3 analogously complement elements contained in the Judges cycle-motif as it occurs within 2:11–3:6. For instance, Judg. 2:3b, which alludes to Deut. 7:16bβ, analogously complements motif element A2a where the latter alludes to Deut. 7:16bα,γ (e.g., Judg. 3:6b). Judges 2:1bδε, by alluding to Deut. 31:16bδε, analogously complements motif A2b where the latter alludes to Deut. 31:16bγ (e.g., Judg. 2:12aα, 13a). Judges 2:1bα restates motif element A2b. Finally, Judg. 2:2aαβ, alluding to Deut. 7:2bβ^i, may complement motif element B2a where the latter alludes antithetically to Deut. 7:2a (e.g., Judg. 2:14aβ; cf. 2:23b, where motif E2a is negated). This complementarity between Judg. 2:1-3 and the Judges cycle-motif in 2:11–3:6 supports the view that the analogous

---

during the period of the judges the House of Joseph included Zebulun, Asher, Naphtali and Dan.

elements of the former passage were designed so as to form a unity with the cycle-motif elements of the latter passage as part of a single stratagem of compilation/redaction, the main concern of which lay with Israel's failure to uphold the standards of YHWH's covenant as expressed in Deuteronomy.

§2. *Prologue-B (2:6–3:6): The Dependence of Cultic Loyalty upon Land Occupation*

After the portrayal of the tribes' wars of occupation in 1:1–2:5, which occur אחרי מות יהושע (1:1aα), Judg. 2:6–3:6 commences with a second reference to Joshua and the period of Joshua's lifetime. Since וישלח יהושע את־העם (2:6a) refers to a period antecedent to that described in 1:1–2:5, it may be translated as a pluperfect ("When Joshua had sent the people ..."; so AV, RV, NIV), though this nuance derives from the context, not from the Hebrew syntax. With the flashback of 2:6a, the reader is introduced to the fact that, in Judges' double prologue, chronology has been reordered. The displacement in Judg. 1:1–3:6 of three consecutive periods seems to reflect a deliberate rhetorical strategy. The three consecutive periods are explicitly delimited in Judg. 2:6–10:

> Period 1: after Joshua's dismissal of the tribes but before his death (Judg. 2:6–7a)
> Transition (Periods 1–2): the death of Joshua (Judg. 2:8–9)
> Period 2: of the generation who outlived Joshua (Judg. 2:7b)
> Transition (Periods 2–3): the death of the generation who outlived Joshua (Judg. 2:10a)
> Period 3: of the generation who arose and knew neither YHWH nor what he had done for Israel (Judg. 2:10b)

In the present arrangement, the book of Judges transposes the chronological order of its contents in the following way:

> Judg. 1:1–2:5[27]   Periods 2 and/or 3
> Judg. 2:6–7a   Period 1

---

[27] While this section may include flashbacks to the time of Joshua (Judg. 1:8, 9, 10-15, 16 or 20), the categorization of 1:1–2:5 under the rubric of 1:1, "After the death of Joshua", seems to have been the compiler/redactor's controlling criterion (see Boling, *Judges* [1975], p. 66). A. E. Cundall, however, reasoned that, "when the book of Judges assumed its present form, the opening words were added not with reference to the section which followed immediately afterwards (*i.e.* 1:1b–2:5) but with a more general application to the whole book as dealing with the situation in the post-Joshua age" (*Judges*, in A. E. Cundall and L. Morris, *Judges and Ruth: An Introduction and Commentary* [TOTC 7, London, 1968], p. 21).

Judg. 2:7b	Period 2
Judg. 2:8-9	Transition (Periods 1–2)
Judg. 2:10a	Transition (Periods 2–3)
Judg. 2:10b–21:25[28]	Period 3

It is crucial to the rhetoric of Judges that this three-period schematization be discerned, because the characterization given each of these periods in the exordium (1:1–3:6) portrays a successive degradation from faithfulness to take possession of the land while forsaking idolatry (Period 1),[29] to coresidence with the natives and toleration of idolatry (Period 2) then to outright idolatry and inability to possess the land (Period 3). The reordering of materials from these periods shows something of the strategy by which the compiler/redactor sought to achieve his/her rhetorical aim. By way of contrast, Josh. 24:28-31 follows the chronological sequence of these periods:

Josh. 24:28	(= Judg. 2:6-7a)	Period 1
Josh. 24:29-30	(= Judg. 2:8-9)	Transition (Periods 1–2)
Josh. 24:31	(= Judg. 2:7b)	Period 2

It was the rhetorical strategy of the Judges compiler/redactor to reorder and extend the periodization, juxtaposing the periods of obedience (Periods 1 and 2 = 2:6-7a, 7b) and the transitions associated with the demise of godly leaders (both Transitions [Periods 1–2 and 2–3] = 2:8-9, 10a), so that the period of the new generation (Period 3) would appear not merely at the end of a chronological sequence but categorically separate from Periods 1 and 2. Important, too, is the function of the newly added material in Judg. 2:6. Whereas Josh. 24:28 had: וישלח יהושע את־העם / איש לנחלתו, Judg. 2:6 has a fuller form: וישלח יהושע את־העם // וילכו בני־ישראל איש לנחלתו לרשת את־הארץ. It is the purpose of the tribes' dismissal to their respective inheritances that figures prominently in Judges' rhetoric: וילכו בני־ישראל...לרשת את־הארץ ("the Israelites went ... to possess the land"). If this were the task for which

---

[28] The temporal arrangement of the book of Judges requires that the episode of Othniel (3:7-11) be regarded as taking place during Period 3. Othniel may be portrayed as an idealized judge and an exception to the more flawed characters who follow, but his generation was the first to do evil in the eyes of YHWH (3:7aα). Thus, the appearance of Caleb and Othniel in 1:11-15 is a case in which characters who may have lived contemporaneously were regarded by the compiler/redactor as representatives of succeeding periods (i.e., Periods 2 and 3). The necessity of the generational distinction between Caleb and Othniel may account for the addition of הקטן ממנו in Judg. 1:13a = 3:9b (cf. Josh. 15:17a).

[29] Cf. Josh. 24:22-24.

the people were being evaluated in Judg. 2:7 (which affirms that they served YHWH during the lifetime of Joshua [Period 1] and the elders who outlived him [Period 2]), then one may surmise that possession of the land (and dispossession of its inhabitants) was the major (though not the only) task of the people during Periods 1 and 2. Accordingly, the contrastive portrayal of Judah versus the northern tribes in Judg. 1:1–2:5—especially of the recurrence, toward its second half, of the negative לא [ל]הוריש (1:19b, 21a, 27a, 28b, 29a, 30a, 31a, 33a; but cf. ויורש [1:20b])—may be significant for discerning which of either Period 2 or Period 3 the contrastive portrayals of 1:1-20 and 1:21-36 were intended to characterize. Indeed, the distinction between 1:1-20 and 1:21-36 may be chronological as well as geographical.

It may be a point of continuity with Judges' ensuing interest in the cycle-motif that 2:6-9/10 recapitulates the death and burial accounts of Joshua, Israel's former leader (motif G1, 2:8; G2, 2:9a), for this starts the cycle of Israel's repeated return to idolatry. Accordingly, Judg. 2:11-3:6 introduces Judges' religious–historical cycle-motif. The vocabulary correspondences in 2:11-3:6 suggest that, besides setting forth elements of Judges' cycle-motif, it may follow a pattern of parallel development (i.e., $A \parallel A^i, B \parallel B^i, C \parallel C^i, D \parallel D^i$):

A	2:11-12a	$\parallel A^i$	2:12b-13
(A1a)	2:11a		
	ויעשו בני־ישראל את־הרע בעיני יהוה		
		(B1)	(2:12b)
			ויכעסו את־יהוה:
(A2a)	2:11b		
	ויעבדו את־הבעלים:		
(A2b)	2:12aαβ	(A2b)	2:13a
	ויעזבו את־יהוה אלהי אבותם		ויעזבו את־יהוה
	המוציא אותם מארץ מצרים		
(A2a)	2:12aγ-ε	(A2a)	2:13b
	וילכו אחרי אלהים אחרים		ויעבדו לבעל ולעשתרות:
	מאלהי העמים אשר סביבותיהם		
	וישתחוו להם		

B   *2:14a*   ‖ **Bⁱ**   *2:14b-15*

(B1)   2:14aα

ויחר־אף יהוה בישראל

(B2a)   2:14aβ[γ]   (B2b)   2:14bα

[וישסו אותם] / ויתנם ביד־שסים   וימכרם ביד אויביהם מסביב

                                  (B3a)   (2:14bβγ)

/ ולא־יכלו עוד
לעמד לפני אויביהם:

                                  (B3a)   (2:15a)

/ בכל אשר יצאו
/ יד־יהוה היתה־בם לרעה
/ כאשר דבר יהוה
וכאשר נשבע יהוה להם

                                  (B3bⁱⁱ)   (2:15b)

ויצר להם מאד:

C   *2:16-17*   ‖ **Cⁱ**   *2:18-19*

(D1)   2:16abα[β]   (D1)   2:18aα

// ויקם יהוה שפטים   / וכי־הקים יהוה להם שפטים

                                  (D2a)   (2:18aβ)

/ והיה יהוה עם־השפט

                                  (D1)   2:18aγ

[מיד שסיהם:] / ויושיעום   / והושיעם מיד איביהם

                                  (F1)   (2:18aδ)

כל ימי השופט

                                  (B3bⁱ)   (2:18b[α]β)

[/ כי־ינחם יהוה מנאקתם]
מפני לחציהם ודחקיהם:

                                  (G1)   2:19aα

2:17aα   / והיה במות השופט

וגם אל־שפטיהם לא שמעו

(A2a)   2:17aβ-δ   (A2a)   2:19aβ-ε

/ כי זנו / אחרי אלהים אחרים   / ישבו והשחיתו מאבותם
וישתחוו להם   / ללכת / אחרי אלהים אחרים

2:17b   לעבדם ולהשתחות להם

סרו מהר / מן־הדרך אשר   2:19b
הלכו אבותם לשמע מצות־יהוה   / לא הפילו ממעלליהם
לא־עשו כן: ומדרכם הקשה:

D   2:20-22   ‖ *D*ⁱ   2:23–3:6

(B1)   2:20a

ויחר־אף יהוה בישראל

- -

2:20b

ויאמר / יען אשר עברו הגוי הזה /
את־בריתי אשר צויתי את־אבותם /
ולא שמעו לקולי:

- -

2:21   2:23a

a   וינח יהוה
b   את־הגוים האלה /

גם־אני לא אוסיף /
להוריש איש מפניהם //   c   לבלתי הורישם מהר //
                              (Negated E2a [‖ B2a]) (2:23b)
מן־הגוים אשר־עזב יהושע <>:   cⁱ   ולא נתנם ביד־יהושע:
                                     3:1aα
                              bⁱ   ואלה הגוים
                              aⁱ   אשר הניח יהוה /
2:22a   3:1aβ
למען נסות בם את־ישראל //   לנסות בם את־ישראל //
                                     3:1b
                                     את כל־אשר לא־ידעו /
                                     את כל־מלחמות כנען:

                                     [3:2]
                              ⎡ רק / למען <> דרות בני־־ישראל /
                              ⎢ ללמדם מלחמה //
                              ⎣ רק אשר־לפנים לא ידעום:
                                     3:3

                                     חמשת סרני פלשתים /
                                     וכל־הכנעני והצידני /
                                     והחוי / ישב הר הלבנון //
                                     מהר בעל חרמון / עד לבוא חמת:
                                     3:4aαβ

                                     ויהיו /
                                     לנסות בם את־ישראל //
2:22b   3:4b
השמרים הם את־דרכ<י> יהוה ללכת בם /   לדעת / הישמעו את־מצות יהוה /
כאשר שמרו אבותם אם־לא: אשר־צוה את־אבותם ביד־משה:
                                     3:5-6a
                              ובני ישראל / ישבו בקרב הכנעני //
                              החתי והאמרי והפרזי /
                              והחוי והיבוסי:
                              ויקחו את־בנותיהם להם לנשים /
                              ואת־בנותיהם נתנו לבניהם //

- -

                              (A2a)   3:6b
                                     ויעבדו את־אלהיהם:

If Judg. 2:11–3:6 were intended to serve as a religious–historical paradigm for the succeeding deliverer accounts (3:7–16:31), it must be significant that it ends with the explanation that Israel's situation was a test of covenant loyalty. Little of the material in the parallel 'D' sections (i.e., 2:20-22, 23–3:6) recurs verbatim in the body of Judges, though its concern with Israel's undulating covenant loyalty anticipates the resurgence of this concern in 6:1, 6-10 and especially 10:6-10, 11-16. Hence, it seems warranted to infer that it is preeminently with concern about Israel's covenant loyalty that the cycle-motif is introduced in Prologue-B (2:6–3:6) and diffused among Judges' deliverer stories. Whereas the individual stories in the body of Judges may have been originally designed to depict how heroes from various tribes, with the help of YHWH, overcame personal limitations to deliver Israel from enemy oppressors, they now serve a scheme that shows how each new cycle functions as a 'test' of Israel's loyalty to YHWH.

The high concentration in 2:11–3:6 of phraseological parallels to biblical passages that focus upon covenantal adherence (particularly Josh. 23–24, Deut. 4–11 and 31:14-29) evidences the compiler/redactor's concern in Prologue-B to have the reader view Israel's conduct against the background of these biblical paraeneses concerning YHWH's covenant and the land. The following table outlines these phraseological parallels:

A 2:11-12a ‖ *A^i 2:12b-13*

A1a	Judg. 2:11a	Deut. 4:25bγ^i?; 9:18bβ^i?; 17:2bβ^i?; 31:29bβ?; ($\neq$ 6:18a; 12:25bβ, 28b$\beta\gamma$; 13:19b; 21:9b)
A2b	Judg. 2:12aα	Josh. 24:16aγ, 20aα	Deut. 31:16bγ?, ($\neq$ 17aα?), [cf. 20bβ]
A2b	Judg. 2:12aβ	Josh. 24:5b-6aα?, 17aβ?	Deut. 4:20a?, 37b?; 5:6β?; 6:12b?, 21b?; 8:14bβ?; 9:26b?
A2a	Judg. 2:12aγ	Josh. 23:16a$\beta\gamma$?; 24:16b?, 20aβ?	Deut. *6:14a; 8:19aγ-ε^i?; 31:18b?; 20bα?
A2a	Judg. 2:12a$\gamma\delta$		*Deut. 6:14
A2a	Judg. 2:12aε	Josh. 23:7bγ?, 16aδ?	Deut. 5:9a?; 8:19aε^{ii}?; 11:16bγ
B1	Judg. 2:12b		Deut. 4:25bγ^{ii}?; 31:29bγ
A2b	Judg. 2:13a	Josh. 24:16aγ, 20aα	Deut. 31:16bγ?, ($\neq$ 17aα?), [cf. 20bβ]

B 2:14a ‖ *B^i 2:14b-15*

B1	Judg. 2:14aα Josh. 23:16bα	Deut. 7:4bα; 11:17aα; 31:17aα?
B2a	Judg. 2:14aβ ≠ Josh. 24:8bα?, 11b?	≠ Deut. 7:2a?

C 2:16-17 ‖ *C^i 2:18-19*

A2a	Judg. 2:17aβγ Josh. 24:16b?, 20aβ?	Deut. 8:19aγ-ε^i?; 31:16bαβ?, 18b?
A2a	Judg. 2:17aδ Josh. 23:7bγ?, 16aδ?	Deut. 5:9a?; 8:19aε^{ii}?; 11:16bγ?
	Judg. 2:17b	Deut. 9:12bαβ?; 31:29aγ?
B3b^i	Judg. 2:18bβ	Deut. 26:7bβ?
A2a	Judg. 2:19aγ-ε^i Josh. 23:7bβ?, 16aβγ?; 24:16b, 20aβ?	Deut. *8:19aγ-ε^i?; 31:20bα?
A2a	Judg. 2:19aε^{ii} Josh. 23:7bβγ, 16aδ?	Deut. 5:9a?; *8:19aε^{ii}; 11:16bγ

D 2:20-22 ‖ *D^i 2:23-3:6*

B1	Judg. 2:20a Josh. 23:16bα	Deut. 7:4bα; 11:17aα; 31:17aα?
	Judg. 2:20bβγ Josh. 23:16aα	
	Judg. 2:21a Josh. 23:13a	
	Judg. 2:22bα	Deut. 8:6?; 10:12bα?; 11:22?; 19:9a?; 26:17bα?; 28:9b?; 30:16aβγ?; cf. 2 Sam. 22:22; 1 Kgs 2:3

Negated E2a (‖ B2a)

	Judg. 2:23b ≠ Josh. 24:8bα?, 11b?	≠ Deut. 7:2a?
	Judg. 3:3 *Josh. 13:3b-5	
	Judg. 3:5	*Exod. 3:8b
	Judg. 3:6a Josh. 23:12b?	Deut. 7:3?
A2a	Judg. 3:6b	Deut. 7:16bα

Altogether missing from 2:11–3:6 are motif elements A1b and C (which also allude to Josh. 23–24 and to Deuteronomy [4–11; 31:14-29), though these are later present in 6:1, 6-10 and 10:6-16.[30] Through allusion to contexts that warn Israel against covenant aberration, Judg. 2:11–3:6 testifies that the ignorant generation of 2:10b epitomized the character of Israel as a wayward nation (cf. Deut. 9:1-6, 7–10:7,

---

[30] Occurrences of motif A1b and C in Judg. 6:1, 6-10 and 10:6-10, 11-16 include:

C	Judg. 6:6b, 7a	Josh. 24:7aα	Deut. 26:7a
C	Judg. 10:10a, 14aβ	Josh. 24:7aα	Deut. 26:7a
A1b	Judg. 10:15aβγ		≠ Deut. 12:8aα/b

10-11) and that in them were fulfilled the prophecies about Israel's apostasy (cf. Deut. 31:16, 20, 27-29; Josh. 24:19).

The allusions of Judg. 2:6–3:6 to Deut. 31:14-29 and Joshua 23–24 correspond to those in YHWH's final denunciation in Prologue-A (Judg. 2:1-3). In both cases there is an implicit rebuke that Israel's failure to conquer is but an expression of their more fundamental failure of covenant disloyalty to YHWH. However, whereas in 1:1–2:5 the greater proportion of material is given to describing Israel's failure to conquer the land, in 2:6–3:6 the greater proportion is given to a depiction of Israel's propensity to covenant disloyalty. Each part of Judges' double prologue is formulated on a recognition of the interdependent relationship between completion of the conquest and covenant loyalty to YHWH but each part emphasizes only one side of this interdependence. Implicit in Judges' double prologue is the idea that, if a solution ever were to be found for the problem of Israel's waywardness, it would have to derive from some camp in Israel where commitment to both the conquest of the land and to the cult of YHWH were mutually steadfast.

In the closing verses of Prologue-B are two rosters of enemy nations. The first mentions four enemies: the five lords of the Philistines, the Canaanite, the Sidonian and the Hivvite (3:3; cf. Josh. 13:3b-5). The second roster lists six: the Canaanite, the Hittite, the Amorite, the Perizzite, the Hivvite and the Jebusite (3:5; cf. Exod. 3:8b).[31] Two names appear in both lists (the Canaanite and the Hivvite). Perhaps significantly, the first name of the first roster (the five lords of the Philistines) and the last name of the last roster (the Jebusite) are enemy nations that appear elsewhere in Judges in connection with descriptions of the failure of the two Israelite tribes most censured in Judges' prologue and dénouement for their failure to occupy the land: Benjamin and Dan. Blame for failure to expel the Jebusite is laid upon the tribe of Benjamin (explicitly in 1:21; implicitly in 19:10-12). Perhaps also, in view of the Danite migration attested in 1:34-36 and 17–18, indirect responsibility for the failure to dislodge the Philistines in the period of Samson (13–16) may be laid upon the tribe of Dan, since, having abandoned their tribal allotment because of Amorite pressure (1:34-36; cf. 18:1), the Danites were no longer present at Zorah and Eshtaol to lend support to Samson (the only judge never to summon a tribe to battle) when he 'engaged' the Philistines (cf. 18:2, 8, 11 with the inclusio formed by 13:25 and 16:31).

---

[31] Cf. the similar roster of nations in Judg. 10:11-12. Like Prologues A and B, Judg. 6:1, 6-10 and 10:6-16 show the interdependence of cultic obligation and land occupation.

§3. *Complementarity between Prologue-A and Prologue-B*

Judges 1:1–2:5 is, from a rhetorical standpoint, an analogous complement to 2:6–3:6. Both sections highlight the deuteronomic interdependence of cultic obligation and land occupation, though each has its own emphasis. In Judg. 1:1–2:5, the greater proportion of narrative is given to portraying the tribes' success in the conquest of the land, yet their relative failure is attributed to cultic disloyalty. In the first verses of Prologue-A (1:1-2), the tribes make cultic inquiry of YHWH to discern how to go about occupying the land. At the end of Prologue-A, however, the tribe's continued cultic disloyalty has resulted in YHWH's threat of continued failure in the conquest of the land (2:3). Although Prologue-A begins with a focus upon the cult (1:1-2), it ends with the Israelites' ironic acknowledgement of cultic failure by making cultic offerings to YHWH (2:4-5).

Likewise, rhetorically, Judg. 2:6–3:6 is an analogous complement to the balance of concern about land and cult in 1:1–2:5. As in Judg. 1:1–2:5, the rhetoric of 2:6–3:6 shows concern about the tribes' occupation of the land, though, unlike 1:1–2:5, the greater proportion of narrative is given to portraying the tribes' cultic disloyalty to YHWH, which is only secondarily related to their failure to occupy the land. In 2:6–3:6, concern about the tribes' occupation of the land is present from the first verse (2:6), and their failure in conquest (2:14-15, 21, 23) is portrayed as the direct consequence of cultic disloyalty (2:11-13, 17, 19-20). Yet, not only is failure to conquer enemy land a consequence of cultic disloyalty (2:14-15, 21, 23), the continued enemy presence in the land has become the basis for expressing their failure to maintain cultic loyalty through holy war (2:22; 3:1-4). Although Prologue-B begins with focus upon land occupation (2:6), it ends with the Israelites' failure to dislodge YHWH's enemies from the land and with Israel forming marriage covenants with these enemies and serving their gods (3:5).

B. JUDGES' DELIVERER ACCOUNTS

The deliverer accounts have been arranged within the book of Judges to advance the compiler/redactor's tribal–political concerns. Yet, besides the concerns implicit in Judges' tribal–political arrangement, one should be able to discern from each account what concerns the compiler/redactor was attempting to address by means of plot-structure and characterization.[32] By focusing upon both plot-structure and the characterization of the tribes' leaders, one may discern what concerns motivated the compiler/redactor's selection of these traditional hero stories and what motivated him/her to present them in their present order.

Besides plot-structure and characterization within each separate account, the issue of theme must be addressed in regard to the aggregate of the deliverer accounts. One needs to determine what themes most accurately reflect the concern of the deliverer accounts. It would appear that, in subservience to the rhetorical concerns of the deuteronomic schema of Judges, the deliverer accounts of Judg. 3:7–16:31 show the following concerns: (1) relating to the deuteronomic concern about Israel's failure to occupy the land, all deliverer accounts portray some tribes' oppression under foreign rulers, from whom the deliverer procures some measure of deliverance; (2) as to deuteronomic concern about intertribal covenant disloyalty, Judges' deliverer accounts portray a disintegrating cooperation among the tribes in matters of covenantal concern; (3) with regard to deuteronomic concern about cultic disloyalty, most deliverer accounts describe some feature of cultic aberration; and (4) relating to the deuteronomic concern about covenant (social) injustice, several deliverer accounts portray at least some form of covenant or social injustice.

In the discussion that follows, I shall attempt to discern the rhetorical concerns of each deliverer account from its plot-structure and characterization. In each case, special effort will be made to understand the effect that the cycle-motif has upon the traditional elements of the story.

§1. *The Account of Othniel (3:7-11)*

The traditional elements in the Othniel account are very sparse. Apart from the personal names, which form part of the cycle-motif formulae, the traditional elements comprise 3:8aδ, 9b and 10aβb. Indeed, among the deliverer accounts in Judges, the Othniel account is unique since only here does the cycle-motif comprise the major portion of the account (i.e., 3:7-8aγ, 8b-9a, 10aαγδ, 11).

The rhetorical concerns reflected by the traditional materials (3:8aδ, 9b, 10aβb) are quite scant: "Othniel, son of Kenaz the youngest

---

[32] In his examination of short stories, R. C. Culley emphasized "the usefulness of describing characters in terms of their roles and actions and in terms of their function in the plot or narrative structure" ("Structural Analysis: Is It Done with Mirrors?", *Int* 28 [1974], p. 173).

brother of Caleb ... went out to battle ... and his hand prevailed over Cushan-Rishathaim", who is called, "king of Aram Naharaim". Nothing about this bears any trace of being taken from a plot-based narrative. The genealogy of 3:9b was already conveyed in 1:13a and perhaps derives from there. The other information fits the genre of report rather than story.

It is chiefly through the cycle-motif elements (3:7-8aγ, 8b-9a, 10aαγδ, 11) that the traditional Othniel materials are formed into a plot-based narrative. Its simple plot-structure may be outlined as follows (with cycle-motif designations appearing in the left column and a broken horizontal line separating the scenes of the development):

Situation Exposition: (3:7-9aα)	
A1a	Israel practiced evil in the eyes of YHWH (3:7aα)
A2b	Israel forgot YHWH (3:7aβ)
A2a	Israel served the Baals and Asherahs (3:7b)
B1	YHWH's anger burned against Israel (3:8aα)
B2b	YHWH sold them into the hand of Cushan-Rishathaim (3:8aβγ)
	king of Aram Naharaim (3:8aδ)
B3a	Israelites served Cushan-Rishathaim eight years (3:8b)
C	Israel cried out to YHWH (3:9aα)
Character Exposition: (3:9aβb)	
D1	YHWH raised up a saviour for the Israelites, and he saved them (3:9aβ)
	Othniel, son of Kenaz the youngest brother of Caleb (3:9b)
Development: (3:10aαβ)	
D2a	YHWH's spirit came upon him (3:10aα^i)
F1	He judged Israel (3:10aα^ii)
— — — — — — — — — — — — — — — — — — —
	He went out to battle (3:10aβ)
Situation Resolution: (3:10aγ-11a)	
E2	YHWH gave Cushan-Rishathaim, king of Aram, into his hand (3:10aγδ)
	His hand prevailed over Cushan-Rishathaim (3:10b)
F2	The land had peace forty years (3:11a)
Character Resolution: (3:11b)	
G1	Othniel, son of Kenaz, died (3:11b)

This is both the first and the simplest plot-based narrative of the book of Judges. Like the Ehud account, it comprises only a single plot-level. Moreover, the account is so lacking in embellishment that it has neither dialogue, reported speech nor anything approaching a dramatic portrayal of events.[33]

The characterization of Othniel is unique among the deliverer accounts in that his is the only portrayal that lacks negative aspects.[34] Nothing is said in this account that could be construed as negatively characterizing Othniel's motives or devotion to YHWH. Without exception, all the subsequent (non-Judahite) deliverers will evince some flaw of character that is paralleled, on an escalated level, by the negative portrayal of the deliverer's tribe or nation.

The theme of YHWH's glorification, evident in all the deliverer accounts, is begun explicitly in the Othniel account through the portrayal of YHWH justly subjecting those who served foreign Baals and Asherahs (3:7b, motif A2a) to serving a foreign king, Cushan-Rishathaim (3:8b, motif B3a). When the Israelites cry to YHWH, however, YHWH is further glorified by raising up a deliverer (motif D1: ויקם יהוה מושיע לבני ישראל ויושיעם, 3:9aβ), by letting his spirit come upon Othniel to 'judge' Israel and thus to instigate them to go to war (motifs D2a/F1: ותהי עליו רוח־יהוה וישפט את־ישראל ויצא למלחמה, 3:10aαβ) and by his giving Cushan-Rishathaim into Othniel's hand (motif E2: ויתן יהוה בידו את־כושן רשעתים מלך ארם, 3:10aγδ).

With the end-rhyme between the mocking appellative ("double wickedness") of 3:8aγ, ביד כושן רשעתים, and the epithet of 3:8aδ, מלך ארם נהרים, the compiler/redactor resumes (from the ridicule of Adoni-Bezek in 1:6-7) what proves to be his/her customary satirization of foreign kings in the book of Judges.[35] Indeed, the royal epithet of Cushan-Rishathaim, "king of Aram [Naharaim]", ostensibly frames the account (3:8aδ, 10aγδ).[36] The characteristic satirization of foreign

---

[33] So Webb, *Judges* (1987), p. 127. Contra Webb, however, there is at least one scene change implied between 3:10aαⁱⁱ and 10aβ (indicated by a broken line in the outline).

[34] Othniel is not, of course, YHWH's only מושיע 'saviour' or 'advocate' (the latter being preferred by J. F. A. Sawyer, "What Was a *mošiaʿ*?", *VT* 15 [1965], pp. 475-86; cf. Judg. 3:9, 15; 12:3). He was, however, the only one without fault.

[35] Most treatments of the Othniel account concern its historicity, and most of these focus upon identifying Cushan-Rishathaim: C. J. Ball, "Cushan-Rishathaim (Judg. iii.7-11)", *ExpTim* 21 (1909-1910), p. 192; J. W. Jack, "Cushan-Rishathaim (כּוּשַׁן רִשְׁעָתַיִם)", *ExpTim* 35 (1923-1924), pp. 426-28; H. Hänsler, "Der historische Hintergrund von Richter 3,8-10", *Bib* 11 (1930), pp. 391-418; 12 (1931), pp. 3-26, 271-96, 395-410; E. I. Täubler, "Cushan-Rishathaim", *HUCA* 20 (1947), pp. 137-42; A. Malamat, "Cushan Rishathaim and the Decline of the Near East around 1200 B.C.", *JNES* 13 (1954), pp. 231-42; cf. Webb, *Judges* (1987), p. 243 n. 5 for a summary of proposed identities.

[36] So Boling, *Judges* (1975), pp. 80-81; Webb, *Judges* (1987), p. 128. Webb inferred that Cushan-Rishathaim thus embodies the institution of foreign kingship just as Othniel embodies the institution of judgeship/saviourhood.

kings in Judges may reflect the compiler/redactor's implicit concern to cast a shadow over Israel's later request to have a king such as the other nations have. It is a rhetoric well-suited to Judges' apparent strategy to offer a standard by which to measure the characterizations of Saul and David in 1 Samuel.

Although Othniel's portrayal is worded similarly to 2:11-19, 20a and 3:6b, thus characterizing him as the embodiment of the institution of judge/deliverer,[37] there are for the reader several first encounters in this deliverer account: (1) excepting perhaps 1:1a$\beta\gamma$, motif element C appears here for the first time (3:9aα);[38] (2) excepting perhaps 2:18aβ, motif element D2a appears here for the first time (3:10aα^i);[39] and (3) motif element F2 appears here for the first time (3:11a).

§2. *The Account of Ehud (3:12-30)*

An analysis of both plot-structure and characterization in the Ehud account reveals that its main tribal–political concerns are to be found in: (1) its satirical portrayal of foreign kingship (i.e., Eglon, king of Moab) in contrast to its glorification of YHWH through the portrayal of YHWH's control of circumstances to bring about Israel's deliverance, (2) its self-promoting, though mostly heroic, characterization of Ehud as a deliverer from Benjamin, and (3) its escalated parallelism between the portrayal of Ehud and tribal Israel as agents of YHWH's expulsion of foreigners from the land. The predominant deuteronomic concern, that of cultic disloyalty, remains implicit in Ehud's failure to remove from the land the twice-mentioned idols that frame the portrayal of Eglon's assassination (3:19a$\alpha\beta$ and 3:26b). This failure to remove the idols characterizes negatively both Ehud (as microcosm) and the tribe whom he delivers (as macrocosm) and ostensibly leads to the religious apostasy that begins the following deliverer account (cf. 4:1).

With the likely exception of the Othniel account, in which there hardly exists a plot-structure, the plot-structure of the Ehud account is the simplest in the book of Judges.[40] Indeed, since the story lacks plot complications, one might deduce that the narrator intended the reader to infer that it was YHWH himself who prevented complications from

---

[37] All the marks of judgeship in ch. 2 apply to Othniel (Webb, *Judges* [1987], p. 127).

[38] However, Israel's inquiry of YHWH in 1:1a$\beta\gamma$ admits neither alarm nor remorse.

[39] So Webb, *Judges* (1987), p. 127.

[40] Even so, it seems fair to say that most literary studies of this account have adhered to an analytical approach that is based upon the scenic principle and have neglected to search for the rhetorical strategy implicit in the plot-structure.

arising in the story world.[41] What adds interest to the development (3:15b-26) is the use of satire and suspense. Satire is achieved through verbal imagery and temporal ordering.[42] Satire achieved through verbal imagery turns on the irony that Eglon the victor fails to discern that he is to become Eglon the victim[43]—victim of Ehud's misdirecting speech, his "double-mouthed" knife and the narrator's contrasting imagery of tribute offering versus sacrifice. Satire achieved through synchroneity (simultaneity) plays a crucial role in ridiculing Eglon's credulous courtiers. Suspense is achieved through Ehud's use of deceptive tactics, both physical (left-handedness, concealing the dagger, making two excursions) and verbal (misdirecting the Moabites through ambiguous speech), and through the same sychroneities by which satire is advanced.[44]

In the following plot-structure analysis of the Ehud account, the left column contains (1) configurations that refer to Judges' cycle-motif elements and (2) vertical lines that connect simultaneous events in the story world. Broken horizontal lines separate scenes in the development section. Letters in the middle column enumerate the repetition or reversal of themes.

Situation Exposition: (3:12-15aα)

A1a		Resumption of Israel's practice of evil (3:12a)
(B2a)		YHWH strengthened Eglon king of Moab over Israel (3:12bα)

---

[41] Despite YHWH's absence from the development, Y. Amit surmised that the narrator left gaps in the stages of narrative development but accumulated data concerning various 'coincidences' that helped Ehud's plan so that the reader would sense YHWH's part in the plot ("The Story of Ehud [Judges 3:12-30]: The Form and the Message", in *Signs and Wonders: Biblical Texts in Literary Focus* [J. C. Exum (ed.), Decatur, Ga., 1989], p. 120; cf. pp. 98, 100, 103; contra Klein, *Triumph of Irony* [1988], p. 38, who inferred from YHWH's absence that he was not in accord with Ehud's deceptive tactics). The attribution of Ehud's success to YHWH reflects a concern of the Judges compiler, since the name יהוה occurs only in the cycle-motif portions of the account, but, whereas אלהים is used in 3:20a (where Ehud is addressing a foreigner), the inference that God helped Ehud probably existed already in the traditional account.

[42] Especially sensitive to the comic and satirical aspects of the Ehud story are L. Alonso-Schökel, "Erzählkunst im Buche der Richter", *Bib* 42 (1961), pp. 149, 150, 153; R. Alter, *The Art of Biblical Narrative* (New York, 1981), pp. 39-40; and Webb, *Judges* (1987), pp. 129-30.

[43] Cf. Webb, *Judges* (1987), p. 130.

[44] R. C. Culley has classed the Ehud account as one of six similarly patterned Hebrew Bible "deception stories"—stories in which deception is the primary means used to accomplish plot resolution ("Structural Analysis" [1974], pp. 177-78; idem, "Themes and Variations in Three Groups of OT Narratives", *Semeia* 3 [1975], pp. 5, 7-9). Along with satire, Webb counted deception as one of the two main characteristics of the Ehud story (*Judges* [1987], pp. 129, 130-32).

A1a	Reason: Israel's practice of evil (3:12bβ)
	Parenthesis: Eglon, allied with the *Ammonites* and *Amalek*, took possession of the *City of Palms* (3:13)
B3a	Israel served Eglon king of Moab eighteen years (3:14)
C	Israel cried out to YHWH (3:15aα)
Character Exposition: (3:15aβ-δ)	
D1	YHWH raised up a saviour (3:15aβ), Ehud, a *left-handed Benjaminite* (3:15aγδ)
Development: (3:15b-28)	
A	Ehud is sent to offer tribute to Eglon king of Moab (3:15b)
aa	Parenthesis: Description of Ehud's previous *preparation and concealment of the dagger* (3:16)
B	Ehud presents the tribute to Eglon king of Moab (3:17a)
bb	Parenthesis: Description of *Eglon as very fat* (3:17b)
C	Ehud's dismisses tribute-bearers after presenting the tribute (3:18) ויהי

---

cc	Ehud *returns from the idols* (3:19aαβ)
	Ehud's direct speech: "a secret matter for you, O king" (3:19aγδ)
	Eglon summons privacy (3:19bα)
dd	Courtiers *go out* (3:19bβγ)

---

ee	Ehud *enters* (3:20aα)
	Parenthesis: Description of Eglon's solitude (3:20aβ)
	Ehud's direct speech: "a divine matter for you" (3:20aγδ)
ff	Eglon *arises* (3:20b)
1/aa	Ehud *takes the dagger from concealment* and stabs Eglon (3:21)
bbⁱ	The effects of stabbing *fat Eglon*: Ehud's dagger hilt *enters*; faeces *come out* (3:22)
1/ee	Ehud *goes out* and locks the doors (3:23)

1/eeⁱ	Ehud *goes out* (3:24aαⁱ)
1/dd	Courtiers *enter* (3:24aαⁱⁱ)

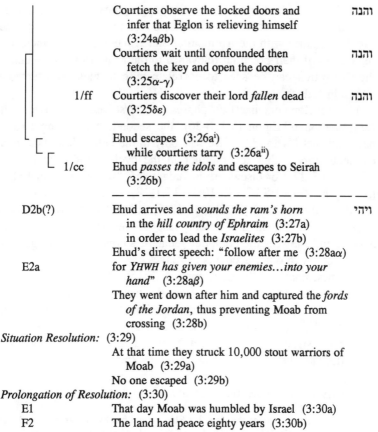

		Courtiers observe the locked doors and infer that Eglon is relieving himself (3:24aβb)	והנה
		Courtiers wait until confounded then fetch the key and open the doors (3:25α-γ)	והנה
	1/ff	Courtiers discover their lord *fallen* dead (3:25δε)	והנה

Ehud escapes (3:26aⁱ)
    while courtiers tarry (3:26aⁱⁱ)

1/cc   Ehud *passes the idols* and escapes to Seirah (3:26b)

D2b(?)   Ehud arrives and *sounds the ram's horn*   ויהי
                          in the *hill country of Ephraim* (3:27a)
                          in order to lead the *Israelites* (3:27b)
                          Ehud's direct speech: "follow after me (3:28aα)

E2a   for *YHWH has given your enemies...into your hand"* (3:28aβ)
                          They went down after him and captured the *fords of the Jordan*, thus preventing Moab from crossing (3:28b)

Situation Resolution: (3:29)
                          At that time they struck 10,000 stout warriors of Moab (3:29a)
                          No one escaped (3:29b)

Prolongation of Resolution: (3:30)
E1   That day Moab was humbled by Israel (3:30a)
F2   The land had peace eighty years (3:30b)

The exposition of the account (3:12-15a), in which the problematic situation is disclosed and the main character introduced, comprises elements of the alienation phase of Judges' cycle-motif and the first element of its restoration phase: YHWH's raising up of a saviour (D1). All the elements of the exposition not included in the cycle-motif also feature elsewhere in the book of Judges ("Ammonites" [3:13] in the Jephthah story, "Amalek" and "City of Palms" [3:13] in *1:16, "left-handed Benjaminites" [3:15aγδ] in 20:16).[45] Although the left-

---

[45] That איש אטר יד־ימינו "a man restricted in [the use of] his right hand" in 3:15aγ indicates left-handedness, not some deformity of the right hand, is supported by the analogy of 3:15aγδ to 20:16. The latter verse refers to seven hundred soldiers of Benjamin who could hardly be expected to load their slings were their right arms infirm. As to Ehud, only if he had use of his right hand could he, by using his left, surprise Eglon. See G. F. Moore, *A Critical and Exegetical Commentary on Judges* (ICC, Edinburgh, 1895), pp. 93-94; C. F. Burney, *The Book of Judges with Introduction and Notes* (London, 2d edn, 1920), pp. 69-70; F. Dexinger, "Ein Plädoyer für die Linkshänder im Richterbuch",

handedness of Ehud and possibly the geographical reference to the City of Palms serve a function in the plot development, the significance of Moab's alliance with the Ammonites and Amalek remains unclear. Yet, regardless of their potential relevance to the Ehud story, all elements of the exposition can be seen to correlate with themes represented elsewhere in Judges.

The development has two phases: the first phase describes Ehud's assassination of Eglon (3:15b-26); the second, his leading Israel into battle against Moab (3:27-28). It is only in the latter phase that thematic elements appear that recur either in the cycle-motif (E2a in 3:28aβ; D2b[?] in 3:27a) or elsewhere in Judges (cf. "hill country of Ephraim" [3:27a] in 2:9, 4:5, 7:24, 10:1, 17:1, 8, 18:2b, 13, 19:1, 16, 18; "fords of the Jordan" [3:28b], in 12:5, 6; cf. "waters of the Jordan", 7:24[2x]).[46] Thus, in this latter phase of the development, as in the exposition, one sees the compiler/redactor's concern for integrating the Ehud story with other accounts in Judges.

The first phase of the development (3:15b-26) appears to be free of accretions. Its integrity appears from the fact that its six main elements conform to a pattern of thematic inversions that pivot at the climactic moment of Eglon's assassination (3:21). However, the result is not a concentric structure (contra Amit) but an asymmetrical development that bifurcates between 3:15b-20 and 3:21-26.[47]

ZAW 89 (1977), pp. 268-69; Alter, Biblical Narrative (1981), p. 38; Gunn, "Joshua and Judges" (1987), p. 115.

Those who have espoused the view that Ehud's right hand was impaired, on the ground that אטר means "crippled", include: Alonso-Schökel, "Erzählkunst" (1961), pp. 148-49; W. Kornfeld, "Onomastica aramaica und das Alte Testament", ZAW 88 (1976), pp. 105-7; J. A. Soggin, Judges: A Commentary (J. Bowden [trans.], OTL, London, 2d edn, 1987), p. 50; idem, "'Ehud und 'Eglon: Bemerkungen zu Richter iii 11b-31", VT 39 (1989), pp. 96-97; HAH, ad loc.; Webb, Judges (1987), p. 245 nn. 26, 27.

Following the Vg and LXX of Judg. 3:15 (LXX: ἀμφοσεροδΔξιον) and 20:16 (LXX: ἀμφοσεροδΔξιοι), H. N. Rösel has surmised that Ehud was ambidextrous ("Zur Ehud-Erzählung", ZAW 89 [1977], p. 270). The context of Judg. 20:16 might allow this interpretation even if the idiom אטר יד־הימין does not require it. Although 1 Chron. 12:2 claims that the Benjaminites who served David were ambidextrous in weapons-handling, the idiom אטר יד־הימין is here rejected for an explicit reference to their use of both right and left hands, מימינים ומשמאלים באבנים ובחצים בקשת. Amit inferred only that Ehud had "excellent command of his left hand" ("Ehud" [1989], p. 106).

[46] All three references in Judges to securing the fords of the Jordan are related to Ephraimite military interventions. They also reflect a lessening degree of cooperation between Ephraim and the other tribes.

[47] Amit proposed the following concentric structure ("Ehud" [1989], pp. 100, 102-3, 119):

The development opens with an interchange between the three stages of Ehud's presentation of Israel's tribute to Eglon (A, 3:15b; B, 17a; C, 18) and two intervening parenthetical descriptions (aa, 3:16; bb, 3:17b). The parenthetical descriptions furnish background for the main plot. The tribute-bearing subplot is not a vehicle for the main plot but camouflage for action that leads to Eglon's assassination. The two parenthetical descriptions (aa, 3:16; bb, 3:17b) anticipate the turning point of Eglon's assassination. Complementing Ehud's preparation and concealment of the dagger in 3:16 (aa) is its sudden use as a weapon in 3:21 (1/aa).[48] Although the mention of Eglon's corpulence appears incidental in 3:17b (bb), in 3:22 (bbⁱ) it facilitates Ehud's escape—the fat that enclosed the dagger may have prevented detectable traces of blood from splattering onto Ehud.[49] The correlation between the 'bb' elements is unique in showing no thematic inversion. Corresponding to

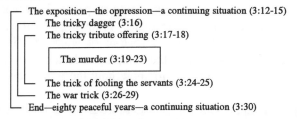

The exposition—the oppression—a continuing situation (3:12-15)
The tricky dagger (3:16)
The tricky tribute offering (3:17-18)

The murder (3:19-23)

The trick of fooling the servants (3:24-25)
The war trick (3:26-29)
End—eighty peaceful years—a continuing situation (3:30)

However, there are few objective data (e.g., theme or vocabulary correspondences) by which to justify Amit's proposal, and her own list of vocabulary collocations between 3:15-17 and 3:21-22 (p. 114) only increases doubt about this concentric analysis.

[48] The dagger is said to be גמד ארכה (3:16aβ), which Tg translates as equivalent to אמה "a cubit". For the *hapax legomenon* גמד, Moore suggested an equivalence to Greek πυγμή "short (cubit)", the distance from the elbow to the knuckles of the fist [ca. thirteen inches] (*Judges* [1895], pp. 93-94; so Burney, *Judges* [2d edn, 1920], p. 70). However, commentators differ as to whether the narrator wanted to emphasize that the dagger was unusually short or long. Some help may be afforded by the amphibology of ויעש לו אהוד חרב (3:16aα), in which לו may indicate either the reflexive "for himself" (so the RSV; NEB; NIV[vid]; Amit ["Ehud" (1989), p. 109], who inferred from this that Ehud acted independently) or, if לו corresponds to the indir. obj. of the previous clause (לעגלון, 3:15b), "[suitable] for him" (so AV, RV, JPSV), namely Eglon, a very fat man (3:17b). The latter alternative might justify Ehud's fashioning an unusually long weapon to have to conceal. Hence, the weapon had to be custom-designed for Eglon: short enough to conceal; long enough to do him in (Alter, *Biblical Narrative* [1981], p. 39).

[49] Rösel, "Ehud-Erzählung" (1977), p. 271; Amit, "Ehud" (1989), p. 113. B. Halpern inferred that there was "no blood" ("The Assassination of Eglon: The First Locked-Room Murder Mystery", *BibRev* 4/6 [1988], p. 41), though this conclusion is rejected as unwarranted by M. L. Barré, "The Meaning of *pršdn* in Judges iii 22", *VT* 41 (1991), p. 7 n. 23.

the commencement of Eglon's attempt to assassinate Eglon by return-ing from the idols in 3:19aαβ (cc) is the completion of his mission in 3:26b (1/cc) when he safely passes the idols.[50] The exit of the courtiers (dd, 3:19bβγ) is inversely complemented by their later entry (1/dd, 3:24aα[ii]). Conversely, the entry of Ehud (ee, 3:20aα) is complemented by his later exit (1/ee, 3:23; 1/ee[i], 3:24aα[i]). Finally, inversely com-plementing Eglon's arising when he is about to be stabbed (ff, 3:20b) is the belated discovery of his fallen corpse by his courtiers (1/ff, 3:25δε).

These six correspondences in the first phase of the development, of which five are inverted, attest a strategy to present Eglon's assassina-tion as the turning point in Israel's fortunes. From this pivotal act, previous actions reverse until, with the plot's resolution, Israel's fortunes are likewise reversed from their state at the close of the exposition. The development achieves the greatest rhetorical effect on the reader through its strategies for heightening suspense. However, it is the position of the development, immediately following YHWH's rais-ing up of Ehud as Israel's deliverer (3:15aβ-δ; of which v. 15aβ is motif D1), that conveys most clearly the compiler/redactor's strategy. The compiler/redactor's strategy was to show how the grand reversal

---

[50] Webb astutely noted that 3:19aαβ, 26b furnishes an inclusio about Ehud's private mission to assassinate Eglon (*Judges* [1987], p. 246 n. 29). Meanings proposed for הפסילים include: (1) "quarries" (so Tg; Psht; AV; RV; JPSV; Amit ["Ehud" (1989), pp. 102, 112, 113, 115, 118]; C. F. Keil and Franz Delitzsch, *Biblischer Commentar über das Alten Testament*, vol. II/1, *Josua, Richter und Ruth*, by C. F. Keil [Leipzig, 1863], ET: *Biblical Commentary on the Old Testament*, vol. 4, *Joshua, Judges, Ruth* [J. Martin (trans.), CFTL 4/VIII, Edinburgh, 1868]; repr. edn, *Commentary on the Old Testament*, 10 vols., vol. 2, *Joshua, Judges, Ruth, I & II Samuel* [Grand Rapids, 1976], p. 296); (2) "boundary stones" (so earlier commentaries by Ralbag [as an alternative], Cornelius à Lapide [1642], Sebastian Schmid [1684] and Paulus Cassell [1865]; also J. Bachmann, *Das Buch der Richter: Mit besonderer Rücksicht auf die Geschichte seiner Auslegung und kirchlichen Verwendung*, vol. 1 [Berlin, 1868–1869], pp. 209-11; Burney, *Judges* [2d edn, 1920], p. 71 [as an alternative]); (3) "sculptured stones" (so Moore, *Judges* [1895], pp. 94, 100; Burney, *Judges* [2d edn, 1920], p. 71 [as an alternative]; RSV; NEB: "carved stones"; Webb, *Judges* [1987], p. 131)—sometimes identified with the twelve stones erected by Joshua (Josh. 4:20; so G. L. Studer, *Das Buch der Richter gram-matisch und historisch erklärt* [Bern, 1835], ad loc.; cf. K. Galling, "Erwägungen zum Stelenheiligtum von Hazor", *ZDPV* 75 [1959], p. 13); or (4) "idols" (so E. G. H. Krael-ing, "Difficulties in the Story of Ehud", *JBL* 54 [1935], p. 206; Rösel, "Ehud-Erzählung" [1977] p. 271; NIV). Whatever may have been the meaning of הפסילים in the traditional account of Ehud, its recontextualization, so as to be interpreted in the light of deuteronomic standards, suggests that it should now be taken to refer to idols (cf. Deut. 4:16-18, 23, 25; 7:25; 12:3).

of Israel's fortunes, which Ehud initiates by assassinating Eglon, redounds to the credit of YHWH, who raised up this saviour.[51]

However, simply to state explicitly that YHWH enabled Ehud to return safely after Eglon's assassination would not have had significant impact on the reader. It is by means of portrayal that the compiler/redactor, who contextualized the development section, sought to make his/her point. Yet, as heroic as is the portrayal of Ehud in the development, his characterization is but a foil for the elevation of YHWH as Israel's true deliverer. In the first phase of the development (3:15b-26), Ehud astutely uses tactics of deception to accomplish his aim: (1) exploitation of his own left-handedness by concealing the dagger on his right thigh, (2) use of his first visit as a ruse of loyalty to remove suspicion at his return, (3) use of misdirecting speech (3:19aγδ, 20aγδ) to induce Eglon's succeeding actions (3:19bα, 20b),[52] (4) refraining

---

[51] Amit has suggested that 3:15aβγ[i] was juxtaposed with 3:15b in order to illustrate the divine–human "double causality" of events in the Ehud account ("Ehud" [1989], p. 105). She emphasized that, while the reader knows that Ehud was raised up by God as a deliverer, the Israelites of the story do not know that Ehud will be their deliverer. Moreover, inasmuch as 3:15aβ-δ is a narrative summary, not a divine revelation within the story world, Ehud himself probably did not know that YHWH had appointed him to deliver Israel until he had succeeded in assassinating Eglon—the fact of his success attesting YHWH's help (3:28aβ; cf. Webb, *Judges* [1987], p. 132).

[52] Several have noticed the repetition with alteration in Ehud's wording from דבר־סתר לי אליך המלך (3:19aδ), by which he gains a private audience with Eglon, to דבר־אלהים לי אליך (3:20aδ), by which Eglon is motivated to rise from his throne (cf. Rösel, "Ehud-Erzählung" [1977], p. 271; Webb, *Judges* [1987], p. 131; Amit, "Ehud" [1989], p. 113). Each speech issues immediately in Eglon acting to facilitate Ehud's plan. In each speech, Ehud uses the ambiguity of דבר, meaning either "word" (i.e., message) or "thing" (i.e., dagger), to misdirect the king and his entourage (so Alter, *Biblical Narrative* [1981], p. 40), but the reader may further sense in Ehud's "I have a secret/divine matter for you [Eglon]" an ironic allusion to his concealed dagger as that which Ehud had made "for him [Eglon]" (3:16aα) (cf. Klein, *Triumph of Irony* [1988], pp. 37-38). Indeed, the duplicity of both speeches' use of דבר may play on a key feature of Ehud's dagger—its double-edgedness (ולה שני פיות, 3:16aβ). E. M. Good recognized the irony attached to the analogy between the description of the dagger as "double-mouthed" and Ehud's misdirecting use of דבר (*Irony in the Old Testament* [London, 1965; repr. edn, BLS 3, Sheffield, 1981], pp. 33-34; cf. Gunn, "Joshua and Judges" [1987], p. 116). Further irony inheres in the pattern of collocations between 3:15b-16 and 3:21 that shows how, in different ways, Ehud had something "in his hand" to present to Eglon (cf. Alonso-Schökel, "Erzählkunst" [1961], p. 152):

וישלחו בני־ישראל בידו מנחה	(3:15bα)	וישלח אהוד את־יד שמאלו	(3:21aα)
ויעש לו אהוד חרב	(3:16aα)	ויקח את־החרב	(3:21aβ)
ויחגר אותה ... על ירך ימינו	(3:16b)	מעל ירך ימינו	(3:21aγ)

Perhaps it is appropriate to observe in this use of דבר the first instance of an implicit theme among the deliverer accounts relating to the efficacy of the word from or directed toward YHWH/God. In the Ehud account, it is the double significance of דבר (i.e., "secret

from withdrawing the dagger to avoid incurring blood stains and (5) locking the doors around Eglon from the outside to delude Eglon's courtiers as to Eglon's safety within.[53] But perhaps one may infer from Ehud's later expression of confidence that YHWH would guarantee victory (כי־נתן יהוה את־איביכם את־מואב בידכם, 3:28aβ) that Ehud already recognized that it was YHWH who had ensured his own success by controlling the consequences of his human tactics: in (1) and (2), by preventing the courtiers' discovery of Ehud's concealed weapon on two occasions; in (3), by ensuring both Eglon's dismissal of his courtiers to furnish Ehud with a private opportunity to strike and Eglon's arising to present an easy target for Ehud's dagger; in (4), by having Eglon's fat envelop the dagger-hilt, perhaps to minimize blood loss; in (5), by ensuring Eglon's accidental discharge so that its odour would decoy his courtiers to tarry while Ehud escaped (cf. 3:24b).[54]

---

word"/"word from God", 3:19aδ, 20aδ) that marks the turning point from Ehud's feigned obeisance to his opposition to Eglon. In the Deborah/Barak/Jael account, it is Deborah's conveyance of a word from YHWH to Barak (4:6-7) that catalyses the main action of the plot. In the Gideon/Abimelech account, God's judgement on Abimelech's crimes is mitigated by a word from Jotham (9:7, 56-57). Ironically, in the Jephthah account, it is the nemesis of the stray word vowed to YHWH (11:30-31) that diminishes Jephthah's house. In the Samson account, the word that catalyses the main action is likewise a stray word (i.e., Samson's riddle instigates the sequence of escalating violence), though, on two occasions, Samson directs an efficacious word of petition toward YHWH (15:18-19; 16:28-30a). Perhaps even the utterances of YHWH's angel/messenger or prophet (2:1-3; 6:8-10; 10:11-14) should be understood as developing the theme of the efficacy of the word from or to YHWH—each is occasioned by Israel's directing words toward YHWH (cf. 2:4-5; 6:7; 10:10). Only in the case of the Othniel account is this theme lacking.

[53] Amit already noted the last three as examples of Ehud's tactics ("Ehud" [1989], pp. 112-13). Ehud's barring the doors around Eglon (so בעדו in בעדו העליה דלתות ויסגר and נעל, 3:23b; cf. הלהב בעד החלב ויסגר, 3:22aβ) so that they could not be reopened without the use of a key (cf. 3:25β) suggests that he barred the doors from the outside by pulling a thong (cf. ונעל, 3:23b and נעלות, 3:24aγ; contra Burney, Judges (2d edn, 1920), p. 74; see Kraeling, "Difficulties" [1935], pp. 208-10).

[54] So Y. Kaufmann, The Book of Judges (Jerusalem, 1961–1962), p. 109 [Hebrew]; Alter, Biblical Narrative (1981), p. 39, who calls it "scatological humor". The hapax legomenon הפרשדנה has been emended by some to הַפֶּרֶשׁ "the faeces" so as to express the subject of the verb (cf. Tg; Vg [statimque per secreta naturae alvi stercora proruperunt]; Luther; T. Nöldeke, Untersuchungen zur Kritik des Alten Testaments [Kiel, 1869], p. 180 n.; K. Budde, Das Buch der Richter [K. Marti (ed.), KHAT 7, Freiburg, i. B., 1897], p. 31; Moore, Judges [1895], pp. 97-98; BDB, p. 832a; Rösel, "Ehud-Erzählung" [1977], p. 272).

Burney (Judges [2d edn, 1920], pp. 72-73) suggested that Akk. parašdinnu, for which the Sumerian KIRRUD.DA (= pa-ra-aš-din-nu) meant 'cavity, opening', offers a possible cognate (so O. Glaser, "Zur Erzählung von Ehud und Eglon (Ri. 3,14-26)", ZDPV 55 [1932], p. 82). For this, Burney cited Friedrich Delitzsch, Assyrisches Handwörterbuch (Leipzig, 1896), p. 546 (cf. F. Buhl [ed.], Wilhelm Gesenius' Handwörterbuch über das Alte Testament [Leipzig, 17th edn, 1915], p. 664; H. Zimmern, Akkadische Fremdwörter

Moreover, the latter three consequences coincide with instances of temporal ordering in the narrative that show how YHWH was in control of the 'coincidences' that led to Ehud's success. Implicit here is a satire on the Moabite courtiers as would-be bodyguards who are three times 'given the slip' during Ehud's well-timed second excursion. The disjunctive syntax that opens 2:20aα sets it in synchroneity with the preceding action of 3:19bβγ—as the courtiers leave Eglon's presence (ויצאו מעליו כל־העמדים עליו) Ehud enters it (ואהוד בא אליו) so that Ehud and Eglon are alone together.[55] This transfer reverses in 3:24aα, where, once again, the disjunctive syntax signals the synchroneity of two actions—while Ehud leaves (והוא יצא) the courtiers come back (ועבדיו באו).[56] Yet, apart from the growing stench, Eglon's condition

---

als Beweis für babylonischen Kultureinfluss [Leipzig, 2d edn, 1917], ad loc.). This etymology and the meaning 'hole' for *parašdinnu* was listed in KB, p. 783, and repeated in *HALAT*, p. 920, though already in 1955 W. von Soden had rejected both the etymology (reading instead, *paraštinnu*) and meaning 'hole' ("Zum akkadischen Wörterbuch, 61-66", *Or* NS 24 [1955], pp. 144-45; cf. *AHw*, vol. 2, p. 832b for Akk. *paraštinnu* = Hittite *parašdu*, 'Knospe?' ['(plant) bud'] = BH *paršdon*).

Rejecting entirely the equation Akk. *paraštinnu* = BH *pršdn*, Barré argued that BH *pršdn* is better equated with Akk. *naparšudu* (root *pršd*) 'to escape, flee' (often parallel to Akk. *[w]aṣû* = BH *yāṣā*ʾ, just as in Judg. 3:22b) ("*pršdn*" [1991], pp. 2-6). Barré allowed that *pršdn* could mean "'the place through which something "escapes" (from the body)'— viz., the anus" (p. 6). On this view, some claim that relaxation of the anal sphincter in a death spasm is said to be a normal bodily reflex when one is struck in the abdomen (cf. Moore, *Judges* [1895], p. 97; Alter, *Biblical Narrative* [1981], p. 39; Halpern, "Assassination" [1988], p. 34; idem, "A Message for Eglon: The Case of Ehud Ben-Gera", in *The First Historians: The Hebrew Bible and History* [San Francisco, 1988], p. 69 n. 3), though this claim is marginalized by Barré on the basis of negative medical evidence ("*pršdn*" [1991], p. 8, n. 25). Barré preferred to argue for a noun meaning 'excrement' and the view that this came from the wound, translating: "and ... the/his excrement came out (of the wound)" (p. 11), though, on this view, Barré must remove either initial ה (definite article) or final ה (3 m. sg suff.) from an allegedly corrupt הפרשדנה.

The latter dilemma may be removed, however, if פרשדן is understood as 'anus' (as etymology allows) and the final ה of הפרשדנה as ה-locative (i.e., "at the anus"). Of course, this leaves a syntax in which there is no explicit subject for the verb ויצא, but, in view of the obviousness of the subject and the evocative force of innuendo (both פרש 'faecal matter' and צאה 'filth, excrement' are paronomastically echoed in ויצא הפרשדנה), its ellipsis need hardly offend us. The difficult ויצא הפרשדנה (3:22b) may therefore mean, "and it [i.e. 'faecal matter'] went out the anus".

[55] Cf. Amit, "Ehud" (1989), p. 115.

[56] Cf. Amit, "Ehud" (1989), p. 116. Against the proposal that Ehud departed undetected through the latrine (Glaser, "Erzählung" [1932], p. 82), it should be argued that Ehud left in the normal manner through the colonnade (so Kraeling, "Difficulties" [1935], p. 208; Rösel, "Ehud-Erzählung" [1977], p. 271; Alter, *Biblical Narrative* [1981], p. 39). That he bypasses the arriving courtiers as he leaves only heightens his cunning, the courtiers' credulity and the reader's suspense.

remains undetected.[57] The concentric pairing of occurrences of יצא and
בוא within the first phase of the development section (3:15b-26) centres
on the climax at 3:21-22—particularly on the gory description of
Eglon's death (3:22b).[58] In 3:26a[i] and 3:26bα one encounters two
examples of disjunction that indicate a change of subject (showing
interchange between the courtiers and Ehud), but these disjunctions
also portray synchroneity showing how, as the courtiers tarried (ויחילו
עד־בוש, 3:25aα; עד התמהמהם, 3:26a[ii]), Ehud escaped (ואהוד נמלט,
3:26a[i]; והוא עבר את־הפסילים וימלט השעירתה, 3:26b).[59]

In contrast to YHWH's glorification, achieved by showing his control
of circumstances in the narrative, Eglon is made the object of satirical
ridicule by means of either ritual tribute offering or sacrificial
imagery.[60] The language of ritual tribute offering and sacrifice is

---

[57] That the attendants waited עד־בוש (lit. "until [the point of] shame", 3:25aα) denotes
only their bewilderment over Eglon's long delay (cf. 2 Kgs 2:17; 8:11; so Moore, *Judges*
[1895], pp. 99, 101; Burney, *Judges* [2d edn, 1920], p. 74). However, through satire
achieved by wordplay, it may also connote their growing embarrassment over the ever
more rank odour emanating from within.

[58] The following concentric analysis, centring on 3:22b, is adapted from Barré,
"*pršdn*" (1991), pp. 8-9:

```
┌─  wysʾw Moabite courtiers (3:19b)
│  ┌─  bʾ Ehud (3:20a)
│  │  ┌─  wybʾ ... wysgr ... bʿd  Ehud's dagger-hilt (3:22a)
│  │  │  ┌─────────────────────────────────┐
│  │  │  │  wyṣʾ  Eglon's excrement (3:22b) │
│  │  │  └─────────────────────────────────┘
│  │  └─  wyṣʾ ... wysgr ... bʿd  Ehud (3:23a)
│  └─  wyṣʾ Ehud (3:24a)
└─  bʾw Moabite courtiers (3:24a)
```

[59] Cf. Amit, "Ehud" (1989), p. 118.

[60] Ancient Near Eastern depictions of tribute-bearers in ritual procession are attested
in: (1) the sarcophagus of Ahiram of Byblos (M. Haran, "The Bas-Reliefs on the Sarcophagus of Ahiram King of Byblos in the Light of Archaeological and Literary Parallels
from the Ancient Near East", *IEJ* 8 [1958], pl. 11 A-B; *ANEP*, no. 458); (2) the gates of
Ashurnasirpal II from Balawat (J. Curtis [ed.], *Fifty Years of Mesopotamian Discovery:
The Work of the British School of Archaeology in Iraq 1932-1982* [London, 1982], fig. 86
[p. 117]); (3) the Black Obelisk of Shalmaneser III (*ANEP*, nos. 351-55; J. Reade,
Assyrian Sculpture [London, 1983], figs. 12 [p. 17], 62-63 [p. 45]; T. C. Mitchell, *The
Bible in the British Museum: Interpreting the Evidence* [London, 1988], pp. 48-49).
These should be distinguished from: (1) depictions of kings reviewing booty taken in
conquest (e.g., on the Megiddo ivory knife handle [Haran, "Bas-Reliefs" (1958), pl. 10
B-C; *ANEP*, no. 332]; or Sennacherib's review of booty from Lachish [*ANEP*, no. 371;
Mitchell, *Bible in the British Museum* (1988), pp. 60-64]); (2) royal banqueting scenes
(e.g., a scene from Karatepe [*ANEP*, no. 849; J. B. Pritchard (ed.), *The Ancient Near
East*, vol. 2, *A New Anthology of Texts and Pictures* (Princeton, 1975), fig. 81]; or Ashurbanipal banqueting [Pritchard (ed.), *The Ancient Near East*, vol. 1, *An Anthology of Texts*

especially prevalent in 3:15b-18.[61] The name עֶגְלוֹן (3:12bα, 14, 15b, 17 [2x]), as that of כּוּשַׁן רִשְׁעָתַיִם (3:8 [2x], 10 [2x]), may be a mocking appellative, "calflike, bovine". It is reminiscent of עֵגֶל 'calf', often used to designate the idolatrous image at Horeb (Exod. 32:4, 8, 19, 20, 24, 35; Deut. 9:16, 21) but sometimes used of sacrifice (Lev. 9:2, 3, 8). It is similarly reminiscent of עֶגְלָה 'heifer', a draught animal (cf. Judg. 14:18) sometimes used for sacrifice (1 Sam. 16:2; cf. Gen. 15:9 [covenant ratification]; Deut. 21:3 [blood-guiltiness]).[62] The nuance is ambiguous: will Ehud make a tribute offering to "Calflike" or slaughter him?[63] Here, the use of panel-writing makes plain the narrator's strategy. Using the pretext of leading a party of bearers to offer tribute to Eglon, Ehud gives the outward impression that he is making an offering to Eglon. This is the pretext set forth by the elements designated A (3:15b), B (3:17a), and C (3:18). Among these clauses are repeated three key expressions of tribute offering: the verb שׁלח 'to send, dismiss'; the noun מנחה 'gift, offering, tribute'; and the verb קרב (in Hi.) 'to present, offer'.

(3:15b) וישלחו בני־ישראל בידו מנחה לעגלון
(3:17a) ויקרב את־המנחה לעגלון
(3:18) ויהי כאשר כלה להקריב את־המנחה וישלח את־העם נשאי המנחה

Alternating with the imagery of ritual tribute offering, the parenthetical remarks that intervene between elements A, B and C (i.e., aa, 3:16; bb, 3:17b) use sacrificial imagery. Like the מנחה, the special doublebladed dagger that Ehud fashioned "for himself" (cf. לוֹ, 3:16a) is, by amphibology, potentially "for him" (i.e., Eglon) but even in the latter case might function ambiguously as either a private gift or, as it turns

---

and Pictures (Princeton, 1958), fig. 122; ANEP, no. 451]); (3) scenes of royal offering to the gods (e.g., an Ashurbanipal relief from Nineveh [Pritchard (ed.), Ancient Near East, vol. 1 (1958), fig. 156; ANEP, no. 626]).

[61] Indeed, it was probably in order to hint at the cultic order—used by Ehud as a ruse for his return visit to Eglon and by the narrator as a clue to the cultic nature of satire against Eglon—that the turning point of the narrative between Ehud's first excursion (to make tribute offering to Eglon) and his second (to sacrifice Eglon) takes place at the idols near Gilgal (3:19a).

[62] That עֶגְלוֹן constitutes an appellative, rather than a personal name, was the view of both M. Noth, who cited Ehud but not Eglon as a proper name (Die israelitischen Personennamen in Rahmen der gemeinsemitischen Namengebung [BWANT III/10, Stuttgart, 1928], p. 146 [on Ehud]), and Soggin ("'Ehud und 'Eglon" [1989], p. 96).

[63] Implicit etymologizing of Eglon's name has been noted by E. I. Täubler, Biblische Studien I: Die Epoche der Richter (H.-J. Zobel [ed.], Tübingen, 1958), pp. 35-36; Alonso-Schökel, "Erzählkunst" (1961), pp. 148-50; Alter, Biblical Narrative (1981), p. 39; Gunn, "Joshua and Judges" (1987), p. 115.

out, a sacrificial knife. Further, Eglon, whose name connotes alternatively an object of illegitimate adoration or of sacrifice, is ברא מאד‎ (Judg. 3:17b). Thus, when Ehud completes his emissary task and dismisses the tribute-bearers at the end of 3:15b-18, one wonders why only the ritual tribute offering course has been fulfilled while hints at a sacrificial course have barely emerged.[64] However, by this means the narrator achieves two rhetorical effects. One effect of this diversionary tactic is to heighten the reader's suspense. A second effect is to set up a foil between the first portrayal of Eglon as a victorious recipient of tribute offering before Ehud's entourage and Eglon's satirical portrayal as a 'sacrificial' victim before YHWH's deliverer Ehud. The satire implicit in the description of Ehud's second excursion is both facilitated and heightened by the dramatic irony that, by granting Ehud complete freedom of movement, Eglon and his attendants show no awareness that the outcome may prove any less profitable for Moab than in Ehud's first excursion. Yet, without disclosing explicitly how a reversal will be effected, already, in the parentheses of 3:16 and 3:17b, one sees its foreshadowing.

Before the close of the first phase of the development (3:15b-26), the narrator inserts an account of the courtiers' delay before discovering the assassination of their king (3:24aβ-25). This description disrupts the connection between the reader and Ehud and thus retards the plot development.[65] The rhetorical aim of this retardation was apparently both to raise suspense and to convince the reader that Ehud, who was simultaneously making his escape, had sufficient time in which to do so.[66] Each of the three statements describing the courtiers' delay begins with והנה‎, which expresses their sense of surprise as they come to each new realization.[67] Inasmuch as it is only the third and final discovery

---

[64] The fact that the description that concludes the course of development involving tribute offering begins with ויהי‎ (C, 3:18) gives it an air of finality. Only once more, when it signals the final phase of the development (3:27-28), does ויהי‎ give weight to the moment.

[65] Alonso-Schökel, "Erzählkunst" (1961), p. 156; Amit, "Ehud" (1989), p. 118.

[66] Amit, "Ehud" (1989), pp. 116, 118.

[67] Täubler, *Biblische Studien I* (1958), pp. 39-40; Alonso-Schökel, "Erzählkunst" (1961), p. 153; Alter, *Biblical Narrative* (1981), p. 40; Amit, "Ehud" (1989), p. 117. On the frequent use of הנה‎ to indicate "free indirect discourse" or surprise, see F. I. Andersen, *The Sentence in Biblical Hebrew* (The Hague, 1974), pp. 94-96; D. J. McCarthy, "The Uses of wěhinněh in Biblical Hebrew", *Bib* 61 (1980), pp. 330-42; M. Sternberg, "Language, World and Perspective in Biblical Narrative Art: Free Indirect Discourse and Modes of Covert Penetration", *Hasifrut* 32 (1983), pp. 88-131, especially pp. 101-2 [Hebrew]; idem, *The Poetics of Biblical Narrative: Ideological Literature and*

that brings them to the truth, the courtiers suffer the ridicule of satire for having been taken in by Ehud's delaying tactics.

With the closing of the first phase of the development, the task of summoning the tribes to battle may begin (leading toward the plot resolution). Ehud, having proven himself a divinely appointed deliverer by virtue of his success (cf. 3:28aβ), sounds the ram's horn to summon the Israelites to battle (3:27). The otherwise difficult sequence of events presented by 3:27-28 may be explained by understanding 3:28abα as a parenthesis designed to embellish the parallel report in 3:27aβb by giving a spiritual motivation for the Israelites' descent. It is perhaps an important question of characterization whether Ehud was seeking to summon the Israelites to battle as a means to attain to leadership among them. If present, the characterization of Ehud as an opportunist is subtle but would parallel that of other deliverers in Judges (cf. the motivation underlying Gideon's request for gold earrings or Jephthah's vow). This implication becomes more pronounced by virtue of the parallel between Ehud's final words, רדפו אחרי "Follow after me" (3:28aα[ii]), and the disjunctive clause of attendant circumstance, והוא לפניהם, "with him leading them" (3:27b[iv]). Ehud's concern that Israel should follow him is surely of secondary importance to the resolution (in which the primary concern is that Israel become liberated from Moabite oppressors) and may be viewed as nothing more than Ehud's encouragement to Israel to take action on the basis of his example. However, the subsequent growing concern of the Judges compiler/ redactor with the leadership qualities of Israel's deliverers leads one, in

---

the Drama of Reading (ISBL, Bloomington, 1985), pp. 52-53; S. Kogut, "On the Meaning and Syntactical Status of הִנֵּה in Biblical Hebrew", in Studies in Bible, 1986 (S. Japhet [ed.], ScrHier 31, Jerusalem, 1986), pp. 133-54. However, see J. Barr's caution against viewing all הִנֵּה clauses as indicating surprise ("[Review:] F. I. Andersen, The Sentence in Biblical Hebrew. The Hague, 1974", JTS NS 27 [1976], pp. 152-53).

The courtiers' surprise at finding Eglon locked in the upper room (3:24aγ) stems from the temporal proximity of Ehud's exit. They are surprised to find the door locked so soon after Ehud's exit, but, to their humiliation, they only gradually realize that there had been foul play. The setting of the murder scene must have been an upper room (designated alternatively עלית המקרה [3:20aβ], העליה [3:23b, 24aγ, 25aβ] and חדר המקרה [3:24bβ]) that had (presumably double) doors (דלתות העליה, 3:23b, 24aγ, 25aβ) and a colonnaded vestibule (המסדרונה, 3:23a) (contra Glaser, "Erzählung" [1932], pp. 81-82, see Kraeling, "Difficulties" [1935], pp. 207-8; Rösel, "Ehud-Erzählung" [1977], pp. 271-72). Because of the matter-of-fact manner in which they draw their mistaken inference, אך מסיך הוא את־רגליו (3:24bβ), there must also have been a toilet within where Eglon customarily relieved himself. On the nature of the toilet, see U. Hübner, "Mord auf dem Abort? Überlegungen zu Humor, Gewaltdarstellung und Realienkunde in Ri 3,12-30", BN 40 (1987), pp. 135-40.

retrospect, to inquire whether Ehud's characterization as a self-promoting saviour is an intended nuance. While Ehud claims YHWH's guarantee of success in 3:28aβ on the basis of his foregoing success, there is something implicitly self-authenticating about it, for by no explicit means had YHWH disclosed this to any character in the story world.[68] Whatever Ehud's motives, Israelites from the hill country of Ephraim do go down (3:28bα) and block the fords of the Jordan to prevent the Moabites from escaping to Transjordan (3:28bβγ).[69]

The plot resolution occurs in two parts. First comes a census of the Moabite soldiers struck down at that time (3:29a), with the claim that, in contrast to Ehud, whom God helped to escape, none of the Moabites escaped (3:29b). Indeed, the apparent hyperbolical claim that not one of them escaped (cf. 4:16bβ) seems to give implicit evidence of YHWH's help, which justifies Ehud's claim in 3:28aβ. Perhaps 3:29 preserves the resolution of the traditional narrative. This resolution is extended, however, by the compiler/redactor's addition of 3:30. Although the similarity of Judg. 3:29aα (ויכו את־מואב בעת ההיא) and 3:30aα (ותכנע מואב ביום ההוא) appears redundant, the latter alone

---

[68] As further evidence of the subtly negative characterization of Ehud, Klein has observed the implicit parallelism between the juxtaposed actions in 3:22b and 3:23a (*Triumph of Irony* [1988], pp. 38-39):

ויצא הפרשדנה	(3:22b)
ויצא אהוד המסדרונה	(3:23a)

The assonance prompts the reader to wonder whether the narrator intended some link between the disgrace associated with the former and the echoing description of Ehud's departure in the latter. Indeed, from this point in the development it is possible to discern that a motive for Ehud's private foray may have been a desire to make himself a leader in Israel. It may be significant in this connection that the Ehud account is one of only two in Judges (cf. that of Gideon) from which the F1 motif ("... judged ... Israel [N years]") is absent.

[69] The ל of למואב (3:28bβ) probably indicates the *dativus incommodi* (dative of disadvantage; GKC, §119s), "against Moab"—Moab standing as a metonymy for the Moabite soldiers (SO RV; JPSV; RSV; NEB; Moore, *Judges* [1895], pp. 102-3; Burney, *Judges* [2d edn, 1920], p. 75). The view that למואב indicates direction "[leading] to Moab" (AV, RV[mg], NIV) seems unlikely, since the same construction occurs also in 7:24aβ (ולכדו את־מעברות הירדן לאפרים ... וילכד) and 12:5a (להם את־המים), where it cannot be explained in this way. Soggin proposed that ל means "from" (i.e. "from [the hands of] Moab"), on analogy with the Ugaritic preposition (*Judges* [2d edn, 1987], p. 52; idem, "'Ehud und 'Eglon" [1989], pp. 97-98). Soggin's analogy to Ugaritic is tenuous but certainly should not lead to his subsequent inference that the Benjaminites' recapture of the fords was aimed at preventing the enemy's crossing towards the west—an inference that founders on the summary of 3:29b, "not one escaped".

recognizes the reversal of Moab's fortune, which is required to resolve the problem of Israel's oppression that was introduced in the exposition. Indeed, 3:30 holds two elements of the compiler/redactor's cycle-motif (E1, F2).

However, as evidence of tribal–political concerns in this account, one should observe two repeated words that, through escalated parallelism, link Ehud's personal triumph with that of tribal Israel. First, one may note the strategic development of the 'hand' motif.[70] It is probably not by accident that the juncture between 3:15a and 3:15b, the climax of the story at 3:21-22, Ehud's speech to rouse the tribes to battle in 3:28a and the closing summary of Israel's success in 3:30 all develop the hand motif. Since Ehud is introduced as איש אטר יד־ימינו (3:15aδ) who is nonetheless a בן־הימיני (3:15aγ), the reader expects that there will be something devious about his characterization. This expectation is not disappointed, for, whereas the account of Ehud's first excursion begins וישלחו בני־ישראל בידו מנחה (3:15bα), the surprising climax of his second excursion shows his sleight of hand through the narrator's turn of phrase וישלח אהוד את־יד שמאלו (3:21aα). Then, in relay fashion, when Ehud returns from Eglon's assassination, he implies that YHWH is transferring the responsibility of victory from his own hand to that of the tribes: כי־נתן יהוה את־איביכם את־מואב בידכם (3:28aβ). Finally, in recognition of the latter, the compiler/redactor recontextualizes the victory of Ehud and the tribes with a national claim (ותכנע מואב ביום ההוא תחת יד ישראל, 3:30a) that furnishes the escalated parallel between the fate of Eglon at the hand of Ehud and that of Eglon's nation under the hand of Ehud's nation.[71]

Another case of repetition links Ehud's assassination of Eglon with Israel's defeat of the Moabites, showing escalated parallelism between the incidents. By a polysemic wordplay, Ehud's strategic blow against Moab (ויתקעה בבטנו, 3:21b; cf. 4:21aβ) may be linked to that of the tribes who are summoned to battle by his blowing on the ram's horn (ויתקע בשופר בהר אפרים, 3:27aβ).[72]

The lack of an explicit statement that the idols (3:19aαβ and 3:26b) were finally removed from the land offers a possible instance of implicit escalated parallelism between the cultic indolence of Ehud and

---

[70] Alonso-Schökel, "Erzählkunst" (1961), p. 149; Webb, *Judges* (1987), p. 245 n. 23; Gunn, "Joshua and Judges" (1987), p. 115; Amit, "Ehud" (1989), p. 120.

[71] Cf. Alter, *Biblical Narrative* (1981), pp. 40-41.

[72] Alonso-Schökel, "Erzählkunst" (1961), pp. 152-53, 157; Alter, *Biblical Narrative* (1981), p. 41.

that of the Israelites whom he summoned to battle. As previously mentioned, this failure to remove the idols subtly, but negatively, characterizes Ehud (as microcosm) and Israel (as macrocosm) and ostensibly leads the latter to the religious apostasy that instigates the following deliverer account (cf. 4:1).

In conclusion, it appears that both plot-structure and characterization serve the rhetorical strategies of satire and suspense. By means of satire, the narrative ridicules Israel's enemy king and his court and glorifies Israel's hero Ehud and god YHWH. Suspense, too, both heightens the heroic characterization of Ehud of Benjamin, who risked his safety to assassinate Eglon, and glorifies YHWH, who controlled circumstances so that they would work out in Ehud's favour. However, the lack of a statement that Israel removed the idols from the land may implicate Israel as a people lacking in cultic devotion to YHWH while under the leadership of the Benjaminite Ehud.

At this juncture it may be appropriate to mention that these observations tell only about the concerns of the Ehud account as it is read in isolation from the book of Judges. With a view to the rhetorical purpose of Judges, however, it is not sufficient to observe in particular that Ehud, as a left-handed Benjaminite, represents an unlikely deliverer whom YHWH, to his own glorification, enabled to outwit and overcome Israel's enemies. Nor is it adequate to observe in general that the compiler/redactor's framework adapts and recontextualizes this story to exemplify YHWH's unmerited grace in delivering the Israelite tribes despite their apparent shortcomings. These are valid observations, but they fail to ascertain what peculiar purpose the Ehud story as a whole was being made to serve within the book of Judges. Whatever may have been the primary rhetorical function of the Ehud story in its traditional context, it does not at first appear, from a reading of the story in isolation, how the Judges compiler/redactor intended it to further his/her overall purpose in Judges. However, insofar as Judges' deliverer stories have been made to serve the book's overall purpose, one may be able to discern this purpose from tracing the development of deuteronomic, tribal–political and monarchical themes shared among the deliverer accounts.[73]

---

[73] See the discussion relating to Judges' deuteronomic and tribal–political schemata in chapter 1 and that relating to Judges' rhetorical strategy of monarchical idealization in chapter 3.

§3. The Account of Deborah/Barak/Jael (4:1–5:31)

As in the Ehud account, plot-structure and characterization are key indicators of rhetorical concerns in the account of Deborah/Barak/Jael. The tribal–political concerns of the latter are evident, first of all, in the satirization of the military commander Sisera as an agent of Jabin's oppressive foreign kingship in contrast to the glorification of YHWH, who controls all circumstances that lead to Israel's deliverance—both those of the temporal order in the prose portrayal and those of the cosmic order, with which Jael's actions are consonant, in the hymnic portrayal. Second, the mixed characterization of Barak in the prose account as a (non-Judahite) tribal leader who is reluctant to fight for YHWH apart from the prompting of a woman of Ephraim and, unable to achieve complete victory without the aid of another woman from a marginal clan (the Kenites) of Judah finds an escalated parallel in the hymnic portrayal of tribal Israel as likewise only partially committed to fighting for YHWH and likewise unable to achieve complete victory without the actions of the Kenite woman. Thus, in both prose and poetry, the halfheartedness of Israel's men is satirized through contrast to the Yahwistic zeal of Israelite women.

The plot-structure of the Deborah/Barak/Jael account is more complicated than that of the Ehud account and initiates a trend in Judges toward more complicated plot-structures. Also, its plot-structure is unique in furnishing a context for Judges' only extended poetic section, the victory hymn of 5:2-31a. The prose account gives context to the hymn (5:2-31a) not only because it frames the hymn (4:1-24; 5:31b) but also because it furnishes information without which the hymn would not achieve its present effect of augmenting the reader's indignation and admiration in regard to the main themes of the prose account.[74] Indeed, the prose and hymnic versions together comprise a rhetoric of entrapment by which, having invited Israel's indignation against Barak for halfheartedness toward YHWH in the prose account,

---

[74] A. Brenner has likewise inferred from the fact that the prose account frames the poem and the fact that information is withheld from both versions that can only be supplied from the other version that Judg. 4 and 5 were designed to complement each other within a single "infrastructure" ("A Triangle and a Rhombus in Narrative Structure: A Proposed Integrative Reading of Judges iv and v", *VT* 40 [1990], pp. 129-30, 136-38). This rhetorical design is tacitly acknowledged by all who fill informational gaps in one version by resorting to the other (e.g., Josephus, *Ant.* V.v.4 §§205-6 [cf. 4:14-15 with 5:4-5, 20-21]; Moore, *Judges* [1895], p. 120 [cf. 4:14 with 5:4-5]; Burney, *Judges* [2d edn, 1920], pp. 79 [cf. 4:14-15 with 5:19], 79, 87-88 [cf. 4:6 with 5:14-15a, 18], 79-80, 93 [cf. 4:21 with 5:26-27], 90-91 [cf. 4:14 with 5:4-5, 20-21], 93 [cf. 4:19 with 5:25]).

the hymn then augments that indignation, directing it against Israel's halfhearted tribes. Hence, it is rhetorically appropriate to allow details of events that are reported in the hymn (e.g., the Kishon flooding the battlefield [5:20-21]) to inform retroactively the prose account.[75]

The plot-structure of Judges 4–5 comprises three plot-levels, each with its own exposition, development and resolution.[76] It is similar in

---

[75] *Pace* B. Lindars ("Deborah's Song: Women in the Old Testament", *BJRL* 65 [1982–1983], pp. 159-60, 161-62; cf. Y. Amit, "Judges 4: Its Contents and Form", *JSOT* 39 [1987], pp. 95, 109 n. 27), since it is my aim to discover the rhetorical purpose of Judges' compiler/redactor, there is no reason to resist comparing details of the hymn with those of its framing prose version, as though to do so would adulterate the original autonomous form of either version. The Judges compiler/redactor evidently intended the two versions to complement each other, and the reader who fails to interpret them as complementary will also fail to discern the compiler/redactor's rhetorical aims (cf. Lindars, "Deborah's Song" [1982–83], p. 159: "it is virtually impossible to tell the story without drawing on *both* accounts, because each has gaps which can be supplied from the other"). Nevertheless, it is important to note where and why the prose account withholds information that is disclosed only later in the hymn.

[76] Proposals on the narrative structure of Judg. 4–5 usually follow the scenic principle, which assumes that a story proceeds along but one plot-level that can be sectioned into blocks according to scene changes. This approach is flawed by its failure to recognize that even a relatively simple story may contain subplots and that, however many subplots, each will have its own exposition, development (perhaps with complications) and resolution (or dissolution). Among several recent proposals on the narrative structure of Judg. 4–5 that follow the scenic principle, that by Alonso-Schökel defined a prologue (4:1-5) and two acts comprising two scenes each (apparently 4:6-13, 14-17 and 4:18-21, 22) but did not include 4:23-24 or 5:31b as part of the story despite the fact that only these verses resolve the problem of Israel's oppression under Jabin, which was raised in 4:1-5 ("Erzählkunst" [1961], pp. 158-59, 160-65).

D. F. Murray, defining the plot-structure according to an alleged convergence between scene changes and narrative disjunctions (vv. 10 ≠ 11, 11 ≠ 12, 16 ≠ 17, 21 ≠ 22), delineated four "episodes" after the introduction (4:4-5): 4:6-10, [11]12-16, 17-21, 22 ("Narrative Structure and Technique in the Deborah–Barak Story [Judges iv 4-22]", in *Studies in the Historical Books of the Old Testament* [J. A. Emerton (ed.), SVT 30, Leiden, 1979], pp. 156-62). Recognizing that 4:11 stands apart from its immediate context, Murray nevertheless had to group it with 4:12-16 because he was following a strictly scenic (or episodic) principle and had no convenient way of relating it to 4:17-21. Judg. 4:11 does not introduce new *dramatis personae* (contra Murray, "Narrative Structure" [1979], p. 161) but, as expositional material, foreshadows the introduction of the new *dramatis persona* Jael (4:17-18). Murray did not treat 4:1-3, 23-24 or 5:31b in his analysis, since he deemed these (not mentioning 5:31b) to be deuteronomic additions that are foreign to the original purpose of the predeuteronomic narrative (cf. "Narrative Structure" [1979], pp. 156 n. 4, 184-85). While this perception seems true, it is precisely to discover in what ways the deuteronomic ideology effects change in the old narrative that I am most concerned to examine the narrative of Judg. 4–5 in its entirety.

Similarly, Lindars, after removing the alleged deuteronomic editing in 4:1, 2b, 3a, 4b-5, 11; the references to Jabin in 4:2a, 17b, 23-24 and the "nine hundred chariots of iron" in 4:3b, 13 (alleged to be mistaken identifications with the account of Jabin in Josh. 11:1-5), outlined three scenes in the predeuteronomic narrative: roughly 4:4a, 6-10; 4:13*-17;

some regards to the telescoping plot-structure of Dénouement-A (17–18) though having fewer levels and a less clearly demarcated presentation of each plot's exposition (e.g., the exposition of Plot B [4:8] is simultaneously the first complication of Plot A; again, the exposition of Plot C is diffused among two foreshadowings [4:9aβ-ε, 11] and a partial exposition [4:17a,b] that are thus not likely to be recognized as comprising this subplot's exposition).[77] The plot-structure of the prose and hymn sections of Judges 4–5 may be outlined as follows (with cycle-motif designations and vertical lines connecting simultaneous events of the narrative in the left column, broken horizontal lines separating scenes in the development and letters and vertical lines indicating repetition patterns in the hymn [5:2-31a]):

> *Plot A:* YHWH's deliverance of Israel from Jabin's military domination by the word of his prophetess Deborah (4:1-7 [8] 9-10a, 12-15a [15b] 16 [17a, 18-20] 21, 23-24; 5:31b)
>
> > *Plot A Situation Exposition:* Introduction of Deborah in response to Israel's repentant cry to YHWH for deliverance (4:1-5)
> >
> > | | |
> > |---|---|
> > | A1a | Resumption of Israel's practice of evil (4:1a) |
> > | <G1> | Reference to the death of Ehud (4:1b) |
> > | B2b | YHWH sold Israel into the hand of Jabin, king of Canaan, who ruled at Hazor (4:2a) |
> > | | His military commander Sisera resided at Harosheth Haggoyim (4:2b) |

and 4:18-22 ("Deborah's Song" [1982–83], pp. 161-64). Because Lindars's study aims to recover the predeuteronomic form of the account, his scenic analysis pertains chiefly to the development section of the account as it is presented in Judges. Nevertheless, Lindars's approach is helpful in that it aims at segregating the additions that gave the account its new form and rhetorical design within the book.

Amit delineated in Judg. 4 an exposition (4:1-5), four scenic units (4:6-9, 10-13, 14-16, 17-22) and a finale (4:23-24) ("Judges 4" [1987], pp. 90-99). Although she chose to work with the form of the account that the Judges compiler/redactor presented, her commitment to the scenic principle resulted in another block-built plot-structure analysis that fails to nuance the ways in which a narrative segment may function at more than one plot-level at a time. Further, her intention to work with the compiler/redactor's version is inconsistent in leaving 5:31b (surely part of the narrative framework) out of consideration.

[77] Murray did observe that the scene that begins with the disjunction in 4:17 is, in fact, adumbrated in 4:9aβ and 4:11 "but in so veiled a manner that its actual occurrence ... is hardly the less unexpected" ("Narrative Structure" [1979], pp. 158-59; cf. pp. 179-83 concerning the rhetorical effects of the foreshadowing in 4:11). Similarly, Amit observed of 4:11 and 4:17b that, "some of the expositional items are scattered throughout the chapter", but, having committed herself to the scenic principle, she could not accommodate this observation into her plot analysis ("Judges 4" [1987], pp. 93, 107 n. 18; cf. p. 90). Culley's treatment of 4:17-24 as "an episode in the larger story" also fails to distinguish different plot-levels within 4:17-24 but does discern that the justification for its hostility "must be derived from the larger story where the Israelites are oppressed by a Canaanite king, Jabin" ("Structural Analysis" [1974], p. 178).

C	Israel cried out to YHWH (4:3a)
	Reason: Sisera had nine hundred chariots of iron (4:3bα)
B3b	Sisera harshly oppressed Israel for twenty years (4:3bβ)
	Deborah was a prophetess, the wife of Lappidoth (4:4a)
F1	She was judging Israel at that time (4:4b)
	She used to sit under the palm of Deborah, between Ramah and Bethel in the hill country of Ephraim (4:5a)
(F1)	Israel would go up to her for judgement (4:5b)

Plot A Character Exposition: Deborah's prophetic summons and instructions to Barak concerning YHWH's plan to deliver Sisera, his chariots and his army into Barak's hand (4:6-7)

Plot B: Deborah's limitation of Barak's glory in battle because of his reluctance to follow YHWH's instructions to deliver Israel (4:8-9, 10b [14a, 15a] 15b-16, 17a, 21-22)

   Plot A Complication/Plot B Exposition: Barak's reluctance to follow YHWH/Deborah's instructions to engage Sisera in battle (4:8)

Plot C: Glorification of the woman who would achieve YHWH's plan to deliver Israel (4:9a, 11, 17-22)

   Plots A & B Development/(Foreshadowing: Plot C Exposition): Deborah limits Barak's glory by predicting that YHWH will deliver Sisera into a woman's hand (4:9a)

   ————————————————————————

   Plots A & B Development: Barak, by returning to Kadesh, begins to execute YHWH/Deborah's instructions, though she had to accompany him (4:9b)

   Plot A Development: Barak, by summoning his troops at Kadesh, continues to execute YHWH/Deborah's instructions (4:10aα)

   ————————————————————————

   Plot A Development: Barak, by ascending [Mount Tabor], continues to execute YHWH/Deborah's instructions (4:10aβγ)

   Plot B Development: Deborah continues to accompany Barak (4:10b)

   ————————————————————————

   Parenthesis (Foreshadowing: Plot C Exposition): Description of Heber the Kenite's departure [from Judah] to dwell near Kedesh (4:11)

   ————————————————————————

   Plot A Development: Sisera, informed of Barak's ascent to Mount Tabor [as per YHWH/Deborah's instructions], summons his troops (4:12-13)

   ————————————————————————

   Plot A Development/Plot B Complication: Deborah's instructions to Barak concerning YHWH's plan to deliver Sisera into Barak's hand (4:14a; contrast 4:9a)

   Plot A Development: Barak, by descending to attack, continues to execute YHWH/Deborah's instructions (4:14b)

Plot A Development/Plot B Complication: YHWH's confusion of Sisera, his chariots and his army before Barak (4:15a)

Plot A Complication/Plot B Development: Sisera descends and flees on foot (4:15b)

Plots A & B Development: Barak, by remaining to pursue Sisera's chariots and army, continues to execute YHWH/Deborah's instructions [unaware of Sisera's escape] (4:16)

Plot A Complication/Plot B Development/Plot C Exposition: Sisera flees on foot to the tent of Jael, the wife of Heber the Kenite (4:17a)

Plot C Exposition: Reason: There were friendly relations between Heber the Kenite and Jabin king of Hazor (4:17b)

Plot A Complication/Plot C Development: Jael invites Sisera into her tent and apparently protects and provides for Sisera (4:18-20)

Plot A Partial Resolution/Plots B & C Resolution: Jael's assassination of Sisera while he slept (4:21)

Plots B & C Dénouement: Jael invites Barak, still pursuing Sisera, into her tent, where he sees Sisera dead (4:22)

Plot A Resolution: (4:23-24)

E1   That day Jabin, king of Canaan, was humbled before Israel (4:23)

              and the hand of Israel continued to weigh against Jabin, king of Canaan, until they destroyed him (4:24)

Prolongation of Plots A & C Resolution: (5:1-31)

              That day Deborah and Barak sang (5:1)

              Hymnic Embellishment of Plot A: (5:2-22)

A   Call to praise (5:2-5)

     a   Summary refrain (5:2)

     b   Summons to kings and rulers to hear (5:3)

     c   An account of YHWH's epiphany (5:4-5)

B   Rehearsal of history (5:6-8)

     −   Decline: Anarchy of routes in Israel (5:6-7a)

     +   Arising of Deborah to call to arms (5:7b-8a)

     −   Decline: Reluctance of Israel to bear arms (5:8b)

A^i   Call to praise (5:9-11a)

     a   Summary refrain (5:9)

     b   Summons to nobles to consider (5:10)

     c   Where YHWH's victories are recounted (5:11a)

B^i   Rehearsal of history (5:11b-13)

       + Descent: People of YHWH (5:11b)

       + Summons of Deborah to arise and sing
           and of Barak to arise and take captives
           (5:12)

       + Descent: People of YHWH (5:13)

C   Postvictory rebuke concerning the rally for
        battle out of regard for intertribal
        covenant loyalty (5:14-18)

       + Willingness of participant tribes
           (5:14-15a)

       − Reluctance of nonparticipant tribes
           (5:15b-17)

       + Willingness of participant tribes (5:18)

C^i   Postvictory rebuke concerning the progress
        of the battle as evidence for the realization
        of YHWH's supremacy (5:19-22)

       − Futility of Canaanite kings' rally for battle
           (5:19)

       + Account of the stars, the river and
           Deborah engaging Sisera in battle
           (5:20-21)

       − Response of Sisera's horses in retreat
           (5:22)

Hymnic Embellishment of Plot C: (5:23-30)

C^ii   Postvictory rebuke concerning the aftermath
        of the battle from the perspective of
        gender-/class-appropriate roles (5:23-30)

       − Curse on nonparticipant citizens of Meroz
           for failing to help YHWH (5:23)

       + Blessing on Jael among tent-dwelling
           women and account of her slaying of
           noble Sisera (5:24-27)

       − Satire on Sisera's mother as a noble
           woman at the window (5:28-30)

Hymnic Embellishment of Plot A: (5:31a)

A^ii   Closing hymnic ejaculation (5:31a)

F2   The land had peace forty years (5:31b)

Plot A (4:1-7 [8] 9b-10a, 12-15a [15b] 16 [17a, 18-20] 21, 23-24; 5:31b; cf. 5:1, 2-22, 31a), which is the main plot of Judges 4–5, throughout bears additions that represent the interests of the compiler/ redactor. At this plot-level, it is YHWH who, in answer to Israel's out-cry, delivers them from Sisera, Jabin's military commander, as a precursor to the complete overthrow of Jabin.[78] The situation exposition (4:1-5) comprises a mixture of cycle-motif elements (4:1-2a, 3a, 3bβ, 4b, 5b) interspersed with character descriptions, which are probably derived from the traditional account. Elements of the alienation phase of the cycle-motif (elements A-C in 4:1a, 2a, 3a, 3bβ) are interspersed with unexpected elements from its restoration phase (i.e., the death notice of Ehud [G1, 4:1b], displaced from the preceding deliverer account, and the descriptions of Deborah judging Israel [F1, 4:4b, 5b], uniquely referring to the giving of judicial decisions).[79] Elements of this situation exposition not comprised by the cycle-motif either appear elsewhere in the account or the book of Judges ("who reigned at Hazor" [4:2aγ] as "king of Hazor" in 4:17bβ, "Sisera, commander of Jabin's army" [4:2bα] in 4:7aβ, "Harosheth Haggoyim" [4:2bβ] in 4:13b, "chariots of iron" [4:3bα] in 4:13aβ but also 1:19bβ) or form the character exposition of Deborah (4:4a, 5a). This seems to lead to the conclusion that only 4:4a and 4:5a were part of the traditional form of the account and that the compiler/redactor interspersed about them an arrangement of cycle-motif elements and materials borrowed from elsewhere in order to establish his/her own expositional situation and problem. The main character exposition of Plot A, however, comprises 4:6-7. The resolution of Plot A (4:23-24; 5:1, 2-31a, 31b) is also composed of both cycle-motif elements (E1, 4:23; F2, 5:31b) and three embellishments: 4:24 (which embellishes Israel's defeat of Jabin in 4:23), the transition at 5:1, which begins ביום ההוא (further embellishing the divine claims of 4:23, which also begins ביום ההוא), and the entire hymn of 5:2-31a (which is the object of ותשר in 5:1 and embellishes the themes of Plots A and C).

Deborah's role in the story is that of a catalyst of action in the plot. She begins in the character exposition (4:6-7) by conveying an oracle of YHWH to Barak (YHWH's designated deliverer) as a means of instigating his actions. She then further catalyses the actions of Barak in the development (4:14a). It is as a mouthpiece for YHWH that Deborah summons Barak to lead the tribes (4:6-7) and announces the day of YHWH's battle (4:14a). It is Barak, not Deborah, who is the

---

[78] While Jabin remains a background character in Judg. 4-5 (Webb, *Judges* [1987], pp. 133, 138), as does Heber, the positions of his mention in the framework (4:2a, 7a, 17b, 23-24[3x]) indicate that YHWH's defeat of Jabin was the controlling concern of the account.

[79] Moore interpreted 4:4b as "she delivered Israel", interpreting this use of שפט in the same sense as that of its uses elsewhere throughout Judges (*Judges* [1895], p. 113; cf. p. 88 on 3:10).

designated deliverer and who ought to have served as the main character of the account. However, because Barak initially proves to be reluctant to serve YHWH, Deborah also acts as a foil to further Barak's negative characterization. Both times Deborah anticipates Barak's reluctance to follow her instructions from YHWH by asking rhetorically, הלא [...] יהוה "Has not YHWH ... ?"[80] If Deborah in her first speech suspects a possible reluctance on Barak's part, Barak's first response confirms her suspicions. In the second instance, the word order emphasizes that YHWH is the true instigator. In this connection, it is significant that the D1 element ("YHWH raised up ... to save them") is lacking from the exposition of Plot A, for it is a unique feature of the Deborah/Barak/Jael account that no one character—least of all Barak (Plot B)—emerges as YHWH's sole deliverer. The subject matter of motif element D1 appears in the development when Deborah calls Barak to deliver Israel (4:6-7), but, as part of the negative characterization of Barak, the D1 keyword קום is used in 4:9b to describe the action of only Deborah when she arose to go with Barak after rebuking him for his reluctance to follow YHWH's instructions (4:9a). Later, it is again Deborah who prompts Barak to arise (קום) and follow YHWH into battle (4:14a) so that Barak comes to be seen as a deliverer who would not "be raised up ... to save" apart from the initiatives and actions of a woman.

Plot B (4:8-9, 10b [14a, 15a] 15b-16, 17a, 21-22) shows how Barak's glory is restricted because of his initial reluctance to obey YHWH's instructions as given by Deborah. It begins in 4:8 with Barak's hesitancy to obey, which is expressed in his condition that Deborah accompany him on his mission. By conditioning his obedience to YHWH upon Deborah's willingness to accompany him, Barak was effectively denying her the authority that YHWH had conferred upon her as a prophetess (4:4a). What Barak's motives may have been is not stated, but it is perhaps safe to surmise that Barak's expectations of Deborah were inappropriate to women, since the counter-response that Deborah deems appropriate is to supplant Barak's future glory with that of a woman (4:9a).[81] From the point of Barak's refusal to follow

---

[80] Cf. F. Gottlieb, "Three Mothers", *Judaism* 30 (1981), p. 195.

[81] Finding a negative characterization in Barak's false echo of Ruth's vow, "Where you go, I will go, and where you stay, I will stay" (Ruth 1:16), Gottlieb suggested that what motivated Barak to insist on Deborah's presence was her renown (Judg. 4:4b, 5b), which could be used to draw the tribes together into battle ("Mothers" [1981], p. 196). However, this view derives from the mistaken notion that in 4:7 Deborah was planning herself to lure Sisera into the trap, whereas, because in 4:6-7 she is presenting an oracle from YHWH, the subject of ומשכתי is YHWH (cf. Murray, "Narrative Structure" [1979],

Deborah's instructions unless she accompanied him (4:8), he earns her rebuke (4:9αβ-ε) so that, while she consents to accompany him (4:9αα), the subsequent repeated mention of her presence with Barak (4:9b, 10b) becomes a strident pedal-note underlying his performance of YHWH's instructions (cf. 4:9b, 10a, 14b with 4:6b).[82] Deborah's ambiguous announcement in 4:14a (זה היום אשר נתן יהוה את־סיסרא בידך; 4:14aβ derives from motif E2a) suggests that, on the basis of Barak's performance of YHWH's instructions, perhaps Sisera would be given into Barak's hand after all, despite the limitation predicted in 4:9αβ-ε.[83] At first, succeeding events seem to follow this course (4:15b). Eventually, however, it is understood that the reference to Sisera in 4:14a was only metonymical (subject [military commander] for adjunct [his chariots and troops]).[84] Deborah's speech in 4:14a was apparently misunderstood by Barak (unless he was deliberately attempting to thwart the outcome of her prediction in 4:9a), for he vainly continues to pursue Sisera to the end (cf. רדף in 4:16a, 22aα).

Plot C (4:9a, 11, 17-22; cf. 5:23-30), which commences with Deborah's prediction of the scheme to transfer Barak's glory to a woman (4:9a), is the plot that shows how YHWH brought glory to this woman. From the reader's standpoint, Deborah's prediction, ביד־אשה ימכר יהוה את־סיסרא (4:9aδε, motif E2b), leaves open the possibility that Deborah herself may be the agent of Sisera's demise until the reader (then Barak) discovers that YHWH had appointed Jael, the wife of Heber the Kenite, to accomplish this feat.[85] Deborah's prediction is

---

p. 169). Lindars proposed that Barak's reluctance to go to war without Deborah was motivated by cowardice ("Deborah's Song" [1982–83], pp. 161, 164).

[82] Contra Murray, who describes 4:9αα as "Deborah's very positive response", her action in 4:9b as a pleonastic expression that "serves to emphasise Deborah's initiative" and 4:10b as a "much more incidental notice of her accompanying Barak" ("Narrative Structure" [1979], pp. 173-74).

[83] Cf. Alonso-Schökel, "Erzählkunst" [1961], pp. 161-62; Murray, "Narrative Structure" [1979], pp. 174-75, 177.

[84] While Murray may be correct in regarding the 3 m. sg suff. (antecedent: Sisera) of ונתתיהו, in 4:7b, as an example of synecdoche (*pars* [Sisera] *pro toto* [Sisera *and* his chariots and troops]) ("Narrative Structure" [1979], p. 174), he seems mistaken in regarding את־סיסרא in 4:14a as the same (p. 177), since, after 4:9a, Deborah would not have intended that Sisera himself should be delivered into Barak's hand. Metonymy involves the literary displacement of associated things (requiring exclusion), whereas synecdoche involves literary representation by membership (requiring inclusion).

[85] While, from the narrator's standpoint, Jael alone is the true referent of אשה in 4:9aδ (so H.-D. Neef, "Der Sieg Deboras und Baraks über Sisera: Exegetische Beobachtungen zum Aufbau und Werden von Jdc 4,1-24", ZAW 101 [1989], p. 34, n. 46), this realization could not yet be expected of a reader who is left with its ambiguity (so Alonso-Schökel, "Erzählkunst" [1961], p. 159; Murray, "Narrative Structure" [1979], p. 177; Gottlieb,

the first of two foreshadowings of Jael (4:9aβ-ε, 11), who is the main character of Plot C.[86] It is significant that Plot C, which leads to Jael's glorification as a foil to Barak's humiliation (Plot B), is foreshadowed by the characterization of Jael's husband (Heber the Kenite) as a covenant malefactor who began his maleficence by departing from the Kenites, who lived in Judah (cf. 1:16).[87] Heber the Kenite is later identified as the husband of Jael (4:17a), and it is the latter who, from zeal for YHWH, acts in defiance of her husband's friendly relations with Jabin (4:17b; cf. Deut. 7:2bβ) to humiliate Sisera and (unwittingly) Barak.

Of the three plot-levels in the Deborah/Barak/Jael account, the only one that proceeds without complication is that which leads to Jael's success (Plot C)—thus demonstrating, as in the problem-free development leading to Ehud's success, that it was YHWH who had controlled the circumstances leading to Jael's success. The straightforward structure of 4:18-21 may be outlined as follows:

Initiating Speeches	*Initiating/Responding Acts*
	Jael acts [intercepts] (4:18aαⁱ)
	ותצא יעל לקראת סיסרא
Jael speaks [invites] (4:18aαⁱⁱβ)	Sisera acts [complies] (4:18bα)
ותאמר אליו /	ויסר אליה האהלה /
סורה אדני סורה אלי אל־תירא //	
	Jael acts [surpasses courtesy] (4:18bβ)
	ותכסהו בשמיכה

———————————————————

"Mothers" [1981], p. 197; Webb, *Judges* [1987], p. 135). Neef's case stands against Murray's assertion that, in the end, "both Deborah and Jael are the *'iššâ* of v. 9: Deborah, by 'subjugating' Barak, effectively achieves the victory over Sisera's forces; Jael, by achieving the victory over Sisera, effectively subjugates Barak" ("Narrative Structure" [1979], p. 178), because 4:9aδε refers only to the woman who would subjugate Sisera himself (not his army).

[86] Although Murray has rightly observed that 4:15b, too, adumbrates the scene with Jael ("Narrative Structure" [1979], pp. 158-59), 4:15b does not furnish expositional material for Plot C in the narrative. Nevertheless, an ironic connection does stand between Barak's troops ascending "at his feet" (ברגליו ויעל, 4:10aβ; cf. ברגליו שלח בעמק, 5:15a), Sisera descending and fleeing "on foot" (ברגליו וינס...וירד, 4:15b) and his fleeing "on foot" to Jael's tent (ברגליו נס, 4:17a) as an adumbration of his coming fall in the scene of 4:18-21 (Murray, "Narrative Structure" [1979], pp. 170-71). However, only in the hymn, is Sisera's fall said to happen "between" Jael's feet (רגליה בין, 2x in 5:27).

[87] If the characterization of Heber is compared to that of the Levites in chs. 17–18 and 19–21, it may be averred that no one in Judges who departs from Judah fares well in Judges. To this consideration may be added the background afforded Judg. 1:16 and 4:11 by Num. 10:29-32, which implies that a prior covenant between the Kenites and Israel should have preempted Heber's friendly relations with a Canaanite (cf. Exod. 23:32; Deut. 7:2bβ). See F. C. Fensham, "Did a Treaty between the Israelites and the Kenites

Initiating Speeches	Initiating/Responding Acts
Sisera speaks [requests] (4:19a)	Jael acts [complies] (4:19b^i)
ויאמר אליה	ותפתח את־נאוד החלב ותשקהו
השקיני־נא מעט־מים כי צמאתי //	
	Jael acts [surpasses request] (4:19b^{ii})
	ותכסהו

Sisera speaks [commands] (4:20)	Jael acts [complies] (implicit)
ויאמר אליה / עמד פתח האהל //	
והיה אם־איש יבוא ושאלך /	
ואמר היש־פה איש ואמרת אין	
	Jael acts [surpasses command] (4:21)
	ותקח יעל אשת־חבר את־יתד האהל
	ותשם את־המקבת בידה /
	ותבוא אליו בלאת /
	ותתקע את־היתד ברקתו /
	ותצנח בארץ //
	[88]והוא־נרדם ויעף וימת

The balance between Sisera's speeches and Jael's acts shows Jael to be
continually acting on her own initiative (4:18aα^i, 18bβ, 19b^{ii}, 21). Only
once does Jael speak (4:18aα^{ii}β), and then only to coax Sisera into the
sphere of her actions. Until the surprise climax of 4:21, the impression
given is that Jael is eager to show hospitality to this official of her husband's ally. Jael gives Sisera a sense of security by inviting him in with
the consolation אל־תירא (4:18aβ)—a consolation ironically borrowed
from the language of the war oracle.[89] It is she who takes the initiative
of covering Sisera and, after giving him milk, of covering him again.[90]

Exist?", *BASOR* 175 (1964), pp. 51-54; Amit, "Judges 4" (1987), p. 108 n. 20; and contrast those who deny Jael Israelite status (e.g., Webb, *Judges* [1987], p. 137; J. W. H.
Bos, "Out of the Shadows: Genesis 38; Judges 4:17-22; Ruth 3", *Semeia* 42 [1988],
p. 58) with those allow it (e.g., Klein, *Triumph of Irony* [1988], p. 43).

[88] Adapted from Alonso-Schökel, who noted the following fixed structure in 4:18-21
("Erzählkunst" [1961], p. 163):

Jael spricht (läde ein)	Sisera handelt (nimmt an)
Sisera spricht (verlangt)	Jael handelt (gibt mehr, als verlant)
Sisera spricht (verlangt)	Jael handelt (tut mehr, als erwartet)

From this structure he inferred, "Diese strenge Stilisierung hält die Handlung gespannt
und führt sie glatt und schnell zur Lösung".

[89] Cf. Murray, "Narrative Structure" [1979], p. 183.

[90] Most favour the view that Sisera is the object of both uses of כסה in 4:18b and
4:19b (so AV; RV; JPSV; RSV; NEB; NIV; Alonso-Schökel, "Erzählkunst" [1961], p. 164).
In support of an alternative interpretation, that the objects of כסה in 4:18b, 19b are the
entrance to the tent and the milk container, respectively, see Bos, "Shadows" (1988),
p. 51. The ambiguity as to the antecedent of the 3 m. sg suffs. on both uses of ותכסהו is
not resolved by previous mention since, while in 4:18b that would be האהלה, in 4:19b it

Indeed, the staging of the phases that lead to Sisera's assassination—the first two ending with Jael's self-motivated acts of covering him (ותכסהו בשמיכה in 4:18bβ; then ותכסהו [without expressed agent] in 4:19b[ii]) and the last ending with a portrayal of her overpowering of him (4:21)—may play on a well-known semantic ambiguity inherent in verbs meaning 'to cover, overwhelm/ overpower'.[91] Thus, while the description of 4:21 does not use the verb ותכסהו in the sense "and she overwhelmed him", the final position of 4:21 in sequence with two preceding portrayals of Jael voluntarily covering Sisera suggests this imagery. Through the ambiguous interplay between Jael's feigned compliance with gestures normally associated with hospitality and her own actions interpreted as aiming to bring about Sisera's defeat, the narrator builds suspense until in 4:21 one reaches the climax—the sudden and surprising resolution of conflicting interests in the story. Indeed, when one reconsiders Jael's first self-motivated action in 4:18aα[i], ותצא יעל לקראת סיסרא, one may now hear overtones reminiscent of the military milieu. All this is designed to show Jael's consummate wit in manipulating Sisera by means of verbal ambiguity and, as in the portrayal of Ehud's manipulation of Eglon and his courtiers, only satirizes him for his gullibility.[92]

However, as in the Ehud account, Jael cannot claim final credit for success in humiliating Israel's enemy. The two foreshadowings of Jael in 4:9aβ-ε and 4:11 seem designed to demonstrate YHWH's control over events in the story. That is, before anyone (character or reader) knew her name or understood her significance, YHWH is seen to have predicted the outcome of Jael's actions through Deborah (4:9aβ-ε) and to have set up the conditions for her humiliation of Sisera (and, unwittingly, Barak) by positioning her tent beside that of her husband on the

---

would be the 3 m. sg suff. of ותשקהו (referring to Sisera). Nor does recourse to an alleged interplay between Jael's covering (ותכסהו בשמיכה) ויסר אליה האהלה ותכסהו, 4:18b), opening (ותפתח את־נאוד החלב, 4:19b) and covering (ותכסהו, 4:19b) and standing at the opening (ויאמר אליה עמד פתח האהל, 4:20a) fully resolve the ambiguity (cf. Bos, "Shadows" [1988], pp. 50-51). However, considerations that lead one to conclude that Sisera is the object are: (1) the circumstance that he bids Jael keep watch at the entrance because he would be sleeping and unable to do so himself and (2) the explicit mention that he was sleeping, as indicated in the circumstantial clause, והוא־נרדם ויעף "now he being fast asleep and exhausted" (4:21bα) (cf. J. Licht, *Storytelling in the Bible* [Jerusalem, 1978], p. 102).

[91] Cf. N. M. Waldman, "The Imagery of Clothing, Covering, and Overpowering", *JANES* 19 (1989), pp. 161-70.

[92] A. J. Hauser, "Judges 5: Parataxis in Hebrew Poetry", *JBL* 99 (1980), p. 36.

route by which Sisera would escape (cf. 4:11, 17).[93] Thus, as with Ehud, the strategies of Jael are seen to work in concert with those of YHWH. What is more, the humiliating effect that Jael's assassination of Sisera has upon Barak (4:22) comes as the result of a strategy outside Jael's interest (and probably awareness) and demonstrates that YHWH, who predicted her actions and positioned her tent, was the one ultimately in control of the circumstances leading to Jael's success.

As to the formal structure of the victory hymn of 5:2-31a, its verse parallelisms and strophic arrangement are patterned on an epanaleptic principle.[94] The effect is one that engenders a sense of escalation. Among the seven triadic strophes of the hymn, repetitions of themes and phraseology between analogous strophes compound to heighten emotion. Between the two triads comprising each 'A' strophe (5:2, 3, 4-5[95] and 5:9, 10, 11a[96]) one may compare the following thematic and phraseological correspondences (summarized above in the plot-structure outline):

9 לבי לחוקקי ישראל / המתנדבים בעם // ברכו יהוה:	2 בפרע פרעות בישראל / בהתנדב עם // ברכו יהוה:

---

[93] That two different tents are implied, one for the husband and another for the wife, may be inferred from the distinction between אהלו "his tent" (4:11), on the one hand, and אל־אהל יעל "to the tent of Jael" (4:17) and אליה האהלה "to her tent" (4:18), on the other. This custom is attested also in the fact that Abraham and Sarah had separate tents (Gen. 18:2 and 6; cf. 24:67), as did Jacob, Leah, Rachel and the two maidservants (Gen. 31:33).

[94] On the use of epanalepsis as a device of poetic parallelism in the hymn, see G. A. Cooke, *The History and Song of Deborah* (Oxford, 1892), p. 27; P. Ruben, "The Song of Deborah", *JQR* 10 (1897-1898), pp. 542, 544, 553, 556. Those who have regarded 5:31a as a liturgical gloss include: J. M. Myers, "The Book of Judges: Introduction and Exegesis", in *IB*, vol. 2, p. 728; J. Blenkinsopp, "Ballad Style and Psalm Style in the Song of Deborah: A Discussion", *Bib* 42 (1961), p. 68; W. Richter, *Traditionsgeschichtliche Untersuchungen zum Richterbuch* (BBB 18, Bonn, 2d edn, 1966), pp. 86-87; H.-P. Müller, "Der Aufbau des Deboraliedes", *VT* 16 (1966), pp. 457-58; M. D. Coogan, "A Structural and Literary Analysis of the Song of Deborah", *CBQ* 40 (1978), p. 144 n. 4; Lindars, "Deborah's Song" (1982-83), pp. 171-72. Arguing for the antiquity of the present hymn's form, however, A. Globe has preferred to retain 5:31a as original along with the other sections generally alleged to be liturgical additions: 5:2-5 and 5:9-11a ("The Literary Structure and Unity of the Song of Deborah", *JBL* 93 [1974], pp. 495, 508). The latter view has been endorsed by Hauser, "Judges 5" (1980), pp. 25 n. 8, 29.

[95] Coogan likewise regarded 5:2-5 as a single strophe ("Song of Deborah" [1978], pp. 145-46).

[96] Judg. 5:9-11a is seen to be a unit also by Globe ("Song of Deborah" [1974], p. 503).

3 שמעו מלכים / האזינו רזנים //   10 רכבי אתנות צחרות /
אנכי ליהוה / אנכי אשירה /   ישבי על־מדין /
אזמר ליהוה / אלהי ישראל: והלכי על־דרך שיחו:

4 יהוה בצאתך משעיר /   11a מקול מחצצים /
בצעדך משדה אדום /   בין משאבים /
ארץ רעשה /   שם יתנו צדקות יהוה /
גם־שמים נטפו //   צדקת פרזנו בישראל //
גם־עבים נטפו מים:

5 הרים נזלו /
מפני יהוה // זה סיני /
מפני יהוה אלהי ישראל:

The similar phraseology and theme of 5:2 and 5:9 are self-evident.[97] It is an important point of the thematic correspondence between 5:4-5 and 5:11a that these final sections of the 'A' strophes offer complementary images of YHWH's control over floodwaters.[98] Whereas, in the epiphanic recital of 5:4-5, YHWH unleashes earthquakes and floodwaters in defence (בצאתך משעיר ‖ בצעדך משדה אדום) of Israel (יהוה אלהי ישראל ‖ יהוה זה סיני), in 5:11a it is those who benefit from the subterranean watering places—places where the waters are now subdued—who should likewise recount the heroic feats of YHWH in Israel. Indeed, the fact that the laudatory 'A' strophes each end with mention of YHWH's power over water sets up the theme of how YHWH's victory was achieved through the agency of water—the key motif of the hymn's 'C' strophes (see below). The remaining structural correspondence between 5:3 and 5:10 suggests that here one finds similar calls to the vanquished kings of Canaan to consider and acknowledge the hymnist's praise of YHWH's victory achieved at their expense.[99] This alleged injunction would be tantamount to a mockery of the very foreign kings and nobles from whom the hymnist solicits attention. Indeed, this sarcastic call to foreign kings and nobles early in the hymn sets the tone for the mockery of foreign kings and nobles in the battle account (5:19, 22) and its aftermath (5:28-30) and furnishes a

---

[97] Cf. Müller, "Aufbau des Deboraliedes" (1966), p. 455; Coogan, "Song of Deborah" (1978), pp. 152, 156; A. J. Hauser, "Two Songs of Victory: A Comparison of Exodus 15 and Judges 5", in *Directions in Biblical Hebrew Poetry* (E. R. Follis [ed.], JSOTS 40, Sheffield, 1987), p. 268.

[98] Cf. Hauser, "Judges 5" (1980), pp. 30-31; idem, "Songs of Victory" (1987), pp. 271-72.

[99] Since 5:2-31a is cast, within the narrative framework, as a hymnic rehearsal of YHWH's victory, this reference to kings and nobles must be viewed as referring to YHWH's now defeated enemies. Cf. Coogan, "Song of Deborah" (1978), pp. 152, 153 n. 65; Hauser, "Judges 5" (1980), p. 28.

foil to the hymn's victorious portrayal of YHWH (5:20-21a) and his allies (5:24-27).[100]

It may be of further significance that the portrayal of YHWH's epiphany from the mountains (Seir || Edom; cf. Sinai) in 5:4-5 is concentric:

YHWH marching from mount PN [*bis*] (5:4a$\alpha\beta$)
  Earth shakes (5:4aγ)
    Heavens drip (5:4aδ)
    Clouds drip water (5:4b)
  Mountains quake[/flow] (5:5aα)
Before YHWH, one of mount PN || YHWH god of Israel (5:5aβb)[101]

The implication is that the one who rescued Israel by cosmic torrents is the one who made covenant with Israel at Sinai.

Besides the thematic and phraseological correspondences between analogous sections in each 'A' strophe (i.e., between 5:2 and 5:9, 5:3 and 5:10, 5:4-5 and 5:11a), two verbal phenomena seem to confirm this structural analysis: (1) the symmetrical distribution of the term ישׂראל among the triadic sections, opening both first sections (5:2, 9), closing both final sections (5:4-5, 11a) and closing the middle section of strophe A (5:3) and (2) the complementary positions of the imperatives (m. pl.) in both middle sections so that שׁמעו opens 5:3 and שׂיחו closes 5:10.

In a similar way, the three sections of the 'B' strophes (5:6-7a, 7b-8a, 8b[102] and 5:11b, 12, 13) correspond thematically:

6	בימי שׁמגר בן־ענת /	11b	אז ירדו לשׁערים עם־יהוה:
	בימי יעל / חדלו ארחות //		
	והלכי נתיבות /		
	ילכו ארחות עקלקלות:		
7a	חדלו פרזון /		
	בישׂראל חדלו //		
7b	עד שׁקמתי דבורה /	12	עורי עורי דבורה /
	שׁקמתי אם בישׂראל:		עורי עורי דברי־שׁיר //
8a	יבחר אלהים חדשׁים /		קום ברק /
	אזל<ו >חמשׁ<י >ערים //		ושׁבה שׁביך בן־אבינעם:

---

[100] Hauser, "Judges 5" (1980), pp. 28-29.

[101] Globe noted the chiasmus in 5:4aγ-5aα ("Song of Deborah" [1974], p. 504).

[102] Globe ("Song of Deborah" [1974], pp. 496, 503) and Coogan ("Song of Deborah" [1978], p. 147) also treated 5:6-8 as a unit.

13   אז ירד שריד / לאדירים   8b   מגן אם־יראה ורמח /
עם // יהוה ירד־לי בגבורים: בארבעים אלף בישראל:

Whereas both the middle sections of the these 'B' strophes (5:7b-8a, 12) give positive portrayals of Deborah (and Barak) arising, the flanking sections present first negative portrayals (5:6-7a, 8b) then positive portrayals (5:11b, 13) of Israel.[103] In view of the correspondence of themes between analogous sections of the 'B' strophes, this shift from negative to positive portrayals of Israel was probably intended to imply that their descent into battle was a result of Deborah's call to action portrayed in the intervening sections (5:7b-8a, 12). As corroboration of the foregoing analysis, one may note two further verbal phenomena: (1) as in the 'A' strophes, there is an even distribution of the term ישראל among the three sections of strophe B and of the complementary designation עם יהוה between the flanking sections of strophe Bⁱ (5:11b, 13) and (2), likewise in the flanking sections of strophe Bⁱ, both clauses open with אז ירד[ו].[104] Further, in strophe B the correspondence between 5:6-7a and 5:8b, both describing the period of anarchy before Deborah's call, implicitly rebukes Israel by contrasting the shamefully weaponless masses of Israel (5:8b) with the courageous individuals Jael (בימי יעל) and Shamgar (בימי שמגר בן־ענת), who both made use of even nonmilitary implements (ox goad [cf. 3:31] and tent peg [4:21; 5:26]) to achieve deliverance for YHWH. Between the 'B' strophes, the flanking sections contrast the military indolence in Israel (5:6-7a, 8b) with the eventual descent of YHWH's people for military action (5:11b, 13). The correspondence between the flanking sections of strophe Bⁱ entails a rallying (אז ירד[ו]) of YHWH's people (עם יהוה [|| שריד in 5:13aα]) "to the gates" (לשערים, 5:11b) and "to the nobles" || "among the warriors" (בגבורים || לאדירים, 5:13).

The 'C' strophes follow the same triadic pattern as the 'B' strophes in that they contrast positive and negative themes by means of a framing pattern that presents one disposition in the flanking sections and its opposite in the centre section. The flanking sections of strophe C (5:14-15a, 18) present positive accounts of the tribes of Israel that rallied at

---

[103] On the inclusio between 5:11b and 5:13, see Boling, *Judges* (1975), p. 111; Globe, "Song of Deborah" (1974), p. 504.

[104] Indeed, the symmetrical arrangement of positive and negative portrayals within the triadic pattern of all 'B' and 'C' strophes (see below) is another stylistic feature of the hymn that raises doubt about the judgement that 5:11b is a gloss based upon 5:13 (see the appendix).

Deborah's summons prior to the battle.[105] They flank the negative description of those tribes that failed to rally (5:15b-17). The rhetorical effect of this framing juxtaposition is to rebuke the tribes that did not respond to Deborah's summons.[106] In this regard, the arrangement of the tribes in the list so as to reverse their geographical situation—tribes situated geographically at the periphery are now made the centre in 5:15b-17—is further evidence that their absence from the rally is the focal concern of the strophe, which serves a rhetoric of rebuke, and further makes for a smoother transition both from the preceding and to the following descriptions (5:13, 19).[107] As further evidence of the rebuke implicit in 5:15b-17, it is probably no coincidence that the exclamation of 5:9aα, לבי לחוקקי ישראל (which corresponds to 5:2a בפרע פרעות בישראל), appears in reversed word order in 5:15bβ חקקי-לב (which forms a framing repetition with 5:16bβ חקרי-לב), thus further characterizing Reuben's failure to rally with other tribes as opposing the ideal (contrast the use of מחקקים in 5:14bβ, describing the rally of Machir).[108]

The framing sections of strophe C[i] (5:19, 22) portray negatively the failing efforts of the Canaanites and their horses in the face of the on-slaught of both divine–cosmic (5:20-21a) and human–military (5:21b)

---

[105] G. Gerleman perceived a triadic structure in 5:14-15, 16-17, 18 in which the outer heroic descriptions flank the description of cowards ("The Song of Deborah in the Light of Stylistics", *VT* 1 [1951], p. 173). Blenkinsopp noted that the inclusion formed between repetitions of Zebulun (5:14, 18) and Naphtali (5:15a [if Barak represents Naphtali?], 18) sets off 5:14-18 as a unit ("Ballad Style" [1961], p. 71; also Coogan, "Song of Deborah" [1978], pp. 149-50, 164-65). While the tribal name "Naphtali" is from the roster in 5:14-15a, which lists the tribes that rallied, and seems to disrupt the correspondence to the mention of both Zebulun and Naphtali in 5:18 (cf. both Zebulun and Naphtali in 4:6b, 10), the mere mention of "Barak" (5:15a) evidences that Naphtali was represented (by synecdoche?; cf. 4:6a). So Täubler, *Biblische Studien I* (1958), pp. 148-49; Blenkinsopp, "Ballad Style" (1961), p. 71; Coogan, "Song of Deborah" (1978), pp. 164-65. Contrast arguments used by those who regard 5:18 as not being a part of the original composition (e.g., H.-J. Zobel, *Stammesspruch und Geschichte: Die Angaben der Stammessprüche von Gen 49, Dtn 33 und Jdc 5 über die politischen und kultischen Zustände im damaligen 'Israel'* [BZAW 95, Berlin, 1965], p. 52; Müller, "Aufbau des Deboraliedes" [1966], pp. 451-52).

[106] Blenkinsopp regarded the denunciation of Reuben in 5:15b-16 as a "taunt-song" ("Ballad Style" [1961], pp. 68, 70 n. 2, 71-72).

[107] Cf. Blenkinsopp, "Ballad Style" (1961), p. 71; Richter, *Richterbuch* (2d edn, 1966), p. 90; Coogan, "Song of Deborah" (1978), p. 164, n. 96.

[108] Another evidence of rebuke in 5:15b-17 inheres in the transfer to the three tribes mentioned there of epithets originally applied to Issachar and Zebulun in Gen. 49:13-14 (see below).

resistance.[109] As in the flanking sections of strophe B[i], so here the flanking sections of 5:19 and 5:22 present clauses that begin with אז + perf. m. pl.[110]

From the correspondence between the flanking sections of strophe C[ii] (5:23, 28-30), one may infer that both denounce feeble opponents of YHWH in the aftermath of the battle: the mother of Sisera (5:28-30) for her thwarted designs against Israel and the citizens of Meroz (5:23) for failing to help during the postbattle mopping-up operations.[111] These frame the positive portrayal of Jael, whose heroic deed is recounted in 5:24-27.[112] The contrast between 5:23 and 5:24 (especially ארו ‖ אורו ארור vs. מנשים ‖ תברך מנשים) suggests that 5:24 goes with the strophe that follows.[113] It was perhaps to point to a reversal of appropriate roles that, whereas the citizens of Meroz (inappropriately) and the court of Sisera's mother's ladies (appropriately) share a predilection for staying at home to wait for news of the battle's outcome, Jael, who has a woman's right to do likewise, is portrayed as going out in military fashion to meet Sisera (ותצא יעל לקראת סיסרא,

---

[109] Both Globe ("Song of Deborah" [1974], pp. 496, 501) and Hauser ("Judges 5" [1980], pp. 32-34; idem, "Songs of Victory" [1987], pp. 268, 272) demarcated 5:19-22 as a unified section. Müller has likewise argued in favour of grouping 5:19-22 into a three-part strophe: "(1) das Heranrücken der 'Könige Kanaans' [19a, 19b] ... (2) die Wende ... 20, 21a, und (3) die panische Flucht der Feinde 22" ("Aufbau des Deboraliedes" [1966], p. 446). While Müller chose not to comment on 5:21b ("Aufbau des Deboraliedes" [1966], p. 448 n. 4), the 1 c. sg suff. on נפשי in the clause תדרכי נפשי עז probably equates to the 1 c. sg forms of אזמר ליהוה in אנכי ליהוה אנכי אשירה אזמר ליהוה in 5:3b—the distributive use of the 1 c. sg in a hymn designed for communal recitation (cf. Müller, "Aufbau des Deboraliedes" [1966], p. 456)—though the narrative transition in 5:1 ties the 1 c. sg ostensibly to Deborah/Barak (cf. 5:12a/b) and the genre of 5:21b echoes the battle cry of 4:14 (cf. again 5:12a/b; Globe, "Song of Deborah" [1974], p. 501). However, as evidence of variation of stance in the poem, note the 2 f. sg form of address in the matching sections 5:7b-8a and 5:12—corroborating the view that the verbs of עד שקמתי דבורה שקמתי אם בישראל (5:7b) preserve the old 2 f. sg form (cf. GKC, §44h; so Moore, Judges [1895], p. 145; Burney, Judges [2d edn, 1920], p. 116; A. Globe, "The Text and Literary Structure of Judges 5,4-5", Bib 55 [1974], p. 171; Coogan, "Song of Deborah" [1978], p. 147 n. 21; Soggin, Judges [2d edn, 1987], p. 86; "you" in JPSV, RSV, Boling [Judges (1975), p. 102]; contra "I" in AV, RV, NEB, NIV, Klein [Triumph of Irony (1988), p. 44]; but cf. the second aor. active indicative 3 c. sg of OG 5:7b [ἐξανέστη ‖ ἀνέστη] with 5:15).

[110] On the correspondence between 5:19 and 5:22, see also Hauser, "Songs of Victory" (1987), p. 275.

[111] So Lindars, "Deborah's Song" (1982–83), p. 170; Sternberg, Poetics (1985), p. 277.

[112] Coogan, "Song of Deborah" (1978), p. 153.

[113] Contra Coogan, "Song of Deborah" (1978), pp. 150, 152, 153.

4:18a)—something the male warriors of Meroz should have done.[114] Similarly, it is perhaps a point of satire on the noble classes that a curse against the city dwellers of Meroz and a satire against the noblewomen of Sisera's mother's court are set in contrast to a blessing on a tent-dwelling woman (5:24-27).[115] While in Jael's tent there takes place a reversal of appropriate gender roles (i.e., a domesticated woman defeats a military commander), the description of Jael's slaying of Sisera also hints at the differences in their social status (cf. מנשים באהל, 5:24b; בספל אדירים, 5:25b; להלמות עמלים, 5:26aβ).

Thus, it may be inferred that the rhetoric of Judges 5 "works by contrasts"[116] and that these contrasts operate within a scheme of strophic triads that pervade the hymn.[117] Also subscribing to the triadic pattern of strophes is the hymn's concern with the portrayal of YHWH's control over the floodwaters. It is significant that each of the middle sections among the 'C' strophes focuses upon images of water in relation to the victory achieved by YHWH. In strophe C, three of the four tribes that are rebuked for staying at home are negatively characterized as preferring to remain beyond or by water bodies—Gilead, beyond the

---

[114] The contrasting character evaluations of 5:23 and 5:24 reflect an analogous concern with appropriate gender roles: בגבורים (m. pl.) vs. מנשים (f. pl.), respectively. On the reversal of gender-appropriate roles in Judg. 4–5, cf. Gottlieb, "Mothers" (1981), pp. 195-98; Sternberg, *Poetics* (1985), pp. 270-83; Webb, *Judges* (1987), p. 135; Klein, *Triumph of Irony* (1988), pp. 47, 218 n. 15; Bos, "Shadows" (1988), pp. 57-58.

[115] Antithetical parallelism between ארר (5:23) and ברך (5:24) has been noted by Globe ("Song of Deborah" [1974], p. 507, n. 32). Further, Müller has shown how the form of the curse in 5:23 ("[1] Aufforderung zum Fluch … [2] die Benennung des Verfluchten … [3] eine berichtende Begründung") is similar to that of the juxtaposed blessing in 5:24-27 ("[1] eine Jussivform von ברך … [2] die etwas erweiterte Benennung des Segensempfängers und [3] ein Bericht der vollbrachten Tat") ("Aufbau des Deboraliedes" [1966], pp. 446-47). When this similarity of form between 5:23 and 5:24-27 is considered together with the fact that each of the 'C' strophes is structured on a triadic pattern in which the flanking sections have the same disposition (whether that be positive [5:11b ‖ 13; 5:14-15a ‖ 18] or negative [5:6-7a ‖ 8b; 5:19 ‖ 22; 5:23 ‖ 28-30]) and the fact that 'C' strophes are thus distributed among three chronological phases (prebattle [5:14-15a, 15b-17, 18], midbattle [5:19, 20-21, 22], postbattle [5:23, 24-27, 28-30]), then it only further supports the view that 5:23 should be grouped with what follows rather than with what precedes (contra Webb [*Judges* (1987), pp. 139-43] and Lindars ["Deborah's Song" (1982-83), pp. 169, 170] to the extent that the latter regarded 5:23 as transitional).

[116] So Gerleman, "Song of Deborah" (1951), pp. 172-73, though he was referring to themes rather than to the correspondence between theme and structure presented in this analysis.

[117] This analysis counters the assertion of Blenkinsopp that "the unity of the poem is not literary but theological" ("Ballad Style" [1961], p. 62).

Jordan; Dan, by ships; Asher, by the seashore (5:17).[118] In strophe Cⁱ, YHWH's victory is achieved by his control of the floodwaters of the Kishon (5:20-21a).[119] Indeed, through both repetition and assonance, the twice-mentioned fighting of the kings of Canaan (נלחמו [2x], 5:19) is appropriately answered by the twice-mentioned fighting of celestial forces (symbolic of YHWH; נלחמו [2x], 5:20) whose agent is none other than the thrice-mentioned river (נחל [3x], 5:21).[120] In strophe Cⁱⁱ, of the two praiseworthy acts of Jael mentioned in the middle section, the first commences with Sisera's now ironic request for water and Jael's subtle refusal through substitution, מים שאל חלב נתנה (5:25a).[121] These developments of the water motif among the 'C' strophes both echo the images of YHWH's epiphanic and benevolent control over water in 5:4-5 and 5:11a, respectively, and lend thematic unity to the hymn.[122]

The moment of climax in both the prose and poetic accounts comes when Jael hammers the peg into Sisera's temple, thus killing him (4:21 of 4:18-21; 5:27 of 5:24-27).[123] That this single act was designed to function as the climax of both accounts is attested by the plot-structure and pace of description in both accounts. While it has been argued that the prose battle description (allegedly 4:14-17) constitutes the narrative climax,[124] 4:18-21 has the advantage of occurring in the normal position for a climax, near the conclusion of the story.[125] Further, 4:21, as the culmination of a prolonged description of Jael's confrontation with Sisera in 4:18-21, offers the slowest paced description of the narrative.[126] Note the deliberation over detail in the portrayal of the action in 4:21a, which leads up to the moment of resolution:

---

[118] Hauser, "Judges 5" (1980), p. 31; idem, "Songs of Victory" (1987), p. 272.

[119] Hauser, "Songs of Victory" (1987), pp. 272-73.

[120] Cf. Hauser, "Judges 5" (1980), p. 33. On the paronomasia between נלחמו and נחל, see Coogan, "Song of Deborah" (1978), p. 159.

[121] Hauser wrote: "the Canaanite chieftain at first has too much water, and then is reduced to begging some from a woman" ("Judges 5" [1980], p. 36); idem, "Songs of Victory" (1987), p. 273.

[122] Cf. Coogan, "Song of Deborah" (1978), pp. 156, 161.

[123] So Müller, "Aufbau des Deboraliedes" (1966), p. 446; Hauser, "Judges 5" (1980), pp. 28, 35, 37, 38; idem, "Songs of Victory" (1987), pp. 275, 278; Coogan, "Song of Deborah" (1978), p. 165; Amit, "Judges 4" (1987), pp. 96-98; Bos, "Shadows" (1988), pp. 54-55. Webb regarded 4:21 as the climax of the prose account (*Judges* [1987], p. 136) but, following Lindars ("Deborah's Song" [1982-83], pp. 169 n. 24, 172), considered the climax of the hymn to be its battle account (*Judges* [1987], pp. 144, 250 n. 74).

[124] Alonso-Schökel, "Erzählkunst" (1961), p. 162.

[125] So Murray, "Narrative Structure" (1979), p. 165 n. 22.

[126] So Licht, *Storytelling* (1978), pp. 99-102; Murray, "Narrative Structure" (1979), pp. 164-65, 183; Amit, "Judges 4" (1987), p. 96.

ותקח יעל אשת־חבר את־יתד האהל
ותשם את־המקבת בידה /
ותבוא אליו בלאת /
ותתקע את־היתד ברקתו /
ותצנח בארץ

It is perhaps noteworthy that three keywords used here to describe
Jael's aggression against Sisera (לקח, יד, תקע) collocate in 3:21, which
is likewise the dramatic climax (and structural apex) of the Ehud
account.[127] The three verbs in 4:21b, והוא־נרדם ויעף וימת, not only
describe the threefold reaction of Sisera to Jael's hammer blow but
echo the three groupings of her actions ... ותכסהו ... ותכסהו
ותקח\ותשם\ותבוא\ותתקע (4:18bβ, 19b, 21a), each concluding an interchange between Sisera and Jael (4:18, 19, 20-21) and each leading
closer to Sisera's death, which is described in 4:21b.[128] Indeed, a consideration of the complementary inaction of Sisera leads to the satirical
inference that the words, והוא־נרדם ויעף וימת, mean that Sisera, being
overwhelmed with sleep (Ni. ptcp m. sg) and exhausted, simply died.

It has similarly sometimes been argued that the climax of the hymn
is furnished by the battle description of 5:19-22.[129] However, the
position of the battle description in 5:19-22 as but the second of three
successive triadic rebukes (i.e., C: 5:14-15a, 15b-17, 18; C^i: 5:19, 20-
21, 22; C^ii: 5:23, 24-27, 28-30) and its faster paced description
(relative to story time) than that of the third and final rebuke (5:23-
30)[130] make it more likely that the intended climax of the poem is in the
central section of strophe C^ii (5:24-27) and, within that section, in the
culminating description of Jael's killing of Sisera (5:27) and, within
that verse, the final word, שדוד "slain, destroyed".[131] As in the prose

---

[127] Cf. Alonso-Schökel, "Erzählkunst" (1961), pp. 151, 154, 165.

[128] *Pace* Alonso-Schökel, who heard in 4:21b an echo of ותכסהו ... ותכסהו ... אין
(4:18bβ, 19b, 20bβ), though its final member lacks symmetry with the preceding f. sg
verbal forms and with the parallel location of these verbs in positions that describe Jael's
acting in excess of the expectations of hospitality ("Erzählkunst" [1961], p. 165).

[129] So Blenkinsopp ("Ballad Style" [1961], p. 69) and Lindars ("Deborah's Song"
[1982–83], pp. 169, n. 24, 172; followed by Webb, *Judges* [1987], pp. 144, 250 n. 74
[though Webb's citations do not correspond to Lindars's references to the climax of the
hymn]). Both considered the battle description the poem's climax because of its alleged
central position within the poem's structure. Lindars also adduced as evidence of the battle
scene's climactic function its compressed description ("Deborah's Song" [1982–83],
pp. 170-71).

[130] Cf. Hauser, "Judges 5" (1980), pp. 36-38.

[131] Hauser observed that שדוד stands out not only because of its final position in the
verse but also because (1), in contrast to the prevalence of 'a' sounds in the verse, it contains the only 'o' sound, and (2), as a passive ptcp, it is the only nonfinite verb in the

description of 4:21a, the description leading up to the cathartic resolution is slow-paced and laden with detail (5:26):

ידה ליתד תשלחנה /
וימינה להלמות עמלים //
והלמה סיסרא
מחקה ראשו /
ומחצה וחלפה רקתו

The series of verbs describing Jael's violent actions (והלמה, תשלחנה, וחלפה, ומחצה, מחקה) is a model of cacophony—the sound of Jael's hammering virtually being driven into the ear of the reader.[132]

Even more than in the prose description of 4:21b, the hymnic version of 5:27 offers a plethora of redundancies at the moment of climax. Its repetition of four finite verbs forms a sevenfold description followed by the predicative Qal passive ptcp, שדוד "slain" (cf. the semantically analogous final verb of 4:21, וימת "and he died"):

בין רגליה / כרע נפל שכב //
בין רגליה   כרע   נפל /
באשר   כרע /
שם   נפל
שדוד[133]

A final justification for regarding 5:24-27 as the structural and thematic climax of the hymn derives from the complementarity between this section and its dénouement foil in 5:28-30 (functioning analogously to the relationship between 4:21 and 4:22 in the prose account). The complementarity between 5:24-27 and 5:28-30 may be seen from the following outline (key words in square brackets):

a Characterization of each woman *vis-à-vis* her domicile:

Blessing on Jael among   Portrayal of Sisera's mother
tent-dwelling women (5:24)   as a woman at her window (5:28a)

b Characterization of each woman *vis-à-vis* Sisera's delay:

Sisera asks [שאל] water;   Sisera's mother asks why [מדוע, 2x]
Jael gives milk (5:25)   the chariots of Sisera delay (5:28b)

---

verse ("Judges 5" [1980], pp. 37 n. 38, 38 n. 41; idem, "Songs of Victory" [1987], pp. 278-79).

[132] Cf. Hauser, "Judges 5" (1980), pp. 36-37, where he also notes (n. 36) the reverberation between והלמה סיסרא "and she hammered Sisera" in 5:26 and אז הלמו עקבי־סוס<י>ם "then hammered horses hooves" in 5:22.

[133] Cf. Alonso-Schökel, "Erzählkunst" (1961), p. 164 n. 1; Hauser, "Judges 5" (1980), pp. 37, 38.

c Charaterization of each woman *vis-à-vis* Sisera's fate:

<table>
<tr>
<td>

α Jael reaches [תשלחנה]
for peg and hammer
(5:26a)

</td>
<td>

α The wisest of the ladies answers
[תעניה]; Sisera's mother
repeats to herself (5:29)

</td>
</tr>
<tr>
<td>

β Jael hammers Sisera
[סיסרא]
crushes his head
[ראשו]
shatters and pierces
his temple [וחלפה רקתו]
(5:26b)
Between her feet [בין רגליה]
he sinks, falls, lies
between her feet [בין רגליה]
he sinks, falls
where he sinks
there he falls
slain (5:27)

</td>
<td>

β A womb or two per warrior's head
[רחם רחמתים לראש גבר]
spoil of dyed stuffs for Sisera
[לסיסרא]
spoil of dyed stuffs with
embroidery [רקמה]
dyed stuff with double-embroidery
[רקמתים]
for the necks of the spoiler
(5:30)

</td>
</tr>
</table>

From comparing the contrasting opening characterizations with the contrasting outcomes one may sense the irony in that, whereas Jael is exalted while yet in her humble dwelling (5:24), Sisera's mother is being humiliated while yet in her palace (5:28a),[134] and this through her satirical portrayal as a "woman at the window".[135] As to Sisera's delay (5:25, 28b), Jael pretends to make a motherly substitution of milk for water so as to lull him to sleep then kill him. Contrariwise, Sisera's mother, worried about his delay, pretends to be unaware of the ominous significance of his failure to return. The contrast between Sisera's real and supposed fates (5:26-27, 29-30) epitomizes Jael as a woman of substance (5:26a) whereas Sisera's mother and her ladies are women of mere words (5:29). Whereas Jael wreaks havoc on Sisera, his head and temples (5:26b), Sisera's mother ironically envisions wombs per warrior's head, booty for Sisera and needlework for his neck (5:30). Whereas the repetitions of 5:30 (שלל, 4x; צבע[י]ם, 3x; רחם רחמתים; רקמתים // רקמה) convey the bounty of booty that Sisera's mother desires, the analogy of 5:27 attests how ill-founded is her avarice. Thus, the ladies of Sisera's court are ridiculed and Jael glorified each in relation to Sisera's demise.

The preference of some to see the climax in the battle descriptions of both the prose and hymn accounts may have been prompted either by a

---

[134] Cf. Richter, *Richterbuch* (2d edn, 1966), p. 101.

[135] Coogan, "Song of Deborah" (1978), p. 154.

consciousness of circumstances within the story world (i.e., the battle would have had epic proportions in contrast to the private encounter between Jael and Sisera)[136] or by a misappropriation of rhetorical conventions governing modulations in the pace of description.[137] On the contrary, the very expectation that the day-long battle against Sisera led by Barak should lead to the climax of the prose account is minimized by its compressed description in contrast to the quick triumph of Jael, which receives the expanded description. Elements of the battle description only complicate the various plot-levels, rather than resolve them, during this period of increasing tension.[138] The posterior position and elongated pace of description given to Jael's baiting and killing of Sisera was clearly designed to subvert the expectation that the chief glory should go to any but the one who is truly zealous for YHWH.

The victory hymn of 5:2-31a does not have a plot-structure *per se*, but it does function as an embellishment on the resolutions of both Plot A and Plot C in the narrative. The whole hymn is the object of ותשר in 5:1; 5:1 stands in apposition to the resolution of Plot A in 4:23 (cf. ביום ההוא in both 4:23 and 5:1), and, since ביום ההוא in 5:1 refers to the day on which Jael killed Sisera, 5:1 also summarizes the resolution of Plot C in 4:21 (i.e., Jabin is defeated by proxy through the defeat of Sisera). Not only does the hymn relate to the resolutions of Plots A and C, through correspondences in the discourse structure, it

---

[136] So, apparently, Alonso-Schökel: "So kommen wir zum Höhepunkt der Handlung: der gewaltige Zussamentstoss zweier Heere, neunhundert Kriegswagen, Pferde, zehntausend israelitische Soldaten" ("Erzählkunst" [1961], p. 162; cf. n. 1 citing A. Schulz, *Erzählungskunst in den Samuel-Büchern* [Biblische Zeitfragen XI/6-7, Munster, i. W., 1923], p. 44). However, on the general reluctance of Hebrew narrators, in contrast to those of other ancient literatures, to indulge in detailed presentation of battles, see Licht, *Storytelling* (1978), p. 101 and n. 10 (cf. Murray, "Narrative Structure" [1979], pp. 164-65, 164 n. 20, 165 n. 24).

[137] So, apparently, Lindars who said of 5:19-22: "This strophe brilliantly compresses the description of the action into a few visual moments of great emotional intensity, fulfilling the expectations built up in the preceding sections of the poem" ("Deborah's Song" [1982-83], p. 170). However, compressed description is not usual at a literary climax, which tends to expand description through portrayal (cf. Licht on the significance of the change of pace between scenes of showing action [i.e., 4:6b-9a, 18-22] and scenes of telling in Judg. 4 [*Storytelling* (1978), pp. 98-102]). Lindars subsequently and accurately observed that "The rest of the poem moves at a slower pace" (p. 170) and, of the expansive description of 5:27, said, "the description at this point is expanded far beyond necessity so as to build up to its climax, the fact that Sisera is dead. ... The whole purpose of this description is to concentrate attention on the annihilation of Sisera ..." ("Deborah's Song" [1982-83], p. 171), yet Lindars was not thereby led to regard 5:27 or 5:24-27 as the climax of the poem (cf. pp. 169, n. 24, 172).

[138] Murray, "Narrative Structure" (1979), pp. 165-66.

also recapitulates the two main themes of Plots A and C: the victory of
YHWH (Plot A) and Jael (Plot C) over the foreign oppressors Jabin
(Plot A) and Sisera (Plots A and C). However, the hymn presents new
information (e.g., 5:20-21a, 28-30) that both embellishes the prose
presentation of these themes and gives them heightened effect. But what
does the hymn make of Plot B in the prose account?

Although the victory hymn does not recapitulate the main theme of
Plot B (i.e., the humiliation of Barak for his reluctance to follow YHWH
whole heartedly), its portrayal of halfheartedness among the tribes of
Israel in 5:14-18 furnishes an escalated parallel to Barak's halfheartedness. Thus, from a comparison between the two portrayals of
reluctance to follow YHWH into battle in Judges 4 and 5, there emerges
an escalated parallelism between the prose ridicule of Barak's
halfheartedness (4:8), in contrast to the zeal for YHWH of Deborah
(4:6-7, 9a, 14a) and especially Jael (4:18-21), and the poetic ridicule of
Israel's tribes for their collective halfheartedness (5:14-18), in contrast
to the zeal for YHWH of Deborah (5:21b) and especially Jael (5:24-27).
In the prose account, Barak's reluctance to go to battle for YHWH
without Deborah's accompaniment is contrasted to Jael's forsaking
even her own husband's friendly relations with Jabin of Hazor (4:17b)
in order to act loyally to YHWH. In the hymn, the absence of four tribal
groups from the rally (5:15b-17) is contrasted both to the zeal of those
tribes that did rally (5:14-15a, 18) and to the zeal of two women: one
who accompanied the troops into battle (5:21b) and another who,
unaccompanied, worked for YHWH's victory (5:24-27). The rhetorical
concern implied by this escalated parallelism is that, through a strategy
of entrapment, Israel (the ostensible reader) is seen to be as halfhearted
as was Barak in regard to having the covenant zeal to conquer foreigners on behalf of YHWH. Further, this escalation of covenant
indifference from an individual to the national level parallels the escalation of emotional intensity between the prose and poetic portrayals of
how YHWH achieved victory over his enemies.

In this connection, it should be noted that just as a shift in disposition
from negative to positive portrayals of Israel between the flanking sections of the 'B' strophes attests a rhetorical design to portray Israel
responding to the arising of Deborah (and Barak), so too the polar shift
in dispositions (positive vs. negative) among the 'C' strophes is rhetorically significant. Among the 'C' strophes, the middle sections
(5:15b-17, 20-21, 24-27) are the focal concern. Whereas the first

triadic 'C' strophe exhibits a positive–negative–positive pattern in which the tribes that failed to rally are the focal concern, the two 'C' strophes that follow reverse this pattern of polarity (negative–positive–negative) so that they focus upon the ideal of YHWH and Deborah's example of zeal (5:20-21a, 21b) in overthrowing foreign powers (5:19, 22) and especially upon the example of Jael (5:24-27), who, out of zeal for YHWH, put to shame both the indolent citizens of Meroz and the indignant noblewomen of Sisera's court (5:23, 28-30).

It is entirely appropriate, then, that the eighth and final strophe of this hymn, which develops principally through patterns of contrast, should conclude in 5:31a with an imprecation and blessing that contrasts the fates of those who either oppose or love YHWH. The very ambiguity of its authorship (as coming ostensibly from Deborah [5:1], from the author of the Deborah/Barak/Jael account(s) or from the Judges compiler/redactor) enjoins the reader's Yahwistic loyalty at all levels and fits the book's strategy of entrapment, since it induces the reader to condemn all who act as enemies of YHWH and implicitly condemns those in Israel who do evil in the eyes of YHWH by failing to show fervent enmity toward YHWH's enemies (as did Barak in Plot B and the tribes in 5:15b-17).

Although plot-structure and characterization in Judges 4–5 are more complex than in the Ehud account, they point to a similar rhetorical strategy. As in the Ehud account, that of Deborah/Barak/Jael employs satire in its plot development. In keeping with the design of Plot A, the narrator satirizes Canaanite kingship and nobility via the ridicule of its military (e.g., the iron chariots of Sisera ironically become a liability in the Kishon's floodplain [cf. 4:13, 15-16; 5:19, 22][139]; again, while fleeing the military men of Israel, the nobleman Sisera ironically finds death through the feigned hospitality of a tent-dwelling woman [4:17-21; 5:24-27][140]). Ridicule of Canaanite nobility is also evident in the

---

[139] Of the prose portrayal, Gottlieb said: "Iron chariots and sheer weight of arms have made the Canaanite army founder in the marsh and it is Sisera's virility that proves his destruction" ("Mothers" [1981], p. 197). Of the hymnic portrayal, Hauser summarized: "The opening words of v 19 are pointed and sarcastic. The double statement that the kings came and fought focuses attention on their military efforts, thereby providing ... the intended sarcasm, since the audience knows that the kings fought to no avail. ... The poet mocks the efforts of the Canaanite kings ...". Of 5:22 he wrote, "The defeat has already been expressed in cosmic terms: now the Canaanites are mocked by picturing them fleeing pell-mell from the battlefield" ("Judges 5" [1980], pp. 32, 34).

[140] Cf. Amit, "Judges 4" (1987), p. 97; Bos, "Shadows" (1988), pp. 53-57.

embellishment on Plot C through satire against its courtly ladies (who ironically credit Sisera's delay to his victory [5:28-30]).[141]

The humiliation of Barak is the key objective of Plot B. Several devices of satire are used toward this end. After Deborah's claim to divine authority (הלא צוה יהוה אלהי־ישראל, 4:6bα), her initial instructions to Barak began לך (4:6bβ). Thereafter, הלך becomes a motif that is repeated seven times more in dialogue and, in all instances, negatively characterizes Barak for his reluctance to go in response to YHWH's commission. His first response is, אם־תלכי עמי והלכתי ואם־לא תלכי עמי לא אלך (4:8). Deborah concedes, הלך אלך עמך (4:9aα), but rebukes Barak with the limitation that the glory for defeating Sisera would be given "into the hand of a woman" (4:9aβ-ε). Is it not then with some intent to ridicule that, when Barak finally meets this woman, she invites him into her tent to see Deborah's prediction fulfilled with the words, לך ואראך את־האיש אשר־אתה מבקש (4:22aδε)?[142]

Perhaps implicitly, Barak again comes under ridicule in the portrayal of his surprise at discovering that Sisera is already dead (והנה סיסרא נפל מת, 4:22bβ; cf. 5:27)—a portrayal worded similarly to that of the courtiers' discovery that Eglon was dead (והנה אדניהם נפל ארצה מת, 3:25γδ).[143] Indeed, in both accounts, the too-late-discovery, which is introduced by והנה, is anticipated by blunders that lead up to the discovery, each introduced by והנה (והנה ברק רדף את־סיסרא, 4:22aα; cf. 3:24aγb-25aα, 25aβ).[144] By design, each portrayal redounds to the ridicule of those who realize too late that victory belongs to those who act with ardour for YHWH.

Another similarity to the Ehud account is the satirical function of simultaneity achieved through disjunctive syntax.[145] In the Deborah/Barak/Jael account, simultaneity increases suspense and conveys the contrast between the vain efforts of Barak, who is caught in the timing of events, and YHWH's control over temporal order in the story world. Judges 4:16 begins וברק רדף to indicate that, while Sisera was fleeing on foot (4:15b), Barak was pursuing the chariots and troops (4:16a). In

---

[141] Cf. Gottlieb: "The progress of the Canaanite armies has been hampered, these women suggest, by sheer weight of booty" ("Mothers" [1981], p. 201).

[142] Alonso-Schökel, "Erzählkunst" (1961), pp. 160-61, 161 n. 1, 165; Murray, "Narrative Structure" (1979), pp. 178-79.

[143] Alonso-Schökel, "Erzählkunst" (1961), p. 166.

[144] Alonso-Schökel, "Erzählkunst" (1961), pp. 153, 166; Murray, "Narrative Structure" (1979), pp. 161-62, 161 n. 15, 172; Amit, "Judges 4" (1987), pp. 96-97, 109 n. 30.

[145] Cf. Alonso-Schökel, "Erzählkunst" (1961), pp. 155, 163, 166.

this connection, the comment, לא נשאר עד־אחד (4:16b*β*; cf. 3:29b), is made with reference to the enumeration of chariots and troops that Barak was chasing (4:16a) and not with reference to Sisera, who had already escaped (4:15b). In that the narrator describes events with reference only to Barak's sphere, it emphasizes the distance between the reader's knowledge that Sisera has already escaped and Barak's ignorance of that fact owing to his preoccupation with chariots and troops. Disjunctive syntax reappears in 4:17a, where the description of Sisera's escape (וסיסרא נס ברגליו אל־אהל יעל אשת חבר הקיני) repeats resumptively the description of his escape in 4:15b (וירד סיסרא מעל המרכבה וינס ברגליו) so that Barak's simultaneous pursuit (4:16) is framed within.[146] The narrative portrayal of simultaneity achieved through resumptive repetition extends further. Barak's pursuit described in 4:16a (וברק רדף אחרי הרכב ואחרי המחנה עד חרשת הגוים) is resumptively repeated in 4:22a*α* (והנה ברק רדף את־סיסרא) so as to enclose the description of the outcome of Sisera's fatal escape to the tent of Jael (4:17-21).[147] Through this interlocking of the two resumptive repetitions in the narrative, the actions of Barak are contrasted, first with those of Sisera, then with those of Jael achieving what Barak had hoped to achieve. Whereas Barak had hoped to thwart Deborah's limiting prediction (4:9) by capturing Sisera (cf. 4:14a), Sisera alone escaped (4:15b, 17a) while Barak pursued chariots and troops (4:16). Again, whereas Barak had hoped to capture Sisera before some woman killed Sisera (4:9), Jael was already accomplishing the deed (4:18-21) while Barak was pursuing (4:16a, 22a).

In the prose account, the tension created between Deborah's prediction that Sisera would be given alternatively into Barak's hand (4:7), then into the hand of a woman (4:9a), then, through an ambiguity fostered by metonymy, into Barak's hand (4:14a) increases suspense as the reader wonders to whom YHWH will finally appoint the task of killing Sisera.[148] This suspense is not resolved until the climax of the narrative in 4:21. In 4:11 the narrator again increases suspense through a delaying tactic, namely, the interruption of the two military groups' movements in preparation for battle (4:10, 12-13) by the information about Heber's movement.[149] Even though the idea of movement is

---

[146] Cf. Murray, "Narrative Structure" (1979), pp. 161, 170-71.

[147] Cf. Murray, "Narrative Structure" (1979), pp. 171-72.

[148] Cf. Murray, "Narrative Structure" (1979), pp. 174-75.

[149] Cf. Alonso-Schökel, "Erzählkunst" (1961), p. 166; Murray, "Narrative Structure" (1979), p. 180.

consistent, it is not at first apparent why this information about Heber is given here. In retrospect, however, it becomes clear that the foreshadowing in 4:11 (Plot C) is strategically positioned to give the reader an impression of elapsed time that corresponds to the story time needed for the report to reach Sisera (4:12a) about the 'ascent' (to Mount Tabor) by Barak, the troops from Zebulun and Naphtali, and Deborah (4:10b).[150] Further, 4:11 is at the centre of a symmetrical presentation of Barak summoning troops (ויזעק ברק ..., 4:10aα), then ascending with Deborah (ויעל ברגליו ... ותעל עמו דבורה, 4:10aβγb), and of Sisera receiving the report that Barak had ascended (ויגדו לסיסרא כי עלה ברק, 4:12b), then himself summoning troops (ויזעק סיסרא ..., 4:13).[151] In this way the actions of Barak and Sisera are seen as evenly matched for a contest in which somehow the information foreshadowed in 4:11 may play a significant role.

The dénouement of the evenly matched contest between Barak and Sisera appears in 4:22 when, in reverse order from the parallel of Sisera preparing for battle (4:12, 13) in response to Barak's preparation for battle (4:10aα, 10aβγ), Barak responds (ויבא אליה, 4:22bα) to Jael's invitation (ותצא יעל לקראתו ותאמר לו לך ואראך את־האיש אשר־אתה מבקש, 4:22a) as a parallel to Sisera's response (ויסר אליה, 4:18bα) to Jael's invitation (ותצא יעל לקראת סיסרא ותאמר אליו סורה אדני סורה אלי אל־תירא, 4:18a).[152] It is this parallelism between the actions of Sisera and Barak, with the foreshadowing (4:11) or description (4:19-21) of Jael's actions intervening, that conveys the similarity of their destinies.[153] Both military leaders are humiliated

---

[150] Alonso-Schökel, "Erzählkunst" (1961), p. 161. He notes also the clever positioning of ויגדו ל– in Judg. 9:7, 42. Cf. also Murray, "Narrative Structure" (1979), pp. 179-80.

With regard to the ellipsis of הר־תבור, the unexpressed object of both uses of עלה in 4:10 (cf. וירד ברק מהר תבור, 4:12b; עלה ברק...הר־תבור, 4:6bβ; לך ומשכת בהר תבור, 4:14bα), Murray has even suggested that an original הר־תבור may have been lost from 4:10c* through a haplography caused by its similarity to the flanking words דבורה (4:10b) and וחבר (4:11aα) ("Narrative Structure" [1979], p. 157 n. 5). However, considering both the absence of textual support and the adequacy of attestation in the context for the ellipsis of הר־תבור in 4:10, an emendation is unwarranted despite "the parallelism it would create between 10b and 12b".

[151] On the parallelism between 4:10 and 4:13, see Murray, "Narrative Structure" (1979), p. 169 and n. 32.

[152] Murray referred to 4:22 as the "true dénouement: the ironic juxtaposition of victor and vanquished" ("Narrative Structure" [1979], p. 159; cf. pp. 161-62, 165, 166, 172). What is ironic in 4:22 is that Barak the 'victor' can look upon Sisera as 'vanquished' only at the cost of realizing that he is also thereby vanquished, for Deborah's prophecy and Jael's actions have succeeded in seizing also his glory.

[153] Murray, "Narrative Structure" (1979), pp. 157, 171, 172, 183.

through the actions of Jael: Sisera, utterly, by her deliberate actions; Barak, partially, by her unwitting cooperation with YHWH's prediction in 4:9a. Indeed, both Sisera and Barak undergo satirization precisely because each, unwittingly, is made the ironic agent of his own undesired fate by playing into the hand of Jael, the agent of YHWH.[154] Further, in that YHWH confirms through Jael Deborah's prediction about יד־אשה, Deborah also triumphs over Sisera and is vindicated over Barak, who initially despised her word from YHWH.

In the development of Plot C, the main object of satire is the military nobleman Sisera, who, contrary to his expectations, is humiliatingly slain by the hand of a tent-dwelling woman whose husband had friendly relations with Sisera's superior, Jabin. Indeed, to the extent that Heber and Sisera are allied, Heber is a character foil for his wife Jael, who proves to be most successful when disregarding her husband's policy of friendship with Israel's enemies (4:17b; cf. Nabal and Abigail, 1 Sam. 25).[155] Satire against Sisera in Plot C may be seen to run along three lines: (1) a reversal of his expectations about appropriate roles for women (4:19; 5:24a, 25a), (2) a reversal of his expectations about class-appropriate roles (perhaps implicit in 4:21 but explicit in 5:24b, 25b, 26; cf. 5:28-30) and (3) a reversal of his expectations (and those of Heber) regarding the showing of hospitality to a guest (4:17, 18bα, 20b; cf. 5:24a).[156]

As mentioned above, the hymn's ridicule of foreign feminine nobility in 5:28-30 offers a foil (if not inclusio) to the ideal of Deborah's 'motherhood' in Israel (5:7b) through a 'woman and the window' type-scene.[157] In the biblical use of this type-scene, one expects to see rhetorically significant variations on its three usual themes of sexual encounter, deception and the threat of death. Working backwards

---

[154] Cf. Murray, "Narrative Structure" (1979), pp. 177, 179.

[155] Klein, *Triumph of Irony* (1988), p. 43.

[156] The dramatic irony of Sisera's instruction to Jael in 4:20b is brought out admirably by Alonso-Schökel ("Erzählkunst" [1961], p. 164). Sisera says, והיה אם־איש יבוא ושאלך ואמר היש־פה איש ואמרת אין "and if someone comes and asks you, 'Is anyone here?' you say, 'There is no one.'" Thus, Sisera has reduced himself to an "anyone" who is soon to become a "no one"—אין being his final word. Cf. Webb, *Judges* (1987), p. 135.

[157] Lindars, "Deborah's Song" (1982-83), p. 172. On the 'type-scene' in general, see Alter, *Biblical Narrative* (1981), pp. 47-62. On the recurrence of the three themes of sexual attraction (or its frustrated potential), deception and the threat of death in the Hebrew Bible 'woman and the window' type-scenes, see R. H. O'Connell, "Proverbs vii 16-17: A Case of Fatal Deception in a 'Woman and the Window' Type-Scene", *VT* 41 (1991), pp. 235-41.

through Judg. 5:28-30 one finds: (1) a pathetically ironic portrayal of Sisera's mother's expectations regarding her son's sexual exploits (5:30), (2) her wilful ignorance of Sisera's fate as she repeatedly consoles herself with the deceiving words of the "wisest of her noble ladies" (5:29) and (3) her latent realization as to the true reason for Sisera's failure to return—his death (5:28). Against this woman's callous designs stand the depictions of two women: Deborah, who, by her summons to battle, averted the continued oppression of Sisera's army and thus became a "mother in Israel" (5:7b; cf. 5:12),[158] and Jael, who, by her actions, averted what Sisera may have intended to do to Israelite women.[159] This makes the words of Sisera's mother, רחם רחמתים לראש גבר (5:30), reverberate with dramatic irony. Not only do they present a farcical foil to Jael's hammering of Sisera's head in 5:26, they also recall that it actually took two women to bring it about—if Deborah's part in YHWH's 'luring' of Sisera across the Kishon floodplain is seen in parallel to Jael's 'luring' Sisera into her tent.[160]

It is an important aspect of the heroic characterization of Jael in Plot C that the portrayal of Sisera's mother is encountered only at the end, in 5:28-30 (i.e., after being withheld from the prose account). Whereas the sympathy evoked for Sisera through Jael's betrayal of his trust (4:18-21; 5:24-27) may have invited repugnance at Jael's methods, in 5:28-30 the callousness of the foreign nobility is exposed for the first time through a 'woman and the window' type-scene. The satire is pointedly anti-Canaanite—the 'woman and the window' motif being prevalent in Levantine iconography—and all the more so because such

---

[158] Lindars, "Deborah's Song" (1982–83), p. 168 and n. 23.

[159] This is an important reason for rejecting Gottlieb's suggestion that "milk" in 4:19, 5:25 is a euphemism for sex or that "between her feet he fell, he lay" means "they made love" (Gottlieb, "Mothers" [1981], pp. 198-200). Such an interpretation may align with some early rabbinic views (e.g., those of Rashi [on the sedative properties of milk], Mṣdt Dvd [on sexual exhaustion], Malbim ["In the place where he fell—to have intercourse with her—there was he killed. Rabbi Yohanan said: 'That wicked wretch had sevenfold intercourse with her at that time, as it says: "At her feet he sunk, he fell, he lay"'" (alluding to the seven verbs of 5:27)]; cf. B. Nazir 23b and Leviticus Rabbah xxiii.10]) and, by analogy, with the portrayal of Judith in the Apocrypha, but it is entirely at odds with the heroic characterization of Jael achieved through satire against the inappropriate class and gender roles of characters around her (cf. Lindars, "Deborah's Song" [1982–83], pp. 173-75; contra Klein, Triumph of Irony [1988], pp. 42, 43, 218 n. 16).

[160] Pace Coogan, "Song of Deborah" (1978), p. 159.

callousness is depicted even among the noble ladies.[161] While there is some poignancy in Sisera's mother seeking comfort against the "agonies of suspense", yet inasmuch as she finds this comfort in a vision of Sisera ravaging Israelite women, the reader's sympathy is frustrated by the realization that she has only suffered the just reversal of her expectations.[162] It is this irony that turns sympathy into repugnance and retroactively dissolves whatever repugnance one may have felt against Jael for betraying the trust of Sisera through her 'inhospitality'. Thus, while Sisera's mother is comforted in her ignorance by the vision of Sisera ravaging Israelite women, the reader now finds satisfaction in knowing that he was at last subdued at Jael's feet (5:27). Nor is it without satirical intent that the vision that plays upon Sisera's mother's ignorance should be put to her by "the wisest of her noble women" (5:29a).[163] The portrayal of Sisera's mother as the epitome of hostility thus becomes a foil for Jael. She softens the reader's revulsion at Jael's inhospitality in slaying Sisera. Whereas the portrayal of Jael threatens to undo her heroic characterization, ironically, it is the portrayal of Sisera's mother that exonerates Jael.

The narrator and poet of Judges 4 and 5 spent such effort on the negative characterizations of Barak and the indolent tribes of Israel and, more so, of Sisera and his mother as representatives of Canaanite kingship and nobility, respectively, so that Deborah and, more so, Jael might attain greater glory.[164] Ultimately, it is to glorify YHWH that

---

[161] On the 'woman and the window' as a Canaanite motif, see W. McKane, *Proverbs: A New Approach* (OTL, London, 1970), pp. 335-36; Coogan, "Song of Deborah" (1978), p. 154.

[162] Says Gottlieb, "It is her lack of fellow feeling that effectively cuts off ours" ("Mothers" [1981], p. 202; cf. p. 200).

[163] Cf. Hauser, "Judges 5" (1980), p. 40.

[164] Gottlieb noted that, while the hymn castigates the men who stayed at home (5:15b-17), it praises Jael for doing just that (5:24) ("Mothers" [1981], p. 198). In this connection, it is worth noting that when formulae are similar between Gen. 49:13-14 and Judg. 5:16-17, the latter applied the formulae to different tribes from those named in the former, thus characterizing negatively the tribes mentioned in Judg. 5:16-17. Note the following transfers in Judg. 5 that show how, in each case, tribes absent from the rally are implicitly rebuked for usurping from tribes that did rally the prerogatives granted them by the blessing in Gen. 49:

Gen. 49:14	יששכר ... רבץ בין המשפתים	Issachar ... reclining between the campfires/sheepfolds
but		
Judg. 5:16a	[ראובן ...] למה ישבת בין המשפתים	[Reuben ...] why did you stay between the campfires/sheepfolds?

Deborah and Jael are made to satirize Barak and Sisera. Moreover, the ridicule of the latter harbours implicit satire on Canaanite kingship, since Sisera merely represents Jabin, king of Canaan, and because the defeat of Jabin is the final concern of the narrative framework (cf. 4:2a, 7a, 17b, 23-24 with 5:31b). Concern with the glorification of YHWH is further evident in two formal features of Judges 4 and 5. First, the change of character focus from Deborah to Barak to Jael among the three plot-levels of Judg. 4:1–5:1, 31b (and variously among the strophes of Judg. 5:2-31a) results in no one human character being present throughout.[165] It is only the theme introduced by the compiler/redactor in the exposition to Plot A that sets the major agenda for Judges 4-5 and determines one's evaluation of the success of its sub-plots (Plots B and C). To the extent that Plots B and C are controlled by the theme of Plot A—that YHWH should deliver Israel from Jabin's domination by the word of his prophetess Deborah—the reader is aware that YHWH guides the events of the story world. In the prose account, Deborah need do no more than convey to Barak YHWH's plan to defeat Sisera (4:6-7), revise that plan (4:9a), then gradually recede (4:9b, 10b, 14a); Barak, after limiting YHWH's original plan with conditions (4:8), need do no more than experience limited success (4:9b-10a, 14b, 16), reappearing only to realize this for himself (4:22); Jael, proving to be fully committed to YHWH, fulfills YHWH's revised plan to defeat Sisera by the hand of a woman (4:18-21) and also unwittingly limits Barak's success (4:22). At the end, as at the beginning, it is YHWH who causes all things to work together so that Israel

---

Gen. 49:13b	[זבולן ...] והוא לחוף אניות	and [Zebulun will] become a haven for ships
but		
Judg. 5:17a	ודן למה יגור אניות	and as for Dan, why did he linger by the ships?
Gen. 49:13a	זבולן לחוף ימים ישכן	Zebulun shall dwell by the seashore
but		
Judg. 5:17b	אשר ישב לחוף ימים	As for Asher, he dwelt by the seashore

Thus, the transfer of epithets in Judg. 5:15b-17 serves a rhetoric of rebuke against the tribes that failed to rally. In the first example (Judg. 5:16a), the rebuke implicit in the transfer to Reuben of an epithet belonging originally to Issachar is heightened by its juxtaposition with the immediately preceding praise of Issachar (cf. A. Globe, "The Muster of the Tribes in Judges 5,11e-18", ZAW 87 [1975], p. 178; Coogan, "Song of Deborah" [1978], p. 164, n. 91). The latter two examples rebuke Dan and Asher through transferring two epithets that belonged originally to Zebulun, the only tribe whose praises frame (5:14, 18) the list of rebuked tribes (5:15b-17).

[165] Murray, "Narrative Structure" (1979), p. 166.

acknowledges that he alone saves (4:1-5, 23-24). Likewise in the hymn, at the beginning and at the end, it is acknowledged that salvation comes only from YHWH (A, 5:2-5; A^i, 5:9-11a; A^{ii}, 5:31a). Both the few who call Israel to arms (B, 5:6-8; B^i, 5:11b-13) and those who rally and fight with YHWH (C, 5:14-15a, 18; C^i, 5:20-21) share in his glory (cf. 5:31aβγ). But those who oppose YHWH (C^i, 5:19, 22; C^{ii}, 5:28-30) and those who do not rally to his cause (C, 5:15b-17; C^{ii}, 5:23) deserve to languish (cf. 5:31aα).

Second, Judges 4 and 5 describe and then laud YHWH's victory achieved by means of floodwater. That Judges' prose and hymnic depictions were designed to parallel the archetypal depiction of YHWH's victory over Pharaoh's army at the sea in the prose and poetic account of Exodus 14-15 has already been suggested.[166] The points of similarity and dissimilarity between these accounts are illustrated in the following correspondences:

	Exodus 14-15	Judges 4-5
Narrative/Poetic Analogy:		
YHWH's plan to defeat Pharaoh/Sisera		
disclosed to/through his prophet/ess		
Moses/Deborah	14:1-4	4:6-7
Pharaoh/Sisera told [נגד] of Israelite		
movements, so he rallies his forces	14:5	4:12-13[167]
Chariots numbered: 600/900	14:7	4:3, 13
Enemy forces:		
"army"		
עם	14:6	
חיל	14:9, 17, 28;	
	15:4a	
צבא		4:2, 7
מחנה		4:15, 16

---

[166] Cf. Blenkinsopp, "Ballad Style" (1961), p. 62-63, 63 nn. 1-2, 64 n. 3, 65; P. Weimar, "Die Jahwekriegserzählungen in Exodus 14, Josua 10, Richter 4 und 1 Samuel 7", *Bib* 57 (1976), pp. 38-73; Hauser, "Songs of Victory" (1987), pp. 265-84; Brenner, "Triangle" (1990), p. 130. Cf. Lindars, "Deborah's Song" (1982-83), pp. 158-59; Webb, *Judges* (1987), pp. 139, 142 and 250 n. 68; and, on the similar usage of אשירה in Exod. 15:1b and Judg. 5:3b, Müller, "Aufbau des Deboraliedes" (1966), p. 456, n. 8.

[167] Weimar, "Jahwekriegserzählungen" (1976), p. 70. The fact that the openings of the "YHWH-war accounts" of Exod. 14:5a and Judg. 4:12a use נגד, whereas those of Josh. 10:1aαbβ and 1 Sam. 7:7aα use שמע, further evidences a link between Exod. 14 and Judg. 4.

	Exodus 14–15	Judges 4–5
"rider/chariot[s]" [רכב]	14:6, 7, 9, 17, 18, 23, 25, 26, 28; 15:1, 4	4:3, 7, 13, 15, 16; 5:28
"horse[s]" [סוס]	14:9, 23; 15:1	5:22
"horseman/men" [פרש/ים]	14:9, 17, 18, 23, 26, 28	—
"officer[s]/commander"		
שלשם	14:7; 15:4b	
שׂר		4:2, 7
Initial reluctance of Israel/Barak and tribes to rely on YHWH	14:10-12	4:8; 5:15b-17
Epiphany of YHWH to defend Israel	14:19-20; 15:13-16	5:4-5, 20-21a
Angel of God/YHWH present at battle	14:19a	5:23
YHWH confused [המם] Egyptian/Canaanite army	14:24b	4:15a
YHWH/stars fighting [לחם] for Israel	14:14, 25	[4:7, 14-15] 5:20
YHWH's use of mud/water to defeat chariots	14:[25] 26-27	4:[14-]15; 5:21a, 22
YHWH/Jael's covering [כסה] of Egyptians/Sisera with water/rug	14:28; 15:5a, 10a	4:18, 19
Fleeing [נוס] of Egyptians/Sisera	14:27	4:15, 17
YHWH's use of human agency (Moses/Jael) to "stretch out [שלח/נטה] ... hand"	14:16, 21, 26, 27; 15:12a	[4:21] 5:26
Except for Pharaoh/Sisera, "not one was left" [לא נשאר ... עד־אחד]	14:28	4:16[168]
Egyptians/Sisera found dead [מת]	14:30	4:22; [5:27]
Narrative summary: "That day [ביום ההוא] YHWH/God ... hand[s] of"	14:30	4:[14] 23-24
Hymn of praise to YHWH [אשירה ... ליהוה]	15:1	5:3
Use of YHWH/Jael's "right hand"	15:6	5:26
Mockery through portrayal of enemy's (Egypt/Canaan) plan to "divide the spoils" [חלק שלל]	15:9	5:[19b] 30

---

[168] Weimar, "Jahwekriegserzählungen" (1976), p. 71. The fact that Exod. 14:28 and Judg. 4:16 use the same expression, which is lacking in the "YHWH-war accounts" of Josh. 10 and 1 Sam. 7, speaks in favour of a deliberate analogy between Exod. 14 and Judg. 4.

	Exodus 14–15	Judges 4–5
Narrative/Poetic Dissimilarity:		
Concern with glory [תפארת/כבד] of YHWH/		
Barak in victory	14:4, 17	4:9
Pursuit by Pharaoh[Egyptians]/Barak	of Israel	of chariots
	14:4, 8 [9,	and army
	23] 15:9	4:16
		of Sisera
		4:22
Israel/Barak 'seeing' the victory of		
YHWH/Jael	14:13, 30-31	4:22
Word of encouragement spoken by		
Moses/Jael: "Fear not"	to Israel	to Sisera
	14:13	4:18

Points of analogy between Exodus 14–15 and Judges 4–5 suggest correlations between the actions of YHWH and Jael, Moses and Deborah,
Moses and Jael, the Egyptian and Canaanite armies, Pharaoh/Egyptians
and Sisera, Pharaoh/Egyptians and Barak, and Israel and Barak. In
each instance, the analogy evoked by the allusion of Judges 4–5 to
Exodus 14–15 heightens the characterization (whether negative or positive) in Judges 4–5. Jael's heroism is increased by association with the
acts of YHWH. Deborah and Jael attain higher status by association with
Moses. In contrast, the defeat of the Canaanite army as paralleling that
of Egypt implicitly mocks the former for failing to learn from the
events recounted in the Exodus tradition (cf. especially 15:13-16). The
negative characterizations of Barak and Sisera increase because of their
analogy to those of Pharaoh and the Egyptians.

Points of dissimilarity between Exodus 14–15 and Judges 4–5
heighten negative characterizations and irony not through analogy but
through contrast. Whereas, in Exodus 14–15, YHWH is expressly concerned to glorify himself by defeating Pharaoh's army, in Judges 4–5
he is expressly concerned to limit Barak's and Israel's glory for their
reluctance to follow his instructions. Pharaoh's mock pursuit of Israel
becomes the model by which Barak pursues Sisera. Again, whereas
Israel in the Exodus was promised that they would "see" (positively)
the victory of YHWH, Barak was brought to "see" (negatively) the victory of YHWH in giving Barak's glory into a woman's hand.[169] With
regard to Moses' and Jael's encouragement, "Fear not", the intertextual change of addressee from Israel (YHWH's people) to Sisera

---

[169] Bos, "Shadows" (1988), p. 57.

(Israel's enemy) enhances the ironic intention of Jael's words (cf. Exod. 15:14-15).

In addition to these points of analogy and dissimilarity, by which both contexts (Exod. 14–15; Judg. 4–5) present accounts of YHWH delivering Israel from enemy chariots by means of water, both hymns are accredited to both male and female singers.[170] In Judges 5, the contrasting uses of water in the final sections of each 'A' strophe (5:4-5, 11a) and among the middle sections of the 'C' strophes (5:15b-17, 20-21, 24-27) offers a satirical echo of YHWH's contrasting uses of the waters of the sea both to save Israel and to defeat Pharaoh's army in Exodus 15.[171] Satire against the Canaanites is also achieved in Judg. 5:19, 30 also by echoing the Egyptians' concern with "spoils" in Exod. 15:9[172] and, perhaps, by the similar imagery of sinking/falling between Judg. 5:27 and Exod. 15:1, 4, 5, 7, 10 [12].[173] The effect of this allusion, evoked through similarity of subject and formal presentation, is to portray the victory of Judges 4–5 as conforming to the archetypal victory of YHWH over Pharaoh's army and to credit Israel's success to YHWH, which further undercuts the acknowledgement of Barak's achievement. The theme of YHWH's triumph over Sisera and Canaan's king(s) is explicit in the victory hymn (5:3, 10, 19, 22, 24-27) and is evident also in the prose account (4:7a, 9, 14, 15, 23). Thus, the present form of Judges 4–5 evinces a clear concern to satirize foreign kingship as a contrast to its glorification of YHWH.[174]

---

[170] Judg. 5:1 says that both Deborah and Barak sang the hymn of 5:2-31a. Exod. 15:20-21a credits to Miriam the prophetess the singing of the refrain (15:21b) that begins the victory hymn (15:1b-18), which was said to have been sung by Moses and the Israelites (15:1a). Although in Exod. 15:1a the singing of the hymn is credited to Moses and the Israelites, it is Miriam who is credited with instigating it when she and other women sang to the accompaniment of tambours. Indeed, the prose–hymn complementarity between 14:1-15:1a and 15:1b-18 is microcosmically echoed between 15:19-21a and 15:21b.

[171] Coogan mentioned specifically the analogy between the situation in Judges 4–5, which implies that the chariots became bogged down in mud, and Exod. 14:25 "clogged their chariot wheels" ("Song of Deborah" [1978], p. 146 n. 14); Hauser, "Songs of Victory" (1987), pp. 270-73.

[172] Hauser, "Songs of Victory" (1987), pp. 273-77.

[173] Hauser, "Songs of Victory" (1987), pp. 277-79.

[174] Although Ps. 68 also has literary affinities with Judg. 5, because its composition was apparently later, it has little direct bearing upon the interpretation of Judg. 5. Nevertheless, since it represents a similar case of literary analogy and uses the victory hymn genre, Ps. 68 offers a useful model for comparison. Whereas Judg. 4–5 seems to have been designed to furnish a broad literary analogy to the previously existing tradition preserved in Exod. 14–15, the close literary affinity between the epiphanies of Judg. 5:4-5 and Ps. 68:8-9 speaks rather of direct (though not mechanical) borrowing. Indeed, there

In summary, two levels of concern are present in the Deborah/
Barak/Jael account. First, on the macrocosmic level, the prevailing
concern to glorify YHWH through the portrayal of his control of circumstances that lead to Israel's deliverance is heightened through the
contrasting satirization of a military commander (Sisera) who is an
agent of (Jabin's) foreign kingship. This concern, raised by the narrative framework, is conveyed, in the prose portrayal, through YHWH's
implicit control of the circumstances that lead to Jael's success and, in
the hymnic portrayal, through YHWH's control of the cosmic forces
with which Jael cooperates. The complementarity between the prose
and hymnic accounts as to the portrayal of YHWH vanquishing a foreign
king by means of a prophetic oracle and water suggests that Judges 4-5
was designed by analogy to the prose and hymnic accounts of Exodus
14-15. Second, on the microcosmic level, there is evident a rhetorical
concern about the performance of covenant responsibilities to YHWH by
individuals, by tribes and according to both gender- and class-
appropriate roles.[175] The fact that Barak is portrayed as a non-Judahite

---

are numerous collocations of vocabulary between Judg. 5 and Ps. 68 that evidence a direct
relationship between these hymns of victory:

Key words/phraseology	Judg. 5	Ps. 68
ברך יהוה\ואלהים	2, 9	27, 36
שיר ‖ זמר	3	5, 33
(various words throughout)	4-5	8-9
שבה שבי	12	19
מני	14 [2x]	32
בנימ[י]ן	14	28
זב[ו]לון	14, 18	28
שרי	15	28 [3x]
נפתלי	18	28
שיר ... זמר	14	32
ישב\שכב בין [המ]שפתים	16	14
דהרות דהרות\ידרון ידרון	22	13
מחק\מחץ ראש	26	22
מחץ רגליהוך	27	24
חלק שלל	30	13

The author of Ps. 68 was alluding to the epiphany of Judg. 5 but in such a way as to adapt
it to his/her concern with the glorification of אלהים, whose victories are viewed apart
from the concerns with human agency that one sees in Judg. 5. Cf. Blenkinsopp, "Ballad
Style" (1961), pp. 67-68; Coogan, "Song of Deborah" (1978), pp. 161-62.

[175] Murray assessed the rhetorical purpose of the traditional narrative in Judg. 4 as follows: "the narrator has an essentially literary rather than historical or quasi-historical
interest. ... The purpose of the narrative in vv. 4-22 cannot originally have been that of
bearing out the historical understanding reflected in the framework passages, vv. 1-3,
23f. ... The narrator is not concerned to give a report of any kind; nor is he primarily
concerned with history as such: his concern is to narrate a story which appeared to him to

male leader who is reluctant to fight for YHWH apart from the prompting of an Ephraimite woman and who, despite the help of those (non-Judahite) tribes that participated in the battle, is unable to complete the victory apart from the divinely decreed actions of a tent-dwelling woman from a marginal clan of Judah suggests an underlying concern to demonstrate the preeminence of even the 'least' of the tribe of Judah (not mentioned among the absentees in 5:15b-17) who is nevertheless wholehearted in zeal for YHWH.[176] The parallel portrayals of the halfheartedness of Barak, in the prose account, and the partial participation by the tribes of Israel, in the poetic account, not only fulfil Judges' pattern of escalated parallelism as they are seen in relation to each other, but, in each of the prose and hymnic accounts, these negative characterizations are contrasted to the idealized portrayal of the Kenite woman Jael.

§4. The Account of Gideon/Abimelech (6:1–9:57)

Like the plot-structure of Judges 4–5, the plot-structure of Judges 6–9 comprises three plot-levels, each with its own exposition, development and resolution.[177] However, the plot-structure of the Gideon/Abimelech

---

comment with telling irony on the roles of two men and two women, and thus on the relationship of men and women in general" ("Narrative Structure" [1979], pp. 184-85). Among the objections to be raised against this assessment are: (1) it fails to appreciate the emphasis that the traditional narrative places upon the religious dimension—each character being evaluated entirely upon the basis of the extent of his or her allegiance to YHWH in battle, and (2) it fails to appreciate the extent to which YHWH's glorification in the prose account depends upon his being seen by the reader as the one in control of the events of history (if not also of the cosmic forces described in Judg. 5).

[176] YHWH's preference for succeeding by means of the zeal of the few (e.g., Ehud, Gideon's 300 [Judg. 7:2, 4], Samson) or the socially marginalized (e.g., Jael, Gideon [Judg. 6:15-16], Jephthah) is a recurring interest not only among the deliverer accounts in Judges but also in 1 Samuel (e.g., Hannah [1 Sam. 2:1-10a]; Saul, at first [9:21; 10:27]; Jonathan [14:6]; David [17:47, cf. 17:34-37]). See the discussion in chapter 3.

[177] Few have undertaken a study of this account using a literary approach, but those who have have tended to follow a scenic delineation of events rather than a stratification of the functions of those events according to their plot-level functions. Their implicit commitment to the scenic principle is evident from the fact that they treat the Abimelech complex of Judg. 8:33–9:57 either as a sequel to that of Gideon in Judg. 6:1–8:32 (e.g., Webb, *Judges* [1987], p. 154) or a self-standing account (e.g., Klein, *Triumph of Irony* [1988], chapter 5). While the Gideon/Abimelech account is more scenically demarcated than most deliverer accounts in Judges, a plot-structure analysis that treats thematic purpose as the main criterion for determining the rhetorical function of the complex of events demonstrates how integral is the Abimelech account to the resolution of themes introduced in the Gideon account.

account is more complicated than that of either the straightforward
Ehud account or the Deborah/Barak/Jael account. The course of the
primary plot (Plot A), from its bifurcated exposition (6:1-6, 11-24),
throughout its development (6:33-35; 7:1, 8b-9, 15b-25; 8:4, 10-12,
18-21?) and to its bifurcated resolution (8:28, 32), is repeatedly
assailed by complications (6:7-10, 25-32, 36-40; 7:2-8a, 10-15a; 8:1-3,
5-9, 13-17, 18-21?, 22-23, 24-27, 29-31). Moreover, the Gideon/
Abimelech account holds the distinction that its subplots (Plots B and
C), introduced as foreshadowing complications in the primary plot,
reach well beyond the resolution of the primary plot. The plot-structure
of Judges 6-9 may be outlined as follows (with cycle-motif designations given in the left column and broken horizontal lines marking
major scene changes):

> *Plot A:* YHWH's deliverance of Israel from the Midianites through Gideon
> (6:1-6 [7-10] 11-24 [25-32] 33-35 [36-40] 7:1 [2-8a] 8b-9 [10-15a] 15b-
> 25; 8:[1-3] 4 [5-9] 10-12 [13-17, 18-21?, 22-23, 24-27] 28 [29-31] 32)
>> *Plot A Situation Exposition:* (6:1-6)

A1a	Resumption: Israel's practice of evil (6:1a)
B2a	YHWH gave Israel into the hand of Midian (6:1b$^{i\text{-}ii}$)
B3a	Seven years (6:1b^{iii})
(B3a)	The hand of Midian prevailed over Israel (6:2a)
Inset^i:	Dispossession and despoilment of Israel by Midianites and Amalekites (6:2b, 3-5, 6a)
C	Israel cried out to YHWH (6:6b)

>> *Plot A Situation Complication:* (6:7-10)

C	When Israel cried out to YHWH [because of Midian] (6:7a[b])
Inset^{ii}:	YHWH's prophetic protest against Israel's disobedience (6:8-10)
(B3b^i)	From the hand of all your oppressors (6:9aβ)
(A1a)	Israel's disobedience (6:10b)

>> *Plot A Character Exposition:* Divine commission(•)/theophanic
>> recognition(○) type-scene (6:11-24)

	(•/○)YHWH's confrontation (6:11-12a)
	(•)YHWH's introductory word (6:12b)
	(•)Gideon's protest (6:13)
	(•)YHWH's commission (6:14)
	(•)Gideon's objection (6:15)
(D1)	"With what could I save Israel?" (6:15aβ)
	(•)YHWH's reassurance (6:16)
	(•)Gideon's request for a confirming sign (6:17)
	(○)Gideon's preparation and presentation of an offertory meal (6:18-19)
	(○)YHWH's theophany (6:20-21)
	(○)Gideon's recognition (6:22)

(○)YHWH's reassurance (6:23)
(○)Aetiology of altar erection (6:24)
Plot B: YHWH's judgement for the failure of Gideon and his tribe to abandon
foreign cultic practices (6:25-32; 8:24-27, 33-34; 9:1-44 [cf. especially
9:4, 6, 27, 37] 46-49, 56-57)
   Plot A Complication/(Foreshadowing: Plot B Exposition): Gideon's
   reluctance openly to confront the Baalists of Ophrah (6:25-32)
                  Night scene 1: YHWH's commission to supplant
                  Baal's altar with an altar to YHWH (6:25-26)

— — — — — — — — — — — — — —

                  Night scene 2(?): Gideon's execution of YHWH's
                  commission to supplant Baal's altar (6:27)

— — — — — — — — — — — — — — — —

                  Morning scene 1: Protest by the Baalists and Gideon's
                  evasion of confronting them; Gideon/Jerubbaal
                  naming aetiology (6:28-30, 31, 32)

— — — — — — — — — — — — — — — — — — —

   Plot A Development: YHWH's spirit prompts Gideon to summon tribes to
   confront Midianite and Amalekite encampment (6:33-35)
                  Midianites and Amalekites cross the Jordan and
                  encamp in the Jezreel plain (6:33)
   D2a   Spirit of YHWH 'clothes' Gideon (6:34a)
   D2b   He sounds the ram's horn (6:34bα)
                  Gideon summons his clan, tribe and the tribes of
                  Asher, Zebulun, Naphtali (6:34bβ-35)
   Plot A Character Complication: (6:36-40)
                  Gideon's request for a second confirming sign
                  (6:36-37)
   (D1)   "If you are going to save Israel by my hand"
                     (6:36bⁱ)
   (D1)   "that you will save Israel by my hand" (6:37bδⁱ)
                  [Night scene 3:] YHWH's concession of the second
                  confirming sign (6:38aα)
                  Morning scene 2: Gideon confirms the sign
                  (6:38aβγb)
                  Gideon's contrasting request for a third confirming
                  sign (6:39)
                  Night scene 4: YHWH's concession of the third
                  confirming sign (6:40a)
                  [Morning scene 3a:] Sign is confirmed (6:40b)

— —

   Plot A Development: Jerubbaal's (Gideon's) encampment opposite
   Midian's camp (7:1)
                  Morning scene 3b: Jerubbaal's (Gideon's) encamp-
                  ment at the Harod spring (7:1a)
                  Relative location of Midian's camp (7:1b)
   Plot A Complication: YHWH's diminution of Gideon's troops (7:2-8a)

First diminution, to 10,000: Dismissal of the fearful
from Mount Gilead (7:2-3)
Second diminution, to 300: Dismissal of those who
knelt to drink to their tents (7:4-8a)

Plot A Development: (7:8b-9)
Resumptive restatement of relative location of
Midian's camp (7:8b; cf. 7:1b)

— — — — — — — — — — — — — — — — —

Night scene 5: (7:9-11a)
YHWH's instruction to attack Midian's camp (7:9)

Plot A Character Complication: (7:10-15a)
YHWH's concession of a fourth confirming sign in
Midian's camp (7:10-11a)

— — — — — — — — — — — — — — — — —

Night scene 6: Gideon's reconnaissance of Midian's
camp (7:11b-15a)

— — — — — — — — — — — — — — — — —

Plot A Development: (7:15b-25)
Night scene 7: Gideon's return, tripartite division of
the 300 and order that they imitate him (7:15b-18)

— — — — — — — — — — — — — — — — —

Night scene 8: Gideon's rout of Midian's camp
(7:19-22)
Gideon again summons his clan, tribe and the tribes
of Asher, Zebulun, Naphtali (7:23)
Gideon summons Ephraim to cut off Midian from the
Jordan (7:24a)
Ephraim cuts off Midian from the Jordan and slays
two Midianite commanders, Oreb and Zeeb
(7:24b-25)

— — — — — — — — — — — — — — — — —

Plot A Complication: (8:1-3)
Ephraimites protest at being excluded from the initial
military rally of tribes (8:1)
Gideon's evasion of confrontation by belittling his
rout in comparison with the Ephraimites' slaying
of Oreb and Zeeb (8:2-3)

— — — — — — — — — — — — — — — — —

Plot A Development: Gideon pursues the Midianites across the Jordan
(8:4)
Plot C: YHWH's judgement for the failure of Gideon, his sons and his tribe
to refrain from covenant (social) injustice (8:5-9, 13-23, 29-31, 35; 9:1-
49a, 50-57)
Plot A Complication/(Foreshadowing: Plot C Exposition): (8:5-9)
aa   Gideon threatens to thresh with thorns the officials of
Succoth (8:5-7)

— — — — — — — — — — — — — — — — —

bb   Gideon threatens to tear down the tower of the "men
                      of the city" of Penuel (8:8-9)

————————————————————————————————————

Plot A Development: (8:10-12)
    cc   Gideon captures the two Midianite kings, Zebah and
                      Zalmunna (8:10-12)

————————————————————————————————————

Plot A Complication/(Foreshadowing: Plot C Exposition): (8:13-23)
    aa^i   Gideon threshes with thorns the seventy-seven
                      officials of Succoth (8:13-16)

————————————————————————————————————

bb^i   Gideon tears down the tower of Penuel and kills the
                     "men of the city" (8:17)
Plot A Development?//Complication/(Foreshadowing: Plot C
    Exposition)?: (8:18-21)
    cc^i   Gideon, failing to coax Jether, his eldest son, to kill
                      Zebah and Zalmunna, himself kills and plunders
                      them (8:18-21)
Plot A Complication/(Foreshadowing: Plot C Exposition): (8:22-23)
                      Israelites request that Gideon and his sons rule them
                      (8:22)
                      Gideon's evasion of the request that he and his sons
                      rule them by deferring to YHWH's rule (8:23)
Plot A Complication/(Foreshadowing: Plot B Exposition): (8:24-27)
                      Gideon requests gold earrings from the Israelites'
                      plunder and makes from them an ephod
                      (8:24-27a$\alpha\beta$)
                      Israel's cultic aberration in worshipping Gideon's
                      ephod (8:27aγb)
Plot A Situation Resolution: (8:28)
    E1   Midian was humbled before the sons of Israel
                      (8:28a$\alpha\beta$)
    F2   The land had peace forty years (8:28b^(i-ii))

————————————————————————————————————

Plot A Complication/Plot C Exposition: Jerubbaal sires seventy sons by
    many wives but Abimelech by a Shechemite concubine (8:29-31)
Plot A Character Resolution: (8:32)
    G1   Gideon the son of Joash died at a good age (8:32a)
    G2   He was buried in the tomb of his father Joash in
                      Ophrah of the Abiezrite(s) (8:32b)
Plot B Exposition: Israel's cultic aberration in worshipping Baal-Berith
    (8:33-34)
    <G1>   As soon as Gideon died (8:33aα[β])
    A2a   The Israelites again whored after the Baals and set up
                      for themselves Baal-Berith as their god (8:33aγ-b)

A2b   The Israelites did not remember YHWH their god,
                     who had rescued them from all their surrounding
                     enemies (8:34)

Plot C Exposition: Israel's failure to act loyally toward the house of
Jerubbaal (Gideon) (8:35)

Plots B & C Exposition: (9:1-22)

a   *People/citizens' action:* Abimelech agitates his
                     brothers (sons of his mother) to incite the citizens
                     of Shechem to overthrow the sons of Jerubbaal
                     (9:1-2)

b   *Report:* Abimelech's offer is told to the citizens of
                     Shechem by his brothers (sons of his mother)
                     (9:3a)

c   Their heart inclines toward Abimelech, since he is
                     their brother (9:3b)

d   *People/citizens supporting violence:* They give
                     Abimelech seventy pieces of silver from the temple
                     of Baal-Berith (9:4a)

e   *Leading to an entrance:* Abimelech hires reckless
                     men, they follow him and he enters his father's
                     home at Ophrah (9:4b-5aα)

——————————————————————

f   *Fatality/depopulation:* Abimelech kills his (paternal)
                     brothers, the seventy sons of Jerubbaal, on a single
                     stone (9:5aβ)
                     Jotham, the youngest son, escapes by hiding (9:5b)

——————————————————————

                     Citizens of Shechem and Beth-Millo make Abimelech
                     king by the great tree and pillar in Shechem (9:6)
                     Jotham curses Abimelech and the citizens of Shechem
                     and Beth-Millo (9:7-21)
                     Jotham addresses the citizens of Shechem from Mount
                     Gerazim (9:7)
                     Jotham's four-part fable and conditional curse on
                     Abimelech and the citizens of Shechem and Beth-
                     Millo (9:8-15, 16-20)

(A1b)   "If you have acted in good faith and honour ..."
                     (9:16)

(A1b)   "If you have acted in good faith and honour ..."
                     (9:19a)
                     Jotham flees in fear from Abimelech (9:21)

(B3b)   Abimelech ruled over Israel three years (9:22)

Plots B & C Development: (9:23-44)

(D2a)   God sent an evil spirit between Abimelech and the
                     citizens of Shechem, who committed treachery, to
                     avenge the sons of Jerubbaal (9:23a, 23b-24)

——————————————————————

Shechem's first treachery: (9:25)

(a)   *People/citizens' action:* Citizens of Shechem ambush travellers in Manasseh (9:25a)

(b)   *Report:* Treachery reported to Abimelech (9:25b)

Shechem's second treachery: (9:26-41)

a^i *People/citizens' action:* Gaal, with his brothers, agitates the citizens of Shechem to overthrow Abimelech son of Jerubbaal (9:26-29)

b^i *Report:* Treachery reported to Abimelech by Zebul, who counsels coming at night with all his people to ambush at morning (9:30-33)

---

c^i *Night scene:* Abimelech's four-part division of his people to lay an ambush against Shechem (9:34)

d^i *Morning scene: People/citizens supporting violence:* Interchange between Gaal and Zebul as Abimelech and his people emerge from ambush (9:35, 36a, 36b, 37, 38)

e^i *Leading to an entrance:* Abimelech slays many while chasing Gaal to the entrance of Shechem (9:39-40)

f^i *Fatality/depopulation:* Abimelech stays in Arumah while Zebul expels Gaal and his brothers from Shechem (9:41)

Abimelech's first act of repression: (9:42-45)

a^{ii} *Next day: People/citizens' action:* The people go out to the field (9:42a)

b^{ii} *Report:* Their vulnerability reported to Abimelech (9:42b)

c^{ii} Abimelech's tripartite division of his people to lay an ambush in the field (9:43a)

d^{ii} *People/citizens supporting violence:* Abimelech [and his people] emerge from ambush (9:43b)

e^{ii} *Leading to an entrance:* Abimelech takes position at the entrance to Shechem while two companies slay those in the field (9:44)

Plot C Partial Resolution: (9:45)

f^{ii} *Fatality/depopulation:* Abimelech captures Shechem that day, killing its people, tearing down the city and sowing it with salt (9:45)

Abimelech's second act of repression: (9:46-49)

Plots B & C *Development:* (9:46-49a)

aⁱⁱⁱ   *People/citizens' action:* Citizens of the tower of
              Shechem enter the stronghold of the temple of
              El-Berith (9:46)

bⁱⁱⁱ   *Report:* Vulnerability of the citizens of the tower
              of Shechem reported to Abimelech (9:47)

cⁱⁱⁱ   Abimelech and his people ascend Mount Zalmon,
              where he cuts off branches and sets them on his
              shoulder (9:48a)

dⁱⁱⁱ   *People/citizens supporting violence:* Abimelech
              orders his people to imitate him, so all the
              people cut off branches (9:48b-49aα)

eⁱⁱⁱ   *Leading to an entrance:* Abimelech, followed by
              his people, sets fire to the stronghold (9:49aβγ)

Plot B *Resolution:* (9:49b)

f ⁱⁱⁱ   *Fatality/depopulation:* A thousand men and
              women of the tower of Shechem die (9:49b)

_____

Plot C *Development:* (9:50-52)

              Abimelech's third act of repression: (9:50)
              Abimelech besieges and captures Thebez (9:50)
              Abimelech's fatal attempt at repression: (9:51-54)

aⁱᵛ   *People/citizens' action:* The men and women and
              the citizens flee to the tower and ascend to the
              roof (9:51)

cⁱᵛ   Abimelech comes to the tower and fights against it
              (9:52a)

eⁱᵛ   *Leading to an entrance:* Abimelech approaches the
              tower entrance to burn it with fire (9:52b)

Plot C *Resolution:* (9:53-55)

              Abimelech's skull is crushed by a stone thrown by
              a woman (9:53)
              Abimelech orders his servant to kill him lest a
              woman be reputed to have killed him (9:54a)

(G1) f ⁱᵛ   *Fatality/depopulation:* Abimelech is stabbed and
              dies (9:54b)

(G1)   The men of Israel see that Abimelech is dead [and
              each returns to his place] (9:55a[b])

Plots B & C *Dénouement:* Thus God recompensed the evil of Abimelech
    for killing his brothers and the evil of the Shechemites, fulfilling the
    curse of Jotham son of Jerubbaal (9:56-57)

Plot A (6:1-6 [7-10] 11-24 [25-32] 33-35 [36-40] 7:1 [2-8a] 8b-9 [10-
15a] 15b-25; 8:[1-3] 4 [5-9] 10-12 [13-17, 18-21?, 22-23, 24-27] 28
[29-31] 32) is the main plot of Judges 6–9 and, though it does not continue beyond 8:32, furnishes the background for a proper rhetorical

evaluation of its subplots (Plots B and C). The cycle-motif elements, which reflect the concerns of the compiler/redactor, are most prevalent in the exposition and resolution sections of Plot A, though recurrences of the 'D' elements appear repeatedly in the characterization of Gideon. This plot-level aims to show how YHWH delivered Israel from the Midianites through Gideon, despite the latter's reluctance finally to shun Canaanite cultic practices or conjugal relations or to restrain himself from exploiting holy war as a means for carrying out personal vendettas.

Apart from cycle-motif elements, the exposition of Plot A comprises a description of the unsettling effects of Midian's and Amalek's incursion into the land of Israel (6:2b-6a) and a hybrid of the biblical divine commission and theophanic recognition type-scenes (6:11-17, 18-24). The cycle-motif in the first part of the exposition (6:1-6) is prevented from leading immediately to YHWH's raising up a deliverer (motif D1) by a complication (6:7-10).[178] The delaying force of 6:7-10 is exaggerated by the fact that it rehearses, in reverse order, themes already given in 6:1-6, which results in a palistrophe that returns to the subject of Israel's failed allegiance to YHWH (A1a).[179] Implicitly, this

---

[178] It is perhaps not surprising that a scribe may have been motivated deliberately to omit 6:7-10 from the MS of 4Q Judges[a] (Boling, *Judges* [1975], p. 40). Such a prophetic condemnation from YHWH is hardly flattering to the scribe's nation. *Pace* A. G. Auld ("Gideon: Hacking at the Heart of the Old Testament", *VT* 39 [1989], p. 263) and J. Trebolle Barrera ("Textual Variants in 4QJudg[a] and the Textual and Editorial History of the Book of Judges", *RevQ* 14 [1989], pp. 236, 245), who assert that the Qumran data speaks against the authenticity of 6:7-10 as an element of the compilation/redaction of Judges, I argue the following: (1) the OG and MT stand together against the omission of 6:7-10 in 4Q Judges[a]—so, while the latter may constitute evidence for the omission of 6:7-10 during scribal transmission, it can scarcely be used as evidence for an addition of 6:7-10 during late editorial stages of Judges' compilation/redaction; (2) Judg. 6:7-10 is justified as intrinsic to the original (deuteronomic) design of its context on three converging lines of evidence: (a) its elaborate thematic preparation in 2:1b-3; 2:14-15; 2:20-3:6 and thematic reappearance in 10:11-14 give strong indication that this was a controlling concern of the Judges compiler/redactor; (b) far from disrupting the flow of its context, it well fits the structure of Judg. 6-8, first, by fitting well into the panelled pattern of exposition (6:1-6)-complication (6:7-10)-exposition (6:11-24)-complication (6:25-32) (see below), and second, by fitting well into the structures that frame Judg. 6-8, whereby the framing portrayals of concern with Gideon's cultic actions in 6:25-27a and 8:24-27aαβ are both framed and thematically paralleled by concerns with Israel's cultic actions in 6:8-10 and 8:27aγb (see below).

[179] Webb has already noted the chiastic order of verse halves at the axis between 6:6 and 6:7 (*Judges* [1987], p. 145; cf. Klein, *Triumph of Irony* [1988], pp. 49-50). The prophetic covenant dispute of 6:7-10 presents the claim of YHWH's innocence (6:8bβ-10aβ) with seven 1 c. sg pron. forms—1 c. sg independent prons. framing the whole (M. Eskhult, *Studies in Verbal Aspect and Narrative Technique in Biblical Hebrew Prose* [AUUSSU 12, Uppsala, 1990], p. 78 n. 54):

delaying tactic raises a question as to whether YHWH will (or should) now raise up a deliverer (D1) as on previous occasions when Israel had cried out to him (C).[180] While the accusation of 6:7-10 is not followed by the threats uttered in Judges' prologue, either that YHWH would not drive out the inhabitants of the land (2:3abα, 20-22; 2:23-3:5) or that the latter's daughters and gods would become a snare (מוקש; 2:3bβγ; cf. 3:6), the omitted threats are nevertheless realized in the subsequent account (cf. מוקש in 8:27b; cf. 8:31; 9:22).[181]

When the expected, but delayed, raising up of a deliverer (D1) does come, in the second phase of the exposition, it takes the form of a divine commission/theophanic recognition type-scene (6:11-17, 18-24). This hybrid type-scene, in which Gideon is both commissioned by (6:11-17) and offers a meal to the angel of YHWH (6:11, 18-24), finds narrative analogy both with other type-scenes of divine commissioning, such as the 'call narrative' of Moses in Exod. 3:1-4:17,[182] and with

---

אנכי העליתי אתכם ממצרים
ואציא אתכם מבית עבדים:
ואצל אתכם מיד מצרים ומיד כל־לחציכם
ואגרש אותם מפניכם
ואתנה לכם את־ארצם:
ואמרה לכם
אני יהוה אלהיכם

It is also significant that, besides the cycle-motif elements (C in 6:7a, [B3b^i] in 6:9aβ and [A1a] in 6:10b), 6:7-10 uses other stock deuteronomic phraseology (e.g., אני יהוה אלהיכם) and contains a collocation of themes and vocabulary that alludes to the account of the Shechem covenant of Josh. 24 (cf. Judg. 6:7a, 8bβγ, 9, 10aγδb with Josh. 24:7a, 8, 12a, 15a, 17a, 24b or Deut. 26:7-9; see the appendix). Nor is it likely to be accidental that this expositional complication, by so alluding to the Shechem covenant, ironically foreshadows the injustices to be perpetrated at Shechem in Judg. 8:31 and 9:1-5a, 25-49. Moreover, inasmuch as 9:6-7 alludes to Josh. 24:26-27 (even if, in 9:6b, מֻצָּב [Ho. ptcp] is not emended to הַמַּצֵּבָה [as Moore, *Judges* (1895), pp. 243-44; BDB, p. 662b; *BHS;* RSV; NIV]), where one likewise finds reference to an assembly at הָאֵלָה of Shechem, one should probably surmise that the Judges compiler/redactor intended these events to be evaluated as acts of covenant abrogation.

[180] The appearance of a prophet (איש נביא, 6:8a) reminds the reader of the analogous expression used of Deborah (אשה נביאה, 4:4) (cf. Webb, *Judges* [1987], pp. 145, 251 n. 80; Klein, *Triumph of Irony* [1988], p. 50). While initially this correspondence raises the expectation that perhaps now YHWH is about to raise up a deliverer, as had Deborah, the expectation is frustrated and delayed while the prophet reproves the nation.

[181] Cf. J. C. Exum, "The Centre Cannot Hold: Thematic and Textual Instabilities in Judges", *CBQ* 52 (1990), p. 417.

[182] On the 'call narrative', see N. Habel, "The Form and Significance of the Call Narratives", *ZAW* 77 (1965), pp. [297-323] 297-305, where, citing Judg. 6:11b-17 and Exod. 3:1-12, he enumerates six elements: (1) divine confrontation (Judg. 6:11b-12a; Exod. 3:1-3, 4a), (2) introductory word (Judg. 6:12b-13; Exod. 3:4b-9), (3) commission (Judg. 6:14; Exod. 3:10), (4) objection (Judg. 6:15; Exod. 3:11), (5) reassurance (Judg. 6:16;

other divine recognition type-scenes involving an offering/hospitality to
YHWH's angel(s), such as that of Gen. 18:1-8 (serving as a foil to
Sodom's inhospitality in Gen. 19:1-9 and being followed by a birth
annunciation type-scene in Gen. 18:9-15) or that of Judg. 13:15-23
(which follows a birth annunciation type-scene, 13:2-14).[183] In the commission scene, each initiative by YHWH (6:11-12b, 14, 16) is opposed
by a protest, objection or request from Gideon (6:13, 15, 17).[184] That

Exod. 3:12a) and (6) sign (Judg. 6:17; Exod. 3:12). Actually, the objections of Moses
continue to meet with reassurances in Exod. 3:13-22; 4:1-9 and 4:10-11 until YHWH
becomes angry with Moses' final objection in 4:13-17. Alternatively, W. Richter, *Die
sogenannten vorprophetischen Berufungsberichte: Eine literaturwissenschaftliche Studie zu
1 Sam 9,1-10,16; Ex 3f. und Ri 6,11b-17* (FRLANT 101, Göttingen, 1970), articulates a
five-element form among the J and E strands of Exod. 3-4; Judg. 6:11b-17 and 1 Sam.
9:1-10:16: affliction, commission, objection, assurance and sign (pp. 138-39). Cf. Auld,
"Gideon" (1989), pp. 257-58.

[183] *Pace* D. R. Ap-Thomas, "The Ephah of Meal in Judges vi 19", *JTS* 41 (1940),
pp. 175-77, who would emend ואיפת in Judg. 6:19 to unapocopated ויאפה "and he baked"
(so Tg), the inordinately large quantity of meal offered in Judg. 6:19 (an ephah) is probably a deliberate point of analogy to Gen. 18:6 (three seahs) in the Abraham version
inasmuch as they are equivalent amounts (ca. 22 litres) (cf. Josephus, *Ant.* VIII.ii.9 §57;
IX.iv.5 §85). Those who have inferred that this מִנְחָה (6:18; OG, σὴν θγσΖαν μογ; Vg,
sacrificium) was thus intended as an offertory meal include: E. Bertheau, *Das Buch der
Richter und Ruth* (KEHAT 6, F. Hitzig et al. [eds.], Leipzig, 1845), p. 113; Ehrlich,
Randglossen, vol. 3 (1910), repr. edn, p. 91; V. Zapletal, *Das Buch der Richter:
übersetzt und erklärt* (EHAT VII/1, Munster, i. W., 1923), p. 106; Burney, *Judges* (2d
edn, 1920), p. 192. If the point of the offering were to verify the identity of the visitor as
YHWH (6:17), there would be little need to argue that meal was not offertory since Gideon
did not realize YHWH's identity until 6:22.

On the correspondence between Judg. 6:11-24 and 13:2-24 (especially 13:15-21), see
W. Böhme, "Die älteste Darstellung in Richt. 6.11-24 und 13.2-24 und ihre Ver-
wandtschaft mit der Jahveurkunde des Pentateuch", *ZAW* 5 (1885), pp. 251-74; S. A.
Cook, "The Theophanies of Gideon and Manoah", *JTS* 28 (1927), pp. 368-83; P. Kübel,
"Epiphanie und Altarbau", *ZAW* 83 (1971), pp. 225-31; Y. Zakovitch, "The Sacrifice of
Gideon (Jud 6,11-24) and the Sacrifice of Manoaḥ (Jud 13)", *Shnaton* 1 (1975), pp. 151-
54, XXV [Hebrew; English summary]; Auld, "Gideon" (1989), pp. 257-58.

[184] All three points of opposition to YHWH reflect character weaknesses of Gideon and
anticipate later plot complications. Gideon's protest in 6:13 questions not only YHWH's
affirmation in 6:12b but the claim in 6:8bβ-9 that YHWH delivers Israel—disclosing a dispassionate disregard for YHWH's primary concern in 6:8bβ-9 about Israel's cultic
disloyalty (anticipating 6:25-32; 8:24-27aαβ). His objection in 6:15 (cf. Exod. 3:11; 4:1,
10; 1 Sam. 9:21; Jer. 1:6) is an attempt to evade personal responsibility for the conquest
because of his clan's smallness (anticipating 7:2-8a; cf. Deut. 7:17-24). His request for a
sign in 6:17 discloses his preoccupation with tangible manifestations of the divine
(anticipating 6:36-37, 39; 7:10-15a; 8:24-27aαβ) (cf. Klein, *Triumph of Irony* [1988],
pp. 63, 65). Indeed, the contrast of characterizations introduced here between YHWH's
patience and Gideon's impetuosity form the background to Gideon's compensatory ruthlessness portrayed in 8:5-9, 13-17 toward those who, like himself (6:15aβ, 36bⁱ, 37bδⁱ),
doubted his ability to capture YHWH's opponents (cf. Klein, *Triumph of Irony* [1988],
p. 62).

the compiler/redactor of Judges intended this commissioning/
recognition type-scene to embellish the D1 cycle-motif element is made
obvious both by Gideon's questioning of the commission (6:15aβ) and
by the compiler/redactor's concern elsewhere to characterize Gideon
by alluding to 'D' elements of the cycle-motif ([D1] in 6:36bⁱ, 37bδⁱ;
D2a in 6:34a; D2b in 6:34bα).

Just as the situational exposition of 6:1-6 is followed by a plot-
delaying complication in 6:7-10, so Gideon's character exposition in
6:11-24 is followed by a delaying complication in 6:25-32, where
YHWH interrupts the concern of Plot A with Midian and Amalek by
sending Gideon to demolish a Baal altar. Perhaps, by means of parallelism between the expositional sections involving Israel (6:1-6) and
Gideon (6:11-24) and similar concerns with cultic disloyalty in the
complications that follow (6:7-10, 25-32), the compiler/redactor has
purposely formed a contrastive interchange between characterizations
of Israel and Gideon.[185] Thus, Judg. 6:1-10, 11-32 would seem to constitute one structurally parallel bifid unit, which the collocation of מדין
ועמלק ובני־קדם in 6:3b and its resumptive repetition at 6:33 appear to
corroborate.[186] The resumptive repetition in 6:33 both restores the
reader's attention to the situation exposed in 6:2b-6a and signals the
first unit of the development proper (6:33-35).

The complication to Plot A presented by Gideon's requests for
contrasting signs with the fleece (6:36-38, 39-40) is introduced by a
recurrence of the D1 motif in the protasis of a conditional sentence
(6:36bⁱ). Since this request is similar to that made in 6:17 (cf. 6:15aβ)
and does little more than reverse the progress of narrative development
after Gideon has already been "clothed" by YHWH's spirit (D2a, 6:34a)
and has sounded the ram's horn   (D2b, 6:34bα), it characterizes
Gideon as an unduly diffident deliverer.[187]

---

[185] Cf. the contrastive interchange between the characterizations of Eli's sons and
Samuel in 1 Sam. 2:12–3:1a.

[186] The designation בני־קדם probably refers generally to the Arab tribes of Transjordan
(Moore, *Judges* [1895], p. 180; cf. BDB, 869b; Eskhult, *Studies in Verbal Aspect* [1990],
p. 74 n. 34; cf. 1 Kgs 5:10; Isa. 11:14; Jer. 49:28; Ezek. 25:4, 10). This usage appears to
be a summarizing appositive: "Midian and Amalek, the easterners" (so Boling, *Judges*
[1975], pp. 124, 125; Webb, *Judges* [1987], p. 250 n. 75; cf. Judg. 8:10a).

[187] Cf. Webb, *Judges* (1987), pp. 150-51. The meaning of ורוח יהוה לבשה את־גדעון
(6:34a) is not, "and the spirit of YHWH put on Gideon"—as though from within (LXX;
Vg; Tg ["a spirit of bravery from before the Lord put on Gideon", so also Rashi and
Ralbag]; Moore, *Judges* [1895], pp. 197-98 [comparing Syr. *lbš* 'take possession of'; so
also BDB, p. 528a 1. f.; RSV; NEB])—but, "and the spirit of YHWH 'clothed/empowered'
Gideon"—from without (Boling, *Judges* [1975], p. 138; cf. "came upon" in AV, RV, NIV).
On the semantic reflexes of לבשה (Qal) that result from syntactical ambiguity in idioms

Plot A develops with each advance toward Israel's final victory over the Midianites: Gideon's summons of tribes to battle (6:33-35), encampment opposite Midian's camp (7:1, 8b), attack on and pursuit of the Midianites (7:9, 15b-25; 8:4), capture of the Midianite kings (8:10-12) and dubiously motivated killing of the kings (8:18-21?). The bifurcated resolution of Plot A is made up essentially of cycle-motif elements (E1 in ·8:28aαβ and F2 in 8:28b^{i-ii}; G1 and G2 in 8:32). The parts of 8:28 that do not correspond to cycle-motif elements may derive from the traditional form of the Gideon story: ... ולא יספו לשאת ראשם בימי גדעון (8:28aγ,b^{iii}). Thus, to the extent that Judges' compiler/redactor established the agenda of Plot A by means of the rhetoric inherent in the cycle-motif, the primary plot ends with the death of Gideon (8:32). The 'loose ends' that remain from those Plot A complications that describe Gideon's cultic aberrations, his relations with a Canaanite woman and his exploitation of a situation of holy war so as to settle a personal vendetta could have been tied up in a dénouement or left undeveloped. However, the compiler/redactor's decision to trace these themes beyond the lifespan of Gideon to their culmination in his heirs shows that he/she had yet to make a major point (through Plots B and C).

Plot B (6:25-32; 8:24-27, 33-34; 9:1-44, 46-49, 56-57) traces the escalation of the evil precipitated by Gideon, in his failure to abandon foreign cultic practices, which is perpetuated by his offspring until YHWH restores justice. Cycle-motif elements occur also in the exposition of Plot B (i.e., G1 in 8:33aα [cf. 8:32a^{i}]; A2a in 8:33aγ-b; A2b in 8:34; and A1b in 9:16, 19a of Jotham's curse) and perhaps in the altered forms that appear in the development of Plots B and C, namely, in the transition showing YHWH's fulfilment of Jotham's curse (B3b [not F1] in 9:22; D2a in 9:23a).[188] Of course, Jotham's curse

---

with double accusative verbs meaning 'to cover/overwhelm' or 'to clothe/overpower/empower', see Waldman, "Imagery" (1989), pp. 163-67.

[188] It is perhaps significant that a hiatus of three years intervenes in 9:22 between the outcry for retribution, implicit in Jotham's parable and curse (9:8-15, 16-20), and God's response in 9:23-24. Some have inferred that this delay issues a concern about the efficacy of the principle of retribution (T. A. Boogaart, "Stone for Stone: Retribution in the Story of Abimelech and Shechem", *JSOT* 32 [1985], p. 56 n. 11) or that it raises questions about divine procedure (Exum, "Centre" [1990], p. 420). Yet this inference is hardly necessary. First, viewed within the hermeneutic fostered by the aggregate structure of Judges' cycle-motif, the period of Abimelech's rule is commensurate with the situations of foreign oppression elsewhere described by motif elements 'B3' so that, contra Exum ("Centre" [1990], p. 420), 9:22 should not be viewed as outside the "deuteronomistic schema" (though Exum elsewhere implies that Abimelech might be equated with Israel's plunderers ["Centre" (1990), p. 419]). Further, an initial ambiguity that 9:22 might be

(9:7bβγ-20) plays the same rhetorical role as the descriptive cycle-motif element C ("Israelites cried to YHWH"), an element otherwise missing from the exposition of Plots B and C in the Abimelech account. Had it been the Judges compiler/redactor who originally inserted Jotham's curse into this account to substitute for cycle-motif element C, this substitution would correspond to that for element D1 in the Gideon story, where discourse (in a divine commission/theophanic recognition type-scene) displaces description (the usual form of D1).

The contest between Gideon and the Baalists (implicitly YHWH versus Baal) introduces a complication into Plot A that, as a foreshadowing of the exposition of Plot B, discloses a reluctance on the part of Gideon openly to shun foreign cultic practices. The fury of the Baalist mob (6:30) is quelled not by Gideon but by the intervention of his father (6:31). Ironically, Gideon's nonconfrontation precipitates his being dubbed "Jerubbaal" (paronomastically etymologized "Let Baal contend with him" [6:32]), which does little more than raise the ever-frustrated expectation that he will finally spurn Baalism.[189] On the contrary, Gideon's reluctance to oppose Baalism openly in 6:25-32 foreshadows the first of three illegitimate actions that spell disaster for Israel in Plot B: Gideon's cultic syncretism, in setting up an ephod in

---

perceived as corresponding to motif element F1 ("... judged ... Israel [N years]") is clarified by its proximity to sequentially related motif elements (*pace* Klein, *Triumph of Irony* [1988], pp. 70, 73, who equates 9:22 with the F1 formula via irony). Second, the regular order of presentation, in which an element 'B3' ("Israelites served/oppressed the Israelites ... N years") precedes element C ("Israelites cried to YHWH"), hardly implies that Israelites began to cry out to YHWH only at the end of each period of oppression. Thus, a delay of YHWH's response is implicit in all the enumerations of Judges' cycle-motif. What is peculiar about the relation of 9:8-20 to 9:22 is that the reversal of normal order makes this delay explicit, doubtless to make the same point as that made in 6:7-10, namely, that God is not inclined quickly to reverse a situation fostered by a people who are inclined quickly to disobey.

[189] In 6:32, ויקרא may represent an indefinite use of the 3 m. sg (often with קרא, cf. GKC, §144d,e) though Moore (*Judges* [1895], pp. 194, 196) recommends a Ni. vocalization. On the probable etymology of ירבעל, see Moore, *Judges* [1895], p. 196; BDB, p. 937b; J. A. Emerton, "Gideon and Jerubbaal", *JTS* NS 27 [1976], p. 290).

R. Gregory has suggested that there is narrative analogy between the scenes of Judg. 6:11-24, 25-32 and that of 1 Kgs 18:20-40, in which Elijah challenges the divine title of Baal (cf. 1 Kgs 18:21, 27 with Judg. 6:31), erects upon a ruined altar a new altar to YHWH to rival that of Baal (cf. 1 Kgs 18:30-33a with Judg. 6:25-27) and summons a theophany to remove doubt as to YHWH's divine claim to allegiance (cf. 1 Kgs 18:22-24, 36-39 with Judg. 6:17-24) (*Irony and the Unmasking of Elijah*, in A. J. Hauser and R. Gregory, *From Carmel to Horeb: Elijah in Crisis* [JSOTS 85, BLS 19, Sheffield, 1990], [pp. 91-169] p. 143). Gideon's reticence is all the more striking in contrast to the tactics of Elijah.

Ophrah (8:24-27a$\alpha\beta$), escalates to cultic apostasy on the tribal level (8:27aγb; cf. 8:33-34; 9:1-22) and invites YHWH's ensuing judgement throughout the remainder of Plot B (cf. 9:23-44, 46-49, 56-57).[190]

A second illegitimate action–consequence that could be construed as stemming from Gideon's Baalist sympathies is his exercise of conjugal privileges with a Canaanite concubine, who bears him the fratricidal son Abimelech (6:31).[191] This complication combines with a third illegitimate course of action, unrelated to Gideon's sympathy for Baalism but equally disastrous: Gideon's ruthlessness in dispensing punishment against his opponents, as though he were serving personal vendettas (8:5-9, 13-23). His sexual relations with a Canaanite and his example of ruthlessness foreshadow, in Plot C (8:5-9, 13-23, 29-31, 35; 9:1-49a, 50-57), the fratricidal rivalry among his would-be heirs (8:30, 35; 9:1-22). That this fratricide escalates to internecine strife between Abimelech and the citizens of Shechem is but the just recompense of YHWH, who brings their evil back upon their own heads (9:23-49a, 50-57). One might wish to notice that besides the verses mentioned where the cycle-motif occurs in the development of Plots B and C, the cycle-motif elements occur also in the resolution of Plot C (G1 in 9:54b^{ii}, 55a^{ii}). Through Plot C, three cities of Manasseh (Ophrah, Shechem, Thebez) undergo a form of foreign domination when Canaanite Baalists, represented in the person of Abimelech, over-come Israelite Yahwists—an emblem of the consequences that inevitably result from the coexistence in the land of Israelites and Canaanites (8:33-9:57; cf. 8:22-23 with 8:24-27).[192]

A further point of rhetorical strategy arises from observing the positioning in the account of the foreshadowings of Plots B and C. The Plot C foreshadowings (8:5-9, 13-17, 18-21?, 22-23) are interwoven only as part of the description of Gideon's pursuit and conquest of the two Midianite kings. Hence, ironically, Gideon's ruthless reprisal against two Manassite cities (Succoth, Penuel) while conquering two

---

[190] Gideon's manufacture, from confiscated gold, of an illegitimate cult object that later becomes an object of Israel's (Manasseh's) cultic aberration foreshadows the scenario involving Micah's making from stolen silver the private cult objects that the Danites come to worship in Judg. 17–18. Cf. Auld, "Gideon" (1989), p. 257; Exod. 32:1-8.

[191] The situation that leads to fratricide need not presuppose that Jerubbaal's sons were actually ruling (*pace* Exum, "Centre" [1990], p. 419), only that "as soon as Gideon died" (8:33aα), there was apprehension among 'non-Israelites' that Jerubbaal's sons might predominate. It is this situation that Abimelech exploited in his appeal to the Shechemites.

[192] Cf. Klein, *Triumph of Irony* (1988), p. 70.

foreign kings is echoed when Abimelech represses two cities in Manasseh (Shechem, Thebez) while ruling as a semiforeign king. The Plot B
foreshadowings (6:25-32; 8:24-27) frame the development of Plot A
and are, in turn, framed by the exposition and resolution of Plot A.
Moreover, it is ironic that Gideon, whose commission to save Israel is
interrupted by YHWH's prerequisite that he desecrate Baal's altar in
Ophrah (6:25-26), later institutes in the same city a cultic emblem by
which the people again corrupt themselves.[193] This offers another
example in Judges of escalated parallelism between the negative characterization of an individual and that of the tribal community (i.e.,
between the cultic syncretism of Gideon and the later full-scale
apostasy of his people). In view of both the strategic positioning in the
Gideon account of the Plots B and C foreshadowings and the escalated
parallelisms that they form between the actions of Gideon and those of
Israel, it is difficult to escape the inference that this is the doing of the
same compiler/redactor who selected and/or designed the Deborah/
Barak/Jael account.[194]

Tribal-political concerns in the account of Gideon/Abimelech are
evident, in 6:35 and 7:23, from Gideon's initial summons to battle of
only the tribes of Manasseh (his own tribe—cf. Judg. 6:11, 15, 34-35;
Josh. 17:2), Asher, Zebulun and Naphtali. An ensuing confrontation
with the late-summoned Ephraimites attests the mounting spirit of
intertribal rivalry in Judges that portends further escalation to intertribal warfare (in the account of Jephthah) and finally pantribal warfare
(in Dénounement-B). The indispensability of Ephraim's participation to
the success of the battle (7:24-25), coupled with Ephraim's ensuing

---

[193] For analogous interruptive/delaying (type-)scenes, where YHWH subversively confronts his own emissary with a death threat warranted by the neglect of some religious
obligation, see Exod. 4:24-26 (where Moses is rescued by his son's circumcised foreskin)
and Num. 22:22-34 (where Baalam is rescued by a donkey that 'sees' reason to fear where
the "seer" does not).

[194] It may be a further indication of the concerns of a deuteronomic compiler/redactor
that there is such close analogy between the themes of Plots B and C in the synthetic
parallelism between 8:34 and 8:35, in the expositions of Plots B and C, respectively.

ולא זכרו בני ישראל את־יהוה אלהיהם
המציל אותם מיד כל־איביהם מסביב:
ולא־עשׂו חסד עם־בית ירבעל גדעון
ככל־הטובה אשר עשׂה עם־ישראל:

The structural analogy between these verses, which form the evaluative transition from the
Gideon account to that of Abimelech, implies that Israel's treatment of YHWH (cultic aberrancy) is analogous to their treatment of the house of Gideon/Jerubbaal (covenant [social]
injustice). The B-cola of both verses seem to refer to the same saving type of deed (cf.
Webb, *Judges* [1987], p. 156; Klein, *Triumph of Irony* [1988], p. 79).

protest at having been neglected until the last (8:1-3), suggests that the compiler/redactor who included this description was concerned to reflect the importance of the cooperation of Ephraim to the welfare of the intertribal community. In this instance, the Ephraimite confrontation complicates the development of Plot A (as in 12:1-6), but the concern registered about Ephraim's cooperation in the intertribal community is ubiquitous in Judges, appearing in Prologue-A (1:29), Prologue-B (2:9), the accounts of Ehud (3:27), Deborah/Barak/Jael (4:5; 5:14), Tola (10:1), Jephthah (10:9; 12:1-6), Abdon (12:15), Dénouement-A (17:1, 8; 18:2, 13) and Dénouement-B (19:1, 16, 18). In 8:1, when the Ephraimites contend with Gideon over his impropriety in summoning them to holy war only after Naphtali, Asher and Manasseh (cf. 7:23-24), Gideon responds with diplomacy and averts a potential intertribal war (8:2-3). Had Gideon acted without due respect for decorum by not summoning all the tribes to holy war, he did so despite the 'clothing' of YHWH's spirit, by which he rallied the tribes for battle (cf. 6:34-35), yet perhaps in line with YHWH's intention to rout the Midianites with a minimal human force (cf. 7:2-8a).

An additional indication of tribal–political concerns may stem from the fact that Gideon is a Manassite (hence, non-Judahite) deliverer with mixed characterization. His diffidence reflects an underlying lack of confidence in YHWH. He is afraid either to confront openly the foreign (Baalist) cult in his home city or to oppose the foreign (Midianite and Amalekite) threat in his tribal region. Indeed, Gideon's inclination toward cultic syncretism (evidenced by his making a golden ephod) and his conjugal union with foreigners (evidenced in the birth of Abimelech to a Shechemite woman) starts two lines of development that escalate in Judges 9 into cultic and social atrocities at Shechem. Inasmuch as this scheme of concerns about tribal politics, cultic aberrancy and covenant (social) injustice results from the merger of the accounts of Gideon (Judg. 6–8*) and Abimelech (Judg. 9*) and is also in harmony with the tribal–political and deuteronomic concerns of Judges' double prologue and double dénouement, one may rightly infer that it was the compiler/redactor of Judges who first joined the originally separate Gideon and Abimelech stories.[195]

There are two dramatic climaxes in the Gideon/Abimelech account. The first comes at the point where Gideon slays with a sword the two kings of Midian (8:21b), ending the third of three vengeful rampages

---

[195] Obvious indications of effort to unite the two accounts appear where the names ירבעל and גדעון have been integrated in the account (e.g., 6:25-32; 7:1aα; 8:29-31).

that Gideon leads against his offenders (cf. 8:5-7 with 8:13-16; 8:8-9
with 8:17; 8:18-19, 21a with 8:20, 21b). This first climactic moment
has been prepared for by mounting tension throughout Gideon's
frenzied pursuit of the Midianites. It begins with the characterization of
Gideon in the scene of 8:1-3, when the Ephraimites ask מה־הדבר הזה
עשית לנו (8:1aβ; reminding one of the Baalists' question מי עשה הדבר
הזה in 6:29aβ).[196] From the point of Gideon's self-effacing evasion of
open confrontation with the Ephraimites (8:2-3), Gideon becomes
obsessed with the capture of the Midianite kings, as though he were
trying to compensate for his own sense of insignificance (cf. 6:15) by a
personal triumph that would surpass even that of the Ephraimites. It is
from this point that YHWH ceases to appear to Gideon and the latter's
expected commitment to covenant (social) justice and cultic loyalty go
awry. Not only does he exercise extreme prejudice against the citizens
of Succoth and Penuel, he usurps the right to vengeance against
YHWH's enemies as a personal right.[197]

The 'aa' and 'bb' members of the parallel series designated aa–bb–
cc–aa^i–bb^i–cc^i in 8:5-21 of the plot outline correspond as to city name
and in the way that mockery and threat correspond to execution of
threat:

aa   Mockery and threat to thresh officials of Succoth (8:5-7)
bb   Mockery and threat to ruin the tower of Penuel (8:8-9)
      ...
aa^i Execution: threshing of officials of Succoth (8:13-16)
bb^i Execution: ruin of Penuel's tower and killing of its "men of the city"
      (8:17)

In both instances of execution, Gideon carries out his threat against
(ranking) citizens who had refused him aid.[198] The 'cc' members of this
series concern the capture of the Midianite kings. The second member
(cc^i) may be quartered into parts that also correspond as mockery and
threat correspond to execution:

---

[196] Cf. Exum, "Centre" (1990), p. 418.

[197] Klein summarizes Gideon's character development: "With the powerful, like the
Ephraimites, Gideon moderates; with the weak, he over-reacts: the coward becomes the
bully" (Triumph of Irony [1988], p. 61).

[198] It is perhaps no small irony that Gideon punishes the officials of Succoth by threshing (דוש, 8:7b, 16b* [read וידש (Psht, Vg, OG) instead of וידע (MT, Tg)]), alluding again
to his occupation (חבט 'beating [out]') when YHWH had called him to deliver Israel from
its oppressors. Moreover, there is ironic foreshadowing in both pairs of members in that
the 'aa' members, Gideon's threshing of seventy-seven elders of Succoth, adumbrate
Abimelech's slaughter of Jerubbaal's seventy sons on a single stone and the 'bb' members,
Gideon's destruction of tower and citizens of Penuel, adumbrate Abimelech's similar
actions against Shechem.

cc   Capture of the Midianite kings Zebah and Zalmunna (8:10-12)

...

cc^i   Killing of the Midianite kings Zebah and Zalmunna (8:18-21)

    a   Mockery of Zebah and Zalmunna about killing Gideon's brothers
       and Gideon's threat to kill them (8:18-19)

    b   Execution: Gideon coaxes his son to kill them (8:20)

    a^i   Mockery of Zebah and Zalmunna (8:21a)

    b^i   Execution: Gideon kills and plunders them (8:21b)

Thus, the climax at 8:21b comes as the culmination of two sets of mockeries and threats together with their corresponding executions of threat. The surprise revelation, in 8:18-19, that Gideon's express motivation for killing the Midianite kings was their killing of his brothers (sons of his mother), not their being enemies of YHWH, discloses Gideon's true perspective on the Midianite affair and is a low point in his characterization. Nor is it any credit to Gideon's company that at this point they make an overture to establish Gideon as their king (8:22a).[199]

The second dramatic climax of the Gideon/Abimelech account comes when Abimelech is struck by the millstone at Thebez (9:53)—a surprise that interrupts the pattern of events, repeated in the previous three descriptions of Abimelech's attacks upon Shechem, and that breaks the tension that has been mounting throughout the increasingly gruesome series of Abimelech's rampages (9:26-41, 42-49, 46-49, 50-52). The sequence followed in each of these four scenes is to some degree a reflection of the sequence outlined in that part of the exposition of Plots B and C in which Abimelech and the citizens of Shechem conspired to slaughter the sons of Jerubbaal (9:1-5a).[200] The delineation

---

[199] As it is a point of negative characterization for both Gideon, who incites his followers to assign him credit for victory like that due YHWH (ליהוה ולגדעון, 7:18bγ), and his followers, who do so (חרב ליהוה ולגדעון, 7:20bβ), that they thus subvert YHWH's intention to bring glory to himself alone (cf. 7:2b), it only furthers this negative characterization that Gideon's followers now credit Gideon alone with delivering them from the hand of Midian (8:22b) and that Gideon, while refusing to usurp YHWH's sole right to kingship (8:23), is loath to deny their premise that he delivered them (cf. Gunn, "Joshua and Judges" [1987], p. 114). As proof that the reader should assess the chief victor as YHWH, Gunn points to 7:7, 9 and especially 7:14, where even a Midianite knows that it is YHWH who is delivering Midian into Gideon's hand ("Joshua and Judges" [1987], p. 114; cf. Exum, "Centre" [1990], p. 419).

[200] Boogaart articulated six correspondences between 9:1-5 and 9:25-41 ("Stone" [1985], pp. 50-51, adapted):

1.	a man comes to Shechem	9:1a	9:26a
2.	the man is accompanied by his brothers	9:1b-3a	9:26a
3.	conspires against the ruler of Shechem	9:2-3a	9:28-29

of each of these five sections into six parts (e.g., a–b–c–d–e–f, in the plot-structure outline above) is not intended to suggest that these sections correspond identically throughout the series, but, to the extent that there is an aggregate of correspondences, it seems valid to assess the five sections as a serial buildup to the climax in 9:53 (and its dénouement in 9:54). The 'a' members correspond in that all portray the citizens of Shechem or Thebez acting in a way that catalyses or invokes Abimelech's subsequent slaughters.

a   Abimelech agitates his brothers (sons of his mother) to incite the
            citizens of Shechem to overthrow the sons of Jerubbaal (9:1-2)

(a)   Citizens of Shechem ambush travellers in Manasseh (9:25a)

a^i Gaal, with his brothers, agitates the citizens of Shechem to over-
            throw Abimelech son of Jerubbaal (9:26-29)

a^{ii} The people [of Shechem] go out to the field (9:42a)

a^{iii} Citizens of the tower of Shechem enter the stronghold of the temple
            of El-Berith (9:46)

a^{iv} The men and women and the citizens [of Thebez] flee to the tower
            and ascend to the roof (9:51)

Members a and a^i correspond in comparing Abimelech's insurrection with that of Gaal. The correspondences of (a), a^{ii}, a^{iii} and a^{iv} rest in the fact that each reports some action by the citizens that will provoke retaliation from Abimelech.

The 'b' members correspond in that each describes a report of some occurrence, usually to Abimelech.

b   Abimelech's offer is told to the citizens of Shechem by his brothers
            (sons of his mother) (9:3a)

(b)   Treachery reported to Abimelech (9:25b)

b^i Treachery reported to Abimelech by Zebul, who counsels coming at
            night with all his people to ambush at morning (9:30-33)

b^{ii} Their vulnerability reported to Abimelech (9:42b)

b^{iii} Vulnerability of the citizens of the tower of Shechem reported to
            Abimelech (9:47)

4.	claims closer genealogical ties with Shechem		
	than those of the ruler	9:2b	9:28
5.	the citizens of Shechem trust the conspirator	9:3b	9:26b
6.	the conspirator encounters the ruler	9:5a	9:30-41

These correspondences of detail evidence a clear intention on the part of the narrator to link the insurrection at Shechem led by Abimelech with that led by Gaal, thus proving the poetic justice of the consequences that ensue between Abimelech and Shechem. However, that God's only purpose for Gaal was to bring Abimelech and Shechem to blows is also evidenced by the fact that, once Gaal has catalysed the debacle, he disappears from the plot (9:41).

There is little ground for inferring thematic correspondences among the 'c' members.

c   Their heart inclines toward Abimelech since he is their brother (9:3b)

c^i Abimelech's four-part division of his people to lay an ambush against Shechem (9:34)

c^{ii} Abimelech's tripartite division of his people to lay an ambush in the field [of Shechem] (9:43a)

c^{iii} Abimelech and his people ascend Mount Zalmon, where he cuts off branches and sets them on his shoulder (9:48a)

c^{iv} Abimelech comes to the tower [of Thebez] and fights against it (9:52a)

Here, correspondence is mostly the result of the regularity of the 'c' members' relative position within the sequence of the aggregate structure 'a–b–c–d–e–f'. Nevertheless, once their correspondence is inferred on formal grounds, the 'c' members show some less obvious points of agreement. There is a certain irony in the correspondence between the first and subsequent 'c' members in that the citizens' initial inclination to conspire with Abimelech is prompted by a regard for him (ויט לבם אחרי אבימלך, 9:3bα) because he was "their brother", whereas subsequent 'c' members show Abimelech acting aggressively against them—c^i, ויארבו על־שכם (9:34bα); c^{ii}, ויארב בשדה (9:43aγ); c^{iv}, וילחם בו (9:52aβ)—just as he had done initially against "his brothers", the sons of Jerubbaal. Against this background, it is perhaps not unwarranted to see a *double entente* in וישם על־שכמו "and he set them against his shoulder/Shechem" (c^{iii}, 9:48aζ). Members c^i and c^{ii} show Abimelech dividing his people into companies (ראשים) (9:34bβ, 43aβ) and members c^{ii} and c^{iii} employ ויקח (9:43aα, 48aγ).

The 'd' members are also thematically diversified, but all, at least implicitly, portray people (citizens of Shechem in d, but Abimelech's personal army in d^i, d^{ii} and d^{iii}) acting in support of Abimelech's policy of violence.

d   [Citizens of Shechem] give [Abimelech] seventy pieces of silver from the temple of Baal-Berith (9:4a)

d^i Interchange between Gaal and Zebul as Abimelech and his people emerge from ambush (9:35, 36a, 36b, 37, 38)

d^{ii} Abimelech [and his people] emerge from ambush (9:43b)

d^{iii} Abimelech orders his people to imitate him, so all the people cut off branches (9:48b-49aα)

As background for Jotham's curse, member d describes the taking of blood money from the temple of Baal-Berith—kindling for a fire of intrigues that eventually consumes all who conspired to do evil. As Abimelech's companies attack, Gaal makes ironic references in member dⁱ to landmarks from which they are attacking: "people are descending from the hilltops" (הנה־עם יורד מראשי ההרים, 9:36aδ; cf. "people are descending from west of the water divide(?)" [הנה־־עם יורד> <ים מעם טבור הארץ, 9:37aγδ]) and "one company is coming from the way to the soothsayer's terebinth" (וראש־אחד בא מדרך אלון מעוננים, 9:37bαβ). Reference to the hilltops may grant an aura of poetic justice to this onslaught against Shechem in that a hilltop overlooking Shechem was the spot from which Jotham first pronounced their doom (9:7a). Reference to the "soothsayer's terebinth" may lend further poetic justice to the attack by alluding to the cultic tree beside which Abimelech was installed as king (9:6) and by drawing from the tree motif of Jotham, whose imagery foreshadows doom (cf. 9:8-15, 37, 48b and especially 9:49aα [dⁱⁱⁱ]).[201] Zebul's remarks in 9:36b, 38 of dⁱ reveal his complicity with Abimelech in the slaughter of the Shechemites over whom, ironically, the former was a leader (cf. 9:30). The phraseology in dⁱⁱ is strikingly similar to Gaal's statements in dⁱ: והנה העם יצא מן־העיר (9:43bβ). Members dⁱ and dⁱⁱ both depict events in which Abimelech attacks from ambush. As to member dⁱⁱⁱ, there can be little doubt that Abimelech's people were aware of the purpose for which they were cutting off branches, as is evident from their complicity in the atrocity that follows.

Most 'e' members concern events in which Abimelech leads his people to entrances with intent to slaughter.

e   Abimelech hires worthless men, they follow him and he enters his
        father's home at Ophrah (9:4b-5aα)
eⁱ   Abimelech slays many while chasing Gaal to the entrance of
        Shechem (9:39-40)
eⁱⁱ   Abimelech takes position at the entrance to Shechem while two com-
        panies slay those in the field (9:44)
eⁱⁱⁱ   Abimelech, followed by his people, sets fire to the stronghold
        (9:49aβγ)
eⁱᵛ   Abimelech approaches the tower entrance to burn it with fire
        (9:52b)

---

[201] Note the terebinth mentioned at the site of YHWH's visitation of Gideon (6:11a) where the latter later erects an altar (6:24). On the cultic tree motif pervading Judg. 6-9, see Klein, *Triumph of Irony* (1988), pp. 53, 71, 72, 75. Cf. Deborah's palm in Judg. 4:5 and see Burney, *Judges* (2d edn, 1920), p. 86.

Members eⁱ, eⁱⁱ and eⁱᵛ—perhaps implicitly also members e and eⁱⁱⁱ—concern the actions of Abimelech that lead him to entrances. Members e and eⁱⁱⁱ similarly employ וילכו אחרי אחריו (9:4bγ) and וילכו אחרי אבימלך (9:49aβ), respectively, and show Abimelech leading a party of killers. Members eⁱⁱⁱ and eⁱᵛ relate to the motif of fire introduced in Jotham's curse.

All the 'f' members, except fⁱ, portray fatal events. Perhaps, the connection that fⁱ has with other members relates to the corollary theme of depopulation.

f	Abimelech kills his (paternal) brothers, the seventy sons of Jerubbaal, on a single stone (9:5aβ)
fⁱ	Abimelech stays in Arumah while Zebul expels Gaal and his brothers from Shechem (9:41)
fⁱⁱ	Abimelech captures Shechem that day, killing its people, tearing down the city and sowing it with salt (9:45)
fⁱⁱⁱ	A thousand men and women of the tower of Shechem die (9:49b)
fⁱᵛ	Abimelech is stabbed and dies (9:54b)

Indeed, fⁱ suggests that Zebul may have prevented Abimelech from carrying out his reprisal against Shechem and, in so doing, incited Abimelech to the compensatory acts of revenge that follow. Thus, perhaps Abimelech, like his father, is shown to be motivated to acts of violence by a profound sense of insecurity.

From the foregoing, it may be inferred that the narrator made an effort to serialize the events leading to Abimelech's demise. While both moments of climax in the Gideon/Abimelech account are prepared for by patterned sequences, the second climax is the more elaborately prepared for. For this reason, and because it is the concluding climax, it seems fair to infer that 9:53 is the main climax of the Gideon/Abimelech account. Further support for this conclusion may be found in the fact that the second climax is also a point of convergence for several stock idioms (i.e., אשה אחת "a certain woman"; פלח רכב "upper millstone" [lit. "riding cleavage-stone"]; על־ראש "upon the head") that here become especially significant for the reader (e.g., the bathos that אשה אחת may mean "*one* woman" [cf. Abimelech's bid to being איש אחד "one man" in 9:2][202]; פלח רכב is both a *single* mill-*stone* [cf. אבן אחת 9:5aβ, 18a] and that which *cleaves* [cf. ותרץ את־גלגלתו "she crushed/fractured his skull" in 9:53b]; על־ראש is

---

[202] Cf. A. D. Crown, "A Reinterpretation of Judges ix in the Light of Its Humour", *AbrN* 3 (1961–1962), p. 96; J. G. Janzen, "A Certain Woman in the Rhetoric of Judges 9", *JSOT* 38 (1987), pp. 34, 36.

literal, but relates to the metonymical use of בראשם in 9:57a). As a result, the poetic justice of this event fulfills the reader's expectation of exact retribution.[203]

In formal structure, the two dramatic climaxes of the Gideon/ Abimelech account parallel the two climaxes of the Deborah/Barak/Jael account, yet, unlike the latter, the two climaxes of the Gideon/ Abimelech account point to two different events. Nevertheless, it is a point of congruence between these deliverer accounts that the second climax of the Gideon/Abimelech account is a rehearsal of images from the climactic event of the Deborah/Barak/Jael account. It is probably more than coincidence that the assault on Abimelech by a woman finds analogy in the account of Jael's slaying of Sisera: both agents are women, both women appear late in the account, both deal a man his deathblow to the head and both thereby evidence YHWH's control of circumstances to bring about military victory (over Sisera or Abimelech) and poetic justice (vis-à-vis Barak or Abimelech).

Within the Gideon story, one finds another example of escalated parallelism. Gideon is moved by divine visitation to tear down his father's asherah and altar to Baal (6:25-27a), yet he ultimately lapses into another form of cultic aberration through the making of an ephod from gold earrings (8:24-27a$\alpha\beta$). Both scenes complicate Plot A and foreshadow the cultic aberrancy depicted in Plot B. This negative characterization, on the grounds of cultic disloyalty, is both structurally framed and thematically paralleled by the portrayal of Israel as a nation that, prompted by divine visitation to repent of worshipping foreign gods (6:8-10), nevertheless relapses into idolatry using the ephod that Gideon had set up in Ophrah (8:27aγb). Ironically, this escalated parallelism within the Gideon account is facilitated by Gideon's manufacture of an ephod from Midianite (Ishmaelite) earrings, described in a scene that offers a narrative analogy to the account of Aaron casting the golden calf from the Egyptians' gold earrings (Exod. 32:1-8).[204] That the narrative analogy was deliberate and designed to characterize Gideon as an instigator of cultic corruption in Israel is apparent from the contrast between the repeated claim of Aaron that it was the cast image that had brought Israel out of Egypt (Exod. 32:4, 8) and the prophetic claim that it was YHWH who had brought Israel out of Egypt

---

[203] Cf. Janzen, "Certain Woman" (1987), pp. 36-37.

[204] Cf. Gunn, "Joshua and Judges" (1987), p. 114, who also cites the prohibition of Deut. 17:17 against a king amassing for himself silver and gold; Auld, "Gideon" (1989), p. 257.

(6:8-9; cf. 1 Kgs 12:28). Hence, is not likely by chance that the Gideon account closes with a corresponding enactment of cultic aberration (i.e., the offering of foreigners' confiscated gold earrings to make an illegitimate cult object for Israel to worship) that parallels the covenant abrogating episode of Aaron and Israel at Sinai.

The parallelism in negative characterization between Israel and their deliverer Gideon extends even further. In despondency, Israel cries out to YHWH for a deliverer (6:6b), and, despite YHWH's patent disappointment in their instability of character (6:8-10), YHWH furnishes one. Yet the deliverer whom YHWH calls is one whose despondency and instability only parallels that of the nation. Gideon, too, is sorely oppressed (6:11b; cf. 6:3-5) and laments the need for deliverance by YHWH (6:13; cf. 6:6b) yet shows the same reluctance as his people to follow YHWH fully. Thus, Gideon, like Barak, is a microcosm of Israel's reluctance to follow YHWH wholeheartedly.[205] Gideon's reluctance to follow YHWH stems both from his fearfulness— a flaw of character made obvious by his nocturnal movements (6:27; 7:11b-15a, 15b-18, 19-22) and preoccupation with confirming signs (6:17, 36-37, 39; 7:10-11a)—and from his unwillingness to shun foreign cultic practices (8:27a). Israel's reluctance to follow YHWH could likewise be construed as stemming from their fearfulness to engage the enemy, exhibited in their retreat to the caves (6:2), and from their unwillingness to shun foreign cultic practices (6:10b). The irony of this characterization is that YHWH raises up a deliverer for Israel who is none other than Israel in miniature (cf. 6:15). So it is little wonder that the outcome of the Gideon story is hardly better than its beginning. A deliverer who acts like Israel can hardly be expected to save Israel from the inclinations that lead them to return to evil.

It has become a standard view to regard Gideon's refusal of kingship (8:23), Abimelech's negative model of kingship (9:1-6, 34-52) and Jotham's mockery of Abimelech's appointment to kingship (9:8-15, 16-20) as evidence of an antimonarchical sentiment in Judges 6-9.[206] In

---

[205] For instances that show that Gideon is a microcosm of Israel in terms of characterization, see Klein, *Triumph of Irony* (1988), pp. 50, 56, 66, 218 n. 5.

[206] Among those who perceive an antimonarchical sentiment in Judg. 6-9 are: M. Buber, *Königtum Gottes* (Heidelberg, 3d edn, 1956), p. 24; Crown, "Reinterpretation" (1961-62), pp. 90-98; W. J. Dumbrell, "'In Those Days There Was No King in Israel; Every Man Did What Was Right in His Own Eyes': The Purpose of the Book of Judges Reconsidered", *JSOT* 25 (1983), pp. 27-28; R. Bartelmus, "Die sogenannte Jothamfabel—Eine politisch-religiöse Parabeldichtung: Anmerkungen zu einem Teilaspeckt der vordeuteronomistischen israelitischen Literaturgeschichte", *TZ* 41 (1985), pp. 97-120;

8:23, the main concern of Gideon is that neither he nor his people should usurp YHWH's right to rule. The issue is not essentially one of the legitimacy of human or hereditary kingship but whether a popular appointment to kingship would be an affront to YHWH's prerogatives as divine king.[207] Abimelech's negative characterization and Jotham's fable and curse certainly point to the faults of choosing a bad king, but this does not entail a rejection of kingship as such.[208] Like Gideon's refusal of kingship, the Jotham fable—indeed, the whole Abimelech context—shows that not kingship *per se* but the ill-motivated popular appointment of a king is the central concern.[209] Of course, the fable by itself ridicules a people who do not know how to choose the right kind of king, and this characterizes negatively both the people who choose and Abimelech their choice.[210] The fable in context, however, functions

U. Becker, *Richterzeit und Königtum: Redaktionsgeschichtliche Studien zum Richterbuch* (BZAW 192, Berlin, 1990), pp. 188-90, 195, 199, 303.

[207] So G. E. Gebrandt, *Kingship according to the Deuteronomistic History* (SBLDS 87, Atlanta, Ga., 1986), pp. 123-29. While G. H. Davies has argued that Judg. 8:23 is an acceptance of kingship "couched in the form of a pious refusal with the motive of expressing piety and of gaining favour with his would-be subjects" ("Judges viii 22-23", *VT* 13 [1963], p. 154), it would be difficult to prove that the compiler/redactor of Judges viewed Gideon in this way, since the Gideon account closes with the same cycle-motif formulae of 2:11-3:6 that characterize the demise of all שפטים (i.e., not מלכים; cf. 2:16, 18-19 with 8:32, 33-34, respectively) (cf. Emerton, "Gideon and Jerubbaal" [1976], pp. 297-98).

[208] Cf. B. Lindars: "The institution of kingship is a presupposition of the fable ... The fact that the fable tilts at a particularly unfortunate situation does not of itself constitute an objection to monarchy as such. ... There is no suggestion that the trees were wrong or foolish to seek for themselves a king" ("Jotham's Fable: A New Form-Critical Analysis", *JTS* NS 24 [1973], p. 365); E. H. Maly, "The Jotham Fable—Anti-Monarchial?" *CBQ* 22 (1960), p. 304; Gebrandt, *Kingship* (1986), pp. 129-34; Webb, *Judges* (1987), p. 159.

[209] Contra Maly, who infers that the original fable was directed against those who refused the burden of leadership ("Jotham Fable" [1960] p. 303; also Lindars, "Jotham's Fable" [1973], p. 366).

[210] Maly has said, "just as in the original fable there was no general condemnation of kingship itself, so, too, in the biblical adaptation there can be found no criticism, on principle, of the rule of a king. It is a criticism, rather, that is directed primarily against those who were foolish enough to anoint a worthless man as king, and, secondarily, against the worthless king himself" ("Jotham Fable" [1960], p. 304).

Two arguments commonly used to show that the earliest elements of the parable (9:8-15a) were intrinsically antimonarchical are: (1) the use of לנוע 'to wave, sway, stagger' in 9:9bβ, 11bβ, 13bβ seems implicitly derogatory (Moore, *Judges* [1895], p. 247; Crown, "Reinterpretation" [1961-62], p. 94); and (2) the use of the perf. החדלתי in 9:9aβ, 11aβ, 13aβ denotes not imminence ("shall I cease ...?"; cf. GKC, §106n [*perfectum confidentiae*]; Moore, *Judges* [1895], p. 247; Burney, *Judges* [2d edn, 1920], pp. 273-74; Soggin, *Judges* [2d edn, 1987], p. 171) but perfective state ("have I ceased ...?"; cf. Bertheau, *Richter und Ruth* [1845], p. 140; Boling, *Judges* [1975], p. 166), which implies that only those who have become unfruitful would deign to be king (so Bartelmus, "Jothamfabel" [1985], pp. 99-100; Becker, *Richterzeit* [1990], p. 139).

to call into question the very legitimacy of the appointment of a king by a people who, as enemies of YHWH living in the land of Israel, are opposed to YHWH's theocracy.

A related issue deserves consideration. Although it has become standard practice to regard the designations בעלי שכם (9:2aα, 3aβ, 6aα, 7bβ, 18bα, 20aγ, 20bα, 23aγ, 23b, 24bδ, 25aα, 26b, 39aβ), בעלי מגדל־שכם (9:46aβ, 47γ) and בעלי העיר (9:51aγ) as "citizens of Shechem" (BDB, p. 127a, 3; RSV [half], NEB and NIV; "men of Shechem" in the AV, RV, JPSV and RSV [half]), "citizens in the tower of Shechem" (NIV; "men of the tower of Shechem" in the RV; "people of the Tower of Shechem" in the RSV; "occupants of the castle of Shechem" in the NEB), and "citizens" (NEB; "they of the city" in the RV; "people of the city" in the RSV and NIV), respectively, the tendency in Judges to bring ridicule against representatives of foreign nobility raises the possibility that such were "citizens" of status.[211] Support for this view is not overwhelming but derives from an accumulation of considerations. First, it is only after Abimelech had killed the people (העם) in the city of Shechem (9:45a) that כל־בעלי מגדל־שכם "all the citizens of the tower of Shechem" entered the stronghold of the temple of El-Berith (9:46aβ). Second, it was to these "citizens" that Abimelech sent his Shechemite maternal halfbrothers to appeal for endorsement (9:2aα), and these "citizens" had authority to finance him

---

However, לנוע need not convey a negative connotation if it be remembered that, in the context of this parable of the trees, it would be the right of a mighty tree to offer shade and protection, both symbols of kingship (cf. Maly, "Jotham Fable" [1960], p. 303 n. 18; Lindars, "Jotham's Fable" [1973], p. 365 n. 2). Rather, the mockery in the parable rests in an *a fortiori* argument: if fruit trees realize that they have not been designed by God for this role (9:9aγ, 13aγ; cf. הטובה את־מתקי ואת־תנובתי, 9:11aβγ), how much less the bramble (cf. צל 'shade, shadow' in 9:15a with Zebul's ironic reference to the same as Abimelech approaches Shechem in 9:36b; *pace* Lindars, "Jotham's Fable" [1973], p. 362). Thus, the parable shares with Gideon's refusal in 8:23 the point that kingship is a matter for God to decide. On the other hand, the mockery of the "cedars of Lebanon" in 9:15b does not conform to the preceding *a fortiori* comparison but, as the highest of trees in the Levant, is an emblem for the extent of destruction in society (i.e., reaching even the arrogant nobility).

As to the perf. tense of החדלתי ("have I ceased …?"), even this presents no compelling case for antimonarchicalism. The perfective form indicates only that nobler trees than that which God had given them to do, and for this reason were prevented from taking up a popular appointment to kingship. The point of the *reductio ad absurdum*, in their addressing the bramble, is that these trees did not know when to leave off seeking a king (i.e., they sought even until they found a tree of no benefit to God or humanity).

[211] So NEB once: "chief citizens of Shechem" (9:2aα). Janzen refers to these בעלי as "lords of …" ("Certain Woman" [1987], pp. 33-35).

from the treasury of the temple of Baal-Berith (9:3-4). Third, the word order of 9:51aβγ, וינסו שמה כל־האנשים והנשים וכל בעלי העיר, would be less redundant if וכל בעלי העיר were taken as, "and all the citizens (of status) of the city", rather than as appositionally specifying the preceding כל־האנשים והנשים to mean, "namely, all the citizens of the city". Moreover, a specifying apposition would normally be presented in the reverse order (so NEB: "and all the citizens, men and women"; RSV: "and all the people of the city fled to it, all the men and women"; cf. 9:49b, כל־אנשי מגדל־שכם כאלף איש ואשה). Thus, there are grounds for arguing that בעלי in Judges 9 designates members of a Canaanite nobility in Shechem. Indeed, they are portrayed as of Canaanite rather than Israelite heritage (cf. 9:3).

This being so, it must seriously affect the course of arguments about the portrayal of choosing a king in Jotham's fable, since it mocks the election by foreign nobles of a foreign, albeit half-Israelite, king.[212] Indeed, if, within the story world, the aim of the fable is to mock the Canaanites' choice of king during his coronation ceremony, it is a mockery both of the folly of Canaanite nobility ("cedars of Lebanon", 9:15b) for choosing such a king and of the type of king such nobility would choose. The negative characterization of Canaanite nobility, which is thus furthered by a satirization similar to that seen in the Deborah/Barak/Jael account, works in tandem with the negative characterization of foreign kingship. Moreover, by means of Jotham's fable and curse, as that part of the exposition of Plots B and C that corresponds to cycle-motif element C, the ensuing recompense of calamity against the citizens of Shechem and Abimelech (cf. the inclusio of 9:23-24, 56-57) redounds to God's glorification.

Indeed, the glorification of YHWH is as much a concern of the Gideon/Abimelech account as it is of the Ehud and Deborah/Barak/Jael accounts. It is a concern already implicit in YHWH's control of circumstances within the Gideon story. The first stage of the diminution of Gideon's troops (7:2-3) corresponds to the conditions for the reduction of fighting men in Deut. 20:5-8, especially for eliminating

---

[212] The criticism of "Israelites" for failing to show loyalty to the house of Jerubbaal (cf. the inclusio in 8:35 [cf. 8:33] and 9:22, which frames the exposition of Plots B and C in 9:1-22) must be taken as a criticism of those Israelite elements of the population who stood idly by, aware of the atrocities that had accompanied Abimelech's rise to power yet unmotivated to oppose the social injustice that had been committed against the house of Jerubbaal. The fact that God himself had to undertake this vindication in 9:25-54 is itself a pathetic comment upon the state of Israelite sensitivity to the requirements of covenant (social) justice in those days.

men by reason of fear (cf. Deut. 20:1, 3, 8). By this selection, based upon inner fortitude, thirty-two thousand troops were reduced to ten thousand 'fearless' men. The second diminution (7:4-8a) selects troops based upon their manner of drinking from the spring water (cf. 7:1). The simile "as a dog laps" (7:5b), viewed with other biblical canine imagery, might bear a negative connotation against those who lapped, though perhaps they could otherwise be commended for refusing to use their hands except to hold their weapons.[213] Regardless of the meaning of this characterization, it is clear that the diminution of troops redounds to the glorification of YHWH, who saves by the few.

It is further to glorify God that he is explicitly credited in 9:23-24 with initiating the dual outcome of Jotham's curse that Abimelech and Shechem should facilitate each other's downfall.[214] It is God who, by a control of circumstances that parallel those leading to Jael's triumph over Sisera, lets the fire consume the cult place of the citizens of Shechem, thus bringing the evil of the Shechemites on their heads (9:57), and it is God who brings the millstone to crush Abimelech's head (9:53, 56).[215] As in the Deborah/Barak/Jael account, plot resolution comes by means of a woman. Thus, in the Gideon/Abimelech account, YHWH's glorification through his control of circumstances is

---

[213] See the discussion in the appendix.

[214] Noting the repetitions of אבימלך and בעלי שכם and the chiastic parallelism in 9:24abαβ^i, the following pattern emerges in 9:23-24:

A	וישלח אלהים רוח רעה בין אבימלך
B	ובין בעלי שכם
B^i	ויבגדו בעלי־שכם
A^i	באבימלך
Axis: a	לבוא
b	חמס שבעים בני־ירבעל
b^i	ודמם
a^i	לשום
A^{ii}	על־אבימלך אחיהם
	אשר הרג אותם
B^{ii}	ועל בעלי שכם
	אשר־חזקו את־ידיו
	להרג את־אחיו:

This pattern shows a clear emphasis upon the control of circumstances by God (in the relation of וישלח to the infs. לבוא and לשום, expressing purpose, result or adverbial means) and a focal concern to show that the enmity that God engineered between Abimelech and the citizens of Shechem (A–B–B^i–A^i) was to compensate an injustice (Axis: b–b^i) by bringing the same (Axis: a–b–b^i–a^i) against its perpetrators (A^{ii}–B^{ii}). Note below the corresponding themes and poetic structure at 9:56-57.

[215] Cf. Blenkinsopp, "Ballad Style" (1961), p. 64 n. 4.

built not so much upon temporal ordering, as in the Ehud and Deborah/ Barak/Jael accounts, as upon his control of outcomes, both of the battle with Midian (using only 300 men) and of Jotham's curse (where Jotham stands alone).[216]

Another means of glorifying YHWH is via his characterization. In the Gideon account, YHWH is shown to be exceedingly gracious and patient toward both parties whom he attempts to persuade to become cultically loyal to him, namely, Israel and Gideon.[217] This grace appears also in the sequel of Judges 9, where, as proof of his loyal love toward Israel, YHWH himself removes foreign lords and cultists from Israel by letting them suffer the effects of their own evil.

Perhaps a further glorification of YHWH in the Gideon/Abimelech account, as in the Deborah/Barak/Jael account, derives from formal ordering. The death of Gideon marks a change of character focus among the plot-levels, a change that results in no human character being present throughout the entire account. By this means, YHWH is seen to be the only constant deliverer of Israel.

S. R. Driver once commented that some narratives of Judges fail to illustrate the theory expounded in Judg. 2:11-19: "a lesson is indeed deduced from the history of Abimelech, 9:24, 56, 57, but not the lesson of 2:11-19".[218] While it is clear that Judges 9 preserves an earlier tradition, which pre-existed Judges' compilation/redaction, one may fairly ask whether the preservation of such vestiges as one finds in 9:24, 56, 57 undercuts the rhetorical purpose of the framework of Judges' compiler/redactor.

In the Abimelech sequel to the Gideon story one encounters not an example of escalated parallelism between deliverer and tribe but a correspondence between covenant offence and divine recompense, which attests a principle of *lex talionis*. The social injustice of

---

[216] Contrast the use of pathetic fallacy in the night scenes of Judg. 6-9 that, as the night scene of Judg. 19, signal moments of negative characterization: hesitation and doubt, on the part of Gideon, and the foreshadowing of Abimelech's approach (note the shade/shadow motif in 9:15a, 36b; cf. 9:9bβ, 11bβ, 13bβ). Yet these characterizations also indirectly glorify YHWH in so far as they darken the portrayal of the human characters around him. Cf. Klein, *Triumph of Irony* (1988), pp. 58-60.

[217] While YHWH speaks to Israel through a prophet in 6:8-10, he speaks to Gideon by means of an angelic theophany, in 6:11-24, and by means of nocturnal visitations, in 6:25-26 and 7:9-11a (cf. 1 Sam. 3:1-15). Ironically, Gideon is the only deliverer to whom YHWH speaks by such visitations, yet it is not these but the ensuing signs that gradually allay his fears (cf. Klein, *Triumph of Irony* [1988], p. 50; Exum, "Centre" [1990], p. 416).

[218] S. R. Driver, *An Introduction to the Literature of the Old Testament* (ITL 1, Edinburgh, 9th edn, 1913), p. 166.

Abimelech's cultlike slaughter of Gideon's seventy sons upon a single
stone is recompensed when an upper millstone falls from the hand of a
woman (an anonymous agent of YHWH) to humiliate Abimelech by
cracking his skull (9:53).[219] Moreover, lest there be any doubt that this
was the narrator's primary concern in including this episode with the
Gideon story, the interpretation of its outcome as divinely ordered is
made explicit in the final evaluation of 9:56-57.[220] As a device for
heightening the sense of *lex talionis*, note also the strategic positioning
of ויגדו ליותם (9:7aα), ויגדו לאבימלך (9:42b) and ויגד לאבימלך
(9:47a).[221] From a rhetorical standpoint, however, it would hardly be
proper to interpret the account of Abimelech separately from its expositional moorings in the account of Gideon (Plots B and C). Its very
purpose is to show how YHWH himself had to resolve two complications that, as an aftermath of Gideon's two corresponding covenant
failings (i.e., his tolerance of cultic syncretism and his conjugation with
a Canaanite woman), show how personal foibles in a tribal leader could
escalate to cause a tribal crisis.

Thus, Driver's view that the Abimelech story goes astray from the
pattern set forth in 2:11-19 is founded, first, on a failure to perceive
how the Abimelech account was designed by the compiler/redactor of
Judges to be a development and resolution of complications introduced
in the Gideon story and, second, on a failure to realize what thematic
analogies there are elsewhere in Judges with the Abimelech story.

---

[219] Once again in Judges, a woman becomes YHWH's agent to exploit a character flaw
in the deliverer (e.g., Deborah and Jael vs. Barak; Jephthah's daughter vs. Jephthah) or to
bring about his downfall (e.g., Delilah vs. Samson).

[220] A chiasmus at 9:56-57 has been noted by both Boogaart, "Stone" (1985), p. 49,
and Eskhult, *Studies in Verbal Aspect* (1990), pp. 69-70, though allowance needs to be
made also for correspondence between the summaries of Abimelech's crime (9:56b) and
God's execution of Jotham's curse (9:57b), as follows:

> A   וישב אלהים (9:56aα)
> > B   את רעת אבימלך (9:56aβ)
> > Axis (crime): אשר עשה לאביו להרג את־שבעים אחיו (9:56b)
> > B^i   ואת כל־רעת אנשי שכם (9:57aαβ)
> A^i   השיב אלהים בראשם (9:57aγ)
> Summary (execution of curse): ותבא אליהם קללת יותם בן־ירבעל (9:57b)

This chiastic structure, whose content corresponds essentially to that of 9:23-24 (see
above), furnishes a nice poetic finish to the scheme of poetic justice that controls this
account.

[221] Cf. Alonso-Schökel, "Erzählkunst" (1961), p. 161.

Perhaps the main problem with Driver's view of Judges 9 is that he was attempting to assess its rhetorical coherence with the book of Judges on the basis of only 2:11-19, rather than on the basis of all the tribal-political and deuteronomic concerns set forth in Judges' double prologue. Thus, while it is true that the Abimelech story extends beyond the confines of the cycle-motif that frames the story of Gideon, the traces of the cycle-motif that frame the Abimelech story are sufficient to show that the latter was designed to be read as a necessary prolongation of the Gideon account—necessary so as to resolve complications introduced by Gideon's misdeeds. Further, it is the escalation of evils begun by the one who delivered Israel from Midian that foments a cultic and social chaos in the land so extensive that YHWH himself must restore order by retributive justice (9:23-24, 56-57). Thus, Judges 9, far from straying from the rhetorical concerns introduced in Judges' double prologue, actually demonstrates how exclusive devotion to YHWH is a necessary condition for the successful expulsion from the land of foreigners (be they Midianites from without or Canaanites from within).[222]

Among the developments in Judges that appear first in the Gideon/Abimelech account, one may list the following:

1. the nature of the oppression is given in detail (6:2b-6a);[223]
2. Israel's cry to YHWH meets with rebuke (6:8-10);[224]
3. the nation's apostasy is reported (perhaps proleptically) before the deliverer has died (8:27aγb);[225]
4. atrocities internal to Israel begin (with Gideon in 8:5-9, 13-17) and escalate (with Abimelech as a Canaanite versus Israelites in 9:1-5a; with internecine Canaanite atrocities in 9:25-49).[226]

Klein further suggested that in Gideon, for the first time in Judges, irony is invested in the character of the deliverer, though his is probably not the first negative characterization of a deliverer of Israel (cf. Barak and perhaps Ehud).[227] However, it should be observed that each of these new developments pertains to a more negative characterization of Israel or its deliverer than has previously occurred in Judges. As

---

[222] Cf. 6:12 with 6:13; cf. 7:2b with 6:36 and 7:18bγ, 20b; cf. 8:23 with 8:22b.
[223] Klein, *Triumph of Irony* (1988), p. 49.
[224] Webb, *Judges* (1987), p. 157.
[225] Webb, *Judges* (1987), pp. 157-58.
[226] Webb, *Judges* (1987), p. 158.
[227] Klein, *Triumph of Irony* (1988), p. 67.

such, it offers a foil to a greater glorification of YHWH than one has yet seen in Judges' deliverer accounts and shows to a greater degree how unmerited was YHWH's continuing beneficence toward Israel.

§5. *The Account of Jephthah (10:6–12:7)*

The plot-structure of the Jephthah account is more complex than that of the accounts of Deborah/Barak/Jael or Gideon/Abimelech, since it comprises not three but four plot-levels.[228] Yet, since, in the Jephthah story, Plots B, C and D extend beyond the resolution of the expositional crisis of Plot A, its overall contour resembles the plot-structure of the Gideon/Abimelech account. As further embellishment, the main plot of the Jephthah account presents a doubly bifurcated exposition (of the situation: 10:6-10, 15-16; and of character: 11:1-3, 5-11), a sporadically interrupted development (10:17; 11:4, 12-29, 32a) and a bifurcated resolution (of the situation: 11:32b-33; and of character: 12:7). This plot-level is interrupted by repeated complications (10:11-14, 18; 11:30-31) and two dissolutions of the situational equilibrium achieved by the resolution (11:34-36, 39a; 12:1-6). The following outline represents the plot-structure of Judg. 10:6–12:7 (with cycle-motif designations or letters enumerating repetition patterns in the left column, while broken horizontal lines mark scene changes):

Plot A: YHWH's deliverance of Israel from Ammon through Jephthah (10:6-10 [11-14] 15-17 [18]; 11:1-29 [30-31] 32-33 [34-36, 39a]; 12:[1-6] 7)

    Plot A Situation Exposition: (10:6-10)

A1a	Resumption of Israel's practice of evil (10:6aαβ)
A2a	They served the Baals and Ashtoreths, the gods of Aram, Sidon, Moab, the Ammonites, the Philistines (10:6aγ-ε)
A2b	They forsook YHWH and did not serve him (10:6b)
B1	YHWH's anger burned against Israel (10:7a)
B2b	He sold them into the hand of the Philistines and the Ammonites (10:7b)

---

[228] Although Webb began with a synopsis of the plot-structure of the Jephthah account ("The Theme of the Jephthah Story [Judges 10:6–12:7]", *RTR* 45 [1986], pp. 34-35; idem, *Judges* [1987], p. 42), he did not allow this initial concern with plot-structure to govern his analysis of the plot-levels of the story. Instead, he offered a division of the Jephthah account into successive "episodes", a strategy that is essentially that of the scenic principle (Webb, "Jephthah Story" [1986], pp. 35, 37, 38, 40, 41, 42; idem, *Judges* [1987], pp. 43, 53, 54, 55, 57, 58, 60, 63, 65, 67, 71, 69, 73-74, 75, 77, 222 nn. 3-4, 228 n. 62; cf. P. Trible, "The Daughter of Jephthah: An Inhuman Sacrifice", in *Texts of Terror: Literary and Feminist Readings of Biblical Narratives* [OBT 13, Philadelphia, 1984], pp. 93, 94, 96, 98, 99, 110 n. 5).

B3b	They crushed and oppressed the Israelites that year, for eighteen years— (10:8abα)
	all the Israelites who were beyond the Jordan in the land of the Amorite, who were in Gilead (10:8bβγ)
	The Ammonites crossed the Jordan to fight also against Judah, Benjamin and the house of Ephraim (10:9a)
B3b^{ii}	Israel was very distressed (10:9b)
C	Israel cried out to YHWH (10:10a)
(A2b)	We have sinned against you, for we have forsaken our god (10:10bαβ)
(A2a)	and served the Baals (10:10bγ)

Plot A Situation Complication: (10:11-14)

(D1?)	YHWH said to the Israelites: Did [I] not [save you] from Egypt, the Amorite, the Ammonites and the Philistines? (10:11)
(B3b^i)	The Sidonians, Amalek and Midian oppressed you (10:12a)
(C)	You cried out to me (10:12bα)
(D1)	I saved you from their hand (10:12bβ)
(A2b)	But you forsook me (10:13aα)
(A2a)	and served other gods (10:13aβ)
	Therefore I will not continue to save you (10:13b)
(C)	Go and cry out to the gods whom you have chosen (10:14a)
(D1)	Let them perform salvation for you (10:14b^i)
B3b^{ii}	in the time of your distress (10:14b^{ii})

Resumption of Plot A Situation Exposition: (10:15-16)

	The Israelites said to YHWH: We have sinned
A1b	Do to us whatever is good in your eyes (10:15aβγ)
	only deliver us this day (10:15b)
(A2a)	They removed the foreign gods from among them (10:16aα)
(A2b)	They served YHWH (10:16aβ)
(B3b^{ii}?)	His soul became exasperated with the hardship of Israel (10:16b)

—————————————————————————————

Plot A Development: (10:17)

	Ammonites are summoned and encamp at Gilead (10:17a)
	Israelites assemble themselves and encamp at Mizpah (10:17b)

Plot B: Consequences of Gilead's failure to uphold covenant loyalty
without ulterior tribe-centred motives and to refrain from covenant
(social) injustice—the oath to Jephthah (10:18; 11:1-3, 5-29 [30-31]
32-39a; 12:1-6)[229]

   Plot A Complication/Plot B Situation Exposition: The officials of
   Gilead propose: Whoever begins to fight against the Ammonites
   will be head of the Gileadites (10:18)

   Parenthesis: Plots A & B Character Exposition: (11:1-3)

             Jephthah the Gileadite was a valiant warrior
               (11:1a$\alpha\beta$)

             son of a prostitute (11:1aγ)

             sired by Gilead yet expelled from his father's
               house by the sons of Gilead's wife (11:1b-2)

             fled to the land of Tob, where reckless men
               gathered themselves to him and went out with
               him (11:3)

   Resumption of Plot A Development: After some days, the
   Ammonites fight with Israel (11:4)

— —

   Resumption of Plots A & B Character Exposition: Analogy to divine
   commission type-scene (11:5-11)

             As soon as the Ammonites fight with Israel, the
               elders of Gilead go to fetch Jephthah from the
               land of Tob (11:5)

             Elders' commission that Jephthah become
               Gilead's commander to fight against the
               Ammonites (11:6)

             Jephthah's objection: Did you not despise me and
               expel me from my father's house? Why have
               you come to me now (11:7abα)

B3b^{ii} as soon as it is distressing for you? (11:7bβ)

             Elders' reassurance: For this reason we have now
               returned to you; (if) you come with us and
               fight against the Ammonites, you will be head
               of the Gileadites (11:8)

             Jephthah's request for a confirming oath: If you
               are going to bring me back to fight against the
               Ammonites and YHWH gives them up before
               me, I alone shall be your head (11:9)

             Elders' oath: YHWH shall be witness between us
               if we do not act according to your terms
               (11:10)

— — — — — — — — — — — — — — — — — — — —

---

[229] While the Jephthah story does not directly mention the covenant, it seems fair to
refer to Gilead's tribe-centredness in terms of cession from covenant obligations, since
Judges' cycle-motif, which forms the framework of this account, makes use of (and,
hence, allusion to) some form of the deuteronomic covenant.

Jephthah returns with the elders (11:11aα)
Gileadites install Jephthah as commander and
provisional head (11:11aβ)
Jephthah states all his terms before YHWH at
Mizpah (11:11b)

- -

Plots A & B Development: (11:12-29)
A Jephthah sends messengers to the king of the
   Ammonites with a disputation (11:12)
   Accusation: Rhetorical question (11:12b)

- -

B Ammonite king's disputation:
   Accusation: Declaration of violations:
    Israel took his land when they came
    up from Egypt (11:13aβ)
    from the Arnon to the Jabbok and to
    the Jordan (11:13aγ)
   Ultimatum: Appeal: Condition of repara- ועתה
   tion: demand of land's return (11:13b)

- -

Aⁱ Jephthah again sends messengers to the king of
   the Ammonites with a disputation (11:14-27):
   Formulaic speech tag (11:15aβ)
   Exoneration of the accused (verbatim denial of
   Ammonite king's claim to the land [contra
   11:13aβ]): Israel took neither the land of
   Moab nor of the Ammonites, but when
   they came up from Egypt, ... (11:15b-16a)
   Exoneration of the accused (substantiation of
   denial): Rehearsal of Israel's conquest of
   the disputed land (11:16b-21aⁱ)
    Israel went through the wilderness to the
    Sea of Reeds and arrived at Kadesh
    (11:16b)
aa   Israel sent messengers to the king of
    Edom requesting safe passage
    (11:17aα)
bb   Edom's king did not listen (11:17aβ)
aaⁱ   Israel sent messengers to the king of
    Moab (11:17aγⁱ)
bbⁱ   Moab's king was unwilling (11:17aγⁱⁱ)
    Israel remained at Kadesh (11:17b)
    Israel circumvented Moab and encamped
    beyond the Arnon without entering
    Moab (11:18)

aa^{ii}	Israel sent messengers to Sihon, king of the Amorites at Heshbon, requesting safe passage (11:19)
bb^{ii}	Sihon's refusal (11:20aα)
	Sihon gathered all his people, encamped at Jahaz and fought with Israel (11:20aβγb)
E2	YHWH, god of Israel, gave Sihon and all his people into the hand of Israel (11:21a^i)

Exoneration of the accused (verbatim denial of Ammonite king's claim to the land [contra 11:13aγ]): Israel struck and dispossessed all the land of the Amorite, from the Arnon to the Jabbok and from the wilderness to the Jordan (11:21a^{ii}b-22)

Counteraccusation: Rhetorical question   ועתה
(appealing to divine right of conquest): YHWH, god of Israel, dispossessed the Amorite before his people Israel, but would you dispossess him? (11:23)

Exoneration of the accused: Right to vindication: Trial by combat (contra 11:13b): Will you not possess what Chemosh dispossesses and we [not] possess what YHWH dispossesses? (11:24)

Counteraccusation: Rhetorical question   ועתה
(appealing to historical precedent): Are you indeed better than Balak son of Zippor, king of Moab? Did he ever dispute with Israel or fight with them? While Israel dwelt for 300 years at Heshbon, Aroer and their environs and in all the cities along the Arnon—why did you not recover them during that time? (11:25-26)

Counteraccusation: Declaration of culpability: It is not I sinning against you but you committing wrong against me by fighting against me (11:27a)

Counterultimatum: Threat (appealing for divine judgement): May judge YHWH judge today between Israel and the Ammonites (11:27b)

— — — — — — — — — — — — — — — — —

B^i Ammonites' king does not listen to the words that Jephthah sent to him (11:28)

— — — — — — — — — — — — — — — — —

D2a   The spirit of YHWH came upon Jephthah
(11:29aα)

He passes through Gilead and Manasseh, passes
by Mizpah of Gilead and passes from Mizpah
of Gilead to the Ammonites (11:29aβb)

Plot C: Consequences of the failure of Jephthah to uphold covenant
loyalty without ulterior motives and of his adoption of foreign cultic
practice—the vow to YHWH (11:30-36 [37-38] 39-40)

   Plots A & B Character Complication/Plot C Exposition: (11:30-31)
           Jephthah vows a vow to YHWH: (11:30a)

E2   If you shall actually give the Ammonites into my
hand (11:30b)

whoever comes forth from the doors of my house
to meet me when I return in peace from the
Ammonites will belong to YHWH, and I shall
offer that one up as a burnt offering (11:31)

Plots A, B & C Development: Jephthah crosses over to the
Ammonites to fight against them (11:32a)

Plot A Situation Resolution/Plots B & C Development: (11:32b-33)

E2   YHWH gave them into his hand (11:32b)

He struck them from Aroer until one comes to
Minnith, twenty cities, as far as Abel
Keramim—a very great onslaught (11:33a)

E1   The Ammonites were humbled before the
Israelites (11:33b)

---

*Plot A Situation Dissolution/Plot B Resolution (implicit)/
Plot C Development:* (11:34-36)

           Jephthah comes to Mizpah to his house
(11:34aα)

cc   His daughter comes forth to meet him   והנה
with timbrels and dancing (11:34aβ)

Now she was his only [daughter], he had neither
son nor daughter besides [her] (11:34b)

dd   When he sees her, he rends his robe, bewails his
degradation and identifies her as his calamity
(11:35a)

He complains that he has opened his mouth to
YHWH and cannot go back (11:35b)

ee   She concedes that, since her father has opened
his mouth to YHWH, he should do to her what
went forth from his mouth—now that YHWH
has done vengeance on his [Jephthah's]
enemies, the Ammonites (11:36)

Plot B Resolution (implicit)/Plot C Complication: (11:37-38)

1/ee	She requests of her father that this thing be done for her: Let go of me for two months that I may go < > upon the mountains and bewail my virginity, I and my companions (11:37)
1/dd	He says: Go; and sends her for two months (11:38a)

1/cc	She goes, she and her companions, and bewails her virginity upon the mountains (11:38b)

Plot A Situation Dissolution/Plot B Resolution (implicit)/
Plot C Resolution: At the end of two months, she returns to her
 father, and he performs on her the vow that he had vowed
 (11:39a)

Prolongation of Plot C Resolution: (11:39b-40)

 She never knew a man (11:39bα)

 She became a tradition in Israel: year by year the
 daughters of Israel would go to commemorate
 the daughter of Jephthah the Gileadite, four
 days a year (11:39bβ-40)

Plot D: Consequences of Ephraim's failure to uphold covenant loyalty
 without ulterior motives and to refrain from covenant (social)
 injustice (12:1-6)

Plot A Situation Dissolution/Plot B Resolution (implicit)/
Plot D Exposition: (12:1-3)

(C)	The men of Ephraim were summoned (12:1aα) and crossed over to Zaphon (12:1aβ)
	Accusation: Rhetorical interrogation: Ephraimites dispute being excluded from the military rally (12:1bαβ)
	Ultimatum: Threat: Ephraimites threaten to burn Jephthah's house upon him (12:1bγδ)
	Exoneration of the accused: (12:2-3a)
	Jephthah remonstrates: I was a man [engaged] in a great dispute, I and my people, with the Ammonites (12:2a)
(C)	I had summoned you (12:2bα)
(D1)	but you did not save me from their hand (12:2bβ)
(D1)	I saw that you were not a saviour (12:3aα) I took my life in my [own] hand and crossed over to the Ammonites (12:3aβ)
E2	YHWH gave them into my hand (12:3aγ)

> *Counteraccusation: Rhetorical question:* Now
> why have you come up against me today to
> fight with me? (12:3b)

_ _

Plot A Situation Dissolution/Plot B Resolution (implicit)/
Plot D Development: Jephthah collects all the men of Gilead and
    fights with Ephraim (12:4a)
Plot A Situation Dissolution/Plot B Resolution (implicit,/
Plot D Resolution: (12:4b*-6)

> The men of Gilead strike Ephraim because they
> had said: *[Ultimatum: Threat:]* You are fugi-
> tives of Ephraim, O Gilead, within Ephraim
> < > (12:4b*)
> Gilead captured the fords of the Jordan for
> Ephraim (12:5a)
> Whenever the fugitives of Ephraim would say,
> "Let me cross", the men of Gilead would say
> to him, "Are you an Ephrathite?" and he
> would say, "No" (12:5b)
> Then they would say to him, "Say,
> 'Shibboleth'", and he would say, "Sibboleth",
> but would not pronounce [it] correctly. Then
> they would seize him and slay him at the fords
> of the Jordan. And that day forty-two thou-
> sand fell from Ephraim (12:6)

Plot A Character Resolution: (12:7)

F1	Jephthah judged Israel six years (12:7a)
G1	Jephthah the Gileadite died (12:7b$\alpha\beta$)
G2	and was buried in his city, < Mizpah > of Gilead (12:7bγ)

Of all the deliverer accounts in Judges, that of Jephthah is the most replete with cycle-motif elements.[230] Within it, all twelve essential elements of the cycle-motif are attested (and at least fifteen of its twenty distinguishable elements). Recurrences of these motif elements make up the two phases of the situation exposition (10:6-10, 15-16), an intervening complication (10:11-14), the situation's initial resolution (11:32b-33), the dissolution of that resolution (12:1-3) and the plot's final character resolution (12:7).

Plot A is the main plot of the account. It traces YHWH's deliverance of Israel from Ammon through the agency of Jephthah (10:6-10 [11-14] 15-17 [18]; 11:1-29 [30-31] 32-33 [34-36, 39a]; 12:[1-6] 7). The

---

[230] This observation runs counter to the claim of J. C. Exum that the cyclical framework of Judges increasingly breaks down as the accounts progress ("Centre" [1990], pp. 411-12).

exposition of this plot (10:6–11:4) seems to preserve two strata of composition: one stratum representing the compiler/redactor's deuteronomic contextualization of the traditional Jephthah account (10:6-7a[b], 8abα[βγ], 9[a]b-16); the other, those elements that preserve the traditional exposition of the account (10:[7b], [8bβγ], [9a], 17–11:3).[231]

The Plot A situation exposition (10:6-10) is a well-defined rhetorical unit, containing motif elements from only the alienation phase of Judges' cycle-motif. After the usual opening motif (A1a), this situation exposition is chiastically framed by repetitions of motifs A2a and A2b:

A2a   (10:6aγ-ε) ויעבדו את־הבעלים ... ואת־אלהי ...
  A2b   (10:6b) ויעזבו את־יהוה

    ...
  (A2b)   (10:10bβ) עזבנו את־אלהינו
  (A2a)   (10:10bγ) ונעבד את־הבעלים

The complication of 10:11-14 is a surprise, since the expected D1 element, which until now has heralded the restoration phase of the cycle-motif, portrays YHWH chiding Israel for presuming that YHWH should restore a nation so repeatedly given to idolatry. The surprise effected on the characters registers also on the reader in that, by now, the reader too may have come to expect that deliverance should follow repentance. YHWH's rebuke thus foreshadows and sets the rhetorical agenda for the Jephthah account, which displays the ironic consequences for Jephthah and the nation of trying mechanistically to manipulate the divine will to serve some private end. It is valuable to notice that YHWH's rebuke in 10:11-14 is made up entirely of phraseology adapted from Judges' cycle-motif, with the exception of his threat in 10:13b (לכן לא־אוסיף להושיע אתכם). Although YHWH's refusal to rescue Israel in 10:13b is not to be taken literally in the context of the Jephthah account, the fact that this exposition (10:6-16) also anticipates the Philistine crisis of the Samson account (cf. 10:7) suggests that it was not merely a rhetorical threat on the part of YHWH.[232]

Following the complication of 10:11-14, the situation exposition resumes in 10:15-16 and shows how Israel put away their idols as a

---

[231] This delineation implies that Amit is incorrect in saying, "the mentioning of the tribal origin of the judge in the exposition stage occurs only in the Samson story (Judg 13:2)" ("Ehud" [1989], p. 106 n. 5). The exposition must include 11:1-3, since the main character, Jephthah the Gileadite, is not introduced until these verses where, in fact, the very legitimacy of his tribal heritage is the point at issue.

[232] The Judges compiler/redactor may have deliberately placed here, in this penultimate deliverer account, YHWH's threat never again to deliver Israel only to make good this threat in the following Samson account, which is the first deliverer account in Judges to lack a statement of Israel's deliverance from their oppressors.

gesture of repentance.[233] With the change of YHWH's disposition toward Israel in 10:16b, one expects that YHWH will at last summon a deliverer. It is important to note not only that elements of or allusions to the cycle-motif are prevalent in the bifid exposition of the situation (10:6-10, 15-16) and in its complication (10:11-14) but that, in the bifid exposition of Jephthah as the main character (11:1-3, 5-11), the cycle-motif is virtually absent (except for B3b[ii] in 11:7b). In other ways, too, Jephthah's emergence as a deliverer is unorthodox.

In the story world, the action of the Plot A development begins simultaneously with that of the Plot A character exposition. The enemy nations pitch camp against each other (10:17)—a development that furnishes the situation for the first plot complication, when the officials of Gilead make the ill-considered oath of 10:18 (Plot B). The main character, Jephthah, is introduced first through a parenthetical flashback (11:1-3),[234] then through a call narrative (11:5-11).[235] These two phases of Jephthah's character exposition are interrupted by a resumption of the Plot A development in 11:4 (cf. 10:17). The resulting pattern of interchange—namely, development (10:17), character exposition (11:1-3), development (11:4), character exposition (11:5-11)—shows under what duress the elders appointed Jephthah their leader. Perhaps from this it is apparent why it is not said of Jephthah that it was YHWH who raised him up to deliver Israel (motif D1). Indeed, its absence reinforces how ill-advised was their oath in 10:18 (the exposition of Plot B) to appoint "whomever" to head their tribe.

As Plot A develops through the portrayal of a disputation in 11:12-29, the reader encounters element E2 of the cycle-motif in the recount of YHWH's giving Sihon into the hand of Israel (11:21a[i]). While this use of the idiom does not describe actions at the level of Plot A, it is Jephthah's concern with the theme of motif E2 that forms the condition for his vow in 11:30.[236] How incriminating for Jephthah's

---

[233] The antithetical correspondence between 10:6aγ-b (ויעזבו ... את־הבעלים) (ויסירו את־אלהי הנכר מקרבם ויעבדו את־יהוה) 10:16a and (את־יהוה ולא עבדוהו) constitutes a framing inclusio that encloses the exposition of 10:6-16 (cf. Webb, *Judges* [1987], p. 42).

[234] Notice the disjunctive *waw* of ויפתח in 11:1 (cf. Webb, *Judges* [1987], p. 50).

[235] The call narrative here (11:5-11) has a form and function (i.e., character exposition) similar to that of the divine commission scene of the Gideon account (6:11-24)—a similarity that suggests that at least one of these scenes may be an innovation of the Judges compiler/redactor.

[236] While it is customary to regard the vow as rash (Klein, *Triumph of Irony* [1988], p. 95) or hastily worded (Boling, *Judges* [1975], pp. 207, 210), it seems better to view it as befitting Jephthah's calculating characterization, an attempt to manipulate the circumstances to his own advantage (Soggin, *Judges* [2d edn, 1987], pp. 215-16; Webb, *Judges*

characterization that, immediately upon his affirmation of YHWH's right to the spoils of victory (11:12-27) and the narrator's comment that the spirit of YHWH came upon Jephthah (11:29aα), Jephthah disrupts the development of Plot A by vowing to perform a human sacrifice if YHWH should give the Ammonites into his hand (Plot C exposition, 11:30-31).[237] Thus, ironically, when Plot A resumes in 11:32a then resolves in 11:32b-33, the act of YHWH's giving the Ammonites into Jephthah's hand (11:32b) implies one thing for Israel and something different for Jephthah. For Israel, it means salvation (i.e., the resolution of the problem of Ammonite oppression in Plot A—note the phraseology of motif E1 in 11:33b); for Jephthah, it means that he must fulfil the macabre obligation of his self-imposed vow. Here is the vexing antinomy introduced into the plot-structure by Jephthah's vow: is Gilead truly saved from foreign oppression when salvation comes at the expense of making a foreign-style sacrifice of one of its number? Ironically, the performance of Jephthah's vow in 11:34-36, 39a, in the aftermath of the resolution of Plot A, only dissolves the situational stability that would have resulted had Jephthah not made the vow. The vow turns Jephthah from a deliverer of Israel into but another oppressor. Jephthah is further negatively characterized through the introduction of another subplot (Plot D, 12:1-6), which further dissolves the situational stability brought about by the resolution of Plot A. Only after Jephthah has catalysed this twofold situational destabilization (at the level of Plot A) is his characterization brought to a close with the final elements of the cycle-motif (F1 in 12:7a; G1 in 12:7bαβ; G2 in 12:7bγ).

[1987], pp. 64, 227 n. 54). Ironically, this shrewd attempt to manipulate YHWH demonstrates both folly and faithlessness in the character Jephthah (Trible, *Terror* [1984], pp. 102, 104, 106, 108).

[237] While the language of 11:31b (והיה ליהוה והעליתהו עולה) would normally refer to animal sacrifice, the description of 11:31a, היוצא אשר יצא מדלתי ביתי לקראתי בשובי בשלום מבני עמון, seems to envision someone welcoming the victor upon his return from battle. In support of the view that the vow intended human sacrifice, see 2 Kgs 3:26-27; Moore, *Judges* (1895), p. 299; Burney, *Judges* (2d edn, 1920), pp. 319-20; Soggin, *Judges* (2d edn, 1987), pp. 215-18; Webb, *Judges* (1987), pp. 64, 227 nn. 51, 52; Klein, *Triumph of Irony* (1988), p. 91 (cf. 221 n. 13); contra those who infer that Jephthah intended to sacrifice an animal: H. W. Hertzberg, *Die Bücher Josua, Richter, Ruth: übersetzt und erklärt* (ATD 9, Göttingen, 1953), pp. 217-18; cf. Boling, *Judges* [1975], p. 208; and contra those who infer that the text is deliberately ambiguous: Boling, *Judges* [1975], pp. 208-9; D. Marcus, *Jephthah and His Vow* (Lubbock, Tex., 1986), pp. 11, 12, 18, 19, 26, 34, 35, 43, 50, 52-53, 54. Note the similarity of the vow formulae in Num. 21:2 and Judg. 11:30-31 (Marcus, *Jephthah* [1986], p. 20).

Plot B traces the consequences of Gilead's failure both to uphold covenant loyalty to YHWH without ulterior (tribe-centred) motives and to refrain from covenant (social) injustice (10:18; 11:1-3, 5-29 [30-31] 32-39a; 12:1-6). This subplot begins with the elders' oath to make a leader of "whoever" would rescue them (10:18) and with the character exposition that shows that it would be a disgruntled Jephthah who would serve in this role (11:1-3, 5-11). Plot B develops as Jephthah prepares to engage in battle with the king of Ammon (11:12-29), is disrupted by Jephthah's insertion of his private agenda (11:30-31), then resumes in the report of Jephthah's victory over the Ammonites (11:32-33). Plot B resolves only implicitly in 11:34-39 and 12:1-6, in the aftermath of Jephthah's victory over Ammon, but the outcome is that Gilead is left with Jephthah as their leader. Ironically, through YHWH allowing Jephthah to triumph, Gilead is granted a leader of their own choosing and character—one whose leadership puts private interests ahead of covenant loyalty to YHWH or concern for the welfare of others. Perhaps the narrator intended that the reader should see in this outcome YHWH's just judgement, for Gilead is thus repaid for their complicity in the sibling rivalry that forms the matrix of Jephthah's character exposition in 11:1-3, 5-11. Indeed, the two-phased outcome that proceeds from the resolution of Plot B, namely, Jephthah's slaughter of his daughter in 11:34-39a and the intertribal slaughter of 12:1-6, is but an escalation of the social injustice spawned by the earlier sibling rivalry that formed the exposition of Jephthah's character in 11:1-3, 5-11. This escalated parallel within Plot B (i.e., that sibling rivalry leads to intertribal rivalry) finds a complement in the escalated parallel between the outcomes of Plots C and B. Just as Jephthah's vow in Plot C leads ironically to a bloody end for Jephthah's own family (11:39-40), so his confirmation as leader according to the elders' vow in Plot B leads to the bloodshed that results from Jephthah's similar pattern of decision making (12:1-6).

Plot C is the subplot that follows the consequences of Jephthah's attempt to manipulate YHWH through the pretext of a vow to perform for him a foreign (nondeuteronomic) cultic rite of human sacrifice (11:30-36 [37-38] 39-40). The vow is promised on the condition that YHWH should grant Jephthah success in battle. Since Jephthah's initial installation as head and commander of Gilead (11:11) was probably provisional, Jephthah would have been concerned to ensure that his appointment not be revoked through his failure to defeat Ammon. This fear motivated his offering to YHWH an extra incentive in 11:30-31 so

as to guarantee victory. The description of this vow begins as did that
in 11:11b (... וידבר יפתח), but here it initiates a new plot-level (Plot C).
The fact that, on the level of Plot A, the reader already knows that
YHWH would have given Jephthah success in battle even without his
vow makes the vow and its negative consequences seem all the more
unnecessary. Hence, it is not without rhetorical warrant that Jephthah's
vow is introduced in 11:30-31 as an interruption in the development of
Plot A toward its resolution.[238] Viewed in this way, the vow achieves
nothing in the story except to mar the accomplishment of YHWH's victory and to characterize Jephthah negatively. It is a callous gesture that
shows Jephthah willing to brutalize even his closest of kin to rule over
a tribe of halfbrothers—a motive not unlike that of Abimelech. Whether
Jephthah anticipated that his daughter would be the victim is perhaps
not essential to his negative characterization. Jephthah swore by a
human life, and that life turned out to be that of his only daughter.[239]
Despite the pathos generated by the reluctance of both daughter and
father to carry out the vow (11:37-38), both eventually submit to it.[240]

---

[238] Webb has observed that the vow of 11:30-31 is marked as an interruption in that it
comes between the final words of 11:29bβγ (וממצפה גלעד עבר בני עמון) and their resumptive repetition in 11:32a (ויעבר יפתח אל־בני עמון להלחם בם) (*Judges* [1987], p. 62).

[239] Perhaps it is the pathetic force of Judg. 11:34b (ורק היא יחידה אין־לו ממנו בן
או־בת), with its use of יחידה in the context of a father sacrificing his only child, that
prompts the allusion to יחיד in Gen. 22:2 and the wider context of Abraham sacrificing
Isaac (cf. Trible, *Terror* [1984], pp. 101, 102, 105, 113 n. 34; Webb, *Judges* [1987],
pp. 68, 228 n. 59; Klein, *Triumph of Irony* [1988], pp. 91, 92, 95, 98, 222-23 n. 18).
Further, both contexts refer to human sacrifice using the same expression: והעלהו...לעולה
in God's command, Gen. 22:2; and והעליתהו עולה in Jephthah's vow, Judg. 11:31bβ.
Yet, the similarity of theme and the collocation alone are probably insufficient to establish
a narrative analogy between Gen. 22 and Judg. 11 (contra E. Leach, *Genesis as Myth and
Other Essays* [London, 1969], pp. 37-38; endorsed by Marcus, *Jephthah* [1986], pp. 38-
40). The allusion merely evokes a contrast between the comic resolution of the situation in
Gen. 22, where YHWH intervenes to save the child, and the pathetic dissolution in Judg.
11, where YHWH is solemnly silent while an outrage is performed in his honour.
Note also the connection suggested between Jacob's vow in Gen. 31:45-54 and
Jephthah's vow in Judg. 11:30-31, between which there is a collocation of the locale
Mizpah of Gilead (Gen. 31:47-50), concern for daughters (Gen. 31:43, 50), an oath
before God (Gen. 31:53) and a sacrifice to ratify the oath (Gen. 31:54) (cf. F. Landy,
"Gilead and the Fatal Word", in *Proceedings of the Ninth World Congress of Jewish
Studies, Jerusalem, August 4-12, 1985: Division A, The Period of the Bible* [Jerusalem,
1986], pp. 39-44). Further, on the ground that the Gileadites' question, האפרתי אתה
(12:5bβ), "could mean 'Are you from Ephratha?'", it is a question that may evoke a connection to the mention of Ephrath, where Rachel was buried, in Gen. 35:16-20.

[240] As evidence of the pathetic reluctance of father and daughter, note how each element of 11:34-36 is temporarily reversed in the complication of 11:37-38 (cc [11:34aβ-b]
vs. 1/cc [11:38b]; dd [11:35] vs. 1/dd [11:38a]; ee [11:36] vs. 1/ee [11:37]). Cf. Trible,
Terror (1984), pp. 98-99.

By one act Jephthah's obligation to his vow is fulfilled and Plot C resolved (11:39a), though, ironically, in sacrificing his daughter, Jephthah extinguishes his own posterity.[241] Strategically, the narrator allows the pathos of this situation to linger, in a prolongation of the resolution, by making this point explicit in 11:39bα, והיא לא־ידעה איש, and by saying that she became memorialized in Israel (11:39bβ-40).[242]

Plot D outlines the consequences of Ephraim's failure both to uphold covenant loyalty without ulterior motives and to refrain from covenant (social) injustice (12:1-6). The accusation and threat of the Ephraimites against Jephthah (12:1b) seems to be borrowed from the milieu of covenant disputation and has the same rhetorical effect as the earlier threat of the king of Ammon (11:13). It is as though, having delivered Gilead from the external threat of the Ammonite king, Jephthah is now faced with an internal threat to the intertribal unity of Israel. However, unlike Gideon in a similar situation (8:1-3), Jephthah is concerned only to exonerate himself (12:2-3a) and again instigates bloodshed in response to a threat against his authority (12:3b). The ensuing slaughter of Ephraim (12:4-6) turns out to be a situation as bad or worse for Israel than that with which the account opened (cf. 10:6-16). It is only after Jephthah reintroduces a situation of instability into Israel that the narrator brings to a close the account of this deliverer (12:7).

According to the principles of plot-structure, the climax of the main plot (Plot A) occurs in 11:32-33, where the expositional problem achieves resolution.[243] Between occurrences of motifs E2 (11:32b) and E1 (11:33b), the narrator gives details of the locale and extent of the onslaught (11:33a): ויכם מערוער ועד־בואך מנית עשרים עיר ועד אבל כרמים מכה גדולה מאד. It is the combination of the summarization in 11:33a with the virtually redundant statements of E2 and E1 that frame it that retards the narrative pace sufficiently to indicate that 11:32-33 describes a moment of dramatic significance in the plot-structure.[244] In

---

[241] Plot C is ostensibly framed between references to the vow in 11:30a (וידר יפתח נדר) and 11:39aγδ (ויעש לה את־נדרו אשר נדר) that use the same cognate accusative expression (cf. Webb, *Judges* [1987], pp. 62-63, 68).

[242] The expression, ותהי־חק בישראל (11:39bβ), seems to convey the idea that Jephthah's daughter became a symbol (i.e., the basis for a custom) in Israel. Cf. the rendering of MT חק by Syr. 'ṯ' 'sign, symbol, standard, pledge, token' in the Psht; Marcus, *Jephthah* (1986), p. 34; Webb, *Judges* (1987), pp. 68, 228-29 n. 63.

[243] Webb regards 11:32a as the climax and 11:33 as the resolution (*Judges* [1987], pp. 42, 60). However, the effect of stating that YHWH gave them into his hand (11:32b) is as resolving to the plot tension as are the two following statements (11:33a, 33b).

[244] It is worthy of note that this is the only account in Judges to use both the E1 and E2 motifs. Cf. the use of the E1 motif elsewhere in this account in 11:21a, 30b; 12:3aγ.

this climactic moment (several hours in the story world) the
expositional problem of Plot A is resolved. But, as in the Gideon/
Abimelech account, the outworking of two subplots (Plots B and C)
extends well beyond the resolution of the situational problem of the
main plot. Moreover, still another complication or subplot (Plot D)
remains to be introduced before the characterization of Jephthah
undergoes closure (12:7). Nowhere is the narrator's rhetorical strategy
in the Jephthah account more evident than in the undercutting of the
situational resolution of Plot A through the events of Plots C and D.

Given the reader's knowledge that Jephthah's vow achieves nothing
toward his success against the Ammonites—knowledge to which
Jephthah was never privy—Jephthah's sacrifice of his daughter can
only be pathetic. It is the pathos of Jephthah's sense of obligation to
sacrifice his only daughter rather than break his unnecessary (indeed,
illegitimate) vow to YHWH that undercuts the reader's sense of relief
after the climax of Plot A. Indeed, the frustration achieved by Plot C is
more emotive than was the sense of climax in Plot A precisely because
it is so unnecessarily horrific.[245] The emotional tension of Plot C arises
first in the surprise for Jephthah (and the reader) that Jephthah's
daughter appears first: והנה בתו יצאת לקראתו (11:34aβ). These words
ironically echo Jephthah's description of the conditions that would
identify the sacrificial victim of his vow: והיה היוצא אשר יצא מדלתי
ביתי לקראתי (11:31aαβ).[246] Once again in Judges, the narrator uses הנה
to convey a sense of surprise on the part of a character—a sense related
to Jephthah's show of emotional recoil when he sees her (11:35a).[247]
Indeed, the narrator augments the pathos of Jephthah's response by
inserting between 11:34aβ and 11:35a the information that she came
forth with timbrels and dancing (בתפים ובמחלות, 11:34aγ) and that she
was Jephthah's only child (ורק היא יחידה, 11:34b).[248] The pathos of the
Plot C development is augmented still further by delay: a subplot
complication is introduced by his daughter's request to go and bewail

---

[245] Cf. Webb, *Judges* (1987), pp. 68, 73.

[246] Cf. Webb, *Judges* (1987), p. 66.

[247] Note the cacophony and assonance among the five words in 11:35a that combine
ויהי כראותו אותה ויקרע את־בגדיו ויאמר אהה בתי הכרע הכרעתני ואת היית :ע/א and ר ,ק/כ
בעכרי. Webb notes especially the wordplay between הכרע הכרעתני and בעכרי (*Judges*
[1987], pp. 67, 227 nn. 55, 56).

[248] For the collocation of יצא, תפים and מחלות in other scenes where women celebrate
military victory, see Exod. 15:19-21; 1 Sam. 18:6-7 (cf. Trible, *Terror* [1984], p. 100).

her virginity (11:37-38).[249] In this request one learns that Jephthah's daughter was and would remain forever childless—more pathos. Indeed, while the resolution of Plot C is short and direct in 11:39a, the prolongation of that resolution in 11:39b-40 achieves nothing if not the generation of yet more pathos over the loss of her progeny and life.[250] So much tragic pathos in Plot C must overshadow the positive emotive effects of the climax and resolution of Plot A, and this hardly reflects positively upon Jephthah as a deliverer of his kinsfolk.[251]

The undermining of the climax and resolution of Plot A can be seen also in the rhetorical effects of Plot D (12:1-6). Here, however, it is not so much the pathos of the situation that achieves the dissolution as the irony that Jephthah now turns his disputational skills, first made evident in 11:12-27 against a foreign enemy, against a fellow tribe of Israel. Thus, whatever gain Jephthah achieved for Israel through his forensic humiliation of the king of Ammon he now undercuts by his application of the same force of rhetoric to destabilize the covenant unity of Gilead and Ephraim (12:1b-3). Given the compiler/redactor's arrangement of deliverer accounts, Jephthah's conduct seems the more reprehensible because it follows Gideon's exemplary avoidance of provoking Ephraim into an intertribal conflict (8:1-3).

The pattern of negative characterization in the Jephthah account is similar to that in previous deliverer accounts: there is an analogy between the deliverer and those delivered as to their foibles. In the Jephthah account, the chief foible highlighted by the rhetoric is that of Israel's utilitarian view of covenant devotion to YHWH. Three converging people groups are characterized as attempting mechanistically to manipulate YHWH in order to serve selfish ends: (1) the Israelites act out a form of repentance in 10:10 and 10:15-16a, the sincerity of which YHWH, in 10:11-14, calls into question; (2) the elders

---

[249] On the meaning of ואבכה על־בתולי (11:37, cf. 38b) vis-à-vis OG καὶ κλαύσομαι ἐπὶ τὰ παρθένιά μου, see K. H. Keukens, "Richter 11,37f: Rite de passage und Übersetzungsprobleme", BN 19 (1982), pp. 41-42.

[250] Besides the framing passages of Judg. 2:4-5 and 20:26; 21:2-4, this is the only situation in Judges where weeping (11:37b, 38b) and sacrifice (11:39; cf. 11:30-31) are closely associated.

[251] The presence of tragic pathos does not make of this episode a tragedy in the classical Greek or Shakespearian sense (contra Boling, Judges [1975], pp. 207, 210; Trible, Terror [1984], pp. 101, 107). See J. C. Exum, "The Tragic Vision and Biblical Narrative", in Signs and Wonders: Biblical Texts in Literary Focus (J. C. Exum [ed.], Decatur, Ga., 1989), pp. 59-83; W. L. Humphreys, "The Story of Jephthah and the Tragic Vision: A Response to J. Cheryl Exum", in ibid., pp. 85-96.

of Gilead, rather than calling upon YHWH for rescue (10:18), defer to
YHWH only when swearing an oath to seal a scheme of their own
devising (11:10); (3) Jephthah attempts to coerce YHWH, through a
vow of human sacrifice, to turn the means of Gilead's deliverance into
an opportunity for self-aggrandizement (11:30-31). All three lines of
attempted divine manipulation generate in the reader the conviction that
Israel's relapses into idolatry reflect their unwillingness to pursue
YHWH with a whole heart.[252]

Many infer that Israel's confession (10:10b) and their removal of
foreign gods (10:16aα) reflect the genuineness of this, the first explicit
instance of true repentance in the book.[253] However, the use of the
same words in YHWH's rebuke (10:12b-13a) indicates that "the putting
away of foreign gods is part of the routine with which he has become
all too familiar from previous experience".[254] YHWH's explicit com-
plaint in 10:12b-13a is not that Israel has failed in the past to remove
foreign gods but that, after every saving intervention, they again forsook YHWH and reverted to serving other gods. Thus, in this instance,
Israel is negatively characterized for attempting again to manipulate
YHWH only to serve their immediate needs (cf. 2:1-3; 6:7-10). The
ensuing portrayals of the elders of Gilead and of Jephthah illustrate
how they, too, are but converging microcosms: the elders of Gilead, a
microcosm of Israel; Jephthah, a microcosm of the elders of Gilead.[255]

---

[252] This negative characterization may reflect the narrator's concern to portray Israel's
failure in terms of the central requirement of the deuteronomic covenant: that they pursue
YHWH with all their heart (Deut. 6:4-5; 10:12-13; 11:13, 22-25; 13:1-4; 26:16; cf. the
exilic concern of 4:29; 30:2, 6, 10). It is perhaps not by chance, then, that the later
portrayal of David as the ideal king defines him deuteronomically as one whose heart was
after YHWH (1 Sam. 13:14; 16:7; cf. 10:9-10; 12:20, 24; 16:13-14; and the characterization of later kings in 1 Kgs 2:4; 3:6; 11:4; 14:8; 15:3-5; cf. the non-Davidic
deuteronomic evaluation of kings in 2 Kgs 10:31; 23:3, 25; and the exilic concern of
1 Kgs 8:48; 2 Kgs 22:19-20). It may be chiefly to this rhetorical end (i.e., the
deuteronomic idealization of David) that deliverers and tribes in Judges are negatively
characterized to substantiate the summary evaluation that they represented a time when
"there was no king in Israel" (17:6a; 18:1a; 19:1a; 21:25a) so that "everyone did what
was right in one's own eyes" (17:6b; 21:25b).

[253] E.g., W. Richter, *Die Bearbeitungen des 'Retterbuches' in der deuteronomischen
Epoche* (BBB 21, Bonn, 1964), p. 23; Boling, *Judges* (1975), p. 193; Exum, "Tragic
Vision" (1989), p. 63; idem, "Centre" (1990), p. 421; Humphreys, "Jephthah" (1989),
p. 94.

[254] Webb, *Judges* (1987), p. 46; cf. pp. 42, 43, 45-46, 48, 222 n. 7.

[255] It is significant that the use of בני ישראל in 10:17, referring to armed men of
Gilead, furnishes a transformation from the use of the same expression throughout 10:6-16
to designate all Israel (albeit as a synecdoche for a part, namely, Gilead). Cf. Webb,
Judges (1987), p. 49.

By comparison of the negative characterizations of Gilead's elders and Jephthah, one comes to see that Jephthah is but a microcosm of the elders of the tribe that he delivers. When the elders of Gilead are faced with imminent military defeat and the resultant loss of their social status, they make the offer: מִי הָאִישׁ אֲשֶׁר יָחֵל לְהִלָּחֵם בִּבְנֵי עַמּוֹן יִהְיֶה לְרֹאשׁ לְכֹל יֹשְׁבֵי גִלְעָד (10:18aβ-b). The phraseology of 10:18aβ-δ is reminiscent of situations of divine inquiry at the beginning and end of Judges, yet no one here calls upon YHWH for a decision about the battle, and no one remonstrates that the one chosen to be leader should be elected by YHWH (cf. Judg. 1:1-2; 20:18, 23, 26-28).[256] Moreover, it may have been further to characterize the elders as irreligious opportunists that they are portrayed in Jephthah's commissioning type-scene (11:5-11) in a role normally played by YHWH.[257] If so, then in the same way that the Gileadite elders are characterized by cultic lax-ness and a spirit of opportunism through their sudden volte-face toward Jephthah (cf. 11:1-3, 6-7), Jephthah, seeing his chance for promotion in Gilead, is likewise characterized as ready to perform an illegitimate cultic vow (11:30-31) to guarantee the military victory he needs to retain the status he has just acquired (11:9-11).[258] The error of Jephthah's vow, like the offer of the elders of Gilead, flows from a character flaw that puts personal ambition above familial loyalty and cultic decorum.[259] In Jephthah, the ambition to achieve status in Gilead, even to the point of sacrificing a family member to secure that ambi-tion, reflects a desperate need to compensate for his sense of public

---

[256] The situation in 10:18aβ-b adumbrates that in 21:5, 8, where the Israelites, dis-couraged by the devastating effects that come of inquiring of YHWH, opt to take counsel only amongst themselves.

[257] The elders initially offer that "whoever" can save them will become "head of all the inhabitants of Gilead" (יִהְיֶה לְרֹאשׁ לְכֹל יֹשְׁבֵי גִלְעָד, 10:18b). In 11:5-11, they make the full offer to Jephthah to become "head of all the inhabitants of Gilead" (וְהָיִיתָ לָּנוּ לְרֹאשׁ לְכֹל יֹשְׁבֵי גִלְעָד, 11:8b), but not before they make the lesser offer to make him "commander" (קָצִין, 11:6a; cf. Josh. 10:24). It is only Jephthah's intervening objection (11:7) that prompts them to raise the offer to its initial level. Indeed, it is their dickering that shows how unprincipled are these opportunists who seek to hire Jephthah's services for less than what they offered a full citizen of Gilead (10:18b). The commissioning type-scene closes with the inauguration of Jephthah as both "head" and "commander" (וַיָּשִׂימוּ הָעָם אוֹתוֹ עֲלֵיהֶם לְרֹאשׁ וּלְקָצִין, 11:11aβ). Cf. Boling, Judges (1975), p. 198; Webb, Judges (1987), pp. 52, 223 n. 23.

[258] Webb rightly infers from these verses that, "By invoking YHWH, ... [Jephthah] elevates victory to the status of divine endorsement" (Judges [1987], p. 52). Once he has so used YHWH's name to aggrandize himself, it is not difficult to see how he rationalizes even human sacrifice as a means to coerce YHWH into giving him his prerequisite victory.

[259] Cf. Webb, Judges (1987), p. 74.

humiliation.[260] But the just recompense of YHWH is carried out against both Jephthah and the elders of Gilead. The elders of Gilead get the leader they deserve, for, like them, he is a person who is willing to utilize "whomever" by whatever means in order to pursue a private agenda.

Not only is the characterization of the elders and Jephthah related as macrocosm to microcosm, the relationship between the effects of the vow of the elders (10:18) and those of the vow of Jephthah (11:30-31) is also one of reduction that leads, in reverse order, to the negative consequences of both vows in the escalating atrocities that end the account—another example of escalated parallelism in Judges.[261] The first element in the escalated parallel may be found in the portrayal of Jephthah, who, for political ambition and as compensation for his sense of public rejection on the basis of illegitimate lineage, makes a vow to perform for YHWH a human sacrifice.[262] Just as Jephthah's vow results in the injustice of the sacrifice of his daughter and his concomitant loss of an heir, so the Israelite league is brought to suffer the consequences of the behaviour of Gilead's leaders in the slaughter of the Ephraimites. Jephthah's slaughter of his daughter (11:39-40) parallels microcosmically Gilead's slaughter of its tribal 'brother' Ephraim (12:1-6). Note the latter's claim that Gilead (like Jephthah) was an illegitimate covenant member of Israel in comparison to Ephraim and Manasseh (12:4). Just as Jephthah through his word (11:30-31) wreaks havoc upon a daughter within his tribe, so Gilead by a word (שבלת/סבלת, 12:6) wreaks havoc upon a fellow tribe within Israel.[263] It should come

---

[260] Compare how the sudden change in Gideon's portrayal that follows his confrontation with Ephraim (8:1-3) seems similarly driven by the narrator's desire to show how violence may be the way that a spiritually flawed character compensates for his sense of inferiority (cf. 6:13, 15). In Jephthah's case, this sense of inferiority stems from his sense of having been victimized by past rejection. The irony is that what Jephthah perpetrates upon his daughter is more violent than the victimization that he had suffered from his brothers. Cf. Trible, *Terror* (1984), p. 96.

[261] Webb notes several instances in the Jephthah account of a "paralleling of situation" (*Judges* [1987], pp. 42, 53-54, 63, 77-78).

[262] That Jephthah counted the elders to have wronged him for their part in supporting his brothers' rejection (11:1-3) is evident from his objection in 11:7abα, but, because he is never said to have been reinstated to his expected birthright, perhaps all were thereafter bound by the finality of their legal decision. Notwithstanding, it would be naive to expect that "the provisions of the Lipit-Ishtar Code were known and in force in Israel at that time" (I. Mendelsohn, "The Disinheritance of Jephthah in the Light of Paragraph 27 of the Lipit-Ishtar Code", *IEJ* 4 [1954], p. 118).

[263] G. von Rad points to the irony of the use of שבלת/סבלת in 12:6 as a "completely empty word on which life and death were made to depend" (*Gottes Wirken in Israel* [Neukirchen–Vluyn, 1974], ET: *God at Work in Israel* [J. H. Marks (trans.), Nashville,

as no surprise that the "justice" wrought upon Ephraim by Gilead is as violent as that which Jephthah, their new ruler, had wrought upon his daughter. As often in Judges, the saviour's personal foibles ironically become the cause of salvation's undoing.

Because of the silence of YHWH after the exposition, the theme of the glorification of YHWH is far from explicit in the Jephthah account, but it may be inferred from a number of correlations in the story world.[264] YHWH becomes angry and sells Israel into the hands of the Philistines and Ammonites (10:7), rebukes Israel (10:11-14), then becomes exasperated with their hardship (10:16b, ותקצר נפשו בעמל ישראל).[265] No doubt, the narrator has juxtaposed the description of

---

1980], p. 41). In this one sees vividly a further escalated parallel between the effects of a misspoken word upon Jephthah's daughter and the Ephraimites. Cf. J. Marquart, "שִׁבֹּלֶת = ephraimitisch סִבֹּלֶת = שִׁבֹּלֶת?", ZAW 8 (1888), pp. 151-55; E. A. Speiser, "The Shibboleth Incident (Judges 12:6)", BASOR 85 (1942), pp. 10-13; reprinted in Oriental and Biblical Studies: Collected Writings of E. A. Speiser (J. J. Finkelstein and M. Greenberg [eds.], Philadelphia, 1967), pp. 143-50; R. Marcus, "The Word Šibboleth Again", BASOR 87 (1942), p. 39; F. Willesen, "The אפרתי of the Shibboleth Incident", VT 8 (1958), pp. 97-98; A. F. L. Beeston, "Hebrew šibbolet and šobel", JSS 24 (1979), pp. 175-77; H. N. Rösel, "The Literary and Geographical Facets of the Shibboleth Story in Judges 12:1-6", in Studies in the History of the Jewish People and the Land of Israel 5 (1980), pp. 33-41 [Hebrew]; P. Swiggers, "The Word šibbōlet in Jud. xii.6", JSS 26 (1981), pp. 205-7; J. A. Emerton, "Some Comments on the Shibboleth Incident (Judges xii 6)", in Mélanges bibliques et orientaux en l'honneur de M. Mathias Delcor (A. Caquot, S. Légasse and M. Tardieu [eds.], AOAT 215, Neukirchen-Vluyn, 1985), pp. 149-57; A. Lemaire, "L'incident de sibbolet (Jg 12,6): Perspective historique", in ibid., pp. 275-81; G. A. Rendsburg, "More on Hebrew Šibbōlet", JSS 33 (1986), pp. 255-58; A. F. L. Beeston, "Šibbōlet: A Further Comment", JSS 33 (1986), pp. 259-61.

[264] Webb interprets the silence of YHWH as a sign of his anger (Judges [1987], pp. 75, 230 n. 75; cf. Klein, Triumph of Irony [1988], p. 95). Exum infers that YHWH's silence is ambiguous and leaves the reader in doubt about his role ("Tragic Vision", [1989] pp. 68, 69, 78; cf. Trible, Terror [1984], pp. 97, 101, 102, 105, 107; Landy, "Gilead" [1986], pp. 41-42).

[265] The use of קצר with either נפש (Num. 21:4-5; Judg. 16:16; Zech. 11:8) or רוח (Job 21:4) as subject is idiomatic, expressing frustration or exasperation (cf. Moore, Judges [1895], p. 282; BDB, p. 894a). It is the idiom that bears this sense, not the verb קצר 'to be short' (contra Webb, Judges [1987], pp. 46-47). YHWH's exasperation is clearly "with/because of Israel's hardship" (בעמל ישראל). Some infer that Israel's hardship refers to their effort in repentance described in 10:16a (e.g., R. M. Polzin, Moses and the Deuteronomist: A Literary Study of the Deuteronomic History, part 1, Deuteronomy, Joshua, Judges [New York, 1980], p. 177; Klein, Triumph of Irony [1988], pp. 85, 220 n. 6). However, the view that their hardship is the ongoing situation of oppression described in 10:8-9 (so Webb, Judges [1987], p. 47) seems better warranted both from the pattern of the cycle-motif and from the function that situations of enemy oppression serve in Judges' deliverer accounts as presenting the crisis that generates the main plot. In the situational exposition of the Jephthah account, this is corroborated by the paronomastic correlation among forms of זעק/צעק after 10:8-9 whereby Israel's cry to YHWH (זעק in

YHWH's exasperation (10:16b) with details of the rally of Ammon for battle (10:17) in order to imply that it was YHWH who set up the circumstances for Jephthah's launch into the role of deliverer.[266] It is sheer desperation that moves the elders to make the open-ended offer that anyone who can save them may govern them (10:18), and it is their mounting sense of urgency (11:4) that drives them to tender the offer even to Jephthah (11:5), one whom they had previously made a social outcast (11:1-3). Yet here is also a recipe for poetic justice: the turn of circumstances results in the reinstatement of an outcast to the highest position in society. Is this Jephthah's vindication from YHWH for the social injustice he had earlier suffered from his halfbrothers? If so, the situation is ironic for the elders of Gilead (cf. the use of motif B3b[ii] in 11:7). YHWH's implicit control of circumstances accrues to his glory even more by the circumstance that, in the commission of Jephthah (11:5-11), it is the elders who are forced by desperation to play a role normally filled by YHWH when summoning a reluctant emissary to fulfil a mission to deliver Israel.[267] Perhaps one may infer that the elders actually presume to take upon themselves this role of YHWH, for, in contrast to Israel's contrition in 10:15, the elders of Gilead act in 10:18 and 11:5-11 without recourse to calling upon YHWH for help. YHWH is to the elders little more than a witness to their offer to Jephthah (11:10; cf. 11:11b). Thus, whatever their motivation or extent of devotion to YHWH, the elders are humbled by circumstances beyond their control (but within YHWH's) to reinstate Jephthah to full citizenship in Gilead, and more, to the position of leading citizen.

The reader will have little difficulty inferring that it was YHWH who controlled the outcome of the battle between Jephthah and the king of Ammon. Those who acknowledge YHWH's role in determining the outcome of the battle include the narrator (11:32b), Jephthah (11:9, 30b, 35b) and Jephthah's daughter (11:36). However, one must wonder

---

10:10a) leads, through YHWH's rebuke of such feigned cries of repentance (צעק in 10:12bα, זעק in 10:14a), to the circumstance that begins their deliverance in 10:17, namely, the Ammonites' summons to battle (the Ni. form of צעק).

[266] Webb suggested that YHWH's control of circumstances is implicit in the irony that, after the Israelites plead with YHWH, "Do to us what is good (הַטּוֹב) in your eyes" (10:15aβγ), YHWH arranges that their deliverer comes from the land of Tob (טוֹב, 11:3a)—ironically, the land to which his Gileadite halfbrothers had unjustly banished him (*Judges* [1987], pp. 50, 223 n. 19).

[267] The form of Judg. 11:5-11 is analogous to that of the divine commission type-scene (also termed a 'call narrative') used in Judg. 6:11-17 and Exod. 3:1-4:17. With God absent, however, Judg. 11:5-11 becomes only a parody of the divine commission type-scene. Cf. the discussion above on Judg. 6:11-17.

why YHWH does not intervene to prevent Jephthah from fulfilling his vow of human sacrifice by killing his only daughter and heiress. The narrator's silence on this point seems at first troubling. Yet, if the reader is supposed to follow the escalating pattern of negative characterization seen in Israel's deliverers to this point in Judges, he/she may infer that in this case Jephthah alone is the agent of violence against his daughter. The vow is not YHWH's doing but the nemesis of Jephthah's arrogance, in attempting to mould YHWH's victory to conform to his own ambition, brings Jephthah's line to an end (11:39bα) and this is an outcome related to YHWH's control of circumstances. Thus, ironically, through Jephthah's seeking to attain permanent social status in Gilead through an act of human sacrifice, the atrocity of that act, coupled with the fact that it is his inaugural act as Gilead's head, forever characterizes him as an agent of atrocity in Gilead (11:39bβ-40).

Perhaps it enhances the glorification of YHWH that Gilead, and later all Israel, comes to reap the consequences of ignoring YHWH's divine right of election. In the Jephthah account, the narrator's concern with YHWH's right to choose Israel's deliverer is made the more significant by its absence. Like Gideon, Jephthah is never explicitly said to be "raised up" by YHWH to deliver Israel (motif D1). However, unlike Gideon, Jephthah is not even expressly commissioned by YHWH to lead Gilead (Israel) to victory. In this, Jephthah's accession (Judg. 11:11) conforms to a pattern evident in the later popular appointment of a king in Israel who would eventually prove to have flawed character—an appointment made in response to Israel's disregard for YHWH's divine right of kingship (cf. 1 Sam. 8; 12). Ironically, it is the combination of YHWH's management of the circumstances that threaten Gilead (10:17; 11:4) together with the narrator's intervening disclosure of information (11:1-3) that apprises the reader as to what extent YHWH is in control of Jephthah's appointment to lead Gilead—and this, while the elders defer to YHWH only to swear by his name (11:5-11). Thus, ironically, those who appoint Jephthah as leader disregard YHWH's divine right of election, while, at the same time, YHWH proves to be in control of the circumstances surrounding their appointment. This pattern has appeared already in the appointment of Abimelech (Judg. 9:6, 16, 19-20, 56-57) and will recur outside Judges in the biblical portrayals of the appointment of Saul (1 Sam. 8:4-22; 10:1, 10:20-11:15) and Jeroboam I (1 Kgs 11:29-39; 12:19-20).[268] Indeed, it may suit the

---

[268] According to 1 Sam. 9:10; 10:1 and 10:20-24, it is YHWH who first chose Saul to be Israel's king, but YHWH's election of Saul came in response to popular demand for a

rhetorical purpose of Judges to characterize negatively any ruler who arises as the result of a popular request motivated apart from concern for YHWH's right of election.

Since it is YHWH who is indirectly responsible for the rise of Jephthah, the conduct of Jephthah in his disputation with the king of Ammon (11:12-28) indirectly redounds to YHWH's credit. Through Jephthah's disputation with the king of Ammon, one sees again in Judges a foreign king and enemy of YHWH subjected to ridicule. The subtle satirization of the king of Ammon results from the fact that, although it was he who initiated with Gilead the conflict over land rights, he is unable to offer a reasonable defence against Jephthah's forensic arguments in 11:12, 14-27. Jephthah's argumentation leaves the Ammonite king speechless (11:28). It may be significant to note that Jephthah's disputation derives from the milieu of royal covenant disputation.[269] Outside the Hebrew Bible, this form of disputation is

---

king (1 Sam. 8:5, 19-20). Thus, it was first the people's choice to prefer a human king over YHWH's kingship (1 Sam. 8:6, 18); YHWH acquiesced to this popular demand knowing that it would only lead to oppression (1 Sam. 8:7-9). Jeroboam I was first elected by YHWH to rule the ten tribes of Israel so as to punish Solomon's infidelity (1 Kgs 11:26-40), but Jeroboam was later appointed king as the result of a popular rebellion against Rehoboam (1 Kgs 12:15, 20).

[269] Exemplars of the covenant disputation form may be found in Deut. 32:1-43; Ps. 50; Mic. 6:1-8; Isa. 1:1-2:5; Jer. 2:5-37. For discussion, see H. Gunkel and J. Begrich, *Einleitung in die Psalmen: Die Gattungen der religiösen Lyrik Israels* (Göttingen, 1933), pp. 329-81; A. Bentzen, *Introduction to the Old Testament* (2 vols., Copenhagen, 1948–1949), vol. 1, pp. 198-200; E. Würthwein, "Der Ursprung der prophetischen Gerichtsrede", *ZTK* 49 (1952), pp. 1-16, reprinted in *Wort und Existenz: Studien zum Alten Testament* (Göttingen, 1970), pp. 111-26; F. Hesse, "Wurzelt die prophetische Gerichtsrede im israelitischen Kult?", *ZAW* 65 (1953), pp. 45-53; B. Gemser, "The *Rîb*- or Controversy-Pattern in Hebrew Mentality", in *Wisdom in Israel and in the Ancient Near East: Presented to H. H. Rowley* (M. Noth and D. W. Thomas [eds.], Festschrift H. H. Rowley, SVT 3, Leiden, 1955), pp. 120-37; H. B. Huffmon, "The Covenant Lawsuit in the Prophets", *JBL* 78 (1959), pp. 285-95; J. Harvey, "Le 'Rîb-Pattern', réquisitoire prophétique sur la rupture de l'alliance", *Bib* 43 (1962), pp. 172-96; G. E. Wright, "The Lawsuit of God: A Form-Critical Study of Deuteronomy 32", in *Israel's Prophetic Heritage: Essays in Honor of James Muilenburg* (B. W. Anderson and W. Harrelson [eds.], New York, 1962), pp. 26-67; H. E. von Waldow, *Der traditionsgeschichtliche Hintergrund der prophetischen Gerichtsreden* (BZAW 85, Berlin, 1963); H. J. Boecker, *Redeformen des Rechtslebens im Alten Testament* (WMANT 14, Neukirchen-Vluyn, 1964; 2d edn, 1970); M. Delcor, "Les attaches littéraires, l'origine et la signification de l'expression biblique 'prendre à témoin le ciel et la terre'", *VT* 16 (1966), pp. 8-25; J. Harvey, *Le plaidoyer prophétique contre Israël après la rupture de l'alliance: Étude d'une formule littéraire de l'Ancien Testament* (Studia 22, Paris, 1967); J. Limburg, "The Root רִיב and the Prophetic Lawsuit Speeches", *JBL* 88 (1969), pp. 291-304; D. J. McCarthy, *Old Testament Covenant: A Survey of Current Opinions* (Richmond, Va., 1972), pp. 38-39; K. Nielsen, *Yahweh as Prosecutor and Judge: An Investigation of the Prophetic Lawsuit (Rîb Pattern)* (F. Cryer [trans.], JSOTS 9, Sheffield, 1978); idem,

known from periods contemporary with or earlier than that of Israel's judges in the following ancient Near Eastern documents: (1) an Assyrian treaty disputation of Tukulti-Ninurta I (1244–1208 BCE) written to the Kassite Kashtiliash IV (1242–1235 BCE);[270] (2) a treaty disputation from Yarîm-Lim of Mari to Yashub-Yahad, king of Dir (ca. 1700 BCE);[271] (3) a letter from King Muwatillish of Hatti (1320–1294 BCE) to a subject Milavata; (4) a disputation against Madduwattash (ca. 1200 BCE); (5) a treaty disputation from the Hittite king to Mita of Pahhawa (ca. 1200 BCE) and (6) a Cappadocian text from King Anum-Hirbi of Mama to King Warshama of Kanish (nineteenth century BCE).[272] The following outline is an aggregate of

---

"Das Bild des Gerichts (RIB-Pattern) in Jes. i-xii: Eine Analyse der Beziehungen zwischen Bildsprache und dem Anliegen der Verkündigung", *VT* 29 (1979), pp. 309-24; M. de Roche, "Yahweh's *Rîb* against Israel: A Reassessment of the So-Called 'Prophetic Lawsuit' in the Preexilic Prophets", *JBL* 102 (1983), pp. 563-74; D. R. Daniels, "Is There a 'Prophetic Lawsuit' Genre?", *ZAW* 99 (1987), pp. 339-60. Cf. Webb, *Judges* (1987), pp. 58-59.

[270] Harvey, "Rîb-Pattern" (1962), pp. 180-88. On the *rîb*-genre within the Epic of Tukulti-Ninurta I (i.e., especially in columns IIA 13'-24' and D obv 9-18-Gap-IIIA 1'-20'), see P. B. Machinist, "The Epic of Tikulti-Ninurta I: A Study in Middle Assyrian Literature", (PhD diss., Yale University, 1978), pp. 40, 76-79, 86-91, 215-19 and 247-48. He outlines IIA 13'-24' as a covenant disputation that parallels the form of the international suzerainty–vassal treaty, upon which it was rhetorically based:

    (1) *13'-14'*   Tikulti-Ninurta's plea to Shamash of his faithfulness to the treaty
                [= Historical prologue]
    (2) *15'-16'*   Historical reminder of the making of the treaty [= Historical prologue]
    (3) *17'-18'*   Praise of Shamash as the vigilant overseer of the treaty [= List of divine
                witnesses and guarantors]
    (4) *19'-21'*   Indictment of Kashtiliash for violating the treaty [= Treaty stipulations]
    (5) *22'-24'*   Call on Shamash for battle that will give victory to the upholder of the treaty
                and defeat to the violator [= Treaty sanctions: curses and blessings]

The form of the segment contained in columns D obv 9-18-Gap-IIIA 1'-20', Machinist gives as follows:

    (1) *1'-8'*   Review of Kashtiliash's treaty violations
    (2) *9'-10'*   Appeal to Shamash against Kashtiliash for his crimes
    (3) *11'-12'* Tukulti-Ninurta's defence of his own treaty loyalty with examples of
                Assyrian goodwill to the Kassites
    (4) *13'-20'* Call for judgement against Kashtiliash by the ordeal of battle

Thus, the aggregate of elements in this work's covenant disputation genre includes: (1) accusation against the offender: declaration of violations, declaration of culpability; (2) exoneration of the offended: (a) claim of initiation of the covenant and of loyalty to the covenant, (b) claim of the right to vindication by combat; (3) ultimatum: threat of total destruction.

[271] Harvey, "Rîb-Pattern" (1962), pp. 183-84.

[272] Harvey, "Rîb-Pattern" (1962), pp. 186-88.

conventional *rîb*-genre variables as they appear in the biblical and
ancient Near Eastern texts presented with the two disputation sections
of the Jephthah account:[273]

I.   Summons to dispute
    A. Call of covenant witnesses
    B. Call to attention of accused
II. Accusation/counteraccusation against the offender
    A. Declaration of obligations/rhetorical interrogation
                  Jephthah: 11:12b, 23, 25-26
                  Ephraimites: 12:1bαβ
                  Jephthah: 12:3b
    B. Declaration of violations
                  King of Ammon: 11:13aβγ
    C. Declaration of culpability
                  Jephthah: 11:27a
    D. Rejection of ritual compensation
III. Exoneration of the offended/falsely accused
    A. Declaration of (covenant) innocence
      1. Initiation of the covenant/*status quo*
              Jephthah: 11:15b-16a (contra 11:13aβ), 21a^{ii}b-21
              (contra 11:13aγ); 12:2-3a
      2. Loyalty to the covenant/*status quo*
        a. Recount of past benefits/conduct
              Jephthah: 11:16b-21a^{i}
        b. Present offer of reinstatement
    B. Declaration of right to vindication
        Trial by combat
              Jephthah: 11:24 (contra 11:13b)
IV. Ultimatum/counterultimatum
    A. Threat
      1. Repeal of covenant benefits
      2. Continued/partial/total destruction
              Ephraimites: 12:1bγδ
      3. Summons to trial by combat
              Jephthah: 11:27b
    B. Appeal
      1. Appeal proper
      2. Motivation
        a. Description of present distresses
        b. Renewal of covenant benefits
      3. Condition
          Terms of reinstatement/reparations
             King of Ammon: 11:13b

---

[273] A form of this outline first appeared in R. H. O'Connell, *Concentricity and
Continuity: The Literary Structure of Isaiah* (JSOTS 188, Sheffield, 1994), p. 42.

The disputation in 11:12b, 14-27 is but a preamble to conflict on the battlefield. In Jephthah's rhetoric there is an invitation to trial by combat from the opening accusation (11:12b) to the final call for divine judgement (11:27b).[274] Thus, while the king of Ammon sues for a peaceful settlement through Israel's forfeiting their land rights, Jephthah's ultimatum contains no such appeal for reconciliation. Despite Jephthah's apparent lack of concern for a peaceful resolution, he recounts Israel's previous disputes with Transjordanian kings (11:16b-21a^i) when Israel sent peaceful appeals (11:17aα, 17aγ^i, 19; marked 'aa' in the plot-structure outline), though the Transjordanian kings refused to comply (11:17aβ, 18, 20aα; marked 'bb'). This alternating pattern in Jephthah's recount sets up the expectation that the present Ammonite king will likewise refuse to listen—and he does (11:28). Moreover, the alternating pattern of 11:16b-21a^i (aa-bb-aa^i-bb^i-aa^{ii}-bb^{ii}) may have been designed to serve as a microcosm of the alternating dialogue in 11:12-28 (A [11:12]-B [11:13]-A^i [11:14-27]-B^i [11:28]) between Jephthah, who, like ancient Israel, begins by sending an appeal (11:12), and the king of Ammon, who, like the ancient Transjordanian kings, refuses to comply (11:28). Jephthah mocks the Ammonite king for contemplating war with a people whose god is YHWH. This mockery only coerces the Ammonite into open conflict and greater humiliation when he, as Sihon before him, is defeated by YHWH. It is perhaps the one positive aspect of Jephthah's mixed characterization that in his argumentation and in his own conduct he never doubts that victory belongs to YHWH (cf. 11:9, 29, 30, 32).

It has sometimes been inferred from the apparent misidentification of Chemosh as the god of Ammon (Judg. 11:24), rather than that of Moab (cf. Num. 21:29; 1 Kgs 11:5, 7, 33; 2 Kgs 23:13; Jer. 48:7, 13, 46), and from the contrast with Balak, king of Moab, (11:25) that: (1) the disputation was originally addressed to a king of Moab and has been imperfectly adapted to address a king of Ammon,[275] (2) the disputation

---

[274] On the rhetorical force of the question מה־לי ולך (11:12bα), see O. Bächli, "'Was habe ich mit Dir zu shaffen?' Eine formelhafte Frage im Alten Testament und Neuen Testament", *TZ* 33 (1977), pp. 69-80, especially pp. 69, 74-75, 79-80. Bächli concludes that, in Hebrew Scripture, this is a formal question used always in the exalted style of diplomatic speech (cf. 2 Sam. 16:10; 19:23; 1 Kgs 17:18; 2 Kgs 3:13; Judg. 11:12; 2 Chron. 35:21; cf. Josh. 22:24; 2 Kgs 9:18-19). The question is always rhetorical and designed to create distance by rendering the addressee uncertain, confused and sensing his guilt for whatever consequences ensue.

[275] Moore, *Judges* (1895), pp. 283, 295 (cf. BDB, p. 484b); Budde, *Richter* (1897), pp. 80-82; W. Nowack, *Richter, Ruth, und Bücher Samuelis* (HKAT I/4, Göttingen,

here made against Ammon (11:12/12-15*, 27) was later conflated with a disputation originally made against Moab (11:13/16-26),[276] (3) the disputation was originally against a king of Ammon who had recently taken part of the Moabite territory and was thus entitled, by diplomatic protocol, to claim Moabite land rights and to defer to Moabite deities[277] and (4) Jephthah is here being deliberately portrayed as ignorant of the facts of tradition.[278] The first two alternatives allege that there is incongruity between the original design and secondary usage of the disputation because it mingles data concerning two gods who are distinguished from one another outside this account, namely, Milcom/Molech, god of Ammon, and Chemosh, god of Moab. However, it seems clear from Jephthah's argument that he views his opponent as the legitimate ruler of both Ammon and Moab, that is, Moab south of the Arnon.[279] First, in reply to his charge, כי־לקח ישראל את־ארצי (11:13b), Jephthah counters, בעלותו ממצרים מארנון ועד־היבק ועד־הירדן (11:15b)—Jephthah thus לא־לקח ישראל את־ארץ מואב ואת־ארץ בני עמון limiting his designation "Moab" to the territory south of the Arnon. Second, the point of stating that the Ammonite king has legitimate right to the land that Chemosh has given him in Moab is to legitimize Jephthah's claim that Israel has equal right to the land that YHWH has given them north of the Arnon (11:24).[280] Finally, Jephthah addresses him as a legitimate successor of the kings of Moab (11:25-26).

1902), p. 100; Burney, *Judges* (2d edn, 1920), pp. 298-99, 310; F. Nötscher, *Das Buch der Richter* (EB 12, Würzburg, 2d edn, 1953), p. 48.

[276] O. Eissfeldt, *Die Quellen des Richterbuches: In synoptischer Anordnung ins Deutsche übersetzt samt einer in Einleitung und Noten gegebenen Begründung* (Leipzig, 1925), p. 26; K. Wiese, *Zur Literarkritik des Buches der Richter* (BWANT 40/2, Stuttgart, 1926), p. 46; W. Richter, "Die Überlieferungen um Jephtah, Ri 10,17–12,6", *Bib* 47 (1966), pp. 524-25; S. Mittmann, "Aroer, Minnith und Abel Keramim (Jdc 11,33)", *ZDPV* 85 (1969), pp. 63-75; M. Wüst, "Die Einschaltung in die Jiftachgeschichte. Ri 11,13-26", *Bib* 56 (1975), pp. 464-79; cf. Soggin, *Judges* (2d edn, 1987), pp. 210, 211-13.

[277] A. Vincent, *Le livre des Juges, Le livre de Ruth* (La Bible de Jérusalem, Paris, 2d edn, 1958), ad loc.; Boling, *Judges* (1975), pp. 203-4; Webb, *Judges* (1987), pp. 56, 225 n. 34.

[278] Klein, *Triumph of Irony* (1988), p. 89.

[279] Cf. Webb, *Judges* (1987), p. 56.

[280] This is essentially parallel to the claim of Num. 21:29, where Chemosh delivers up the people of his land (Moab) to its new ruler (Sihon). Compare how Cyrus, king of Persia, claims that he received benefactions from the Babylonian god Marduk as a result of conquering Babylon (A. L. Oppenheim, "Cyrus [557–529]", in *The Ancient Near East*, vol. 1, *An Anthology of Texts and Pictures* [J. B. Pritchard (ed.), Princeton, 1958], pp. 206-8). In view of the parallel between Judg. 11:24 and the Phoenician ʿAzzibaʿal inscription, J. Obermann argues that the emphasis in Judg. 11:24 is not upon the divine

If one assumes the rhetorical coherence of the disputation with its narrative context, the question of the relationship of this disputation to the satirization of the Ammonite king has a bearing upon one's determination of the narrator's disposition toward Jephthah as a negotiator. If the narrator is attempting to ridicule the Ammonite king, his strategy could hardly be made effective by restating the illegitimate arguments of an inept negotiator.[281] However, given the narrator's apparently deliberate structural analogy between the alternating dialogue of 11:12-28 and the alternating pattern of Israel's historic negotiations with Transjordanian kings in 11:16b-21a[i], it seems difficult to infer that one is dealing with anything other than a strategy designed to mock not Jephthah but the Ammonite monarch.[282] Thus, from a rhetorical standpoint, the most coherent explanation of the apparent factual incongruities of the disputation would be that of alternative (3), namely, that the disputation was addressed to a king of Ammon who had recently taken Moabite territory and was thus entitled to claim Moabite land and to defer to Moabite deities.[283]

A subtle satirization of the Ammonite king in Judg. 11:12-28 is further corroborated by other considerations. First, as with the king of Edom (11:17a), the king of Ammon is not even granted the recognition of being named. His anonymity in the present context contrasts starkly with the fame of Sihon, whose notoriety derives from Israel's conquering of his land—a matter now being disputed by the Ammonite king (11:19-21). Even Balak, king of Moab, attains notoriety here by his alleged compliance with Israel's military supremacy (11:25). Second, further satirization of the Ammonite king seems implicit in the intertextual relationship between Jephthah's recount of Israelite traditions in Judg. 11:15b-26a and the narratives of Numbers 20-24 and

---

element but upon maintaining the geopolitical *status quo* between Israel and Ammon/Moab—though Jephthah's legitimation of Chemosh as a peer of YHWH is hardly in line with deuteronomic theology ("An Early Phoenician Political Document: With a Parallel to Judges 11:24", *JBL* 58 [1939], pp. 237-39).

[281] On Jephthah's prowess as a negotiator, see Webb, *Judges* (1987), pp. 57-58, 71, 74.

[282] For the view that Jephthah is inept as a negotiator, see Exum, "Tragic Vision" (1989), pp. 73-75, 77, 90, 91; Humphreys, "Jephthah" (1989), p. 91.

[283] This argument is not meant to imply that either of alternatives (1) or (2) listed above is an impossible explanation of the origin of the disputation, but alternative (4) is inconsistent with the subtle satirization of foreign kingship in this account.

Deuteronomy 2–3.[284] The important issue for determining the rhetoric of Jephthah's disputation (i.e., whether or not it is ironic) is not whether Judg. 11:15b-26a is directly dependent upon other written traditions of Israel's dealings with Edom, Moab, Ammon or the Amorites but whether the prominent affirmations that Jephthah presents as tradition are in accord with the consensus of those other written records. One may observe the following points of congruence among Israel's records of tradition:

	Num. 20–24	Deut. 2–3	Judg. 11
Israel avoided Ammon/Moab	21:10-20, 24b	2:9, 13-18 19, 37	11:15b
Israel came out of Egypt and went via the Reed Sea to Kadesh			11:16
Israel refused by king of Edom	20:14a, 17aα, 20-21	2:4-6; cf. 2:29a	11:17aαβ
Israel refused by king of Moab		cf. 2:29a	11:17aγ
Israel stayed at Kadesh			11:17b
Israel avoided Edom/Moab	21:4a, 10-13	2:8, 13	11:18
Israel sent to Sihon	21:21-22	2:24a, 26-28, 29b	11:19
Israel refused and warred at Jahaz	21:23	2:30a, 32	11:20
Israel defeated Sihon	21:24a	2:30b-31, 33	11:21a
Israel possessed Sihon's land	21:24bαβ	2:34a, 36	11:21b-22
Land taken by Israel/ given by YHWH	cf. 21:30-31		11:23a, 24b
Land given by Chemosh to Sihon/king of Ammon	cf. 21:29		11:24a
Balak, king of Moab, avoids land taken from Sihon (cf. Josh. 24:9-10)	22:4b (2a)		11:25a

---

[284] J. Van Seters argues generally that Deut. 2:24–3:11 and Judg. 11:19-26 were composed prior to Num. 21:21-35 and Jer. 48:45-46 and specifically that Num. 21:21-25 conflates Deut. 2:26-37 with Judg. 11:19-26 ("The Conquest of Sihon's Kingdom: A Literary Examination", *JBL* 91 [1972], pp. 182-97). See the rebuttal by J. R. Bartlett, "The Conquest of Sihon's Kingdom: A Literary Re-examination", *JBL* 97 (1978), pp. 347-51; and Van Seters's rejoinder, "Once Again—The Conquest of Sihon's Kingdom", *JBL* 99 (1980), pp. 117-19. Cf. D. M. Gunn, "The 'Battle Report': Oral or Scribal Convention?", *JBL* 93 (1974), pp. 513-18; Webb, *Judges* (1987), pp. 57, 225 n. 37.

	Num. 20–24	Deut. 2–3	Judg. 11
Israel settled in Heshbon, environs and towns along Arnon	21:25, 26bγ (27, 30-31)		11:26aαβ

The question of the relative priority of these accounts is significant,[285] yet it is less a determining factor in the rhetoric of Judg. 11:15b-26 than whether it harmonizes with the consensus of written records about Israel's early traditions. Thus, while Jephthah affirms that messengers were sent to Moab (11:17aγ), there are no data elsewhere to confirm his claim (but cf. Deut. 2:29a). On the other hand, there is nothing in either Numbers 20–24 or Deuteronomy 2–3 to contradict the salient claims presented by Jephthah in Judg. 11:15b-26a.[286] Hence, Jephthah's disputation cannot be said to satirize Jephthah as a negotiator who cannot get his facts right.[287] Rather, the satirization is aimed against the present king of Ammon, who responds no differently to Jephthah's messages than did former Transjordanian kings.

At the end of Jephthah's disputation, and in confirmation of the justice of his mission, the spirit of YHWH comes upon him (11:29aα). Everything in the characterization of Jephthah to this point indicates that YHWH has been at work to vindicate himself against the enemies of Israel and to vindicate Jephthah before those who expelled him from Gilead. Ironically, the shift from a positive to a negative characterization of Jephthah begins only after, and despite the fact that, the spirit of YHWH had come upon him (11:29aα). Jephthah begins appropriately in 11:29aβb with actions that imply that he was summoning an army more substantial than the force rallied in 10:17b and engaged by the Ammonites in 11:4:

---

[285] E.g., note the deuteronomic phraseology of יהוה אלהי־ישראל in Judg. 11:23a and of יהוה אלהינו in 11:24b where such is lacking from the corresponding account of Numbers, thus suggesting that the Judges rendering is secondary.

[286] The presentation of Israel as בארץ מואב (Deut. 1:5a) and בשדה מואב (Num. 21:20a) should be understood as an example of analepsis, referring to regions whose designation derives from the circumstance that this land was formerly a part of Moab—a circumstance recently altered by Sihon's conquest of that part of Moab north of the Arnon and by Israel's more recent taking of that same part of former Moab from Sihon the Amorite (cf. Num. 21:21-31).

[287] Contra Exum, "Tragic Vision" (1989), pp. 73-75, 77, 90, 91.

ויעבר את־הגלעד ואת־מנשה
ויעבר את־מצפה גלעד
²⁸⁸וממצפה גלעד עבר בני עמון

The threefold repetition of עבר indicates his passing through Gilead
and (Half-)Manasseh (11:29aβ), returning to Mizpah (11:29bα), then
passing on to confront the Ammonites (11:29bβγ; cf. 11:32a).²⁸⁹
However, once Jephthah summons Gilead and (Half-)Manasseh
(11:29aβb), the reader encounters a turning point in Jephthah's characterization. The turn comes not with Jephthah's reception of the spirit of
YHWH but with his making the vow of human sacrifice (11:30-31).
From this point onward, Jephthah becomes an instrument of irony in
the narrative. Ironically, though Jephthah conquers a foreign king, he
himself comes to be crushed under his self-imposed obligation to fulfil
a foreign rite of human sacrifice (11:34-40). Likewise ironically,
Jephthah, who uses his disputational skill to such advantage in his contest with the king of Ammon, will for selfish reasons turn this skill
against his kinsfolk in Israel (12:1-6). To be sure, the Ephraimites'
approach is bellicose from the outset (12:1b),²⁹⁰ but Jephthah's
response to them (12:2-3) is as unconciliatory as was his response to
the king of Ammon. Further, while the Ephraimites' threat in 12:1bγδ
is against Jephthah personally, Jephthah's identifying himself with his
tribe in 12:2a (אני ועמי) escalates the dispute from a personal to an
intertribal level.²⁹¹ With the belated information given in 12:4b*, the
reader comes to understand Jephthah's motive for engaging the
Ephraimites: their taunt, "You are fugitives of Ephraim, O Gilead,
within Ephraim", strikes a sore spot in Jephthah, who has only just
been received back after having been cast out by his brothers. Little

---

²⁸⁸ The relative position of these actions, immediately after the spirit of YHWH had
come upon Jephthah, coincides with the actions of Israel's previous deliverers: e.g.,
Othniel 'judges' Israel and goes out to battle (3:10aαⁱⁱ) immediately after the spirit of
YHWH comes upon him (3:10aαⁱ); Gideon rallies troops (6:34b-35) immediately after
being 'clothed' by YHWH's spirit (6:34a). Each instance implies the summoning of troops
(so Webb, *Judges* [1987], pp. 61-62).

²⁸⁹ Webb, *Judges* (1987), pp. 61, 226 n. 44. The narrator conveys the close succession
of Jephthah's actions through the close repetition of עבר and anadiplosis (cf. E. W.
Bullinger, *Figures of Speech Used in the Bible* [London, 1898; repr. edn, Grand Rapids,
1968], pp. 251-55).

²⁹⁰ Their offended sense of self-importance is emphasized by the clause-initial position
of ולנו in 12:1bβ (ולנו לא קראת ללכת עמך), and their threat in 12:1bγδ (ביתך נשרף עליך
באש) is essentially the same as that of the Philistines in 14:15 (cf. 15:6). Cf. Webb,
Judges (1987), p. 70.

²⁹¹ Webb, *Judges* (1987), p. 71.

wonder that the compensatory vengeance he wreaks upon the "fugitives of Ephraim" is brutal in the extreme (12:5b-6).

In the final subplot of the Jephthah account the reader encounters one of the tribal–political concerns of the Judges compiler/redactor. This concern seems evident in the negative characterization of Ephraimite leadership. The key difficulty is the claim of Jephthah in 12:2:

איש ריב הייתי אני ועמי ובני־עמון מאד
ואצעק אתכם ולא־הושעתם אותי מידם:

Jephthah makes the claim that he was a man in disputation—not an inappropriate claim in view of the *rîb*-genre underlying the form of 11:12-28). If one assumes that this claim is a legitimate one, it furnishes Jephthah with ground for exoneration from the Ephraimites' accusation that Jephthah had failed to conduct his military affairs with due consideration for the covenant obligation of other tribes. After Ephraim accuses Jephthah of failing to summon them to battle—a claim having the appearance of zeal for intertribal covenant unity, though it may have been little more than tribal self-interest—Jephthah makes a counteraccusation against Ephraim. He claims that he had summoned them, though they had not come to his rescue—a claim making their accusation seem unfounded. If Ephraim's accusation against the leader of Gilead is that he had failed to rally Israel's other tribes to fulfil their military obligation to the covenant, it is perhaps ironic that this implied military obligation was earlier in the period (though later in the book of Judges) turned against Jabesh-Gilead for their failure to rally when summoned (Judg. 21:5, 8b-12). Of course, any negative character-ization of Ephraim does little to diminish the negative characterization of Jephthah for his part in the general lack of diplomacy, especially when his conduct in 12:1-6 is contrasted with that of Gideon in a similar situation (8:1-3).

There are a number of formal correspondences between the account of Gideon/Abimelech and that of Jephthah that evidence a similar pattern of mixed characterization. Both accounts are prefaced by plot-delaying statements of YHWH's reluctance to save Israel (6:7-10; 10:11-14). In both, the exposition of the main character begins with some form of the divine commission type-scene: YHWH commissions Gideon in 6:11-17, but it is the elders who summon Jephthah in 11:5-11. In both character expositions, the deliverer is designated גבור חיל (6:12b; 11:1a). Like Gideon, Jephthah rallies troops for battle from adjacent tribal regions immediately after the spirit of YHWH has come upon him (6:35; 11:29aβb). Similarly, both then seek a guarantee of success even after the spirit of YHWH has come upon them (6:36; 11:30).[292] In both accounts, one born illegitimately becomes the rival of his halfbrothers (8:31; 9:2; 11:1-3) and, through a series of intrigues, becomes the agent of cultic violence against the heir(s) of a deliverer in Israel (9:5; 11:30-31, 34-40). Both the Gideon and Jephthah accounts describe a confrontation with the Ephraimites (8:1-3; 12:1-6). Finally, both Gideon (by making an ephod) and Jephthah (through human sacrifice) reintroduce foreign forms of cultic aberration into Israel. These formal correspondences seem to result from an attempt to illustrate, between these successive accounts, a pattern of escalation in the decay of cultic loyalty to YHWH and of intertribal covenant unity.

The following are the main developments in Judges that appear first in the Jephthah account:

1. the detailing of cycle-motif C ("Israelites cried to YHWH") both before and after an intervening complication to show what form the repentance took (10:10a, 15-16);[293]
2. for the first time since 2:1-3, and using a threat similar to that of YHWH in 2:3, YHWH speaks directly to Israel in the framework (10:11-14);[294]
3. human sacrifice as a form of cultic aberration (11:30-31, 39a);
4. intertribal warfare (with the Gileadites' slaughter of Ephraimites in 12:4-6).

Perhaps it is rhetorically significant that the last two new developments in Judges, each representing a new kind of atrocity in Israel, constitute the main escalated parallel in this deliverer account.

§6. The Account of Samson (13:1-16:31)

The plot-structure of the Samson account comprises four plot-levels, as does that of the Jephthah account.[295] However, unlike the plot-

---

[292] Cf. Exum, "Centre" (1990), p. 417.

[293] Webb, *Judges* (1987), p. 44.

[294] Exum, "Centre" (1990), p. 421.

[295] As in the study of other plot-based deliverer accounts in Judges, studies of the structure of the Samson account have been dominated by the scenic (or episodic) principle. See, e.g., J. A. Wharton, "The Secret of Yahweh: Story and Affirmation in Judges 13-16", *Int* 27 (1973), pp. 54-56; J. L. Crenshaw, "The Samson Saga: Filial Devotion or Erotic Attachment?", *ZAW* 86 (1974), pp. 478, 485, 487, 495-96, 498, 502; J. C. Exum, "Promise and Fulfillment: Narrative Art in Judges 13", *JBL* 99 (1980), pp. 43-59; idem, "Aspects of Symmetry and Balance in the Samson Saga", *JSOT* 19 (1981), pp. 10-18 (cf. idem, "The Theological Dimension of the Samson Saga", *VT* 33 [1983], p. 34). Following the analysis of Exum, Webb speaks of the structure of the Samson account only in terms of "two major movements" in chs. 14-15 and ch. 16 and of ch. 13 as comprising "three major units" (Webb, *Judges* [1987], pp. 163, 168, 171, 173). Even the study of Blenkinsopp, while overtly concerned with plot-structure, fails to delve beyond the scenic

structures of the accounts of Gideon/Abimelech and Jephthah, the subplots of the Samson account (Plots B, C and D) do not extend beyond
the resolution of the situational crisis that was introduced in the exposition of Plot A. Indeed, unlike other deliverer accounts in Judges,
Plot A of this account is never fully resolved.[296] The account of
Samson presents a double exposition (of the situation, in 10:7bα[β] and
13:1; of character, in 13:2-24), a sporadically interrupted development
(13:25; 14:4-6, 8-9, 12-19aα; 15:1-2, 6, 9-14; 16:2, 7-9, 11-12, 13b-
14, 22, 28-30aαβ) and a sporadically interrupted series of partial
resolutions (of the situation: 14:19aβb; 15:3-5, 7-8, 15-17; 16:3,
30aγ-ε; of character: 15:20; 16:30b-31). Interrupting Plot A are
repeated complications (13:8-23; 14:1-3, 7, 10-11; 15:18-19; 16:1, 4-6,
10, 13a, 15-21, 23-27), most of which are developments within either
Plot C or D. There is no dissolution of Plot A, simply a lack of resolution in that Samson's slaughter at Gaza does not represent Israel's final
triumph over the Philistines.[297] The following is a plot-structure
analysis of Judges 13-16 (with cycle-motif designations or letters
enumerating repetition patterns in the left column and broken horizontal lines marking scene changes):

> *Plot A:* YHWH's deliverance of Israel from the Philistines through Samson
> (13:1-7 [8-23] 24-25; 14:[1-3] 4-6 [7] 8-9 [10-11] 12-19; 15:1-17 [18-19]
> 20; 16:[1] 2-3 [4-6] 7-9 [10] 11-12 [13a] 13b-14 [15-21] 22 [23-27]
> 28-31)
>> *Plot A Situation Exposition:* (< 10:7bα[β] > ; 13:1)
>>> < B2b   He sold them into the hand of the Philistines
>>>   (10:7bα[β]) >

---

principle to trace how events have been arranged to achieve a single purpose
(J. Blenkinsopp, "Structure and Style in Judges 13-16", *JBL* 82 [1963], pp. 65-69).

[296] Since this unique feature of plot-structure occurs only in the last deliverer account
of the book, it may reflect a deliberate strategy on the part of the Judges compiler/redactor
to anticipate the continuing situation of Philistine oppression that forms the background to
1 Samuel—a further evidence of rhetorical continuity between Judges and 1 Samuel.

[297] It could be argued that, since the exposition portrays Samson as one who would
only begin to deliver Israel from the Philistines (13:5b), the main plot may resolve in his
final and greatest act of deliverance (16:30b) despite the continuance of Philistine domination. However, while it is fair to say that the exposition never anticipates a complete
resolution of the situational crisis introduced in the exposition (13:1), the continuance of
the Philistine oppression beyond the death of Samson is disappointing because it fails to
continue the pattern set up by all the preceding deliverer accounts in which at least the
main plot comes to be resolved (even if later to be dissolved, as in the Jephthah account).
Regardless of the fact that the character exposition anticipates only partial success on the
part of Samson, the crisis introduced in the situational exposition (10:7bα[β] and 13:1) is
never fully resolved.

A1a   Resumption of Israel's practice of evil (13:1a)
B2a   He gave them into the hand of the Philistines
                 (13:1b^{i-ii})
B3a   forty years (13:1b^{iii})
Plot B: YHWH's provision of a son to the barren wife of Manoah (13:2-7 [8-
23] 24a)
  Plot A Character Exposition/Plot B Exposition: Barrenness of the wife of
  Manoah, a Danite from Zorah (13:2)
  Plot A Character Exposition/Plot B Development: Angelic birth
  annunciation(•)[298]/theophanic recognition(○) type-scene [13:3-23][299]
  (13:3-7)
    a   Angel of YHWH appears and announces the birth of a
                 son (13:3-5)
    α   (•/○)Angelic appearance (13:3a)
    β   (•)Introductory annunciation (13:3b)
    γ   (•)Annunciation proper: prohibitions and oracles
                 (13:4-5)
                 Prohibition against mother's having wine, fer-
                   mented drink or unclean food; oracle of birth
                   of a son (13:4-5aα)
                 Prohibition against shaving son's head; oracle
                   of the boy's Nazirite status (13:5aβγ)
    (D1)   Oracle of boy's role as one who would begin to
                 deliver Israel from the Philistines (13:5b)
    ────────────────────────────────────
    b   (•)Wife recounts to Manoah the angel's appearance
                 and birth annunciation (13:6-7)
  Plots A & B Complication: Angelic birth annunciation(•)/theophanic
  recognition(○) type-scene [continued] (13:8-23)
    c   (•)Manoah prays for an angelic visitation to give
                 instruction as to their conduct concerning the boy
                 (13:8)
    ────────────────────────────────────
    a^i α   (•/○)Angel reappears to Manoah's wife in Manoah's
                 absence (13:9)
    b^i (•)Wife reports to Manoah the angel's reappearance
                 (13:10)
    c^i (•)Manoah goes and inquires as to the angel's identity
                 and what customs should apply to the boy
                 (13:11-12)

---

[298] Cf. the similarity of concern with Israel's covenant waywardness among the angelic visitations of YHWH in 2:1-3; 6:8-10 and 10:11-14. On the annunciation type-scene in Judg. 13, see Blenkinsopp, "Judges 13–16" (1963), pp. 66-68; Crenshaw, "Samson Saga" (1974), pp. 476-77; Webb, *Judges* (1987), pp. 164, 174.

[299] On the theophanic recognition type-scene in Judg. 13:3-23, see Wharton, "Secret" (1973), pp. 57-58; Crenshaw, "Samson Saga" (1974), p. 477.

a^{ii} γ   (•)Angel recounts the prohibitions announced
               previously to Manoah's wife (13:13-14)
          (○)Manoah's preparation and presentation of an
               offertory meal (13:15-19a)
          (○)YHWH's theophany (13:19b-20a)
          (○)Manoah's recognition (13:20b-22)
          (○)Wife's reassurance (13:23)

Plot A Character Exposition/Plot B Resolution: Birth and naming of Samson (13:24a)
Plot A Character Exposition: Boy's growth and blessing by YHWH
     (13:24b)
Plot A Development: (13:25)
D2a   Spirit of YHWH began to impel Samson (13:25aαβ^i)
               in Mahaneh Dan, between Zorah and Eshtaol
               (13:25aβ^{ii}b)

Plot C: Samson's quest for a Philistine wife from Timnah (14:1-3 [5-6] 7
[8-9] 10-11 [12-20; 15:1-2, 6])
Plot A Complication/Plot C Exposition: (14:1-3)
aa   Samson went down to Timnah, saw a Philistine
               woman and asked his parents to get her as his wife
               (14:1-3abα)
(A1b)   Reason: for she/it is right in my eyes (14:3bβ)
Parenthesis: Plot A Development: His parents did not know that she/it
     was from YHWH, for he was seeking an opportunity against the
     Philistines; at that time the Philistines were ruling Israel (14:4)

Plot A Development/Plot C Complication: (14:5-6)
               Samson went down < > and was attacked by a lion
               at the vineyards of Timnah (14:5)
D2a   Spirit of YHWH came upon him (14:6aα)
               He barehandedly tore the lion as one tears a kid
               (14:6aβγ)
               He did not tell his parents what he had done (14:6b)

Plot A Complication/Plot C Development: (14:7)
               He went down and spoke to the woman (14:7a)
(A1b)   Summary: she was right in Samson's eyes (14:7b)

Plot A Development/Plot C Complication: (14:8-9)
               When Samson returned to take her, he turned aside
                 and found in the lion's carcass bees and honey,
                 which he ate as he went; and he gave some to his
                 parents so that they ate (14:8-9a)

He did not tell his parents from where he got the honey (14:9b)

Plot A Complication/Plot C Development: (14:10-11)

Samson's father went down to the woman (14:10a)

Samson made a feast, as was customary, and, at their seeing him, was given thirty companions (14:10b-11)

Plot A Development/Plot C Complication: (14:12-19aα)

Samson propounds a wager of thirty sets of garments if within seven days they could not solve his riddle (14:12-14a)

For three days they could not solve his riddle (14:14b)

− bb On the fourth day the Philistines threaten to burn Samson's bride and father's household if she does not entice her bridegroom to tell the riddle (14:15)

cc Samson's bride laments that he has not told her the riddle (14:16a)

Samson retorts that he has not told even his parents, so should he tell her? (14:16b)

dd Because she pressed him for seven days, he told her the riddle, and she told her people (14:17)

ee Before sunset on the seventh day, the people of the city told Samson the riddle (14:18a)

Samson rebuked them for having solved the riddle by coercing his wife (14:18b)

D2a ff *Sanction/empowerment:* Spirit of YHWH came upon him (14:19aα)

Plot A Partial Situation Resolution/Plot C Complication: (14:19aβb)

+ gg He went down to Ashkelon, struck down thirty men, took their belongings (14:19aβγ)

---

and gave their sets of garments to those who told the riddle (14:19aδε)

(B1) His anger burned (14:19bα)

He went up to his father's house (14:19bβ)

Plot C Dissolution: Samson's bride was given to the friend who attended his wedding (14:20)

Plot A Development/Prolongation of Plot C Dissolution: (15:1-2)

Samson visits his wife to consummate his marriage (15:1a)

—   Her father refuses, explains that he had given her to the friend and offers instead her younger sister (15:1b-2)

_____

Plot A Greater Partial Situation Resolution: (15:3-5)

ff[i]   *Sanction/empowerment:* Samson asserts his innocence when he does mischief with them this time (15:3)

+   gg[i]   He captures 300 jackals,[300] ties them tail to tail, sets a torch between each pair of tails, sets fire to the torches, sends them into the standing grain of the Philistines and sets fire to shock, standing grain, vineyard and olive grove (15:4-5)

_____

Plot A Development/Plot C Greater Dissolution: (15:6)

—   Philistines go up and burn Samson's wife and her father (15:6)

_____

Plot A Greater Partial Situation Resolution: (15:7-8)

ff[ii]   *Sanction/empowerment:* Samson asserts his right to revenge (15:7)

+   gg[ii]   and attacks them hip over thigh with a great slaughter (15:8a)

_____

then goes down and stays in the cave of the rock of Etam (15:8b)

_____

Plot A Development: (15:9-14)

—   d   Philistines go up, encamp in Judah and spread out at Lehi, and the men of Judah say, "Why have you come up against us?" (15:9-10a)

e   They say, "We have come up to bind Samson to do to him what he did to us" (15:10b)

_____

d[i]   Three thousand men from Judah go down to the cave in the rock of Etam and say to Samson, "Do you not realize that the Philistines are ruling us? What is this you have done to us?" (15:11a)

e[i]   He said, "What they did to me, I did to them" (15:11b)

_____

[300] It is still a point of dispute whether the reference is to jackals, as indigenous to the Philistine plain (so Blenkinsopp, "Judges 13–16" [1963], p. 74; G. G. Cohen, "Samson and Hercules: A Comparison between the Feats of Samson and the Labours of Hercules", *EvQ* 42 [1970], p. 138; cf. BDB, p. 1043b), or to foxes, as reflecting the legendary traditions underlying the Samson saga (so Crenshaw, "Samson Saga" [1974], pp. 478-80, 483 and especially p. 496; cf. R. Hartmann, "Simsons Füchse", *ZAW* 31 [1911], pp. 69-72; KB, p. 956b; G. von Rad, *Gottes Wirken* [1974], ET: *God at Work* [1980], pp. 44, 45).

f	They say, "We have come down to bind you and to give you into the hand of the Philistines" (15:12a)
g	Samson says, "Swear to me lest you yourselves confront me" (15:12b)
f^i	They say, "No, we will only bind you and give you into their hand" (15:13aαβ)
g^i	"but we will not put you to death" (15:13aγ)
	They bind him with two new cords and bring him up from the rock (15:13b)

	When he arrived at Lehi, the Philistines shouted victoriously at meeting him (15:14a)
D2a ff^{iii}	*Sanction/empowerment:* Spirit of YHWH came upon him (15:14bα)
	The cords on his arms became like charred flax and his bindings disintegrated from his hands (15:14bβ-δ)

Plot A Greater Partial Situation Resolution: (15:15-17)

+ gg^{iii}	He found a fresh jawbone of an ass, reached out, took it and with it slaughtered a thousand men (15:15)
	Samson propounds a victory saying (15:16)
	Geographical aetiology: When he finished speaking, he threw the jawbone from his hand and called that place Ramath Lehi (15:17)

Plot A Complication: (15:18-19)

(C) hh	⌐ He became very thirsty and called to YHWH, "You have given this great victory into the hand of your servant, but now I shall die of thirst and fall into the hand of the uncircumsized" (15:18)
	YHWH split open the crater at Lehi, water came out from it and he drank (15:19aαβ)
(D2a)/(ff^{iv})	*Sanction/empowerment:* His spirit returned, and he revived (15:19aγ)
	⌐ Geographical aetiology: Therefore he called it Ein Haqqore, which is at Lehi to this day (15:19b)

Plot A Partial Character Resolution: (15:20)

F1	He judged Israel twenty years (15:20^{i,iii})
	in the days of the Philistines (15:20^{ii})

Plot D: Philistine plot to kill Samson in retaliation for his exploit at Gaza (16:1-6 [7-9] 10 [11-12] 13a [13b-14] 15-21, 23-27 [28-30a])

Plot A Complication/Plot D Exposition: (16:1)

aa^i	Samson went down to Gaza, saw there a harlot and went in to her (16:1)

Plot A Development/Plot D Exposition: (16:2)

–	< It was told > to the Gazaites that Samson had come there, so they encircled and lay in ambush for him

all night at the city gate; they kept quiet all night,
saying, "At morning light we will kill him"
(16:2)

Plot A Greater Partial Situation Resolution/Plot D Exposition: (16:3)

+ Samson slept until midnight, arose at midnight, seized the doors of the city gate with its two posts and bar, pulled them out, set them on his shoulders and brought them up to the hilltop facing Hebron (16:3)

— —

Plot A Complication/Plot D Development: (16:4-6)

Samson loved a woman named Delilah in the Sorek Valley (16:4)

− bb^i The Philistine tyrants went up and bribed Delilah with eleven hundred silver pieces to entice Samson to show the source of his great strength and how they could overpower and bind him so as to subdue him (16:5)

— —

cc^i Delilah asks Samson the source of his great strength, how he may be bound so as to be subdued (16:6)

Plot A Development/Plot D Complication: (16:7-9)

h Samson misdirects Delilah, saying, "If one ties me with seven fresh thongs, I will become weak like any man" (16:7)

i The Philistine tyrants brought her seven fresh thongs with which she tied him, and, with the ambush by her in the room, she said to him, "The Philistines are upon you, Samson!" (16:8-9a)

(+) j He snapped the thongs as a strand of tow snaps when it touches fire (16:9b)

— —

Plot A Complication/Plot D Development: (16:10)

cc^{ii} Delilah rebukes Samson for mocking and lying to her and again asks how he may be bound (16:10)

Plot A Development/Plot D Complication: (16:11-12)

h^i Samson misdirects Delilah, saying, "If one ties me with new cords, I will become weak like any man" (16:11)

i^i She tied him with new cords, and, with the ambush by her in the room, she said to him, "The Philistines are upon you, Samson!" (16:12a)

(+) j^i He snapped them from his arms as thread [snaps] (16:12b)

— —

Plot A Complication/Plot D Development: (16:13a)

ccⁱⁱⁱ   Again Delilah rebukes Samson for mocking and lying to her and asks how he may be bound (16:13a)

Plot A Development/Plot D Complication: (16:13b-14)

hⁱⁱ   Samson misdirects Delilah, saying, "If one weaves the seven locks of my head with the warp < and tightens it with the pin, I will become weak like any man > " (16:13bc*)

iⁱⁱ   < Delilah lulled him to sleep, weaved the seven locks of his head with the warp >, tightened it with the pin and said to him, "The Philistines are upon you, Samson!" (16:14a*)

(+)   jⁱⁱ   He awoke from his sleep and pulled out the pin of the loom and the warp (16:14b)

— — — — — — — — — — — — — — — — — —

Plot A Complication/Plot D Development: (16:15-20)

cc^{iv}   Delilah rebukes Samson for not loving and confiding in her, for mocking her three times and for not telling her the source of his great strength (16:15)

ddⁱ/hⁱⁱⁱ   Because she pressed him and nagged him every day with her words, he became exasperated to [the point of] death, so he told her everything and said, "No razor has come upon my head, for I am a Nazirite to God from birth. Were I shaved, my strength would leave me, and I would become as any man". When Delilah saw that he had told her everything, she summoned the Philistine tyrants, "Come up once again, for he has told me everything". The Philistine tyrants went up to her with the silver in their hand (16:16-18)

eeⁱ/iⁱⁱⁱ   She lulled him to sleep on her lap, summoned the man, shaved the seven locks of his head and thus began to subdue him (16:19abα)

(D2a)1/ff   His strength departed from him, (16:19bβ) and she said, "The Philistines are upon you, Samson!" (16:20a)

jⁱⁱⁱ   He awoke from his sleep and said, "I shall go forth as on previous occasions and shake myself free" (16:20bαβ)

(D2a)1/ffⁱ   Parenthesis: He did not know that YHWH had departed from him (16:20bγδ)

Plot A Complication/Plot D Partial Resolution: (16:21)

          Philistines seized him (16:21aα)

(A1b)   and gouged out his eyes (16:21aβ)

— — — — — — — — — — — — — — — — — —

They brought him down to Gaza, bound him with
bronze shackles, and he became a grinder in prison
(16:21b)

Parenthesis (Foreshadowing: Plot A Development):

(ff ^{v})   *Sanction/empowerment:* The hair of his head began to
grow after it was shaved (16:22)

— —

Plot A Complication/Plot D Greater Partial Resolution: (16:23-27)

The Philistine tyrants assembled to make a great
sacrifice to Dagon their god and to celebrate,
saying, (16:23abα)

(B2a/E2)   "Our god has given into our hand
Samson our enemy" (16:23bβγ)

When the people saw him, they praised their god,
saying, (16:24abα)

(B2a/E2)   "Our god has given into our hand
our enemy (16:24bβ)
the devastator of our land
and the multiplier of our slain" (16:24bγδ)

Philistines summon Samson from prison to entertain
them, and he performs before them (16:25abαβ)

They make Samson stand between the pillars, and he
says to the servant holding his hand, "Let me stand
where I can feel the pillars on which the temple
rests so that I may lean against them"
(16:25bγ-26)

Parenthesis: The temple was filled with men and
women—all the Philistine tyrants were there and
on the roof were about 3000 men and women—
watching Samson's performance (16:27)

Plot A Development/Plot D Complication: (16:28-30aαβ)

(C)   hh^i ⌐Samson called to Yʜᴡʜ, (16:28a)
      "Lord Yʜᴡʜ, now remember me,
      now strengthen me just this once, Elohim
      (16:28bα)
      that I may avenge with one act of revenge
(A1b)   my two eyes on the Philistines" (16:28bβ)
      └Samson turned to the two central pillars on which the
temple rested, braced himself against them, one on
his right and one on his left, and said, "Let me die
with the Philistines" (16:29-30aαβ)

Plot A Partial Situation Resolution/Plot D Dissolution: (16:30aγ-ε)

+   gg^{iv} He pushed with strength, and the temple fell on the
tyrants and all the people (16:30aγ-ε)

Plot A Character Resolution: (16:30b-31)

G1   The dead he put to death at his death
exceeded those he put to death in his life (16:30b)

	His brothers and paternal household went down and unearthed him (16:31aα)
G2	then went up and buried him between Zorah and Eshtaol in the grave of Manoah his father (16:31aβ-δ)
F1	He judged Israel twenty years (16:31b)

Perhaps as many as ten of the twelve essential cycle-motif elements are attested in the Samson account (and twelve of its twenty distinguishable elements), though they are less recognizably formulaic and function in a way that is more intrinsic to the narrative than has been the case in the preceding deliverer accounts. For example, whereas Israel never cries out (זעק) to YHWH (motif C),[301] Samson twice calls (קרא) to YHWH because of personal affliction (15:18; 16:28a).[302] Again, while Israel's enemies are never delivered into their hand (motif E2), the Philistines boast that their god has given Samson into their hand (16:23bβγ, 24bβ; cf. motif B2a)—ironically, just moments before YHWH implicitly delivers them into Samson's hand. Cycle-motif elements constitute the situation exposition (13:1) and most of the two character resolutions (15:20; 16:30b-31). Elsewhere they appear sporadically throughout (in the Plot A character exposition [13:5b], development [13:25aαβ¹; 14:6aα, 19aα; 15:14bα; 16:28a, 28bβ], complications [14:3bβ, 7b; 15:18, 19aγ; 16:19bβ, 20bγδ, 21aβ, 23bβγ, 24bβ] and partial resolutions [14:19bα; 15:20ⁱ,ⁱⁱⁱ]). Although cycle-motif element B2b is lacking, its function as an expositional element for the Samson account is foreshadowed already in 10:7bα(β). Since the mention of the Philistines in 10:7bα(β) serves no rhetorical purpose within the Jephthah account, it must be understood to serve as an anticipatory expositional element for the Samson account that, because of its placement beside the B2b element in the situational exposition of the Jephthah account, may imply the simultaneity of the Ammonite and Philistine oppressions.[303]

---

[301] Cf. Webb, *Judges* (1987), p. 163.

[302] In this, perhaps Samson is portrayed as a microcosm of Israel. Webb notes further that, in answer to Samson's first call, he is granted life (15:18-19), but, in answer to his second call, he is granted death (16:31) (*Judges* [1987], pp. 167, 171-72).

[303] Webb has observed a reversal between the order "into the hand of the Philistines and the Ammonites", in 10:7b, and the order represented by, first, the Ammonite oppression of the Jephthah account, then, the Philistine oppression of the Samson account (*Judges* [1987], pp. 162-63). It is doubtful that this is highly significant, however, since the order of mention of these paired foreign nations continuously alternates in 10:6, 7b and 11.

Plot A, the main plot of the account, governs the full extent of chs.
13–16 (13:1-7 [8-23] 24-25; 14:[1-3] 4-6 [7] 8-9 [10-11] 12-19; 15:1-17
[18-19] 20; 16:[1] 2-3 [4-6] 7-9 [10] 11-12 [13a] 13b-14 [15-21] 22
[23-27] 28-31) and traces action leading toward YHWH's deliverance of
Israel from the Philistines through Samson—though this plot lacks a
complete resolution. The exposition of the Samson account conforms
most closely to the expositional pattern of the Gideon/Abimelech
account in that it comprises cycle-motif elements (13:1; cf. 6:1-6) and
its character exposition (and complication) (13:2-7 [8-23] 24) contains a
hybrid of two type-scenes (13:3-23; cf. 6:11-24). The character exposition and its complication, which centre on the problem of the
barrenness of Manoah's wife (Plot B), do not disclose Samson's
character so much as that of his parents. To this end, the delaying
strategy of twice presenting the elements of the annunciation type-scene
(cf. the designations $a\alpha\beta\gamma$–b–c, $a^i\alpha$–b^i–c^i, $a^{ii}\gamma$ in the outline) shows
how Samson's father, Manoah, on the pretence of showing religious
zeal, only comically obstructs and delays YHWH's progress.[304] Since,
by means of the angelic annunciation, Samson is appointed a Nazirite
deliverer from birth, the reader is induced to hope that this deliverer
might prove to be the awaited ideal deliverer. Yet, the birth annunciation only proves to augment Samson's negative characterization when
the reader realizes that, in the book of Judges, he is the deliverer who
is least interested in being a deliverer.[305] Samson is portrayed as a
self-gratifying brute whose acts of deliverance are rarely better than
by-products of his spiteful nature. Nevertheless, this will also redound
to YHWH's glory, for, through his control of circumstances, YHWH
manages the affairs of this prankish womanizer so as to accomplish for

---

[304] The angel's second visitation reveals nothing except the unwillingness of Manoah to
believe the first annunciation made to his (unnamed) wife. Indeed, the function of the succeeding theophanic recognition type-scene (13:3, 9, 15-23) serves no purpose in the plot
other than to portray Manoah as one who misapprehends the motives of YHWH and who
obstructs and delays YHWH's progress. Ought the reader to regard Manoah's characterization as designed to foreshadow the characterization of Samson, who, while disregarding
the angelic commission that he should perpetually be a Nazirite, nevertheless unwittingly
fulfils its purpose?

[305] Barak is initially halfhearted about obeying YHWH's summons to join battle with
the Canaanites but eventually does so, Gideon serves YHWH in battle but eventually
exploits the situation to serve a personal vendetta against the Midianites and Jephthah
attempts to coerce YHWH into making his victory an opportunity for self-aggrandizement,
but never do these deliverers so completely ignore the interests of YHWH regarding the
welfare of the tribes of Israel as does Samson, who, even in his final prayer, seeks only
personal revenge.

Israel a measure of relief—even comic relief—from the oppression of their Philistine overlords.[306] Perhaps it is for this reason that one is reminded in 13:24b, the only clauses of the Plot A character exposition that are unrelated to Plot B, that Samson was blessed by YHWH.

The development of Plot A begins with the statement that YHWH's spirit began (חלל) to impel (פעם) Samson in Mahaneh Dan, between Zorah and Eshtaol (13:25).[307] Both the words חלל and פעם become important *Leitwörter* in the account, but this is the only sentence in which they occur together. The development of Plot A progresses intermittently, being complicated whenever it comes into conflict with Plots C and D. Already, with the notice that Samson asks his parents to get for him a Philistine wife from Timnah (14:1-3, Plot C exposition), Plot A is complicated by the revelation that Samson is determined to pursue a course at odds with both his parents' social preferences (14:3a) and his divine election to begin to deliver Israel from the Philistines (13:5b). Yet, in the parenthesis of 14:4, the narrator assures the reader (with information to which Samson's parents were not privy) that Samson's social aberration and religious apostasy were in accord with YHWH's control of circumstances leading to Israel's deliverance from the Philistines. With every step that he makes toward securing the Timnite woman as his wife (14:7, 10-11), Samson disregards YHWH's enmity with the Philistines. Yet, it is by YHWH's control of

---

[306] On the role of the trickster in the sociology of literature, see B. Babcock-Abrahams, "'A Tolerated Margin of Mess': The Trickster and His Tales Reconsidered", *JFI* 11 (1975), pp. 147-86; on Samson as trickster, see S. Niditch, "Samson as Culture Hero, Trickster, and Bandit: The Empowerment of the Weak", *CBQ* 52 (1990), pp. 608-24.

[307] Since the location of the Mahaneh Dan mentioned in 18:12 is specific and west of Kiriath Jearim in Judah, whereas this Mahaneh Dan is related to a location between Zorah and Eshtaol, one may infer alternatively: (1) that there were two specific locations called Mahaneh Dan, one by Kiriath Jearim and one between Zorah and Eshtaol (so Bertheau, *Richter und Ruth* [1845], p. 179; Soggin, *Judges* [2d edn, 1987], p. 236); (2) that there was but one location called Mahaneh Dan (most naturally, that in Judah) and that the mention of Mahaneh Dan in 13:25a is a spurious insertion into the text (so Moore, *Judges* [1895], p. 326; Burney, *Judges* [2d edn, 1920], p. 353); (3) that the reference in 13:25a is not a proper name but simply a reference to "a Danite camp between Zorah and Eshtaol" (so Boling, *Judges* [1975], p. 225) or (4) that there were two locations called Mahaneh Dan, one a specific place west of Kiriath Jearim and one the general enclave wherein were settled the remnants of the tribe of Dan (subsequent to the migration of Judg. 18) and within which were located the villages of Zorah and Eshtaol. In the latter two instances, one would have to infer that the term מחנה was being used differently in 13:25 and 18:12 yet so as to furnish a link between the accounts of Samson and the migration of the Danites.

circumstances that Samson is confronted by a lion, which he slays by
the empowerment of YHWH's spirit (14:5-6), and that there is a swarm
of bees in the lion's carcass when he returns to see it (14:8-9). It is
these divinely ordained circumstances that furnish the makings of
Samson's prankish riddle (14:12-14), which leads the Philistines to
coerce Samson's bride (14:15-18a), which furnishes Samson with his
first reason for revenge against the Philistines, which he wreaks, ironically, by the empowerment of YHWH's spirit (14:18b-19).[308] Thus,
while Samson is in control of his vengeful responses, he is not in control of the circumstances that YHWH has designed to bring Samson into
conflict with the Philistines. Even the subsequent escalating confrontations between Samson and the Philistines (15:3-5, 6, 7-8, 9-14a,
14b-17; 16:2, 3) are a consequence of YHWH's control of circumstances that remain beyond the control of Samson (i.e., 14:20-15:2).
Not until the dénouement-like incident of Samson's thirst (15:18-19) is
Samson humbled into acknowledging in prayer that it is YHWH, not he,
who controls the circumstances of his life.

Yet, Samson does not infer from the incident at Ein Haqqore that he
is obligated to serve YHWH's interests before his own. Indeed, Plot D
of ch. 16 is catalysed by a return venture into Philistine territory to
satisfy his seemingly insatiable appetite for Philistine women (16:1). In
parallel with the interplay between Plots A and C in chs. 14-15,
Plots A and D in ch. 16 develop intermittently, each being complicated
by the development of the other. No sooner does Samson extricate himself from the Philistine ambush at Gaza (16:2-3) than the Philistines are
again seeking to ambush him in Delilah's chamber (16:4-6, 10, 13a,
15-20). In all but the last instance, Samson evades his would-be captors
(16:7-9, 11-12, 13b-14), which only adds to their frustration and
humiliation. Yet, even when Samson's assailants succeed at last in
humiliating him (16:21, 23-27), the narrator offers a parenthetical

---

[308] On the interpretation of the riddles in the Samson story, see H. Bauer, "Zu
Simsons Rätsel in Richter Kapitel 14", *ZDMG* 66 (1912), pp. 473-74; H. Schmidt,
"Miscellen: 4. Zu Jdc 14", *ZAW* 39 (1921), p. 316; J. R. Porter, "Samson's Riddle:
Judges xiv. 14, 18", *JTS* NS 13 (1962), pp. 106-9; H.-P. Müller, "Der Begriff 'Rätsel' im
Alten Testament", *VT* 20 (1970), pp. 465-89, especially pp. 465-70; Crenshaw, "Samson
Saga" (1974), pp. 488-94; Y. David, "Simsons Rätsel nach der Auffassung des Moses
Hayyim Luzzato", *Semitics* 5 (1977), pp. 32-35; E. L. Greenstein, "The Riddle of
Samson", *Prooftexts* 1 (1981), pp. 237-60; S. Segert, "Paronomasia in the Samson Narra-
tive in Judges xiii-xvi", *VT* 34 (1984), pp. 455-56; P. Nel, "The Riddle of Samson (Judg
14,14.18)", *Bib* 66 (1985), pp. 534-45; O. Margalith, "Samson's Riddle and Samson's
Magic Locks", *VT* 36 (1986), pp. 225-34, especially pp. 225-29.

comment that suggests that his strength may return and Plot A may thus continue (16:22). Indeed, it does, in a greater though partial resolution (16:30aγ-ε), but not before Samson has once again been forced to acknowledge in prayer his dependence upon YHWH (16:28-30aαβ; cf. 15:18-19). Only then does the character resolution follow, in 16:30b-31 (complementing 15:20).

While many view the incident involving the harlot at Gaza (16:1-3) as unrelated to that of Delilah (16:4-30a), the former furnishes the Philistines with the motive for seeking vengeance on Samson through their intrigues with Delilah. The view that 16:1-3 and 16:4-30a form a continuous subplot may be justified by the fact that the eight-member sequence of chs. 14-15 (i.e., aa-bb-cc-dd-ee-ff-gg-ff^i-gg^i-ff^{ii}-gg^{ii}-ff^{iii}-gg^{iii}-hh-ff^{iv}) parallels that of ch. 16 only if 16:1-3 and 16:4-30a are continuous (cf. aa^i in 16:1; bb^i-cc^i-cc^{ii}-cc^{iii}-cc^{iv}-dd^i-ee^i-1/ff-1/ff^i-ff^v-hh^i-gg^{iv} in 16:5-30a).[309] Moreover, the fact that the Philistines seek to humiliate Samson at the city of Gaza (16:21b) suggests that, through Delilah, they were seeking an opportunity to retaliate in particular for the humiliation that they had suffered when Samson one night carried off Gaza's city gates (16:3).[310]

Plot B, which portrays YHWH's provision of a son to the barren wife of Manoah, is contained within 13:2-24a. Apart from its prolonged complication (13:8-23), it functions to introduce the character Samson, the primary human actor in the development of Plot A. The development and complication of Plot B (13:3-7 [8-23]) comprise an amalgamation of elements from two biblical type-scenes: that of the angelic birth annunciation (13:3-14) and that involving recognition of a

---

[309] Cf. presentations of the parallel structures of chs. 14-15 and ch. 16 in Exum, "Symmetry" (1981), pp. 3-9; Webb, *Judges* (1987), pp. 163-64. However, Exum's attempt to demonstrate structural parallelism between chs. 14 and 15, on the basis of sections marked off by "introductory formulae" (i.e., uses of ירד, הלך and עלה in 14:1, 5, 7, 10; 15:4, 6b, 9), seems unconvincing because: (1) there are in chs. 14-15 many uses of these verbs that Exum does not count as "introductory", and (2) there is nothing sufficiently distinctive or regular about the verbal clauses to indicate that their usage here is formulaic (pp. 10-16; cf. some points of similarity to Blenkinsopp, "Judges 13-16" [1963], pp. 66-67). Neither is the similarity between the four allegedly parallel "episodes" (i.e., 14:1-4 ‖ 15:1-3; 14:5-6 ‖ 15:4-6a; 14:7-9 ‖ 15:6b-8; 14:10-20 ‖ 15:9-19) sufficient to indicate that parallelism was deliberate (contra Exum, "Symmetry" [1981], pp. 16-18).

[310] Not only do the episodes of 16:1-3 and 16:4-30a culminate in material destructions at the same city, Gaza, but there is perhaps a paronomastic correspondence in the irony that the Philistines' failure to ambush Samson at night (cf. the four uses of הלילה in the night scene of 16:2-3) foreshadows their four subsequent attempts to capture him through Delilah (cf. the seven uses of דלילה in 16:4, 6, 10, 12, 13 <14> 18).

theophany (13:3a, 9, 15-23). I have already described a similarly structured hybrid of two type-scenes in the divine commission/theophanic
recognition type-scene of Judg. 6:11-24. The divine commission type-
scene is also the model for the elders' commission of Jephthah in
11:5-11. Although Judg. 13:3-23 contains none of the elements characteristic of the divine commission type-scene, its overall function, as
determining Samson's lifelong appointment to deliver Israel from the
Philistines (13:4-5, 13-14), is ostensibly that of a commissioning type-
scene.[311] Furthermore, motif element D1, the rhetorical function of
which parallels that of the divine commission type-scenes of 6:11-17
and 11:5-11, occurs in 13:5b (cf. 6:15aβ).

In the angelic annunciation type-scene of 13:3-14, Manoah's wife is
a foil to Manoah. When Manoah prays for another angelic visitation so
that he may inquire how they should treat the boy to be born (c, 13:8),
he unnecessarily delays the development of Plot B (as well as the
exposition of Plot A) just because he is unwilling to trust his wife's
testimony. Consequently, the angel reappears to his wife (a$^i\alpha$, 13:9; cf.
aα, 13:3a), she again goes and tells her husband (b^i, 13:10; cf. b, 13:6-
7), he again inquires about the boy (c^i, 13:11-12) and the angel again
explains what had already been communicated to Manoah's wife (a$^{ii}\gamma$,
13:13-14; cf. aγ, 13:4-5). Thus, in contrast to his wife, Manoah
obstructs the development of Plot B by requiring that the annunciation
scene be performed again for his own verification (cf. the sequence
a$\alpha\beta\gamma$–b–c, a$^i\alpha$–b^i–c^i, a$^{ii}\gamma$). Manoah is characterized as being
incredulous, if not cynical, about the angelic visitation—a negative
characterization that is protracted in the theophanic recognition type-
scene.

It is in Judg. 13:3a, 9, 15-23 that one finds the components of a
theophanic recognition type-scene. Manoah's hospitality to the angel of
YHWH in Judg. 13:15-23 is analogous to the pattern of Gideon's
hospitality to YHWH in 6:11-24, which was analogous to Abraham's
hospitality to YHWH in Genesis 18 (itself a foil to Lot's hospitality to
the two angels in Gen. 19). However, while the theophanic recognition
type-scene of 13:3a, 9, 15-23 has most of the expected elements, this
version lacks the expected altar aetiology (cf. 6:24), and, in place of a
reassurance from YHWH (cf. 6:23), the reassurance that they will not
die comes from Manoah's wife (13:23), who thus chides Manoah for
misapprehending the purpose of the divine visitation.

---

[311] Cf. Wharton, "Secret" (1973), p. 61; von Rad, *Gottes Wirken* (1974), ET: *God at
Work* (1980), pp. 44-45.

The birth and naming of Samson (13:24a) provides the resolution of Plot B, which had opened with an exposition of the problem of Manoah's wife's barrenness (13:2). Thus, the angelic birth annunciation and theophanic recognition type-scenes, which form the development and complication of Plot B (13:3-7 [8-23]), are enclosed by the barest elements of exposition and resolution needed to form a subplot.

Plot C (14:1-3 [5-6] 7 [8-9] 10-11 [12-20; 15:1-2, 6]), the subplot that traces the outworkings of Samson's quest for a Philistine wife from Timnah, is contained within chs. 14-15, though reprisals related to its dissolution extend to 16:2. Thus, while Plot C does not extend beyond 14:1-15:6, it is a catalyst for the confrontations between Samson and the Philistines in 15:7-16:2. The development of Plot C, wherein Samson attempts to secure a bride from among the Philistines, competes with the development of Plot A, wherein YHWH attempts to deliver Israel from the Philistines through Samson. Thus, throughout Judges 14-15, wherever Plot C develops it complicates the development of Plot A and vice versa. Since Samson never consummates his marriage to the Timnite woman, Plot C never comes to resolution. Indeed, once the father gives the bride to Samson's companion (14:20), the plot is dissolved, though, so long as there remained a possibility that she might be restored to Samson (e.g., through the death of her Philistine husband), there was hope that Plot C might recover from this state of dissolution. However, even this hope is finally removed when the Philistines burn Samson's wife (as the narrator regards her) and her father in 15:6. From the similarity of the testimonies of the Philistines (15:10b) and of Samson (15:11b), that each was retaliating for what the other had done, one discerns that the alternating pattern of reprisal and counterreprisal on the part of Samson (15:7-8a, 15-17) and the Philistines (15:9-10, 14a; 16:2) is but the consequence of the irreversible dissolution of Plot C in 15:6.

Plot D (16:1-6 [7-9] 10 [11-12] 13a [13b-14] 15-21, 23-27 [28-30a]) is contained entirely within ch. 16 and traces the Philistine plot to kill Samson in retaliation for his exploit at Gaza. Its exposition (16:1-3) presupposes that the Philistines already had reason to retaliate against Samson (16:2). However, after Samson humiliates the Gazaites by his feat of strength in carrying off their city gates (16:3), they become preoccupied more specifically with discovering the secret of his strength so that they, in turn, might humiliate him (16:5; cf. 16:6-7,

10-11, 13, 15-17). Hence, in contrast to Plot C, where it is the purpose of Samson that initially opposes but eventually catalyses the development of the main plot, in Plot D it is the Philistines' actions that complicate the development of Plot A. Nevertheless, it must be recognized that Plot D could not have come about were it not for its being catalysed by Samson's two further ventures after Philistine women (16:1, 4).

Just as the development of Plot C was intermittently interrupted by the series of incidents pertaining to Samson's riddle (14:5-6, 8-9, 12-19), so the development of Plot D is intermittently interrupted by the sequence made up of Samson's misdirections and Delilah's frustrated attempts to bind him (cf. h–i–j, 16:7-9; hⁱ–iⁱ–jⁱ, 16:11-12; hⁱⁱ–iⁱⁱ–jⁱⁱ, 16:13b-14). Only in the fourth and final segment of the series is the pattern broken, when Samson consents to tell Delilah the secret of his strength (hⁱⁱⁱ–iⁱⁱⁱ–jⁱⁱⁱ, 16:16-18, 19-20a, 20bαβ).[312] The latter development in Plot D culminates in a partial resolution in 16:21, where, in retaliation for Samson's seizing Gaza's city gates (ויאחז בדלתות שער־העיר ובשתי המזוזות, 16:3), the Philistines seize Samson (ויאחזוהו, 16:21aα), gouge out his eyes (וינקרו את־עיניו, 16:21aβ) and return him bound to Gaza (16:21b).[313] Considering the significance of cycle-motif element A1b in the book of Judges, there may be poetic justice in Samson's loss of the eyes in which his Philistine women had seemed so right (14:3bβ, 7b). Yet, ironically, just when it seems that Plot D has resolved in the Philistine ridicule of Samson (and YHWH) (16:23-27), it is Samson's desire to avenge the loss of his eyes that motivates him to complicate Plot D with another call to YHWH for strength (16:28-30aαβ; cf. 15:18-19). The result is not just the devastation of the devotees of Dagon but the final dissolution of Plot D (16:30aγ-ε).

Like the deliverer accounts of Deborah/Barak/Jael, Gideon/Abimelech and Jephthah, the Samson account has more than one dramatic climax. Indeed, the Samson account has nine moments that achieve at least a partial resolution at the level of Plot A (indicated in the plot-structure outline by the siglum '+'), each climactic moment

---

[312] On this use of the 3+1 numerical sequence, see Blenkinsopp, "Judges 13–16" (1963), pp. 67, 73-75. It is also worth noting how segments of two different series, 'h–i–j' and 'dd–ee–ff', coincide in 16:16-20 (i.e., ddⁱ/hⁱⁱⁱ, 16:16-18; eeⁱ/iⁱⁱⁱ, 16:19-20a [including 1/ff, 16:19bβ]; jⁱⁱⁱ, 16:20bαβ; 1/ffⁱ, 16:20bγδ).

[313] Note the irony inherent in the paronomasia between Samson's expectation, expressed in ואנער "and I shall shake myself [free]" (16:20b), and the result, expressed in the Philistine's action וינקרו "and they gouged" (16:21a).

building upon the intensity of those that precede (14:19aβγ; 15:4-5, 8a, 15; 16:3, [9b, 12b, 14b] 30aγ-ε).[314] Of these, three climaxes involve the destruction of some object of material or cultural worth to the Philistines: the burning of their wheat crop (15:4-5), the destruction of the gate at Gaza (16:3) and the destruction of Dagon's temple at Gaza (16:30aγ-ε). Four climaxes entail the killing of Philistines: thirty men at Ashkelon (14:19aβγ), a great slaughter (at Timnah?) (15:8a), a thousand men at Ramath Lehi (15:15) and all the 'tyrants' and people at the temple of Gaza (16:30aγ-ε). Only in the last climax do both material destruction and mass homicide combine so that the last climax of the account is unmistakably the most intense. Indeed, it is explicitly described by the narrator as being Samson's greatest slaughter (16:30b) and is further intensified by being prepared for by two sequences: it comes as the long-awaited compensation for the disappointment of the last segment of the 'h-i-j' sequence (cf. 16:7-9b, 11-12, 13b-14 vs. 16:16-19abα, 20bαβ),[315] and it is the delayed fulfilment of the expected

---

[314] Most scholars find only two major climaxes in the Samson account (which, indeed, is the case in the accounts of Deborah/Barak/Jael, Gideon/Abimelech and Jephthah). Wharton regards 15:14-19 as "the logical climax" of chs. 14–15 ("Secret" [1973], p. 62) but specifies that "with Samson's bloodthirsty cry [15:16] ... the story that began with the woman at Timnah has reached its climax" (p. 56). Similarly, within ch. 16, Wharton considers Samson's prayer (16:28 or 30aαβ?) the climax ("Secret" [1973], p. 61). Exum infers that the allegedly parallel passages of 15:12-13 and 16:23-24 anticipate the climaxes that begin at 15:14 and 16:25, respectively ("Symmetry" [1981], pp. 6, 19); however, Exum is later more definitive: "At the point where Samson appears defeated, both accounts reach their climax. Resolution comes when Samson calls (qr') on Yhwh and Yhwh answers Samson's petition (xv 18-19, xvi 28-30)" ("Theological Dimension" [1983], p. 34). Webb finds the major climaxes in 15:14-20 and 16:31, each closing a major movement in the story (Judges [1987], pp. 163, 166, 168, 170, 171, 172), yet elsewhere contradicts this by stating that "the Samson story reaches its climax in the great festival of Dagon in 16.23-30" (p. 165). Crenshaw speaks only broadly of "the climactic encounter between Samson and Delilah" ("Samson Saga" [1974], pp. 480, 487). However, if one allows plot function, rather than emotional tension or intensity of action, to determine where climaxes should fall, in chs. 14–15, one may discern more precisely that it is only in the account of the slaughter of Philistines in 15:15 that there is sufficient partial resolution of the expositional problem to consider this a climax at the level of Plot A. Similarly, in ch. 16, not until Samson slaughters the Philistines of Gaza in 16:30aγ-ε does he again resolve partially the situational problem that propels the action of the main plot.

[315] Blenkinsopp seems to be mistaken in regarding 16:15-21 as the main climax of Judg. 16 ("Judges 13-16" [1963], pp. 67, 74). In fact, it is only 16:21 that serves as a dramatic climax, and that only at the level of Plot D (cf. Crenshaw's similar sense of climax at the resolution of Plot B in 13:24[a] ["Samson Saga" (1974), p. 476]). The latter climax, having been prepared by the sequence of minor climaxes within Plot A that are designated elements j (16:9b), j^i (16:12b) and j^ii (16:14b), coincides with the anticlimax of element j^iii (16:20bαβ). In any case, 16:21 is only the penultimate climax of the account.

but displaced element gg^{iv} of the series aa^i–bb^i–cc^i–cc^{ii}–cc^{iii}–cc^{iv}–dd^i–ee^i–1/ff–1/ff^i–ff^v–hh^i–gg^{iv}.[316] But the final climax of 16:30aγ-ε has the ironic distinction of being the moment of Samson's suicide.

One might also observe that in Judges there is a pattern of escalation among the deliverer accounts as to the number of dramatic climaxes per account. The Othniel and Ehud accounts had but one climax each, there were dual climaxes in three of the deliverer accounts (Deborah/Barak/Jael, Gideon/Abimelech and Jephthah)—making a further six—and the number of climaxes in Plot A of the Samson account is nine.

Besides the gradual escalation of intensity among the climactic moments of the Samson account, the parallel sequencing of events between chs. 14–15 and ch. 16 offers another example in Judges of escalated parallelism. Elements designated above by double letters in the plot-structure outline are presented essentially in parallel order (i.e., aa–bb–cc–dd–ee–ff–gg–ff^i–gg^i–ff^{ii}–gg^{ii}–ff^{iii}–gg^{iii}–hh–ff^{iv} roughly parallels aa^i–bb^i–cc^i–cc^{ii}–cc^{iii}–cc^{iv}–dd^i–ee^i–1/ff–1/ff^i–ff^v–hh^i–gg^{iv}). Also to be considered is the fact that both sequences end in a recurrence of the F1 motif (15:20^{i,iii}; 16:31b). Indeed, it may have been awareness of the parallel sequencing of events between chs. 14–15 and ch. 16 that prompted the compiler/redactor to insert the partial character resolution of 15:20 so as to anticipate rhetorically, and to parallel structurally, that of 16:31b.[317]

As further evidence of deliberate parallel sequencing between chs. 14–15 and ch. 16, one may consider the recurrence of *Leitwörter* related to the lexeme אסר: לאסור (15:10b), לאסרך (15:12a), לא כי־אסר נאסרך (15:13a), ויאסרהו (15:13b), אסוריו (15:14b), ואסרנחו (16:5), במה תאסר (16:6), אם־יאסרני (16:7), ותאסרהו (16:8), ובמה תאסר (16:10), אם־אסור יאסרוני (16:11), ותאסרהו (16:12), במה תאסר (16:13a), מבית האסירים (16:25b), בתית האסירים (16:21bγ), ויאסרוהו (16:21bβ). What strikes one as being more than coincidental is the fact that it is only in the final uses of both episodes that one finds a change from verbal forms to nominal forms (15:14b; 16:21bγ, 25b).

---

[316] The delay of the 'gg' element in the second series is felt more intensely because it was an element that four times followed element 'ff' in the preceding parallel series: aa–bb–cc–dd–ee–ff–gg–ff^i–gg^i–ff^{ii}–gg^{ii}–ff^{iii}–gg^{iii}–hh–ff^{iv}. Compare the similar sequential preparation of both climaxes in the Gideon/Abimelech account (8:5-21a leading to 8:21b; 9:1-5aβ, 25-49, 51-52 leading to 9:53).

[317] Exum, "Symmetry" (1981), p. 9; Webb, *Judges* (1987), p. 257 n. 131.

Even beyond the parallel sequencing of events in chs. 14–15 and ch. 16, there are three sets of inclusios that indicate that chs. 14–16 were intended to be read in conjunction with each other and as distinct from the exposition of ch. 13. One inclusio, framing chs. 14–16, may be seen in the references to Zorah and Eshtaol in 13:25aβ^{ii}b and 16:31aβ-δ.[318] Another, surrounding the entire saga, is to be found in the references to Samson's father, Manoah, and Zorah in 13:2 and 16:31aβ-δ.[319] A third inclusio, framing ch. 13, may be found in the only references to the Danites in the account: the reference to "the clan of the Danites" in 13:2 and to "Mahaneh Dan" in 13:25aβ^{ii}b. Moreover, it may be a result of deliberate design that these three inclusios are triangulated among three verses (13:2, 25aβ^{ii}b; 16:31aβ-δ) so that each verse contains only two inclusio elements.

There may be an escalated parallelism between the characterization of Samson and that of the tribes of Israel in that, just as Samson repeatedly neglects his Nazirite obligations to YHWH by engaging in impure acts and relations with foreign women, so the tribes of Israel, in general (e.g., Judah [15:11-13] and "Israel" in element A1a [13:1a]; cf. A1a, A1b, A2a and A2b throughout Judges), and Dan, in particular (cf. Judg. 18), prove to be negligent of their obligations to YHWH as an elect people by engaging in cultically disloyal acts and by neglecting to expel foreigners from the land.[320] This escalated parallelism rests only

---

[318] Cf. Exum, "Symmetry" (1981), pp. 5, 9; Webb, *Judges* (1987), p. 164. Moreover, these geographical references also form an important link to the account of Judg. 18, which describes the prior migration of the Danites from Zorah and Eshtaol (i.e., 18:2, 8, 11). In this connection, perhaps greater attention should be given to the demarcating function of geographical references in the plot-structures of deliverer accounts of Judges: e.g., the references to the פסילים in the Ehud account (3:19aαβ, 26b), to (the site of) the tent of Heber or Jael in the Deborah/Barak/Jael account (4:11, 17a, 18b and 20a [as framing 4:18-20]; 5:24b), to Ophrah in the Gideon account (6:11a; 8:27aαβ, 32b) and to Mizpah (of Gilead) in the Jephthah account (10:17b; 11:11b, 29b [*bis*], 34aα).

[319] Webb, *Judges* (1987), p. 164.

[320] The explicit negative characterization of Judah, in 15:11-13, is not only representative of "Israel", but shows, by contrast with the preeminence of Judah both in the framework (1:1-20; 20:18) and as the first tribe to put forth a deliverer (Othniel, 3:7-11), the extent to which intertribal covenant zeal has degenerated since the deliverer accounts of Judges began (cf. Webb, *Judges* [1987], p. 163). Indeed, some infer that Samson is portrayed as the polar opposite of Othniel, whose marriage was exemplary, who summoned Israel to holy war and who delivered Israel into an era of peace (so Boling, *Judges* [1975], p. 83; Webb, *Judges* [1987], p. 170). As to the negative characterization of the Danites, the reason why Samson is the first deliverer not to summon his tribe to battle against the Philistines seems to derive from the fact that his family represents a part of only a small remnant of the Danite tribe that, in a preceding generation, had migrated northward from the same general locale (cf. Judg. 13:25aβ^{ii}b; 16:31aβ-δ; 18:2, 8, 11). Ostensibly, it is the Danites' prior abandonment of their tribal land that prevented "Israel"

upon an implicit similarity between the portrayal of Samson and those of Israel or the tribe of Dan within the Samson account (for, beyond 13:2, 25aβ[ii]b, there is no reference to the Danites in the account). It is perhaps appropriate that the Samson account comes as the last in the series of deliverer accounts. By its final position, Samson's portrayal signals what may be a culminating expression of Israel's inability to put forth a deliverer who would guide both tribe and nation into a new age of obedience to YHWH. In any case, by his failure to fulfil his divine commission as a Nazirite, Samson is a microcosm of the Danite tribe and of Israel for their respective failures to fulfil their obligations to YHWH.[321] Thus, given the present context of the Samson account, Samson's struggle between loyalty to his parents and erotic attraction to foreign women is an effigy of the struggle of his tribe and his nation between religious devotion to YHWH and attraction to foreign cults.[322]

The glorification of YHWH is a rhetorical concern of the Samson account as much as of the previous deliverer accounts. The first event to accrue to YHWH's glorification is that of his removal of barrenness from Manoah's wife in answer to Israel's need of a deliverer.[323] Indeed, YHWH's theophanic annunciation of Samson's birth comes in answer to the distress of Israel and, implicitly, of Manoah's barren wife, though neither party explicitly cries out to YHWH for help.[324] YHWH's readiness to help overtly demonstrates that his kindness alone, and not the nation's repentance, is the ultimate basis for Israel's hope of deliverance in the events that follow.

The Samson account resembles preceding deliverer accounts in that YHWH is here again glorified through his portrayal as controlling all

---

from being summoned by Samson to engage the Philistines in battle and, presumably, from totally defeating them as had "Israel" under previous deliverers.

[321] Webb says, "Samson is virtually incontinent, wilful Israel personified and is scarcely recognizable as a saviour-judge" (*Judges* [1987], p. 158; cf. pp. 172, 258 nn. 139, 140). Cf. Wharton, "Secret" (1973), pp. 53, 60; Crenshaw, "Samson Saga" (1974), p. 479; J. B. Vickery, "In Strange Ways: The Story of Samson", in *Images of Man and God: Old Testament Short Stories in Literary Focus* (B. O. Long [ed.], BLS 1, Sheffield, 1981), p. 62; Greenstein, "Riddle" (1981), p. 247.

[322] In this way one may integrate the seemingly opposed viewpoints of Crenshaw ("Samson Saga" [1974], pp. 471, 472, 478, 484, 486-87) and von Rad (*Gottes Wirken* [1974], ET: *God at Work* [1980], p. 46) as to the central struggle in the Samson account.

[323] Cf. Wharton, "Secret" (1973), pp. 472, 473-74.

[324] Crenshaw asserts that pathos inheres in the theme of barrenness in Israel and that this pathos in ch. 13 is only augmented by the angelic birth annunciation ("Samson Saga" [1974], pp. 473, 475, 477; on Crenshaw's notice of pathos elsewhere in the Samson account, see pp. 486, 499, 502).

circumstances of the account. Although, in Judges 13–16, Samson is portrayed as repeatedly putting personal ambitions ahead of YHWH's interests, YHWH controls circumstances so that Samson becomes an unwitting (if not unwilling) agent of counterattack upon the Philistines.[325] Since the Nazirite obligation imposed upon Samson by YHWH is the essential information disclosed about Samson in the character exposition (13:5a$\beta\gamma$, 7), it sets the standard for evaluating his subsequent abdications of duty. According to Num. 6:1-21, one who had taken a Nazirite vow was to refrain from eating anything from the vine, from drinking wine or other fermented drink (Num. 6:1-4), and from cutting his hair for the duration of the vow (Num. 6:5-8) and was to avoid the presence of a dead body (6:9-12). The fact that Samson's mother was told to avoid consuming anything from the vine, fermented drink or anything unclean (Judg. 13:4, 7, 14) suggests that these restrictions applied to her because, during pregnancy, her body would be nourishing Samson in the womb. The only Nazirite restriction explicitly applied to Samson is that his hair should not be cut (13:5a$\beta\gamma$; 16:17), though it may also follow that, after his birth, he would remain under the same obligations that had been imposed upon his mother.[326] Only twice in the account does Samson apparently break his Nazirite obligation: once in chs. 14–15 (i.e. 14:8-9a) and once in ch. 16 (i.e. 16:16-20a). Samson violates the obligation to avoid eating anything unclean when he eats honey from the carcass of the lion (14:8-9a).[327] The reader is never explicitly told that Samson drank fermented brew at his wedding feast (cf. 14:10b-11),[328] but 16:17 portrays Samson

---

[325] Cf. Wharton, "Secret" (1973), pp. 479, 501-2.

[326] Blenkinsopp has inferred that the difference from Num. 6 of the order of Nazirite prohibitions mentioned in Judg. 13, where Samson's prohibition against shaving comes climactically at the end, evidences a concern for plot ("Judges 13–16" [1963], p. 66). Cf. Burney, *Judges* (2d edn, 1920), pp. 342-43; Webb, *Judges* (1987), pp. 170, 257 n. 127.

[327] Even if one concedes that 13:5 is a later insertion into the traditional account (so Wharton, "Secret" [1973], pp. 59-60; Crenshaw, "Samson Saga" [1974], p. 476), yet, contra Wharton (p. 57; cf. pp. 57-60), an assumption of Samson's Nazirite status, as revealed in 13:5, 7b, is necessary for understanding chs. 14–15. Samson's Nazirite status was not a secret to his parents (13:4-5a, 7b, 13-14) nor even to Samson himself (16:17), so what other explanation should be offered as to Samson's motive for keeping secret from his parents the fact that he had come into contact with a lion's carcass (14:6b, 9b, 16b)? For a treatment of the theme of the broken Nazirite vow in the Samson saga, see Blenkinsopp, "Judges 13–16" (1963), pp. 65, 66 n. 7, 67, 69, 73.

[328] It is neither valid nor fair to the narrator's purpose to infer from the etymology of מִשְׁתֶּה 'feast' (14:10b, 12, 17) that Samson drank fermented drink on this occasion (contra Burney, *Judges* [2d edn, 1920], p. 344; Blenkinsopp, "Judges 13–16" [1963], p. 66). Contrast with this, Crenshaw, "Samson Saga" [1974], pp. 480-81 (following John Milton, *Samson Agonistes*, ll. 541-45, 558-59).

recklessly disclosing the secret that his hair should not be cut. Through YHWH's control of circumstances, both of Samson's abdications of responsibility in regard to his Nazirite status lead to situations of conflict with the Philistines—indeed, the first and last such situations in the account. Perhaps, the critical role that these framing confrontations play in the story makes it seem that Samson would never have attained triumph over the Philistines except at the cost of violating his Nazirite obligations.[329] Concomitantly, Samson's very resistance to YHWH's commission redounds to the glorification of YHWH, who manages to achieve his purpose not in spite of, but by means of, Samson's resistance.[330]

As in some preceding deliverer accounts, in which cultic concerns are prevalent (e.g., the idols of the Ehud account, the altar of Baal, the ephod and Shechemite temple in the Gideon/Abimelech account and the cultic rites of sacrifice in the Jephthah account), there is a pervasive concern with cultic matters in the Samson account. Besides concern with the Nazirite vow, evidence of a cultic concern begins with Manoah's offering of a kid (גדי העזים, 13:19) to the angel of YHWH.[331] Later, Samson seems intent on making a similar offering, though perhaps only as a gesture of reconciliation (15:1).[332] Finally, Samson himself is mocked by the Philistines as a captive of their god, Dagon.[333] As viewed against YHWH's denunciation of Israel's serving the gods of the Philistines in 10:6aγ-ε, the destruction of the temple of

---

[329] It is perhaps this observation that prompted Blenkinsopp to propose that the plot of the Samson story revolves around the theme of the broken Nazirite vow ("Judges 13-16" [1963], pp. 65-69).

[330] While correct in perceiving that YHWH's purpose to humiliate the Philistines through Samson is the main purpose of Judg. 13-16, Wharton seems nevertheless mistaken in describing this purpose as "secret" ("Secret" [1973], pp. 55-58, 60-61). In fact, it is a purpose that is made explicit in 13:5b [motif D1] to both reader and characters (at least to Samson's mother). True, the means by which YHWH seeks an occasion against the Philistines comes as a surprise to Samson's parents (14:4a), no less than to Samson (cf. 14:18b; 15:3), but the fact that YHWH purposed that Samson should achieve a partial Philistine defeat is no secret.

[331] Between Manoah's offering in 13:19 and Gideon's offering in 6:18-19 there is a reverse order collocation of מנחה and גדי העזים. Perhaps the assonance in 13:19 between the offerer (מנוח) and the offering (מנחה) was deliberate. Note a similar offering to Baal, son of Dagon, in the Ugaritic Krt text (CTA 14 ii 66-70). Cf. Blenkinsopp, "Judges 13-16" (1963), p. 67 n. 10; Wharton, "Secret" (1973), p. 62.

[332] Cf. Crenshaw, "Samson Saga" (1974), p. 481.

[333] Cf. Wharton, "Secret" (1973), p. 62. Implicitly, the triumph of Dagon is less over Samson than over Samson's god, YHWH.

Dagon in the final scene of the Samson account (16:23-30a) has the aura of religious polemic.[334]

The Judges compiler/redactor may not have needed greatly to modify the Samson traditions in order to adapt them to his/her concern to satirize foreign kingship. Mockery of the Philistines is so intrinsic to the parallel accounts of chs. 14–15 and ch. 16 that it may even have been the main point of the original, perhaps secular, traditions.[335] However, whether by the author's or compiler/redactor's design, the Philistine tyrants (סרן) are mentioned seven times in the present form of ch. 16 (16:5, 8, 18 [bis], 23a, 27, 30a), and the last of these comes at the moment of climax—a coincidence that seems hardly fortuitous in the general scheme of Judges to satirize foreign kingship.

Besides the satirization of the Philistine rulers at the end of Judges 16, the Philistine populace as a whole is subjected to satire at every moment of climax in Plot A (14:19aβγ; 15:4-5, 8a, 15; 16:3, [9b, 12b, 14b] 30aγ-ε). Besides this, the initial instigation of conflict between Samson and the Philistines, through the verbal contest of the riddles of 14:12-19a (i.e., 14:14aβγ, 18aγδ, 18bβγ), initiates a series of increasingly negative characterizations of the Philistines as inclined to coercion (14:15), covenant disloyalty (15:1b-2), violence (15:6), increased violence (15:9-10a), murderous ambush (16:2) and bribery (16:5)—all the passages marked with the siglum ' − ' in the plot-structure outline. Indeed, for every negatively characterized action on the part of the Philistines (siglum ' − '), Samson carries out a poetically just recompense against them (the moments of climax marked ' + '). Note how each of the first five negative acts of the Philistines are matched by an act of retaliation from Samson:

Philistine injustice	Samson's retaliation
14:15	14:19aβγ
15:1b-2	15:4-5
15:6	15:8a
15:9-10a	15:15
16:2	16:3

---

[334] Cf. Webb, *Judges* (1987), pp. 167-68. It must remain a matter of ambiguity whether YHWH's seemingly positive response to Samson's final prayer was motivated by concern to avenge the loss of Samson's eyes or to avenge himself against the implicit religious mockery of the Philistine devotees of Dagon. In any case, here, as in the Jephthah account, YHWH seems both silent and inactive when Samson offers himself as a human sacrifice (cf. Webb, *Judges* [1987], p. 170). Nothing explicit is said about the source of his strength when he topples the pillars of Dagon's temple—only his revenge is in view (cf. how Samson's feats are sometimes said to be motivated by revenge, as in 15:3, 7;

The last of the negative Philistine acts is followed by a prolonged series comprising three minor moments of climax and the delay describing Samson's capture before the great and final climax of the account:

Philistine injustice	Samson's retaliation
16:5	16:[9b, 12b, 14b] 30aγ-ε

From this scheme it is apparent that, so far as the plot-structure is concerned, it is the acts of injustice by the Philistines that are the main cause of the escalation of violence in the account and that justly culminate in the destruction of Gaza's temple, the Philistine rulers and their subjects.[336]

Alter has called attention to a motif of fire in chs. 14–16, which may be seen in the following: the Philistine threat of death by fire made against Samson's bride (14:15), Samson's reprisal of burning the Philistines' fields for their reneging upon his marital contract (15:4-5), the Philistines' counterreprisal of burning Samson's ex-bride and ex-father-in-law (15:6) and the simile that likens Samson's strength in snapping cords to fire burning flax (15:14).[337] I have already remarked on the rhetorical functions of the *Leitwort* פעם (verb: 'pound' > 'impel'; noun: 'step' > 'occasion') in Judg. 13:25aαβ¹; 15:3; 16:18, 20, 28 and its connection with the motif that uses the verb חלל (Hi. 'to begin') in 13:5b.[338]

Developments in Judges that first appear in the Samson account include:

1. the angelic annunciation of the birth of the deliverer (13:3-14);
2. the instigation of conflict (and the exposure of character) through a verbal contest using enigmatic sayings (14:12-19a, i.e., 14:14aβγ, 18aγδ, 18bβγ);[339]
3. the fact that no tribe is summoned by the deliverer to join battle with the foreign oppressors of Israel;

16:28bβ; and sometimes said to be empowered by YHWH's spirit [cycle-motif D2a], as in 14:6aα, 19aα; 15:14bα).

[335] Cf. Blenkinsopp, "Judges 13–16" (1963), p. 68; Wharton, "Secret" (1973), pp. 52, 53, 54, 60; Crenshaw, "Samson Saga" (1974), p. 479; von Rad, *Gottes Wirken* (1974), ET: *God at Work* (1980), p. 44.

[336] On the question of the relation between vengeance, retaliation and poetic justice, see Crenshaw, "Samson Saga" (1974), p. 483.

[337] Alter, *Biblical Narrative* (1981), pp. 94-95.

[338] See the discussion in chapter 1 concerning motif D2a.

[339] One should note, however, that the disputation of Jephthah against the king of Ammon (11:12-28) performs a similar function of humiliating through satire an enemy of Israel.

4. the fact that there is no final removal from the land of the foreign oppressors.

Both the first and the last two of these new developments in Judges show how marked a contrast there is between the heightened expectations that the reader has for Samson as a divinely appointed Nazirite deliverer at the beginning of the account and the disillusionment that comes at the end, when no tribe is summoned to battle and no decisive victory is won to expel the foreigners from the land. Thus, even though Samson fulfilled YHWH's intention that he only begin to deliver Israel from the Philistines, the positioning of this partially resolved story as the last of Judges' series of deliverer accounts elicits disappointment.

C. JUDGES' DOUBLE DÉNOUEMENT

In the first section of this chapter, I described the distinct role that each part of Judges' double prologue plays in the book's overall aim of orienting its readers to a pro-Judah tribal–political standard of inter-tribal leadership and to a deuteronomic religious standard of behaviour in Israel. In both parts of the double prologue, these higher standards resemble the normative standards of YHWH's covenant with Israel as set forth in the book of Deuteronomy. The tribes' toleration of foreigners in the land and their propensity toward idolatry, which are disclosed in Prologue-A, are serially exemplified in each situation that forms the main crisis in the deliverer accounts (3:7–16:31). Moreover, each deliverer account exemplifies the cycle-motif pattern introduced in Prologue-B. Hence, although the accounts of Judges illustrate, indeed escalate, problems of covenant loyalty that were introduced in the double prologue, they never furnish a solution for Israel's most fundamental problem. Nevertheless, Prologue-A may hint that a solution should be expected to emerge from the tribe of Judah, since this tribe's characterization is the most favourable of the tribes depicted in 1:1–2:5. Prologue-A may further hint that Jebus/Jerusalem, which features prominently in the structure of 1:1–2:5 and which plays a prominent role in the contrasting characterizations of Judah versus Benjamin, may be a token of YHWH's favour. Both Prologue-A and Prologue-B together hint that, if a solution should be found for the problem of Israel's covenant waywardness, it will have to derive from some place in Israel where a commitment to the conquest of the land and to the cult of YHWH is steadfast.[340] However, no explicit resolution emerges to solve the problem of Israel's covenant disloyalty except that which is implicit in the negative characterization of the period of the judges when viewed from the perspective of the monarchy (17:6; 21:25). Indeed, Judges 17–18 and 19–21, while illustrating the most blatant violations of the covenant ideals endorsed by Judges' compiler/ redactor, clarify for the first time what appears to be the rhetorical purpose of the book of Judges in regard to both covenant and monarchical idealization.

The dénouement accounts of Judges 17–18 and 19–21 are framed and punctuated by a monarchy motif (17:6a; 18:1a; 19:1a; 21:25a) that, in its first and last occurrences, is followed by motif A1b (17:6b; 21:25b). Apparently, the A1b motif of Judges 17–21 was intended to complement thematically the A1a motif, which introduces each recurrence of the cycle-motif in Prologue-B and the deliverer accounts. Given this relationship between motifs A1a and A1b in Judges, it seems significant—especially for the interpretation of Judges' double dénouement—that formulae that antithetically resemble Judges' A1b and A1a motifs are elsewhere found in collocation only in Deut. 12:1– 13:19 (i.e., the antithesis of A1b in Deut. 12:8aα/b; the antithesis of A1a in 12:25bβ, 28bβγ and 13:19b; [cf. elsewhere: 6:18a; 21:9b; but A1a properly in 4:25bγ^i, 9:18bβ^i, 17:2bβ^i and 31:29bβ]).[341] When this collocation is considered with other thematic and phraseological correspondences between Judges 17–18 and Deuteronomy 12, on the one hand, and between Judges 19–21 and Deuteronomy 13, on the other, the probability increases that Judges' compiler/redactor intended 17–18 and 19–21 to be read in the light of the covenant regulations endorsed by Deuteronomy 12 and 13, respectively. It is my aim to demonstrate that, whatever other narrative analogies may exist between Judges 17– 18 and 19–21 and other biblical narratives (e.g., Num. 12:16–14:25

---

[340] Such hints are not obvious upon first reading Judges' double prologue, but they become apparent after reflecting upon the significance of the monarchical idealization introduced in the double dénouement of chs. 17–18 and 19–21. Indeed, Judges' overall concern to promote an ideal king as the means of insuring the stability of both intertribal justice and the cult remains concealed until its closing five chapters.

[341] In regard to Judg. 17:6 and 21:25, F. E. Greenspahn commented, "Whatever the relationship between this statement and the stories which it punctuates, its literary affinities are clear. To 'do good in the eyes of ...' (ʿśh yśr bʿyny) is common and even characteristic in deuteronomic literature" ("An Egyptian Parallel to Judg 17:6 and 21:25", JBL 101 [1982], p. 129). Cf. M. Weinfeld, Deuteronomy and the Deuteronomic School (Oxford, 1972), p. 335.

and Gen. 19:1-11, respectively), their correlation with Deuteronomy 12 and 13 also controls, at least to some extent, the rhetorical strategy of the Judges compiler/redactor.[342]

§1. *Dénouement-A (17:1-18:31): Failure to Occupy the Land Promotes Cultic Disloyalty*

Prologue-B and Dénouement-A share a number of parallel features, which suggests that they were designed to frame symmetrically Judges' main body of deliverer stories. In support of the view that Judg. 2:6-3:6 and 17-18 were intended to frame symmetrically the book of Judges, Gooding proposed three allegedly intentional correspondences between these sections: (1) Israel's multigenerational degeneration into idolatry (2:10, 17, 19) and Micah's inducement to idolatry by his mother (17:1-6); (2) concern to test Israel's covenant (cultic) loyalty to YHWH as prescribed by Moses (2:12-3:4) and the aberration from cultic loyalty to YHWH by Moses' own descendant (17:7-12; 18:2b-6, 18-20, 30b); (3) Israel's national apostasy from YHWH's cult (2:11-13, 19) and the Danites' tribal apostasy from YHWH's cult (18:14-26, 30a, 31).[343] Indeed, both sections concern cultic disloyalty in Israel and a subsidiary concern about occupation of the tribal territories. However, whereas in Judg. 2:6-3:6 YHWH withholds territory from Israel because of cultic disloyalty, in Judges 17-18 Dan succumbs to cultic

---

[342] Few have acknowledged more than a tacit correspondence between the narrative portions of Judg. 17-18 and the stipulations enjoined in Deut. 12, perhaps because the latter are generally assumed to have arisen first in connection with the centralization of the cult at Jerusalem under the monarchy of Judah. However, many have noted correspondences between Judg. 19:1-21:24 and Deut. 13, e.g., Moore, *Judges* (1895), pp. 440 and 442 (on Judg. 20:40; Deut. 13:17), 444 (on Judg. 20:48; Deut. 13:15-16); S. Niditch, "The 'Sodomite' Theme in Judges 19-20: Family, Community, and Social Disintegration", *CBQ* 44 (1982), p. 372; Webb, *Judges* (1987), p. 232 n. 15 (on Judg. 20:48; Deut. 13:16-17). No one has yet commented on the implicit incrimination that this correspondence levels against Israel when the plot-structure of Judg. 19:1-21:24 is read against the covenant requirements of Deut. 13 (see below).

Richter argued that Deut. 13 and 17:2-7 furnished the covenant-legal background of both Judg. 2:11-19, Judges' framework (Rdt₁) and the *Beispielstück* of 3:7-11 (Rdt₂) (*Retterbuches* [1964], pp. 78-79, 81-86). However, in view of the widespread phraseological correspondences between elements of Judges' cycle-motif and Deuteronomy (which Richter cited in his own table, p. 78; also, see above the table citing correspondences between Judg. 2:11-3:6, Joshua and Deuteronomy), it may have been ill-advised for him to have attempted to isolate Deut. 13 and 17:2-7 as the key passages influencing Judges' cycle-motif.

[343] D. W. Gooding, "The Composition of the Book of Judges", in *Eretz-Israel: Archaeological, Historical and Geographical Studies*, vol. 16, *Harry M. Orlinsky Volume* (Jerusalem, 1982), p. 76*.

disloyalty in the course of compromising their obligation to occupy their territory.

In addition to these parallel themes between Prologue-B and Dénouement-A, the arrangement of Dénouement-A attests a clear rhetorical focus upon concern about cultic disloyalty. The plot-structure of Judg. 17:1–18:31 begins with an account of Micah's family cult (an aberration from the ideal of one intertribal cult enjoined by Deut. 12), becomes complicated by the Levite's quest for a priestly position apart from YHWH's cult, becomes further complicated by the Danites' departure from their tribal territory and culminates in the promotion of Micah's family–cult apostasy to the level of tribal–cult apostasy by the Danites (Judg. 18:30a, 31).[344] This plot-structure 'telescopes' so that each new plot develops by escalating the complications of previous plots. Furthermore, each major development is signalled by the recurring notice that the action takes place "at Micah's house in the hill country of Ephraim" (17:1, 8b; 18:2b, 13, [22a]).

Four plot-levels may be traced through Judg. 17:1-5, 7-13; 18:1b-31: (1) the plot that concerns the outcome of Micah's mother's curse upon the thief who stole her silver (17:1-2a [2b] 3a [3b] 4a [4b-5, 8b-13; 18:13-17, 22-26, 30a, 31]) (Plot A); and the three mediating plots by which the complication of Plot A is carried forward: (2) the plot that shows the Levite's illegitimate quest for a place of employment other than in the cult of YHWH (17:7-12; 18:[2b-6, 13-17] 18-20, 30b) (Plot B); (3) the plot showing the Danites' illegitimate quest for a place to settle other than in the region of their tribal inheritance (18:1-2a [2b-6] 7-12 [13-19] 21 [22-26], 27-29) (Plot C); (4) the plot showing the Danites' illegitimate adoption of a cult (objects and priesthood) other than that of YHWH (18:2b-6, 13-20, 22-26, 30a, 31) (Plot D).[345] The plot-structure of the narrative may be outlined as follows:

---

[344] The suggestion of Klein, that the meaning of Dan ("judge" from דין) may be a point of irony in Judg. 17–18 (*Triumph of Irony* [1988], p. 159), is dubious, since this nuance is not made explicit, as is the ironic play on Benjamin ("son of the right") in Judg. 20:16 (cf. 3:15).

[345] Webb described a three-part plot-structure (17:1-5, 7-13; 18:1b-30) with 17:6 and 18:1[a] at "nodal points" in the development of the single plot (*Judges* [1987], pp. 182-83, 260 n. 2). Y. Amit has discerned "three episodes" in Judg. 17–18, of which the first two (17:1-5, 7-13) provide the exposition for the third (18:1b-30) in that "They furnish supplementary information for the reader about the sanctuary at the Mountain of Ephraim ... introducing the characters, furnishing details about the scene of the action and the customary behaviour of the world of the personages" ("Hidden Polemic in the Conquest of Dan: Judges xvii–xviii", *VT* 40 [1990], pp. 5, 15-16). Actually, the first two episodes are not the complete exposition for the third because they do not introduce the Danites nor the problem that they seek to overcome (i.e., their need for new territory).

Plot A: Execution of the curse against the thief who stole Micah's mother's silver (17:1-2a [2b] 3a [3b] 4a [4b-5, 8b-13; 18:13-17, 22-26, 30a, 31])

    Plot A Exposition: Micah's confession from fear of his mother's curse upon the thief who stole her silver (17:1-2a)

    Plot A Complication: Mother's blessing of Micah (17:2b)

    Plot A Partial Resolution: Micah's return of stolen silver (17:3a)

    Escalation of Plot A Complication: Mother's consecration to YHWH of a votive idol (17:3b)

    Plot A Partial Resolution: Resumptive statement of Micah's return of stolen silver (17:4a)

    Escalation of Plot A Complication: [Mother's] deposit of the idol in Micah's house (17:4b)

    Escalation of Plot A Complication: Micah's institution of an idol shrine and family priest (17:5)

Plot B: Levite's illegitimate quest for employment elsewhere than in the cult of YHWH (17:7-12; 18:[2b-6, 13-17] 18-20, 30b)

    Plot B Exposition: Levite's quest for new employment (17:7-8a)

    Escalation of Plot A Complication/Plot B Development: Micah induces the Levite to become his family priest (17:8b, 9-10)

    Escalation of Plot A Complication/Plot B Partial Resolution: Levite's acceptance and installation as family priest (17:11, 12)

    Escalation of Plot A Complication: Micah's confidence of YHWH's blessing (17:13)

Plot C: Danites' illegitimate quest for a settlement elsewhere than in their tribal allotment (18:1-2a [2b-6] 7-12 [13-19] 21 [22-26], 27-29)

    Plot C Exposition: Danites' quest for new territory (18:1-2a)

Plot D: Danites' illegitimate quest for a cult other than that of YHWH (18:2b-6, 13-20, 22-26, 30a, 31)

    Plots B & C Complication/Plot D Tacit Exposition: Danite spies' inquiry of God through Levite priest (18:2b-6)

    Plot C Development: Danite spies explore and report; Danites depart for new territory (18:7, 8-10, 11-12)

    Escalation of Plot A Complication/Plots B & C Complication/

    Plot D Exposition and Development: Danites steal Micah's idols (18:13-14, 15-17)

    Plots B & D Development/Plot C Complication: Danites induce Levite to become tribal priest (18:18-19)

    Plots B & D Partial Resolution: Levite's acceptance of and complicity in stealing Micah's idols (18:20)

Rather, the third episode has its own exposition (18:1-2a) and plot, which becomes complicated only when confronted by the characters and circumstances of the previous two episodes (18:2b-6, 13-17). It is the complication that results from the entanglement of the previous three plot-levels that tacitly serves as the exposition for the fourth plot-level (i.e., the Danites' quest for a cult other than that of YHWH). This fourth plot-level emerges only as a result of the telescoping of all three previous plot-levels.

Plot C Development: Danites resume journey to new territory (18:21)
Plots A & C Complication/Plot D Development: Micah vainly protests
  Danites' theft of his idols and priest (18:22-26)
Plot C Resolution: Danite conquest of new territory (18:27-29)
Escalation of Plot A Complication/Plot D Resolution: Danite institution
  of idol shrine (18:30a)
Plot B Resolution: Levite's installation as tribal priest (18:30b)
Escalation of Plot A Complication/Plot D Resolution: Danite institution
  of idol shrine (18:31)

Some parallelism may be adduced among Plots A, B, C and D. Indeed,
the most significant elements of the plot-structure are those that are
shared among the four plots. Repetitions of these shared elements
sometimes bear phraseological similarity. The following table lists plot
elements shared among actions involving: (1) Micah and the Danites,
(2) Micah's idol or son and the Levite and (3) the Levite and either
Micah or the Danites:

	Plot A	*Plot A/B*	*Plot A/B/C/D*
(1) Micah and Danites:			
Theft of silver/idols	17:1-2a	[18:20aβγ]	18:13-14, 15-17
Family/tribal idol shrine			
ויעשׂהו פסל ומסכה	17:4bβ		
בית אלהים // ויעשׂ אפוד ותרפים	17:5abα		
את־הפסל			18:30a
את־פסל מיכה אשר עשׂה ... בית־האלהים			18:31
Micah's confidence/vain protest	17:13		18:22-26
(2) Micah's idol/son and Levite:			
Idol/Levite at Micah's house			
ויהי בבית מיכיהו	17:4bγ		
ויהי בבית מיכה		17:12b	
Son/Levite installed as priest			
וימלא את־יד אחד מבניו			
ויהי־לו לכהן	17:5bβ		
וימלא מיכה את־יד הלוי			
ויהי־לו הנער לכהן		17:12a	
(3) Levite and Micah/Danites:			
Levite/Dan's illegitimate quest		17:7-8a	18:1-2a
Micah/Dan induces Levite		17:9-10	18:18-19
ויאמר לו מיכה שׁבה עמדי			
והיה־לי לאב ולכהן		17:10aαβ	
ויאמרו לו ... לך עמנו			
והיה־לנו לאב ולכהן			18:19a
Levite accepts Micah/Dan's offer		17:11	18:20aαb
Levite installed by Micah/Dan		17:12a	18:30b

Because Judges 17-18 opens and closes with phraseological parallels between the actions of Micah and/or the Danites ([1] above), one may infer that the issue of the idol shrine is of greatest significance to the narrator. Since concern with the private installation of a Levite in either a family or tribal shrine is treated in the intermediary position in the narrative ([2] and [3] above), one may infer also that this concern is subsidiary for the narrator. The same proportions of emphasis—a major concern for the shrine with a minor concern for the Levitical priesthood—are evident in Deuteronomy 12, which lends support to the possibility that Deuteronomy 12 forms a basis of the rhetorical strategy of the author of Dénouement-A. Deuteronomy 12 focuses upon the issue of the legitimacy of one cult centre for YHWH and incidentally mentions the obligation to support the Levites who were responsible for the upkeep of YHWH's shrine (Deut. 12:12, 18-19).

In Plot C are several elements that bear analogy to the spy story of Num. 12:16-14:45 and Deut. 1:19-46. Indeed, there appears to be deliberate narrative analogy between the account of the Danites' migration in Judges 18 and the events that precipitated Israel's day of provocation in Num. 12:16-14:45 and Deut. 1:19-46:[346]

---

[346] Cf. A. Malamat, "The Danite Migration and the Pan-Israelite Exodus-Conquest: A Biblical Narrative Pattern", *Bib* 51 (1970), pp. 2-7; however, Malamat speaks of narrative "typology", which presupposes that an ideal basic structure underlay the narrative formation. At least deliberate narrative analogy is demonstrable between the spy stories of Num. 12:16-14:45; Deut. 1:19-46 and Judg. 18. However, Malamat admits: "Whereas the typology of the 'spy story' is lucid, that of the other themes is less articulate" ("Danite Migration" [1970], p. 7). Thus, Judg. 18 cannot be said to exemplify narrative analogy to any one account of Israel's conquest, since there is no single self-contained account of the latter by which collocation of vocabulary with Judg. 18 can be demonstrated (Malamat cites: Exod. 12:37; 13:20; 17:1; 19:2 with Judg. 18:11-13; then Exod. 15:23; 17:7; Num. 11:3, 34 with Judg. 18:12 [though naming-aetiology *per se* is hardly a motif]; Exod. 12:37-38 with Judg. 18:21; Exod. 12:37; Num. 11:21 with Judg. 18:11, 16, 17; Num. 27:21 with Judg. 18:5; Exod. 25ff. with Judg. 18:13ff.; and Exod. 32[:4, 8] with Judg. 18:14, 17, 18, 20). However, if it is valid to designate the relationship between the spy story elements of Judg. 18 and both Num. 12:16-14:45 and Deut. 1:19-46 as illustrating narrative analogy, then the shaping of Dan's conquest of Laish in terms reminiscent of Israel's conquest of Canaan may also be termed narrative analogy so long as one understands that this is a much broader type of narrative analogy than that usually so termed (cf. R. P. Gordon, "Simplicity of the Highest Cunning: Narrative Art in the Old Testament", *SBET* 6 [1988], p. 76). Cf. P. E. Satterthwaite, "Narrative Artistry and the Composition of Judges 17-21" (PhD diss., University of Manchester, 1989).

	Num. 12:16–14:45	Deut. 1:19-46	Judg. 18
Narrative Analogy:			
Situation without land	12:16	1:19-21	18:1 (11-12)
Dispatch to spy out/			
explore the land	13:2a, 3a, 16a, 17a (18-20) 25 (14:36a)	1:22a(b) (24)	18:2a (5-6)
Selection of tribal/			
clan representatives	13:2b, 3b	1:23bβ	18:2a
Number of spies	13:4-15	1:23bα	18:2a
Arrival in hill country	13:17b	1:24	18:2b
Northern extent	13:21		18:28
Positive report:			
about land	13:27; 14:7-8	1:25b	18:(7b) 9, 10b
about inhabitants	13:30; 14:9	1:29-31	18:(7a) 10a (27a, 28)
Narrative Contrast:			
Negative report (about inhabitants)	13:28, 31-33 (14:36b-37a)	1:28b	—
Negative response	expressed 14:1-4, 10a (36b)	expressed 1:26-28a, 32-33	averted (18:9bβ)
Aftermath A: provoking	explicit (14:11-12, 21-23, 25, 26-30a, 32-35)	explicit (1:34-35, 37, 40)	implicit (18:30-31; cf. 1:34-36)
Aftermath A: weeping	14:39	— (cf. 1:41a)	— (but cf. 2:4)
Aftermath B: conquest	failed (14:40-45)	failed (1:41b-44, 46)	succeeded (18:27-29)
Aftermath B: weeping	—	1:45	— (but cf. 20:23, 26; 21:2, 6)
Aftermath C: conquest	succeeded (14:24, 30b-31, 38)	succeeded (1:36, 38-39)	failed (18:30b)

The points of analogy to Plot C are significant insofar as they articulate similar characterizations of Israel and Dan in their sending of spies. These characterizations similarly portray Israel and Dan as being willing to forsake their covenant obligation to conquer the land through reliance upon YHWH (cf. Deut. 7). What is most significant, however, are not the points of analogy but the differences highlighted by the analogy at the point in Plot C where the Danites take action in response to the spies. The Danite spies give no negative report about the inhabitants of their prospective territory, as had Israel's spies, and this highlights the incongruity of Dan's subsequent actions. With repeated emphasis upon the security and defencelessness of their victims (18:7bα, 10aα, 27aδ), the narrator portrays the Danites and their spies not only as too fearful to conquer their own territory (cf. 1:34-36) but as unscrupulous as well (i.e., willing to conquer a defenceless territory [18:7bβ-δ, 10aβ, 28aαβ] and to victimize weaker Micah [18:14-26]). Hence, unlike the Israelites, the Danites respond to the spies' report without hesitation (18:9bβ), but this only heightens their negative characterization as eager perpetrators of injustice. Whereas the Israelites' reluctance to conquer the land provoked YHWH to reject them openly on the day of provocation, YHWH's view of the Danites remains unexpressed in the narrative of Judges 18, though his provocation seems implicit in the compiler/redactor's assessment in 17:6 and 18:1a. Indeed, since 17:6b (motif A1b) alludes to Deut. 12:8aα/b, which evokes the whole context of Deuteronomy 12, it may be against this covenant (cultic) background that the rhetorical concerns of Plots A, B and D are best assessed.

In regard to the rhetorical concern of Plot A, the citation of motif A1b in Judg. 17:6b (which alludes antithetically to Deut. 12:8aα/b) immediately after the institution of Micah's shrine marks the completion of Micah's shrine with an implicit declaration of its illegitimacy. Even before the Levite has entered the story, this is the implicit evaluation of the narrator, who evokes Deuteronomy 12 as a judgement upon Micah's cult. Thus, the mere existence of a cult that is not endorsed by Deuteronomy 12 is the point of the complication of Plot A.[347] It is a

---

[347] Dumbrell ("Those Days" [1983], p. 32 n. 9) suggested that,

> Deut. 12:8 provides ... [a] suggestive context by which Judges 17:6 and 21:25 might be compared, namely with the use of the phrase ['every man did what was right in his own eyes'] in connection with a call for the avoidance of pagan worship in order that divine rest in the land, which is the aim of the settlement (Deut. 12:9), might be realized. But in Judges it is to the disorders of the period that reference is being made and not to the many acts of apostasy by which it was characterized; we should therefore take the phrase at Judges 21:25 as referring to the extreme individualism which stamped the times.

First, the concern of Deut. 12 is not with "pagan worship" *per se* but with worship at various sites, as opposed to one divinely appointed site. In the context of Judg. 17–18, Judg. 17:6 relates to the same concern as Deut. 12:8, in its context of Deut. 12, namely, worship at sites other than the one appointed by YHWH. It is probably no accident that Judg. 17–18 concludes with a reference to the legitimate בית־האלהים בשלה (18:31b)—thus implicitly condemning Micah's illegitimate בית אלהים (17:5a) and the cult objects "that he made" (cf. 17:5b) by means of contrast with the Danites' enshrinement of the same (18:30a, 31a). Concern about avoidance of idolatry is also present in Judg. 17–18, as throughout the book of Judges (whose framework shows clear dependence upon

point of irony, therefore, that Micah's mother 'blesses' her son (17:2b) by offering thanksgiving to YHWH through commissioning an illegitimate idol (17:3b, 4b) that becomes the point of departure for her son's and the Danites' cultic aberrancy (17:5; 18:30-31). This concern with illegitimacy of cult in Judges 17-18 becomes more focused as its telescoping plot-level series unfolds.

Plot B focuses upon a Levite's aberrancy from expected norms of behaviour in that it resolves with this Levite fulfilling his quest for employment (17:7-8a) through his agreement to be installed as priest at a private cult (17:11; 18:20aαb)—a cult other than the national cult endorsed in Deuteronomy 12. Further, the eagerness of Micah and the Danites to employ the Levite (17:9-10; 18:18-19) only compounds their previous aberrancy from cultic ideals endorsed by Deuteronomy 12— Micah's aberrancy in manufacturing illegitimate cult objects (17:5), Dan's aberrancy in deserting their tribal allotment for a remote settlement (18:1-2a, 7-12) and in stealing Micah's cult objects (18:13-17). Deuteronomy 12 is evoked not only by the allusive force of 17:6 but by the fact that this account is also terminated by a repetition of the monarchy motif (18:1a), which reminds the reader of its occurrence in 17:6a, which was juxtaposed with motif A1b (17:6b), which had evoked a recollection of the context of Deut. 12:8aα/b.[348] Thus, the citation of the monarchy motif in Judg. 18:1a, immediately after the installation of the Levite as Micah's private priest, implicitly declares its illegitimacy. Moreover, because Deuteronomy 12 already contains explicit prescriptions concerning the popular obligation to support the Levites by maintaining the central cult shrine (Deut. 12:12, 18-19), what the closing verse of Judg. 17:7-13 reveals is only a development of the irony of Micah's self-delusion in expecting YHWH's 'blessing' (cf. 17:2b) for employing a Levite in his private shrine. Ironically, while thinking they are doing right, both Micah and his mother have

---

deuteronomic phraseology and idealization), but its focus is upon the legitimacy of any shrine other than that at Shiloh. Second, the clause "every man did what was right in his own eyes" in Judg. 21:25 probably does not refer merely to "the extreme individualism which stamped the times". Judg. 19-21 shows a specific concern with covenant injustice and presents this concern in terms of the atrocity of Gen. 19:1-11 and an implicit contrast with the procedures for executing covenant justice against an apostate city as prescribed in Deut. 13 (despite the fact that the procedures in Deut. 13 are related to a different apostasy, namely, worshipping of other gods).

[348] Amit also regarded the repetition of the monarchy motif in 18:1a as sufficient to remind the reader of the statement of 17:6b (motif A1b), with which the monarchy motif of 17:6a was previously contiguous ("Hidden Polemic" [1990], pp. 5-6).

performed the antithesis of YHWH's cultic requirements as prescribed in Deuteronomy 12. If this negative evaluation of Micah's exclusive cult and employment of the Levite is implicit in 17:7-13, then, as Plot B develops in 18:1b-31, this negative evaluation carries over also to the Danites' exclusive cult and employment of the Levite.

In this connection, Plot D (which absorbs the concerns of both Plots A and B into the sphere of the Danites' illegitimate migration [Plot C]) focuses upon the escalation of apostasy from a family to a tribal level. The implicit negative evaluation of Plot D is to be expected in that Plot D merely escalates the aberrancies of Plots A and B; however, it may also devolve upon the whole of 18:1b-31 by virtue of the transitional nature of the monarchy motif in 18:1a.[349] In any case, there can be little doubt that the implicit rhetorical force of the concluding comparisons of 18:30-31 is to present the Danites' cult (both objects and priesthood) as antithetical to the legitimate cult of YHWH at Shiloh.

Judges 17-18 contains several thematic elements and concerns in common with Deut. 12:1-13:1, though the former usually portrays them antithetically, as follows:

	Deut. 12:1-13:1	*Judg. 17-18*
Cult sites on hills	to be destroyed (12:2)	constructed (17:1-5)
Idols	to be cut down (12:3aδ)	manufactured
(ופסילי אלהיהם)		
(פסל ומסכה)		(17:3bβ, 4bβ)
Ideal of central shrine	repeatedly endorsed (12:4-7, 11, 13-14, 17-18aγ, 18b, 26-27)	repeatedly and ironically ignored (17:2b-5, 13; 18:31b)
What is right in ... own eyes	prohibited (12:8aα/b)	practised (17:6b)
Popular support of Levites	at central shrine (12:12, 18aδ, 19)	at private shrine (17:7-13; 18:19-20, 30b)

---

[349] Both Dumbrell ("Those Days" [1983], pp. 23-24) and Amit ("Hidden Polemic" [1990], pp. 5-6) regard 17:6 and 18:1a as transitional, both concluding the preceding episode and introducing the next.

	Deut. 12:1–13:1	*Judg. 17–18*
Inheritance not yet settled	Israel excused (12:9-10a)	Micah (settled)/ Danites (unsettled) unexcused (17:1; 18:1b [cf. 1:34-36])
YHWH to let live in safety (וישבתם־בטח) (*יושבת־לבטח ... שקט ובטח)	future Israel (12:10b)	not Dan but Laish (18:7bα*, 10aα, 27aδ)
YHWH to extend territory (כי־ירחיב ... את־גבולך) (*והארץ רחבת ידים / כי־נתנה אלהים בידכם (בעמק אשר לבית־רחוב)	future Israel (12:20aα)	not Dan but Laish (18:7bβ-δ, 10aβ*) (18:28aαβ)

Each point of antithesis between Judges 17–18 and Deuteronomy 12 heightens the rhetorical point that, in doing what was right in their own eyes, the characters of this account were acting in defiance of the cultic ideals set forth in Deuteronomy 12. It is probably not just fortuitous that Judges 17–18 concludes and culminates (18:30-31) with a contrast between the Danite cult and the cult of YHWH at Shiloh, the only cult endorsed by the narrative of chs. 17–21 (cf. 21:19).

As evidence of thematic continuity of Judges 17–18 with its preceding context, several points of similarity may be noted between Judges 13–16 and Judges 18 (Plot C) that illustrate the mutual integration of these chapters in their concern about the Danites' illegitimate migration: both make reference to Zorah and Eshtaol as a point of origin or termination (13:2, 25; 16:31a; 18:2, 8, 11), both make reference to Mahaneh Dan as a point of departure (13:25 [between Zorah and Eshtaol]; 18:12 [W of Kiriath-jearim]) and both accounts present complications resulting from the Danites' failure to conquer their tribal region (cf. 1:34-36). Indeed, the events of ch. 18 (Plot C) historically precede and furnish background for those of chs. 13–16. Judges 1:34-36 and ch. 18 (Plot C), on the one hand, and chs. 13–16, on the other, culminate in a portrayal of Dan's tribal and Samson's individual foibles, respectively. Both protagonists practise covenant compromises in carrying out their conquests (against Micah and Laish or the Philistines), and both eventually give in either to Canaanite cult practices (ch. 18, Plot D) or to Philistine sexual relations. Points of dissimilarity are also present between ch. 18 and chs. 13–16. Dan moves from a position of military weakness to one of strength, albeit at the expense of cultic loyalty; Samson, from physical strength to weakness because of ritual impurity. While the Danites seemed to get away with doing what was right in their own eyes, Samson (who did likewise) suffered the loss of both eyes. However, both eventually fall prey to the consequences of their own self-interest: Samson in destroying a false cult (16:23-30), the Danites in establishing one (18:30-31).

§1.1. *Failure to Occupy the Land*

It is only Plot C of Judges 18 that focuses concern upon Israel's failure to occupy their allotted territory. This deficiency was foreshadowed by the description of Dan's weakness before the Amorites in 1:34-36 and becomes a point of negative characterization as the Danites of Judges 17-18 become bullies toward the weaker Micah and the citizens of Laish. Doubtless the key rhetorical motivation underlying the narrative analogy of the Danites' migration vis-à-vis the account of Num. 12:16–14:25 is the similarity between the unfaithfulness of Israel and Dan in forsaking their obligation to conquer their allotted territory. Dan's failure is thus a microcosm of that of the nation. Plot C, concerning the Danites' illegitimate quest for new territory, resolves and culminates in the conquest of Laish (18:27-29), which is the antithesis of the ideal of Dan purging their allotted territory of its native inhabitants. The compiler/redactor's concern with the Israelite tribes' failure to occupy their allotted territories, expressed in Prologue-A (1:1–2:5), is an undeniable aspect of the portrayal of Dan's migration in Judges 18. However, insofar as interest in the Danites' failure to occupy their tribal inheritance does not emerge in ch. 17, this rhetorical concern probably does not represent the controlling concern of Dénouement-A. Rather, Plot C is complementary to the development of the narrator's main concern with aberrancy from cultic ideals.

§1.2. *Cultic Disloyalty*

The common rhetorical focus of Plots A, B and D is their apparent mutual concern with disloyalty to the cultic ideals expressed in Deuteronomy 12. The interest of the narrative of Judges 17-18 in the context of Deuteronomy 12 is made evident not only by the antithetical allusion of Judg. 17:6b to Deut. 12:8aα/b but by the convergence of its inverted portrayals of the ideals enjoined in Deuteronomy 12 (e.g., concern about the legitimacy of alternative cultic shrines [Judg. 17:3b, 4b, 5; 18:13-17, 30a, 31a vs. Deut. 12:4-7, 8-14, 17-18, 26-27], concern about the Levites' means of support [Judg. 17:7-13; 18:18-20, 30b vs. Deut. 12:12b, 18aγ, 19], concern about naming the shrine site [Judg. 18:29 vs. Deut. 12:5, 11, 21] and concern about intertribal support of the one central shrine [Judg. 18:31 vs. Deut. 12:5aα]). The Danites, who properly should have destroyed Micah's cult (cf. Deut.

12:2-3), instead find it worthy of acquisition, even if by means of theft (18:15-17).

Since concern about cultic disloyalty permeates Judges 17–18, it may be inferred that this is the controlling concern of Dénouement-A. This is further corroborated by the fact that the culminating point of the narrative is an implicit condemnation not of the Danites' conquest of Laish (18:27-29) but of their tribal endorsement of Micah's idol and its attendance by a Levitical priesthood (18:30-31). It is for the matter of cultic disloyalty that the narrator reserves his/her final word.

§2. Dénouement-B (19:1–21:25): Failure of Intertribal Covenant Loyalty Promotes Covenant (Social) Injustice

Certain parallel features of Prologue-A and Dénouement-B suggest that these sections were intended to frame symmetrically the book of Judges. Boling proposed that Achsah's prowess, displayed in her domination by submission over the male characters in the pericope of 1:12-15, finds its contrasting counterpart in the rape of the Shiloh maidens in Judges 21.[350] Boling also discerned a framing function in the analogous emphasis upon pan-Israelite holy war in Judges 1 and 19–21.[351] Gooding likewise inferred that the compiler/redactor of Judges intended a structural correspondence between the story of how Othniel got his wife (1:11-15) and the story of how the remainder of the Benjaminite men got their wives (21:1-25).[352] Other thematic links inferred by Gooding in support of the view that Prologue-A and Dénouement-B were intended to frame symmetrically the book of Judges include: the Israelite invocation of YHWH to ask who should go up first and his reply, "Judah" (1:1-2; 20:18); the incrimination of the Benjaminites for failing to expel the Jebusites from Jebus (1:21; 19:1-30) and the Israelites' weeping and sacrificing before YHWH in connection with violations of YHWH's covenant (2:1-5; 20:26-28). Inasmuch as these features are paralleled in the framing sections of Judges, they can be expected to play a prominent role in serving the compiler/redactor's rhetorical aims for his/her readers.

Not only the correspondence between Prologue-A and Dénouement-B, but the arrangement of materials within Dénouement-B itself helps

---

[350] Boling, *Judges* (1975), p. 64.

[351] More precisely, Boling has presented the framing sections of Judges as poles in a tragicomic movement from "Israel disintegrating", in Judg. 1, to "Israel, reunited at last in the wake of a tragic civil war", in Judg. 19-21 (*Judges* [1975], pp. 36-38).

[352] Cf. Gooding, "Composition" (1982), pp. 76*-78*.

in determining its rhetorical focus. The plot-structure of Judg. 19:1b–21:24 begins with an account of Gibeah's social atrocity (19:1b-9, 10aγ-28; the latter being a narrative analogue to Gen. 19:1-11),[353] becomes complicated by Benjamin's refusal to cooperate with other tribes of Israel in executing judgement upon Gibeah (19:29-20:13), leads to Benjamin's near extinction (20:14-18, 19-23, 24-28, 29-48) and becomes further complicated by three abrogations of covenant justice. These covenant injustices include: (1) Israel's refusal to execute justice by exterminating Benjamin (21:1-3, 23b-24, which escalates to the national level the crime committed earlier by the Benjaminites in regard to Gibeah), (2) Israel's deflection of the sanctions of holy war to a scapegoat, Jabesh-Gilead, through a justice of expedience (21:4-11, 12-14) and (3) Israel's toleration of Benjamin's abduction of Israelite women for sexual ends (21:15-23a, which escalates to the tribal level the crime committed earlier by the Gibeahites).[354] Since every major plot complication in Judg. 19:29-21:24 depends upon a knowledge of the policies of holy war against an apostate city, endorsed by Deut. 13:2-19, it seems fair to suggest that Judg. 19:29-21:24 was designed to function as a narrative reflection (though not an analogue) of the concerns of Deut. 13:2-19 for executing justice against a city of Israel. Thus, the point of connection between Judges 19-21 and Deuteronomy 13 is not related to the specific situations of apostasy that they describe, for the former relates to a city that commits social injustice but the latter to a city that worships other gods. Rather, the connection relates to the question of the proper procedure for executing justice against a city that apostasizes, whatever the cause.

Israel's inversion of the standards of covenant justice, through misplaced priorities, is mimicked in the reverse order presentation of

---

[353] On narrative analogy between Judg. 19:10aγ-26 and Gen. 19:1-11, see M. Güdemann, "Tendenz und Abfassungszeit der letzten Kapitel des Buches der Richter", *MGWJ* 18 (1869), pp. 357-68; R. C. Culley, *Studies in the Structure of Hebrew Narrative* (Philadelphia, 1976), pp. 54-59; Niditch, "'Sodomite' Theme" (1982), pp. 365, 375-78; S. Lasine, "Guest and Host in Judges 19: Lot's Hospitality in an Inverted World", *JSOT* 29 (1984), pp. 37-41. On narrative analogy between Judg. 19:29-20:48 and 1 Sam. 11:1-11, see Lasine, "Guest and Host" (1984), pp. 37, 41-43. For a less plausible case of narrative analogy, cf. J. Unterman, "The Literary Influence of 'the Binding of Isaac' (Genesis 22) on 'the Outrage at Gibeah' (Judges 19)", *HAR* 4 (1980), pp. 161-66.

[354] It may be a point of irony in Judg. 19-21 that those set forth as heroes of Benjamin ("son of the right") are left-handed (20:16; cf. 3:15). In Judg. 3:12-30 this anomaly becomes the key to Ehud's successful deception. In 20:16, however, it is the motive for which Benjamin is warring with the other tribes that draws out the ironic amphibology of the boast about left-handed Benjaminites who could sling ולא יחטא ("and not miss/sin").

plot resolutions. The Three plot-levels can be traced through 19:1b–21:24: (1) the recovery of the Levite's concubine from Bethlehem to a city in the hill country of Ephraim, which is dissolved by the Gibeahites' atrocity and the death of the concubine (19:1b-9, 10aγ-28) (Plot A); (2) the bringing of judgement against the Gibeahites and the Benjaminites, their defenders, for their crime against the Levite and his concubine (19:10aγ-28; 19:29–20:48), which is dissolved by the restoration of Benjamin's remnant to their cities (21:23b) (Plot B) and (3) the illegitimate concern to restore the remnant of Benjamin lest they suffer extinction, the only plot to achieve resolution, albeit by perverted means (21:1-3, 4-14, 15-23a) (Plot C). The plot-structure of this narrative may be outlined as follows:

Plot A: Recovery of the Levite's concubine (19:1b-10aβ [10aγ-28])
    Plot A Exposition: The concubine's flight (19:1b-2)
    Plot A Development: The Levite's pursuit of his concubine (19:3-4):
      Days 1–3:

A	Arising to depart for Bethlehem (19:3a)	... ויקם אישה וילך
B	Father offers hospitality (19:3b-4aα)	ויראהו אבי הנערה / וישמח לקראתו:
		ויחזק־בו חתנו אבי הנערה /
C	Levite receives hospitality (19:4aβb)	וישב אתו שלשת ימים //
		ויאכלו וישתו / וילינו שם:

    Prolongation of Plot A Development: (19:5-10aβ)
      Day 4:

Aⁱ	Arising to depart from Bethlehem (19:5a)	ויהי ביום הרביעי /
		וישכימו בבקר ויקם ללכת //
Bⁱ	Morning: Father offers hospitality (19:5b)	ויאמר אבי הנערה אל־חתנו /
		סעד לבך פת־לחם ואחר תלכו:
Cⁱ	Morning: Levite receives hospitality (19:6a)	וישבו / ויאכלו שניהם יחדו וישתו //
D	Afternoon: Father offers hospitality (19:6b)	ויאמר אבי הנערה אל־האיש /
		הואל־נא ולין ויטב לבך:
Aⁱⁱ	Arising to depart from Bethlehem (19:7a)	ויקם האיש ללכת
Dⁱ	Afternoon: Father offers hospitality (19:7bα)	ויפצר־בו חתנו /
E	Afternoon: Levite receives hospitality (19:7bβ)	וישב וילן שם:

Day 5:

Aⁱⁱⁱ   Arising to depart from Bethlehem (19:8aα)

וישכם בבקר ביום החמישי ללכת

Bⁱⁱ   Morning: Father offers hospitality (19:8aβ-δ)

ויאמר אבי הנערה /

סעד־נא לבבך / והתמהמהו עד־נטות היום //

Cⁱⁱ   Morning: Levite receives hospitality (19:8b)

ויאכלו שניהם:

A^{iv}   Arising to depart from Bethlehem (19:9a)

ויקם האיש ללכת ...

Dⁱⁱ   Afternoon: Father offers hospitality (19:9b)

ויאמר לו חתנו אבי הנערה

הנה נא רפה היום לערב /

לינו־נא הנה חנות היום לין פה וייטב לבבך /

והשכמתם מחר לדרככם / והלכת לאהלך:

1/E   Afternoon: Levite refuses hospitality (19:10aα)

ולא־אבה האיש ללון /

A^v   Arising to depart from Bethlehem (19:10aβ)

ויקם וילך

Plot B: Execution of justice against Gibeah/Benjamin (19:10aγ–20:48
[21:1-3, 23b-24])

   Plot A Complication and Dissolution/Plot B Exposition: Journey home
   by the Levite and his concubine (19:10aγ-28)

      Day 5/6 sunset until daylight: Crisis: Lodging for the evening of the
      sixth day (19:10aγ-26):[355]

         1/Eⁱ   Afternoon: Levite refuses Jebusite hospitality
                        (19:10aγ-13)

         1/D   Evening: Gibeahites refuse to offer hospitality
                        (19:14-15)

                   Evening: Old Ephraimite and Levite negotiate lodging
                        (19:16-19)

         Dⁱⁱⁱ   Evening: Old host offers hospitality (19:20)

         Eⁱ   Evening: Levite receives hospitality (19:21)

         1/Eⁱⁱ   Evening: Levite receives inhospitality (19:22-26)

      Day 6 after daylight: Return home by the Levite and his concubine
      (19:27-28)

         A^{vi}   Arising to depart from Gibeah (19:27a)

ויקם אדניה בבקר / ויפתח דלתות הבית /

ויצא ללכת לדרכו //

                   Levite discovers his ravaged concubine
                        (19:27b-28bα)

         A^{vii}   Arising to depart from Gibeah (19:28bβγ)

ויקם האיש / וילך למקמו:

---

[355] See the table below on the narrative analogy between Gen. 19:1-11 and Judg.
19:10aγ-26.

Plot B Development: Punishing Gibeah/Benjamin (19:29–20:48)
(Day 6 plus intervening days): (19:29–20:18)

aa	Levite dismembers and distributes his concubine among Israel's tribes (19:29)
bb	Israelites demand an explanation (19:30a)
bbⁱ	Levite's leading of Israel to demand an explanation (19:30b*)[356]
cc	Assembly of Israel "as one man" at Mizpah (20:1)
dd	Census: Leaders of 400,000 Israelites [without Benjamin] (20:2)
1/cc	Benjamin hears of assembly of Israel at Mizpah (20:3a)
bbⁱⁱ	Israelites demand an explanation (20:3b)
aaⁱ	Levite explains dismembering and distributing his concubine among Israel's tribes (20:4-6)
Aᵛⁱⁱⁱ	Levite claims Gibeahites arose to kill him (20:5)

ויקמו עלי בעלי הגבעה / ויסבו עלי את־הבית לילה //
אותי דמו להרג / ואת־פילגשי ענו ותמת:

Levite summons Israel to judge Gibeah (20:7)
Israel resolves to judge Gibeah (20:8-11) [inclusio]:

Aⁱˣ ccⁱ	Arising "as one man" to refuse to depart from Gibeah (20:8)

ויקם כל־העם / כאיש אחד לאמר //
לא נלך איש לאהלו / ולא נסור איש לביתו:

ccⁱⁱ	Assembly "as one man" against Gibeah (20:11)

ויאסף כל־איש ישראל אל־העיר / כאיש אחד חברים:

Israel summons Benjamin to judge Gibeah (20:12-13a)
Benjamin refuses to comply with Israel (20:13b)

1/ccⁱ	Assembly of Benjamin at Gibeah (20:14)
1/dd	Census: 26,000 Benjaminites + 700 Gibeahites—700 left-handed slingers who do not "miss" (20:15-16)
ddⁱ	Census: 400,000 Israelites without Benjamin (20:17)
Aˣ ee	Arising to inquire of YHWH at Bethel: who should lead battle against Benjamin? (20:18)

ויקמו ויעלו בית־אל וישאלו באלהים /
ויאמרו בני ישראל /

---

[356] On the MT haplography in Judg. 19:30b*, which may be retroverted from the LXX, see the note on 19:30 in the appendix. The following is an English translation of Judg. 19:30 with the haplography restored:

> And it would happen that everyone who saw would say: "Nothing like this has ever happened or been seen from the day the sons of Israel came up from the land of Egypt until this day", for he would command the men whom he sent, saying, "Thus say to every man of Israel: 'Has anything like this happened since the day the sons of Israel came up from the land of Egypt until this day? Consider among yourselves, take counsel and speak.'"

מי יעלה־לנו בתחלה / למלחמה עם־בני בנימן //
ויאמר יהוה יהודה בתחלה:

Siege Day 1:

A^{xi}a   Arising to besiege Benjaminites at Gibeah (20:19)

ויקומו בני־ישראל בבקר // ויחנו על־הגבעה:

  b   Israelites take up battle position (20:20)

  c   Benjaminites go out (20:21a)

  d   Census: 22,000 Israelites destroyed (20:21b)

  bⁱ   Israelites reposition as on the first/former day (20:22)

  e   Inquiry of YHWH (20:23)

Siege Day 2:

  aⁱ   Approaching the Benjaminites (20:24)

ויקרבו בני־ישראל אל־בני בנימן ביום השני:

  cⁱ   Benjaminites go out (20:25aα)

  dⁱ   Census: 18,000 Israelites destroyed (20:25aβ-b)

  eⁱ   Inquiry of YHWH (20:26-28)

  αα   Israel sets up an ambush (20:29)

Siege Day 3:

  aⁱⁱ   Rising up against the Benjaminites (20:30a)

ויעלו בני־ישראל אל־בני בנימן ביום השלישי //

  bⁱⁱ   Israelites reposition as formerly (20:30b)

  cⁱⁱ   Benjaminites go out (20:31a)

  dⁱⁱ   Census: 30 Israelites struck down (20:31b)

  ββ   Benjaminites' delusion of victory (20:32a)

ויאמרו בני בנימן / נגפים הם לפנינו כבראשנה //

  ααⁱ   Israel's reliance on ambush (20:32b)

ובני ישראל אמרו / ננוסה ונתקנהו /
מן־העיר אל־המסלות:

S	A^{xii} bⁱⁱⁱ	Arising to position a counterattack (20:33a)

וכל איש ישראל / קמו ממקומו / ויערכו בבעל תמר //

U		
M	γγ	Ambush attacks from its position (20:33b)
M	1/d	Census: 10,000 choice Israelites (20:34aα)
A	ββⁱ	Benjaminites' ignorance of defeat (20:34aβb)
R		YHWH defeats Benjamin before Israel (20:35aα)
Y	1/dⁱ	Census: 25,000 Benjaminites destroyed (20:35aβ-b)

  ββⁱⁱ   Benjaminites' delusion of victory (20:36a)[357]

ויראו בני־בנימן כי נגפו //

---

[357] E. J. Revell has demonstrated from narrative structure that the subject of נגפו in 20:36a must be Israel, contrary to the view of most commentators (e.g. Moore, *Judges* [1895], p. 438) and English translations (e.g., the AV, RV, RSV, NEB, NIV, NRSV and REB) that the subject is Benjamin ("The Battle with Benjamin [Judges xx 29-48] and Hebrew Narrative Techniques", *VT* 35 [1985], pp. 430-31, n. 20). Among EVV, only the NAB anticipated Revell's view.

$\alpha\alpha^i$ Israel's reliance on ambush (20:36b)

ויתנו איש־ישראל מקום לבנימן / כי בטחו אל־הארב /
אשר שמו אל־הגבעה:

$\gamma\gamma^i$ Ambush attacks and strikes Gibeah (20:37)

$\delta\delta$ Smoke to signal turning of Israel (20:38-39a)

והמועד / היה לאיש ישראל עם־הארב // <> /
להעלותם משאת העשן מן־העיר:
ויהפך איש־ישראל במלחמה //

d^{iii} Census: 30 Israelites struck down (20:39bα)

ובנימן החל להכות חללים באיש־ישראל כשלשים איש /

$\beta\beta^{iii}$ Benjaminites' delusion of victory (20:39bβ-δ)

כי אמרו / אך נגוף נגף הוא לפנינו / כמלחמה הראשנה:

$\delta\delta^i$ Smoke signal (20:40a)

$\varepsilon\varepsilon$ Turning of Benjamin (20:40b)

$\delta\delta^{ii}$ Turning of Israel (20:41aα)

ואיש ישראל הפך /

$1/\beta\beta$ Benjaminites' realization of defeat (20:41aβb)

ויבהל איש בנימן // כי ראה / כי־נגעה עליו הרעה:

$\varepsilon\varepsilon^i$ Turning of Benjamin toward the desert (20:42aα)

$1/c$ Israel's pursuit of Benjamin (20:42aβ)
      Those from the city were destroying Benjamin in the
      midst (20:42b)

$1/c^i$ Israel's pursuit of Benjamin to the vicinity of Gibeah
      (20:43)

$1/d^{ii}$ Census: 18,000 Benjaminites fallen (20:44)

$\varepsilon\varepsilon^{ii}$ Turning of Benjamin toward the desert (20:45aα)

$1/d^{iii}$ Census: 5,000 Benjaminites struck down (20:45a$\beta\gamma$)

$1/c^{ii}$ Israel's pursuit of Benjamin to Gidom (20:45bα)

$1/d^{iv}$ Census: 2,000 Benjaminites struck down (20:45bβ)

$1/d^v$ Census: 25,000 Benjaminites fallen (20:46)

$\varepsilon\varepsilon^{iii}$ Turning of Benjamin toward the desert (20:47aα)

d^{iv} Census: 600 Benjaminites escaped (20:47aβb)
      Israelites return to execute covenant justice on the
      cities of Benjamin (20:48)

Plot C: Restoring wives to Benjamin's remnant (21:1-23a)
   Plot B Complication/Plot C Exposition: Weeping for Benjamin before
   YHWH (21:1-3)

α Israel's oath precluding giving daughters to Benjamin
      (21:1)

β Israel's lament for Benjamin (21:2-3)

Plot C Development: Evasion of justice against Benjamin (21:4-9)
   Siege Day 4 (plus intervening days):
      Sacrifice to appease YHWH (21:4)

$1/e$ Inquiry [but not of YHWH] (21:5-23a)

γ Inquiry as to who failed to assemble (21:5a)

δ   Israel's oath that whoever failed to assemble at
         Mizpah should be put to death (21:5b)
βⁱ   Israel's lament for Benjamin (21:6-7a)
αⁱ   Israel's oath precluding giving daughters to
         Benjamin (21:7b)
γⁱ   Inquiry as to who failed to assemble at Mizpah
         (21:8a)
δⁱ   Discovery that Jabesh-Gilead failed to assemble
         (21:8b-9)
Plot C Partial Resolution: Procuring wives for Benjamin (21:10-14a)
ε   Scheme to capture maidens by holy war against
         Jabesh-Gilead (21:10-12)
ʓ   Maidens given to Benjamin at Shiloh (21:13-14a)
Plot C Complication: Insufficient wives for Benjamin (21:14b)
Plot C Resolution: Procuring wives for Benjamin (21:15-23a)
βⁱⁱ   Israel's lament and inquiry for Benjamin
         (21:15-17)
αⁱⁱ   Israel's oath precluding giving daughters to
         Benjamin (21:18)
εⁱ   Scheme to let maidens be captured by Benjamin at
         Shiloh (21:19-22)
Annual Festival of YHWH:
ʓⁱ   Abduction of maidens during the festival of YHWH
         (21:23a)
Plot B Dissolution: Return of Benjamin and Israel (21:23b-24)
         Benjaminites return to rebuild their cities (21:23b)
         Israelite tribes return to their inheritances (21:24)

Plots A and B (but, significantly, not Plot C) are punctuated and demarcated by the 'arose' motif (וַיָּקֻם), designated 'A' in the outline. Important, too, for symbolic reasons, is the structure delineated by the reports of the successive days by which Plot A unfolds.

The model hospitality enjoyed by the Levite while in Bethlehem is the foil against which the conduct of the Gibeahites is to be evaluated. Its redundancy is designed to convey the potentially endless hospitality that the Levite may have enjoyed had he chosen to remain in Bethlehem of Judah.[358] It is his decision to leave the security of this

---

[358] Lasine's inference that "it is the father-in-law's excessive hospitality", an example of comic repetition, "which forces the Levite to be dependent on the citizens of Gibeah for hospitality", is unnecessarily pejorative toward the father-in-law ("Guest and Host" [1984], pp. 56-57 n. 34). The father-in-law is greatly (not excessively) hospitable, and, in any case, his hospitality is not set forth by the narrative as a culpable cause of the outrage at Gibeah. Niditch, who likewise observed that the father-in-law's delays explain why the man was only halfway home by nightfall, nevertheless rightly observed that the chief aim of the repetitions in Judg. 19:4-9 is to portray the father-in-law as a model of hospitality ("'Sodomite' Theme" [1982], pp. 366-67). Lasine's inference minimizes the fact that what

environment and pass through the region of Benjamin that breaks the pattern of social grace with the irruption of moral atrocity. If the hospitality of Bethlehem is one foil to the atrocity at Gibeah, then the Levite's aversion to Jebus, a non-Israelite enclave to be avoided, is implicitly a second foil. It is a significant point in the narrative that the rapists are Israelites.[359] This concern is registered by the compiler/ redactor in motif A1b (in 19:24aγδ, at the point of decision to betray the women to the mob, and in 21:25b). Ironically, by this decision the two men, both Ephraimite outsiders in this Benjaminite town (19:1bαβ, 18aβ, 16aγ; cf., analogously, Gen. 19:9a), become a microcosm of the townspeople's betrayal of their own obligation to safeguard sojourners among them.[360]

Plot A dissolves and Plot B unfolds in the account of the rape at Gibeah on the evening of the sixth day (19:10aγ-26). It is an important point of pathetic fallacy that the rape takes place during the dark hours. Indeed, the narrator took pains to signal the ominous approach of darkness at the time of the decision to pass by Jebus (19:11-13) and to mark sunset and daybreak as signposts that frame the atrocity itself: night falls upon arrival at Gibeah (19:14); daybreak marks the end of both scandal and victim (19:26).

The elements describing the lodging for the evening of the sixth day (19:10aγ-26) are presented in a manner analogous to Genesis 19 so as to highlight the contrasting outcomes of these two incidents:[361]

Hospitality amidst injustice	*Gen. 19:1-11*	*Judg. 19:(10aγ-13) 14-28 (29-21:24)*
Narrative contrast:		
Ironic foil to wicked city	—	Jebus (19:10aγ-13)
Narrative analogy:		
Arrival at sunset	19:1aα	19:14b
Turning aside (סור)	19:2aβⁱ	19:15aα

---

caused the Levite's party to go on to Gibeah was their decision to bypass Jebus because it was a foreign city (19:11-12). Since the foreign status of Jebus implicitly redounds to the discredit of Benjamin (cf. 1:21) and this discredit is compounded by the irony that, in seeking to avoid the potential inhospitability of a foreign city, the Levite's party suffers at Gibeah that very fate, indirect blame for the atrocity at Gibeah seems better laid upon Benjamin than upon the Levite's father-in-law.

[359] Niditch, "'Sodomite' Theme" (1982), p. 369.

[360] Cf. Niditch, "'Sodomite' Theme" (1982), p. 371.

[361] Cf. Burney, *Judges* (2d edn, 1920), p. 444; Culley, *Structure of Hebrew Narrative* (1976), pp. 56-57; Niditch, "'Sodomite' Theme" (1982), pp. 369, 376; Lasine, "Guest and Host" (1984), p. 39; V. Matthews, "Hospitality and Hostility in Genesis 19 and Judges 19", *BTB* 22 (1992), p. 9; K. Stone, "Gender and Homosexuality in Judges 19: Subject-Honour, Object-Shame?", *JSOT* 67 (1995), pp. 88, 93.

	Gen. 19:1-11	Judg. 19:(10aγ-13) 14-28 (29-21:24)
Sojourning host (גור)	19:9aβ [cf. 13:12b]	19:16aδ
Entering house (בוא אל־/לביתו)	19:2aβ[ii], 3aγ	19:21aα
Gestures of hospitality:		
Washing feet (רחץ רגלים)	19:2aβ[iii]	19:21bα
Refusal to let men pass the night in the street (ברחוב ללון)	19:2aβ[iv]	19:[15], 20b
Provision for a meal	19:3bα	19:20a
Eating [and drinking] (ויאכלו [וישתו])	19:3bβ	19:21bβ
Men of the city: (אנשי העיר אנשי סדם/בני־בליעל)	19:4aβ[i] [cf. 13:13]	19:22aβ [cf. 20:13aα]
Surround the house (נסבו על־/את־הבית)	19:4aβ[ii]	19:22aγ [cf. 20:5aβ]
Call to the host: Demand he expel guest(s)	19:5aα	19:22bαβ
(האנשים אשר־באו אליך הוציאם אלינו)	19:5aβbα	
(הוצא את־האיש אשר־בא אל־ביתך)		19:22bγδ[i]
Threat of homosexual rape (ונדעה אתם/ונדענו)	19:5bβ	19:22bγδ[ii]
Host exits (ויצא אליהם)	19:6a	19:23aαβ
Host protests disgracing hospitality (to men) (אל־נא אחי תרעו)	19:7	
(אל־אחי אל־תרעו נא)		19:23aδ [cf. 20:3bγ, 12bα]
(אחרי אשר־בא האיש הזה אל־ביתי אל־תעשו את־הנבלה הזאת)		19:23b [cf. 20:6b, 10b]
(רק לאנשים האל אל־תעשו דבר כי־על־כן באו בצל קרתי)	19:8b	
(ולאיש הזה לא תעשו דבר הנבלה הזאת)		19:24b
Host offers to substitute virgin daughter(s)—two women (הנה־נא לי שתי בנות אשר לא־ידעו איש אוציאה־נא אתהן אליכם)	19:8aα-γ	
(הנה בתי הבתולה ופילגשהו אוציאה־נא אותם וענו אותם)		19:24aαβ
Allusion to covenant injustice (ועשו להן/ם כטוב בעיניכם)	19:8aδε	19:24aγ

	Gen. 19:1-11	*Judg. 19:(10aγ-13)*
		14-28 (29–21:24)
Narrative contrast:		
Consequence of substitution	angels help	Levite allows
	family escape	concubine's rape
		and ravage
	19:9-11	19:25-26, 27-28
Aftermath: city destruction		
and perpetual ruin	fulfilled	frustrated
	(19:12-29)	(19:29–21:24)

Plot A is complicated by the rape in Judg. 19:10aγ-26, 27-28. Then, the concubine's death irrevocably obstructs the resolution of Plot A in which the Levite, having been reconciled to his concubine, should have returned in peace to his home in the hill country of Ephraim. Plot A does, in fact, end with the return of both Levite and concubine to Ephraim but with the macabre twist that she is dead—hardly a desirable resolution to the problem introduced in the exposition of Plot A (19:1b-2). The dissolution of Plot A in Judg. 19:10aγ-26, 27-28 serves simultaneously as the exposition of Plot B. Somehow the injustice of the Gibeahites must be requited.

The development of Plot B, like that of Plot A, is punctuated and demarcated by the 'arose' motif (וֹקם) and, as with Plot A, is structured by reports of the successive days during which the plot unfolds. Apparently, the author intended that these elements of Plot B should 'answer' the day-motif structure of Plot A that had ended in disaster—a motif structure designed to evoke the pathos of *lex talionis*.

Judges 19:29-20:13a evidences the transference of concern for justice from the Levite to Israel's leaders and emphasizes the extent to which the leaders were willing to investigate and bring justice to bear on the Gibeahite offence (cf. 19:30-20:3, 12-13a). The procedure for placing Gibeah under the ban derives from a law recorded in Deut. 13:13-19, and the author of Judg. 19:29-20:48 seems to take pains to present the measures taken against Gibeah and Benjamin as adhering to the terms enjoined by this legislation.[362]

Although it was the Levite's intention in 20:4-7 to arouse the indignation of Israel against Gibeah, it was perhaps not thought

---

[362] While it is true that the offence presupposed by the sanctions of Deut. 13:13-19 is that of idolatry (cf., similarly, Deut. 17:2-7), Niditch is probably correct in concluding that, "the abomination wrought by the men of Gibeah is understood as contrary to proper covenantal behavior. Anti-social behavior breaks the covenant with God as much as idolatry" ("'Sodomite' Theme" [1982], p. 377).

important enough for him to mention that the mob had originally expressed sexual desires toward him.[363] What was thought important, however, is reflected in his emphasis upon the fact that the mob had originally intended to kill him (a Levite).[364] It is also significant that the point of the offence, in the Levite's report of the incident at Gibeah, is introduced with a recurrence of the 'arose' motif (20:5). This heightens the pathos of *lex talionis* and anticipates the recurrences of the 'arose' motif that introduce Israel's retaliations against Gibeah and Benjamin (20:8, 18, 19, 33a; cf. 20:24, 30a).

Judges 20:8-13a shows how concern about justice against Gibeah passes from the Levite to the leaders of Israel. The succeeding verses (20:13b-48) give an account of the reprisals against Benjamin for their failure to comply with the standards of covenant justice. Judges 20:19-23, 24-29, 30-31 outline, in a repeated sequence (elements 'a–b–c–d–e'), the events of three successive days of siege against Benjamin at Gibeah. Each of the five elements of the sequence occurs once for each siege day except element 'b', which is repeated on siege day 1 but is lacking for siege day 2, and the final element 'e' (where Israel should make inquiry of YHWH; but cf. 21:5a, 8a, 16), which is lacking for siege day 3. However, before the final element 'e' the narrator has inserted a protracted account of the turn of events that led to Benjamin's near extinction (20:32-48).

The account of Judg. 20:32-48 is marked by resumptive repetitions.[365] Two cases of resumptive repetition seem especially significant in the outline of the development of the passage: the repetitions of element 'd' in 20:31b and 20:39bα, which frame the account of how

---

[363] Lasine suggested that the Levite may have avoided mentioning the mob's sexual intention because of "his shame at being the object of such desires" ("Guest and Host" [1984], p. 57 n. 38). Cf. Niditch, "'Sodomite' Theme" (1982), p. 371.

[364] Note the emphatic word order of the first clause and the disjunctive word order of the second: אוֹתִי דִמּוּ לַהֲרֹג / וְאֶת־פִּילַגְשִׁי עִנּוּ וַתָּמֹת: "[It was] me they intended to kill, but they raped my concubine and she died". It seems also appropriate to infer that the Levites, despite suffering a possible general neglect by Israel in the book of Judges (cf. Deut. 12:12, 18-19 with Judg. 17:7-8a, 9b; 19:1bαβ?, 18aβ?), still enjoyed elevated social status as a priestly caste (17:10, 13; 18:19, 30b).

[365] Cf. the analysis of resumptive repetition by E. J. Revell, "Battle" (1985), pp. 426-33. On the various functions of resumptive repetition, see S. Talmon, "The Presentation of Synchroneity and Simultaneity in Biblical Narrative", in *Studies in Hebrew Narrative Art through the Ages* [J. Heinemann and S. Werses (eds.), ScrHier 27, Jerusalem, 1978], pp. 9-26. On the rhetorical effect of the temporal reordering implied by resumptive repetition in this passage, see P. E. Satterthwaite, "Narrative Artistry in the Composition of Judges xx 29ff.", *VT* 42 (1992), pp. 80-89.

Benjamin's delusion of victory led to surprise defeat (20:32-39a), and the repetition of paired elements $\beta\beta$ + $\alpha\alpha$ in 20:32 and 20:36, which frame the summary of how Israel's ambush led to Benjamin's surprise defeat (20:33-35). It is only because 20:33-35 presents an overview of the ambush that element '1/d' (concluding that 25,000 Benjaminites fell, 20:35aβ-b and 20:46) is repeated. It is not an example of resumptive repetition. For the same reason, neither are the repetitions of element $\gamma\gamma$ in 20:33b and 20:37 resumptive.

The pathos of *lex talionis* is present where the repetitions of the census of Israel's fallen soldiers (elements 'd': 20:21b, 25aβ-b, along with the resumptive repetitions in 20:31b and 39bα) are answered by repetitions of the censuses of Benjamin's fallen soldiers (elements '1/d': 20:44, 45a$\beta\gamma$, 45bβ, framed by the sums in 20:35aβ-b and 20:46).

In the plot outline of Judg. 19:29–20:48, Plot B traces a scenario to bring the injustice of the night at Gibeah to resolution by means of holy war. However, Plot B never comes to complete resolution. Indeed, the requirements of holy war could not be met until the last remnant of Benjamin (20:47aβb) had been exterminated.[366] Israel returned to the region of Benjamin to set about this task, and, according to the requirements of covenant justice, all was going as it should (cf. Judg. 20:48 with Deut. 13:16-17). But just at this point Israel, moved to pity by misplaced priorities, introduced a complication into the development of Plot B. With the departure from concern for *lex talionis* in Plot B, there is also a departure from the pattern of recurrences of the 'arose'

---

[366] On holy war in Israel, see C. H. W. Brekelmans, *De Herem in het Oude Testament* (Nijmegen, 1959); R. de Vaux, *Les Institutions de l'Ancien Testament* (2 vols., Paris, 1958, 1960), ET: *Ancient Israel: Its Life and Institutions* (J. McHugh [trans.], 2 vols., London, 2d edn, 1965), s.v., part 3, chapter 5, "The Holy War", vol. 1, pp. 258-67; G. von Rad, *Der Heilige Krieg im alten Israel* (Zurich, 3d edn, 1958); ET: *Holy War in Ancient Israel* (M. J. Dawn [trans. and ed.], Grand Rapids, 1991); R. Smend, Jr, *Jahwekrieg und Stämmebund: Erwägungen zur ältesten Geschichte Israels* (FRLANT 84, Göttingen, 2d edn, 1966), ET: *Yahweh War and Tribal Confederation* (Nashville, 1970); F. Stolz, *Jahwes und Israels Kriege: Kriegstheorien und Kriegserfahrungen im Glauben des alten Israel* (ATANT 60, Zurich, 1972); M. Weippert, "'Heiliger Krieg' in Israel und Assyrien: Kritische Anmerkungen zu Gerhard von Rads Konzept des 'Heiligen Krieges im alten Israel'", *ZAW* 84 (1972), pp. 460-93; P. D. Miller, Jr, *The Divine Warrior in Early Israel* (HSM 5, Cambridge, Mass., 1973); G. H. Jones, "'Holy War' or 'Yahweh War'?", *VT* 25 (1975), pp. 642-58; P. C. Craigie, *The Problem of War in the Old Testament* (Grand Rapids, 1978); M. C. Lind, *Yahweh is a Warrior: The Theology of Warfare in Ancient Israel* (Scottdale, Pa., 1980); G. H. Jones, "The Concept of Holy War", in *The World of Ancient Israel: Sociological, Anthropological and Political Perspectives* (R. E. Clements [ed.], Cambridge, 1989), pp. 299-321.

motif (וְקָם) and the reports of the successive days during which the plot unfolds.

With the exposition of Plot C, all that is appropriate to the requirements of covenant justice becomes misdirected through Israel's rationalizations in ch. 21. The expected resolution of Plot B is frustrated by the introduction of Israel's remorse for the remnant of Benjamin.

Judg. 21:1-23a comprises a series of paired elements (designated $\alpha + \beta$, $\gamma + \delta$, $\varepsilon + \zeta$ in the plot-structure outline). The pairing of these elements undergoes embellishment: (1) the reversal of the order of pair $\alpha + \beta$ (i.e., α-β $\parallel$ β-α $\parallel$ β-α) and (2) the alternation of the occurrence of a city name between the other pairs: (a) "Mizpah", alternatively in either the γ or δ elements, (b) "Shiloh", alternatively in either the ε or ζ elements. Judges 21:4 and 21:14b stand out from this structure: the former, as describing Israel's first scheme of rationalized disobedience to the covenant stipulations against Benjamin; the latter, as describing the complication to Israel's first scheme of rationalization (21:5-14a), which leads them into yet a second scheme of rationalization (21:15-23a).

Siege day 4 begins with Israel's attempt to appease YHWH's demand for the extermination of Benjamin by a substitution of sacrifices (20:4; cf. 1 Sam. 15:8-23). Then follows, in 21:5-23a, Israel's long-delayed inquiry (element 'e') deriving from the repetition sequence of siege days (20:19-23, 24-29, 30-31). The inquiries in 21:5-23a (vv. 5a, 8a, 16) reverse expectations, however, inasmuch as they are not made of YHWH. In their attempt to evade the requirements of covenant justice, Israel searches for a scapegoat and does not continue to inquire of YHWH (21:5a, 8a). Instead, they conduct their own inquiry by taking a census to ascertain who had failed to assemble at Mizpah (21:9). Thus, of the four inquiry accounts that occur after Benjamin's disobedience of Judg. 20:13b, the last account is the longest and most complex (3+1 pattern; cf. 20:18, 23, 26-28; 21:1-23a) and discloses Israel's attempt to evade the responsibilities of covenant justice.[367] However, the epitome of covenant injustice is reserved for the final verses of Plot C, where the abduction of Israelite maidens during the annual festival of YHWH is said to have been sanctioned.

The interruption of Plot B, through Plot C's misdirection of justice motivated by Israel's pity on the remnant of Benjamin, is finally

---

[367] On the customary prebattle preparation of seeking a favourable divine oracle, see Jones, "Concept" (1989), pp. 301, 303.

brought to a close, though not a resolution, in Judg. 21:23b-24. These closing verses of the narrative illustrate the antithesis of adherence to the requirements of covenant justice.

With the restoration of Benjamin to their allotment and the rebuilding of their cities (including, as history knows, Gibeah), Plot B comes to ultimate dissolution. The requirements of covenant justice, that criminal cities—and in this instance, criminal tribes—be exterminated, burned and left in perpetual ruin (Deut. 13:17), have not been met by Israel by the end of the account.

The clause ונבערה רעה מישראל in Judg. 20:13aβ alludes to various prohibitions and sanctions within Deuteronomy 12-26 that use this expression (e.g., Deut. 13:6b; 17:7b, 12bβ; 19:13b, 19b; 21:9aβ, 21aβ; 22:21b, 22b, 24b; 24:7bβ). However, because of collocation with several other points of Judg. 19:29-21:24, Deut. 13:2-19 seems to be the context to which this allusion points. Indeed, Deut. 13:13-19 furnishes a covenant precept that is most significant to a rhetorical reading of Judg. 19:29-21:24. The following points of convergence exist between these contexts:

Just Holy War	Deut. 13:13-19	Judg. 19:29-21:24
Summons to Israel's tribes	[assumed]	dividing concubine 19:29 [cf. 19:30b*; 20:7]
Scope of investigation	extensive 13:15a	Levite's testimony; 19:30b; 20:3b summons to Benjaminites 20:12-13a
Object of scorn:		
(התועבה)	13:15b	
(הרעה)		20:3bγ, 12bα [cf. 19:23aδ]
(זמה ונבלה/הנבלה)		20:6bα, 10bγ [cf. 19:23b, 24b]
אנשים בני־בליעל	13:14aα	20:13aα [cf. 19:22aβ]
בער [ה]רעה	[cf. 13:6b, 17:7b]	20:13aβ
Object of destruction:	evil city	Gibeah/Benjamin/ Jabesh-Gilead(?)
(הכה תכה / את־ישבי העיר ההוא לפי־חרב // החרם אתה ואת־כל־אשר־בה ואת־בהמתה לפי־חרב)	13:16	

	Deut. 13:13-19	*Judg. 19:29–21:24*
(ויכום לפי־חרב /		
מעיר מתם עד־בהמה /		
עד כל־הנמצא)		20:48aα[ii]-γ
(ויצוו אותם לאמר /		
לכו והכיתם את־יושבי		
יבש גלעד לפי־חרב /		
והנשים והטף:)		21:10b
(ואת־כל־שללה /		
תקבץ אל־תוך רחבה /		
ושרפת באש את־העיר /		
ואת־כל־שללה כליל /		
ליהוה אלהיך)	13:17a	
(גם כל־הערים הנמצאות		
שלחו באש:)		20:48b
Aftermath: perpetual ruin	prescribed	frustrated
(והיתה תל עולם /		
לא תבנה עוד:)	13:17b	≠ 21:23b
לעשות הישר /		
בעיני יהוה אלהיך	13:19b	[but cf. 19:24a]
		[but cf. 21:25b]

The resonance between the plot-line of Judg. 19:29–20:48 and the pre-scriptions of Deut. 13:13-19 is such that the reader is initially led to the expectation that, in contrast to the antithesis between Deut. 12:1–13:1 and the preceding account of Judges 17–18, Israel is here performing YHWH's commands to the letter. This is perhaps why the final verse of the section (19:29–20:48) is reserved for the report that, in accordance with Deut. 13:16-17a, the cities of the rebellious Benjaminites were incinerated.

However, at just this point the direction reverses abruptly to emphasize that, by choosing to do what was right in their own eyes, the tribes acted in defiance of the ideals of covenant justice set forth in Deut. 13:2-19. It is hardly accidental that, after the intervention of Plot C (21:1-23a), the final verses of the account (21:23b-24) portray the dissolution of Plot B with a description of their defiance of the law of Deut. 13:17b, a law that states that rebellious cities should remain a perpetual ruin and never be rebuilt.

In terms of negative characterization, Judg. 19:29–21:24 never makes overt the sense of bereavement that one should expect of the Levite. Instead, he is portrayed as taking actions that show concern to bring judgement upon Gibeah, and the tribes of Israel initially adopt the Levite's concern for covenant justice. Ironically, in contrast to the min-imization of any sense of bereavement on the part of the Levite, the tribes suddenly come to feel pity and a sense of bereavement for Benjamin, introducing Plot C (21:1-23a) at just the point where Israel is about to fulfil the covenant requirement to render Benjamin extinct. Indeed, Plot C intervenes in order to obstruct the fulfilment of both Deut. 13:16-17a and 13:17b.

This feature of characterization in the account may reflect a deliberate inversion of appropriate expressions of bereavement so as to undergird the framing evaluation that everyone did what was right in one's own eyes. Compassion emerges in the account only where Israel refuses to carry out the responsibility of holy war to exterminate the tribe of Benjamin (after 21:1). Israel comes to sense bereavement for Benjamin the covenant-breaker. Indeed, it may be valid to suggest that the account of Dénouement-B portrays an inverted world, for, after the Levite's departure from Bethlehem, few of the main scenarios in the plot resolve in a way that would be appropriate to the occasion.[368]

§2.1. *Intertribal Covenant Disloyalty*

Niditch has lately argued that "Judges 19-20 is about community and unity".[369] Thus, while deferring to recent qualifications of and dissent from M. Noth's classic theory of Israelite amphictyony,[370] she affirmed:

> the unity-theme [is] central to the narrative; the tale builds to this theme in a stylistically elegant way. Without this theme the work loses its *raison d'être*. In this way literary analysis tends to support the notion that tribal confederation was a key concept to the author. ... We cannot be sure what constituted

---

[368] On the comic dimensions of the "inverted world" (especially in Judg. 19), see Lasine, "Guest and Host" (1984), pp. 37, 50 n. 1 and *passim*.

[369] Niditch, "'Sodomite' Theme" (1982), p. 372.

[370] On M. Noth's theory of the amphictyony, see *Das System der zwölf Stämme Israels* (BWANT IV/1, Stuttgart, 1930; 2d edn, 1966). For subsequent qualifying and dissenting views, see N. P. Lemche, *Israel i dommertiden: En oversigt over diskussionen om M. Noths "Das System der zwölf Stämme Israels"* (TT 4, Copenhagen, 1972) [Danish]; A. D. H. Mayes, *Israel in the Period of the Judges* (SBT II/29, London, 1974); C. H. J. de Geus, *The Tribes of Israel: An Investigation into Some of the Presuppositions of Martin Noth's Amphictyony Hypothesis* (SSN 18, Assen, 1976); O. Bächli, *Amphiktyonie im Alten Testament: Forschungsgeschichtliche Studie zur Hypothese von Martin Noth* (Basel, 1977); H. Seebass, "League of Tribes or Amphictyony? A Review of O. Bächli, *Amphiktyonie im Alten Testament: Forschungsgeschichtliche Studie zur Hypothese von Martin Noth*. Basel, 1977", *JSOT* 16 (1980), pp. 61-66; N. P. Lemche, "The Greek 'Amphictyony'—Could It Be a Prototype for the Israelite Society in the Period of the Judges?", *JSOT* 4 (1977), pp. 48-59; B. Lindars, "The Israelite Tribes in Judges", in *Studies in the Historical Books of the Old Testament* (J. A. Emerton [ed.], SVT 30, Leiden, 1979), pp. 95-112; N. P. Lemche, *Early Israel: Anthropological and Historical Studies on the Israelite Society before the Monarchy* (SVT 37, Leiden, 1986).

"all-Israel" for this author, but that he had such an ideal concept seems unquestionable. Our analysis while using different critical methods from those of Martin Noth and beginning in fact with quite different presuppositions and interests ends up agreeing with Noth's basic insight about Judges 19–20 that the narrative is about community, cooperation, and unity among Israelites, the *Gesamtleben* of the Israelite tribes.[371]

Nevertheless, while the disunity of the premonarchic period may have provided the *raison d'être* for Judges 19–21, it must be conceded (in view of the monarchy motif framing Judg. 19–21) that this concern remained relevant during the early schismatic period of the monarchy.[372] The problem of tribal disunity is a key concern of the compiler/redactor, who used Judges 19–21 to convey this concern.[373] However, it is not intertribal unity *per se* that is the narrator's (or compiler/redactor's) concern but intertribal conformity to the ideal of covenant justice. Had Benjamin, along with the rest of the tribes of Israel, yielded to the exigencies of covenant justice, Gibeah would have been put under the ban and there would have been no further complications after Plot B.[374] Beginning with Benjamin's refusal to cooperate with the other tribes, the narrator's ultimate concern with intertribal unity begins to come into focus: Benjamin, by siding with Gibeah, disrupts the unity of all Israel's commitment to the sanctions of Deut. 13:13-19.

---

[371] Niditch, "'Sodomite' Theme" (1982), p. 373.

[372] Niditch, "'Sodomite' Theme" (1982), p. 374.

[373] As Dumbrell asserted ("Those Days" [1983], pp. 24-26):

> Pan-Israelite concerns ... engaged the editor of the Book of Judges. This is demonstrable in the Shiloh episodes of Judges 21 and clear from the interconnections established between the material of Judges 17–21. ...
>
> To be sure, Judges is very much an *editorial* unity with a pan-Israelite ideal in mind. ...
>
> As an editorial unity, the main thrust of the book is to present the concept of a united Israelite confederacy.

[374] While it is strictly true that Deut. 13:13-19 concerns sanctions against apostasy expressed in the form of idolatry, rather than social injustice, it is implicit in the allusion of Judg. 19:29–21:24 to Deut. 13:13-19 that such deuteronomic prescriptions were understood to apply to other forms of apostasy as well. This would be analogous to the manner in which the extent of application of sanctions may vary for the same offence depending on whether the crime was committed by an entire city (Deut. 13:13-19) or by only one member of the city (Deut. 17:2-7)—in the case of Judg. 19:29–20:48 the sanctions are extended to include an entire tribe. Departure from strict adherence to the wording of laws when applying them is at variance with the modern notion of legal precedent but in keeping with the ancient Near Eastern notion that case (casuistic) laws were essentially paradigmatic and designed to be adapted. Cf. J. J. Finkelstein, *The Ox that Gored* (TAPS 71/2, Philadelphia, 1981).

The reason the Levite cut his concubine into twelve parts was so that one part could be sent to each of the (ostensibly twelve) tribes of Israel (cf. 21:3b). Presumably, the Benjaminites were sent one part, though they chose not to respond to the summons. Judges 20:3a reflects Benjamin's indolence and foreshadows their blatant defiance of the obligations of intertribal covenant unity in 20:13b. When Israel later conducts similar sanctions against Jabesh-Gilead on the pretext of the latter's failure to respond to the intertribal summons to conduct sanctions against Benjamin (cf. 21:5a, 8-9), Israel is doing so in order to try to preserve the remnant of Benjamin. Thus, the analogy between these situations furnishes the irony that united Israel exterminates Jabesh-Gilead of all but virgin females for the very covenant crime of which Benjamin had earlier been guilty and does so in order to evade exterminating Benjamin from the nation.[375] As a result, intertribal unity is preserved at the cost of loyalty to the terms of YHWH's covenant.

The final verse of the narrative, Judg. 21:24, picks up the phraseology of Judg. 2:6, the first verse of Prologue-B (2:6–3:6). Since Joshua does not appear at the council of tribes (20:1-7), one may infer that this event took place after his dismissal of the tribes each to its own inheritance (i.e., 2:6) and after his death (1:1a; 2:8). However, inasmuch as Phinehas, son of Eleazar, son of Aaron, is said to have been present (20:27b-28aβ[ii]), the incident ostensibly occurred not long after Joshua's death.[376] Indeed, the scenario of Judges 19-21, portrayed as one of the earliest incidents of Judges, offers a paradigm of the degradation that would characterize the entire period covered by the book. It discloses a prototypical characterization of the tribes of the period, but, because this information is withheld until the end of the book of Judges, it represents a culminating point for the compiler/ redactor.[377] The Benjaminites' essential problem was that they let

---

[375] If no remnant had been left alive in Jabesh-Gilead (cf. 21:10-11, 14a), one might infer that the later residents of Jabesh-Gilead (i.e., the contemporaries of Saul and David, according to 1 Sam. *11:1-11 [which should include the addition between MT 10:27 and 11:1 attested by 4QSam[a] and Josephus, *Ant.* VI.v.1 §§68-71]; 1 Sam. 31:11-13; 2 Sam. 2:4b-7) descended from Gileadites who repopulated the city.

[376] Even if Judg. 20:27b-28aβ[ii] had been inserted into the book after its main compilation, the information furnished by this addition may yet be accurate. However, in this case one would need to recognize that, since this information was not furnished by the main compiler, it should be taken into consideration only inferentially (i.e., as an inference that the intended readers could be expected to have drawn for themselves).

[377] Both parts of Judges' double dénouement portray events that are chronologically antecedent to events of preceding accounts in the book. The events of Judg. 17-18 likely precede those of chs. 13-16, Jonathan being ostensibly the grandson of Moses (18:30b),

individual tribal concerns take precedence over concern about national adherence to the terms of YHWH's covenant. Thus, in matters of holy war, the tribes of this early period proved no more committed to purging themselves of evil than would be the intertribal league as a whole to expelling the Canaanites and idolatry thereafter. There is, hence, an escalated parallelism between Judg. 1:1–2:5, which focuses upon the failure of Benjamin to exterminate the Jebusites from Jebus (1:21), and chs. 19–21, which focuses upon the failure of Israel to exterminate the Benjaminites from the land of Israel.

§2.2. Covenant (Social) Injustice

It is never made a point of comment that the Levite waited four months before going to retrieve his concubine. Perhaps he did not know where she had gone and only heard from her father in due course; perhaps he did not care enough to act sooner. As events turn out, although it would appear that the Levite was interested in retrieving his concubine, he was not necessarily concerned for her welfare—he never explicitly speaks to her until she is ravaged and does not appear to have lost much sleep during the night of her ruin. It is seemingly to his credit that, having endured a threat against his person (or so he claims) and having suffered the loss of his concubine, he acted to bring justice out of chaos—albeit by a means as grotesque as the crime he seeks to redress. However, the Levite's speech to the tribes reveals that it was concern about his own suffering that motivated him to summon the tribes "to purge the evil from Israel" (cf. 20:5bα).

The expression וּבִעַרְתָּ רָעָה מִיִּשְׂרָאֵל, used in Judg. 20:13aβ, refers in Deuteronomy to purging Israel of idolaters (Deut. 13:6b; 17:7b); those in contempt of the rule of priests, Levites or judges (17:12bβ); murderers (19:13b; 21:9aβ); false witnesses (19:19b); rebellious sons (21:21aβ); the sexually immoral (22:21b, 22b, 24b) and kidnappers (24:7bβ). It is often contiguous with the expression of three concerns related to the execution of covenant justice: (1) the right of the victim in being the first to execute justice (Deut. 13:10aβb; 17:7a), (2) the importance of executing justice without pity (Deut. 13:9b-10aα; 19:21a) and (3) the benefit to Israel in learning to fear covenant justice (Deut. 13:12; 17:13; 19:20; 21:21b). In one form or another, each of these concerns is reflected in the narrative of Judg. 19–21.

---

and the events of Judg. 19–21, Phinehas being a contemporary of Othniel (3:7-11), are antecedent to all episodes portrayed as subsequent to that of Othniel (i.e., 3:12–16:31).

The national inquest and siege of Benjamin in Judg. 20:8-48, 20:18 seems intrinsic to the development of the story, since it introduces a series of three such inquiries of YHWH prior to holy war against Benjamin (20:23, 26-28; but cf. 21:2-5) and illustrates the propriety of allowing that tribe whose native citizen was victimized (i.e., the concubine of Bethlehem) to commence the holy war against Benjamin (cf. Deut. 13:10aβb; 17:7a).

Two violations of covenant justice were committed by Gibeah and Benjamin, respectively, in Judg. 19:2–20:7: the Gibeahites' rape of the Levite's concubine and Benjamin's refusal to rally against Gibeah with the other Israelite tribes. During the tribes' inquest, these emerge in the same order: first, the inquest into Gibeah's offence (20:8-13a), then, the refusal of Benjamin to cooperate with the other tribes to fulfil the requirements of covenant justice (20:13b-14). The course of the holy war against Benjamin (20:15-48) was ostensibly to punish both crimes. The account of Israel's inquest and of its holy war is presented as having been in conformity to Deut. 13:13-19. However, in the course of destroying Benjamin, the Israelite tribes began to feel remorse and pity for Benjamin (against the prohibition of Deut. 13:9b-10aα; 19:21a), and it is this that led them to renege on their obligation to execute justice for YHWH.

Israel's concessions to the requirements of covenant justice are presented in reverse order from that in which the offences occurred: first, in 21:1-14 Israel compromises the principle whereby they should punish Benjamin for refusing to cooperate with the other tribes by rallying for holy war; then, in 21:15-23a, Israel compromises the principle whereby they should punish Gibeah for ravaging the Levite's concubine. These reversals of justice, which occur in reverse order from the crimes of city and tribe, respectively, illustrate how Israel put Benjamin's interests above the nation's commitment to YHWH's covenant laws.

As mentioned above, when Israel laid siege to Jabesh-Gilead to provide wives for the male remnant of Benjamin (21:1-14), Israel was punishing Jabesh-Gilead for a crime of which the Benjaminites themselves had been guilty (cf. 20:3a, 21:5a, 8-9). It is therefore no minor point of irony that all Israel, by finally siding with Benjamin, perverts the ideal of covenant justice by deflecting the sanctions of holy war from Benjamin to a scapegoat, the city of Jabesh-Gilead. Israel punishes one offender in order to ameliorate the circumstances of another who has committed the same crime. Ironically, Benjamin's crime of harbouring criminals has now become escalated to a national level. Israel shows preferential treatment to Benjamin over Jabesh-Gilead presumably because Benjamin is a tribe of Israel whereas Jabesh-Gilead is merely a city (and a city of Gilead at that) whose extinction is preferable to that of a tribe.[378] Indeed, this situation offers a parallel to that in which the Levite of ch. 18 perverts justice toward an individual (i.e., Micah) in order to gain the acceptance of a tribe (i.e., Dan). This instance of the inversion of a principle of justice is then immediately followed by a second (21:15-23a): Israel's allowing the abduction and ostensible rape of the Shiloh maidens to furnish wives for the remaining men of Benjamin. Israel now sanctions the same crime of forced sexual rape against the maidens of Shiloh as Benjamin had earlier sanctioned against the Levite's concubine. The license that Benjamin gave the Gibeahites, Israel now gives Benjamin.

Judges 21:23b shows that Israel's perversion of justice is the narrator's greatest concern. The account of Judg. 20:8-48, which presents an idealized portrayal of adherence to the instructions of Deut. 13:13-19, is subverted by Israel's intervening abrogations of justice in 21:1-14 and 21:15-23a (each commencing with an expression of grief over the idea of exterminating Benjamin). With the statement in 21:23b, however, the very policy of Deut. 13:13-19 is overturned: Benjamin, in defiance of Deut. 13:17b, returns to their inheritance to rebuild the towns that had been burned and were to remain in ruins. Thus, the whole of chs. 19–21 portrays a situation involving national abandonment of YHWH's standards of justice for the sake of one tribe. Hence, whatever sense of covenant justice the remaining tribes of Israel may have learned from the ruins in Benjamin evaporates with the rebuilding of their cities (cf. Deut. 13:12; 17:13; 19:20; 21:21b).

It may be to the discredit of the Levite in this account that his description of the Gibeahite offence (20:4-7) does not include the self-incriminating fact that it was he who had thrown his concubine to the mob in order to save himself (cf. 19:25).[379] Nevertheless, neither the mention nor omission of this detail should diminish the propriety of Israel's becoming indignant against Gibeah (20:8-11). Gibeah, by their conduct, had brought guilt upon themselves, a guilt that Israel thought was deserving of the sanctions of holy war, a guilt that the narrator portrayed as commensurate with that of Sodom. Lasine's regard of the

---

[378] For evidence that premonarchical Gilead was a tribal and dialectal backwater of Cisjordan, see B. Halpern, *The Emergence of Israel in Canaan* (SBLMS 29, Chico, Calif., 1983), pp. 166-70.

[379] Lasine, "Guest and Host" (1984), pp. 49, 57 nn. 39, 40.

punishment executed against Benjamin as "excessive revenge" is therefore unwarranted if, to the contrary, the aim of the author were to show in Judges 19–21 how Israel came to compromise the sanctions of holy war prescribed in Deut. 13:13-19.[380] Nor did Israel necessarily "ask the wrong question" in Judg. 20:18 if it were the aim of the author to present Israel following proper procedure by selecting, in order to initiate retaliation, a tribe whose citizen (i.e., the concubine) had been victimized (cf. Deut. 13:10aβb; 17:7a).[381]

§3. *Complementarity between Dénouement-A and Dénouement-B*

Besides the references to the absence of monarchy (17:6a; 18:1a; 19:1a; 21:25a) and the recurrences of the A1b motif (17:6b; 21:25b), several points of analogy between the narratives of Judg. 17:1-5, 7-13, 18:1b-31 and 19:1b–21:24 suggest that these accounts, in their present form, were designed to be read as analogous:

1. Both dénouement accounts portray a Levite as the catalyst in escalating cultic aberrations or covenant injustices from a family or city level (17:3-5 ‖ 19:25b) to a tribal or national scale (18:30a, 31 ‖ 21:23a). It is to this end that the Levite in each account receives negative characterization.[382]

2. In both cases, the Levite departs from Bethlehem in search of a place to stay and meets with complicating circumstances that lead to his becoming a collaborator in or instigator of tribal or national covenant violations (17:7-8a, 9b [cf. 18:19-20, 30] ‖ 19:10-13 [cf. 20:1-7, 8-11, 12-13a; 21:1-2, 23b-24]).

3. Both accounts portray priestly functionaries of YHWH employing a mantic device to discern from YHWH the outcome of circumstances, but, in each case, the actual outcome runs contrary to expectations because of covenant compromise (18:5-6 [but cf. 18:14, 18-20, 30-31] ‖ 20:27-28 [cf. 20:18, 23; but also 21:2-5a, 8a, 9]).

4. Both accounts describe a military contingent of six hundred men whose alienation from their tribal allotment brings about compromises in cult and/or covenant justice (18:11, 16, 17b, 25 ‖ 20:47; 21:7a, 12a, 14, 16-17, 23).

---

[380] Lasine, "Guest and Host" (1984), p. 49.

[381] Lasine, "Guest and Host" (1984), p. 50.

[382] The Levite in Judg. 17-18 is negatively characterized both to the extent that he prostitutes himself for hire at private and tribal shrines that depart from the one national cult envisaged by Deut. 12 and to the extent that he is so coldly dispassionate toward Micah when departing to serve as priest for the tribe of Dan. On the negative characterization of the Levite in Judg. 19, see Lasine, "Guest and Host" (1984), pp. 37-38, 42, 43-50. Lasine contended that in Judg. 19 it was the narrator's aim to condemn the Levite, though one is not told what specific function this negative characterization serves in the strategy of chs. 19-21 or in the compiler/redactor's strategy for the book of Judges.

5. In both accounts, sanctions of holy war are executed against a city as a means to finding a final solution to the alienation of the six hundred warriors (18:1-2, 27aγb-28a ‖ 21:10-11).
6. Both accounts culminate in a reference to Shiloh that is used implicitly to condemn the tribe and/or nation featured in the context (18:31b ‖ 21:12b, 19, 21).

Perhaps the most significant analogy between Judges 17–18 and 19–21 rests in the rhetorical strategy of their plot-structures. Both dénouement sections contain a narrative analogy to a symbolic event of rebellion against YHWH: Judg. 18:1-10 is analogous to the account of Israel's sending of the twelve spies in Num. 12:16–14:45 and Deut. 1:19-46, and Judg. 19:14-28 is analogous to the description of Sodom's rebellion in Gen. 19:1-11. The function of the narrative analogies in both dénouement sections is to set up a foil by which to contrast their resulting aftermaths. Hence, whereas Num. 12:16–14:45 and Deut. 1:19-46 end in Israel's military defeat and exclusion from the land, Judges 18 (Plot C) ends in Dan's military victory and settlement, albeit with the irony that they have compromised the conquest of their traditional allotted tribal region. Likewise, whereas Gen. 19:1-11 ends with innocent Lot's escape and Sodom's destruction, Judges 19–21 ends with guilty Benjamin's escape, the destruction of Jabesh-Gilead as a scapegoat and the abduction of maidens from both Jabesh-Gilead and Shiloh, the latter event imitating the Gibeahites' abduction of the Levite's concubine. Moreover, the aftermaths of both dénouement sections epitomize violations of deuteronomic legislation: Judges 18 closes with Dan establishing an illegitimate sanctuary, in violation of Deuteronomy 12, and Judges 21 closes with Benjamin rebuilding rebellious cities, in violation of the procedure enjoined by Deuteronomy 13.

These points of analogy between Judges 17–18 and 19–21 are further reinforced by the analogous symmetry that they share in regard to the repetition of the monarchy motif (17:6a; 18:1a; 19:1a; 21:25a) and the A1b motif (17:6b; 21:25b) whereby these different motif elements appear in contiguity only in the outermost repetitions of the monarchy motif (17:6; 21:25). The symmetry of the repetition pattern thus encloses 17–21 so as to suggest that the compiler/redactor intended that these accounts be read as rhetorically complementary.

D. CONCLUSION

It is with the addition of chs. 17–21 that the overall purpose of Judges comes into focus. Implicit in the repeated references to the monarchy in 17:6; 18:1; 19:1a; 21:25 is the endorsement of Israel's king as the agent of Judges' desired higher standards of cultic and social order in Israel. When the monarchical endorsement of chs. 17–21 is read in connection with hints furnished by Judges' double prologue that YHWH favours Judah as the tribe to lead all Israel (cf. 1:1-2 and 20:18) or that the conquest of Jerusalem should be seen as an emblem of divine favour (cf. 1:8 with 1:21; 19:11-14), one might infer that the Judges compiler/redactor was implicitly endorsing a Judahite king enthroned in Jerusalem. If so, it may be inferred that the Judges compiler/redactor thought that Israel's neglect of YHWH's commission to expel the Canaanites from the land and their consequent relapses into idolatry could be overcome only by their united endorsement of a Judahite king loyal to YHWH's covenant ideals. Hence, it would appear that the primary rhetorical purpose of the book of Judges was to enjoin "all Israel" to endorse that king from Judah who exemplified loyalty to the ideals of land occupation, intertribal unity, cultic order and social justice prescribed by YHWH's covenant.

This monarchical idealization points to a solution to the increasingly problematic situations portrayed throughout the body of the book of Judges, whether those situations were caused by the tribes' disinterest in ridding the land of foreigners or their cult, their growing intertribal disunity, their own cultic disintegration or their climate of social injustice. Only in the case of the first deliverer, Othniel from Judah, is the characterization free of implicit condemnation in regard to the international, intertribal, cultic and social ideals of the book. Thereafter, the quality of leadership in each tribal hero successively worsens. Accordingly, the character of the king implicitly endorsed in the final five chapters of Judges stands in contrast to the mixed characterizations of both non-Judahite tribal heroes and, by recurring escalated parallelisms, the tribes or nation that these heroes either sought or were charged to deliver.

Moreover, frequent interest among the deliverer accounts in the glorification of YHWH reflects another aspect of the rhetorical concern of the Judges compiler/redactor. Often the elevated characterization of YHWH is set off against a satirization of foreign rulers. Indeed, the resulting contrastive combination may have been designed to set up a standard by which to measure the wisdom of the Israelite people's later request, in 1 Samuel 8 and 12, that in place of YHWH Samuel should appoint for them a king such as all the other nations have. Certainly there are other indications in the book of Judges and in 1 Samuel that suggest that the Judges compiler/redactor had in mind some of the issues and circumstances relating to Saul's rise to kingship as opposed to that of David.[383]

---

[383] See the discussion in the succeeding chapters.

CHAPTER THREE

THE RHETORICAL STRATEGY OF JUDGES

There are many aspects of Judges' double dénouement that lead to unexpected implications for the reader. By the close of Judges' series of deliverer accounts, the reader has already tacitly made decisions about ideals of leadership in Israel. Then, in the final five chapters, the monarchical and cultic perspectives of its compiler/redactor appear for the first time. Indeed, it makes sense that, if Judges were a work designed to inculcate new political and religious ideals, it would employ subtle strategies of idealization, refraining from making direct references to the cause that it endorses until a new consciousness of the situation had been established. Once one has encountered the explicit monarchicalism of the dénouement sections of Judges, one can see in retrospect both explicit and implicit strategies of monarchical idealization throughout the book. It is chiefly by means of a strategy of entrapment that Judges achieves its implicit rhetorical purpose of idealizing the monarchy of Judah at the expense of that of Benjamin.[1]

Perhaps the only resolution to the problem of Israel's covenant disloyalty, repeatedly expressed in the cyclical deuteronomic schema of Judges, is that implied by the compiler/redactor's explicit monarchicalism in Judg. 17:6 and 21:25. The monarchical idealization of Judges is a reflex of the compiler/redactor's implicit negative evaluation of the premonarchical period, which is contrasted to the period of the monarchy.[2]

---

[1] This carries with it the implication that the ostensible situation of composition for the book of Judges is that of the rivalry between the houses of David and of Saul at a time when the legitimacy of David's rule over all Israel was still open to dispute (e.g., the situation portrayed in 2 Sam. 1-4). See the discussion in chapter 4.

[2] Of the studies that focus upon the significance of the monarchical motif in Judges, those that favour monarchical idealization include: M. Noth, "Der Hintergrund von Richter 17-18" (1962); reprinted in vol. 1, *Archäologische, exegetische und topographische Untersuchungen zur Geschichte Israels*, in *Aufsätze zur biblischen Landes- und Altertumskunde* (2 vols., H. W. Wolff [ed.], Neukirchen-Vluyn, 1971), pp. 133-47, ET: "The Background of Judges 17-18", in *Israel's Prophetic Heritage: Essays in Honor of James Muilenburg* (B. W. Anderson and W. Harrelson [eds.], The Preachers' Library, London, 1962), pp. 68-85; A. E. Cundall, "Judges—An Apology for the Monarchy?", *ExpTim* 81 (1969-1970), pp. 178-81; F. E. Greenspahn, "An Egyptian Parallel to Judg 17:6 and 21:25", *JBL* 101 (1982), pp. 129-30; M. Brettler, "The Book of Judges: Literature as Politics", *JBL* 108 (1989), pp. 395-418. Those who deny monarchical idealization

A. Explicit Monarchicalism in Judges' Double Dénouement

From the references to a premonarchical period in 17:6a; 18:1a; 19:1a; 21:25a, it is evident that Judges was finally compiled/redacted subsequent to the establishment of the monarchy in Israel.[3] The fact that

include: S. Talmon, "In Those Days There Was No King in Israel", in *Proceedings of the Fifth World Congress of Jewish Studies, Jerusalem 1969* (5 vols., P. Peli et al. [eds.], Jerusalem, 1971), vol. 1, pp. 135-44 [Hebrew; English summary: vol. 1, pp. 242-43]; W. J. Dumbrell, "'In Those Days There Was No King in Israel; Every Man Did What Was Right in His Own Eyes': The Purpose of the Book of Judges Reconsidered", *JSOT* 25 (1983), pp. 23-33.

[3] The proposal of Talmon (following Qimḥi on Judg. 18:1), that in Judges the titles שֹׁפֵט and מֶלֶךְ are essentially synonymous ("Those Days" [1971], vol. 1, pp. 242-43 [Hebrew; English summary]), has been endorsed by L. R. Klein (*The Triumph of Irony in the Book of Judges* [JSOTS 68, BLS 14, Sheffield, 1988], pp. 141, 229 n. 2). This leads to the view that Judg. 17:6a; 18:1a; 19:1a and 21:25a do not connote the absence of a 'king' but merely of a 'ruler, leader'. Thus, the concern expressed in this motif would be with apostasy during the leaderless interims of the period of the judges rather than with the absence of the monarchical period to come.

Against Talmon's equation of שֹׁפֵט and מֶלֶךְ in Judges one may list the following observations. First, Gideon refuses to establish hereditary 'rule' (מָשַׁל, 8:22-23). Second, Abimelech is denounced for usurping such 'rule' (מָשַׁל, 9:2) as 'king' (מלך, 9:6, 8, 10, 12, 14, 16, 18—not 'judge' שֹׁפֵט), and the Judges compiler/redactor avoids referring to the period of his 'rule' using the standard (F1) motif וישפט את־ישראל but uses instead וישר אבימלך על־ישראל (9:22). Third, a distinction is made in 2 Kgs 23:22 between שֹׁפֵט and כי לא נעשה כפסח הזה מימי השפטים אשר שפטו את־ישראל וכל ימי מלכי ישראל ומלכי יהודה) that, although outside Judges, reflects a concern to differentiate the periods of the 'judges' from those of the 'kings' by employing distinct technical terms for their differing roles as rulers (so M. S. Rozenberg, "The *šōfᵊṭīm* in the Bible", in *Eretz-Israel: Archaeological, Historical and Geographical Studies*, vol. 12, *Nelson Glueck Memorial Volume* [Jerusalem, 1975], p. 82*; cf. Greenspahn, "Egyptian Parallel" [1982], p. 129 n. 5). Rozenberg concluded that, because the titular use of שֹׁפֵט never appears outside Judges' framework, it was not original to the traditions that the Judges compiler/redactor used but reflects his/her concern to distinguish the type of leadership inherent in the premonarchical period from that of the monarchy (pp. 82*, 85*; so T. Ishida, "The Leaders of the Tribal Leagues: 'Israel' in the Pre-Monarchic Period", *RB* 80 [1973], pp. 521, 529-30). Thus, Klein's citation of Ishida's and Rozenberg's studies as though in agreement with Talmon's equation of שֹׁפֵט and מֶלֶךְ may be misleading (*Triumph of Irony* [1988], p. 229 n. 2). Fourth, most examples of parallelism between שֹׁפֵט and מֶלֶךְ (or some other synonym for 'king') occur outside the former prophets (i.e., the so-called Deuteronomistic History): (1) שֹׁפֵט ‖ מֶלֶךְ: Hos. 7:7; Pss. 2:10; 148:11 (cf. Isa. 33:22); (2) שֹׁפֵט ‖ שַׂר: Exod. 2:14; Amos 2:3; Mic. 7:3; Zeph. 3:3; Prov. 8:16; 2 Chron. 1:2; (3) שֹׁפֵט ‖ מֶלֶךְ and שַׂר: Hos. 13:10 (cf. Ps. 148:11); (4) שֹׁפֵט ‖ רֹזֵן*: Isa. 40:23 (cf. מֶלֶךְ ‖ רֹזֵן*: Judg. 5:3) (see Ishida, "Leaders" [1973], p. 520). Nor does the Ugaritic parallelism between *ṭpṭ* (sometimes synonymous with *dyn*) and *mlk* or *zbl* offer any regulation on how שֹׁפֵט should be understood in Judges and the former prophets (Ishida, "Leaders" [1973], p. 518; cf. J. Blenkinsopp, "Structure and Style in Judges 13–16", *JBL* 82 [1963], p. 69 n. 16). Uses of שֹׁפֵט that are generally taken to mean 'ruler' from context alone also occur outside the former prophets (Mic. 4:14; Dan. 9:12). Thus, nowhere in the former prophets can a

this monarchical perspective on the period is disclosed only at the end of the book suggests that its disclosure was designed to achieve a retroactive rhetorical effect. This retroactive effect conforms to a rhetorical pattern of entrapment found in other contexts of the Hebrew Bible whereby the text delays specifying the situation of comparison until the hearer has already endorsed the principle that will apply to that situation.[4] Nothing in the preceding chapters of the book has prepared for the late disclosure in 17:6 and 21:25 that the book has been compiled/redacted with the purpose of demonstrating how, with the exception of Othniel, Israel's leadership prior to the monarchy had fallen short of the tribal–political and deuteronomic ideals that would come to be exemplified by a later king in Israel. However, subsequent to the explicit disclosure of the compiler/redactor's monarchist perspective, the reader must reevaluate retroactively the framework and deliverer accounts of Judges so as to discern whether the compiler/redactor had already there implicitly prepared for this monarchical idealization.

B. IMPLICIT MONARCHICALISM IN JUDGES' TRIBAL-POLITICAL CONCERNS

When viewed from the monarchist perspective of Judges' double dénouement, two features of the tribal–political arrangement of the book stand out: first, the framing positive portrayal of Judah as the tribe divinely elected by YHWH (1:1-2; 20:18)—in both contexts, the portrayal of Judah being juxtaposed with a negative portrayal of Benjamin (1:1-21; 19–21); second, both the priority of Judah in the order of tribes (in Prologue-A and among the deliverer accounts) and the uniquely positive portrayal of Othniel among Judges' deliverers. These features, when read against the monarchist perspective of the closing chapters of Judges, indicate that the book may have been composed to endorse implicitly a divinely elected Judahite as the ideal king of Israel.

---

synonymity between שֶׁפֶט and מֶלֶךְ be clearly demonstrated, and the fact that, in the former prophets, verbal (nontitular) uses of שפט appear in contiguity with the title מֶלֶךְ (e.g., 1 Sam. 8:5, 6, 20; 2 Kgs 15:5 = 2 Chron. 26:21) shows only that שפט may mean 'to rule, lead', but this offers no help in determining the specific denotation of the title שפט either in this corpus generally (e.g., שׁפט in 2 Sam. 7:[7 (MT: שִׁבְטֵי)], 11 = 1 Chron. 17:6[?], 10 may apply to 'judges' or 'kings' who are said "to shepherd" Israel) or in the book of Judges specifically.

[4] Cf. 2 Sam. 12:1-10; 14:4-17; Isa. 5:1-7. Indeed, Jotham's fable (Judg. 9:7-20) is a microcosm of the strategy of entrapment used in the book of Judges as a whole.

§1. The King as the Divine Elect

As just stated, a portrayal of Judah as YHWH's elect tribe frames the book of Judges (1:1-2; 20:18). In both contexts, Judah's positive portrayal is juxtaposed with a negative portrayal of Benjamin (1:1-21; 19–21). In the light of the monarchical idealization that closes the book of Judges, one could infer that it would be a king from Judah, as opposed to one from Benjamin (or any other tribe), who would serve ideally as king of Israel. From Gideon's refusal of rulership in Judg. 8:23, it is apparent not that hereditary kingship *per se* is denounced but that rulership should not come by means of a popular election, by usurping YHWH's prerogative as ruler of Israel.[5] Ironically, the only occasion in Judges when a ruler is appointed is that when Gideon's son Abimelech is made 'king' (9:6), though, on that occasion, Jotham curses Abimelech and Shechem for colluding in the murder of Abimelech's halfbrother rivals (9:7-20). Since it is God who is said to have carried out Jotham's curse (9:56-57), it is implicit that the narrator concurs with his judgement of those who murder to attain (or retain) a kingship that has been renounced by God's spokesperson. Indeed, the only position to which YHWH is said to have appointed any leader in Judges is that of deliverer. Sometimes a deliverer is appointed by a prophetic or angelic call, as when Deborah summoned Barak or when Samson was appointed to become a Nazirite deliverer through an angelic birth annunciation, but most often YHWH's election of a deliverer is expressed in the recurrences of the D1 cycle-motif element ("YHWH raised up ... to save them") and of element D2a ("YHWH's spirit ... upon"). It is not coincidental that Abimelech, as the only 'king' in Judges, lacks any indication of divine election. On the contrary, according to Judg. 9:23a, YHWH is said to have sent an evil spirit between Abimelech and the citizens of Shechem. If the Judges compiler/redactor's monarchical idealization at the end of the book were designed to characterize the evil of the usurpation of kingship, then it would need to be evident that the king whom he/she endorsed was divinely elected—whether because he was chosen from the elect tribe of Judah, was appointed by a prophet or angel of YHWH, was a recipient of YHWH's spirit, or all the above.[6]

---

[5] Note that the verb used in Judg. 8:23 is משל 'to rule', not מלך 'to reign, be king'.

[6] For a discussion of the parallel imagery used in Judges and 1 Samuel to contrast the characterizations of Saul and David as YHWH's elect, see chapter 4.

§2. *The King as Representative of Judah*

The preeminence of Judah as first in the order of Israel's tribes in Prologue-A (Judg. 1:1-20) and as represented first among the deliverer accounts (3:7-11) is probably not accidental. Further, among the tribes mentioned in Prologue-A, Judah is portrayed as the most successful in expelling foreigners from the land,[7] and, among the deliverers of Israel in 3:7-16:31, the portrayal of Othniel is uniquely positive. Since Othniel is the only deliverer from the tribe of Judah, his positive representation may be construed as a symbolic endorsement of leadership from the tribe of Judah.[8] Thus, if on the basis of both priority of mention and characterization the Judges compiler/redactor were intent on characterizing one tribe as preeminently qualified to put forth a leader for Israel—a leader who, according to the monarchical idealization of Judg. 17:6 and 21:25, should be king—then that tribe would be Judah.[9]

C. IMPLICIT MONARCHICALISM IN JUDGES' DEUTERONOMIC CONCERNS

Four aspects of the portrayal of characters in the book of Judges offer evidence that the compiler/redactor was implicitly evaluating the characters in the light of deuteronomic standards. These evidences of deuteronomic monarchicalism in Judges' include the portrayal of characters against the ideal of the king: (1) as holy-warrior, (2) as executor of intertribal covenant loyalty, (3) as supreme patron of the cult and (4) as arbiter of covenant (social) justice. In the following discussion, certain evidences that the deuteronomic patterns conform to monarchist ideologies elsewhere evident in texts from the ancient Near East may be cited when deemed relevant.

---

[7] Cf. Brettler, "Judges" (1989), pp. 401-2.

[8] All the major deliverers, with the exception of Othniel, are portrayed with at least some negative aspect of character—whether as indifferent to cultic syncretism (e.g., Ehud, re the idols; Gideon, re the ephod), as self-promoting opportunists (e.g., perhaps Ehud, who acts independently to attain leadership of the tribes; Jephthah, who tries to manipulate YHWH through a vow) or as reluctant when divinely appointed to some duty (e.g., Barak and Gideon, as deliverers; Samson, as a Nazirite). It is the deliverers' stance toward YHWH and toward YHWH's concern with the welfare of Israel that sets the standard by which one measures each deliverer's character in response to YHWH's calling.

[9] On the implicit contrast between Saul as rejected and David as elected in the contrast between Judges' denunciation of Gibeah/Benjamin and its portrayal of Judah as the elect of YHWH, see the discussion in chapter 4.

§1. The King as Holy-Warrior par excellence

In some ancient Near Eastern texts, national warfare was interpreted as the manifestation of the divine. Comparative material supporting an ideology of holy war is available from the period contemporary with ancient Israel from Ugarit, Mari, Hatti, Neo-Assyria, Egypt and Arabia.[10] Kings of the ancient Near East are commonly portrayed as laying claim to divine endorsement in battle. Of Sargon's rule it was claimed that, "Enlil did not let anyone oppose Sargon".[11] Sargon also asserted that Nergal is "the all-powerful among the gods, who goes at my side, guarding my camp".[12] Mesha, king of Moab claimed, Chemosh "saved me from all the kings and caused me to triumph over all my adversaries".[13] National enemies were enemies of the god, no less than of the king, and "reprisals had to be taken against them because they had broken 'the oath sworn by the great gods'".[14]

That military victory is a supreme manifestation of YHWH's control of circumstances is clearly a perception that the compiler/redactor of Judges wished to emphasize. Israel's recognition of this theme marks the turning point in each occurrence of the deuteronomic cycle-motif (forming the transition from motif C to motif D1) and frequently recurs as a theme intrinsic to the narrative traditions of the deliverer accounts. Thus, whatever ideal of monarchical military prowess the Judges compiler/redactor may have wished to contrast with Israel's deliverers,

---

[10] See A. Musil, *Arabaia Petraea III* (Vienna, 1908); idem, *The Manners and Customs of the Rwala Bedouins* (New York, 1928); T. Fish, "War and Religion in Egypt and Mesopotamia", *BJRL* (1939), pp. 387-402; R. Labat, *Le caractère religieux de la royauté Assyro-Babylonienne* (Études d'Assyriologie, Paris, 1939), pp. 253-74; H. W. F. Saggs, "Assyrian Warfare in the Sargonid Period", *Iraq* 25 (1963), pp. 145-48; W. von Soden, "Die Assyrier und der Krieg", *Iraq* 25 (1963), pp. 137-44; A. Glock, "Warfare in Mari and Early Israel" (PhD diss., University of Michigan, 1968); J.-G. Heintz, "Oracles prophétiques et 'guerre saint' selon les Archives Royales de Mari et l'AT", in *Congress Volume, Rome 1968* (SVT 17, Leiden, 1969), pp. 112-38, 4 figs. (against Heintz, see P.-E. Dion, "The 'Fear Not' Formula and Holy War", *CBQ* 32 (1970), pp. 565-70; M. Weippert, "'Heiliger Krieg' in Israel und Assyrien: Kritische Anmerkungen zu Gerhard von Rads Konzept des 'Heiligen Krieges im alten Israel'", *ZAW* 84 (1972), pp. 460-93; P. D. Miller, *The Divine Warrior in Early Israel* (HSM 5, Cambridge, Mass., 1973), pp. 8-63. Cf. G. H. Jones, "The Concept of Holy War", in *The World of Ancient Israel: Sociological, Anthropological and Political Perspectives* (R. E. Clements [ed.], Cambridge, 1989), pp. 299-302.

[11] *ANET*, p. 267b.

[12] D. D. Luckenbill, *Ancient Records of Assyria and Babylonia* (2 vols., Chicago, 1926-1927), vol. 2, p. 99.

[13] *ANET*, p. 320b.

[14] *ANET*, p. 285b; so Jones, "Concept" (1989), p. 300.

he/she would not have intended to diminish YHWH's right to glorify himself in the affairs of war. Neither the guile of Ehud, nor Barak's halfheartedness to serve YHWH on the battlefield, nor Gideon's perversion of an occasion of holy war to serve a personal vendetta, nor the opportunism of Jephthah, nor the egocentricism of Samson can assuage or lessen the judgement that it is YHWH alone who grants military victory against the enemy. Thus, whereas almost all the deliverers of Judges (Othniel excepted) hold less than a full measure of zeal for YHWH's glory in military victory, the foundation is laid for the assessment that an ideal military leader in Israel would be one who was intensely motivated by a zeal for YHWH's glory on the field of battle.[15]

It is customarily portrayed in ancient Near Eastern texts that, prior to battle, kings would repair to a shrine to invoke the deity for help in battle.[16] Imprecations such as "rip him open in the fight, as one rips open a bundle; let loose upon him a tempest, an evil wind" were summoned against the enemy.[17] The Hittite "Ritual before Battle" indicates that sacrifices were offered at the border of enemy territory.[18] Mantic devices would also customarily be consulted to obtain omens about the outcome of the battle. Some used astrological phenomena such as the moon and stars;[19] others, hepatoscopy.[20] A favourable oracle guaranteed the king's military success.[21]

In the prebattle preparations of Judges, invocations of YHWH are not necessarily to be considered manifestations of a lack of confidence in YHWH's ability to save. Such invocations could be read as tokens of a desire for divine direction as to how to engage the enemy (e.g., Judg. 1:1-2; 20:18). On the other hand, an excessive concern with confirming signs as to whether or not to engage battle could be construed as evidence of a lack of confidence in or commitment to YHWH's purpose (e.g., Judg. 6:17, 36-37, 39; or 20:23, 26-28; 21:2-4, respectively). In one instance, a reluctance to follow prophetic directives to engage in battle could be interpreted only as testing the patience of YHWH (Judg.

---

[15] E.g., Jonathan in 1 Sam. 14:6, 12b or, more so, David in 1 Sam. 17:25-26, 29-32, 34-37a, 45-47.

[16] *ANET*, pp. 268a, 285b, 289b.

[17] Luckenbill, *Ancient Records* (1926–27), vol. 2, pp. 331-32.

[18] *ANET*, pp. 354b-355a.

[19] Labat, *Le caractère religieux* (1939), p. 255.

[20] Labat, *Le caractère religieux* (1939), p. 256; Fish, "War and Religion" (1939), p. 395.

[21] *ANET*, pp. 277, 294b.

4:6-8). If the compiler/redactor of Judges were intent on portraying Israel's deliverers (Othniel excepted) as less than ideal holy-warriors, the implied standard by which they would be measured would be one that required unyielding commitment to divine directives in expelling foreigners from the land (cf. the references and allusions to Deut. 7 in the framework). Concomitantly, were the ideal king, referred to by Judg. 17:6 and 21:25, to furnish an appropriate contrast to the negatively characterized deliverers of Judges, he would have to be a king who did not compromise in cultic preparations for battle.[22]

In the depictions of some ancient Near Eastern texts, during the course of battle, emblems representing the gods were carried before the troops. Hammurapi had a reddish-gold emblem and disc representing Assur that he fashioned and carried into battle on a chariot.[23] In battle, the deity was also thought to stand beside the king to empower his weaponry.[24] The gods of Esarhaddon promised, "We will march with you".[25] The king might describe the various deities of battle: "butting my enemies with her mighty horns ... cutting the throats of my enemies with his sharp point",[26] raining flames upon his foes[27] or turning them into panicked madmen.[28]

According to the deuteronomic traditions, fashioning an idol or effigy of the god who saves Israel was not a sanctioned practice (Deut. 9:7-10:11; cf. Exod. 32:4, 8). Yet, in at least one biblical tradition, the ark of the covenant is portrayed as the counterpart to pagan effigies of the god who accompanies troops into battle (Josh. 5:13-6:27). Despite this precedent, however, the ark of the covenant is not mentioned in the book of Judges until 18:30b* (see the appendix), where it is described as going into captivity, and 20:27b, where it is described as the place where YHWH was consulted before battle. Therefore, never during the period of the judges is the ark portrayed as a vehicle of Israel's god of war.[29] Indeed, the fact that it is mentioned so late in the book and in a

---

[22] For a discussion of the contrast between the less-than-exemplary cultic preparations of Saul to engage battle (1 Sam. 10:8; 13:2-14; 14:24, 36-37, 44-46; 28:4-19) and the appropriate preparations of Jonathan (1 Sam. 13:23-14:12) or David (23:2, 4; 30:3-8), see chapter 4.

[23] Cf. figs. in Labat, *Le caractère religieux* (1939), p. 260; *ANET*, p. 270a.

[24] Luckenbill, *Ancient Records* (1926-27), vol. 2, pp. 116, 139, 234.

[25] *ANET*, p. 289b.

[26] *ANET*, p. 300a.

[27] Luckenbill, *Ancient Records* (1926-27), vol. 1, p. 72.

[28] *ANET*, p. 289b; Luckenbill, *Ancient Records* (1926-27), vol. 2, p. 83.

[29] The only occasion after the conquest of Jericho when YHWH's ark was pressed into military service was one of disaster for Israel's priests and troops (1 Sam. 4:1b-11).

parenthesis (20:27b-28aα, which may have been the compiler/ redactor's addition) signals a general neglect of the ark throughout the period portrayed in Judges. Thus, were an idealized king, such as the one referred to in Judges' double dénouement, to compensate for the neglect of the ark characteristic of the period of the judges, he would need to be one who venerated the ark of the covenant of God.[30]

Sometimes ancient Near Eastern texts attest that, after significant battles, commemorative stelae were erected at the battle site to honour the king's deity.[31] Perhaps it was a desire to erect a memorial to YHWH's prowess in battle that motivated Gideon to take the booty of Midianite gold earrings to make from them an ephod and to erect the ephod in his home town (8:24-27a). There can be little doubt, however, that this was regarded by the Judges narrator as an act of cultic aberrancy that could not be condoned (8:27b). Whether or not one should see in the same light Jephthah's vow to offer up a human sacrifice to YHWH is open to dispute. However, it is in the light of the 'appropriateness' of such offerings in contemporary pagan cultures (cf. 2 Kgs 3:26-27) that the narrator's focus upon the commemoration of the slaughter of Jephthah's daughter (Judg. 11:34-40) becomes the more ironic, for its pathos undermines Jephthah's ostensible intent thus to honour the god who had given him victory. According to the compiler/redactor of Judges, whatever means an idealized holy-warrior might use to commemorate a victory achieved by YHWH, he would need to avoid both taking booty that belonged to YHWH and slaughtering the innocent.[32]

---

[30] Nowhere in 1 Samuel is Saul portrayed as concerned for the welfare of the ark of God (barring MT 1 Sam. 14:18, which may be spurious; see below). Indeed, the attention given to the portrayal of the ark in the chapters preceding the portrayal of Saul (i.e., 1 Sam. 3:3; 4:3-6; 4:11-7:2) stands in marked contrast to the silence about the ark until David ascends the throne of all Israel (2 Sam. 6:2-7:2; 11:11; 15:24-29).

[31] ANET, p. 293a.

[32] Contrast Saul's retention of banned animals under the ruse of offering them up as a sacrifice to YHWH (1 Sam. 15:9, 12-26 [especially the reference to Saul erecting a monument "to him(self?)" in 15:12]) and his 'pious' vow (1 Sam. 14:24) that not only fatigued his troops and tempted them to sin (14:31-35) but led him to the brink of slaughtering his own son Jonathan (14:44-45). Perhaps it was the humiliation of being defied by his troops that led Saul to break off pursuit of the battle (1 Sam. 14:46). In retrospect, even YHWH's silence condemns him (1 Sam. 14:36b-37). Later, Saul would repeatedly attempt to kill David (1 Sam. 18:10-11, 17, 21; 19:1, 9-10, 11, 15; 20:30-33; etc.) and would even order the slaughter of the priests and all the living beings of Nob in what proved to be a sinister misapplication of YHWH's policy of holy war (22:16-19). While David was living among the Philistines, he kept the livestock taken from raids upon the Geshurites, Girzites and Amalekites (1 Sam. 27:6-9) but distributed some of the Amalekite plunder among the elders of Judah (30:26-31). Unlike Saul, David preferred to take the shewbread of YHWH

§2. *The King as Executor of Intertribal Covenant Loyalty*

In the accounts of Ehud, Deborah/Barak/Jael, Gideon/Abimelech, Jephthah and Samson, there is evidence of disintegrating relationships in the intertribal league of Israel and of a growing disinterest in upholding the deuteronomic stipulation to expel foreigners from the land (cf. Deut. 7). After the Othniel account, there is scarcely an occasion in Judges when all the tribes of Israel cooperate in a military endeavour. Ehud summons only the inhabitants of the hill country of Ephraim (3:27); Barak rallies only the men of Zebulun and Naphtali (4:10; cf. 5:14b, 18—though 5:14-15a includes some from Ephraim, Benjamin, Makir and Issachar); Gideon summons to battle the Abiezrites, Manasseh, Asher, Zebulun, Naphtali (6:34b-35) and, only during the pursuit, Ephraim (7:24), for which the Ephraimites raise an objection (8:1); Jephthah leads only the Gileadites and perhaps half-Manasseh into battle (11:29b), causing the Ephraimites to object so vehemently (12:1) that the controversy leads to the first Israelite civil war (12:4-6); and Samson, who never summons any tribe to battle, is instead handed over to the Philistines by the men of Judah (15:9-13)—constituting what may be another negative characterization of Judah in the book (cf. 1:19b). It would appear that none of the deliverers are portrayed as agents of a pan-Israelite summons to obey the covenant stipulation to expel foreigners from the land saving, perhaps, Othniel, who is not said to have summoned a particular tribe but to have judged "Israel" and gone out to war (3:10). Thus, at least on a literary level, Othniel alone could be said ostensibly to have rallied all Israel.

The ostensible disintegration of intertribal loyalty to the deuteronomic covenant reaches its nadir in the dual portrayal of Judges' double dénouement: both the cultic aberration of the Ephraimite Micah and later the Danites (17–18) and the social injustice of the Benjaminites and later all Israel (19–21) are portrayed as violations of the stipulations of Deuteronomy 12 and 13, respectively. Indeed, since an implicit concern with the covenant loyalty of pan-Israel is evident in the framing accounts of Judges (1:1; 2:4; 20:1, 2; 21:5) and passages that seem to form part of the editorial framework (e.g., 8:27aγb), one might do well to infer that a concern for intertribal covenant loyalty was a preeminent concern of the compiler/redactor,

---

rather than allow his troops to go hungry (1 Sam. 21:3-6) and proved unwilling to harm even his potential adversaries (whether the citizens of Keilah, in 23:9-13; Saul, in 24:1-22 and 26:1-25; or Nabal, in 25:4-39a).

who was apparently seeking to portray the period of the judges as fomenting a situation of intertribal disintegration. Thus, if an ideal king were to resolve the problem of intertribal disintegration (as Judges' double dénouement implies that he would), such a king would have to be committed to promoting intertribal loyalty to the covenant.[33]

§3. The King as Patron of the Cult

Since, in some texts of the ancient Near East, the king's strategies were considered a reflection of the divine sphere, ultimate victory was credited to the gods.[34] This recognition is a prominent feature of the royal hymns of victory.[35] The Hittites would observe an elaborate "Festival of the Warrior-God".[36] Assyrian and Babylonian kings regularly offered sheep sacrifices after battle as a gesture of thanksgiving.[37] According to some ancient Near Eastern texts, certain kings exacted from the conquered a 'sacrificial dues' for the patron deity of the king.[38] A king might sometimes erect a new temple or furnish and expand an existing one with spoils taken in battle.[39]

While the book of Judges indeed has its own victory hymn to YHWH (5:2-30), there are in the deliverer accounts several instances of a deliverer's aberration from standards of cultic worship that are endorsed by the compiler/redactor of Judges (e.g., Ehud's toleration of

---

[33] From the moment of his election to kingship, Saul is portrayed as self-conscious about his Benjaminite heritage (1 Sam. 9:21). His later obsession with keeping the kingship in his own family, even at the cost of committing murder (1 Sam. 20:30-31), seems to derive from the same intractable narcissism. But perhaps the climax of the negative characterization of Saul as a king comes when he is portrayed as inciting the Benjaminites both to be disloyal to YHWH's anointed royal heir (1 Sam. 22:6-8) and to slaughter YHWH's priests at Nob (22:17-18). Though they refused, Saul was successful in inciting Doeg the Edomite to decimate the town of Nob according to sanctions applied only in cases of holy war (22:17-19). David, on the other hand, was concerned to repair intertribal rifts enough to elicit loyalty even from the most devoted subjects of the Saulide dynasty (cf. 1 Sam. 10:27c*-11:11 [including the plus attested in 4QSamᵃ, Josephus *Ant.* VI.v.1 §§68-71 and the NRSV]; 31:11-13; 2 Sam. 2:4b-7). Indeed, David's portrayal throughout the incidents of 2 Sam. 1-4 is noticeably void of actions that might implicate him for moving directly against Saul, his house or his loyalists (despite the explicit notice of 2 Sam. 3:1, 6 that the houses of Saul and David were at war for a long time).

[34] *ANET*, p. 281b. Cf. Jones, "Concept" (1989), p. 302.

[35] *ANET*, pp. 373-78. On the function of the victory hymn, see P. C. Craigie, "Ancient Semitic War Poetry" (PhD diss., University of Aberdeen, 1968), pp. 121ff.

[36] *ANET*, pp. 358-61.

[37] *ANET*, pp. 276b, 278a.

[38] *ANET*, p. 293a. Cf. Jones, "Concept" (1989), p. 302.

[39] Fish, "War and Religion" (1939), p. 398.

the idols mentioned in 3:19aαβ, 26bα; Gideon's making a gold ephod that later leads to idolatry [Judg. 8:27]; Jephthah's sacrificing his daughter; Samson's disregard for his Nazirite status). In Dénouement-A, Micah's mother ironically thinks that she is honouring YHWH by commissioning the making of the idol that Micah sets up in a shrine (Judg. 17:3-5, 6; contra Deut. 12:4-14). Micah proves to be the patron of a Levite from Bethlehem (Judg. 17:8b-12), which leads to the irony that Micah thinks that YHWH will bless him for employing a Levite in his shrine (17:13; contra Deut. 12:12, 17-19). However, he proves to be anything but a patron of the cult as it is idealized by Deuteronomy 12. The situation only worsens when the Danites induce Micah's Levite to become priest at the shrine they establish at Dan (Laish). This situation eventually leads to the Danite's enticement to steal and erect this shrine at Dan (18:30-31; contra Deut. 12:4-14). Although Shiloh had allegedly served as Israel's central cult site during the period (cf. Jer. 7:12, 14),[40] it is not mentioned in the book of Judges until 18:31, which suggests that it was not only neglected by the Danites but was scarcely venerated by the other tribes of Israel (cf. 21:12, 19-23). Similarly, the ark of the covenant of God is not mentioned until Judg. 20:27b.

In the light of the monarchical idealization inherent in Judg. 17:6 and 21:25, perhaps these cases of cultic aberration or neglect were intended to serve as negative characterizations that would cast in a more positive light a king who would endorse a deuteronomically legitimate form of the worship of YHWH. If the compiler/redactor of Judges were intent on portraying the period of the judges as one in which people did what was right in their own eyes, then any king who would offer a solution to this aberrancy would have to endorse and patronize the legitimate sanctuary of YHWH.[41]

---

[40] Cf. J. Day, "The Destruction of the Shiloh Sanctuary and Jeremiah vii 12, 14", in *Studies in the Historical Books of the Old Testament* (J. A. Emerton [ed.], SVT 30, Leiden, 1979), pp. 87-94.

[41] Every instance of Saul's association with an altar results in his further negative characterization. His offerings in 1 Sam. 13:7b-10 were in disobedience of YHWH's instructions (cf. 10:8; 13:13) and were motivated less by devotion to YHWH than by expediency (13:11-12). Later, Saul's retention of banned livestock from the Amalekite raid (1 Sam. 15:9), while ostensibly motivated by a desire to serve the cult of YHWH (15:15, 21), was repudiated by Samuel as having defied YHWH's instructions (cf. 15:2-3, 10-11, 18-19, 22-23). On only one occasion did Saul build an altar to YHWH (1 Sam. 14:34-35), and that was only to assuage YHWH's wrath against the troops whom Saul had famished to the point that they fell upon the livestock and ate meat with blood (cf. 14:24, 31-33; Deut. 12:15-16, 20-25). Saul's slaughter of the priests of Nob (1 Sam. 22:17-19)

§4. *The King as Arbiter of Covenant (Social) Justice*

Whether wittingly or not, all the main characters of Judges serve YHWH's purpose by becoming deliverers in Israel. However, as one encounters each successive deliverer, one finds that, to an increasing degree, each suffers implicit ridicule for retarding or subverting, by the foibles of his own character, his achievement of deliverance.[42] Under a rhetorical strategy of entrapment, it is the retroactive reassessment prompted by motif A1b ("everyone did what was right in one's own eyes") in the double dénouement that confirms the suspicion that, along with Israel's explicit negative characterization (cf. 2:16-17, 18-19), an implicit negative characterization of Israel's leaders has been brewing throughout Judges' deliverer accounts.[43] Thus, one should expect that any positive characterization of the king, according to the perspective afforded by Judg. 17:6 and 21:25, would have to offer an antithetical complement to the negative characterization of Judges' deliverers in regard to standards of social justice.[44]

---

proves to be the greatest manifestation of his contempt for the priesthood of YHWH. Only after David's accession to the throne of Israel would he prove to be a patron of YHWH's sanctuary (2 Sam. 6:1-7:2). In 2 Samuel 7, David's intention to build a sanctuary for YHWH received YHWH's confirmation in the promise of a perpetual dynasty. David is never portrayed as a model patron of the Levites or priesthood in the books of Samuel, though his dealings with the priests of Nob (1 Sam. 21:1-9; 22:20-23) offers a contrast to those of Saul.

[42] So Klein, *Triumph of Irony* (1988), p. 46.

[43] U. Hübner has discerned the extent to which readers may vary in their estimation of a character's behaviour depending upon whether the ethics of an action are viewed on a political or theological level ("Mord auf dem Abort? Überlegungen zu Humor, Gewaltdar-stellung und Realienkunde in Ri 3,12-30", *BN* 40 [1987], p. 131). Disavowals of the legitimacy of putting ethical questions to the Ehud account, such as those made by J. A. Soggin ("ʾEhud und ʿEglon: Bemerkungen zu Richter iii 11b-31", *VT* 39 [1989], p. 95) and B. G. Webb (*The Book of the Judges: An Integrated Reading* [JSOTS 46, Sheffield, 1987], p. 131) on the ground that its satirical character precludes questioning of this kind, reflect an evaluation made from Judges' tribal-political standpoint, not from the deuteronomic evaluation that "everyone did what was right in one's own eyes". While Hübner has recognized that the *'schwarzen' Humor* in this account advances its strategy to satirize Israel's political enemy ("Mord" [1987], pp. 132, 134), he has done a service in alerting us to the possibility of posing ethical questions from alternative perspectives in the book. Similar ethical equivocations are put upon the reader by Jael's tactics (cf. Klein, *Triumph of Irony* [1988], pp. 43, 46-47, 218 n. 14).

[44] When the people entrust Saul with doing what is right in his eyes (1 Sam. 14:36a, 40b), they have to intervene in order to rescue Jonathan from his hands (14:45).

D. IMPLICIT MONARCHICALISM ACHIEVED THROUGH
NARRATIVE ANALOGY

Not only in the compiler/redactor's superimposed tribal–political and deuteronomic schemata (introduced in Judges' double prologue) but also among the deliverer accounts and double dénouement there is evidence of an implicit strategy of pro-Judahite monarchical idealization. The Judges compiler/redactor evidently selected deliverer accounts the internal rhetorical concerns of which supported his/her own tribal–political and deuteronomic agendas. Moreover, there seem to be several points of narrative analogy between the mixed characterization of deliverers in Judges and the characterizations of Saul versus David in the books of Samuel.[45] S. Dragga has already suggested a number of possible narrative analogies between accounts in the book of Judges and episodes in the life of Saul as depicted in 1 Samuel.[46] Dragga's thesis is that the portrayal of Saul in 1 Samuel was designed to show how Saul's failure was in alignment with Judges' negative assessment of the non-Judahite deliverers.[47] Justification for this is already explicit in 1 Sam. 12:9-15, where Samuel's speech draws a parallel between Israel's situation under Saul and that under the judges Jerubbaal, Barak, Jephthah and Samson, who rescued Israel from their enemies Sisera, the Philistines and the king of Moab.[48] Thus, the covenant ultimatum that Samuel expounds (1 Sam. 12:14-15) takes its justification from the tradition preserved in the deliverer accounts of Judges,

---

[45] On biblical narrative analogy, see R. C. Culley, *Studies in the Structure of Hebrew Narrative* (Philadelphia, 1976); P. D. Miscall, *The Workings of Old Testament Narrative* (Philadelphia, 1983); R. Alter, *The Art of Biblical Narrative* (New York, 1981). On the use of narrative analogy in 1 Samuel, see M. Garsiel, *The First Book of Samuel: A Literary Study of Comparative Structures, Analogies and Parallels* (P. Hackett [trans.], Ramat-Gan, 1985).

[46] S. Dragga, "In the Shadow of the Judges: The Failure of Saul", *JSOT* 38 (1987), pp. 39-46.

[47] Dragga wrote: "It is clear that 1 Samuel is severally linked to the book of Judges. ... The books possess a unity of analogous episodes and comparative and contrastive characterizations. And it is this artistic linking which clarifies a critical issue of interpretation: though Saul's failure is a religious failure of obedience, it is equally a political failure to satisfy heightened expectations, a failure to eclipse charismatic predecessors, a failure to escape the shadow of the judges" ("Shadow" [1987], pp. 43-44).

[48] Contra P. K. McCarter (*I Samuel: A New Translation with Introduction, Notes and Commentary* [AB 8, Garden City, N.Y., 1980], p. 211), on 1 Sam. 12:11, read "Barak" with the OG and Psht; the MT has "Bedan", whose form בדן closely resembles that of ברק. Also in 1 Sam. 12:11, read "Samson" with the OG and Psht; the MT has "Samuel". See the discussion in chapter 4.

from the precedent of disasters that inevitably came upon a disobedient people.[49]

Not all the narrative analogies between Judges and the books of Samuel find their correspondence in Saul, however, for there is analogy between the opening formulae, the themes of barrenness and the birth annunciation in accounts of the births of Samson (Judg. 13:2-23) and Samuel (1 Sam. 1:1-18).[50] Both Samson and Samuel are born under the obligations of a Nazirite vow (Judg. 13:4-5, 7, 14; 1 Sam. 1:11, 15), and both bring about a monumental defeat of the Philistines (cf. Judg. 13:5; 16:30 and 1 Sam. 7:13).[51] One could postulate a correspondence between the portrayals of Samson and the ark: humiliation occurs when they are captured by the Philistines (Judg. 16:21; 1 Sam. 4:10-22), and both achieve victory in the temple of Dagon (Judg. 16:23-30; 1 Sam. 5:1-8). Deborah's role as prophetic judge in the vicinity of Bethel and Ramah (Judg. 4:4-5) is analogous to Samuel's role in the same vicinity (1 Sam. 7:15-17).[52] Yet, while there may be a variety of points of analogy between Judges and the books of Samuel, the focus of concern in the discussion that follows is with those analogies that characterize the kingship of Saul versus that of David.[53]

§1. *Analogy to Prologue-A (1:1–2:5)*

Besides the positive characterization of Judah and the negative characterization of Benjamin in Prologue-A,[54] there are at least two further points of analogy between Judg. 1:1–2:5 and 1 Samuel. The first is phraseological, the second, based upon scenario. As to the phraseological analogy, just as it is said that "YHWH was with Judah" (1:19a; cf. 1:22b re Joseph) and it is never said that YHWH was with Benjamin

---

[49] For further discussion of the relationship between 1 Sam. 12:9-15 and the book of Judges, see chapter 4.

[50] Cf. J. A. Wharton, "The Secret of Yahweh: Story and Affirmation in Judges 13-16", *Int* 27 (1973), p. 58; Alter, *Biblical Narrative* (1981), pp. 49, 51, 81-86, 101; Garsiel, *First Book of Samuel* (1985), pp. 35-37, 55, 144 n. 10.

[51] Garsiel, *First Book of Samuel* (1985), p. 55.

[52] Garsiel, *First Book of Samuel* (1985), pp. 54-55.

[53] It may be admitted from the outset that, although some of the suggested points of analogy in the following sections and tables may not be as convincing as others, it is the cumulative weight of similarities between characterizations in Judges and those of the books of Samuel that justifies the inference that the book of Judges was designed to serve as a paradigm by which to measure the performances of Saul versus David in 1 Samuel. Hence, even marginal points of analogy that have been observed by scholars are included here in the interests of forming a comprehensive judgement.

[54] See the discussion in chapter 1.

(1:21), so 1 Samuel portrays YHWH as being with David (of Judah) but as having departed from Saul (of Benjamin) (cf. 1 Sam. 16:13-14; 18:12, 14-15, 28-29).

The narrative analogy that is based upon a similarity of scenario relates to Judg. 1:11-13. This account portrays Othniel emerging as a holy-warrior from an incident at Hebron, the capital of a region of Anakite giants (cf. Num. 13:28b, 32-33; Deut. 1:28; 9:1-2 and especially Josh. 11:21-22), in response to Caleb's offer of his daughter in marriage (Judg. 1:12). This narrative parallels that of Saul inviting someone to conquer the giant Goliath (cf. 1 Sam. 17:4-7) through the offer of his daughter in marriage (and of privileged status for the victor's family, 1 Sam. 17:25).[55] As a result of both offers, a hero emerges from the tribe of Judah: Othniel in Judg. 1:13, David in the protracted description of 1 Sam. 17:26-58 (closing with the recognition of the victor's family) and in the complicated marriage account of 18:17-19, 20-27.[56] It may be that this correspondence of scenarios between the account of Othniel of Judah, the first and only idealized deliverer in Judges (cf. 3:7-11), and the account of the arrival at court of David of Judah, the only king of Israel idealized in the books of Samuel, was intended by the compiler/redactor of Judges who introduced this account into the book.

§2. *Analogy to the Account of Othniel (3:7-11)*

There is little phraseological material that offers clear analogy between the deliverer account of Othniel and the books of Samuel. Only in the vaguest sense can it be argued that the idealization of Othniel in Judges is analogous to the mostly idealized characterization of David in the books of Samuel. Yet, when this is viewed together with Judges' idealization of the tribe of Judah, as both elect of YHWH (1:1-2; 20:18) and as first in order among the tribes (in Prologue-A and the deliverer accounts), it seems plausible that the Judges compiler/redactor intended that Othniel represent the advantages of Judahite rule. Only in retrospect—i.e., from the promonarchical perspective afforded by Judges' double dénouement—could one infer that Othniel had been

---

[55] So G. F. Moore, *A Critical and Exegetical Commentary on Judges* (ICC, Edinburgh, 1895), p. 27; J. J. Slotki, "Judges: Introduction and Commentary", in H. Freedman and J. J. Slotki, *Joshua and Judges* (A. Cohen [ed.], SBB, London, 1950), p. 159.

[56] Saul's offer of the right to marry the king's daughter and privileged status for the family (1 Sam. 17:25), are fulfilled in reverse order in 17:58 and 18:17-19, 20-27.

intended to represent positively the Judahite monarchy. Indeed, it stands to reason that the compiler/redactor of Judges would not want to disclose too soon the precise identity of those parties whom he/she wished either to glorify or to vilify were he/she intent on pursuing a rhetorical strategy of entrapment.

§3. *Analogy to the Account of Ehud (3:12-30)*

There is a similar vagueness of correspondence between the character-ization of the Benjaminite Ehud in Judges and that of the Benjaminite Saul in 1 Samuel. Indeed, were it not for the general antipathy of the Judges compiler/redactor toward the Benjaminite tribe, evident in the negative characterization Benjamin receives in the framework (1:21; 19-21), one might at first find no further similarity between Ehud and Saul than that of their common tribal heritage. Yet both tribal heroes find their initial rise to power in summoning Israel to engage in battle a Transjordanian aggressor: Ehud by delivering the inhabitants of the hill country of Ephraim from Eglon of Moab and his Ammonite and Amalekite allies (3:12-13, 26-30), Saul by delivering the citizens of Jabesh-Gilead from Nahash of Ammon (1 Sam. 10:27c*-11:15). Further, if fault may be levelled against Ehud for allowing the 'idols' near Gilgal to remain standing (Judg. 3:19, 26), there may be some degree of correspondence to the fact that Saul was later confirmed as king at Gilgal and that both transgressions that disqualified Saul from kingship were likewise cultic: the first again at Gilgal (1 Sam. 13:7b-14) and the second for sparing the life of the Amalekite king (1 Sam. 15:1-31). Incidentally, the references to the 'idols' in the Ehud account (3:19, 26) form an inclusio that frames the description of Ehud's assas-sination of the Moabite king in much the same way that the accounts of Saul's cultic transgressions in 1 Sam. 13:7b-14 and 15:1-31 form an inclusio that frames the account of Saul's disqualification. Perhaps this rather loose analogy between situations involving Moabites, Ammonites and Amalekites might go some way in explaining the other-wise token mention of the allegiance of the Ammonites and Amalekites with Moabites in the Ehud account (3:13).

When these correspondences are viewed in conjunction with Judges' negative characterization of the tribe of Benjamin, the fact that Benjamin is mentioned second in tribal order in both Prologue-A and the deliverer accounts and that their failures are most starkly contrasted with the successes of Judah (1:1-20 vs. 1:21; 19:10-20:17 vs. 20:18) seems hardly coincidental. Indeed, it is plausible that the Judges compiler/redactor intended that the Benjaminite Ehud should be the first in the series of deliverers who depict the disadvantages to Israel of serving under non-Judahite leadership. Viewed from the monarchical perspective of Judges' double dénouement, one could retrospectively infer that Ehud was intended to represent the incipient, premonarchical form of a later Benjaminite monarchical experiment. Were the compiler/redactor of Judges intent on pursuing a rhetorical strategy of entrapment, one should expect that he/she would be initially vague in forming associations between Ehud and Saul—especially, if he/she did not want to identify prematurely the dynasty to be discredited.

§4. *Analogy to the Account of Deborah/Barak/Jael (4:1-5:31)*

The degree of correspondence between the deliverer account of Deborah/Barak/Jael (Judg. 4:1-5:31) and the account of the battle of Saul against the Amalekites (1 Sam. 15:1-33) suggests that narrative analogy may have been deliberate. The focus of the analogy seems to be one between matters that characterize similarly the actions of Barak and Saul:[57]

Characteristic	Barak	Saul
Main national enemy	Canaanites	Amalekites
Prophetic summons	Judg. 4:6 (by Deborah)	1 Sam. 15:1-3 (by Samuel)
Kenite role	Judg. 4:11, 17, 21 (Jael betrays peace with Jabin)	1 Sam. 15:6 (separated from Amalek; cf. Judg. 1:16*)
Hero fails to slay the enemy leader	Judg. 4:17, 22 (Sisera eludes Barak)	1 Sam. 15:9, 20 (Agag spared by Saul)
Substitute slayer	Judg. 4:21; 5:26-27 (Jael)	1 Sam. 15:32-33 (Samuel)
Sonless mother	Judg. 5:28 (Sisera's mother)	1 Sam. 15:33a (Agag's mother)

Deborah's prophetic summons of Barak to fight against the Canaanites (Judg. 4:6) finds analogy in Samuel's prophetic summons of Saul to conduct a holy war against the Amalekites (1 Sam. 15:1-3). In both accounts, Kenites appear near the battle site: it is Jael, the wife of a Kenite, who slays Sisera (Judg. 4:11, 17, 21); Saul, before engaging the Amalekites, warns the Kenites to depart from the area (1 Sam. 15:6).[58] The aftermaths of these battle accounts are analogous in that in

---

[57] Cf. Garsiel, *First Book of Samuel* (1985), p. 55.

[58] Garsiel, *First Book of Samuel* (1985), p. 55.

neither case does the Israelite commander succeed in slaying the enemy commander (Judg. 4:21; 5:26-27; 1 Sam. 15:33b). In Barak's case, failure to slay Sisera (Judg. 4:17, 22) is the result of Deborah's rebuke (Judg. 4:9a); in Saul's case, the decision to spare Agag (1 Sam. 15:9, 20) results in Samuel's rebuke (15:17-18, 26). Finally, both accounts associate the death of the enemy commander with the bereavement of his mother (Judg. 5:28; 1 Sam. 15:33a).[59] Although the negative characterization of Saul in 1 Samuel 15 is evident even apart from narrative analogy to Judges 4-5, the analogy casts a darker shadow over Saul's actions. Indeed, the analogy evokes all the more indignation because, in accordance with Samuel's words in 1 Samuel 12, the reader has been explicitly invited to assess Saul's performance on the basis of the performance of Judges' deliverers.

§5. *Analogy to the Account of Gideon/Abimelech (6:1-9:57)*

There seem to be many points of analogy between the account of Gideon/Abimelech in Judges and that of Saul in 1 Samuel. Of course, not all the points of analogy between Judges 6-9 pertain directly to Saul. For example, both Gideon and Jonathan go to the edge of the enemy camp, each accompanied by a single servant, where an enemy utters a word that may be interpreted as a sign of victory from YHWH (Judg. 7:10-15a; 1 Sam. 13:23-14:12).[60] Yet even here the contrast between the analogous actions of Gideon and Jonathan, who trust YHWH to save by few (Judg. 7:2-8a; 1 Sam. 14:6), and the actions of Saul, who does not trust YHWH enough to save by few (1 Sam. 13:7b-12), redounds to the discredit of Saul. The following table outlines some points of analogy (chiefly between Judg. 6:1-8:32 and 1 Sam. 13:2-14:46) that show how the characterization of Gideon's actions as judge may have been designed to form the basis for a negative evaluation of Saul's actions as judge and king.

Characteristic	*Gideon/Jerubbaal*	*Saul*
Main national enemy	Midianites	Ammonites/Philistines/ Amalekites
Man of valour (גבור חיל)	Judg. 6:12b	= 1 Sam. 9:1b[61]

---

[59] Garsiel, *First Book of Samuel* (1985), p. 55.

[60] Garsiel, *First Book of Samuel* (1985), p. 91.

[61] N. Habel, "The Form and Significance of the Call Narratives", *ZAW* 77 (1965), p. 299.

Characteristic	Gideon/Jerubbaal	Saul
Initial self-effacement	Judg. 6:15	= 1 Sam. 9:21[62]
Empowering by YHWH's spirit	Judg. 6:34a	= 1 Sam. 10:6[63]
Holy war: Division of column	Judg. 7:16	= 1 Sam. 11:11[64]
Israelites hide in caves	Judg. 6:2	= 1 Sam. 13:6[65]
Holy war (cont'd): Mustering troops by blowing ram's horn	Judg. 6:34b	= 1 Sam. 13:3-4[66]
Enemy superiority	Judg. 7:12	= 1 Sam. 13:5[67]
Trembling troops	Judg. 7:3 (חרד) (removed)	1 Sam. 13:7b (חרד)[68] (flee)
Test of commander's self-control	Judg. 7:4-8	1 Sam. 13:6-7a, 8-14[69]
Number of troops	Judg. 7:8	1 Sam. 13:15[70]
Panic of enemies	Judg. 7:22	= 1 Sam. 14:2[71]
Ephraimites' pursuit	Judg. 7:24-25	= 1 Sam. 14:22[72]
Fatigue of troops	Judg. 8:5, 8 (Gideon requests food)	1 Sam. 14:24[73] (Saul forbids food)

[62] Habel, "Call Narratives" (1965), p. 300 n. 10; P. R. Ackroyd, *The First Book of Samuel* (CBC, Cambridge, 1971), p. 79.

[63] Ackroyd, *First Book of Samuel* (1971), p. 84.

[64] Ackroyd, *First Book of Samuel* (1971), p. 92. Cf. 1 Sam. 13:17. McCarter, who saw 1 Sam. 10:27b–11:11 as a single narrative unit embraced by notices of national response to Saul's kingship (10:26-27a; 11:12-15), considered this unit analogous to the episodes of Israel's major judges (Judg. 3:7–16:31) except that: (1) all Israel was summoned to the defence of Jabesh-Gilead [cf. Judg. 21:5-9, where Jabesh-Gilead was the only district of all Israel not summoned], and (2) Saul becomes king (*I Samuel* [1980], pp. 205-7).

[65] Garsiel, *First Book of Samuel* (1985), pp. 89-90, 91.

[66] Garsiel, *First Book of Samuel* (1985), pp. 89, 91.

[67] Garsiel, *First Book of Samuel* (1985), pp. 89, 91.

[68] Garsiel, *First Book of Samuel* (1985), pp. 90, 91.

[69] Cf. 1 Sam. 10:8 (where Samuel commands Saul to wait at Gilgal a full seven days before Samuel offers sacrifices) with 13:13-14.

[70] Ackroyd saw the similarly small numbers of troops as indicative of mutual heroism between Saul (with 600 men) and Gideon (with 300) (*First Book of Samuel* [1971], p. 107). Dragga contested that there is a contrast here in that Saul, though blessed with twice the troops, is not half as obedient as Gideon ("Shadow" [1987], pp. 41, 45 n. 8; so also Garsiel, *First Book of Samuel* [1985], pp. 90, 92).

[71] Garsiel, *First Book of Samuel* (1985), pp. 90, 91.

[72] Garsiel, *First Book of Samuel* (1985), pp. 90, 91.

[73] Garsiel, *First Book of Samuel* (1985), pp. 90, 91.

Characteristic	Gideon/Jerubbaal	Saul
Making of cult object	Judg. 8:27 (ephod to commemorate YHWH's victory)	1 Sam. 14:35[74] (altar to assuage YHWH's wrath)
Slaughtering Israel	Judg. 8:5-9, 13-17 At Succoth/Penuel (for not aiding Israel's troops)	1 Sam. 21:1-6; 22:18-19 At Nob (for aiding David's troops)
Sparing enemy king(s)	Judg. 8:10-12, 18-21	= 1 Sam. 15:9, 20, 32-33
Offer of kingship	Judg. 8:22-23 (popular offer rejected by Gideon as sin)	1 Sam. 8:5-22; 9:16; 10:1*;[75] 11:12, 14-15; 12:2, 17, 19-20; 13:1[76] (popular offer accepted by YHWH though a sin)

Among the many points of analogy listed above, those between the account of Gideon's battle against the Midianites and Saul's first battle against the Philistines at Michmash (1 Sam. 13:2–14:46) offer the greatest concentration of correspondences. One may mention the similar descriptions of the Israelites hiding in caves (Judg. 6:2; 1 Sam. 13:6), of mustering troops (Judg. 6:34b; 1 Sam. 13:3-4), of the enemy's numerical superiority (Judg. 7:12; 1 Sam. 13:5), of trembling troops leaving (Judg. 7:3; 1 Sam. 13:7b), of the panic in the enemy camp such that "each man's sword was against his companion" (Judg. 7:22; 1 Sam. 14:2), of the Ephraimites joining in pursuit (Judg. 7:24-25; 1 Sam. 14:22) and of the fatigue of the Israelite troops (Judg. 8:5, 8; 1 Sam. 14:24).[77] Several of the preceding points of analogy between the portrayals of Gideon and Saul cast Saul in the more negative light. For example, when Gideon blows the ram's horn (6:34b), he is summoning the troops from which he would cull his three hundred for battle (7:6, 8). By contrast, Saul's sounding the ram's horn (1 Sam. 13:3-4) summons troops besides his standing army of three thousand (1 Sam. 13:2). By this analogy, Saul is characterized as lacking the faith of Gideon, who, like Jonathan, believed that nothing could hinder

---

[74] Garsiel, *First Book of Samuel* (1985), p. 90.

[75] Restore MT 1 Sam. 10:1 with the plus in the OG and Vg, which appears to have fallen out by homoeoteleuton (so the REB).

[76] Cf. G. H. Davies, "Judges viii 22-23", *VT* 13 (1963), p. 151.

[77] Garsiel, *First Book of Samuel* (1985), p. 91.

YHWH from saving "whether by many or by few" (1 Sam. 14:6; cf.
Judg. 7:2-8a). Again, while Gideon, by requesting food for his troops
(Judg. 8:5, 8), seeks to remedy their fatigue, Saul causes fatigue by
prohibiting his troops from eating (1 Sam. 14:24).

Besides these parallels to Saul's first battle against the Philistines, the
mixed characterization of Gideon parallels that of Saul in the early
episodes of the latter's emergence as a deliverer in Israel. Perhaps the
specific mention of Amalekites in connection with the Midianites (6:3,
33), whose kings Gideon would have spared but for his personal
vendetta (Judg. 8:10-12, 18-21), is a further indication of an attempt by
the Judges compiler/redactor to link this event with that in which Saul
would have spared the king of the Amalekites but for Samuel's executing him (1 Sam. 15:9, 20, 32-33).[78] Yet, ironically, both Gideon and
Saul willingly execute the sanctions of holy war against cities in Israel
(Judg. 8:5-9, 13-17; 1 Sam. 21:1-6; 22:18-19).[79] If Gideon is to be held
accountable for slaughtering Israelites at Succoth and Penuel because
they failed to support Israel's troops (Judg. 8:5-9, 13-17), how much
more should one hold accountable Saul, who ordered the brutal
slaughter of the priests and citizens of Nob in reprisal for their willingness to give bread to Israel's troops (1 Sam. 21:1-7; 22:9-19).

A similar degree of analogy may be found between the accounts of
Gideon's battle against the Midianites and Saul's final battle against the
Philistines at Gilboa (1 Sam. 28–31; cf. 2 Sam. 1:21).[80]

Characteristic	Gideon/Jerubbaal	Saul
Main national enemy	Midianites	Philistines
Geographical locale:		
Israelite camp	Judg. 7:1a, 4	= 1 Sam. 28:4b[81]
	(by/on Mount	(on Mount Gilboa)
	Gilboa)	
Enemy camp	Judg. 7:1b, 8b	= 1 Sam. 28:4a[82]
	(NE of Mount	(W slope of Mount
	Moreh, at En-Dor;	Moreh, at Shunem)
	cf. Ps. 83:11)	

---

[78] Cf. Klein, *Triumph of Irony* (1988), p. 62.

[79] Cf. Deut. 20:13 (Klein, *Triumph of Irony* [1988], p. 62).

[80] Garsiel, *First Book of Samuel* (1985), pp. 94-97.

[81] Cf. A. Malamat, "The Battle of Gideon against Midian", in *The Military History of the Land of Israel in Bible Times* (J. Levor [ed.], Tel Aviv, 1964), pp. 110-23 [Hebrew]; Garsiel, *First Book of Samuel* (1985), p. 95.

[82] Garsiel, *First Book of Samuel* (1985), pp. 95-96.

Characteristic	Gideon/Jerubbaal	Saul
Prebattle fear:		
Of the troops	Judg. 7:3 (חרד)	= cf. 1 Sam. 13:7b (חרד)
Of the leader	Judg. 7:10-11a	= 1 Sam. 28:5 (חרד)[83]
Prebattle omens:		
Dew	Judg. 6:36-38, 39-40 (two signs)	cf. 2 Sam. 1:21[84] (no dew on Mount Gilboa)
Dream	Judg. 7:10-11a (YHWH offers)	1 Sam. 28:6[85] (YHWH refuses)
Night reconnaissance to En-Dor	Judg. 7:11b-15a (promising omen)	1 Sam. 28:7-25[86] (menacing omen)
Another, commanded to slay king(s), disobeys out of fear	Judg. 8:20	= 1 Sam. 31:4a[87]

The events of both battle accounts take place in the vicinity of Mount
Gilboa and Mount Moreh, and, in both accounts, there is either
reference or allusion to the spring of Harod and En-Dor.[88] Once again,
several points of analogy show Saul to be more negatively characterized than Gideon: whereas Gideon's troops tremble (חרד) in the
vicinity of the spring of Harod (עין חרוד) (Judg. 7:1, 3), before Saul's
last battle it is Saul himself who trembles (חרד) (1 Sam. 28:5); whereas
YHWH offers the sign of the dream and its interpretation to Gideon to
help him overcome his fear (Judg. 7:10-15a), YHWH refuses to answer
Saul's requests for a dream or sign (1 Sam. 28:6) except for the
menacing omen pronounced by Samuel's ghost (1 Sam. 28:7-25);
finally, whereas, when Gideon commands his son to slay the Midianite
kings, he refuses out of fear (Judg. 8:20), when Saul's armour bearer

---

[83] Garsiel, *First Book of Samuel* (1985), pp. 96, 97.

[84] Garsiel, *First Book of Samuel* (1985), pp. 96, 97.

[85] Garsiel, *First Book of Samuel* (1985), p. 96.

[86] Garsiel, *First Book of Samuel* (1985), pp. 95-96.

[87] D. M. Gunn, "Narrative Patterns and Oral Tradition in Judges and Samuel", *VT* 24
(1974), pp. 297-301, though Gunn attributed the analogy to the use of stock patterns in
oral tradition; Garsiel, *First Book of Samuel* (1985), pp. 96, 97, 155 n. 12. In support of
the view that the compiler/redactor(s) of the Gideon/Abimelech account and of the books
of Samuel worked from written documents, see Garsiel, *First Book of Samuel* (1985),
p. 99.

[88] Cf. Y. Aharoni and M. Avi-Yonah, *The Macmillan Bible Atlas* (New York, rev.
edn, 1977), pp. 54 (map 75), 64 (map 96); Garsiel, *First Book of Samuel* (1985),
pp. 95-96.

likewise refuses, it is because he is afraid to slay Saul, the Israelite king (1 Sam. 31:4a).[89]

The preceding hints of narrative analogy between Judg. 6:1–8:32 and the descriptions of Saul in 1 Samuel seem to invite the judgement that Saul is being characterized as standing in the shadow of the judges—a judgement that 1 Samuel 12 in fact explicitly invites. Hence, just as Gideon and his heir Abimelech commit acts of cultic disloyalty and covenant (social) injustice that invite God's judgement, so does Saul. Just as Gideon's role undergoes a transformation through his son Abimelech, when the latter becomes king, so Saul's role undergoes a transformation when Israel makes him king. However, it is perhaps the differences between Gideon and Saul that induce the reader to view Saul's offences as the more heinous. One of the main rhetorical points to which the narrative analogy between the accounts of Gideon/Abimelech and Saul leads is that of affirming the sole right of YHWH to elect Israel's leaders, whether judges or kings. What Gideon refuses in Judg. 8:23 is not kingship *per se* but kingship by popular appointment (Judg. 8:22).[90] This may be an important rhetorical aspect of the contrast between the analogy of YHWH's election of Gideon to judgeship (despite Gideon's protest in Judg. 6:15) and YHWH's election of Saul to be anointed נגיד 'leader' (1 Sam. 9:16; 10:1; despite Saul's protest in 1 Sam. 9:21), on the one hand, and the analogy of the pathological quest of Gideon's son Abimelech for kingship (Judg. 9) and Saul's pathological quest to retain kingship (1 Sam. 18–26), on the other. Thus, Gideon's refusal to accept popular appointment to kingship (Judg. 8:22-23) and YHWH's reluctant concession to Israel's sinful request for "a king like [those of] other nations" (cf. 1 Sam. 8:4-22; 9:16; 10:1* [with the OG and Vg plus]; 11:12, 14-15; 12:2, 17, 19-20; 13:1) characterize such popular requests for kings such as these (i.e., Abimelech and Saul) as undesirable from the outset. Thus, it is a negative characterization of this kind of popular request for kingship in Judg. 6:1–8:32 and 1 Sam. 8:1–13:1 that lays the foundation for the negative characterization of Abimelech, in Judg. 8:33–9:57, and of Saul, in 1 Sam. 13:2–31:13, respectively.

Several correspondences may be offered in support of the view that there may be narrative analogy between the account of Abimelech, in Judg. 8:33–9:57, and that of Saul, in 1 Sam. 13:2–31:13 (as fulfilling 8:4-22; 12:1-25):

---

[89] Garsiel, *First Book of Samuel* (1985), pp. 95-97.
[90] Contra Garsiel, *First Book of Samuel* (1985), p. 99.

Characteristic	Abimelech	Saul
Personal enemy	Judg. 9:2 (halfbrothers as rival rulers)	= 1 Sam. 20:30-31; 22:7-8 (David as rival claimant to throne)
Motivated by "evil spirit" from YHWH	Judg. 9:23	= 1 Sam. 16:14b[91]
Slaughtering Israel	Judg. 9:5 (70 sons of Jerubbaal)	= 1 Sam. 22:18[92] (85 priests of YHWH)
	Judg. 9:40, 45, 49b (citizens of Shechem)	= 1 Sam. 22:19[93] (citizens of Nob)
	Judg. 9:5b, 21 (escape of Jotham alone)	= 1 Sam. 22:20[94] (escape of Abiathar alone)
Prophetic rebuke	Judg. 9:7-21 (curse of king and subjects in Jotham's fable of the trees)	= 1 Sam. 8:4-22; 12:1-25 (curse of king and subjects in Samuel's speeches at Ramah and Gilgal)
		= 1 Sam. 24:8-22;[95] 26:13-25 (curse of king in David's figure of Saul searching for a dead dog/flea)
Suicidal command to armour bearer	Judg. 9:54 (obeyed)	1 Sam. 31:4a[96] (disobeyed)

---

[91] Garsiel, *First Book of Samuel* (1985), pp. 98 (noting that the expression רוח רעה is peculiar to these passages), 155 n. 15; J. C. Exum, "The Centre Cannot Hold: Thematic and Textual Instabilities in Judges", *CBQ* 52 (1990), p. 420. On YHWH's sending the "evil spirit" as a sign of divine retribution, see T. A. Boogaart, "Stone for Stone: Retribution in the Story of Abimelech and Shechem", *JSOT* 32 (1985), p. 56 n. 12.

[92] Garsiel, *First Book of Samuel* (1985), p. 98.

[93] Garsiel, *First Book of Samuel* (1985), p. 98.

[94] Garsiel, *First Book of Samuel* (1985), p. 98.

[95] Garsiel, *First Book of Samuel* (1985), p. 98.

[96] Cf. Gunn, "Narrative Patterns" (1974), pp. 297-301; Garsiel, *First Book of Samuel* (1985), pp. 98-99, 155 n. 16. Commenting upon 1 Sam. 31:4, Ackroyd wrote, "the story implies that this is a heroic and courageous action, like that of the rather shoddy character Abimelech in Judg. 9:54" (*First Book of Samuel* [1971], pp. 227-28). It was motivated, he said, by Saul's desire to avoid the same mockery of the Philistines as was suffered by Samson in Judg. 16. Dragga contended, however, that Ackroyd missed the irony in Saul's avoidance of the "dishonour" that led to Samson's greatest victory by echoing the suicidal request of one of Judges' villains ("Shadow" [1987], pp. 45-46).

Between the accounts of Abimelech and Saul, the points of analogy seem to lead to a sharper condemnation of Saul. In a situation of perceived rivalry for the throne (Judg. 9:2; 1 Sam. 20:30-31; 22:7-8), Abimelech slaughters his seventy halfbrothers, all sons of Gideon (Judg. 9:5), and the 'citizens' of the Canaanite city Shechem (9:40, 45, 49b); Saul, however, slaughters eighty-five priests of YHWH and the citizens of the Israelite city Nob (1 Sam. 22:18-19). YHWH's sending of an "evil spirit" between Abimelech and the citizens of Shechem (Judg. 9:23) seems well deserved; however, the "evil spirit" sent to torment Saul (1 Sam. 16:14b) exaggerates the judgement that YHWH's spirit had departed from him (1 Sam. 16:14a; cf. Judg. 16:20). The "evil spirit" sent by God is the prime catalyst of the debacle that accompanies Abimelech's rule of Shechem (9:23-24), as it is of that which accompanies Saul's rule of Israel (1 Sam. 16:13-14). At the inauguration of both kings, a spokesman appears to curse those who have chosen such a man to be king: Jotham, in the Abimelech account (Judg. 9:7-21); Samuel, twice in the Saul story (1 Sam. 8:4-22; 12:1-25). Of course, there is also a sense in which Jotham's role parallels that of David: Jotham is the youngest of his siblings, as was David; he eludes Abimelech's death threat (9:21), as David does Saul's; he gives retribution into the hand of God, as does David, who does not take personal revenge against Saul. When Abimelech and Saul finally die, they are portrayed as bearing the retribution of God, who thus vindicates Jotham and David, respectively. Moreover, the fact that the description of the death of Saul so closely resembles that of the death of Abimelech (1 Sam. 31:4a; Judg. 9:54) further suggests that the parallelism between the two portrayals may have been intentional. These indications lead to the inference that Abimelech's portrayal was intended to present "a type of the abuse of royal power later 'predicted' by Samuel".[97]

§6. *Analogy to the Account of Jephthah (10:6–12:7)*

The points of analogy between the portrayals of Saul and Jephthah are not as pervasive as those between Saul and either Gideon or Abimelech. However, the following correspondences may be adduced to show possible narrative analogy between the incidents related to Jephthah's vow (Judg. 11:30-40) and those related to the vow that Saul

---

[97] E. H. Maly, "The Jotham Fable—Anti-Monarchial?", *CBQ* 22 (1960), p. 299 (cf. p. 305).

made on the occasion of his first battle against the Philistines (1 Sam. 14:24-46):

Characteristic	Jephthah	Saul
Main national enemy	Ammonites	Philistines
Man of valour (גבור חיל)	Judg. 11:1	= 1 Sam. 9:1b[98]
Self-centred vow	Judg. 11:30-31	= 1 Sam. 14:24[99]
Ostensible motive:		
Vengeance on foes	Judg. 11:36 (נקמות מאויביך)	= 1 Sam. 14:24[100] (ונקמתי מאויבי)
Unwitting offer of offspring	Judg. 11:34a	= 1 Sam. 14:25-28[101]
Cause of trouble (עכר)	Judg. 11:35 (Jephthah says, "my daughter")	1 Sam. 14:29[102] (Jonathan says, "my father")
Spirit of compliance:		
Father	Judg. 11:35, 36-40 (remorseful)	1 Sam. 14:39, 44[103] (callous)
Daughter/son	Judg. 11:36 (compliant)	1 Sam. 14:43b[104] (compliant)[105]

---

[98] Habel, "Call Narratives" (1965), p. 299.

[99] Cf. P. D. Miscall, "The Jacob and Joseph Stories as Analogies", *JSOT* 6 (1978), p. 30; R. P. Gordon, "David's Rise and Saul's Demise: Narrative Analogy in 1 Samuel 24-26", *TynBul* 31 (1980), p. 52; Garsiel, *First Book of Samuel* (1985), p. 93.

[100] Garsiel, *First Book of Samuel* (1985), p. 93.

[101] Garsiel, *First Book of Samuel* (1985), p. 93.

[102] P. Trible, *Texts of Terror: Literary and Feminist Readings of Biblical Narratives* (OBT 13, Philadelphia, 1984), p. 113 n. 37; Garsiel, *First Book of Samuel* (1985), p. 93; F. Landy, "Gilead and the Fatal Word", in *Proceedings of the Ninth World Congress of Jewish Studies, Jerusalem, August 4-12, 1985: Division A, The Period of the Bible* (Jerusalem, 1986), p. 43.

[103] Saul's eagerness to execute the penalty of his vow, "even if it lies with [his] son Jonathan", shows how self-centred he had become since the day he rescued those who had first opposed his anointing as king. Whereas Saul, motivated by concern to act in concert with YHWH's rescue of Israel (cf. 1 Sam. 11:13), then rescued men from "the people", ironically, Saul's men, motivated by a similar concern to act in accord with YHWH's rescuing of Israel by Jonathan (1 Sam. 14:45), now need to rescue Jonathan from Saul. On the inviolability of the vow spoken to the deity, see Trible, *Terror* (1984), pp. 103 (cf. Num. 30:3; Deut. 23:22-24), 114 n. 41.

[104] Trible, *Terror* (1984), p. 114 n. 43.

[105] So 1 Sam. 14:43b in the RSV, REB; contra the NIV: "I merely tasted a little honey with the end of my staff. And now must I die?"

Characteristic	Jephthah	Saul
Fulfilment of vow	Judg. 11:39	1 Sam. 14:45[106]
	(executed)	(frustrated)
Aftermath: remaining		
offspring	Judg. 11:34b	1 Sam. 14:49[107]
	(none)	(five)

After the elders of Gilead make the conditional offer to Jephthah that, should he prove successful in battle, they would make him their permanent tribal leader, Jephthah attempts to secure his victory by vowing to offer up to YHWH a human life (Judg. 11:30). Jephthah proves to be so mechanistically devoted to the self-imposed conditions of his vow that he prefers to sacrifice his only daughter rather than renege, and that despite his remorse. This scenario may foreshadow the incident of 1 Sam. 14:24-46 in which Saul, having likewise sworn by a human life, prefers to sacrifice his offspring rather than renege on his public vow (cf. 14:44). However, despite the fact that, in Saul's case, the Israelites rescue Jonathan, Saul's attitude remains so unremorseful that the greater negative characterization accrues to him.[108]

§7. *Analogy to the Account of Samson (13:1–16:31)*

Certain correspondences between the portrayals of Samson (Judg. 13–16) and Saul (1 Sam. 16:14a; 31:4aβ, 4b) may be cited in support of the view that their analogy may have been deliberate.

---

[106] Trible, *Terror* (1984), pp. 113 n. 37, 114 nn. 41, 43. K. W. Whitelam attempted to resolve the apparent dilemma in Saul's judicial authority by arguing that Saul's authority here stemmed only from military, not purely regal, prerogatives (*The Just King: Monarchical Judicial Authority in Ancient Israel* [JSOTS 12, Sheffield, 1979], pp. 73-83). Nevertheless, it cannot be contested that this portrayal seriously undermines the legitimacy of Saul's status as a spokesman for YHWH's justice. On the absence of protest in Judg. 11:39, see Trible, *Terror* (1984), p. 105. Thus, the vow involving the taking of human life in Judg. 11 stands between the portrayals in Gen. 22 and 1 Sam. 14 as an example of the extremes achieved when neither God nor community intervenes.

[107] Dragga ascertained that Saul, blessed with five times the number of Jephthah's children, proves less worthy a character than Jephthah ("Shadow" [1987], p. 49).

[108] Contrasting this portrayal with Saul's conduct in the incident of 1 Sam. 28:22-25, where, before Saul's last battle, he reneges on his own vow not to eat, one may infer that Saul is characterized as both a hypocrite and one who did not know when it was, and when it was not, appropriate to fulfil a vow involving fasting.

Characteristic	Samson	Saul
Main national enemy	Philistines	Ammonites/Amalekites/ Philistines
Repeated empowering by YHWH's spirit	Judg. (13:25); 14:6, 19; 15:14	= 1 Sam. 10:6, 10; 11:6 1 Sam. 19:23
Departure of YHWH's spirit	Judg. 16:20	= 1 Sam. 16:14a[109] 1 Sam. 16:14b
Subjected to enemy ridicule	Judg. 16:25 (actual)	1 Sam. 31:4aβ (potential)
Voluntary suicide	Judg. 16:30a (great victory)	1 Sam. 31:4b[110] (great defeat)

In the pattern of correspondences between the accounts of Samson and Saul, it is the latter whose characterization is the worse for the comparison. Some points of analogy, such as the pattern of repeated references to YHWH's spirit empowering, are unique to the portrayals of Samson and Saul, though, in Saul's case, the final instance of this 'empowering' (1 Sam. 19:23) disables Saul from pursuing David. Again, whereas both Samson and Saul suffer the departure of YHWH's spirit (Judg. 16:20; 1 Sam. 16:14a), only Saul is then said to have been sent an "evil spirit" from YHWH (16:14b). Blenkinsopp has remarked that the Samson story has in common with the stories of Abimelech, Saul and Zimri a heroic pattern whose central action involves passion and death.[111] Yet, whereas Samson's suicide seems heroic, in that it became the means for his greatest victory (Judg. 16:30b), Saul's 'suicide' was anything but heroic and came about during the course of his greatest military defeat.[112]

---

[109] Ackroyd, *First Book of Samuel* (1971), p. 134; Garsiel, *First Book of Samuel* (1985), p. 155 n. 15; Dragga, "Shadow" (1987), pp. 42-43.

[110] Cf. J. L. Crenshaw, "The Samson Saga: Filial Devotion or Erotic Attachment?", *ZAW* 86 (1974), pp. 502-3.

[111] Blenkinsopp, "Judges 13-16" (1963), p. 70.

[112] Inasmuch as Samson was more often spirit-filled than any judge (Judg. 13:25; 14:6, 19; 15:14), it is noteworthy that, after the closing summary of the first part of his episode (Judg. 15:20; cf. 16:31), Samson is never again explicitly said to be spirit-filled after YHWH's departure (Judg. 16:20)—though one might infer that he was so empowered for his final feat of slaughter. In Saul's case, however, YHWH's departure seems to have been irreversible (1 Sam. 19:23 notwithstanding) so that, in comparison, Saul's suicide seems the less condonable.

§8. Analogy to Dénouement-A (17:1–18:31)

As in the case of the accounts of Othniel and Ehud, few phraseological correspondences can be offered as evidence of narrative analogy between Dénouement-A of Judges and the books of Samuel. However, one may infer from Dénouement-A an implicit scenario that finds correspondence to a situation portrayed in the books of Samuel. The most salient concern of Dénouement-A is the negative characterization of a citizen of Ephraim (Micah), of his exploitation of a compromising Levite and of the Danites for their part in promoting an illegitimate cult in Israel to the neglect of the central shrine at Shiloh (cf. Judg. 18:30-31).[113] In Dénouement-A, this situation is seen to derive from the fact that, in the period of the judges, there was no king to prevent such cultic aberrations from occurring (Judg. 17:6a; 18:1a).[114] Furthermore, the Danites are portrayed as forsaking their traditional allotment to subject a single city (Laish) to holy war (Judg. 17:27aγ-b). Hence, if a narrative analogy to Judges 17–18 were intended to be found in the books of Samuel, one should expect it to show concern with a less-than-ideal king, a disregard for legitimate cult and a misapplication of the sanctions of holy war. If such an analogy were to be found, it would also likely correspond to the actions of tribes that "did what was right in their own eyes" (Judg. 17:6b) to the detriment of intertribal covenant loyalty to the true cult of YHWH (cf. Deut. 12:8). Inasmuch as the false cult of Dénouement-A was instigated in Ephraim and established at Dan (Laish), one may also infer an implicit criticism of the tribes of northern Israel that severed loyalty to the true cult of YHWH.[115]

On first evaluation, the most obvious narrative analogy to Judges 17–18 does not seem to occur in the books of Samuel but in the books of Kings. Indeed, those who have attempted to identify a situation of composition for Judges 17–18 usually find it in the aftermath of the schism of the cult that resulted from the schism of the kingdom between Rehoboam and Jeroboam I (1 Kgs 12:1-24 [schism of kingdom]; 12:25-33 and 13:33 [schism of cult]).[116] This association seems to have the

---

[113] On the role of the shrine at Shiloh as Israel's cult centre prior to the assignment of this role to the cult site at Jerusalem, see Day, "Shiloh Sanctuary" (1979), pp. 87-94.

[114] So Y. Amit, "Hidden Polemic in the Conquest of Dan: Judges xvii-xviii", *VT* 40 (1990), p. 8.

[115] Amit, "Hidden Polemic" (1990), p. 7.

[116] Cf. Noth, "Hintergrund" (1962), ET: "Background" (1962), pp. 68-85; Brettler, "Judges" (1989), p. 417; Amit, "Hidden Polemic" (1990), pp. 14, 19 ("our story was written in the intermediate stage after the destruction of Dan [732 B.C.] and before the

advantage of associating concern about the establishment of an illegitimate shrine at Dan (Judg. 18:30-31) with that surrounding the erection of Jeroboam I's illegitimate cult in the same vicinity.[117] Yet, there is in this association no commensurate denunciation of the cult at Bethel.[118] Moreover, the cultic aberration instigated by Jeroboam I in 1 Kgs 12:25-33 goes astray of the point being made in Judg. 17:6a and 18:1a that, had there been a king in Israel (at least a deuteronomically legitimate one), such cultic aberrations would not have occurred. Indeed, it is the kings of both Judah and Israel whose actions precipitate the schism, both of the monarchy (for which blame falls chiefly upon Rehoboam) and of the cult (for which blame falls upon Jeroboam I). The situation in 1 Kings 12 reflects well on neither the Judahite nor the non-Judahite monarchies in Israel. Finally, the whole scheme of associating Judges 17-18 with the portrayal of 1 Kings 12 and 13:33 seems out of keeping with the ostensible strategy of the

---

openly undertaken deeds of Josiah [622 B.C.]", p. 19). The establishment of Jeroboam I's rule at Shechem and his fortification of Penuel (1 Kgs 12:25) suggest further ties to Judges: Jeroboam I thus reverses Abimelech's destruction of Shechem and Gideon's destruction of Penuel.

[117] Noth, of course, inferred that the original tradition of Judg. 17-18 was designed to polemicize the cult of Micah in order implicitly to legitimize the royal cult site established by Jeroboam I at the expense of the original Danite shrine ("Hintergrund" [1962], ET: "Background" [1962], pp. 78, 81-82). However, apart from the similar locale and theme of illegitimate cult, the Danite shrine of Jeroboam I is not necessarily implied in Judg. 17-18, because: (1) Jeroboam I's cult was not Levitical, (2) it concerned a golden calf not Micah's cultic vessels and (3) it lacked continuity with Micah's cult (so Judg. 17-18 was not its aetiology).

[118] Amit attempted to answer this objection by arguing that the polemic against Bethel's cult had to remain "hidden" so long as Bethel was an active cult site, even though the polemic against the cult at Dan could be "open" because it no longer existed after the destruction of Dan in 732 BCE ("Hidden Polemic" [1990], pp. 18-19). However, it is difficult to substantiate that the author intended all that Amit inferred in favour of an implicit polemic in Judg. 17-18 against the cult at Bethel ("Hidden Polemic" [1990], pp. 12-16). Even if Bethel were implied in the name "Mount Ephraim" (|| "Dan") in Jer. 4:15, should Bethel therefore be implied in the regional name "hill country of Ephraim" in Judges? Indeed, concern with the hill country of Ephraim in Judges can be accounted for as serving interests other than as a synonym for Bethel. Is the allegation of paronomasia in the reference to Micah's בית אלהים (Judg. 17:5) sufficient to identify Micah's shrine with Bethel? Should one assume, on the basis of the association of Bethel and Dan elsewhere (1 Kgs 12:26-33; 2 Kgs 10:29), that the mention of Dan implies an association with Bethel in Judges? Is it fair to associate Micah's appointment of a son and Levite as priests (Judg. 17:5, 12) with Jeroboam I's appointment of anyone but Levites as priests at Bethel and elsewhere (1 Kgs 12:31-32; 13:23)?

remainder of Judges to furnish legitimation for the monarchy of Judah while negatively characterizing that of Benjamin.

A less problematic analogy to Judges 17–18, and one that seems more in keeping with the overall rhetorical purpose of Judges, may be found in 1 Samuel's portrayal of Saul's neglect of the ark of God (MT 1 Sam. 14:18, notwithstanding), his slaughter of YHWH's priesthood and his subjection of the city of Nob to the sanctions of holy war (1 Sam. 22:6-19).[119] Indeed, the respectful and protective conduct of David toward the priests of Nob (1 Sam. 21:1-9; 22:20-23) contrasts markedly with the atrocities that Saul wreaks upon them. Since the problem of the decentralized cult in Israel ostensibly continued until David's attempt to recentralize the cult by bringing the ark to Jerusalem (2 Sam. 6), it is possible that the Judges compiler/redactor intended to suggest an analogy between Judges' portrayal of the Ephraimite leagues' disregard for YHWH's cult while the ark and temple remained at Shiloh and the more negative portrayal, in the books of Samuel, of Saul's disregard for YHWH's cult while the ark remained at Kiriath-Jearim[120] and the tabernacle at Nob.

§9. *Analogy to Dénouement-B (19:1-21:25)*

Several features of Judg. 19:29–20:48; 21:1-24 and 1 Sam. 10:27c*– 11:11; 15:1-9 + 22:6-19 suggest that the former two sections were designed to furnish narrative analogies to the events recorded in the latter. Saul's turn for the worse, implicit in a comparison of the contrasting characterizations of these passages in 1 Samuel, depicts a shift from a noble concern with the welfare of Jabesh-Gilead (inspired by YHWH's spirit) to an illegitimate concern with the preservation of his

---

[119] The MT of 1 Sam. 14:18 has Saul ordering Ahijah: הגישה ארון האלהים כי־היה ארון האלהים ביום ההוא ובני ישראל "Bring the ark of God (for the ark of God was [with] the Israelites in those days)", though it seems that the original text (reflected in the LXX and one OLat MS [115]) had *הגישה האפוד כי הוא היה נשא האפוד ביום ההוא לפני ישראל "Bring the ephod (for he was carrying the ephod that day before Israel)". So S. R. Driver, *Notes on the Hebrew Text and the Topography of the Books of Samuel, with an Introduction on Hebrew Palaeography and the Ancient Versions, and Facsimiles of Inscriptions and Maps* (Oxford, 2d edn, 1913; repr. edn, Winona Lake, Ind., 1984), p. 110. Contra P. R. Davies, "Ark or Ephod in I Sam. xiv. 18?", *JTS* NS 26 (1975), pp. 82-87; idem, "The History of the Ark in the Books of Samuel", *JNSL* 5 (1977), pp. 14-16; G. W. Ahlström, "The Travels of the Ark: A Religio–Political Composition", *JNES* 43 (1984), pp. 145-46.

[120] The ark allegedly remained at Kiriath-Jearim for the period between that ending the twenty years prior to the battle of Mizpah (cf. 1 Sam. 7:1-2) and the time when David took it to Jerusalem (cf. 2 Sam. 6:2-3, 9-17).

own dynasty (inspired by an evil spirit; cf. 1 Sam. 16:14b). Saul's turn for the worse finds analogy in Judg. 19:29–21:24 precisely where the plot shifts from concern with the execution of covenant justice (Plot B) to Israel's concern with preserving the tribe of Benjamin (Plot C, Judg. 21:1–23a). Had the Israelites been obedient and exterminated the tribe of Benjamin, presumably no descendants should have remained. The inference for the compiler/redactor's audience would be that it is only because of Israel's unwillingness to carry out YHWH's ban that any from Benjamin survived until their day. This implication of Judg. 19:1b–21:24, read within the framing repetitions of the monarchy motif (19:1a; 21:25a), suggests that interest in the legitimacy of the survival of Benjamin and Gibeah (cf. 21:23b) relates to the later royal status held by this tribe and city. It is perhaps not surprising, therefore, that the similarity between Judg. 19:29 and 1 Sam. 11:7 should invite an intertextual comparison between Judg. 19:29–21:24 and an account of the similar event that led to Israel's confirmation of Saul's kingship.[121]

Three points of characterization regarding the Levite and Israel in Judg. 19:29–20:48; 21:1-24 correspond to three analogous characterizations of Saul in 1 Sam. 10:27c*–11:11; 15:1-9 + 22:6-19. All three analogous characterizations are based upon conduct in holy war: (1) instances of just summons to holy war, (2) instances when just conditions of holy war are reneged upon and (3) instances of selfishly motivated holy war. These may be compared as follows:

Just summons to holy war	Levite & non-Benjaminite tribes (Judg. 19:29–20:48)	Saul [of Benjamin] (1 Sam. 10:27c*–11:11; 13:1-15)
Method of summons	Levite divides his concubine (19:29)	Saul divides his oxen (11:7)[122]
Popular response to method of summons	revulsion (19:30)	dread (11:7bα)
Assembly "as one man"	20:1	11:7bβ
Muster of opposing ranks	20:2-3a (cf. 20:14-17)	11:8
Sending of messengers to threatened party	20:12-13	11:9
Object of vindication	covenant justice(?)	Jabesh-Gilead[123]
Object of destruction	Gibeah(?)/Benjamin(?)	Ammonites

---

[121] On the circumstance that Saul was already king, though his popularity as king was not yet acknowledged by all, see 1 Sam. 10:17-27; cf. S. Lasine, "Guest and Host in Judges 19: Lot's Hospitality in an Inverted World", *JSOT* 29 (1984), pp. 42, 55 n. 24.

[122] Cf. Lasine, "Guest and Host" (1984), p. 37; Brettler, "Judges" (1989), pp. 412-13.

[123] Brettler, "Judges" (1989), pp. 412-13.

Just summons to holy war	*Levite & non-Benjaminite tribes (Judg. 19:29– 20:48)*	*Saul [of Benjamin] (1 Sam. 10:27c*– 11:11; 13:1-15)*
(Aftermath	—	[1] people's confirmation of Saul's kingship [1 Sam. 11:12-15]
	—	[2] Samuel's rebuke of people for requesting a king [1 Sam. 12]
	remnant of 600 men from Gibeah who will return to rebuild their cities [20:47; cf. 21:1-23]	[3] remnant of 600 men from Saul's army at Gibeah [1 Sam. 13:15; cf. 13:2])

Just conditions of holy war reneged upon	*Non-Benjaminite tribes (Judg. 21:1-24)*	*Saul [of Benjamin] (1 Sam. 15:8-23)*
Reneged object of destruction	remnant of Benjamin	Amalekite king (15:8-9) best of animals (15:9)
Rationalization	exception made for tribe [vs. city] (21:2-3, 6-7a, 15-17)	exception made for king [vs. people] (15:20; cf. 15:35a but 15:11, 35b)
	sacrifice offered to appease YHWH instead (21:4)	sacrifice thought to please YHWH instead (15:15, 21; but cf. 15:22-23)
(Aftermath	—	[1] YHWH's rejection of Saul's kingship [1 Sam. 15:24-33]
	Benjaminites return to their cities [21:23b]	[2] Saul returns to Gibeah [15:34]
	—	[3] YHWH's rebuke of Samuel through anointing of David as king [1 Sam. 16:1-13])

Selfishly motivated holy war	*Non-Benjaminite tribes (Judg. 21:1-24)*	*Saul [of Benjamin] (1 Sam. 22:6-19)*
Object of destruction	near total slaughter of Jabesh-Gilead	Davidic kingship via (supposed) total slaughter of priesthood at Nob
Object of vindication	remnant of Benjamin via maidens of Jabesh-Gilead (cf. 21:1, 7b with 21:5, 8-9)	Saulide kingship
Rationalization	interests of a tribe take precedence over those of a city	rivalry of Saulide kingship versus Davidic kingship

Lasine argued that it was ironic that, "the Levite's dismembering of his concubine almost leads to the annihilation of the very town [Jabesh-Gilead] which is later saved because Saul dismembers the oxen".[124] However, it would be mistaken to see in this any implicit blame for the Levite, for it is only Israel's sudden remorse for Benjamin (20:1-3; contra Deut. 13:13-19) that leads them to compromise covenant justice and to exact from Jabesh-Gilead a justice of convenience that also furnishes wives for the Benjaminites. Further, while there is some evidence of negative characterization of the Levite, especially in regard to his respect for his concubine and his method of summoning Israel to council by using the divided parts of her body, there is no censure against the Levite for the fact of his summoning Israel to council for holy war.[125] Thus, whatever implicit execration there may be against the Levite in Judges 19-21, it does not preclude the inference that Judges 19-21 is also implicitly an execration against the Saulide dynasty of Gibeah, the dynasty of one who summons Israel to holy war from a city that should have remained a ruin of holy war (contrast Judg. 21:23b with Deut. 13:17). There is perhaps no small irony in the correspondence between the six hundred fugitives from the battle of Gibeah who return to rebuild their cities (cf. Judg. 20:47; 21:23) and the remnant of six hundred men from Saul's standing army at Gibeah (1 Sam. 13:15; cf. 13:2).

---

[124] Lasine, "Guest and Host" (1984), p. 42; cf. p. 55 n. 23.

[125] Cf. Lasine's comment: "The intended contrast with Saul's dismembering of the oxen highlights the grotesqueness of the Levite's action" ("Guest and Host" [1984], p. 45). But S. Niditch's suggestion that the dismembered body is also a potent symbol of Israel's twelve-member body, which is now called to unite through dividing the concubine's body, invites reflection ("The 'Sodomite' Theme in Judges 19-20: Family, Community, and Social Disintegration", *CBQ* 44 (1982), p. 371).

That the Judges compiler/redactor ends with an account of the most extreme atrocities in Israel, atrocities that clearly cast a shadow over Gibeah, seems hardly fortuitous. Its points of analogy to negative portrayals of Saul in 1 Samuel show by implication that the rhetorical purpose of Judges 19–21, as that of the book as a whole, may have been to demonstrate to Israel its need of an ideal king from Judah.[126]

E. Conclusion

While it has been the inference of many scholars that the continuation of the 'judges' formula after the book of Judges (e.g., 1 Sam. 4:18; 7:15) implies that "the pre-deuteronomic book must have concluded with the discourse of 1 Samuel 12",[127] the narrative analogies between portrayals of deliverers in Judges and that of Saul in 1 Samuel suggest a continuity of a different kind. In the light of Judges' rhetoric of entrapment, whereby its monarchical idealization is made explicit only at the end of the book, both the tribal–political and deuteronomic concerns expressed or implied in Judges lead to the inference that the compiler/redactor of Judges was intent on establishing a standard of characterization whereby his/her readers could evaluate the performance of subsequent leaders in Israel, especially as they are portrayed in 1 Samuel 1–2 Samuel 4.[128] The possibility remains that Judges and an earlier compilation of the materials that now appear in 1 Samuel 1– 2 Samuel 4 were assembled by one and the same individual. Perhaps certain phrases and characterizations were imported into the accounts of one or the other book interactively so as to create analogy between them. Such a hypothesis might go some distance in explaining the

---

[126] Cf. Brettler, "Judges" (1989), pp. 413-14.

[127] Blenkinsopp, "Judges 13–16" (1963), p. 69. See Moore, *Judges* (1895), pp. xxii-xxiv, 276; and M. Noth, *Überlieferungsgeschichtliche Studien, I. Die sammelnden und bearbeitenden Geschichtswerke im Alten Testament* (Schriften der Königsberger Gelehrten Gesellschaft, 18. Jahr.; Geisteswissenschaftliche Klasse, Heft 2; Halle, 1943, pp. 43-266; Tübingen, 2d edn, 1957), ET of 2d edn, pp. 1-110: *The Deuteronomistic History* (JSOTS 15, Sheffield, 1981), pp. 42-53.

[128] It is interesting to note that, for all the alleged monarchical idealization in the book of Judges that draws upon deuteronomic standards, seemingly nothing in Judges reflects an awareness of the stipulations of Deut. 17:14-20 concerning the conduct of the king in Israel. Perhaps one may account for this fact by suggesting that, at the time of Judges' compilation/redaction, the portrayal of ideal Israelite kingship found in Deut. 17:14-20 was not yet to be found among the traditions that now form the book of Deuteronomy. Indeed, it is probable that Deut. 17:14-20 was added only later by a redactor in order to legitimate the negative portrayal of Solomon to be found in 1 Kgs 8:10-11:40.

compatibility between the rhetorical design of Judges to idealize Judah and the monarchy while vilifying Benjamin and the actual idealization of the Davidic dynasty and vilification of the Saulide dynasty in 1 Samuel 1–2 Samuel 4.

CHAPTER FOUR

THE RHETORICAL SITUATION IMPLIED BY JUDGES

The concern of this chapter is to discern the ostensible religious-political situation that best suits the rhetorical design of the book of Judges. In particular, I will test the hypothesis that the book of Judges should be interpreted in the light of the political and religious situation described in 2 Samuel 1–4, a situation that had seen neither the rule of David extended to include the Ephraimite league of tribes nor the centralization of the cult in Jerusalem. Corollary to this is the question of Judges' success as a rhetorical design if the book is to be understood as aimed at persuading Saulide loyalists and devotees of the false shrines to support the incipient Davidic monarchy and its cult.

Various suggested identifications of the book's religious–political situation of compilation/redaction include:

(1) that described in 1 Samuel 1–11/12, a situation in which Saul had established a monarchy that had not yet fallen into disfavour (ca. 1053 BCE[1]);[2]

(2) that described in 2 Samuel 1–4, a situation that had not yet seen the rule of the Davidic monarchy extended to include the Ephraimite league of tribes (ca. 1011–1004 BCE);[3]

(3) a situation subsequent to the beginning of David's rule over all Israel from Jerusalem (post-1004 BCE);[4]

---

[1] Although the authenticity of the verse is disputed, I emend MT 1 Sam. 13:1 on the basis of the OG, OLat and conjecture to read בֶּן שְׁלִישִׁים שָׁנָה שָׁאוּל בְּמָלְכוּ אַרְבָּעִים וּשְׁתַּיִם שָׁנָה מָלַךְ עַל־יִשְׂרָאֵל "Saul was *thirty* years old when he became king. He reigned over Israel *forty*-two years" (cf. Acts 13:21; S. R. Driver, *Notes on the Hebrew Text and the Topography of the Books of Samuel, with an Introduction on Hebrew Palaeography and the Ancient Versions, and Facsimiles of Inscriptions and Maps* [Oxford, 2d edn, 1913; repr. edn, Winona Lake, Ind., 1984], pp. 96-97).

[2] E.g., C. F. Keil and Franz Delitzsch, *Biblischer Commentar über das Alten Testament*, vol. II/1, *Josua, Richter und Ruth*, by C. F. Keil (Leipzig, 1863), ET: *Biblical Commentary on the Old Testament*, vol. 4, *Joshua, Judges, Ruth* (J. Martin [trans.], CFTL 4/VIII, Edinburgh, 1868); repr. edn, *Commentary on the Old Testament*, 10 vols., vol. 2, *Joshua, Judges, Ruth, I & II Samuel* (Grand Rapids, 1976), p. 248(?); C. J. Goslinga, *Richteren-Ruth* [KVHS, Kampen, The Netherlands, 3d edn, 1966], ET: *Joshua, Judges, Ruth* (R. Togtman [trans.], BSC, Grand Rapids, 1986), p. 219.

[3] E.g., Keil, *Richter* (1863), ET: *Judges* (1868), repr. edn, vol. 2, p. 248(?).

[4] E.g., A. E. Cundall, *Judges*, in A. E. Cundall and L. Morris, *Judges and Ruth: An Introduction and Commentary* (TOTC 7, London, 1968), pp. 26-27.

(4) the aftermath of the division of the monarchy in which Jeroboam I established a calf cult at Dan and Bethel and a non-Levitical priesthood at various cult centres (post-931 BCE, cf. 1 Kgs 12);[5]

(5) the aftermath of Tiglath-pileser III's subjugation in 734 BCE of all the northern kingdom of Israel except Samaria;

(6) the aftermath of the fall of Samaria in 722 BCE;

(7) a pre-exilic situation subsequent to Josiah's reform of 621 BCE (i.e., a 'deuteronomic' compilation/redaction);[6]

(8) the exilic aftermath of the 587 BCE deportation to Babylon (i.e., a 'deuteronomistic' compilation/redaction;[7] or a 'postdeuteronomistic' compilation/redaction[8]); and

(9) a postexilic situation of the 5th or 4th C. BCE (i.e., a redaction of JE [by Rje] and D [the 'deuteronomic redactor'];[9] or of Rp [the 'priestly redactor']]).[10]

Since, in this chapter, my aim is to describe the 'ostensible' situation of the compilation/redaction of Judges as implied by its rhetorical design, I shall concern myself more with the *Sitz im Text* of the books of the former prophets (i.e., the situation implied within the world[s] of the texts of Joshua, Judges, 1–2 Samuel, 1–2 Kings) than with any attempt to discern Judges' actual historical situation(s) of compilation/redaction.[11] With this end in view, of the various alternatives listed

---

[5] E.g., M. Brettler, "The Book of Judges: Literature as Politics", *JBL* 108 (1989), p. 417.

[6] F. M. Cross, *Canaanite Myth and Hebrew Epic: Essays in the History of the Religion of Israel* (Cambridge, Mass., 1973), pp. 250-54, 287-89 (re Dtr[1] in Judges); R. G. Boling, *Judges: Introduction, Translation and Commentary* (AB 6A, Garden City, N.Y., 1975), pp. 30, 35, 36 (re Dtr[1] in Judges).

[7] E.g., M. Noth, *Überlieferungsgeschichtliche Studien, I. Die sammelnden und bearbeitenden Geschichtswerke im Alten Testament* (Schriften der Königsberger Gelehrten Gesellschaft, 18. Jahr.; Geisteswissenschaftliche Klasse, Heft 2; Halle, 1943, pp. 43-266; Tübingen, 2d edn, 1957), ET of 2d edn, pp. 1-110: *The Deuteronomistic History* (JSOTS 15, Sheffield, 1981), pp. 42-53; Boling, *Judges* (1975), pp. 30, 35, 36-37 (re Dtr[2] in Judges); Cross, *Canaanite Myth* (1973), pp. 287-89 (re Dtr[2] in general); R. D. Nelson, *The Double Redaction of the Deuteronomistic History* (JSOTS 18, Sheffield, 1981), pp. 43-53, 120, 122-23, 124 (re Dtr[2] in Judges).

[8] E.g., A. D. H. Mayes, *Judges* (OTG 3, Sheffield, 1985), pp. 15, 33; W. J. Dumbrell, "'In Those Days There Was No King in Israel; Every Man Did What Was Right in His Own Eyes': The Purpose of the Book of Judges Reconsidered", *JSOT* 25 (1983), p. 29.

[9] E.g., G. F. Moore, *A Critical and Exegetical Commentary on Judges* (ICC, Edinburgh, 1895), pp. xxxiv, xxxv.

[10] E.g., C. F. Burney, *The Book of Judges with Introduction and Notes* (London, 2d edn, 1920), p. 1 of the introduction; J. Gray, *Joshua, Judges, Ruth* (NCBC, Basingstoke, 2d edn, 1986), p. 232.

[11] For a similar disclaimer, see Brettler, "Judges" (1989), pp. 397-99. This literary perspective of the world of the text as providing a valid context for describing the

above, it seems that the situation described in 2 Samuel 1–4 offers the greatest number of correspondences to the ostensible situation of Judges' compilation/redaction. The primary considerations for discerning that the implied situation of Judges' compilation/redaction was contemporary with David's rule from Hebron, prior to his rule of all Israel from Jerusalem, are: (1) Judges' situational analogy to the circumstances of 1 Samuel that lead up to the situation portrayed in 2 Samuel 1–4, and (2) Judges' internal sense of recency, its chronological references and its historical scope. I shall discuss these points of Judges' rhetoric in what follows.

A. The Rhetorical Situation Implied by Judges' Strategy

It would be difficult to understand how Judges functions as an exemplar of monarchical idealization apart from its canonical context. Viewed as a work of monarchical idealization, its genre intelligibility depends upon its being read in contiguity with both Deuteronomy and the books of Joshua and, especially, Samuel.[12] The period of Israel's history covered by the book of Judges fills the gap between the book of Joshua (which ends with the death of Joshua) and 1–2 Samuel (which commences with the emergence of the monarchy during the time of Samuel). Yet, there are also aspects of Judges that show that it was intended to function somewhat independently of these other books. For instance, the verbatim repetition in Judg. 1:10-15; 2:6-9 of material found also in Josh. 15:13-19; 24:28, 31, 29-30 suggests that the compiler/redactor of Judges intended his/her work to function semi-independently of the book of Joshua.[13]

On the other hand, an awareness of Israel's history as portrayed by Deuteronomy, Joshua and 1–2 Samuel not only enhances the reading but also discloses to the reader, by means of canonical contextualization, a framework for appreciating the rhetorical function of Judges. Indeed, the reader depends upon all the books of this corpus for

---

'ostensible' situation of composition seems the more justified if one regards the book of Judges as forming an integral part of the so-called Deuteronomistic History.

[12] Mayes describes the prologue and epilogue of Judges as serving the interests of "monarchic propaganda" (*Judges* [1985], p. 15).

[13] One need not thereby assume that all materials common to Joshua and Judges were borrowed by the compiler/redactor of Judges from the book of Joshua. The compiler/redactor(s) of these books may have had access to other sources from which to supplement them. Cf. Moore, *Judges* (1895), p. 6.

information about the ostensible situation in which Judges was composed. Reference to incidents that occurred in the birthplaces of both Saul and David (Gibeah of Benjamin and Bethlehem of Judah, respectively) in the closing account of Judges (19–21) shows how an understanding of the rhetorical design of Judges depends upon a prior knowledge of the events described in 1–2 Samuel, at least up to 2 Samuel 4.[14]

From Judges' references to a premonarchical period (17:6a; 18:1a; 19:1a; 21:25a) it is evident that the book was compiled subsequent to the establishment of the monarchy in Israel. Were the dénouement the only source of information about Judges' idealization of the monarchy, it would be difficult to ascertain which king, if any one in particular, the Judges compiler/redactor may have had in mind. However, several implications, drawn from points of narrative analogy to portrayals of Saul and David in 1–2 Samuel, seem to delimit the aims and circumstances under which the book was ostensibly compiled/redacted. By its comparative denunciation of the premonarchical period of the judges, the book of Judges indirectly idealizes the rule of a king in Israel. But exactly which king the compiler/redactor of Judges was idealizing must be inferred from a consideration of two thematic lines in the book: (1) the implicit standard by which the deliverer accounts were selected and arranged and (2) the peculiar set of concerns that form the fingerprint of Judges' monarchical idealization. In what follows, I shall treat successively these two thematic lines.

§1. *The* Sitz im Text *Implied by Judges' Narrative Analogies to 1 Samuel*

Besides the narrative analogies between accounts in Judges and those in Genesis, Exodus, Numbers, Deuteronomy and Joshua (see chapter 2), Judges has a great many points of analogy to 1 Samuel. The sheer number of correspondences to 1 Samuel invites the inference that the compiler/redactor who arranged the accounts of Judges and the compiler of the Saulide accounts in 1 Samuel may have been one and the same individual, whose design it was to implicate Saul's dynasty and legitimize David's dynasty. This inference seems corroborated in that Samuel's argument in 1 Samuel 12 depends upon a prior knowledge of the events portrayed in the book of Judges (see below) and that neither

---

[14] Correspondingly, some of the materials in 1 Samuel, e.g., Samuel's argument in 1 Sam. 12, require a prior knowledge of the events described in the book of Judges.

Judges' rhetoric of entrapment nor its implicit monarchical idealization find definition apart from Judges' network of analogies to 1 Samuel.

Of the plot-based accounts in Judges, Dénouement-B (Judg. 19–21) and most deliverer accounts find clear points of analogy to portrayals of Saul in 1 Samuel. In most instances, the analogy invites the conclusion that the more negative characterization belongs to Saul. Of the less salient instances of narrative analogy (i.e., those between the accounts of Othniel, Ehud, Dénouement-A and the accounts of 1 Samuel), one may at least infer that they correspond in a general way: Othniel, as an idealized representative of Judah, corresponds to the Judahite David in 1 Samuel; Ehud, as a representative of Benjamin, corresponds to Saul of Benjamin in 1 Samuel; as portrayed in Dénouement-A, the association of the themes of the abuse of cult and priesthood by Micah (representing Ephraim) and by the Danites and of the Danites' holy war against a single city (Laish), correspond to Saul's abuses of cult (1 Sam. 13:1-15; 15:8-23), slaughter of the priests of YHWH and subjection of the city Nob to the sanctions of holy war (1 Sam. 22:6-19).

The degree of correspondence between the allegedly analogous accounts of heroes/deliverers in Judges and of Saul in 1 Samuel may be summarized as follows:

	Judges	*1 Samuel*	*(Deuteronomy)*
1.	1:19a vs. 1:21	16:13-14; 18:12, 14-15, 28-29	
2.	1:12, 13	17:4-7, 26-58; 18:17-19, 20-27	
3.	4:6, 11, 17, 21-22; 5:26-28	15:1-33	(7)
4.	6:2, 12, 15, 34, 36-40; 7:1, 3-8, 10-16, 22, 24-25; 8:5-23, 27	8:5-22; 9:1–14:35; 15:9, 20, 32-33; 21:1-6; 22:18-19; 28:4-25; 31:4	
5.	9:2, 5, 7-21, 23, 40, 45	8:4-22; 12:1-25; 16:14; 20:30-31; 22:6-20; 24:8-22; 26:13-25; 31:4	
6.	11:1, 30-31, 34-40	9:1; 14:24-49	
7.	(13:25); 14:6, 19; 15:14; 16:20, 25, 30	10:6, 10; 11:6; 16:14; 19:23; 31:4	
8.	17–18	22:6-19	(12)
9.	19:29–20:48	10:27c*–11:11; 13:1-15	(13)
10.	21:1-24	15:8-23; 22:6-19	(13)

In principle, it would seem to be easier to find stories about various individuals to furnish analogies to events of one life than to find episodes from the life of one person to furnish analogies to a pre-existing anthology of stories about various individuals. This principle alone might lead to the inference that the book of Judges was arranged subsequent to the portrayal of Saul in 1 Samuel so as to present analogies to Saul's life that would negatively characterize him. However, the relation of dependence between Judges and 1 Samuel is not that clear. It is clear only that both Judges and the analogous accounts of 1 Samuel must have been written subsequent to the events of the life of Saul to which they allude or refer.[15] It may never be possible to demonstrate whether the book of Judges was compiled/redacted before the analogous accounts of 1 Samuel or vice versa. A demonstration of the priority of either Judges or proto-Samuel (especially those accounts of the books of Samuel that find analogy in Judges) depends upon the extent to which dependence can be demonstrated between the arrangement of accounts in Judges and the arrangement of accounts in 1 Samuel. Perhaps the safest inference to be drawn at this time is that the evidence of dependence works simultaneously in both directions.[16]

§2. The Sitz im Text Implied by Judges' Monarchicalism

When the book of Judges is read from the perspective of the monarchical idealization of 17:6a, 18:1a, 19:1a and 21:25a, it is difficult to escape the implication that Judges was designed to endorse a Judahite monarchy and to denounce one deriving from the tribe of Benjamin. Further, when Judges is read with sensitivity to the network of analogies that it forms with portrayals in the books of Samuel, it is likewise difficult to escape the implication that the ostensible situation of Judges' composition is one analogous to a situation of rivalry between the dynasties of Saul and David. My contention is that, at least so far as

---

[15] Cf. S. Lasine's inference ("Guest and Host in Judges 19: Lot's Hospitality in an Inverted World", *JSOT* 29 [1984], p. 41):

> The dismemberment of the concubine in Judges 19.29 is usually assumed to be 'influenced by the tradition of Saul's action' (Martin, 1975: 206). It is much more accurate to say that Judges 19.29 presupposes the reader's awareness of the incident recorded in the given text of Samuel, and requires that awareness in order to be fully appreciated.

Yet from this Lasine infers that "the contrast between 1 Sam. 11.7 and Judg. 19.29 is designed to highlight the perversity of the Levite's act" ("Guest and Host" [1984], p. 55 n. 21).

[16] It must be emphasized that this inference pertains to the *Sitz im Text*, the 'ostensible' situation implied in the world of the texts of Judges and the books of Samuel, rather than to the actual historical situation of compilation/redaction of either Judges or the books of Samuel.

the *Sitze im Text* of Judges and the books of Samuel are concerned, this literary situation best corresponds to that presented in 2 Samuel 1-4, a situation in which David had not yet come to rule all Israel (2 Sam. 5:1-5), had not yet conquered Jerusalem (2 Sam. 5:6-16), had not yet fully defeated the Philistines (2 Sam. 5:17-25; 8:1, 11-12; 19:9; 21:15-22) and had not yet brought the ark of God to Jerusalem (2 Sam. 6).[17]

The book of Judges seems to give prominence to political and religious concerns that suit the time of rivalry between David's house, when David ruled Judah from Hebron, and the house of Saul, when Ish-Bosheth ruled the Ephraimite league from Mahanaim (cf. 2 Sam. 2:8-9; 3:1). Many of these political and religious concerns pertain to the idealization of Israel's monarchy and may be seen to offer contrasting characterizations of the dynasties of David and Saul. In what follows, I shall examine a number of the issues that relate the implicit monarchicalism of Judges to its ostensible situation of compilation/redaction.

§2.1. *Return to National Ideals*

What is important to the establishment of the legitimacy of any new political order, such as that brought about by the displacement of the Saulide dynasty with that of David, is that it be perceived to represent not a departure from but a return to the founding ideals of the nation. Correlations between the implicit monarchicalism of Judges and the religious and political situation of 2 Samuel 1-4 intimate that David's rule represented such a return.

---

[17] Of course, the actual situation of Judges' compilation/redaction may be seen to require a historical date of composition later than the events portrayed in 2 Sam. 5-6. This may be inferred from: (1) the prominence given to Jerusalem/Jebus (Judg. 1:8, 21; 19:10-12), which would have become important only after Jerusalem had become Israel's capital; (2) the reference to the ark of God as having been at Bethel "in those days" (20:27b-28a), which may be taken to imply that it was already in Jerusalem (though it could as well imply some other location); (3) the reference to Samson as having only begun to deliver Israel from the Philistines, which could imply that the compiler/redactor knew of the time when the Philistines had finally been ousted from Israel (though the implied Philistine defeat could as well have been seen as that of 1 Sam. 7:13-14). The presentation of the ark's removal to Jerusalem in 2 Sam. 6 (though the event probably took place later than David's first year of rule, ca. 977 BCE; cf. E. H. Merrill, "The 'Accession Year' and Davidic Chronology", *JANES* 19 [1989], pp. 101-12) and the importance of its association with the rejection of the dynasty of Saul (2 Sam. 6:21-23) show that the compiler/redactor of these accounts of 2 Samuel was still sensitive to the rivalry between the dynasties of Judah and Benjamin, but the rhetorical situation of Judges does not extend to the time when the ark was brought to Jerusalem.

§2.1.1. *Importance of Conquest to the Ideal That Israel's Leader Be YHWH's Holy-Warrior*. The most consistent component of the heroic characterization of Judges' deliverers is that they initiate holy war against the enemies of YHWH. All the deliverers are venerated as deliverers because of the triumphs they achieve against foreign leaders or militia: Othniel defeats Cushan-Rishathaim, Ehud slays Eglon then leads an attack against the Moabites, Barak defeats the troops of Sisera while Jael kills Sisera himself, Gideon leads his troops to defeat the Midianites, Jephthah's men rout the Ammonites and the Nazirite Samson slays Philistine soldiers and leaders. In every instance, it is a special calling or spiritual empowerment by YHWH that gives the tribal hero his/her victory. Thus, the tribal heroes of Judges are portrayed as holy-warriors acting at YHWH's bidding with YHWH's enabling against YHWH's enemies.

Initially, Saul is characterized as a deliverer of the same order as those of Judges (1 Sam. 10:27c*–11:11). By saving Jabesh-Gilead, Saul came to be acknowledged as a holy-warrior of YHWH and, as such, deserving of kingship (1 Sam. 11:12-15). Saul's characterization changes, however, precisely because he disqualifies himself as a representative of YHWH, whom he repeatedly disobeys (1 Sam. 13:2-15; 15:1-35). From that point on, David emerges as the one specially endowed by YHWH to serve as Israel's holy-warrior. This is evident in the portrayal of David's triumph over Goliath (1 Sam. 17) and especially in the portrayal of his military successes as preeminent over those of Saul: "Saul has slain his thousands, / and David his tens of thousands" (1 Sam. 18:7; cf. 21:11). The statement that "YHWH was with David" (1 Sam. 16:13; 18:12, 14, 28) so that he was successful in all his military endeavours (1 Sam. 18:5, 13-16) offers a clear analogy to a statement in Judges that "YHWH was with the men of Judah" (1:19). Comparing the military success of the Joseph tribes, of whom it is also said that "YHWH was with them" (Judg. 1:22), with the fact that Benjamin, in 1:21, conquered nothing, one may be justified in inferring that YHWH was not with the latter. Thus, the portrayals of Judah versus Benjamin in Judges as regards their prowess in holy war may offer an analogy to the portrayals of David versus Saul as holy-warriors in 1 Samuel.

Perhaps it is appropriate to mention here another possible means for idealizing David: the characterization of David through the characterization of the cities from which he would rule. Since Gibeah, the city from which Saul would later rule, is negatively characterized in Judges 19–21, it may be that both Hebron and Jerusalem, the cities from which David would later rule, are positively characterized in Judges. Hebron is represented in Judges as having been conquered by an idealized holy-war hero, Caleb of Judah. Hebron, by tradition, had been granted to Caleb by YHWH and by Joshua (cf. Josh. 14:13-15; 15:13-14). Thus, when YHWH later chooses Hebron to become David's city (2 Sam. 2:1), it is already a city associated with Judah's founding warrior heroes Caleb and Othniel (cf. Judg. 1:10-15 with Josh. 15:13-19). David is thus portrayed as legitimate heir to the city of Caleb, the slayer of the Anakites. Indeed, the analogy to Caleb, the giant slayer, is not wasted on David, who himself is portrayed in 1 Samuel 17 as having slain Goliath (nor, for that matter, is the complementary negative analogy between Israel's fear of the Anakites [cf. the parenthetical additions of Num. 13:22, 28b, 33] and the 'giant' Saul's reluctance to engage Goliath [cf. 1 Sam. 9:2; 10:23-24 with 17:4, 11]).

The reference in Judg. 1:21 to the fact that Jerusalem had not been conquered by the Benjaminites and remained in Jebusite hands "until this day" offers an ostensible *terminus ad quem* for the composition of this verse (if, indeed, it refers to sole Jebusite occupation before David's conquest rather than later Jebusite presence in Jerusalem; cf. 2 Sam. 24:18).[18] That is, according to the ostensible situation of Judges' composition (i.e., that implied by its canonical context), Jerusalem had not yet been conquered by David. Nevertheless, there is elsewhere in Judges a clear concern with conquering Jerusalem/Jebus (Judg. 1:8) and the problem of its foreign occupancy (Judg. 19:10-12), a concern that implicitly redounds to the discredit of Benjamin for failing to conquer that city (1:21).[19] This situation comports with that

---

[18] Of course, the use of עד היום הזה in Judg. 1:21 offers no firm evidence for the actual historical time of Judges' final compilation/redaction (cf. 2 Chron. 5:9).

[19] From a historical point of view (i.e., with concern for Judges' actual situation of compilation/redaction), the Judges compiler/redactor's concern with the political status of Jerusalem would most likely have arisen after its conquest by David, which offers a viable historical *terminus a quo* for the compilation/redaction of Judges, but such a concern offers no viable historical *terminus ad quem*, since Jerusalem remains a political centre of concern throughout the remainder of the biblical corpus and history of Israel. Of course, David's conquest of Jerusalem would later become a central aspect of his idealization as YHWH's holy-warrior and of his right to rule Israel. The capture of Jerusalem and the establishment of a palace there (2 Sam. 5:6-16) would be viewed as YHWH's confirmation of David's divine right to rule (cf. the ideology in the Ugaritic *Palace of Baal* and 2 Sam. 5:10, "YHWH the warrior god was with him" [cf. Judg. 1:19] with 2 Sam. 5:12 [David's recognition of YHWH's election] and 5:14 [concerning dynastic offspring]). Contrast the portrayal of the divine election of Judah, the tribe (of David) that conquered Jerusalem (Judg. 1:8), with the portrayal of Benjamin, the tribe of Saul that could not conquer Jerusalem/Jebus (Judg. 1:21). Despite these considerations, however, it remains that

described by 2 Samuel 1-4, during which David ruled Judah from Hebron.

§2.1.2. *Importance of Ephraim's Endorsement to the Ideal of Intertribal Covenant Loyalty.* The following factors seem to support the hypothesis that the book of Judges was designed with the aim of elevating the status of Judah (i.e., the house of David) in the estimation of the Ephraimite league of tribes. According to the tribal correspondences between the prologue and dénouement, it is the Joseph tribes (among whom Ephraim was preeminent) that represent the northern, non-Judahite tribes. Ephraim is a tribe whose *Leitmotif* reappearance throughout the body of the book serves only to emphasize the prominent role that this tribe plays in the strategy of the Judges compiler/redactor as representing the non-Judahite tribes of Israel (cf. 3:27; 5:14; 7:24-8:3; 10:1; 12:1-6, 15; 18:22-26 [cf. 17:1]).[20] On this basis, it may be argued that members of the Ephraimite league were the implied readers for whom Judges was written in order to sway their allegiance from the Benjaminite dynasty of Saul (under Ish-Bosheth) to the Judahite monarchy of David. The analogy between Judges' concern with intertribal covenant disloyalty, implicit in the Ephraim motif, and the Ephraimite league's persistence in following Saul's heir Ish-Bosheth, in the portrayal of the Israelite civil strife of 2 Sam. 2:8-4:12, conforms to the general rhetorical design of the Judges compiler/ redactor to present an endorsement of David's rule as the means to ameliorate the problem of intertribal disintegration.

§2.1.3. *Importance of Veneration for the Ark to the Ideal of the Centrality of YHWH's Cult.* The concern in 1 Sam. 4:1-7:2 to correct Israel's disregard for the ark of YHWH/God is not apparent in 2 Samuel 1-4 (though it emerges as the central concern in 2 Sam. 6). Since, in the ostensible situation of Judges' compilation/redaction, Jerusalem was still in Jebusite hands (1:21), and since, in the analogous situation of 2 Samuel 1-4 (i.e., before David had conquered Jerusalem; 2 Sam. 5:6-13), David had not yet brought the ark to Jerusalem (2 Sam. 6),

---

Judges' literary context implies a situation of compilation/redaction when as yet David's conquest of Jerusalem had not taken place (cf. Judg. 1:21).

[20] J. J. Slotki inferred from Judges that "the tribe of Ephraim claimed the hegemony because of its possession of the principal city, its central position, the situation within its territory of the Tabernacle at Shiloh, and the fact that Joshua had belonged to this tribe" ("Judges: Introduction and Commentary", in H. Freedman and J. J. Slotki, *Joshua and Judges*, A. Cohen [ed.], SBB, London, 1950, p. 154). Brettler inferred that Ephraim, in Judges, represents northern kingship after the division of the monarchy ("Judges" [1989], pp. 408, 416-17).

one may infer that, for the Judges compiler/redactor, the ark had not yet come to play a significant role in the idealization of David. On the contrary, disregard for the ark in the analogous situations of Judges and 1 Samuel 1–2 Samuel 4 negatively portrays the period of the judges as one similar to that of Saul's rule for its neglect of the ark. In the analogous situation of 2 Samuel 1–4, David is portrayed as divinely elected to rule from Hebron (2 Sam. 2:1) and the ark as already within the region of Judah, at Kiriath-Jearim (Josh. 15:60). In other words, David would not have needed to be concerned about the relocation of the ark until after he had become king also of the other tribes of Israel (2 Sam. 5:1-5). Only then would it have become politically expedient to move the ark from Judah proper to a more cosmopolitan locale, the royal city of David (cf. 2 Sam. 5:7, 9).

§2.1.4. *Importance of Integrity to the Ideal of Social Justice.* Implicit in the monarchical idealization of Judg. 17:6a, 18:1a, 19:1a and 21:25a is the idea that, had there been a king in Israel, such cultic aberrations and social injustices as one finds in Judges 17–18 and 19–21 would not have occurred. Since, even under monarchy, one finds instances of social injustice, such as that implied in the Judges accounts that are analogous to those in 1 Samuel that portray Saul's acts of injustice, it must have been the Judges compiler/redactor's aim to commend not just any king but a king in Israel who would not tolerate such injustices. If Judges' analogies to Saul disqualify Saul from being considered as the king referred to by Judg. 17:6a, 18:1a, 19:1a and 21:25a, then one must consider whether the compiler/redactor of Judges had in mind another king. It is perhaps not by coincidence that David, in 1 Samuel 18–26, is portrayed as consistently restraining himself from serving personal vengeance (24:5-7; 25:32-34; 26:8-11) whereas Saul consistently pursues it (18:10-11, 17, 21; 19:1, 9-10, 11, 15, 19-24; 20:30-31; 22:11-19; 23:7-8). According to the *Sitz im Text* of Judges and the books of Samuel, therefore, the just king in Israel implicitly endorsed by Judges is likely to have been David of Judah.[21]

§2.2. *Present Crisis of National Leadership*
In the cycle-motif of Judges, YHWH's raising up of a deliverer and empowering him/her to act (motif elements D1 and D2a) feature prominently as the turning points in the deliverer accounts. Two formulaic

---

[21] For a treatment of the theme of justice in the idealization of Israelite kingship, see K. W. Whitelam, *The Just King: Monarchical Judicial Authority in Ancient Israel* (JSOTS 12, Sheffield, 1979).

expressions seem to function in this capacity within the framework of Judges: D1 "YHWH raised up ... to save them" (2:16abα, 18aα,γ; 3:9aβ, 15aβ; [6:15aβ]; 10:1aα, 3aα; [10:12bβ, 14b^i; 12:2bβ, 3aα]; [13:5b]) and D2a "YHWH's spirit ... upon ..." ([2:18aβ]; 3:10aα^i; 6:34a; 11:29a; 13:25aα-β^i; 14:6aα, 19aα; 15:14bα, [19aγ; 16:19bβ, 20bγδ]). Yet, despite the importance of these formulae as indicating the turning point in each account, only three deliverer accounts feature a semblance of both formulae (those of Othniel, Gideon and Jephthah), and one lacks either (that of Barak). Moreover, in several deliverer accounts (e.g., those of Barak, Gideon, Jephthah and Samson), the emergence of the deliverer is delayed or prolonged by the initial reluctance of the deliverer to act in that capacity. This offers an important clue to another rhetorical concern of the Judges compiler/redactor: a concern to associate the portrayal of national calamity with that of a crisis of national leadership.

In the Ehud account, the tribes never rally to battle until summoned to do so by Ehud (3:15, 27-28). In the poetic version of the Deborah/ Barak/Jael account, the prevailing situation before Deborah arose to summon Barak is one of a crisis of leadership (cf. 5:6-8, 11b-13). In the corresponding prose account, the designated leader Barak delays the plot by his reluctance to obey YHWH's word (4:8). Ironically, Barak's halfheartedness will undercut his own military success (4:9), opening him up to the embarrassment that Jael would succeed where he had failed (4:22). Moreover, the parallel contrast between the rebuke of the tribes who had failed to rally for battle (5:15b-17) and the blessing of Jael (5:24-27) escalates, to the tribal level, the problem of Israel's crisis of leadership.

It is only after a sequence of dialogues between YHWH and Gideon that YHWH's spirit induces Gideon to summon the tribes to rally for battle (6:34-35). Then follows a similar sequence of dialogues that end with Gideon summoning the tribes to engage in battle (7:23-25).[22] Thus, the obstacle of Israel's crisis of national leadership seems to have been surmounted. In Judg. 8:1-21, however, Gideon's initiative begins to move independently of YHWH's direction, which results in Gideon's

---

[22] The first sequence of dialogues comprises Judg. 6:11-23 (Gideon's response in 6:24) and 6:25-26 (Gideon's response and its consequences in 6:27-32). Then YHWH's spirit induces Gideon to rally the tribes for battle (6:34-35). The second sequence comprises Judg. 6:36-40 (Gideon's response in 7:1), 7:2-3a (consequence in 7:3b), 7:4 (Gideon's response in 7:5a), 7:5b-7 (Gideon's response in 7:8) and 7:9-11a (Gideon's response and its consequences in 7:11b-21). The culmination of the second sequence is not reached until Gideon takes the initiative in summoning Israel's tribes to engage in battle (7:23-25).

unjust exploitation of a situation of holy war to serve a personal vendetta. In the dénouement to the latter section (8:22-27)—a dénouement that juxtaposes the problem of popular appointment to kingship with that of cultic disloyalty to YHWH—Gideon unwittingly misdirects the people. The nemesis of these themes—social injustice, cultic disloyalty and popular appointment to kingship—reemerges in the Abimelech account. Indeed, in Judges' double dénouement, a similar combination of concerns for proper cult (chs. 17-18), social justice (chs. 19-21) and ideal kingship (17:6a; 18:1a; 19:1a; 21:25a) is in the foreground.

A similar tactic of delay may be found in the accounts of the emergence of Jephthah and Samson as deliverers of Israel. Jephthah insists upon dickering with the elders of Gilead before accepting their offer to make him leader (11:4-10), and the emergence of the deliverer Samson, who never fully accepts his calling to be a Nazirite deliverer, is long delayed by the account of his birth annunciation (13:2-23).

Finally, it should be noted how the direct confrontations between YHWH and Israel in the Gideon account (in 6:8-10) and in the Jephthah account (in 10:11-14) are interposed between Israel's pleas for deliverance (6:7; 10:10) and retardations or embellishments of YHWH's expected response of providing a deliverer (6:15, 34a; 11:29a). The discomfort that these confrontations emote through their rhetoric of rebuke is heightened by the fact that their very interposition retards the narrative movement to the expected deliverance motifs. Moreover, the theme of these confrontations is, in both instances, one of rebuke for religious aberration in the form of the worship of foreign idols. This feature of the confrontations between YHWH and Israel implies that there may be a correlation between Israel's crisis of leadership and their ritual infidelity. Perhaps this correlation was implied from the outset of Judges by the fact that the first of YHWH's three confrontations of Israel correlate Israel's cultic disloyalty with their military deficiencies (2:1-3).

The return of such crises of national leadership that require YHWH's electing a national leader is a dominant concern in the book of Judges. The implication that Israel's want of a willing or ideal leader was the source of their religious and political problems becomes increasingly evident in the portrayals of the deliverers. Yet it is the monarchical idealization implicit in 17:6a, 18:1a, 19:1a and 21:25a that makes it evident that the Judges compiler/redactor always had in mind a solution to the problem of Israel's crisis of national leadership.

The ostensible situation of the compilation/redaction of Judges as one befitting a time in which tribes of Israel were lacking a leader corresponds more readily to that following Ish-Bosheth's murder (cf. 2 Sam. 3:8-19; 5:1-5) than to any subsequent time during the monarchy, when, whether because of hereditary dynastic rights, coregencies or usurpation, the northern tribes never lacked for a pretender to the throne. This situation seems corroborated by its parallels with four further aspects of the ostensible situation of Judges' compilation/redaction, which include: a continued military threat from the Philistines, intertribal disunity resulting from rivalry between factions that favour either Judah or Benjamin, tribal disregard for the cult of YHWH and social injustices in Israel.

§2.2.1. *Present Military Threat of the Philistines.* One of Noth's indicators that the deuteronomistic form of Judges was not closed by the present ending of the book was the inconsistency between the forty-year oppression of the Philistines, mentioned in Judg. 13:1, and the twenty-year judgeship of Samson (cf. 15:20; 16:31).[23] Two assumptions controlled Noth's chronology of the times of Dtr's (the Deuteronomist's) alleged compilation: (1) the assumption that, from the perspective of the compiler, the period of Philistine oppression succeeded that of the Ammonite oppression rather than having been partly contemporaneous with it and (2) the assumption that, from the perspective of the compiler, the forty-year period of Philistine oppression mentioned in Judg. 13:1 marks the full extent of the period of Philistine oppression, which extended over Samson's, Eli's and part of Samuel's judgeships, rather than marking that part of the period of Philistine oppression that came before Israel's deliverers "began" to throw off their rule (cf. 13:1, 5; 14:4b; 15:11).

As to the first assumption, Noth thought that the compiler of Judges, who had linked the Ammonite and Philistine oppressions in 10:7 in reverse order from that in which they are described in 10:8-12:7 and 13-16, was mistaken.[24] Apparently, Noth did not consider that the arrangement may have been a narrative means of indicating

---

[23] Noth, *Überlieferungsgeschichtliche Studien, I* (1943), ET: *Deuteronomistic History* (1981), pp. 21-22. Noth also later refers to "the Deuteronomistic Book of Judges" (p. 118 n. 4).

[24] Noth argued: "The Philistines are mentioned before the Ammonites in v.7 because of an error, possibly simply the result of the juxtaposition of the two names at the end of v.6" (*Überlieferungsgeschichtliche Studien, I* [1943], ET: *Deuteronomistic History* [1981], p. 120 n. 23).

synchroneity.[25] Thus, when the oppression of the Philistines is mentioned again in 13:1, it may resume the summary introduction of 10:7, which was perhaps intended to link the Jephthah and Samson episodes chronologically.

As to Noth's second assumption, perhaps Noth should have considered the possibility that the forty-year Philistine oppression had been intended to refer to a period prior to Samson's twenty-year judgeship, which only "began" to deliver Israel from the Philistines (13:5). Indeed, it is only by analogy to the relationship between foreign oppressions and periods of judgeship in previous deliverer accounts that one can know whether, in this instance, the situation of Philistine oppression should continue into the period of Samson's judgeship.[26]

As to Noth's assumption that, from the perspective of the compiler, the forty-year period of Philistine oppression (13:1) marks the full extent of the Philistine oppression of Israel,[27] it should be noted that the ostensible situation of the Judges compiler/redactor moves against this assumption. From the implied vantage point of the compiler/redactor of Judges, there are indications that the Philistines were still regarded as a potential military threat. The Philistines, who pose the last foreign threat against Israel among the deliverer accounts of Judg. 3:7–16:31, are not said to have been entirely defeated by Samson.[28] If the notion of recency is any indication of the compiler/redactor's concerns, the mere continuation of the Philistine threat beyond the final deliverer account of Judges would suggest an ostensible situation of compilation/ redaction in which the Philistine threat was still present.[29] Since the

---

[25] Cf. S. Talmon, "The Presentation of Synchroneity and Simultaneity in Biblical Narrative", in *Studies in Hebrew Narrative Art through the Ages*, J. Heinemann and S. Werses (eds.), ScrHier 27, Jerusalem, 1978, pp. 9-26.

[26] The defeat of Sisera, portrayed in Judg. 4–5, was similarly portrayed as only a partial step toward the complete removal of Jabin (cf. 4:24), though the situation of Jabin's oppression that had lasted twenty years (4:3) ostensibly ended with the events described in Judg. 5 whereby the land had peace forty years (5:31b).

[27] See Noth, *Überlieferungsgeschichtliche Studien*, *I* (1943), ET: *Deuteronomistic History* (1981), pp. 47, 52-53.

[28] There is neither a statement to the effect that the land had peace N years (motif F2) nor does the statement that Samson would only "begin to deliver Israel from the hands of the Philistines" (Judg. 13:5b) allow that there should be.

[29] Moreover, a consideration of the chronological displacement of Judg. 13–16 and 17–18 implies that the reason Samson is the only judge never to have rallied Israel to battle is because his own tribe had already abandoned the charge to rid their region of foreigners (cf. the Danites' similar failure to oust the Amorites, in 1:34-36). Thus, for the compiler/redactor, Judah had come under Philistine threat (15:9-11) not so much because Samson was a troublemaker (the perception of Judah, 15:11) but because the Danites had

Philistines continued to pose a threat throughout the premonarchical and early monarchical periods—during the judgeships of Eli (cf. 1 Sam. 4:1b-18) and Samuel (1 Sam. 7:2-17) and the kingships of Saul (1 Sam. 13:1–14:52; 17; 27–29; 31:1-10) and David (2 Sam. 1:20; 5:17-25; 7:1, 9, 11; 8:1, 11-12; 19:9; 21:15-22)—one may infer that the putative compiler/redactor may have completed Judges anytime prior to the final defeat of the Philistines.

The vantage point of the author of the comment, "At that time the Philistines were ruling over Israel" (14:4b; cf. 15:11a), is evidently from a time after they had ceased to rule Israel. However, it would be mistaken to infer from this comment that the Philistines had ceased to pose a military threat to Israel just because they had ceased to rule Israel directly. This is precisely the situation that ensues after Samuel had defeated the Philistines at the battle of Mizpah/Ebenezer (1 Sam. 7:2-14). The careers of Saul and David in 1–2 Samuel should be ample evidence of the continuation of a Philistine threat even after they had ceased to rule Israel.[30]

According to the *Sitz im Text* of Judges and the books of Samuel, the Philistines were the primary threat to Israel during the judgeships of Samson, Eli and Samuel and during the rules of Saul and David. Thus, while there is no incontrovertible evidence here to support the association of the ostensible situation of Judges' compilation/redaction with the situation described in 2 Samuel 1–4, neither is there evidence that would preclude the possibility that the ostensible situation of the compilation/redaction of Judges equates to that portrayed in 2 Samuel 1–4, which then leads to that of 2 Sam. 5:17-25 (cf. 2 Sam. 1:20; 3:18). Indeed, 2 Sam. 5:17-25 shows how, as a result of David's anointing as king over all Israel, he was able to defeat and expel the Philistines from the region of Benjamin.

§2.2.2. *Present Intertribal Disunity Resulting from Rivalry between Judah and Benjamin*. From an analysis of the tribal–political arrangement of Judges it is apparent that the tribes or representatives of Judah and Benjamin are juxtaposed in three contexts: 1:1-20, 21; 3:7-11,

---

reneged upon their covenant responsibility. Perhaps it was the mere presence of the Philistine threat that prompted the Judges compiler/redactor to give such prominence to the negative portrayals of the Danite tribe (cf. the final position of 1:34-36 and chs. 13–16 within Prologue-A and the main body of Judges, respectively).

[30] Contra J. A. Wharton, who inferred that, because the Philistines had ceased to rule Israel by the time of the compilation/redaction of Judg. 13–16, they were "no longer a threat" ("The Secret of Yahweh: Story and Affirmation in Judges 13–16", *Int* 27 [1973], p. 54).

12-30; and 19-21. Because the tribal–political schemata of Judges in 1:1-2:5 and 3:7-16:31 are roughly parallel (see chapter 1), the priority of Judah over Benjamin in both sections seems hardly accidental. It appears that the compiler/redactor of Judges put these tribes together in 1:1-2:5 and 3:7-16:31 and pitted them against each other in chs. 19-21 so as to intensify their contrasting characterizations. Such a design might reflect an ostensible situation of compilation/redaction in which the tribes of Judah and Benjamin were viewed by the Judges compiler/ redactor as political rivals.

Attempting to describe the supposed historical situation of Judah's portrayal in Judg. 1:1-20, Boling lamented the difficulty in assessing the precise historical role of Judah in the emergence of Israel.[31] One could infer that the paucity of archaeological data that would cor- roborate the presence of Judah in the hill country prior to the widespread upheaval in the late thirteenth to early twelfth centuries BCE is complemented by the apparent absence of Judah from the materials that make up what appear to be the oldest traditions of the book of Judges (i.e., excluding the accounts of Othniel, possibly Jephthah [cf. 10:9] and Samson [where the first and last instances of Samson's empowering in Judah occur; cf. 13:25 and 15:9-13 with 18:12]). Yet, the presence in 1:1-20 of materials not found elsewhere in the Hebrew Bible (e.g., 1:4-7, 8, 16, 17, 18) suggests that the tribe of Judah was ancient enough to have had their own premonarchical traditions about the conquest of their land. These considerations notwithstanding, what is of greatest import for intimating the rhetorical situation of Judges' compilation/redaction (its *Sitz im Text*) is Judah's priority of mention, prolixity of description and divine endorsement in 1:1-20. The negative characterization of Benjamin in the succeeding verse (1:21) presents a stark contrast to the generally positive portrayal of the achievements of Judah.

The absence from the body of Judges of a bona fide tribal account about a hero from Judah (that of 3:7-11 being too schematic to qualify) could be accounted for on the rhetorical level as reflecting an inten- tional reticence to speak too extensively about an individual hero of Judah who might outshine the one implicitly being endorsed, namely, David. Perhaps this is why the account of 3:7-11 reuses Othniel's name (cf. 1:13-14) instead of introducing the name of some other hero from the tribal lore of Judah. The account of Othniel offers a heroic counterpart to David whose antiquity does more to enhance David's

[31] Boling, *Judges* (1975), p. 64.

legitimacy as a Judahite than to compete with it. It is probably not accidental that the idealized portrayal of Othniel is followed immediately by the mixed portrayal of the Benjaminite deliverer Ehud, who, having triumphed over Israel's enemies by means of deception, allows the idols at the border of the land to remain standing (3:12-30).

The closing episode of Judges 19-21 portrays an internecine rivalry between Benjamin and the other tribes of Israel with Judah leading them (cf. 20:18). This context, by its contrasting characterizations of Gibeah (the later birthplace and capital of Saul) and Bethlehem (the later birthplace of David), reflects a situation of intense rivalry between most of tribal Israel (with Judah at its head) and the tribe of Benjamin.

From a consideration of the three contexts in Judges where Judah and Benjamin are presented together, it may be inferred that Judges was arranged so as to address a situation of political rivalry between Judah and Benjamin. Moreover, the presentation of this rivalry in the context of accounts that concern other tribes suggests that it may have been those tribes whose endorsement the Judges compiler/redactor was seeking for Judah. This would explain why, in both instances when the tribes of Israel are portrayed as asking YHWH to choose which of them should lead—even when that means leading them against Benjamin— YHWH chooses Judah (1:1-2; 20:18). This portrayal in Judges presents a situation parallel to that depicted in 2 Samuel 1-4. In both contexts it is Judah that is portrayed as the preeminent rival of Benjamin. One may also note how, in 2 Sam. 3:17, the elders of Israel (presumably non-Benjaminite; cf. 3:19) do not share the Benjaminite's antagonism toward the Judahite (Davidic) monarchy.[32]

§2.2.3. *Present Cultic Disorders.* The prevalence of concern in Judges for cultic aberrations suggests that the rhetorical situation of Judges' compilation/redaction was one in which Israel may have been guilty of such. The narrative framework of Judges is often explicit in describing Israel's idolatry (2:11-13, 17, 19; 3:6b, 7, 12a; 4:1a; 6:1a; 8:33; 10:6, 16; 13:1a). There are frequent evidences of the idolatrous practices in the land (3:19, 26; 6:25-26, 28-32; 9:4, 6, 27; 17:3-5, 14, 17-18, 20, 30-31). Several times YHWH or a prophet rebukes Israel for cultic disloyalty (2:1-3; 6:7-10; 10:11-14). This prevalence of concern

---

[32] Indeed, the role of the elders from the time of the judges, with elders of Israel making all national policy decisions, was still shared with the king during the reign of David from Hebron (cf. Judg. 11:11 with 2 Sam. 3:17, 21; 5:1, 3) and Jerusalem (2 Sam. 17:4, 15; cf. 19:11). After the governmental reforms of Solomon (1 Kgs 4:1-19), the elders seem to serve only as executives of the king, offering him counsel but unable to surmount his authority (cf. 1 Kgs 12:6, 8, 13).

with instances of cultic infidelity needs to be weighed against the implied neglect of the tabernacle of YHWH at Shiloh (18:31; note the need to give directions to Shiloh, in 21:19) and of the ark of God, mentioned only once in the book (20:27b). Indeed, the fact that the tabernacle and ark are not mentioned in Judges until the final chapters suggests that the neglect of YHWH's cult was of concern to the compiler/redactor (and may suggest that he/she had ties to the cult of YHWH). It seems fair to infer from this concern with Israel's cultic aberrations and relative neglect of the cult of YHWH that Judges was compiled/redacted to address a situation in which a similar situation prevailed.

I have already observed that a situation of disregard for the ark of YHWH and his tabernacle prevailed in Israel throughout the period of the judges and reached its nadir during the rule of Saul. This is evident in Saul's neglect of the ark of God (MT 1 Sam. 14:18, notwithstanding), his slaughter of YHWH's priesthood and his relegation of Nob, the city of priests, to the sanctions of holy war (1 Sam. 22:6-19). Moreover, during the period that David ruled Judah from Hebron (2 Sam. 1-4), the ark remained in the Judahite city of Kiriath-Jearim. The problem of the decentralized cult ostensibly continued in Israel all the time that the tribes of Israel remained disjoined. Only after David came to rule all Israel (2 Sam. 5:1-5) did he subsequently bring the ark to Jerusalem (2 Sam. 6) and ostensibly restore the ark to its former role as the central cult object of the tribes of Israel.

§2.2.4. *Present Social Injustices.* The book of Judges bristles with descriptions of social injustice. What is notable about the arrangement of these examples is that their severity generally increases as the book progresses. Whereas at the beginning of Judges, the account of Othniel is free of descriptions of injustice, Ehud, Jael and Samson are portrayed as achieving victory over foreigners by violent betrayals of the social mores of hospitality incumbent upon guest or host.[33] The accounts of Gideon/Abimelech and Jephthah, however, cite instances of violence committed against Israelite cities, an Israelite woman and a tribe of Israel.[34] Yet, the most vile series of social injustices in Judges

---

[33] Cf. D. J. Chalcraft's sociological justification of the inhospitality of Jael, Ehud and Samson as having been directed against outsiders, enemies of Israel ("Deviance and Legitimate Action in the Book of Judges", in *The Bible in Three Dimensions: Essays in Celebration of Forty Years of Biblical Studies in the University of Sheffield* [D. J. A. Clines, S. E. Fowl and S. E. Porter (eds.), JSOTS 87, Sheffield, 1990], pp. 182-88).

[34] Cf. Chalcraft, "Deviance" (1990), pp. 189-96.

is that which begins with the Gibeahites' abduction and rape of the Levite's concubine (Judg. 19-21). This violence escalates into an internecine civil war between the Benjaminites, who unjustly harbour the criminals, and the other tribes. Ironically, the threat of Benjamin's extinction prompts the other tribes to compromise their obligation to carry out the sanctions of holy war against Benjamin and induces them both to wipe out the citizens of the Israelite town of Jabesh-Gilead (save 400 virgins) and to abduct a further 200 Israelite virgins from Shiloh. Thus, the account of Judges 19-21 combines into one account all the types of violence done within Israel that one finds distributed between the accounts of Gideon/Abimelech and Jephthah (i.e., violence done against an Israelite woman, Israelite cities and a tribe of Israel).

The fact that the most concentrated series of social injustices in Judges is said to have been precipitated by violence at Gibeah (cf. 19:30; 20:3b, 6b, 10b, 12-13a) implicitly undermines the legitimacy of Gibeah's later claim of a right to rule Israel. Since the book of Judges ends with this portrayal of the negative repercussions for Israel of the Gibeahite offence, one could infer that the negative repercussions of the rule of Israel from Gibeah under Saul was the ostensible motivating concern at the time of Judges' compilation/redaction. This ostensible concern generally comports with that appropriate to the situation of civil war between the Benjaminite loyalists of Saul and the Judahite loyalists of David described in 2 Samuel 1-4.

§2.3. Beneficence toward Old Order Loyalists

Were it the purpose of 1 Samuel 1-2 Samuel 4 to engender a loyalty to the dynasty of David in those who had once been loyalists of the dynasty of Saul, one would expect to find in David's portrayal indications of his innocence of any possible violent usurpation of the throne and of a conciliatory spirit toward old order loyalists. In Judges, this would be evident in a rhetorical repudiation of violent usurpation and in a policy that pays honour to loyalists of the former dynasty.[35]

§2.3.1. *Importance of Demonstrating Innocence of Usurpation*. The closing summary of Judg. 9:56-57, which credits God with vindicating Gideon's sons by carrying out retribution against their assassins,

---

[35] Later, David's kindness to Mephibosheth because he was a descendant of Jonathan would further characterize David as beneficent toward even the offspring of Saul's dynasty (2 Sam. 9) and would further exonerate David of possible charges of ill will toward the house of Saul. However, this portrayal offers no analogy to the ostensible situation of Judges' compilation, despite the notice of 2 Sam. 4:4 that Jonathan was survived by his son Mephibosheth.

suggests that the Judges compiler/redactor found a special satisfaction in the fact that God so guided events as to bring about justice by fulfilling Jotham's curse (cf. 9:7-20). Indeed, this is probably the main point of Judg. 8:33–9:57 (cf. 8:35). This incident is unique in the book of Judges but finds a possible analogy to two portrayals of David in 2 Samuel 1–4 where he acts justly against those who perpetrated violence against the house of Saul. The first concerns David executing the Amalekite who confessed to having assassinated Saul (2 Sam. 1:1-16; especially 1:15-16). The second such incident is that in which David carried out justice against the assassins of a member of Saul's house, Ish-Bosheth (2 Sam. 4:1-12; especially 4:9-12). It is probably no accident that these two accounts frame 2 Samuel 1–4, whose intervening materials describe the just actions of David during the period of rivalry between the houses of Saul and David after Saul's death.

The intervening accounts of David's lamentation over Saul's death (2 Sam. 1:17-27) and of his declaration of innocence and lamentation over Abner's death (2 Sam. 3:22-39; especially 3:28, 33-34) are recessed within the framing accounts of David's execution of the assassins and, in turn, frame two pairs of corresponding accounts: that of David's rule from Hebron (2 Sam. 2:1-7; 3:1-5) and that of the attempts of Abner to bring reconciliation between the warring tribes of Benjamin and Judah (2:8-32; 3:6-21)—the latter arranged in a panelled structure.

A		David's just retaliation against an assassin of a member of the house of Saul (Saul) 1:1-16
B		David's lament over the death of Saul and Jonathan in battle 1:17-27
	C	David's accession to rule Judah from Hebron 2:1-7
	D	Abner's first attempt to end the rivalry between the tribes of Benjamin and Judah 2:8-32
	C^i	David's increase during his rule of Judah from Hebron 3:1-5
	D^i	Abner's second attempt to end the rivalry between the tribes of Benjamin and Judah 3:6-21
B^i		David's lament over the death of Abner at the hands of Joab 3:22-39 (especially 3:33-34)
A^i		David's just retaliation against the assassins of a member of the house of Saul (Ish-Bosheth) 4:1-12

The impression given is that the primary rhetorical concern of the compiler of 2 Samuel 1–4 was that of vindicating David against possible allegations that he had usurped the throne by violence.

§2.3.2. *Importance of Honouring Jabesh-Gilead*. Perhaps the most loyal subjects of Saul's house, besides the Benjaminites, were the citizens of Jabesh-Gilead, whom Saul had rescued from Nahash the Ammonite (1 Sam. 10:27c*–11:11). Inasmuch as the Jabesh-Gileadites never afterward forsook their loyalty to the house of Saul (cf. 1 Sam. 31:11-13; 2 Sam. 21:12b), one may interpret David's commendation of the Jabesh-Gileadites' loyalty to Saul (2 Sam. 2:4b-6) as designed to woo them as formerly devoted Saulide loyalists to the side of David (2 Sam. 2:7). Indeed, since, according to the books of Samuel, Saul remains unvindicated until David executes the Amalekite who ostensibly assassinated him (2 Sam. 1:1-16; cf. 1 Sam. 31:4-5) and the heroism of Saul and his sons remains unsung until David lauds it (2 Sam. 1:17-27), David himself is portrayed as a loyalist of Saul.[36] Thus, both the Jabesh-Gileadites and David are portrayed as honouring Saul and his sons after their deaths at the hands of the Philistines.

The compiler/redactor of Judges intimates an awareness of the role that Jabesh-Gilead played in the political situation of 2 Samuel 1-4. In Judg. 21:8-14, Jabesh-Gilead is portrayed as a passive abetter of Gibeah's offence, since its citizens were not willing to join with Judah and the other tribes in executing YHWH's sanctions against Gibeah— later to become Saul's capital. Thus, to the extent that the citizens of Jabesh-Gilead in the period of the judges did not join with Israel under the leadership of Judah, they were culpable before YHWH. This scenario finds analogy in the situation intimated by 2 Samuel 1-4 in which David implicitly summons the Jabesh-Gileadites to transfer their loyalty from Saul to him as the rightful claimant to the throne of Israel: "Now, let your hands be strong, and become sons of valour, for your lord, Saul, is dead and it is me that the house of Judah has anointed as king over them" (2 Sam. 2:7).

§2.4. *Evidence of Divine Favour*
Certain contrasting parallels between Judges and 1 Samuel 1– 2 Samuel 4 suggest that both were designed to demonstrate how divine favour is a *sine qua non* of legitimate leadership in Israel. These parallels entail contrasting portrayals of YHWH's election and empowering of leaders and contrasting portrayals of leaders making inquiry of YHWH.

---

[36] Later, David would further venerate the bones of Saul and Jonathan by returning them from Jabesh-Gilead to be buried in the tomb of their father Kish at Zela in Benjamin (2 Sam. 21:11-14), though this would not have been a concern in the ostensible situation of Judges' compilation.

§2.4.1. *Importance of* YHWH's *Election and Empowering*. Much of the imagery used in Judges to portray YHWH's election and empowering of deliverers is used again in 1 Samuel in the contrasting characterizations of Saul and David. When Saul was anointed to be king by YHWH's prophet Samuel (1 Sam. 10:1), the spirit of God/YHWH empowered him for his royal role (10:6aα, 10bα; 11:6aα)—alluding to Judges' cycle-motif element D2a as it appears in the Samson account (Judg. 14:6aα, 19aα; 15:14bα)—yet later Saul was rejected from being king (13:13-14; 15:22-23; 16:1a) and, like Samson, suffered the departure of YHWH's empowering spirit (16:14a). Immediately after the spirit of God/YHWH departed from Saul, an evil spirit from God/YHWH came to torment him (1 Sam. 16:14b-15, 23; 18:10; 19:9)—alluding to Judg. 9:23 as indicating God's intention to bring retribution against Abimelech. Saul was never again empowered by God's spirit except on the occasion when God was intervening to protect David (1 Sam. 19:23). When David was anointed to become king by Samuel the prophet (1 Sam. 16:1b, 11-13aαβ), the spirit of God/YHWH empowered him for his royal role (16:13aγ)—again alluding to the form of Judges' cycle-motif element D2a used in the Samson account—though, in this instance, the narrator added that YHWH's spirit would remain with David "from that day on" (16:13aδ). Thus, unlike Saul's election and empowering, David's election and empowering were never to be revoked.

Besides the parallel images in the books of Samuel that contrast portrayals of Saul and David with respect to YHWH's election and empowering, there is an implicit parallel between the contrasting characterizations of Gibeah/Benjamin and Judah, in Judges, and Saul and David, in the books of Samuel. On both occasions in Judges when Israel inquires of YHWH which tribe should lead the confederation into holy war, Judah is chosen by YHWH—once in each of the framing sections of the book (1:1-2; 20:18). No other tribe attains this distinction in Judges. It is apparent, then, that the Judges compiler/redactor was attempting to cast Judah in a prominent role in relation to the other tribes of Israel. It is probably not coincidental that the compiler/redactor ends the book of Judges with an account in which Judah is portrayed as divinely elected to execute justice against the tribe of Benjamin for crimes committed at Gibeah (later the birthplace and capital of Saul). Once this negative portrayal of the citizens of Gibeah is viewed against the generally positive portrayal of the hospitality of a

Bethlehemite in 19:3-9 (the later birthplace of David), one senses from the Judges parallels that the compiler/redactor of Judges may have been foreshadowing the later contrasting circumstances of Saul and David.

Moreover, if one weighs the negative characterization of the tribe of Benjamin, who both failed to conquer Jerusalem/Jebus (1:21; 19:10, 11) yet protected the perpetrators of the atrocity at Gibeah (20:13), against the positive portrayal of the tribe of Judah, as divinely elect both to lead the conquest against foreigners in the land (1:1-2; once, conquering Jerusalem [1:8]) and to lead YHWH's war against the Benjaminites (20:18), one gains the impression that the ideal of kingship being endorsed in Judg. 17:6 and 21:25 is not an ideal in sympathy with the Benjaminite dynasty of Saul but with the Judahite dynasty of David. Indeed, the very rebuilding of Gibeah, implicit at the end of the account (21:23b), is portrayed as violating a policy espoused by Deut. 13:17. As an implicit condemnation of the later capital city of Saul (1 Sam. 10:26; 13:15; 15:34; 23:19; 26:1), this negative characterization of Gibeah in Judg. 19-21 could hardly be more scathing.

§2.4.2. *Importance of the Ability to Make Direct Inquiry of YHWH.* Three times in the Gideon account, Gideon asks YHWH for signs to confirm YHWH's commission to engage in battle (Judg. 6:17, 36-37, 39), and, whether or not these requests imply that Gideon lacked confidence in YHWH, YHWH performs the signs. Further, YHWH even offers Gideon a sign, that of the dream and its interpretation, to assuage his fear (Judg. 7:10-15a). Perhaps the closest analogies in the books of Samuel to these portrayals in Judges may be found in YHWH's confirmation of requests for prebattle confirming signs from Jonathan (1 Sam. 13:23–14:12) and David (23:2-4; 30:3-8). The depictions of YHWH's willingness to encourage Gideon, Jonathan and David by confirming signs evidences YHWH's favour upon these individuals whom he had chosen to work deliverance for Israel.

Contrariwise, the fact that, after a sequence of inquiries of YHWH about war with Benjamin (Judg. 20:18, 23, 26-28), the tribes of Israel break off the sequence to find a scapegoat of their own choosing (21:2-9) redounds to the negative characterization of the tribes who preferred to ignore YHWH rather than to reduce Benjamin to extinction. Concomitantly, it is perhaps not by accident that YHWH is portrayed as not answering Saul's prebattle requests for a confirming sign (1 Sam. 14:37; 28:6; cf. 28:15) except to condemn him by the omen of Samuel's ghost (1 Sam. 28:12-25). YHWH's silence condemns Saul, particularly because it is seen to result from Saul's acts of rashness and disobedience in matters of warfare (cf. 1 Sam. 10:8; 13:2-14; 14:24, 36-37, 44-46; 28:4-19). Thus, through the contrasting portrayals of YHWH's silence versus responsiveness to requests for confirming signs, both Judges and the books of Samuel demonstrate YHWH's contrasting dispositions toward the disobedient tribes versus Gideon, in Judges, or Saul versus Jonathan and David, in the books of Samuel.

Moreover, in Judges, the descriptions of tribes asking YHWH which of them should lead Israel into battle are similarly worded (cf. Judg. 1:1-2; 20:18). This similarity corroborates the view that they were designed to serve as a framing device in the book. Each description pertains to the question of tribal priority in the engagement of battle. YHWH's approval of Judah, in each instance, evidences that Judah was his favoured agent. Perhaps it was by design that the wording of these inquiries bears some resemblance to that of David asking whether he should go up to Judah (2 Sam. 2:1a). Once again, YHWH responds by approving Judah and the result of David's going up is that David is anointed king of Judah at Hebron (2 Sam. 2:4). One may infer that the portrayals of characters making inquiry of YHWH was another means for positively or negatively characterizing those whom YHWH had approved or rejected, respectively, and that in Judges and 1 Samuel 1–2 Samuel 4 these play a significant role in characterizing the rivalry between the dynasties of David and Saul.

B. THE RHETORICAL SITUATION IMPLIED BY JUDGES' RECENCY, CHRONOLOGICAL REFERENCES AND HISTORICAL SCOPE

While it is not my task to define the actual historical situation of Judges' compilation/redaction, there are a number of historical aspects of the book that help one to form judgements about the rhetorical intention of Judges. These include such considerations as Judges' implied recency, its chronological references and its historical scope.

§1. Implied Recency in Judges' Polemic Rehearsal of History

One possible strategy for the establishment of a new world order is the demonstration of a persistent downward trend of history leading up to the present moment of crisis. In biblical literature, this could be termed a "polemic rehearsal of history". Through a polemic rehearsal of history, the rhetorician would impress upon his/her readers the inevitability of the continuance of a worsening trend unless it were averted through the establishment of the new order. It would be important to such a rhetorical strategy that the polemic rehearsal of history lead right up to the present moment and that it account for present undesirable circumstances. Otherwise, there would be no justification for claiming that the time for change had come.

Such is the rhetorical aim of the historical prologue of Joshua's covenant renewal at Shechem (Josh. 24:2-13), a rehearsal showing YHWH's control of events leading up to Israel's presence in the land at Shechem (in ostensible fulfilment of Deut. 11:26-32).[37] There are also indications in the book of Judges that the period of the judges was being polemicized from the vantage point of a crisis situation in the subsequent period of the monarchy.[38]

In an Egyptian account of the chaos that preceded the accession of Setnakhte (ca. 1184-1182 BCE), Harris Papyrus no. 1 states that "the land of Egypt had been overthrown with every man being his own standard of right (*s nb m ᶜk3.f*) since they had no leader (*r ḥry*) for many years in the times of others".[39] Not only does this furnish an ideological parallel to Judges' motif A1b (איש הישר בעיניו יעשה)— indeed, Eg. *ᶜk3* 'straightness, right'[40] conveys a similar notion of conformity to norm as does BH ישר 'straightness, uprightness, right'—but it serves the interests of polemicizing the present order as a result of the previous period of history. Commenting upon this Egyptian parallel to Judg. 17:6b, 21:25b, Greenspahn said,

> Although this exact statement is unique, Egyptian pharaohs often contrast their own effectiveness with that which had come before. Nor can there be any question as to the beneficiary of this contrast. Ramses IV, in whose reign the text was written, describes his father subsequently as *r ḥry* (lit., "chief mouth"), precisely what we have been told Egypt lacked during its anarchic period. Moreover, the establishment of authority under Setnakhte is said to have restored the land to "its normal condition" (*sḥr.f mtry*). The text thus tells us that the coming of the twentieth dynasty brought to a close the period

---

[37] In the New Testament, too, there are examples of the polemic rehearsal of history used inferentially to rebuke a present-day audience (e.g., Stephen's last speech before being stoned). Jesus' reference to two instances of YHWH's rejection of Israel in Luke 4 does not constitute a rehearsal of history, though it does serve the same rhetorical function as Stephen's rehearsal: to rebuke faithless ethnocentrics (i.e., the citizens of Nazareth) for adhering to a pattern (not a trend) of faithlessness in Israel.

[38] Cf. Brettler: "The redactor of Judges uses the reconstructed past ... to legitimize the present order" ("Judges" [1989], p. 418).

[39] Harris Papyrus 1:75, 2-4. See W. Erichsen, *Papyrus Harris I* (Bibliotheca Aegyptiaca V, Brussels, 1933), p. 91; F. E. Greenspahn, "An Egyptian Parallel to Judg 17:6 and 21:25", *JBL* 101 (1982), pp. 129-30.

[40] Cf. A. Erman and H. Grapow, *Wörterbuch der ägyptischen Sprache* (5 vols., Leipzig, 1926-1931), vol. 1 (1926), pp. 233-35; A. H. Gardiner, "A Pharonic Encomium (II)", *JEA* 42 (1956), p. 15.

of chaos when, in the absence of strong leadership, each person had acted according to his own standards.[41]

Although no case should be made for direct dependence between Judges and this Egyptian parallel, two points may be made in regard to its similarity to Judg. 17:6b and 21:25b: (1) the characterization of the preceding period as one in which everyone followed his/her own standard of right is a negative characterization,[42] and (2) it is claimed that the contemporary dynasty is the source of order that has brought an end to the anarchy of the preceding period. Other examples of negative characterization by Egyptian pharaohs against preceding periods, dynasties or pharonic rules are extant.[43]

The four references in Judges 17–21 to the existence of a king in Israel (17:6a; 18:1a; 19:1a; 21:25a) and their implicit idealization of the king as the solution to the problems that characterized the period of the judges reflect the primary rhetorical concern of the Judges compiler/redactor. It is because of the monarchy motif that one can perceive the compiler/redactor's monarchist viewpoint. Since the monarchy and A1b motifs most likely reflect the compiler/redactor's innovations to the accounts of 17:1-5, 7-13; 18:1b-31 and 19:1b-21:24, whatever other interests may have motivated the composition of these accounts, the compiler/redactor thus made them subservient to his/her aim to contrast Israel's covenant disobedience before the monarchy with what Israel's conduct became, or should have become, under the monarchy.

Were the only consideration the fact that Judges contrasts the period of the judges with that of the monarchy, several kings might qualify as

---

[41] Greenspahn, "Egyptian Parallel" (1982), p. 130.

[42] This analogy may be used beside the argument, from biblical usage, that to do right in one's own eyes (Deut. 12:8) is, *ipso facto*, not to do right in the eyes of YHWH (Deut. 6:18a; 12:25b, 28b; 13:19b; 21:9b; cf., antithetically, 4:25b; 9:18b; 17:2b; 31:29b). Judges motifs A1a and A1b should be interpreted in the light of their usage in Deuteronomy, contra Boling, who said that Judg. 21:25 meant, "the time had arrived once again for every man to do what was right before Yahweh without any sacral political apparatus to get in the way" (*Judges* [1975], p. 293); also contra Dumbrell, "Those Days" (1983), pp. 29-33. Both Boling and Dumbrell interpret Judg. 17:6 and 21:25 as essentially positive characterizations because they attempt to read these verses from an exilic perspective and apart from the covenantal ideology of Deuteronomy that is basic to the rhetorical strategy of Judges.

[43] Cf. R. O. Falkner, "Egypt: From the Inception of the Nineteenth Dynasty to the Death of Ramses III", in *The Cambridge Ancient History*, vol. II/2 (Cambridge, 3d edn, 1975), pp. 240-41; J. H. Breasted, *Ancient Records of Egypt* (5 vols., Chicago, 1906-1907), vol. 2, §§305, 307, 845, 883; vol. 3, §§103, 270.

a contemporary of the compiler/redactor (and be the object of his/her monarchical idealization). The weight of probability, however, rests upon the likelihood that the negative characterization of a preceding period—indeed, its very periodization—reflects the view that there has been a recent turning point in the world order. Thus, from the vantage point of the compiler/redactor of Judges, it would be the emergence of a new monarchical order that represents this crucial event. The fact that the account of Judg. 19:1b–21:24 contrasts the inhospitality of Gibeah, the ancestral home and birthplace of Saul, with the hospitality of Bethlehem, the ancestral home and birthplace of David, seems hardly superfluous to the compiler/redactor's strategy of monarchical idealization. Several scholars have regarded the negative characterization of Gibeah in Judges 19 as an implicit anti-Saulide polemic, and, from this, some have surmised that the account of 19:1b–21:24 was composed during the reign of David.[44]

Certainly, for those who knew the status of Gibeah under Saul, there would have been, in the account of Judg. 19:1b–21:24, an implicit but pointed polemicizing of Saul's dynasty. Saul is thus implicated for having set up as Israel's capital a city that had been the epicentre of a breech of covenant justice that incriminated both Benjamin (for defending Gibeah against Israel) and Israel (for allowing Benjamin to rebuild it). Since the restoration of the Benjaminites to their allotment and the rebuilding of the Benjaminite cities (including Gibeah) are both the final points made in the narrative of 19:1b–21:24 and the culminating focus of rhetorical concern, the narrative achieves its maximal relevance if read as having been intended to address a situation in which the legitimacy of Gibeah's status (or, indeed, the status of Benjamin) should be called into question.

§2. *Chronological References in Judges*

A number of chronological references, mostly contained in framing sections of the book (Judg. 1:1-36; 17–21), indicate an ostensible period of composition (at least for the framework) during the period of David's seven-year rule from Hebron. First, in Judg. 1:21b the narrator remarks parenthetically, וישב היבוסי את־בני בנימין בירושלם עד היום הזה, which would indicate that, from the narrator's vantage point,

---

[44] So B.-Z. Luria, "The Account of the Outrage at Gibeah", in *Studies in the Book of Judges* (PIBS 10, Jerusalem, 1966), pp. 463-94 [Hebrew]; J. Unterman, "The Literary Influence of 'the Binding of Isaac' (Genesis 22) on 'the Outrage at Gibeah' (Judges 19)", *HAR* 4 (1980), pp. 161 n. 2, 162, 164-65.

David had not yet captured and annexed Jerusalem as his royal city (cf. 2 Sam. 5:6-10).[45]

Second, Judg. 18:31b indicates that the Danites worshipped the idols of Micah during the remainder of the period in which the "shrine of God" was at Shiloh (ostensibly, while the ark was also there, ca. 1399–1104 BCE).[46] Judges 18:31b does not therefore imply that the Danites ceased to worship Micah's idols when God's shrine had ceased to be at Shiloh. However, because Judg. 18:31b contrasts the illegitimacy of Dan's shrine with the legitimacy of Shiloh's shrine without mentioning Jerusalem, at least from the vantage point of the note's implied author, either: (1) Jerusalem had not yet been established as Israel's only legitimate cult centre or (2) the question of the legitimacy of Dan's worship of Micah's idols was no longer relevant by the time Jerusalem had become established as Israel's cult centre for, by then, Dan no longer

---

[45] On the rhetorical level, the parenthetical clarification of 'Jebus' in 19:10, היא ירושלם "that is, Jerusalem", may indicate only that, at the time of Judges' compilation/redaction, the city was no longer called Jebus by Israelites. It is not impossible that the toponymic equivalent 'Jerusalem' constitutes a later scribal clarification, suggesting that 'Jerusalem' became the name of the city only after its conquest and annexation by David, but Judg. 1:8, where Judah is said to have attacked 'Jerusalem' (not 'Jebus'), suggests that 'Jerusalem' was in some places original to Judges' framing narrative (cf. 1:7). In any case, the reference in 1:21 states that the city was in Jebusite hands at the time of its author (and, ostensibly, the compiler/redactor) regardless of its designation.

[46] This chronology follows the internal chronology of the Hebrew Bible as a system constructed by its compilers/redactors (cf. 1 Kgs 6:1; Exod. 40:17; Num. 10:11; 14:33-34; Josh. 14:7, 10, 15b; 18:1-2; so E. H. Merrill, *Kingdom of Priests: A History of Old Testament Israel* [Grand Rapids, 1987], pp. 146-51, 176-78). It is not here intended to serve as a system of absolute dating.

It warrants mention that Y. Aharoni attributed a small amount of Late Bronze pottery found by the Danish expedition at Shiloh to an early Israelite settlement, which persuaded him that Israel's settlement had begun already in the thirteenth or even fourteenth C. BCE (Y. Aharoni, "The Ten Thousands of Ephraim and the Thousands of Manasseh", in *Eretz Shomron: The Thirtieth Archaeological Convention, September 1972* [J. Aviram (ed.), Jerusalem, 1973], p. 46 [Hebrew]; Y. Aharoni, V. Fritz and A. Kempinski, "Excavations at Tel Masos (Khirbet el-Meshâsh): Preliminary Report on the Second Season, 1974", *TA* 2 [1975], p. 121). However, I. Finkelstein concluded from a gap in occupation at the end of Late Bronze Shiloh that there is no justification for dating Israel's arrival there as early as the thirteenth C. BCE (I. Finkelstein, S. Bunimovitz, Z. Lederman in I. Finkelstein [ed.], "Excavations at Shiloh 1981-1984: Preliminary Report", *TA* 12 [1985], pp. 165, 167). Finkelstein averred that, in the Late Bronze Age, Shiloh was occupied solely by a cult place whose devotees did not live at the site but apparently brought offerings to the cult site from elsewhere (Finkelstein-Bunimovitz-Lederman, "Shiloh 1981-84" [1985], pp. 166-67) and that, in Iron Age I, Shiloh's twelve-dunam site flourished as a cult centre for supratribal Israel for the fifty years from the end of the twelfth to the mid-eleventh centuries BCE (pp. 168-69).

worshipped Micah's idols.[47] In any case, the implicit claim of Judg. 18:31b that Shiloh was the only legitimate cult centre of Israel in the period of the judges is made independently of any claim that Jerusalem would later become the successor of Shiloh as Israel's cult centre. The point is that Judg. 18:31b does not attest any 'deuteronomistic' notion of the cultic succession from Shiloh to Jerusalem.

In this connection, Jer. 7:12, 14 and Ps. 78:59-64 offer valuable indications as to the vantage point of the ostensible author of Judg. 18:31b. Both Jer. 7:12, 14 and Ps. 78:59-64 make the claim that Jerusalem's temple was the legitimate successor of the central shrine status of Shiloh's temple and that this succession took place after the abandonment of Shiloh as a cult centre. Against the once-prevailing scholarly view that Jer. 7:12, 14 refers to the Philistine destruction of the Shiloh sanctuary (ca. 1050 BCE),[48] R. A. Pearce adduced archaeological and historical arguments that these verses refer primarily to the disaster fomented by the Assyrians in either 734 or 722 BCE and only secondarily include a reference to the earlier disaster.[49] Soggin likewise concurred that excavations at Shiloh had not yet

---

[47] While it is true that, when Jeroboam I is portrayed as establishing calf idols at Dan and Bethel, there is no mention of Levitical priests at Dan (1 Kgs 12:28-30), it is only with reference to the high places of Bethel (1 Kgs 12:32) and the towns of Samaria (1 Kgs 13:32) that Jeroboam I is said to have appointed non-Levitical priests (cf. 1 Kgs 12:31-32; 13:32-34). Thus, the possibility remains that Levitical priests had been in attendance at the shrine of Dan until 931 BCE.

[48] The view that Shiloh was captured by the Philistines in the eleventh C. BCE was supported by: M. Noth, *Geschichte Israels* (Göttingen, 2d edn, 1954), p. 154, ET: *The History of Israel* (London, 2d edn, 1960), pp. 166-67; O. Eissfeldt, "Silo und Jerusalem", in *Volume du Congrès, Strasbourg 1956* (SVT 4, Leiden, 1957), p. 138; R. de Vaux, *Les Institutions de l'Ancien Testament* (2 vols., Paris, 1958, 1960), vol. 2, p. 136, ET: *Ancient Israel: Its Life and Institutions* (J. McHugh [trans.], 2 vols., London, 2d edn, 1965), vol. 2, p. 304. Exegetical arguments were supported by the archaeological dating of the destruction of Shiloh House A (later designated Hall 306) to the mid-eleventh C. BCE by H. Kjaer ("The Excavation of Shiloh", *JPOS* 10 [1930], p. 105) and W. F. Albright ("New Israelite and Pre-Israelite Sites: The Spring Trip of 1929", *BASOR* 35 [1929], p. 4).

[49] R. A. Pearce, "Shiloh and Jer. vii 12, 14 & 15", *VT* 23 (1973), pp. 105, 107-8. Previous dissent from the view that Jer. 7:12, 14 refers primarily to the Philistine destruction of Shiloh had been expressed by F. Buhl, *Geographie des alten Palästina* (Leipzig, 1896), p. 178; J. N. Schofield, "Judges", in *Peake's Commentary on the Bible* (H. H. Rowley and M. Black [eds.], London, 1962), p. 314 §269g; and M.-L. Buhl in M.-L. Buhl and S. Holm-Nielsen, *Shiloh: The Danish Excavations at Tall Sailun, Palestine, in 1926, 1929, 1932 & 1963* (Copenhagen, 1969), p. 34, who redated the destruction of Shiloh House A to the eighth C. BCE.

revealed a destruction in the late eleventh century BCE.[50] However, J. Day has demonstrated, on archaeological and exegetical grounds, that an eleventh-century BCE date for the destruction of the sanctuary at Shiloh is most likely.[51] First, Buhl's assessment of the archaeological evidence supporting an eighth-century BCE date for the destruction of Shiloh House A (Hall 306) was founded upon an erroneous typology of the large collared-rim jars (which are analogous to collared-rim jars of Early Iron I sites)[52] and, furthermore, failed to note that none of the other undisturbed sherds found in the debris belong to Early Iron II.[53] Second, given the 'deuteronomistic' assumption of Jer. 7:12, 14 that there was only one legitimate place where YHWH caused his name to dwell (cf. Deut. 12:14) and that, after the tenth century BCE, this place was Jerusalem, the reference in Jer. 7:12 to the ruin of Shiloh's sanctuary, the place where YHWH "at first" caused his name to dwell, can refer only to one prior to the establishment of Jerusalem's temple in the tenth century.[54] On the literary level, Ps. 78:59-64 comports with the description of the Philistine victory at Aphek (1 Sam. 4) and further supports the view that Shiloh's loss of national cult status took place in the eleventh century BCE, not the eighth.[55] Inasmuch as the narrator in Judg. 18:31b does not express any awareness of a cultic succession from Shiloh to Jerusalem, his/her vantage point could be (and ostensibly was) later than the eleventh-century BCE date for the ruin of Shiloh's shrine but before the establishment of Jerusalem's temple as Israel's cultic centre.[56] In any case, Shiloh's destruction (ca. 1050 BCE)

---

[50] J. A. Soggin, *Judges: A Commentary* (J. Bowden [trans.], OTL, London, 2d edn, 1987), pp. 276-77.

[51] J. Day, "The Destruction of the Shiloh Sanctuary and Jeremiah vii 12, 14", in *Studies in the Historical Books of the Old Testament* (J. A. Emerton [ed.], SVT 30, Leiden, 1979), pp. 87-94.

[52] Cf. R. Amiran, *Ancient Pottery of the Holy Land* (Jerusalem, 1969), pp. 232-33, pl. 77.

[53] Y. Shiloh, "[Review:] Marie-Louise Buhl and S. Holm-Nielsen, *Shiloh: The Danish Excavations at Tall Sailun, Palestine, in 1926, 1929, 1932 & 1963.* Copenhagen, 1969", *IEJ* 21 (1971), pp. 67-69; idem, "The Camp at Shiloh", in *Eretz Shomron: The Thirtieth Archaeological Convention September 1972* (J. Aviram [ed.], Jerusalem, 1973), pp. 10-18 [Hebrew]; cf. Day, "Shiloh Sanctuary" (1979), p. 88, n. 9. Finkelstein and Bunimovitz concurred that the Iron Age I settlement of Shiloh was destroyed by a conflagration (Finkelstein–Bunimovitz–Lederman, "Shiloh 1981-84" [1985], pp. 127, 133, 173-74) that Albright and Kjaer had earlier attributed to the Philistines (pp. 126, 130, 173).

[54] Day, "Shiloh Sanctuary" (1979), pp. 88-90.

[55] Day, "Shiloh Sanctuary" (1979), pp. 90-91.

[56] Cf. Day, "Shiloh Sanctuary" (1979), pp. 93-94.

was not necessarily contemporaneous with the capture of the ark (ca. 1104 BCE), nor is this association claimed in 1 Samuel 4 (or Jer. 7:12, 14; or Ps. 78:59-64), nor is it the concern of Judg. 18:31.

Third, Judg. 18:30b says that Jonathan son of Gershom, the son of Moses, and his sons were priests for the tribe of Dan "until the day of the exile of the land" (עַד־יוֹם גְּלוֹת הָאָרֶץ), which some have understood to refer to the conquests of Tiglath-pileser III (734–732 BCE, cf. 2 Kgs 15:29) or Shalmanezer V (722 BCE, cf. 2 Kgs 17:5-6).[57] Thus, Judg. 18:30b either constitutes a post-eighth–century BCE gloss or indicates that Judges 17–18/21 was appended after the Assyrian conquest. Others have understood 18:30b, read in relation to the period in which God's temple remained at Shiloh (18:31), to refer to some earlier captivity of the land, such as that following the Philistine defeat of Israel at Ebenezer (1 Sam. 4:11).[58] In either case, because Judg. 18:30b lacks further specificity, it could be assessed in the light of the aggregate of historical references within Judges that indicate the ostensible situation of its compilation/redaction.[59] The otherwise consistent concern of Judges' framework with the ostensible religious–political situation after the fall of Shiloh but antecedent to David's capture of Jerusalem and the proximity of this qualification of the duration of the Danite Levitical priesthood (18:30b) with a reference to the duration of Dan's use of Micah's idols (18:31)—both references reflecting concern with events of the preceding story and both thereby providing historical background that enhances the rhetoric of Judges—might lead one to conclude that the deportation to which 18:30b refers was one associated

---

[57] For a date of 734 BCE, see Rashi; Moore, *Judges* (1895), p. 400; Soggin, *Judges* (2d edn, 1987), p. 269; Gray, *Judges* (2d edn, 1986), p. 347. For a date of 722/1 BCE, see Boling, *Judges* (1975), p. 266; Dumbrell ("Those Days" [1983], p. 29). For either date, see E. Sellin, *Einleitung in das Alte Testament* (Evangelisch-theologische Bibliothek, Leipzig, 1910; 3d edn, 1920), ET of 3d edn: *Introduction to the Old Testament* (W. Montgomery [trans.], London, 1923), p. 105; J. D. Martin, *The Book of Judges* (CBC, Cambridge, 1975), p. 196. Cf. B. G. Webb, *The Book of the Judges: An Integrated Reading* (JSOTS 46, Sheffield, 1987), pp. 202-3 nn. 47-49.

[58] So Keil, *Richter* (1863), ET: *Judges* (1868), repr. edn, vol. 2, pp. 439-42; Burney, *Judges* (2d edn, 1920), p. 415. Comparing גלה כבוד מישראל in 1 Sam. 4:21-22, so also E. W. Hengstenberg, *Beiträge zur Einleitung in das Alte Testament* (3 vols., Berlin, 1831-1839), vol. 2, pp. 153ff.; and H. A. C. Hävernick, *Handbuch der historische-kritischen Einleitung in das Alte Testament* (3 vols., Erlangen, 1839-1856), vol. 2, part 1, p. 109.

[59] Unless the use of גלה in the expression גלות הארץ can be unequivocally shown to have limited reference to the Assyrian captivity, comparison with גלות ירושלם in Jer. 1:3 (e.g., Pearce, "Shiloh" [1973], p. 107 n. 1) should perhaps not control the interpretation of the referent of גלה in Judg. 18:31.

with the Philistine incursion into Ephraim after Saul's defeat upon Mount Gilboa even though there is no other record of such a deportation to Philistia.[60]

All the foregoing interpretations of Judg. 18:30b depend upon the text: עד־יום גלות הארץ (so the MT and all ancient versions). However, the interpretation that Judg. 18:30b refers to the Philistine defeat of Israel at Aphek/Ebenezer (1 Sam. 4:11) has also given rise to the suggestion that גלות הארץ is a textual corruption from original גל(ו)ת הארו(ן) "exile of the ark" (cf. 1 Sam. 4:11).[61] Support for this emendation comes from a number of considerations: scribal, historical and rhetorical.[62] The emendation, if accepted, supports the view that Judg. 18:30b refers to the Philistine defeat of Israel at Ebenezer (1 Sam. 4:11) and, concomitantly, removes the only textual evidence in Judges by which one should infer that the book's final form postdates the Assyrian exile of 734 or 722 BCE.

Fourth, the parenthetical reference describing the location of Shiloh as אשר מצפונה לבית־אל מזרחה השמש למסלה העלה מבית־אל שכמה ומנגב ללבונה (Judg. 21:19aβγb) gives directions to this sanctuary as though it were a place whose location was, at the time of writing, no longer well known in Israel. The most likely explanation for this would be that these directions were written many years subsequent to the decline of Shiloh, which came about after the Philistine capture of the ark at the

---

[60] The historical reference in 18:30b to the "deportation of the land" ("land" = "inhabitants" by metonymy) could be read as a comment that refers not to the termination of the Danite Levitical priesthood (as, e.g., Boling, *Judges* [1975], p. 266; Martin, *Judges* [1975], p. 196) but to the fact that this priesthood continued after the Philistines had "deported [the inhabitants of] the land" of Ephraim. Thus, it would be to the experience of the compiler/redactor and those whom he/she was addressing that this notice of exile would appeal, not to the experience of Danites in the north who remained unaffected by the Philistine conquest.

[61] So K. F. Houbigant, *Biblia Hebraica cum notis criticis et versione latina ad notas criticas facta* ... (4 vols., Paris, 1753), ad loc. on the basis of Qimḥi's view that "the capture of the land" referred to the capture of the ark and its sequel; F. Bleek, *Einleitung in das Alte Testament* (J. F. Bleek and A. Kamphausen [eds.], J. Wellhausen [rev.], Berlin, 4th edn, 1878), p. 349; E. Riehm, *Einleitung in das Alte Testament* (A. Brandt [rev. and ed.], 2 vols., Halle, 1889–1890), vol. 1, p. 396; Burney, *Judges* (2d edn, 1920), pp. 414-15, 435; J. J. Slotki, *Judges* (1950), p. 152; J. Blenkinsopp, *Gibeon and Israel: The Role of Gibeon and the Gibeonites in the Political and Religious History of Early Israel* (SOTSMS 2, Cambridge, 1972), p. 77; R. van der Hart, "The Camp of Dan and the Camp of Yahweh", *VT* 25 (1975), pp. 722-23 n. 7. Ralbag, however, understood Judg. 18:30b to refer to the exile of the Danites alone in the time of Jabin king of Canaan (cf. Judg. 4:2-3).

[62] See the note to Judg. 18:30b in the appendix.

battle of Aphek/Ebenezer (ca. 1104 BCE, cf. 1 Sam. 4:1-11; 6:1; 7:1-2).[63] On the other hand, 1 Kgs 11:29 refers to Ahijah of Shiloh, indicating that the city was inhabited (reinhabited) during the reign of Solomon. The ignorance of Shiloh's geographical location implied by Judg. 21:19aβγb suggests further that this parenthetical note was composed sometime during the interval of Shiloh's eclipse as an occupied site, namely, between its decline as a cult centre and destruction by the Philistines (ca. 1104–1050 BCE), on the one hand, and its rehabitation under Solomon (after ca. 970 BCE), on the other. Thus, both the parenthetical note of Judg. 21:19aβγb and the parenthetical note of Judg. 18:31b seemingly antedate the establishment of Jerusalem's temple as Israel's cult centre.

§3. *The Historical Scope of Judges and the Argument of 1 Samuel 12*

The fact that the historical period treated by the book of Judges spans that from the death of Joshua (Judg. 1:1; cf. 2:6) to the death of Samson, at the time when the Philistines ruled Israel (13:1; 15:11; cf. 13:5), indicates something about the concern of the Judges compiler/redactor. I have already described the extent of rhetorical interdependence between Judges and 1 Samuel 1–2 Samuel 4. Since the

---

[63] The decline of Shiloh as the cult centre of Israel after ca. 1104 BCE may have antedated the final destruction of that city by some fifty years (cf. Jer. 7:12, 14; 26:6, 9; so Merrill, *Kingdom* [1987], p. 176 n. 83). The city of Shiloh, if referred to during the period of David's rule from Hebron (ca. 1011–1004 BCE), would already have been in ruins for almost fifty years. Following its capture ca. 1104 BCE, the ark allegedly stayed seven months among the Philistines (1 Sam. 6:1) and a further twenty years at Abinadab's house at Kiriath-Jearim (1 Sam. 7:12; i.e., until ca. 1084 BCE). The close of this twenty-year interval ostensibly coincided with the incident of Samuel's rallying of Israel at Mizpah (1 Sam. 7:3-6), whereupon, after the ensuing battle (1 Sam. 7:7-11), the Philistines were so demoralized as not to be able immediately to counterattack Israelite territory (7:12-13), though later they would. After the battle at Mizpah, the ark would have remained at Abinadab's house a further 107 years until the incident of 2 Sam. 6:1-11, 12-23, seven years before the close of David's reign (ca. 977 BCE; so Merrill, *Kingdom* [1987], pp. 242-48). On this occasion, in 2 Sam. 6:23, the narrator substantiates David's assessment of YHWH's rejection of Saul's dynasty (2 Sam. 6:21) by noting Michal's life-long barrenness. The emphasis here is not upon the longevity of her barrenness thereafter, but upon the fact that her lifelong barrenness was proof of YHWH's rejection of Saul's dynasty.

It would be inconsistent with internal biblical chronology to presume, on the basis of 1 Sam. 7:2, that the ark was at Kiriath-Jearim for only twenty years prior to its removal to Jerusalem (*pace* Day, "Shiloh Sanctuary" [1979], p. 92). Twenty years is insufficient time for the intervening incidents leading to the ark's removal to Jerusalem (even within David's lifetime), and, in any case, 1 Sam. 7:2 makes reference neither to the incident of 2 Sam. 6:1-11, 12-23 nor to Jerusalem.

historical period covered by Judges spans that between what closes the book of Joshua and what begins 1 Samuel 1–2 Samuel 4, one could infer either that Judges and 1 Samuel 1–2 Samuel 4 were together designed to resume the account of Israel's history after the book of Joshua or that Joshua was written after Judges to fill in the gap left between the death of Moses, recorded at the end of Deuteronomy (cf. Josh. 1:1), and the death of Joshua, described at the beginning of Judges (cf. Judg. 1:1). However, since most of the phraseological links between Judg. 1:1–3:6 and Joshua 15, 17 and 24 indicate that the form of the material in Judges is secondary,[64] it seems best to infer that the form of Joshua that included chs. 15, 17 and 24 preceded the form of Judges that included 1:1–3:6 (even if one infers that both books' compilations/redactions represent the work of one individual).

What is perhaps of greatest importance for determining the ostensible situation of Judges' compilation/redaction, however, is the relationship between the historical scope of Judges and the argument of 1 Samuel 12. The argument ascribed to Samuel in 1 Samuel 12 refers to the situations of national oppression and the Israelite deliverers described in the book of Judges as though they were well-known events and persons in the story world of Samuel. Thus, underlying Samuel's argument in the story world seems to be an assumption that there was, by the time of Samuel's address, an awareness of the presentation of events and persons now described in Judges. Samuel ostensibly refers not just to the period of the judges but to a form of its presentation that appears in the literary traditions now contained in the book of Judges.[65] Hence, if there were an intended correspondence between the circumstances portrayed in 1 Sam. 12:9-15 that accompanied Saul's rise to kingship and the circumstances described in the book of Judges, Samuel's argument in 1 Samuel 12—especially its periodization of leaders from the death of Joshua to the rise of Saul—becomes very

---

[64] Cf. the redaction-critical notes in the appendix on the relationship between Judg. 1:10-11 and Josh. 15:13-15, between Judg. 1:12-15 and Josh. 15:16-19, between Judg. 1:20 and Josh. 15:13-14, between Judg. 1:21 and Josh. 15:63, between Judg. 1:27-29 and Josh. 16:10; 17:11-13, between Judg. 2:6-9 and Josh. 24:28-31, and between Judg. 3:3 and Josh. 13:3b-5.

[65] Of course, rhetorical inferences of this kind, which are based upon situations alleged in the story world, are not necessarily historically valid, especially if one assumes with Noth that the speech of 1 Sam. 12 was composed by a seventh-century BCE deuteronomistic editor and was anachronistically put into the mouth of Samuel in the same way that the chapter itself was inserted into the midst of the traditional stories that now constitute 1 Samuel.

important for determining the ostensible situation of Judges' compilation/redaction because it suggests that Samuel knew a form of Judges that included stories about Jerubbaal, *Barak, Jephthah and *Samson and about Israel being rescued from Sisera, the Philistines and the king of Moab.[66] The character Samuel thus implicitly draws parallels between Israel's situation under Saul and that under the judges described in the book of Judges. The name "Barak" corresponds to "he sold them into the hand of Sisera" (1 Sam. 12:9bα) and alludes to Judges 4–5. The name "Samson" corresponds to "into the hands of the Philistines" (1 Sam. 12:9bβ) and alludes to Judges 13–16 (unless to Judg. 3:31). Mention of the "king of Moab" (1 Sam. 12:9bγ) alludes to Judg. 3:12-30 (i.e., to Ehud). References to Jerubbaal and Jephthah allude to Judges 6–8(9) and 10:6–12:7, respectively. Thus represented by these allusive references in 1 Sam. 12:9, 11 are the following deliverer accounts of the book of Judges:

Enemy	Deliverer	Book of Judges
King of Moab		3:12-30
(Philistines)		(3:31)
Sisera	*Barak	4–5
	Jerubbaal(/Gideon)	*6–8
	Jephthah	10:6–12:7
Philistines	*Samson	13–16

None of the judgeships contained in the book of Judges for which enemies are unspecified (namely, those of Tola, Jair, Ibzan, Elon, Abdon) is mentioned in 1 Sam. 12:9, 11. Concomitantly, all the judgeships of Judges for which enemies are identified are here represented except one: that of Othniel of Judah. Indeed, the latter seems a significant omission in the light of the pro-Judahite (pro-Davidic) stance of both Judges and 1 Samuel 1–2 Samuel 4. When this is considered together with the fact that 1 Sam. 12:9-11 uses two formulae from Judges' cyclical framework (i.e., "sold them into the hand of ..." and "they cried out to YHWH"), it appears that, for the author of 1 Sam. 12:9-15, some form of the materials constituting the body of the

---

[66] *Pace* P. K. McCarter on 1 Sam. 12:11, read "Barak" with the OG and Psht (*I Samuel: A New Translation with Introduction, Notes and Commentary* [AB 8, Garden City, N.Y., 1980], p. 211). The consonantal form of MT "Bedan", in Aramaic script בדן, probably derives secondarily from the similar form ברק. Many now restore "Barak" (so the RSV; NEB; NIV; REB; NRSV; J. Day, "Bedan, Abdon or Barak in 1 Samuel xii 11?", *VT* 43 [1993], pp. 461-64; cf. BDB, p. 96a 1; D. T. Tsumura, "Bedan, a Copyist's Error?", *VT* 45 [1995], pp. 122-23). Also in 1 Sam. 12:11 read "Samson" with the LXX-AII MSS and Psht; the MT and LXX-AI,B-group have "Samuel".

book of Judges was already in existence—a form that attested at least these two formulae of Judges' cyclical framework.

Upon further consideration, one might infer alternatively that Judges was designed with the purpose of anticipating the argument of 1 Samuel 12. The fact that most of the foreign rulers in Judges (i.e., Adoni-Bezek, Eglon, Sisera [in proxy for Jabin], the two kings of Midian, the king of Ammon and the rulers of the Philistines) are subjected to satirization implicitly mocks the people's resolve in 1 Samuel 8–12 to secure for themselves "a king like those of other nations" (1 Sam. 8:5, 20; cf. 8:6, 10, 18; 10:19; 12:1-2, 12-13, 17, 19).[67] It does not seem fortuitous that, after referring to the preceding judges, Samuel's ultimatum in 1 Sam. 12:14-15 echoes the ultimatum made by Jotham (Judg. 9:16, 19-20) at the coronation of Abimelech (Judg. 9:6; cf. 1 Sam. 11:14-15). Samuel's analogous ultimatum thus forebodes disastrous consequences for Israel under the leadership of the king of their choosing (1 Sam. 12:1-2, 12-13; cf. 10:24-27 with 11:12-15).

However, the contrast between Judges' overall characterization of the premonarchical period as one in which "everyone did what was right in one's own eyes" also sets up the irony that, in 1 Samuel 12, Samuel rebukes Israel for "the evil [they] did in the eyes of YHWH when [they] asked for a king" (1 Sam. 12:17; cf. 12:19, 20).[68] If, in Judges, the monarchy is presented as an ideal, why in 1 Samuel is Israel rebuked for seeking to establish a monarchy? Evidently, it was not monarchy in principle that was being held up to scorn by Samuel but the kind of king that Israel was seeking, namely, "a king like those of other nations". Hence, while Samuel's ultimatum in 1 Sam. 12:14-15 rightly forebodes the problems that Israel would experience under the leadership of a king of their choosing (1 Sam. 12:1-2, 12-13; cf. 10:24), this should not be taken to imply a rejection of monarchy in principle. Yet, the idealized monarchy that the book of Judges sets in contrast to the period of the judges would have to be realized in a king who, in contrast to the king of Israel's choosing (i.e., a king like those of other nations), would be a king of YHWH's choosing (i.e., a king

---

[67] Judges does not assess monarchy *per se* as an unacceptable institution except when foreign models of kingship are presented. Cf. Webb, *Judges* (1987), pp. 119, 128 (of Cushan-Rishathaim), 130 (of Eglon), 138 (of Jabin), 159 (of Gideon/Abimelech); G. E. Gebrandt, *Kingship according to the Deuteronomistic History* (SBLDS 87, Atlanta, Ga., 1986), pp. 171-86.

[68] YHWH's supernatural confirmation of Samuel's assessment in 1 Sam. 12:18 shows that, on this negative evaluation of Israel's request for a king, Samuel and YHWH concur.

whose heart is right in the eyes of YHWH [cf. 1 Sam. 16:1-13; 1 Sam. 9:1-2, 15-17 and 10:1, 24 notwithstanding]).

C. CONCLUSION

From a consideration of the matters discussed above, it would appear that the ostensible religious–political situation of Judges' compilation/ redaction best aligns with that described in 2 Samuel 1–4. The strategy of Judges, which entails an anti-Benjaminite but pro-Judahite rhetoric of entrapment, implicitly spurns the monarchy of Saul but idealizes the monarchy of David. The *Sitz im Text* implied by Judges' many points of narrative analogy to 1 Samuel leads to the inference that the Judges compiler/redactor shaped his/her materials on the basis of portrayals of Saul in 1 Samuel ostensibly to address the situation that succeeded that of 1 Samuel (i.e., that of 2 Sam. 1–4). Judges' monarchicalism aligns with the ostensible situation of 2 Samuel 1–4 as to: (1) national ideals such as those of holy-warrior, intertribal covenant loyalty, the centrality of YHWH's cult and social justice; (2) the portrayal of a present crisis precipitated by a Philistine threat, by rivalry between Judah and Benjamin, by cultic disorders and by social injustices; (3) the portrayal of the lack or presence of beneficence in regard to usurpation or showing honour to old order loyalists and (4) demonstrations of YHWH's favour, whether by his election and empowering or by one's being able to inquire of YHWH. Finally, the implied recency, chronological references and historical scope of Judges likewise seem to suggest that its ostensible rhetorical situation was that described in 2 Samuel 1–4.

CONCLUSION

The four lines of evidence offered in the chapters of this study lead to the conclusion that the rhetorical purpose of the book of Judges is ostensibly to enjoin its readers to endorse a divinely appointed Judahite king who, in contrast to foreign kings or non-Judahite deliverers in Israel, upholds such deuteronomic ideals as the need to expel foreigners from the land and the need to maintain intertribal loyalty to YHWH's cult and his regulations concerning social justice.

As described in chapter 1, the tribal–political and deuteronomic schemata offer two lines of evidence that support Judges' rhetorical purpose. The south-to-north tribal–political schema of Prologue-A (1:1–2:5) sets forth the preeminence of Judah among the tribes of Israel. The twelve-part religious–historical cycle, introduced in Prologue-B (2:6–3:6), recurs among all the deliverer accounts and provides the framework for the main plot of each. The aggregate structure of Judges' cycle-motif schema is bifurcated to distinguish the portrayal of Israel's alienation (using deuteronomic terminology) from that of their restoration to blessing in the land (stated without deuteronomic language). Together, the double prologues emphasize the need to expel foreigners from the land and the need to maintain intertribal loyalty to YHWH's cult. As an evaluative framework, the cycle-motif portrays Israel's departure from YHWH in deuteronomic language perhaps to emphasize Israel's covenant waywardness. YHWH's restoration of Israel to blessing in the land is expressed without deuteronomic language in terms that show YHWH exceeding his obligations to the covenant.

Chapter 2 presented a new approach to Judges' plot-based narratives in which plot-structure and characterization are made to form the basis for observations about rhetorical concerns in the deliverer accounts and the accounts of the double dénouement. In that chapter appeared a new approach to plot-structure analysis that gives preeminent consideration to plot-levels (rather than scenes) as the controlling criterion for determining the rhetoric of plot-based narratives. I noted the evaluative role that rhetorical devices such as satire and narrative analogy play in portraying characters—noting especially the mixed characterization of non-Judahite deliverers and tribes, the negative characterization of foreign kings and the glorification of YHWH. In the plot-based narratives, there is also a regular pattern of escalated parallelism in the characterization of the deliverers and of the people whom they deliver. The pervasiveness of this pattern among the deliverer accounts suggests that it was the Judges compiler/redactor who designed this scheme in order to demonstrate the similarity of character foibles between non-Judahite tribes and their deliverers.

Chapter 3 discussed Judges' strategy of entrapment and its function to foreshadow evaluatively, through narrative analogy, the portrayals of Saul and David in 1 Samuel. The controlling purpose of the book of Judges may be discerned from the relationship between its tribal-political and deuteronomic schemata and the monarchist perspective disclosed in the double dénouement (in 17:6; 18:1; 19:1; 21:25). Moreover, the compiler/redactor's concern for cult, evident in Judges' belated interest in the ark, Levites and Shiloh, alerts the reader to Israel's deficit of attention to cult throughout the period. Such matters, first revealed in Judges double dénouement, engage the reader in a reassessment of standards of leadership by which those of the period of the judges measured themselves and prompt the reader to see the need for a new order. The compiler/redactor's patterning of events and phraseology to furnish analogies to the portrayals of Saul in 1 Samuel serves an implicitly polemic function. Most of Judges' proleptic narrative analogies offer negative characterizations of Saul and furnish evidence that the Judges compiler/redactor was concerned not only to elevate the status of the Davidic monarchy, through a portrayal of Judah's preeminence, but also to lower the status of the Saulide monarchy.

Finally, in chapter 4, I noted the relationship between the 'ostensible' situation of Judges' compilation/redaction, its chronology and its historical scope, on the one hand, and the ostensible situation of 2 Samuel 1-4, on the other. It seems that the Judges compiler/redactor shaped the book's stories to create a deuteronomic idealization of Judahite kingship so that the intended readers would endorse the dynasty of David over that of Saul. Since the Judges compiler/redactor combined both traditional hero stories and covenant ideals borrowed from deuteronomic traditions to construct a standard of kingship for Israel, it appears that the compiler/redactor's rhetorical purpose in Judges was probably to furnish a background by which to evaluate, through tribal-political and deuteronomic foreshadowing, the portrayals of Saul and David in 1 Samuel 1-2 Samuel 4.

COMPILATION, REDACTION AND THE RHETORIC OF JUDGES

In view of the evidence for different regional dialects of Hebrew between various episodes of Judges, it would be naive to suggest that the book was composed throughout by a single author, unless, of course, one were able to demonstrate that this divergence was intended to serve some rhetorical function such as verisimilitude (cf. Judg. 12:6).[1] Regional dialectal divergencies in Hebrew are well attested from Hebrew epigraphic texts.[2] Therefore, an empirical approach must

---

[1] Such regional dialectal characteristics, evident in inscriptions and BH, may include:

Grammatical Form	Northern Cisjordan	Southern Cisjordan
Different orthography = different consonantal articulation(?)	תנה 'recount' Ug. ṯny; Judg. 5:11 יְתַנּוּ; 11:40 לְתַנּוֹת (cf. Ps. 8:2?)	שׁנה 'repeat, recount'
Diphthong contraction *ay > N Heb.: [ê] / S Heb.: [ay]	לֵשֶׁם (< לַיְשָׁם*) nom. loc. Josh. 19:47 (EHO, pp. 57, 68; cf. pp. 19, 42 n. 20)	לַיִשׁ nom. loc. (Egypt. lus(i) ca. 1850–1825 BCE) Judg. 8:7, 14, 27, 29
Prose relative pron.	‑שֶׁ, ‑שָׁ, ‑שְׁ Judg. 6:17; 7:12; 8:26; (poetic in 5:7 שַׁקַּמְתִּי [2x] but 5:27 בַּאֲשֶׁר) elsewhere always poetic (GKC, §§36, 138a n. 1; BDB, p. 979a)	אֲשֶׁר
m. pl. termination	‑ין Judg. 5:10 מִדִּין 'carpets, blankets' (GKC, §87e)	‑ים
abs. f. sg ending N Heb.: ‑ת / S Heb.: ‑ה	שׁת 'year' Phoen., Moab., N Israel (cf. EHO, p. 36 #6)	שְׁנַת 'year' (cstr)
2 f. sg pron.	אַתִּי Judg. 17:2; cf. 1 Kgs 14:2; 2 Kgs 4:16, 23; 8:1; Jer. 4:30; Ezek. 36:13 (GKC, §32h; BDB, p. 61b)	אַתְּ
2 f. sg perf.	‑תִּי Judg. 5:7 קַמְתִּי; 17:2 אָלִיתִי (not L); Ruth 3:3, (GKC, §44h n.; EHO, p. 67)	‑תְּ

[2] Cf. W. R. Garr, *Dialect Geography of Syria–Palestine, 1000–586 B.C.E.* (Philadelphia, 1985). Garr's possible evidences for regional dialectal distinctions in first M. BCE Hebrew epigraphic texts include: (1) *ay > N Heb. [ê] / S Heb. [ay] (pp. 38–39,

begin by recognizing in Judges the presence of different regional traditions that have been integrated into its composite form. Some type of compilation, therefore, must be at the heart of the literary structure of Judges. For the literary critic the difficulty is to account for the historical and rhetorical processes by which these traditions came into their present literary framework.[3]

When one discusses theories of the process of Judges' formation, one needs to distinguish 'compilation' from 'redaction'. The former refers only to a process of selecting excerpts from sources and of combining and arranging them into a coherent framework through prefacing, interposing and appending newly composed material. However, to argue that Judges was initially compiled in this way

---

41); similarly, m. pl. cstr ending *-ay > N Heb. [-ê] / S Heb. [-ay], e.g., בני (Arad 16:5; 49:1, 2, etc.), ספרי (Lach. 6:4), דברי (Lach. 6:5) (p. 93); similarly, particle of non-existence אין attested only in S Heb. [ʾayn] (Silwan B 1; Lach. 4:5, 7/8 [+ pron. suff.]; Arad 40:13/14 [partially restored; + pron. suff.]), whereas N Heb. would have been *[ʾên] (p. 115); (2) aphaeresis of א in S Heb. in the first M. BCE[?], e.g., נחנו (Lach. 4:10/11) (pp. 51-52; cf. GKC, §§19h, 32d; BDB, p. 59b; but אנחנו in Judg. 9:28; 19:18); (3) only the 1 c. sg pron. אני is attested and only in S Heb.[?] (Arad 88:1; Beit Lei A 1 [partly restored]) (p. 79; so Judg. 1:3; 6:10; 8:23; 13:11; 15:3; never אנכי in Judges; cf. GKC, §32c-e; BDB, pp. 58b-59b); (4) only the prose relative pron. אשר and only in S Heb. (Lach. 3:5; Arad 40:5, etc.; Mur. 17 A 2; Silwan B 1.2; etc.)[?] (pp. 85-87) (there is no evidence of the relative pron. -ש in Heb. epigraphic texts; evidence of אשר from a broken Samaria text [N Heb.] is uncertain, pace E. L. Sukenik, "Note on a Fragment of an Israelite Stele Found at Samaria", PEFQS [1936], p. 156); (5) the abs. f. sg ending in N Heb.: -ת / S Heb.: -ה [?], e.g., שת < *šant 'year' Phoen. (KAI 19:5; 52:4; 60:1; etc.), Moab. (Mesha 2:8), N Heb. (Sam. Ost., passim; העשרת [hā-ʿśīrīt] 'the tenth' (Sam. Ost. 1:1, etc.); but S Heb.: רבעת [rĕbīʿīt] 'fourth' (Lach. 29) (pp. 93-94); (6) the 2 m. sg possessive suff. ך- attached to pl. nouns and some preps., e.g., לפניך (Arad 7:6), אליך (Mur. 17 A 2), אלהיך (Lach. 6:12/13); but יכה- only from S Heb., e.g., אלהיכה (Beit Lei A 1) (p. 106). Some of these dialectal distinctions, evident in Hebrew by the first M. BCE, may already have featured in the latter half of the second M. BCE. Indeed, the linguistically isolative effects of physical geography, religion and politics should be expected to have begun exerting influence immediately after the Israelite settlement (cf. Garr, Dialect Geography [1985], pp. 232-34). Garr refers to ירחו (Gezer Calendar, lines 1.1.2) as an example of the old nom. case ending in N Heb.[?] (Dialect Geography [1985], p. 63), though this view may founder if the ו here designates final -ô, which cannot denote the old nom. case ending (contra GKC, §90k,o) as can final -û. Moreover, there is still a dispute whether the Gezer Calendar is a Heb. (so EHO) or a Phoen. inscription.

[3] Despite the difficulty of establishing empirical criteria for a diachronic (historical-critical) analysis of composite texts such as the book of Judges, problems of literary coherence that arise through this approach actually serve to complicate and thereby enhance the interpretative task for the rhetorical critic. Cf. S. Boorer, "The Importance of a Diachronic Approach: The Case of Genesis–Kings", CBQ 51 (1989), pp. 195-208.

implies nothing about the duration of time over which the process took place, the number of possible reworkings of the developing whole or the aims of various individuals under whom the book may have been processed. The term 'redaction' seems better reserved for describing only those alleged systematic reworkings of the book subsequent to its initial compilation.

That Judges is the product of the compilation of originally separate tribal traditions is, in this study, taken to be self-evident. That it bears evidence that it was also subjected to one or more subsequent redactions and that remnant traces of the layers of these redactions may be critically isolated is a proposition that has been disputed among scholars. I shall first consider various literary theories that have been applied to Judges and then shall consider how a diachronic approach to Judges may serve the interests of understanding Judges' rhetoric.

A. DIACHRONIC APPROACHES TO JUDGES' LITERARY FORMATION

The ensuing discussion outlines various scholarly studies of the formation of Judges under two categories of the diachronic approach, source criticism and redaction criticism, the latter being affected by three significant advances: (1) M. Noth's hypothesis of a 'Deuteronomistic History' spanning Joshua–Kings, (2) W. Richter's discovery of a '*Retterbuch*' underlying Judges and (3) R. Smend's perception of other 'deuteronomists' in Judges (chiefly DtrN, the '*nomistiche*' deuteronomist). First, I shall consider the models of Judges' compilation/redaction proposed by the source critics, for these furnished the foundation for the later redaction-critical studies.

§1. *Source Criticism and Judges*

Among the first significant studies of Judges to discover and describe the composite character of the book were the commentaries by G. L. Studer and E. Bertheau.[4] Their approach to Judges was representative of an emerging consensus among scholars as to the growth of the entire biblical tradition by a process of accretion of originally separate literary sources. Yet the consensus was by no means fully formed in this period. Many commentaries appeared contemporaneously that,

---

[4] G. L. Studer, *Das Buch der Richter grammatisch und historisch erklärt* (Bern, 1835); E. Bertheau, *Das Buch der Richter und Ruth* (KEHAT 6, F. Hitzig et al. [eds.], Leipzig, 1845).

while thoroughly analytical, nevertheless resisted treating Judges as part of a comprehensive source-critical theory.[5]

Among the more important examples of works that did support the source-critical agenda should be mentioned the introductions or commentaries by A. Kuenen, J. Wellhausen, R. Kittel, K. Budde, G. F. Moore and C. F. Burney. Although these scholars sometimes disagreed on the dating and provenance of alleged sources, they nevertheless achieved a remarkable degree of consensus as to the compilational/ redactional stratigraphy of Judges.

A. Kuenen proposed three major phases in the compositional history of Judges: a predeuteronomic, a deuteronomic and a post-deuteronomic.[6] Concerning the postdeuteronomic stratum, Kuenen wrote that Judg. 1:1–2:5 (which presents a very old account of the conquest) and 17–18; 19–21 (which contain old narratives that were later thoroughly interpolated) were united with the deuteronomic version of 2:6–16:31 only by Judges' final redactor.

Kuenen's deuteronomic Judges allegedly held all the stories now contained in Judg. 2:6–16:31 except that of Shamgar (3:31), including those of Othniel and the 'minor' judges. He inferred that the work of the deuteronomic redactor in Judges (i.e., Judg. 2:6–16:31; 1 Sam. 7–12) and the promonarchical sections of Samuel resembled the work of the pre-exilic redactor (Rd^1) in the books of Kings. He argued that 2:6–3:6 was, as a whole, the work of the deuteronomic redactor of the book.

Kuenen argued that the predeuteronomic book of Judges lacked accounts for Othniel and Shamgar and counted both Abimelech and Samuel among the twelve judges. This book, which lacked the deuteronomic historical cycle, arranged the hero stories as a series of portraits anachronistically designed to show YHWH's preservation of a unified Israel.

Kuenen's stratification was typical of early source-critical approaches to Judges before there was a scholarly consensus in regard

---

[5] E.g., C. F. Keil and Franz Delitzsch, *Biblischer Commentar über das Alten Testament*, vol. II/1, *Josua, Richter und Ruth*, by C. F. Keil (Leipzig, 1863); J. Bachmann, *Das Buch der Richter: Mit besonderer Rücksicht auf die Geschichte seiner Auslegung und kirchlichen Verwendung*, vol. 1 (Berlin, 1868-1869).

[6] A. Kuenen, *Historisch-critisch Onderzoek naar het Onstaan en de Verzameling van de Boeken des Ouden Verbonds* (3 vols., Leiden, 1861-1865; Amsterdam, 2d edn, 1885-1892), GT: *Historisch-kritische Einleitung in die Bücher des Alten Testaments* (T. Weber [trans.], 3 vols., Leipzig, 1887-1892), vol. 1, pp. 88-100. Kuenen was the first to propose that, on analogy with the book of Judges, the books of Kings were originally compiled in the pre-exilic period and underwent final redaction only during the exile.

to the place of Judges relative to the formation of the biblical traditions as a whole. With the publication of J. Wellhausen's monumental theory of the history of Israelite literary traditions there was subsequently an agreed upon standard for the critical treatment of Judges.[7]

Wellhausen took the established position that Judg. 1:1–2:5 and 17–21 were postdeuteronomistic additions to a traditional deuteronomistic core in 2:6–16:31 and that the deuteronomistic work was the product of an antimonarchical redaction that had been foisted upon the predeuteronomistic, promonarchical traditions in the book. Wellhausen later affirmed that the predeuteronomistic book of Judges, contained entirely within Judg. 2:6–16:31, existed as a complete book containing the accounts of Ehud, Deborah–Barak, Gideon (Abimelech), Jephthah and Samson.[8] To this predeuteronomistic version Wellhausen ascribed

---

[7] J. Wellhausen, *Geschichte Israels*, vol 1 (Berlin, 1878); republished as *Prolegomena zur Geschichte Israels* (Berlin, 2d edn, 1883).

[8] J. Wellhausen, *Die Composition des Hexateuchs und der historischen Bücher des Alten Testaments* (Berlin, 2d edn, 1889), p. 219. Wellhausen also recognized, chiefly within the stories of Deborah–Barak and Gideon, vestiges of divergent old traditions that antedated even the predeuteronomistic compilation. He alleged that the old Deborah–Barak account was made up of two accounts: a primary poetic account (ch. 5) and a secondary prose account (ch. 4) that distinguished themselves from each other in five ways (pp. 220-23):

Judges 5	Judges 4
1. Sisera was head king (5:19-20, 28-29, 30 [שָׁלָל[2] > שֵׁגָל consort, queen])	Sisera was Jabin's army commander (4:2bα)—though Sisera had his own residence (4:2bβ) and Jabin of Hazor had already appeared (Josh. 11)
2. Anonymous enemies disturbed road and village in the land (5:6-8)	Canaanites severely oppressed the Israelites (4:2-3)
3. All tribes adjacent to the Jezreel Plain took part—Ephraim, Benjamin, Machir, Zebulun, Naphtali, Issachar—the latter, the tribe of both Deborah and Barak (5:15)	Only Zebulun and Naphtali were summoned to battle (4:6b, 10)—Barak deriving from Kadesh of Naphtali (4:6a)
4. Sisera collapsed to the ground after Jael struck him with a hammer blow (5:26-27)	Sisera died motionlessly in his sleep after a tent peg was driven through his temple (4:21)
5. Deborah's husband's name is not mentioned	Deborah's husband, Lappidoth (4:4; cf. Exod. 20:18, where a derivate of the same root is used), reminds one (midrashically) of Barak's fear-filled character

Wellhausen saw, likewise in the Gideon story, a combining of two originally distinct accounts that antedated even the predeuteronomistic redaction of Judges (pp. 223-28).

Israel's introductory cries to YHWH (3:15; 4:3; 6:6), the conclusions that record how enemy oppressors (Moab, Canaan, Midian, Ammon) were humbled under Israel's hand (3:30; 4:[23-]24; 8:28; 11:33) and the generalization "all Israel" to describe events that often concerned only this or that tribe.

Wellhausen averred that it was not the deuteronomistic editor who first combined the separate tribal accounts into a coherent work. Among the stories, the deuteronomistic editor allegedly added only that of Othniel (3:7-11). Otherwise, he[/she] was responsible for: (1) Judges' chronological schema, (2) its religiously pragmatic framework (including the introduction of 2:6-3:6) and (3) the moral confrontations of 6:1, 7-10 and 10:6-16.[9] Against Bertheau, Wellhausen argued that Judg. 6:2-6 could not be attributed to the deuteronomist since these verses were presupposed by 6:11-13. The introduction of Judg. 2:6-10, which should be connected with Josh. 24:28-31, allegedly did not presuppose Judg. 1:1-2:5 (of which ch. 1 shows no trace of deuteronomistic redaction).[10]

According to Wellhausen, the accounts of the six 'minor' judges (including Shamgar) were later added to the original six major judges only so as to make a full dozen.[11] For this he found corroboration in the supposition that the 70 years required for five of their judgeships (23 + 22 + 7 + 10 + 8 = 70 [cf. Judg. 10:2, 3; 12:9, 11, 14], no figure being given for Shamgar) was designed to coincide with the 71 years of Israel's five interregnal oppressions (8 + 18 + 20 + 7 + 18 = 71 [cf. Judg. 3:8, 14; 4:3; 6:1; 10:8]).[12] Wellhausen argued that Judges 17-18, which was previously thought to reflect two originally separate accounts of the manufacture of cult objects, was simply an old account corrupted by various glosses (e.g., 17:2-4; 18:14-18 *passim*; 18:30).[13] Judges 19-21, which present a centralized Israel, derive from very different concerns from those presented in the rest of the book.[14] The clause, "In those days there was no king in Israel" (17:6; 18:1; 19:1; 21:25), Wellhausen understood to derive from a supplementary redaction that took place when 17-18 and 19-21 were combined.

---

[9] Wellhausen, *Composition* (2d edn, 1889), pp. 218-19.

[10] Wellhausen, *Composition* (2d edn, 1889), p. 215.

[11] Wellhausen, *Composition* (2d edn, 1889), p. 217.

[12] Wellhausen set aside from this schema the Samson account, since it represented a forty-year Philistine oppression (Judg. 13:1).

[13] Wellhausen, *Composition* (2d edn, 1889), pp. 232-33.

[14] Wellhausen, *Composition* (2d edn, 1889), pp. 233-37.

Contrary to many contemporary source critics, however, Wellhausen did not affirm the continuation into Judges of the J and E sources found in the Hexateuch (except perhaps within the preredactional strata of the Gideon story).[15]

R. Kittel denied altogether the existence of a predeuteronomic book of Judges.[16] He thought that it was the deuteronomic author (Ri) who first drew from unknown ancient collections the stories of 2:6–16:31 and melded them into his[/her] schematic religious and chronological framework. A later deuteronomic redactor (R), whose style resembled more closely that of E in the Hexateuch than that of Ri, was credited with introducing several glosses and some longer additions, including those of 1:1–2:5 and 17–21. Although Kittel's view was not widely accepted in his own time, his was thus the first double deuteronomic redaction theory to be applied to Judges.

Most of K. Budde's compositional stratigraphy of Judges was presented in his study of the sources of Judges and Samuel, though a concise summary of his stratigraphy of Judges appeared in the introduction to his commentary.[17] Since Judg. 2:6 was thought to bear a connection to the book of Joshua, he considered 1:1–2:5 to be an insertion separate from the design of the author of what follows.[18] Similarly, since the editorial framework that characterizes 2:11–16:31 ceases before chs. 17–21, he isolated the latter as a double appendix to the former stories of the judges.

Budde's predeuteronomistic Judges combined materials from the J and E sources to include (minus the deuteronomistic elements) materials now contained in 1:1–2:5 (except 2:1b–5a); *2:6–3:6; *3:12–30; *4–5; *6–9; *10:6–12:7; *13–16 and some of *17–21 (pp. XII–XV). Budde designated this redaction 'Rje' (p. XII). It was apparently this work that became the basis of the later deuteronomistic redaction of Judges.

Budde's deuteronomistic Judges included only the framework introduction, *2:6–3:6 (2:11–19 minus 2:17) and accounts of the so-called major judges: Othniel, Ehud, Deborah–Barak, Gideon, Jephthah

---

[15] Wellhausen, *Composition* (2d edn, 1889), pp. 226-27.

[16] R. Kittel, "Die pentateuchischen Urkunden in den Büchern Richter und Samuel", *TSK* 65 (1892), pp. 44-71; idem, *Geschichte der Hebräer* (2 vols., Gotha, 1888-1893), I/2 (1892), pp. 1-22.

[17] K. Budde, *Die Bücher Richter und Samuel: Ihre Quellen und ihr Aufbau* (Giessen, 1890); idem, *Das Buch der Richter* (K. Marti [ed.], KHAT 7, Freiburg, i. B., 1897), pp. IX-XXIII. See his table of Judges' compilational strata (pp. XXI-XXIII).

[18] Budde, *Richter* (1897), p. IX. Subsequent page citations refer to this work.

(10:17[6]–12:7) and Samson. The fact that the Abimelech story (Judg. 9) lacks the deuteronomistic framework prompted Budde to infer that it had been removed from the source used by the deuteronomistic redactor (Rd). Indeed, 8:33-35 seemed to Budde to have been created by this deuteronomist specifically to compensate for his[/her] excluding the Abimelech story from the Gideon account (p. XI).

Budde's postdeuteronomistic priestly redactor (Rp) framed the deuteronomistic book with 1:1–2:5 and 17–21, copied from predeuteronomistic sources and added the 'minor' judge accounts of 10:1-5 and 12:8-15 (p. X). Budde isolated the 'minor' judge accounts from the deuteronomistic redaction because they do not agree with the guiding principles set up in the foundational passage of the deuteronomistic framework (2:11-19) (p. IX) and because they seem to have been created by Rp from materials other than those used by the deuteronomistic redactor (p. XI). Further, since 10:1 presupposes the presence of the Abimelech sequel to the Gideon story, Judges 9 was probably introduced into the deuteronomistic work by Rp from the same predeuteronomistic source from which the deuteronomistic redactor had drawn the Gideon account (p. XI). Budde reasoned that the account of Shamgar (3:31) had been introduced (from 5:6?) by a post-Rp redactor to compensate for the presence of Abimelech, whom this redactor considered too evil to be included in the reckoning of the twelve judges (pp. IX, X; cf. p. XI n. 1).

G. F. Moore, too, regarded Judg. 2:6–16:31 as forming an older stratum of compilation/redaction than that which included the framing passages of 1:1–2:5 and 17–18.[19] Moore endorsed the view shared by Kuenen, Wellhausen, Budde and others that the author of 2:6–16:31 used "a pre-Deuteronomic Book of the Histories of the Judges".[20] Moore believed that the old form of Judges included materials originally contained in the J and E sources.[21] Moore considered Judg. 9, 16, 17–18, and *19–21 to derive from the same predeuteronomic collection (Rje), though he alleged that they had been omitted from the deuteronomic redaction as unsuited to its purpose.[22]

---

[19] G. F. Moore, *A Critical and Exegetical Commentary on Judges* (ICC, Edinburgh, 1895), pp. xix-xxxvii. Moore acknowledged that he adopted his view of Judges' formation from K. Budde (*Richter und Samuel* [1890]; cf. Moore, *Judges* [1895], p. xxxvi). See also Moore in *SBOT*, vol. 7 (1900).

[20] Moore, *Judges* (1895), p. xxi.

[21] Moore, *Judges* (1895), pp. xxiv-xxviii, xxx.

[22] Moore, *Judges* (1895), p. xxii; but cf. pp. xxxvi-xxxvii. Moore contended that the original order of the stories may have varied from that presented in the deuteronomic book

He therefore inferred that "Rje may with greater justice than D [the deuteronomic redactor] be regarded as the true author of the book".[23] Moreover, on the basis of formulaic similarities between Judges and 1 Samuel (e.g., [1] Judg. 10:2, 3; 12:7, 9, 11, 14; 16:31 = 1 Sam. 4:18; 7:15; [2] Judg. 3:30; 8:28; 11:33 = 1 Sam. 7:13a; [3] Judg. 2:18 = 1 Sam. 7:13b), Moore concurred with Budde that the predeuteronomic Judges included the accounts of Eli and Samuel and ended with 1 Samuel 12, which contains a retrospect of the period of the judges (1 Sam. 12:7-11).[24]

C. F. Burney regarded the accounts of Ehud (3:12-30), Gideon (6:1–8:28), Abimelech (9), Jephthah (10:17–12:7), Micah (17), the Danites (18) and the Benjaminite civil war (19–21) as composites of the J and E documents.[25] These documents, he alleged, continued as far as 1 Samuel 12[26] and were subject to two predeuteronomic redactions: one by Rje and a second by Re$_2$.[27]

Burney saw in 2:6–3:6 both the true sequel to Joshua 24 (E$_2$) and the original introduction to the book of Judges.[28] He regarded this introduction as composed by the same editor (Re$_2$) as was responsible for the framework of the following narratives, which extended no further than that of Samson (p. xxxvii). Burney concurred with the view of Budde and Moore that this original editor of Judges had deleted chs. 9 (substituting 8:33-35) and 16 from the older "history-book" and that these chapters were only later reinserted, perhaps by the same editor who inserted 1:1–2:5 and added the 'minor' judge accounts of 10:1-5;

---

of Judges—especially chs. 17, 18 and 19-21, which should appear earlier since their present position in the "days of the Philistines", between Samson and Eli, is anachronistic (p. xxii).

[23] Moore, *Judges* (1895), p. xxxiv.

[24] Moore, *Judges* (1895), pp. xxii-xxiii, xxxiv. Cf. Budde, *Richter und Samuel* (1890). Kuenen had previously argued that this was true of the deuteronomic Judges (*Historisch-critisch Onderzoek*, vol. 1 [1861], pp. 338-67).

[25] C. F. Burney, *The Book of Judges with Introduction and Notes* (London, 2d edn, 1920), pp. xxxvii, xlix.

[26] Burney, *Judges* (2d edn, 1920), pp. xxxviii-xxxix. Burney agreed with Moore and others that 1 Sam. 1-12 stood in connection with Judges as a precursor to the institution of the monarchy and that "examination of the old narrative of Judg. cannot be carried out apart from some consideration of these earlier chapters of 1 Sam." (p. xxxviii, n.; cf. p. xl). Indeed, Burney alleged that most of Judges' framework motifs were modelled upon 1 Sam. 12, other sections of E$_2$ or, at least, some similar source (pp. xlviii-xlix).

[27] Burney, *Judges* (2d edn, 1920), p. xlix.

[28] Burney, *Judges* (2d edn, 1920), pp. xxxv, xxxvi. Subsequent page citations refer to this work.

12:8-15 (p. xxxvii). Burney inferred that, although Judg. 1:1–2:5 was made up of old J materials, it "cannot originally have stood as the proper sequel of the closing chapter of Josh. [24]" (p. xxxv). He took Joshua 23 to be a later deuteronomic insertion that the deuteronomic redactor (Rd) substituted for Joshua 24, the original (E_2) conclusion of Joshua.[29] Because Burney likewise inferred that the closing narratives of Judges (17; 18; 19–21) fail to illustrate the scheme of the original editor (Re_2) and altogether lack traces of his[/her] hand, he was compelled to conclude that they were not a part of the original book of Judges (p. xxxvii). The notice of Shamgar (3:31) was apparently also added later.

Although subsequent source-critical studies continued to differ over the dating and derivation of sources used in Judges, they found significant agreement as to Judges' compilational/redactional stratigraphy. Most were agreed that the accounts of Ehud (3:12-30), Deborah–Barak (*4–5), Gideon (*6–8), Abimelech (*9), Jephthah (*10:17–12:7) and perhaps Samson (*13–16) first appeared in traditional literary corpora that also included the accounts of Eli and Samuel that now appear in 1 Samuel 1–12. The earliest form of Judges was redacted from this traditional corpus by prefixing some form of the framework introduction of *2:6–3:6 and by omitting the Samuel materials, the account of Abimelech (whose place was taken by Judg. 8:33-35) and perhaps ch. 16 of the Samson account. The latest stages of Judges' compilation/ redaction are generally taken to include the addition (from ancient sources, often J or E) of 1:1–2:5, 17–18 and 19–21 along with the (re)insertion of chs. 9, 16, and the accounts of the 'minor' judges (10:1-5; 12:8-15) and Shamgar (3:31). This broad stratigraphy remained the consensus expressed in source-critical studies whether they were as cautious and reserved as those by S. R. Driver[30] and E. Sellin[31] or as innovative and highly nuanced as those by O. Eissfeldt[32] and C. A. Simpson.[33]

---

[29] Burney, *Judges* (2d edn, 1920), pp. xliii-xlv. A modification of this view was later proposed by R. Smend (see below).

[30] S. R. Driver, *An Introduction to the Literature of the Old Testament* (ITL 1, Edinburgh, 1891; 9th edn, 1913), pp. 160-72.

[31] E. Sellin, *Einleitung in das Alte Testament* (Evangelisch-theologische Bibliothek, Leipzig, 1910; 3d edn, 1920), ET of the 3d edn: *Introduction to the Old Testament* (W. Montgomery [trans.], London, 1923).

[32] O. Eissfeldt, *Die Quellen des Richterbuches: In synoptischer Anordnung ins Deutsche übersetzt samt einer in Einleitung und Noten gegebenen Begründung* (Leipzig, 1925); idem, *Einleitung in das Alte Testament unter Einschluss der Apokryphen und*

§2. Redaction Criticism and Judges

Building upon the work of many source critics in Deuteronomy, Joshua, Judges, Samuel and Kings, M. Noth mounted the thesis that these books were first assembled into their present arrangement by a sixth-century BCE compiler who intended thereby to form a comprehensive history of Israel, the so-called 'Deuteronomistic History'.[34] The approach used by Noth and his successors was thoroughly redaction-critical and therefore deserves separate treatment from that of the source critics, yet the present concern remains to understand how the formation of a 'Deuteronomistic History' may serve as a literary-theoretical model that accounts for the compilation/redaction of Judges.

In favour of the presence of a controlling literary-historical scheme for the 'Deuteronomistic History' were two important considerations:

1. the unbroken chronological continuity between major periods extending from Moses' commission to possess the land in Deuteronomy, through the conquest of Joshua and settlement problems of Judges and to the problems of the monarchy in Samuel and Kings
2. the recurrence of speeches/summaries that develop deuteronomic themes at major transitions between the heterogeneous portrayals of historical periods featured in this corpus.

There are important observations within these considerations, but some have done well to admit that the observations need not lead to the inference either that the essential arrangement of the Joshua–Kings corpus was exilic or that the positions of the inserted deuteronomistic speeches is indicative of some earlier stage of development among these books. In regard to the first point, that there is a historical scheme uniting Joshua–Kings, it may be countered that since the original traditions relating to successive periods may in any case have

---

Pseudepigraphen (Tübingen, 1934; 3d edn, 1964), ET of 3d edn: *The Old Testament: An Introduction including the Apocrypha and Pseudepigrapha, and also the Works of Similar Type from Qumran* (P. R. Ackroyd [trans.], Oxford, 1965).

[33] C. A. Simpson, *Composition of the Book of Judges* (Oxford, 1957). Ironically, the ultraprecision of Simpson's source and redaction analyses served only to reduce confidence in the credibility of his results (cf. P. R. Ackroyd's review, *JTS* NS 10 [1959], pp. 103-6). B. G. Webb criticized Simpson for general insensitivity to narrative strategy (*The Book of the Judges: An Integrated Reading* [JSOTS 46, Sheffield, 1987], p. 221 n. 108; cf. pp. 223-24 n. 24).

[34] M. Noth, *Überlieferungsgeschichtliche Studien, I. Die sammelnden und bearbeitenden Geschichtswerke im Alten Testament* (Schriften der Königsberger Gelehrten Gesellschaft, 18. Jahr., Geisteswissenschaftliche Klasse, Heft 2, Halle, 1943), pp. 43-266; (Tübingen, 2d edn, 1957), ET of 2d edn, pp. 1-110: *The Deuteronomistic History*, JSOTS 15, Sheffield, 1981.

been presented in chronological sequence there is, on that basis alone, no need to argue for a systematic re-presentation according to the grand scheme that Noth envisioned for the single compiler of the 'Deuteronomistic History'. Israel's historical traditions may periodically have been gathered into 'books' by successive 'historians' who deliberately added to what they knew was a growing corpus without any systematic attempt on their part to meld the books into a coherent theory of Israel's history.[35]

Noth's second observation seems more cogent but requires that one first agree with his view that the deuteronomistic 'speeches' in Deuteronomy–Kings originally functioned as literary transitions in a deuteronomistic corpus. If one assumes that these speeches were once literary transitions, then the 'periods' between the speeches can be legitimated as literary boundaries even though this periodization otherwise cuts across the literary boundaries established by the present books of Joshua, Judges, Samuel and Kings.[36]

I turn now to a consideration of Noth's work with Judges in particular. From the outset of his study, Noth admitted to having a special concern for disproving the argument of W. Rudolph that the materials that conclude Joshua and begin Judges are incompatible with each other under the thesis of a unified deuteronomistic compilation of Joshua–

---

[35] The thesis that it is possible to discern a guiding thematic unity in the Deuteronomistic History may be called into question by comparison of the major themes, patterns of presentation and rhetorical aims inherent in Joshua and Judges, as opposed to those of Samuel and Kings—and this need not be limited to their final forms. These books not only describe different religious–political situation(s) but seem to reflect further the concerns of each book's compiler/redactor's religious–political situation. Noth's disclaimer that divergences of style and rhetorical aim between the books resulted from variations among the sources compiled is hardly sufficient to account for the differences among the editorial formulae and frameworks of these books and could as profitably be used to prove the essential autonomy of Joshua, Judges, Samuel or Kings except insofar as each was related to antecedent compilations. At least it is a point in favour of the originality of the former prophet book divisions that these are the only forms in which the books have come down to us. Contrariwise, verification of Noth's hypothesis requires substantial remodelling, especially of Judges.

[36] Noth alleged that the periods of Israel's history were originally demarcated by the protagonist speeches of Moses (Deut. 1–3), Joshua (Josh. 1:12-18 [F. M. Cross prefers 1:11-15 (see below)]; 12; 23), Samuel (1 Sam. 12:1-24), Solomon (1 Kgs 8:14-53 [Cross prefers 8:12-51]) and by deuteronomistic summaries such as those concerning the judges (Judg. 2:11-19 [Cross prefers 2:11-22]) and the fall of Samaria (2 Kgs 17:7-23 [Cross prefers 17:7-18, 20-23]). D. J. McCarthy has proposed that the oracle of Nathan (2 Sam. 7:1-16) and the prayer of David (2 Sam. 7:18-29) should also have been included in Noth's list of speeches ("II Samuel 7 and the Structure of the Deuteronomic History", *JBL* 84 [1965], pp. 131-38).

Judges.[37] Noth understood that a correct criticism of the materials that mark the transition from Joshua to Judges was a linchpin in his thesis of a unified deuteronomistic compilation.[38] Rudolph had proposed to segregate two separate strands that formed an original 'deuteronomistic' conclusion to Joshua (comprising Josh. 23:1-16; Judg. 2:6-10, 13, 20-22; 3:1a, 3-4, 6) and an original deuteronomistic introduction to Judges (comprising, in order, Judg. 1:1-2:5, 23; 3:5; 2:11-12, 14-16, 18-19), while Judg. 2:17 and 3:1b-2 he considered late glosses. According to Rudolph, the former (Joshua) strand permits Israel's moral decline only after Joshua's generation and describes foreign inhabitants on the border of Israel's land; the latter (Judges) strand portrays Joshua's generation initiating Israel's moral decline and allows some foreign inhabitants even within Israelite territory.

Noth judged that Rudolph's need to transpose Judg. 2:23 and 3:5 before 2:11-12 showed how forced were the latter's efforts to discover two independent strands in 2:11-3:6 through segregating doublets, formal inconsistencies and incompatibilities in subject matter (pp. 7, 101 n. 9). Further, Noth rejected Rudolph's use of the distinct subject matter of Judges 1 as evidence for a deuteronomistic editor different from the deuteronomistic editor of Joshua precisely because Noth contended that Judges 1 was not 'deuteronomistic' at all (p. 8). By means of this assessment of Judges 1, Noth was able to remove from the 'Deuteronomistic History' those parts of Joshua and Judges that marked these books as distinct literary entities and was then able to infer that

> the speech by Joshua with which Dtr. ends his account of the Conquest (Jos. 23) is directly linked with the transition, also composed by Dtr., to the history of the period of the "judges", set forth in Judg. 2:6-11, 14-16, 18-19. ... Afterwards, in the style similar to that of Dtr., the Deuteronomistically edited passages Jos. 24:1-28 ... and Judg. 2:1-5 were added after the final chapter of the book of Joshua, chapter 23, and—later still—without any Deuteronomistic revision, the mass of old traditional fragments, which form the present Judg. 1 [p. 8].

Noth therefore concluded that "every passage between Jos. 23 and Judg. 2:6 which points to a division between Joshua and Judges was

---

[37] W. Rudolph, *Der 'Elohist' von Exodus bis Josua* (BZAW 68, Giessen, 1938), pp. 240-44; Noth, *Überlieferungsgeschichtliche Studien, I* (1943), ET: *Deuteronomistic History* (1981), pp. 6-9.

[38] Noth, *Überlieferungsgeschichtliche Studien, I* (1943), ET: *Deuteronomistic History* (1981), pp. 8-9. Subsequent page citations refer to the English translation.

brought in after Dtr." and that "the same is true of the passages at the end of Judges" (p. 9). It should be apparent that Noth's desire to regard Judges 1 as a postdeuteronomistic addition was a reflex of his need to remove materials common to Joshua and Judges so as to prove an original cohesion between these books. Yet, even if the materials in Judges 1 could be shown to have been added after the compilation of 2:6–12:15, one wonders whether this would necessarily support Noth's equation of the hand that compiled Judg. 2:6–13:1 with that which compiled the final form of Kings in the sixth century BCE.[39]

The same impulse to recognize where the literary boundaries of Israel's historical traditions may have been moved appears also in Noth's treatment of the transition from Judges to 1 Samuel. Like many source critics before him, Noth proposed that there had been a deuteronomistic book of Judges that was aligned in content with a historical period of the 'judges' and that it had included various materials now found in Judg. 2:6–12:15 and 1 Sam. 1–12.[40] Thus, with respect to the Judges materials, Noth concluded that the "old tradition" that served as Dtr's source included only Judg. 3:15b-30a, 31; 4:1b, 3b-4a; 4:5–5:31a; 6:2-6a; 6:11–8:27a; 9:1-57; 10:2-5, 17; 11:1-11; 11:29–12:15, to which Dtr prefixed an introduction (2:6-11, 14-16, 18-19). Noth argued that some elements in Dtr's framework, such as the designation 'judges' in Judg. 2:16, (17), 18, derive from the "(minor) judge" accounts, though, since the figure Jephthah allegedly appeared both in the "(minor) judges" source and in the original hero story, there need have been no incompatibility between being a military hero and being called a 'judge' (pp. 43-44).

---

[39] Both G. von Rad and F. M. Cross later argued against the probability of a single redactor for the whole of Joshua–Kings on the basis of incompatibilities between Judges and Kings as to their method of presentation and theological themes (see below). Moreover, the prevalence in the books of Kings of statements that derive from a pre-exilic point of view (e.g., using "to this day" [whether 'archivally' or 'editorially'] in reference to: [1] the poles of the ark, 1 Kgs 8:8 [but cf. 2 Chron. 5:9]; [2] the conscription of foreigners, 9:20-21 [but cf. 2 Chron. 8:7-8]; [3] Israel's rebellion against the house of David, 12:19 [but cf. 2 Chron. 10:19] and [4] Edom's rebellion against Judah, 2 Kgs 8:22 [but cf. 2 Chron. 21:10]) would allow that these passages that were composed before the exile may likewise have been compiled then. Thus, it could be argued that even the books of Kings existed in some form prior to their exilic redaction. Hence, demonstrably later references such as that to Jehoiachin's release from prison (ca. 562 BCE, 2 Kgs 25:27-30) may have been added to a preexisting corpus.

[40] Noth, Überlieferungsgeschichtliche Studien, I (1943), ET: Deuteronomistic History (1981), pp. 42-43; p. 118 n. 4. Noth recognized that, in alleging an original amalgamation of these two segments, Dtr would have drawn from and combined "two different traditions", only the latter of which presupposed a Philistine oppression.

A noteworthy gap in Noth's treatment of the present form of Judges was his omission of a detailed discussion of chs. 17–21.[41] This was only partially ameliorated in his study of the tradition history of chs. 17–18.[42] Yet, given the extent to which Noth's understanding of the deuteronomistic period of the judges (portrayed in Judg. 2:6–12:15; 1 Sam. 1–12) depended upon the dismissal of the last five chapters of the present Judges, it should have been more fully explained how he came to regard Judges 17–18 and 19–21 as rhetorically and historically incompatible with the deuteronomistic form of the book.

The implications of Noth's grand thesis were far-reaching though not without problems. Not long after Noth's epoch-making work, G. von Rad published his tradition-historical study of the deuteronomic traditions.[43] The first six chapters were foundational to the seventh chapter, in which he attempted to articulate the deuteronomist's theological claim through a study of themes in the books of Kings. Von Rad justified confining his analysis of the themes of the Deuteronomistic History to Kings by claiming that, "a new section begins for the Deuteronomist with Solomon, and it is only then that the histories come to their real subject".[44] Inherent in the claim that this limitation of scope was justified by the special subject of the books of Kings was von Rad's conscious realization that the aim underlying the

---

[41] Cf. Noth, *Überlieferungsgeschichtliche Studien, I* (1943), ET: *Deuteronomistic History* (1981), p. 121 n. 29.

[42] M. Noth, "Der Hintergrund von Richter 17–18" (1962); reprinted in vol. 1, *Archäologische, exegetische und topographische Untersuchungen zur Geschichte Israels,* in *Aufsätze zur biblischen Landes- und Altertumskunde* (2 vols., H. W. Wolff [ed.], Neukirchen–Vluyn, 1971), pp. 133–47, ET: "The Background of Judges 17–18", in *Israel's Prophetic Heritage: Essays in Honor of James Muilenburg* (B. W. Anderson and W. Harrelson [eds.], The Preachers' Library, London, 1962), pp. 68–85. In this study Noth concludes that Judg. 17–18 (except the later glosses 18:30, 31b; pp. 82–85) is an "essential literary unity" ("Hintergrund" [1962], ET: "Background" [1962], p. 69) that was written in support of the royal Israelite sanctuary at Dan established by Jeroboam I (pp. 81–82).

[43] G. von Rad, *Deuteronomium-Studien* (FRLANT 58, Göttingen, 1947; 2d edn, 1948), ET: *Studies in Deuteronomy* (D. M. G. Stalker [trans.], SBT 9, London, 1953).

[44] Von Rad, *Deuteronomium-Studien* (1947; 2d edn, 1948), ET: *Studies in Deuteronomy* (1953), p. 75 n. 2. F. M. Cross argued similarly: "We desire first to analyse the latter part of the Deuteronomistic history, especially the Book of Kings. Here we should find the climactic section of the history. As the historian draws closer to his own times, we expect him to express his intent most clearly both in specifically theological or parenetic sections which would constitute his framework and in the shaping of special themes which unify his work" (*Canaanite Myth and Hebrew Epic: Essays in the History of the Religion of Israel* [Cambridge, Mass., 1973], p. 278).

varied treatments of covenant and royal ideology were not homogeneous throughout the Deuteronomistic History. Yet the main issue in
question was whether a grand theological scheme could be discerned
for the whole of Joshua–Kings. While recognizing the incompatibilities
of themes and methods of presentation between Judges and Kings,
von Rad (like Cross after him) nevertheless continued to speak of a
thematically unified Deuteronomistic History—albeit, in the case of
Cross, a pre-exilic history that had undergone an exilic redaction.[45]
Moreover, the rhetorical incongruities between Judges and Kings noted
by von Rad (e.g., cycles of apostasy and repentance versus an essentially downward trend of apostasy; idealization of the monarchy versus
the idea that monarchy usually corrupts the nation; tacit assessment of
the judges versus explicit judgement against the kings; YHWH's controlling of history through judges' charismata versus history as the
fulfilment of YHWH's prophetic word; guilt of those opposed to judges
[Judg. 2:17] versus guilt of the moral disposition of kings) were not
fully accounted for even by Cross' hypothesis of a double redaction of
the Deuteronomistic History.[46] Following von Rad, G. Fohrer called
into question the sufficiency of Noth's theory of the unity of Joshua–
Kings by arguing that different 'deuteronomistic' hands, at various
times, must have edited the various books that constitute the
Deuteronomistic History.[47] Nevertheless, a majority of scholars
continue to uphold Noth's model of a unified Deuteronomistic History
with the modification that the work is now generally recognized to have
been revised at least one or more times after the pre-exilic
deuteronomist and that the present structure of Judges is consonant
with this redactional history.[48]

---

[45] G. von Rad, *Theologie des Alten Testaments*, vol. 1: *Die Theologie der
geschichtlichen Überlieferungen Israels* (Munich, 1957), ET: *Old Testament Theology*,
vol. 1: *The Theology of Israel's Historical Traditions* (D. M. G. Stalker [trans.], London,
1962), pp. 346-47; Cross, *Canaanite Myth* (1973), p. 278.

[46] H. W. Wolff further noted "stylistic tensions" between Deut. 4 and 1 Kgs 8—both
being speeches that Noth assigned to the same deuteronomist (*Bibel—Das Alte Testament:
Eine Einführung in seine Schriften und in die Methoden ihrer Erforschung* [Stuttgart,
1970], ET: *The Old Testament: A Guide to Its Writings* [K. R. Crim (trans.), London,
1974], p. 52).

[47] G. Fohrer, *Einleitung in das Alte Testament* (Heidelburg, 1965), ET: *Introduction to
the Old Testament* (D. Green [trans.], Nashville, 1968), pp. 192-95.

[48] E.g., A. D. H. Mayes wrote that whatever differences there are between Judges and
Kings, "one must weigh against the clear indications of unity in the history which prohibit
any such division between the various books; and this in turn suggests the possibility that
where differences exist they belong to different levels within what must in general terms
continue to be seen as a uniform and single work. In other words, the cyclic pattern of

W. Richter contributed an important redaction-critical study of Judges proposing that remnants of an original *Retterbuch* ("Book of Saviours") were to be found among some of Judges' main episodes.[49] These alleged remnants are present in the episodes concerning: Ehud (3:15b-26), the only account preserved intact; Jael (4:17a, 18-21, [22]) and Gideon (7:11b, 13-21; 8:5-9, 14-21a; 9:56[?]). Richter further isolated within Judges four strata that he assigned to subsequent redactional phases through which the *Retterbuch* passed: (1) a redactional stratum that transformed the wars of saviours into holy wars of YHWH (i.e., 3:13, 27-29; 4:4a, 6-9, 11, 17b; 6:2b-5, 11b-17, 25-27a, 31bβ-34; 7:1, 9-11a, 22-25; 8:3-4, 10-13, 22-23, 29, 31; 9:1-7, 16a, 19b-21, 23-24, 41-45, 56-57); (2) an early 'deuteronomic' stratum that inserted the earliest framework elements (i.e., 3:12, 14, 15a, 30; 4:1a, 2-3a, 23-24; 5:31 [except the number]; 6:1 [except the number], 2a; 8:28 [except the number]; and possibly 9:16b-19a, 22, 55); (3) a later 'deuteronomic' insertion of a *Beispielstück* (i.e., 3:7-11a except the number and formulae of 3:8, 10-11); (4) a stratum inserted during the first compilation of the Deuteronomistic History (2:7, 10-12, 14-16, 18-19; 4:1b; 10:6-16). Richter assigned the old collection of the *Retterbuch* to prophetic circles of the north in the time of Jehu; the final two deuteronomistic editions, which provided the framework and *Beispielstück*, he connected with Josiah's restoration of the popular army. This deuteronomistically edited form of the *Retterbuch* was allegedly designed to legitimize the traditional ideal of holy war.[50]

---

presentation of history in Judges is a fundamental characteristic of a stage of development of that book which is not to be set on the same level as the linear presentation of history in Kings" (*Judges* [OTG 3, Sheffield, 1985], p. 12).

[49] Richter's main work was published in two parts: *Traditionsgeschichtliche Untersuchungen zum Richterbuch* (BBB 18, Bonn, 1963; 2d edn, 1966); and *Die Bearbeitungen des 'Retterbuches' in der deuteronomischen Epoche* (BBB 21, Bonn, 1964). For reviews, see L. Alonso-Schökel, "Dos obras recientes sobre el libro de los Jueces", *Bib* 45 (1964), pp. 543-50 [on Richter's *Richterbuch* (1963)]; W. J. Moran, "A Study of the Deuteronomic History", *Bib* 46 (1965), pp. 223-28 [on Richter's *Retterbuches* (1964)]; J. A. Soggin, "[Review:] W. Richter, *Die Bearbeitungen des 'Retterbuches' in der deuteronomischen Epoche*", *AION* 25 (1965), pp. 299-302. I. Schlauri gives a summary of Richter's work ("W. Richters Beitrag zur Redaktionsgeschichte des Richterbuches", *Bib* 54 [1973], pp. 367-403). There are also shorter summaries in D. N. Knight, *Rediscovering the Traditions of Israel* (SBLDS 9, Missoula, Mont., rev. edn, 1975), pp. 182-86; A. D. H. Mayes, *The Story of Israel between Settlement and Exile: A Redactional Study of the Deuteronomistic History* (London, 1983), pp. 58-80; and J. A. Soggin, *Judges: A Commentary* (J. Bowden [trans.], OTL, London, 2d edn, 1987), pp. 5-6.

[50] Richter, *Richterbuch* (2d edn, 1966), pp. 336-43. Cf. Mayes, *Story* (1983), p. 164 n. 47.

Because most of Judges' framework elements in the Jephthah story occur in its introduction (10:6-16), Richter considered the actual account of Jephthah (10:17-12:6) to lie outside the original *Retterbuch* and therefore treated it elsewhere.[51] Here Richter argued that the Jephthah tradition had an independent history. The old Jephthah tradition (Judg. 11:1-11, 34-36) originally told of a family feud and was only later set into the context of a dispute between Gilead and Ammon. The aetiology of Judg. 11:37-40 was added secondarily to account for the origin of a custom in Israel. The 'shibboleth' incident of 12:5-6 and Jephthah's message to the Ammonite king in 11:15-26 were added at a later stage. Editorial passages, which combined these units and brought them into unity with the *Retterbuch*, include: 10:17-18; 11:4, 11b, 12-14, 27-29, 32-33.

R. Smend, too, introduced an important departure in the treatment of the Deuteronomistic History that has since been developed by W. Dietrich and T. Veijola.[52] With respect to Joshua–Judges, Smend proposed that Judg. 2:10 originally continued Josh. 24:31 in the Deuteronomistic History, in which Josh. 24:1-31 was original and Joshua 23 a later insertion by DtrN ("*nomistische*" Dtr).[53] DtrN inserted Judg. 2:17, 20-21, 23 into the deuteronomistic introduction to Judges and prefaced the whole with the preexisting materials of Judg.

---

[51] See W. Richter, "Die Überlieferungen um Jephtah, Ri 10,7-12,6", *Bib* 47 (1966), pp. 485-556. Cf. R. Smend, Jr, *Die Entstehung des Alten Testaments* (Theologische Wissenschaft 1, Stuttgart, 1978), p. 127; Mayes, *Story* (1983), pp. 64-65. Against Richter's view that Jephthah was not a deliverer but a 'minor' judge, the speech of Samuel explicitly mentions Jephthah together with Jerubbaal and *Barak (< Bedan) as deliverers of Israel (1 Sam. 12:11) (so T. Ishida, "The Leaders of the Tribal Leagues: 'Israel' in the Pre-Monarchic Period", *RB* 80 [1973], p. 521).

[52] R. Smend, Jr, "Das Gesetz und die Völker: Ein Beitrag zur deuteronomistischen Redaktionsgeschichte", in *Probleme biblischer Theologie: Gerhard von Rad zum 70. Geburtstag* (H. W. Wolff [ed.], Munich, 1971), pp. 494-509 [on Joshua–Judges]; idem, *Entstehung des Alten Testaments* (1978), pp. 110-39 [on Joshua–Kings]; T. Veijola, *Die ewige Dynastie: David und die Entstehung seiner Dynastie nach der deuteronomistischen Darstellung* (AASF B/193, Helsinki, 1975) [on 1 Kgs 1-2; 1 Sam. 25; 20:12-17; 2 Sam. 21-24]; idem, *Das Königtum in der Beurteilung der deuteronomistischen Historiographie: Eine redaktionsgeschichtliche Untersuchung* (AASF B/198, Helsinki, 1977) [on Judg. 17-21; 1 Sam. 10:17-11:15; 8; 9:1-10:16; 12; Judg. 8:22-23; 9:7-21]; W. Dietrich, *Prophetie und Geschichte: Eine redaktionsgeschichtliche Untersuchung zum deuteronomistischen Geschichtswerk* (FRLANT 108, Göttingen, 1977) [on Kings].

[53] Smend, "Das Gesetz und die Völker" (1971), p. 506; idem, *Entstehung des Alten Testaments* (1978), p. 115. Earlier, J. N. M. Wijngaards had likewise reasoned that Josh. 24:3-13 was predeuteronomic and Josh. 23:12-16 deuteronomic (*The Dramatization of Salvific History in the Deuteronomic Schools* [P. A. H. de Boer (ed.), *OTS* XVI, Leiden, 1969], pp. 58-59).

1:1-2:5.[54] Accordingly, DtrN then inserted Judg. 2:6-9 (which restates Josh. 24:28, 31, 29-30) to preserve the original connection between Josh. 24:31 and Judg. 2:10.[55] Smend later assigned redactional materials found in the body and conclusion of Judges to the various redactional strata that he and his students had proposed.[56] In Judges were found no passages from the 'prophetic' redactor (DtrP) proposed by W. Dietrich for the books of Kings.

R. D. Nelson, building upon the proposal of Cross, developed lines of argument for a double deuteronomistic redaction of Joshua–Kings similar to those made earlier by source critics such as Kuenen.[57] Nelson made the case that passages such as Judg. 2:1-5 and 6:7-10 derive from an exilic editor of the pre-exilic Deuteronomistic History. He compared features that characterize these allegedly exilic insertions with similar features in 2 Kgs 17:7-20, 23b, 24-40; 21:1-18—passages that can be shown to be secondary to Kings on other grounds.[58]

Two more recent diachronic studies relating to the compositional history of Judges, those by A. D. H. Mayes and B. Pekham, offered presentations of the chronology and provenance of the book's literary traditions but neither so significant as to alter the broad consensus among the source and redaction critics described above as to the relationship among the various strata of Judges. Mayes, for example, described a predeuteronomic book of Judges in the collection of

---

[54] Smend, "Das Gesetz und die Völker" (1971), pp. 504-6, 506-8; idem, *Entstehung des Alten Testaments* (1978), pp. 115-16. Smend credited to DtrN the concept that victory over "the remaining nations/land" was dependent upon obedience to "the book of the law" (cf. Josh. 1:8; 13:2-6; 23:4, 6-8, 12-13; Judg. 1:1-2:5, 20-21)—a concept that DtrN may have derived from Judg. 1:1-2:5 (pp. 508-9). In Joshua, Smend assigned to DtrN: Josh. 1:7-9 (pp. 495-97); 13:1bβ-6 (pp. 497-500) and ch. 23 (pp. 501-4).

[55] Smend, "Das Gesetz und die Völker", (1971) p. 506; idem, *Entstehung des Alten Testaments* (1978), p. 115.

[56] Smend, *Entstehung des Alten Testaments* (1978), pp. 115-18.

[57] Kuenen, *Historisch-critisch Onderzoek* (1861-65; 2d edn, 1885-92); F. M. Cross, "The Structure of the Deuteronomic History", *Perspectives in Jewish Learning* 3 (1968), pp. 9-24; reprinted as chapter 10: "The Themes of the Book of Kings and the Structure of the Deuteronomistic History", in *Canaanite Myth* (1973), pp. 274-89; R. D. Nelson, "The Redactional Duality of the Deuteronomistic History" (PhD diss., Union Theological Seminary, Va., 1974); revised as *The Double Redaction of the Deuteronomistic History* (JSOTS 18, Sheffield, 1981).

[58] Nelson, *Double Redaction* (1981), pp. 43-98; see especially pp. 45-46 [on Judg. 2:1-5] and pp. 48-49 [on Judg. 6:7-10]. Other passages from Kings that Nelson alleged were secondary include: 1 Kgs 8:44-51; 9:6-9; 2 Kgs 23:31-25:30 and segments of 2 Kgs 22:15-20; 23:1-30. Outside Kings, his exilic additions include Deut. 4:19-20 and Josh. 24:1-28.

premonarchical deliverers in 2:11–16:31 wherein the cause of external threats to Israel are assigned to Israel's inner covenant unfaithfulness.[59] He offered a five-stage model of the compositional history of this predeuteronomic book. Following Richter, Mayes reasoned that an old "pre-framework collection", the earliest core of the book of Judges, included the stories of Ehud, Deborah–Barak and Gideon(–Abimelech) and was concerned to present events in which deliverers conducted holy wars by which YHWH delivered his people (pp. 62-63, 72-73). In the next edition of these three stories, a sixfold framework was added that, according to Mayes, accounts for the fact that the complete form of the framework is preserved only in these stories. The third stage in the development of Judges was the addition of Judg. 3:7-11, which Mayes took to be a story composed as a model of the entire period of the judges (i.e., Richter's *Beispielstück*) (pp. 66, 73). The fourth stage of Judges' formation saw the addition of the basic layer of 2:11–3:6, the basic layer of 10:6-16 (and 11:33), the Jephthah account of 10:17–12:6 together with its framing 'minor' judge lists in 10:1-5 and 12:7-15 and, because of the anticipatory reference to the Philistines in 10:7, probably also the Samson stories of 13–16 (p. 73). Mayes segregated within 2:11–3:6 a basic narrative (2:11-12aα, 13b, 14-16 [omitting 15aβ], 18aβb, 19aαb) from its later editorial layer (pp. 67-69, 76). Similarly, in 10:6-16 a basic text, 10:6aα, 7-9, was supplemented with 10:6aβb, 10-16 (pp. 69, 76). The fifth and final stage of the editing of Judges' central division involved only the editing of 2:11–3:6 (adding 2:12aβb-13a, 17-18aα, 19aβ, 20-21, 23; 3:5-6) and 10:6-16 (adding 10:6aβb, 10-16) (pp. 68-69, 74). Nowhere in the primary collection of the deliverer stories of Ehud, Deborah–Barak, Gideon(–Abimelech) nor, at its second stage, in its sixfold (cycle-motif) framework, nor, at its third stage, in the accretion of 3:7-11 could Mayes find contact with any of the three stages of deuteronomistic editing elsewhere evident in Deuteronomy and Joshua (p. 74). Only in the chronological scheme of 2:11–16:31, which shows harmonization with the 480 years of 1 Kgs 6:1, does the framework point beyond the otherwise closed collection of deliverer stories. In view of the fact that the statements that the land had rest occur elsewhere without accompanying chronological indications, Mayes took these chronological statements in Judges to be later additions to the framework (p. 75).

As to the deuteronomic phases of Judges' redaction, Mayes proposed that Judg. 1:1–2:5 continued only the third of three redactional layers

---

[59] Mayes, *Story* (1983), p. 61. Subsequent page references refer to this study.

evident in Deuteronomy and Joshua.[60] He argued that this hand is to be identified with that which added Josh. 24:1-28 to the book of Joshua, since Judg. 2:1-5, the section by means of which the materials in Judges 1 were incorporated into the book, is, like Josh. 24:1-28, "an abrupt introduction of materials of uncertain origin" having "strong concern with covenant and ritual" wherein "there is a strong concern with Israel's obedience to covenant law" (p. 60). Mayes regarded the epilogue of Judges 17–21 similarly as illustrating Israel's internal instability and held these chapters to present one literary unit bound together by the monarchical motif of 17:6; 21:25; 18:1; 19:1 (p. 79). He disputed claims that deuteronomistic editing is evident in these chapters. Indeed, Mayes perceived that chs. 17–21 disrupt the original connection between the Samson and Samuel narratives that are introduced by the anticipation of Ammonite oppression in 10:6aα, 7-9. Thus, chs. 17–21 were introduced later than the deuteronomistic layers, yet they show close connections with 1:1–2:5 (pp. 79-80).

B. Peckham proposed the following five-stage sequence for the formation of the Deuteronomistic History: (1) the composition of a history of Israel by J; (2) the compilation of a history (with special interest in the Judahite monarchy) by Dtr[1], who knows, quotes and expounds J; (3) a nationalistic revision of J by P designed to balance and correct the revision of J by Dtr[1]; (4) the supplementation of J, Dtr[1], and P by E, who enunciates the regional complexity of Israel; (5) the amalgamation of the diverse national and theocratic viewpoints of all foregoing histories by Dtr[2] into one universal history of Israel.[61] Following Noth, Peckham understood Judges to have been composed *in toto* from older sources by a single compiler, but his handling of the materials in Judges (as in the books of Joshua, Samuel and Kings) seems marred by his cautionless reduction of their formal arrangement into a series of illusory concentric structures.

Perhaps the more rhetorically significant of two redaction-critical studies of Judges to have appeared in recent years is that by L. G. Stone.[62] Stone argued that the materials of Judges generally relegated

---

[60] Mayes, *Story* (1983), pp. 58-60. The redactional layers proposed are: (1) that of the deuteronomistic historian, (2) that of a later deuteronomistic editor and (3) that of a later nondeuteronomistic editor.

[61] B. Peckham, *The Composition of the Deuteronomistic History* (F. M. Cross [ed.], HSM 35, Atlanta, Ga., 1985), pp. 1, 73.

[62] L. G. Stone, "From Tribal Confederation to Monarchic State: The Editorial Perspective of the Book of Judges" (PhD diss., Yale University, 1988), pp. 113-29. Another recent redaction-critical study of Judges is that by U. Becker, *Richterzeit und Königtum:*

to the final stage of redaction (i.e., 1:1–2:5; 3:31; 6:7-10 and 10:10-14; portions of 8:22-35; 9; the 'minor' judge lists of 10:1-5 and 12:8-15; 16; and 17–21) as well as the model account of Othniel (3:7-11) should be seen as part of a deliberate and coherent redactional programme designed to bring the previous form of Judges into line with the promonarchical and pro-Judahite perspective shared among these passages.[63] Thus, Stone's hypothesis as to the editorial perspective of Judges' final redactor relates quite well to the rhetoric of the final form of Judges that I have presented in this study.

B. Rhetorical Aspects of Judges' Literary Formation

Disenchanted with a perceived "crisis in biblical scholarship" resulting from over a century of bias toward historical-critical analysis, R. M. Polzin undertook to apply the analytical techniques of Russian formalism to the first part of the Deuteronomistic History (i.e., Deuteronomy–Judges) as a means of escaping the tedium of historical criticism.[64] Polzin treated Judges as though it were a distinct literary unit yet "a major turning point in the narrative" comprising Deuteronomy–Kings.[65] Polzin noted that Judges' prologue does not simply continue the Joshua narrative but "recapitulates" it before interpreting the period that followed the death of Joshua (cf. Judg. 1:1a), just as Joshua's opening recapitulated the salient features of

---

Redaktionsgeschichtliche Studien zum Richterbuch, BZAW 192, Berlin, 1990. Becker's approach, worked out along lines established by the "Göttingen school" of Smend and his students, takes the position that an antimonarchical Dtr(H) was the original compiler of Judges (*2:11–16:31) rather than the author of Richter's *Retterbuch*, that an antimonarchical moralist (DtrN) added to the former another framework (1:21, *27-35; 2:1-5, 12aα, 13-14a, 16b-17, *18aα, 19-21; 3:5-6; 8:24-27; 9:16b-19a, 24, 56-57; 17-18*), and that a pro-Judahite, promonarchical redactor from the priestly school (Rp) was responsible for a third (though not the final) redactional stratum (including *1:1-18, *22-26; 17:6; 18:1a, 31b; *19-21). See my review of Becker's work in *VT* 43 (1993), pp. 133-34.

[63] Stone, "Tribal Confederation" (1988), pp. 113-29.

[64] R. M. Polzin, *Moses and the Deuteronomist: A Literary Study of the Deuteronomic History*, part 1, *Deuteronomy, Joshua, Judges* (New York, 1980), pp. 1-24. On Judges, see pp. 146-204, 210-12, 213-18. Members of the Russian formalist and sociological schools that Polzin cited include: V. N. Voloshinov, M. M. Bakhtin and B. Uspensky (p. 214 n. 6). He further cited the rhetorical and frame-analytical insights of W. Booth and E. Goffman, respectively, as beneficial to his approach. Cf. Webb, *Judges* (1987), pp. 32-33.

[65] Polzin, *Moses and the Deuteronomist*, part 1 (1980), pp. 161-62. The following page citations refer to this study.

Deuteronomy before interpreting the period that followed the death of Moses (cf. Josh. 1:1a) (pp. 147-48). Judges aims to show that Israel's failure to complete the conquest is the major cause for all later negative consequences. In the body of Judges, Polzin focuses upon the unifying dimension of implicit symbolic patterns that underlie the repeated surface patterns of the book. Important to the alleged function of Judges as a turning point in the narrative of Deuteronomy–Kings is the development, from Ehud to Samson, of the characterization of the judge who achieves YHWH's aim in an apparently unknowing fashion (p. 160). Finally, according to Polzin, the rhetorical design implied by the contrastive repetition in 20:18 of the tribes' initial inquiry of YHWH's oracle in 1:1-2, coupled with the contrasting interest of their contexts' interest in civil war and wars of occupation, respectively, shows that "the narrator [was] intent upon intensifying the doubt and confusion in Israel with which he began his story in Judges 1" (p. 202).

While assessing the aims of Judges' pattern of recurrence within the context of the Deuteronomistic History, G. W. Trompf called for a qualification of "the linear–cyclical dichotomy" (i.e., a limitation of the forced contrast between "straight-line" and "cyclical" views of history).[66] Biblical models of either pattern of historical recurrence may be subsumed under a stable rubric of retributive justice. Thus, according to Trompf, the historical paradigm of Judges 2 does not present merely "a monotonously recurring cycle"[67] but an alternation between low and high points brought on by Israel's undulation between disobedience and obedience, respectively, under a fixed scheme of recurrent retribution.[68] Trompf acknowledged that, "although the rest of [the deuteronomist's] work lacks the symmetry of Judges, he was remarkably consistent in proving for his readers that transgression (that is, disobedience against the law delivered to Moses ... and rejection of Yahweh's dĕbārîm uttered through the prophets) must needs be requited by God, and faithfulness, in turn, be rewarded".[69]

For the purposes of the present rhetorical study of Judges it is less important to comment upon the provenance and dating of compositional

---

[66] G. W. Trompf, "Notions of Historical Recurrence in Classic Hebrew Historiography", in *Studies in the Historical Books of the Old Testament* (J. A. Emerton [ed.], SVT 30, Leiden, 1979), p. 229.

[67] So C. R. North, *The Old Testament Interpretation of History* (London, 1946), pp. 96-97.

[68] Trompf, "Notions" (1979), pp. 220-21.

[69] Trompf, "Notions" (1979), pp. 221-22.

strata in the book than upon the effect of there being discernible editorial layers in the structure of Judges. For the most part, I support the inferences of Stone as to the need to recognize the broad consensus among scholars concerning the compositional strata of Judges.[70] Moreover, Stone's insight that the materials allegedly included at the final stage(s) of the book's compilation/redaction should be seen to set the agenda for Judges harmonizes nicely with what appears to be the main design of Judges' final form on rhetorical grounds. This is especially true of the framing sections, 1:1–2:5 and 17–21, but also highlights the rhetorical importance of passages that stand out from their contexts whether because of uncommon language and portrayals of oracular events (e.g., 2:1-5; 6:7-10; 10:10-14) or because they break up the otherwise homogeneous use of plot-based narrative accounts that derive from traditional lore (e.g., 3:7-11; 3:31; 10:1-5; 12:8-15).[71]

The compositional stratification of Judges presented in the appendix of this study assigns the materials in Judges to one of three categories: (1) materials that derive from the hand of a compiler/redactor, (2) materials that relate to traditions found also in known biblical books (chiefly Numbers, Deuteronomy or Joshua) and (3) materials that appear to derive from other sources available to the compiler/redactor. The question of whether Judges is entirely the product of a single compiler (as Noth thought) or of a compilation with subsequent redactions (as most others have thought) is of little consequence in the assignment of materials to the hand of a compiler/redactor. However, in deference to the scholarly consensus about Judges' formation, I have presented in the right margin of the appendix a single vertical line to indicate what may have been included in the penultimate form of Judges and a double line to indicate what may have been additions made during the final redaction of the book.

---

[70] Stone, "Tribal Confederation" (1988), pp. 113-20.
[71] Stone, "Tribal Confederation" (1988), pp. 121-29.

SCRIBAL DEVELOPMENTS AND THE RHETORIC OF JUDGES

Textual criticism in the Hebrew Bible comprises many simultaneous and mutually interdependent operations, but its general aims remain: (1) to classify the Hebrew and versional MSS according to their textual families or subgroups,[1] (2) to compare the variants among readings of the textual families and subgroups so as to account for their divergencies whether through translation tendencies or scribal heritage, (3) to aggregate the best variants among the MS families, (4) to compare the best variant(s) of the versions with that/those of the Hebrew MSS so as to account for the origin of secondary readings and, concomitantly, (5) to decide upon the earliest reading of the Hebrew text according to the extant evidence even if that requires retroverting a Hebrew form on the basis of versional evidence.

This excursus is concerned chiefly with scribal developments in the Hebrew text of Judges. Hence, the data presented here relate to translation tendencies among the versions or with recensional problems in the Greek text of Judges only insofar as these matters bear upon the elucidation of the history of the Hebrew text. To that end, the following considerations regarding the classification of MS families and of the characterization of the versions are significant.

A. MANUSCRIPT FAMILIES OF THE VERSIONS

For matters of MS classification in Targum Jonathan (Tg), the Peshiṭta (Psht) and Jerome's Vulgate (Vg) one may refer to the modern major editions.[2] In the case of the Septuagint (LXX), however, there is not

---

[1] Cf. W. R. Bodine, *The Greek Text of Judges: Recensional Developments* (HSM 23, Chico, Calif., 1980), pp. 2-3.

[2] The editions of Judges used in the text-critical notes to the appendix of this book include: for the Tg, A. Sperber, *The Bible in Aramaic*, vol. 2, *The Former Prophets according to Targum Jonathan* (Leiden, 1959); for the Psht, P. B. Dirksen, *Judges*, in *The Old Testament in Syriac according to the Peshiṭta Version*, vol. II/2 (Leiden, 1978); and idem, "10c4–Judges and I/II Samuel (II,2)", in *The Peshiṭta: Its Early Text and History: Papers Read at the Peshiṭta Symposium Held at Leiden, 30-31 August 1985* (P. B. Dirksen and M. J. Mulder [eds.], MPIL 4, Leiden, 1988), pp. 270-72; for the Vg, *Biblia Sacra iuxta latinam vulgatam versionem ad codicum fidem iussu Pii PP. XI, cura et studio monachorum Abbatiae Pontificiae Sancti Hieronymi in urbe ordinis Sancti Benedicti edita*, vol. 4, *Iosue, Iudicum, Ruth* (Rome, 1939).

yet a critical edition of the Greek Judges. However, much of the work of sorting the LXX MSS of Judges has already been carried out, and it is now generally agreed that the Greek Judges displays two main MS groups, one of which comprises three subgroups:

> Group A   I. the (hexaplaric) Alexandrinus family [AI = AGabcx, k]
>   II. the Lucianic family [AII = KZgln(o)w, (d)ptv]
>   III. a third (mixed) family [AIII = MNyb$_2$, h]
>
> Group B   the (*Kaige*) Vaticanus family [B-group = B(d)efsz, irua$_2$ and, secondarily, jm(o)q].[3]

The Lucianic family (AII) was considered by Lindars to consist of a text relatively free of the hexaplaric additions found in MS A and its congeners (AI).[4] Even so, Billen earlier observed that MSS dpt of this family should be regarded as later and of less purity than KZgln(o)w,

---

For discussions of the grouping of the Psht MSS of Judges into families, see P. B. Dirksen, *The Transmission of the Text in the Peshiṭta Manuscripts of the Book of Judges* (MPIL 1, Leiden, 1972); idem, "The Relation between the Ancient and the Younger Peshiṭta MSS in Judges", in *Tradition and Re-Interpretation in Jewish and Early Christian Literature: Essays in Honour of Jürgen C. H. Lebram* (J. W. van Henten et al [eds.], Leiden, 1986), pp. 163-71; and especially idem, "The Ancient Peshiṭta MSS of Judges and Their Variant Readings", in *The Peshiṭta* (1988), pp. 127-46 (note corrections to the edition: nn. 7, 10). On the distinctiveness of old versus new Psht MSS, see the remarks in idem, "Peshiṭta Institute Communication xix: East and West, Old and Young, in the Text Tradition of the Old Testament Peshiṭta", *VT* 35 (1985), pp. 475, 478-79.

[3] The MS sigla are those of A. E. Brooke and N. McLean, *The Old Testament in Greek according to the Text of Codex Vaticanus* (Cambridge, 1906–1940). The designations AI, AII, AIII and B-group are those of I. Soisalon-Soininen, *Die Textformen der Septuaginta-Übersetzung des Richterbuches* (AASF, B72, I, Helsinki, 1951).

Soisalon-Soininen built upon the MS groupings of A. V. Billen ("The Hexaplaric Element in the LXX Version of Judges", *JTS* 43 [1942], p. 12-13 [i.e., Aabcx KZglnow,dpt MNyb$_2$ Befjqsz]). Billen subdivided the Lucianic grouping of O. Pretzl ("Septuaginta-Probleme im Buch der Richter: Die griecheschen Handschriftengruppen im Buch der Richter untersucht nach ihrem Verhältnis zueinander", *Bib* 7 [1926], p. 233 [i.e., AGabckx KZdglnoptvw MNhyb$_2$ B(d)efij(o)qrsuza$_2$]). Soisalon-Soininen's groupings have been endorsed more recently by B. Lindars ("Some Septuagint Readings in Judges", *JTS* NS 22 [1971], pp. 1-2; idem, "A Commentary on the Greek Judges?", in *VI Congress of the International Organization for Septuagint and Cognate Studies, Jerusalem 1986* [C. E. Cox (ed.), Atlanta, Ga., 1987], pp. 167-200) and Bodine (*Greek Text of Judges* [1980], pp. 2-3], though the subgrouping of the Vaticanus family here follows Bodine's article, "*Kaige* and Other Recensional Developments in the Greek Text of Judges", *BIOSCS* 13 (1980), p. 45. Cf. the reviews of Soisalon-Soininen's work by W. G. Lambert (*VT* 2 [1952], pp. 184-89), P. Walters [Katz] (*TLZ* 77 [1952], cols. 154-58) and J. R. Porter (*JTS* NS 4 [1953], pp. 57-59).

[4] Lindars, "Septuagint Readings" (1971), p. 1. Many of the MT pluses are marked with the obelus in LXX MS G and in the Syh.

since the former included many more hexaplaric readings and conflate readings than the latter.[5]

Bodine's dissertation clarified the hypothesis of D. Barthélemy that the B family of Judges derives from the *Kaige* recension and may be expected to contain many reflexes of the proto-Masoretic text. Bodine showed that, though the B-group (especially irua$_2$) is part of the *Kaige* family and exhibits many *Kaige* characteristics, it is also distinct in that it presents characteristics that do not appear elsewhere in the *Kaige* recension.[6] Bodine concluded that the clearest preservation of the OG in Judges is likely to be found first among the Lucianic family (AII), then in the OLat and especially where both agree.[7] The Alexandrinus family (AI) of Judges is a relatively full text influenced primarily by the insertions of Origen's Hexapla, while the AIII family presents a form of the OG that was subject to mixed influences, agreeing mostly with AI, AII, Syh and OLat against the B-group, yet agreeing with the B-group more often than do the others.[8] Taking into consideration Bodine's observations, a genealogy of the recensions of the Greek text of Judges might then look as follows:

---

[5] Billen, "Hexaplaric Element" (1942), pp. 12-13.

[6] Bodine, *Greek Text of Judges* (1980), pp. 30, 185 but especially p. 77; "*Kaige*" (1980), pp. 45, 51 but especially p. 47.

[7] Bodine, *Greek Text of Judges* (1980), p. 185; "*Kaige*" (1980), pp. 47-48. A. Sáenz-Badillos and J. Targarona have argued that Judges LXX-AII[(KZ)glnw], often characterized as 'proto-Lucianic', are historically 'pre-Lucianic' (i.e., prior to Lucian of Antioch in the late third C. CE) and that ptv, which show more hexaplaric influence, can be distinguished as being from Lucian himself ("Some Contributions to the Text-History of the Greek Judges", *BIOSCS* 8 [1975], pp. 14-15 [abstract]). Lindars, however, differed with their view ("Commentary on the Greek Judges?" [1987], p. 172). Lindars retained for glnw the designation 'proto-Lucianic' and cautioned against the claim that glnw are largely free of hexaplaric readings.

[8] Bodine, *Greek Text of Judges* (1980), pp. 185-86; "*Kaige*" (1980), p. 48.

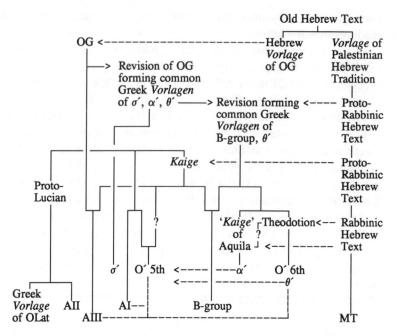

The preceding diagram illustrates the genealogy of recensions yet should not be taken to preclude the possibility of the random cross-pollination of variant readings between genealogically distant MSS.[9] Nevertheless, some general principles for classifying the variants of the LXX of Judges that have been followed in this study are:[10]

Principles for isolating the OG:

(1) If AII ≠ rell	then AII = OG or Lucian
(2) If OLat ≠ rell	then OLat = OG or OLat translator
(3) If AII = OLat (= Syh) ≠ rell	
(especially MT)	then AII & OLat (& Syh) = OG

---

[9] See the remarks of Z. Talshir concerning "double translations" in LXX-B (e.g., Judg. 1:14b; 15:14) that allegedly show direct dependence upon LXX-AI ("Double Translations in the Septuagint", in *VI Congress of the International Organization for Septuagint and Cognate Studies, Jerusalem 1986* [C. E. Cox (ed.), Atlanta, Ga., 1987], pp. 48-50. In the absence of corroborating evidence, however, one must beware of viewing all such doublets as though they represent double translations of the same Hebrew *Vorlage*, for such may preserve only inner Greek variants placed side by side (cf. Lindars, "Commentary on the Greek Judges?" [1987], p. 172).

[10] Adapted from Bodine, *Greek Text of Judges* (1980), pp. 94-95, 134-36, 140-41, 147, 150, 152-54, 154-57, 185-86.

Principles for isolating Kaige:

(4) If B-group = MT ≠ AII = OLat   then B-group = *Kaige*
(5) If B-group = Syh (unless SyhX)   then B-group & Syh = *Kaige*

Principle for Isolating Origen (hexaplaric additions):

(6) If Syh (or SyhX) = MT ≠ OG   then Syh = Origen

Given the preceding classifications of the MS families among the versions, I shall now turn to the question of the characterization of the main versions: the Tg, Psht, Vg and LXX. On the continuum of literal versus paraphrastic rendering, two tendencies of translation are evident in Tg Judges. Most of Tg Judges exhibits a literal translation of the Hebrew text, deviating only to elucidate the meaning of a phrase or to demonstrate a principle of rabbinic interpretation (especially where the text speaks of divine activity).[11] However, a freer midrashic style of rendering is evident throughout Judges 5 (as in other poetic sections, e.g., 1 Sam. 2:1-10; 2 Sam. 22:1-23:7).[12]

B. CHARACTERIZATION OF THE VERSIONS

The Hebrew text-type that underlay Tg Judges evidently belonged to the tradition of the MT. According to P. Churgin, most of Tg Judges' deviations from MT Judges exhibit one of three characteristics of its translation.[13] First, there are many cases where the Tg attests an unquestionably different reading from that of the MT (though the preponderance of such cases can be attributed to a difference only in the vocalization of the Hebrew consonantal text).[14] Second, the Tg

---

[11] D. J. Harrington and A. J. Saldarini, *Targum Jonathan of the Former Prophets: Introduction, Translation and Notes*, in *The Aramaic Bible*, vol. 10 (M. McNamara [ed.], Edinburgh, 1987), pp. 3-4.

[12] D. J. Harrington, "The Prophecy of Deborah: Interpretive Homiletics in Targum Jonathan of Judges 5", *CBQ* 48 (1986), pp. 432-42.

[13] P. Churgin, *Targum Jonathan to the Prophets* (YOSRes 14, New Haven, 1927), pp. 52-54; reprinted in L. Smolar and M. Aberbach, *Studies in Targum Jonathan to the Prophets* and P. Churgin, *Targum Jonathan to the Prophets* (LBS, New York, 1983), pp. 280-82. Smolar–Aberbach, however, grouped the translation tendencies of the Tg under three general headings: Halakha, Historical and Geographical Allusions and Theological Concepts.

[14] Churgin commented that a similar phenomenon is evident in Aquila since it too emanated from the period when there were doubts about certain words in the consonantal text (*Targum Jonathan* [1927], p. 53). Some of these variants are supported by the LXX or Psht. Churgin cited the following examples of translations in Tg Judges that are based upon an unquestionably different Hebrew *Vorlage* (*Targum Jonathan* [1927], pp. 55-56):

exhibits a noticeable tendency to eliminate the more striking cases of grammatical incongruence (in gender or number) within a sentence.[15] Third, the Tg tends to render similar sentences, which differ only in particulars, in one and the same way.[16] Therefore, variants manifesting these tendencies would not necessarily involve the translation of a Hebrew text different from that of MT.

		MT	Tg	Read	
Judg.	3:2	לא ידעום	לא הוו ידעין	ידעו,	Psht
	9:9	החדלתי את דשני	דמניה מיקרין ...		
		אשר בי	וביה מתפנקין	בו,	cf. 9:13
	11:34	אין לו ממנו	מינה	ממנה,	Qimḥi
	14:15	הלירשנו קראתם לנו	הלמסכנותא קריתון		
		הלא	יתנא הלכא	הלם,	2 MSS
	19:9	לינו נא הנה חנות	ביתו כען הכא לחוד	הנה,	OG
		היום	יומא דין		
	20:34	מנגד לגבעה	מדרום לגבעתא	מנגב,	mlt MSS
	21:10	נגרע היום שבט אחד	איתמנע	נגרע,	mlt MSS

[15] Churgin (*Targum Jonathan* [1927], p. 53) has remarked that the LXX and Psht also exhibit this tendency to some extent. Although in most cases where grammatical incongruence occurs in the Hebrew text the Tg does not attempt to impose grammatical congruence, when it does, there is no consistent pattern whereby the incongruence is resolved. It may be resolved in conformity with the first, last or middle grammatical form in the sentence. Examples that Churgin cites include (*Targum Jonathan* [1927], p. 66):

		MT	Tg	Following	
Judg.	2:14	ביד שסים	בידיהון	ביד אויביהם	
				לפני אויביהם	
	2:22	את דרך	אורחן דתקנן	ללכת בם,	Psht
	20:37	והאורב החישו	אוחי ואתנגד	וימשך האורב ויך	
		ויפשטו			

[16] Churgin said that this was also a tendency in the Samaritan text, to some extent in the LXX and to a greater extent in the Psht (*Targum Jonathan* [1927], pp. 53-55). In most cases the Tg translator was evidently concerned to eliminate factual divergencies and, though no definite rule can be discerned, the second passage is more often made to conform to that preceding (e.g., Judg. 7:7 [MT: בְּיָדְךָ = Tg: בידך], 7:18, 20 [MT: וּלְגִדְעוֹן; but Tg: עַל יְדֵי גדעון [וּנצחנא] "and [victory] *by the hands of* Gideon"]). Churgin cited also: Judg. 5:8 (Tg: דמקרב אתעבידא דלא איתעסקו בהון אבהתכון "which were made nearby, with which your fathers had not occupied themselves", which follows Deut. 32:17); Judg. 7:7 (Tg: בידיהון לפומהון "with their hands to their mouth", which follows Judg. 7:6; so also Psht); Judg. 7:18 (Tg: חרבא "a sword", which follows Judg. 7:20; so also Psht); Judg. 20:38 (Tg: יטור "column", which follows 20:40); and Judg. 20:40 (Tg: תננא "the smoke", which follows Josh. 8:20) (*Targum Jonathan* [1927], pp. 70-71).

More recently, Harrington–Saldarini have added a further eight translation characteristics of the Tg for which examples may be found in Tg Judges. The following is adapted from their list.[17]

1. The Tg usually changes the Hebrew collective singular into a plural (e.g., Judg. 1:4, 21, 29, 30; 3:30; 8:28).

2. The Tg often gives the contemporary name for a place (e.g., Judg. 1:16, MT: מעיר התמרים "from the city of palms" = Tg: מקרתא יריחו "from the city of Jericho"). If the place is unknown to the targumist, an identification with a known place is sometimes suggested, sometimes inaccurately (e.g., [1] Judg. 11:16, MT: קדשה "to Kadesh[-Barnea]" = Tg: לרקם "to Rekam" [in Transjordan]; cf. Josh. 10:41; 14:6, 7; [2] Judg. 20:33, MT: בבעל תמר "at Baal-Tamar" [near Gibeah] = Tg: במישרי יריחו "in the plains of Jericho" [through midrash]). Sometimes a place name was not recognized as such, so the Tg translated it as a nominal form (e.g., [1] Judg. 9:31, MT: בתרמה "at Tormah" = Tg: ברז "in deceit, in secret" [Tg construed MT as a noun]; [2] Judg. 7:1, MT: המורה "Moreh" = Tg: דמסתכיא "which faces, which overlooks" [the Tg construed the MT as a participle]).

3. The Tg makes regular specifying additions (e.g., Judg. 3:11, 30, MT: הארץ "the land" = Tg: ארעא דישראל "the land of Israel"). The Tg regularly substitutes vocabulary (e.g., [1] Judg. 11:17,[18] MT: ולא שמע "but he did not hear" = Tg: ולא קביל "but he did not accept"; cf. Josh. 1:18; [2] Judg. 3:30, MT: ותכנע "and [Moab] was subdued" and 8:28, MT: ויכנע "and [Midian] was subdued" = Tg: ואתברו "and [PN pl.] were shattered" [to indicate defeat in battle]). The Tg also tends to make clarifying interpolations (e.g., [1] Judg. 6:4, MT: מחיה "life-means, sustenance" = Tg: מזון לקימא נפש "food to sustain life"; [2] Judg. 6:19, MT: ויעש ... ואיפת־קמח מצות "he prepared ... and unleavened cakes from an ephah of flour" = Tg: ומכילתא דקמחא אפא "he baked a measure of unleavened flour"; [3] Judg. 6:25, MT: ופר השני שבע שנים "a second ox seven years old" = Tg: ותורא תנינא דאתפטים שבע שנין "a second ox that has been fattened up for seven years"; [4] Judg. 17:3, MT: את־אלף־ומאה הכסף "the one hundred eleven in silver" = Tg: ית אלף ומאה סלעין דכסף "the one hundred eleven selas of silver" [supplying the unit of currency]).

4. The Tg sometimes interprets an obscure term in the MT in an attempt to make it clear (e.g., [1] Judg. 2:3, MT: לצדים "opponents, adversaries" [cf. Arab. ḍiddun "contrary, opposed, adverse"] = Tg: למעיקין "oppressors"; [2] Judg. 9:37, MT: מעם טבור "from the navel" [where navel is a metonymy for "centre"] = Tg: מן תקפא "from the strength" [taking navel as a metonymy for "strength"]).[19]

---

[17] Following Harrington–Saldarini, *Targum Jonathan* (1987), pp. 4-13.

[18] Harrington–Saldarini mistakenly cited Judg 3:17 (*Targum Jonathan* [1987], p. 6).

[19] In Harrington–Saldarini, the reference to Judg 3:23 (*Targum Jonathan* [1987], p. 7) confuses MT Judg. 3:22b: הפרשדנה [*hapax legomenon*] "faeces, excrement" [BDB, p. 832a; cf. BH פֶּרֶשׁ I. 'faecal matter' (BDB, p. 831b), Aram. פרתא 'dung'] = Tg: אכליה

5. The Tg modernizes archaic items or customs (e.g., [1] Judg. 7:8, MT: לאהליו "[each] to his tent" and 19:9,[20] לאהלך "to your tent" = Tg: לקרוהי "to his city" and לקרוך "to your city", respectively; [2] Judg. 1:28a, 30b, MT: למס "forced labour" = Tg: למסקי מסין "bearers of tribute" [since taxes later replaced forced labour]; [3] Judg. 1:15, MT: ברכה "a blessing" = Tg: אחסנתא "an inheritance";[21] [4] Judg. 3:20a, 24b, MT: המקרה [בעלית/בהדר] "[in the upper chamber/privy of] coolness" = Tg: בית קיטא [בעלית/באדרון] "[in the upper chamber/privy of] the summer house" [reflecting a Hellenistic custom of the wealthy];[22] [5] Judg. 19:6, MT: וישבו [ויאכלו] "and they sat [to eat]" = Tg: ואסחרו [ואכלו] "and they reclined [to eat]" [reflecting Hellenistic and Roman custom]; [6] Judg. 2:16 and *passim*, MT: שפטים "judges" = Tg: נגודין "leaders" [whose contemporary meaning better fit the activities of these "judges"]; [7] Judg. 4:5, MT: תחת־תמר "under the palm" = Tg: בקרתה "in her city" [since cities were the place of courts in later times]; [8] Judg. 14:10, MT: וירד אביהו אל־האשה "and his father went down to the woman" = Tg: ונחת אבוהי על עיסק אתתא "and his father went down regarding the matter of the woman" [since proper procedure was for parents to confer]; [9] Judg. 8:24, MT: ישמעאלים "Ishmaelites" = Tg: ערבאי "Arabs" [since Arabs were regarded as descendants of Ishmael]).

6. The Tg tends to render figurative language more literally (e.g., [1] Judg. 14:18, MT: חרשתם בעגלתי "you plowed with my heifer" = Tg: בדקתון באתתי "you examined my wife"). Proverbs are changed to discursive prose (e.g., Judg. 8:2, MT: הלוא טוב עללות אפרים מבציר אביעזר "Is not the gleaning of the grapes of Ephraim better than the vintage of Abiezer?" = Tg: הלא טבין חלשיא דבית אפרים מתקפיא דבית אביעזר "Are not the weak ones of the house of Ephraim better than the strong ones of the house of Abiezer?").

7. The Tg tends to emphasize both divine transcendence (avoiding anthropomorphism when referring to God) and monotheism (avoiding legitimation of the existence of other gods). Means used to emphasize God's transcendence include: (1) modifying expressions of divine activity (e.g., [a] Judg. 1:22, MT: ויהוה עמם "and YHWH was with them" = Tg: ומימרא דיוי בסעדהון "and the Word of the Lord was at their aid"; [b] Judg. 3:20, MT: דבר־אלהים לי אליך "I have a word of God for you" =

שפיך "his faeces pouring" with the *hapax legomenon* המסדרונה "porch" [so the AV; BDB, p. 690b ('porch, colonnade'); the RV; NEB; NIV] in MT Judg. 3:23a = Tg: לאכסדרא "to the hall"). Likewise, Harrington–Saldarini, *Targum Jonathan* (1987), p. 64 n. 29 referred to the wrong term in the text. In the latter text, the Tg renders both terms in a sensible manner despite the possibility that the MT may preserve duplicate *hapax legomena* (cf. *BHS*).

[20] Harrington–Saldarini mistakenly cited Judg 1:14 (*Targum Jonathan* [1987], p. 7).

[21] Indeed, the Tg interpretatively links MT Judg. 1:14 השדה "the field" with MT Judg. 1:15 ברכה "blessing" by translating both terms with אחסנתא "inheritance".

[22] This is a dubious case, however, since the NEB translates the term in MT Judg. 3:20a, 24b: "summer palace" and the NIV, alternatively, "summer palace" and "house".

Tg: פתגמא דיוי אית לי למללא עמך "I have a message of the Lord to speak with you"; [c] Judg. 4:14, MT: הלא יהוה יצא לפניך "Is not YHWH going out before you?" = Tg: הלא מלאכא דיוי נפיק לאצלחא קדמך "Is not the angel of the Lord going forth to ensure success before you?" [substituting an intermediary being for YHWH]); (2) rendering anthropomorphisms of Hebrew idiom in an indirect way (e.g., [a] Judg. 4:1, MT: בעיני יהוה "in the eyes of YHWH" = Tg: קדם יוי "before the Lord"; [b] Judg. 2:15, MT: יד־יהוה היתה־בם "the hand of YHWH was against them" = Tg: מחא מן קדם יוי הות בהון "the slaughter from before the Lord was upon them"; [c] Judg. 2:2, MT: ולא־שמעתם בקלי "but you did not obey my voice" = Tg: ולא קבילתון למימרי "but you did not accept my Word" [substituting the metonymical effect for its cause]); (3) expressing human relations with God as forms of prayer (e.g., [a] Judg. 2:12a, MT: ויעזבו את־יהוה "and they abandoned YHWH" = Tg: ושבקו ית פלחהא דיוי "and they abandoned the service of the Lord"; [b] Judg. 2:18, MT: כי־ינחם יהוה מנאקתם "YHWH was moved to pity by their groaning" = Tg: יוי ממא דאמר ומקביל צלותהון ופריק להון "the Lord was turning from what he said and was receiving their prayers and was saving them"); (4) altering the portrayal of God as the object of human activity (e.g., [a] Judg. 1:1, MT: וישאלו בני ישראל ביהוה "and the Israelites inquired of YHWH" = Tg: ושאילו בני ישראל במימרא דיוי "and the Israelites inquired of the Word of the Lord"; [b] Judg. 2:12b, MT: ויכעסו את־יהוה "and they provoked YHWH" = Tg: וארגיזו קדם יוי "and they made provocation before the Lord"). Means used to emphasize God's uniqueness (monotheism) include: (1) distinguishing the God of Israel from a generic use of "god" (e.g., [a] Judg. 1:7, MT: אלהים = Tg: יוי [changing "God", in the speech of a foreigner, to "Lord (= YHWH)"; cf. Judg. 3:20]; [b] Judg. 2:3, MT: ואלהיהם "and [as for] their gods" = Tg: וטעותהון "and their idols" [designating foreign gods "idols"; cf. Judg. 2:12; 5:8; 10:14a; 17:5a]); (2) distinguishing a priest of YHWH (כהן) from a priest of foreign gods (כומרא) (e.g., [a] Judg. 17:5b, MT: לכהן = Tg: לכומרא [so Bomberg; לכוהן, Antwerp Polyglot; לכהין, rell; cf. Judg. 17:13]; [b] Judg. 17:12, MT:לכהן = Tg: לכומרא [so British Museum MS Add. 26899; לכהין, rell]); (3) distinguishing altars of YHWH from altars of foreign gods (e.g., Judg. 6:25, MT: את־מזבח "the altar [of Baal]" = Tg: ית איגורא "the mound [of Baal]"; contrast 6:26 מדבחא "altar [before the Lord]" and cf. 6:28 [both terms]); (4) rendering the portrayal of foreign gods using contrary-to-fact clauses (e.g., Judg. 10:14, MT: המה יושיעו לכם בעת צרתכם "Let them deliver you in the time of your distress" = Tg: האם יכלן למפרקכון בעדן עקתכון "whether they are able to save you in your time of distress").

8. The Tg sometimes makes midrashic additions, an example of which is Tg Judges 5, which manifests targumic interpretative homiletics through filling out its terse poetic wording and clarifying its meaning for contemporary readers. The Tg "turned Judges 5 into an illustration of

Israel's relationship with God: Whenever Israel rejects the Law, its enemies triumph; whenever it returns to the Law, it triumphs over the enemies".[23] The Tg sometimes harmonizes a passage with later halakhic (legal) practices (e.g., Tg Judg. 11:39 both states a law against child sacrifice and surmises that, had Jephthah consulted Phinehas the priest, he would have been instructed how to redeem his vow). The Tg sometimes makes theologically motivated alterations (e.g., [1] removal of the theophoric element בעל from Judg. 3:3 or of בעלי "masters, occupants" from 9:2; [2] attribution of Judah's inability to occupy the plain to their prior sin [Judg. 1:19];[24] [3] substitution of "quarries" in Judg. 3:19, 26 for "carved idols", as legitimate landmarks in Israel; [4] substitution of "the prophet of[/by commission from before] the Lord" in Judg. 2:1, 4, 5:23 for "the angel of YHWH"; [5] interpretation of the name כושן רשעתים in Judg. 3:8 [2x], 10 [2x] as כושן חיבא "Cushan the sinner").

Variants between the MT and Tg manifesting the foregoing translation tendencies would therefore probably not imply that the Tg was translating from a Hebrew *Vorlage* different from that of the MT.

The Psht is best represented by its oldest (pre-ninth C. CE) MSS 6h7, 8a1, 8a1ᶜ, 9c1/10c1/10c4, 7a1, 7g1 and 9a1.[25] Among the main translation tendencies enumerated by Dirksen should be mentioned:[26]

1. If "into the hand of" is followed by a noun, the Psht usually translates with the singular (e.g., Judg. 2:4; 10:7). If, however, it is followed by a suffix, the Psht usually translates with the plural (e.g., Judg. 3:28; 7:15; 8:3, 10). Exceptions include Judg. 16:23, 24 (*bidan* in most MSS) (p. 135).

2. The tendency of MS 6h7 (and its congeners—in declining order: 8a1, 8a1ᶜ, 9c1/10c1/10c4) is to improve the Syriac (p. 134). The *Vorlage* of MS 6h7 shows a tendency to adapt the text to better Syriac idiom and assimilation to the context or another passage (e.g., the additions in Judg. 1:15; 3:25; 8:10, 25; 9:47; 11:3; 19:1; the variants in Judg. 1:1; 4:5; 16:23; 20:46) (p. 144).

Excluding from consideration inner Syriac variants and errors, which bear no relation to the Hebrew *Vorlage*, four variants within the Psht may be of interest to the textual criticism of the Hebrew text of Judges:

---

[23] Harrington–Saldarini, *Targum Jonathan* (1987), p. 11.

[24] Harrington–Saldarini ill-advisedly attributed this inability to Joshua (*Targum Jonathan* [1987], p. 12).

[25] Cf. Dirksen, "Ancient Peshiṭta MSS" (1988), pp. 128-30.

[26] The following page citations refer to Dirksen, "Ancient Peshiṭta MSS" (1988). This study does not take into consideration the many instances in which the Psht MSS unanimously differ from the MT. These would have to be considered in an evaluation of the *Tendenz* of the Psht as a witness to its Hebrew *Vorlage*.

the addition/omission at Judg. 2:7 and the differences within Psht at Judg. 14:4; 15:20; 18:29.[27]

The major conclusion about the value of the Psht for the criticism of the Hebrew text of Judges is that

> we have at our disposal the text which underlies the available Syriac MSS of Judges, except for a small number of cases in which no decision as to textual priority can be made, and that only in a very small number of cases the difference between two readings is of interest to the textual critic. To be remembered is that readings peculiar to one MS are not covered by this conclusion.[28]

It has been nearly a century since significant scholarly attention was focused upon examining the character of the Vg translation of the Hebrew text of Judges.[29] Nevertheless, the important study of B. Kedar-Kopfstein that examined the *Tendenz* of the Vg in relation to the Hebrew Bible as a whole often draws illustrations from the Vg text of Judges.[30] The following characteristics of the Vg translation of Judges may be noted:

1. The Vg freely renders idiomatic Hebrew verbal constructions that are unidiomatic in Latin or difficult to correlate to Latin constructions (e.g., [1] Judg. 11:39, where the MT cognate accusative of ויעש לה את נדרו אשר נדר "And he did to her the vow that he had vowed" is avoided in the Vg: *fecit ei sicut voverat* "he did to her as he had vowed"; [2] Judg. 9:8, where the MT infinitive absolute הלוך הלכו העצים "the trees went about" is disregarded by the Vg: *ierunt ligna* "the trees went"; [3] Judg. 11:3, where the paratactic repetition in the MT: ויאמר אל זבל...ויאמר אליו זבל "And he said to Zebul ... and Zebul said to him" is converted into hypotaxis in the Vg by means of a relative pronoun: *dixit ad zebul cui ille respondit* "He said to Zebul ... to whom he answered"; [4] Judg. 11:14, where the MT verbal construction ויסף עוד ... וישלח מלאכים "And he added again ... and sent messengers" = the Vg adverbial rendering: *per quos rursum mandavit* "By the same he again sent word ...") (pp. 256, 258, 265, 22, respectively).

2. When the Vg augments the Hebrew by explanatory additions, it tends to do so in order to render potentially obscure idiomatic or figurative

---

[27] Dirksen, "Ancient Peshiṭta MSS" (1988), p. 145.

[28] Dirksen, "Ancient Peshiṭta MSS" (1988), p. 146; cf. p. 128.

[29] Cf. B. Neteler, *Das Buch der Richter der Vulgata und des hebräischen Textes übersetst und erklärt* (Munster, i. W., 1900).

[30] B. Kedar-Kopfstein, "The Vulgate as a Translation: Some Semantic and Syntactical Aspects of Jerome's Version of the Hebrew Bible" (PhD diss., Hebrew University, Jerusalem, 1968). All page citations below refer to Kedar-Kopfstein, "Vulgate as a Translation" (1968).

language into plain relief (e.g., [1] Judg. 8:25, where MT: ויפרשׂו את־השׂמלה "and they spread out a mantle" = Vg: *expandentesque super terram pallium* "and spreading out on the ground a cloak"; [2] Judg. 5:31aβγ, where the MT simile ואהביו כצאת השׁמשׁ בגבורתו "but [may] his devotees [be] like the going forth of the sun in its strength" = Vg: *sicut sol in ortu suo splendet ita rutilent* "and may those who love you shine out glorious as the sun in its rising"; [3] MT Judg. 10:6 ... ויסמׂו לעשׂות הרע "and they again ... did evil" = Vg: *peccatis veteribus iugentes nova fecerunt malum* "joining new sins to their old they did evil") (pp. 69 [cf. 156, 157], 33 [cf. 245], 137 [cf. 207], respectively).

3.　The Vg often freely deviates from the Hebrew vocabulary and syntactical constructions even where a greater degree of formal correspondence was otherwise possible (e.g., [1] MT Judg. 19:21b-22a: ויאכלו וישׁתו המה מתיבים את־לבם "and they ate and they drank. And while they were making their hearts merry" = the redundant Vg rendering: *recepit eos in convivium. Illis epulantibus et post laborem itineris cibo et potu reficientibus corpora* "and he received them with a meal. There while feasting and, after the toil of their journey, refreshing their bodies with food and drink"; [2] Judg. 3:31, where two Hebrew words in the MT: מלמד הבקר "cattle prod" = one term in the Vg: *vomer* "ploughshare"; [3] Judg. 20:32, where the direct speech of the MT: ויאמרו בני בנימין נגפים הם לפנינו כבראשׁנה ובני ישׂראל אמרו ננוסה "The sons of Benjamin said, 'We are striking them before us as at first.' But the sons of Israel said, 'Let us flee'" = indirect speech in the Vg: *putaverunt enim solito eos more cedere qui fugam arte simulantes* "they thought they would kill them in their accustomed manner who cunningly pretended to flee"; [4] MT Judg. 18:7 ויראו את־העם ... שׁקט ובטח ואין־מכלים דבר בארץ "And they saw the people ... quiet and secure with no one humiliating anything in the land" is rendered by the ablative absolute construction in the Vg: *videruntque populum ... securum et quietum nullo ei penitus resistente* "And they saw the people ... secure and quiet, no one at all resisting her [i.e., the city]") (pp. 35-36, 100, 178, 232, respectively).

4.　Sometimes the Vg specifies from the context a more precise meaning than that of the Hebrew word (e.g., [1] MT Judg. 11:10 כדברך "according to your word" = Vg: *promissa* "as promised" [rather than a form of *verbum*]; [2] MT Judg. 9:28 ויאמר = Vg: *clamans(/te)* "(by) crying aloud" [rather than a form of *dicere* "to say"]; [3] MT Judg. 15:2 אמר אמרתי "I said" = Vg: *putavi* "I thought"; [4] MT Judg. 9:27: בית אלהיהם "house of their god" = Vg: *fanum dei sui* "sanctuary of their own god") (pp. 112 [*bis*], 113, 115, respectively).

5.　Contrariwise, the Vg sometimes exhibits a tension between the usual sense of a word in context and its etymology, presumed or real (e.g., MT Judg. 15:5: ועד קמה "even to the [standing] grain" = Vg: *adhuc stantes in stipula* "even that which yet stood in the stalk") (p. 103).

6.　When an idiomatic use of parts of the human body occurs in Hebrew, the Vg may render the term literally and transfer it to a seemingly more appropriate place (e.g., MT Judg. 9:36 מראשׁי ההרים...את צל ההרים

אתה ראה כאנשים "from the summits of the hills ... the shadow of the hills are you seeing as though [they were] men" = Vg: *de montibus ... umbras montium vides quasi capita hominum* "from the mountains ... shadows of the mountains you see as though heads of men") (p. 120).

7. Where physical gestures differ between the Hebrew and Jerome's cultures, the Vg may substitute that of the latter (e.g., MT Judg. 18:19 שׁים ידך על פיך "put your hand over your mouth" = Vg: *pone digitum super os tuum* "put a finger upon your mouth") (p. 122).

8. Occasionally the Vg simply grafts (transliterates) the Hebrew word into the sentence without translation (e.g., [1] MT: תרפים "(mantic) figurines" in Judg. 17:5, 18:14, 17 = Vg: *theraphim* [but cf. the translation *idola* "idols" in 18:18, 20]; [2] MT: שׁכר "(intoxicating) drink; beer" in Judg. 13:4, 7, 14 = Vg: *sicera* in contexts where BH שׁכר parallels יין "wine"—otherwise being translated *vinum* "wine" [Num. 28:7; Ps. 69:13]) (pp. 95, 96, respectively).

One would be well advised to check for possible instances of these translation characteristics before assuming that the Vg was based upon a divergent Hebrew *Vorlage*. Concomitantly, it would be mistaken to conclude that Jerome's translation always reflects a direct dependence upon a single Hebrew *Vorlage*, for Jerome used during his lifetime a number of divergent, and some nonstandard, Hebrew MSS.[31] Moreover, many Latin variants in the Vg may be directly dependent upon the OLat translation. Jerome himself declared that it was his policy to leave intact as many of the OLat elements as possible, especially where the latter had become sanctified by tradition or dogma. Hence, where the Vg may seem to agree with the text-type represented in the Lucianic MSS of the LXX, it may simply reflect the dependence of the OLat upon that Greek tradition.[32] In sum, the Vg may sometimes blur the distinction between divergent Hebrew text-types, on the one hand, or between Hebrew text-types and the text-type represented by the OLat translation, on the other. The most significant variants of the Vg, therefore, will be those that diverge from both the OLat and the MT, though even in this instance the aggregate of such unique variants may derive either from separate Hebrew text-types or from Jerome's free translation style.

In the absence of a critical edition of the LXX in Judges, by which one may learn of the OG translator's *Tendenz*, a characterization of the OG Judges would be premature. A special study by J. Schreiner

[31] Kedar-Kopfstein, "Vulgate as a Translation" (1968), p. 71.
[32] Kedar-Kopfstein, "Vulgate as a Translation" (1968), pp. 58-59.

offered, lists of characteristic expressions in LXX Judges.[33] What is needed, however, is an aggregation of the tendencies reflected among the distinctive readings of each major recension as they are interpreted in the context of each separate recension. Accordingly, Lindars, in a recently published study on the text of Judges, provided a rationale for a study of the Greek Judges in its own right.[34] Lindars commented that, when the OG translator on occasion (e.g., Judg. 1:14; 16:13-14; 18:8) failed to understand his/her Hebrew *Vorlage*, his/her mistranslation often engendered further variants concerned to establish closer relations to the exegesis reflected in the developing Hebrew text but, equally, showed concern to present a Greek text that made sense.[35] However, whatever dogmatic interests Lindars observed in the LXX (e.g., with reference to the angel of YHWH in 2:1; 6:14, 16; and to mixed marriage in 21:22) seem not to derive from the OG *per se*.

C. MANUSCRIPT FAMILIES AND CHARACTERIZATION OF THE HEBREW TEXT

The Judges MS fragments found in Qumran caves 1 and 4, of which only those from cave 1 have yet been published , are scant and make a small contribution to an understanding of the developing Hebrew text during the last centuries BCE and the first CE.[36] Understandably, it is

---

[33] J. Schreiner, *Septuaginta-Massora des Buches der Richter: Eine textkritische Studie* (AnBib 7, Rome, 1957). Cf. the review by P. Walters [Katz] in *TLZ* 86 (1961), cols. 829-32.

[34] Lindars, "Commentary on the Greek Judges?" (1987).

[35] Lindars, "Commentary on the Greek Judges?" (1987), p. 193.

[36] The 1QJudg fragments were first published in D. Barthélemy and J. T. Milik (eds.), *Qumran Cave I* (DJD I, Oxford, 1955), pp. 62-64, pl. XI. A cursory summary of the contents of 4QJudg[a] and 4QJudg[b] is offered in R. G. Boling, *Judges: Introduction, Translation and Commentary* (AB 6A, Garden City, N.Y., 1975), p. 40. More recently, J. Trebolle Barrera has offered an assessment of the place of 4QJudg[a] in Judges' history of transmission ("Textual Variants in 4QJudg[a] and the Textual and Editorial History of the Book of Judges", *RevQ* 14 [1989], pp. 229-45). The *editio princeps* of the Judges MSS from cave 4 promises to appear shortly (E. Ulrich [ed.], *Qumran Cave 4: IX: Deuteronomy, Joshua, Judges, Kings* [DJD XIV, Oxford, 1996]).

The following sections of the book of Judges have been identified and catalogued among the Qumran fragments:

Judg. 6:3-13	4QJudg[a]
6:20-22	1QJudg 1
8:1(?)	1QJudg 2
9:1-4	1QJudg 3
9:4-6	1QJudg 4
9:28-29	1QJudg 5
9:29-31	1QJudg 6

difficult to characterize the text-type of 1Q Judges, though F. M. Cross, in Boling's commentary, reported that 4QJudgᵃ "does reflect the type of text in the better Septuagint tradition"—presumably referring to the Lucianic text-type represented by LXX-AII.[37]

Among the historical books, MT Judges is a relatively stable text-type, though it is not entirely free from the errors coincident with transcription.[38] Variants among the MT MSS seldom offer improvements on these errors, and few materially affect the sense. The differences in Kethib–Qere readings are often inconsequential (e.g., the Qere supplies either a ו or י missing in the orthography of the Kethib: 1:27; 21:20; the Qere substitutes a Paʿil for a Kethib Paʿul noun: 7:13; or the reverse: 16:21, 25).[39] Accidental scribal variations are probably reflected in the Kethib–Qere where: Qere cites a variant that has preposition כ for Kethib ב in 19:25 (pp. 71, 144); Qere cites a variant in which *waw* consecutive stands for י of the prefix conjugation in 6:5 (pp. 73, 145); Qere either cites a variant or corrects to לִי the Kethib לָהּ²—probably a dittography from לָהּ¹ in the preceding line (pp. 82, 152). According to Gordis, instances where the Kethib may be preferred include: 7:21, where Kethib–Qere reflect different conjugations (p. 134); 9:8, 12, where the Kethib preserves the older form of the imperative (p. 108); 13:18 (p. 124); 19:3, where Kethib–Qere show gender variation because of different agreements (p. 139). Equally justifiable to Gordis were the Kethib–Qere readings in 11:37 (pp. 42, 124); 13:17 (pp. 61, 136); 16:25 (K: כִּי טוֹב; Q: כְּטוֹב) (pp. 81, 151); 19:21 (pp. 60, 136), 25 (pp. 71, 144); 20:13 (pp. 78, 147).

Some Qere readings reflect attempts to interpret difficulties in the text. The Kethib preserves the 2 f. sg pronoun אַתִּי in 17:2 and the 2 f. sg perfect ending ־תִּי in 17:2 אָלִיתִי (not in L).[40] That the Qere

---

9:40-42	1QJudg 7
9:40-43	1QJudg 8
9:48-49	1QJudg 9
16:5-7	4QJudgᵇ 1
21:12-25	4QJudgᵇ 2

[37] Boling, *Judges* (1975), p. 40.

[38] G. F. Moore, *A Critical and Exegetical Commentary on Judges* (ICC, Edinburgh, 1895), p. xliii; cf. n. *.

[39] See R. Gordis, *The Biblical Text in the Making: A Study of the Kethib-Qere* (New York, 2d edn, 1971), pp. 7, 8, 96, 97; pp. 34, 117; and pp. 35, 118, respectively. All subsequent page citations refer to Gordis, *Biblical Text* (2d edn, 1971).

[40] Gordis, *Biblical Text* (2d edn, 1971), pp. 17, 102. Gordis wrote: "In Ju 17:2 K ואתי אליתי; Q וְאַתְּ אָלִית; LXX reads 'and you beswore me' eq. וְאַתִּי אָלִית the K, with אָלִית interpreted in a causative sense" (p. 57).

probably did not intend to correct here, only to explain or to cite a variant, may be proven from comparison with the same phenomenon in 5:7 קַמְתִּי, where no Kethib–Qere exists. MT Judges preserves no instance where diphthong 'ai' was preserved in the Kethib without י, except in the standard form of the place name ירושלם (e.g., 1:8, 21).[41] The Qere in 16:26 reflects not a scribal metathesis but a Rabbinic comment showing paronomasia between the Kethib וְהֵימִשֵׁנִי "and let me touch [the columns]" and the Qere וַהֲמִישֵׁנִי "and let me remove [the columns]" (cf. Mic. 2:3).[42]

In conclusion, the Hebrew text of Judges reflects a relatively reliable history of scribal transmission, and this makes the goal of establishing the earliest form of the text less problematic than it would be for some other books of the Hebrew Bible (e.g., the books of Samuel and Jeremiah). The textual problems selected for analysis in the text-critical notes to the appendix are those deemed most relevant to the rhetoric of the book of Judges. Of course, it is sometimes difficult to draw hard lines between either scribal or editorial motivations that may underlie the present form of the text, but the examples selected should furnish the reader with ample illustrations of the character and of the problems of the transmission of the Hebrew text of Judges.

---

[41] Gordis, *Biblical Text* (2d edn, 1971), p. 100.
[42] Gordis, *Biblical Text* (2d edn, 1971), pp. 33, 116.

APPENDIX

A COMPILATIONAL STRATIGRAPHY OF
THE TEXT OF JUDGES

JUDGES 1:1–2:5[i] [1]

S ◇	N/D/J ◇	C/R

1 1 ויהי אחרי מות יהושע / וישאלו בני
ישראל / ביהוה לאמר // מי יעלה־לנו
אל־הכנעני בתחלה להלחם בו[ii]:
2 ויאמר יהוה יהודה יעלה[iii] // הנה
נתתי את־הארץ בידו:

3 ויאמר יהודה לשמעון אחיו עלה אתי
בגורלי / ונלחמה בכנעני / והלכתי
גם־אני אתך בגורלך // וילך אתו שמעון:

4 ויעל יהודה /

ויתן יהוה

את־הכנעני ו־

הפרזי בידם // ויכום בבזק / עשרת
אלפים איש:
5 וימצאו את־אדני בזק בבזק / וילחמו
בו // ויכו

את־הכנעני ו־

את־הפרזי:

6 וינס אדני בזק / וירדפו אחריו // ויאחזו
אתו / ויקצצו / את־בהנות ידיו ורגליו:
7 ויאמר אדני־בזק / שבעים מלכים
בהנות ידיהם ורגליהם מקצצים / היו
מלקטים תחת שלחני / כאשר עשיתי / כן
שלם־לי אלהים //
ויביאהו ירושלם וימת שם: ‪-פ-‬

8 וילחמו בני־יהודה בירושלם / וילכדו
אותה / ויכוה לפי־חרב // ואת־העיר
שלחו באש:

9 ואחר / ירדו בני יהודה / להלחם
בכנעני // יושב ההר / והנגב והשפלה:
10 וילך יהודה / אל־הכנעני היושב
בחברון[iv] [2] / ושם־חברון לפנים קרית
ארבע[v] //
ויכו את־ששי ואת־אחימן ואת־תלמי[vi]:

11 וילך[3] משם / אל־יושבי דביר[vii] //
ושם־דביר לפנים קרית־ספר[viii]:

S ◇   N/D/J ◇   C/R

12 ויאמר כלב / אשר־יכה
את־קרית־ספר ולכדה // ונתתי לו
את־עכסה בתי לאשה:
13 וילכדה עתניאל בן־קנז / אחי כלב
הקטן ממנו[ix] //
ויתן־לו את־עכסה בתו לאשה:
14 ויהי בבואה / ותסיתהו[4] לשאול
מאת־אביה <>שדה[5] / ותצנח מעל
החמור // ויאמר־לה כלב מה־לך:
15 ותאמר לו הבה־ל[x]י ברכה / כי ארץ
הנגב נתתני / ונתתה לי גלת מים //
ויתן־לה כלב[6] / את גלת עלית / ואת
גלת תחתית[xi]: ‒פ‒

16 ובני קיני חתן משה[7] עלו מעיר
התמרים את־בני יהודה / מדבר <>[8] /
אשר בנגב <במורד>[9] ערד // וילך[10] וישב
אתה< >עמ<לק>[11]:
17 וילך יהודה את־שמעון אחיו / ויכו
את־הכנעני יושב צפת // ויחרימו אותה /
ויקרא את־שם־העיר חרמה:

18 וילכד[12] יהודה את־עזה ואת־גבולה /
ואת־אשקלון ואת־גבולה // ואת־עקרון
ואת־גבולה[13]:

19 ויהי יהוה את־יהודה / וירש
את־ההר // כי לא להוריש[14] את־ישבי
העמק / כי־רכב ברזל להם[15]:
20 ויתנו לכלב את־חברון / כאשר דבר
משה[xii] //
ויורש משם / את־שלשה בני הענק[16][xiii]:

21 ואת־היבוסי ישב<י>[17] ירושלם / לא
הורישו בני בנימן // וישב היבוסי
את־בני בנימן בירושלם / עד היום
הזה[xiv]: ‒ס‒

22 ויעלו בית־יוסף[18] גם־הם בית־אל //
ויהוה[19] עמם:

23 ויתירו[20] בית־יוסף[21] בבית־אל //
ושם־העיר לפנים לוז:
24 ויראו השמרים / איש יוצא מן־העיר //
<ויאחז[ו]הו>[22] ויאמרו לו / הראנו נא
את־מבוא העיר / ועשינו עמך חסד:
25 ויראם את־מבוא העיר / ויכו את־העיר
לפי־חרב // ואת־האיש ואת־כל־משפחתו
שלחו:

S ◇	N/D/J ◇	C/R

26 וילך האיש / ארץ החתים // ויבן[23]
עיר / ויקרא שמה לוז / הוא שמה / עד
היום הזה: ‎-פ-

27 ולא־הוריש מנשה / את־בית־שאן
ואת־בנותיה ואת־תענך ואת־בנתיה /
ואת־ישב<י>[24] דור ואת־בנותיה /
ואת־יושבי יבלעם ואת־בנתיה /
ואת־יושבי מגדו ואת־בנותיה[xv] //
ויואל הכנעני / לשבת בארץ הזאת[xvi]:

28 ויהי כי־חזק ישראל / וישם
את־הכנעני למס // והוריש לא
הורישו[xvii]: ‎-ס-

29 ואפרים לא הוריש / את־הכנעני
היושב בגזר // וישב הכנעני בקרבו
בגזר[xviii]: ‎-פ-

30 זבולן / לא הוריש את־יושבי קטרון /
ואת־יושבי נהלל // וישב הכנעני
בקרבו / ויהיו למס: ‎-ס-

31 אשר / לא הוריש את־ישבי עכו /
ואת־יושבי צידון // ואת־אחלב ואת־אכזיב
ואת־חלבה / ואת־אפיק ואת־רחב:
32 וישב האשרי / בקרב הכנעני ישבי
הארץ // כי לא הורישו: ‎-ס-

33 נפתלי / לא־הוריש את־ישבי
בית־שמש ואת־ישבי בית־ענת / וישב
בקרב הכנעני ישבי הארץ // וישבי
בית־שמש ובית ענת / היו להם למס: ‎-ס-

34 וילחצו האמרי את־בני־דן ההרה //
כי־לא נתנו לרדת לעמק:
35 ויואל האמרי לשבת בהר־חרס /
באילון ובשעלבים //

ותכבד יד בית־יוסף / ויהיו למס:

36 וגבול האמרי[25] / ממעלה עקרבים //
מהסלע ומעלה: ‎-פ-

2 1 ויעל מלאך־יהוה מן־הגלגל
אל־הבכים[26] // ויאמר
אעלה אתכם ממצרים[xix] / ואביא אתכם
אל־הארץ[xx] / אשר נשבעתי
לאבתיכם[xxi] / ואמר / לא־אפר בריתי
אתכם לעולם[xxii]:
2 ואתם / לא־תכרתו ברית ליושבי
הארץ הזאת[xxiii] / מזבחותיהם
תתצון[xxiv] //

S ◇   N/D/J ◇   C/R

ולא־שמעתם בקלי מה־זאת עשיתם:

3 וגם אמרתי / לא־אגרש אותם

מפניכם[xxv] // והיו לכם לצדים[27] /

ואלהיהם / יהיו לכם למוקש[xxvi]:

4 ויהי / כדבר מלאך יהוה את־הדברים

האלה / אל־כל־בני[28] ישראל // וישאו

העם את־קולם ויבכו:

5 ויקראו שם־המקום ההוא בכים //

ויזבחו־שם ליהוה: ‎-פ-

JUDGES 2:6–3:6

S ◇   N/D/J ◇   C/R

2 6 וישלח יהושע את־העם //

וילכו בני־ישראל

איש לנחלתו

לרשת את־הארץ[xxvii]:

7 ויעבדו העם[xxviii] את־יהוה / כל ימי

יהושע // וכל ימי הזקנים / אשר

האריכו ימים אחרי יהושע / אשר

ראו[xxix] /

את כל־מעשה יהוה

הגדול[xxx] /

אשר עשה לישראל[xxxi]:

8 וימת יהושע בן־נון עבד יהוה //

בן־מאה ועשר שנים[xxxii]:

9 ויקברו אותו בגבול נחלתו /

בתמנת־חרס[xxxiii] בהר אפרים[xxxiv] //

מצפון להר־געש[xxxv]:

10 וגם כל־הדור ההוא / נאספו

אל־אבותיו // ויקם דור אחר אחריהם /

אשר לא־ידעו את־יהוה / וגם

את־המעשה / אשר עשה לישראל: ‎-ס-

11 ויעשו בני־ישראל את־הרע בעיני

יהוה[xxxvi] //

ויעבדו את־הבעלים:

12 ויעזבו את־יהוה אלהי אבותם[xxxvii] /

המוציא אותם מארץ מצרים[xxxviii] /

וילכו אחרי אלהים אחרים[xxxix] / מאלהי

העמים אשר סביבותיהם[xl] / וישתחוו

להם[xli] // ויכעסו את־יהוה[xlii]:

13 ויעזבו את־יהוה[xliii] //

ויעבדו לבעל ולעשתרות:

14 ויחר־אף יהוה בישראל[xliv] / ויתנם

ביד־שסים[xlv] /

S ◇   N/D/J ◇   C/R

וישסו אותם // וימכרם ביד אויביהם
מסביב / ולא־יכלו עוד / לעמד לפני
אויביהם:
15 בכל אשר יצאו / יד־יהוה היתה־בם
לרעה /
כאשר דבר יהוה / וכאשר נשבע יהוה
להם //
ויצר להם מאד:

16 ויקם יהוה שפטים // ויושיעום / מיד
שסיהם:
17 וגם אל־שפטיהם לא שמעו /
כי זנו / אחרי אלהים אחרים[xlvi] /
וישתחוו להם[xlvii] / סרו מהר / מן־הדרך
אשר הלכו אבותם לשמע מצות־יהוה
לא־עשו כן[xlviii]:

18 וכי־הקים יהוה להם שפטים / והיה
יהוה עם־השפט / והושיעם מיד
איביהם / כל ימי השופט // כי־ינחם
יהוה מנאקתם /
מפני לחציהם ודחקיהם[xlix]:
19 והיה במות השופט / ישבו והשחיתו
מאבותם /
ללכת / אחרי אלהים אחרים / לעבדם[l] /
ולהשתחות להם[li] //
לא הפילו ממעלליהם / ומדרכם הקשה:
20 ויחר־אף יהוה בישראל[lii] //
ויאמר /
יען אשר עברו הגוי הזה / את־בריתי
אשר צויתי את־אבותם[liii] /
ולא שמעו לקולי:
21 גם־אני לא אוסיף / להוריש איש
מפניהם[liv] //
מן־הגוים אשר־עזב יהושע <>[29]:
22 למען נסות בם את־ישראל //
השמרים הם את־דרכ<>י־[30] יהוה ללכת
בם[31] [lv] /
כאשר שמרו אבותם אם־לא:
23 a וינח יהוה
b את־הגוים האלה /
c לבלתי הורישם מהר //
cⁱ ולא נתנם ביד־יהושע[lvi]: –פ–
3 1 bⁱ ואלה הגוים
aⁱ אשר הניח יהוה /
לנסות בם את־ישראל // כל־אשר
לא־ידעו / את כל־מלחמות כנען:

S ◇   N/D/J ◇   C/R

2 רק / למען <>[32] דרות בני־ישראל /
ללמדם מלחמה // רק אשר־לפנים לא
ידעום:

3 חמשת סרני פלשתים[lvii] /
וכל־הכנעני[lviii] והצידני[lix] /
והחוי[lx] / ישב הר הלבנון[lxi] //מהר בעל
חרמון[lxii] / עד לבוא חמת[lxiii]:

4 ויהיו / לנסות בם את־ישראל //
לדעת / הישמעו את־מצות יהוה /
אשר־צוה את־אבותם ביד־משה:

5 ובני ישראל / ישבו בקרב הכנעני //
החתי והאמרי והפרזי / והחוי והיבוסי[lxiv]:

6 ויקחו את־בנותיהם להם לנשים /
ואת־בנותיהם נתנו לבניהם[lxv] // ויעבדו
את־אלהיהם[lxvi]: –פ–

JUDGES 3:7-30

S ◇   N/D/J ◇   C/R

3 7 ויעשׂו בני־ישׂראל את־הרע בעיני
יהוה / וישכחו את־יהוה אלהיהם //
ויעבדו את־הבעלים ואת־האשרות:

8 ויחר־אף יהוה בישׂראל / וימכרם /
ביד כושן רשעתים / מלך ארם נהרים //
ויעבדו בני־ישׂראל את־כושן רשעתים
שמנה שנים:

9 ויזעקו בני־ישׂראל אל־יהוה / ויקם
יהוה מושיע לבני ישׂראל ויושיעם //

את עתניאל בן־קנז / אחי כלב הקטן
ממנו[lxvii]:

10 ותהי עליו רוח־יהוה וישפט
את־ישׂראל /

ויצא למלחמה /

ויתן יהוה בידו / את־כושן רשעתים
מלך ארם //

ותעז ידו / על כושן רשעתים:

11 ותשקט הארץ ארבעים שׁנה // וימת
עתניאל בן־קנז: –פ–

12 ויספו בני ישׂראל / לעשׂות הרע
בעיני יהוה //

ויחזק יהוה את־עגלון מלך־מואב
על־ישׂראל /

על כי־עשׂו את־הרע בעיני יהוה:

13 ויאסף אליו / את־בני עמון ועמלק //
וילך / ויך את־ישׂראל / ויירשׁו[33] את־עיר
התמרים:

S ◇	N/D/J ◇	C/R

14 ויעבדו בני־ישראל את־עגלון
מלך־מואב / שמונה עשרה שנה: ‪-ס-‬
15 ויזעקו בני־ישראל אל־יהוה / ויקם
יהוה להם מושיע /

את־אהוד בן־גרא בן־הימיני / איש אטר
יד־ימינו //
וישלחו בני־ישראל בידו מנחה / לעגלון
מלך מואב:
16 ויעש לו אהוד חרב / ולה שני פיות
גמד ארכה // ויחגר אותה מתחת למדיו /
על ירך ימינו:
17 ויקרב את־המנחה / לעגלון מלך
מואב // ועגלון איש בריא מאד:
18 ויהי כאשר כלה / להקריב
את־המנחה // וישלח את־העם / נשאי
המנחה:
19 והוא שב / מן־הפסילים אשר
את־הגלגל / ויאמר / דבר־סתר לי אליך
המלך // ויאמר הס / ויצאו‪[34]‬ מעליו /
כל־העמדים עליו:
20 ואהוד בא אליו / והוא־ישב בעלית
המקרה אשר־לו לבדו / ויאמר אהוד /
דבר־אלהים לי אליך // ויקם מעל הכסא:
21 וישלח אהוד את־יד שמאלו / ויקח
את־החרב / מעל ירך ימינו // ויתקעה
בבטנו:
22 ויבא גם־הנצב אחר הלהב / ויסגר
החלב בעד הלהב / כי לא שלף החרב
מבטנו // ויצא הפרשדנה:
23 ויצא אהוד המסדרונה // ויסגר דלתות
העליה בעדו ונעל:
24 והוא יצא ועבדיו באו / ויראו / והנה
דלתות העליה נעלות // ויאמרו / אך
מסיך הוא את־רגליו בחדר המקרה:
25 ויחילו עד־בוש / והנה איננו פתח
דלתות העליה ויקחו את־המפתח
ויפתחו / והנה אדניהם / נפל ארצה מת:
26 ואהוד נמלט עד התמהמהם // והוא
עבר את־הפסילים / וימלט השעירתה:
27 ויהי בבואו /
ויתקע בשופר בהר אפרים // וירדו עמו
בני־ישראל מן־ההר והוא לפניהם:
28 ויאמר אלהם רדפו‪[35]‬ אחרי /
כי־נתן יהוה את־איביכם את־מואב
בידכם //
וירדו אחריו /

S ◇	N/D/J ◇	C/R

וילכדו את־מעברות הירדן למואב /
ולא־נתנו איש לעבר:
29 ויכו את־מואב בעת ההיא / כעשרת
אלפים איש / כל־שמן וכל־איש חיל //
ולא נמלט איש:

30 ותכנע מואב ביום ההוא / תחת יד
ישראל // ותשקט הארץ שמונים
שנה36: ־ס־

JUDGES 3:31–5:31

S ◇	N/D/J ◇	C/R

31 3 ואחריו היה

שמגר בן־ענת / ויך את־פלשתים
שש־מאות איש / במלמד הבקר //

וישע גם־הוא את־ישראל: ־ס־

4 1 ויספו בני ישראל / לעשות הרע
בעיני יהוה // ואהוד מת:
2 וימכרם יהוה / ביד יבין מלך־כנען /
אשר מלך בחצורlxviii // ושר־צבאו
סיסראlxix / והוא יושב בחרשת
הגויםlxx:
3 ויצעקו בני־ישראל אל־יהוה // כי
תשע מאות רכב־ברזל לוlxxi / והוא לחץ
את־בני ישראל בחזקה עשרים
שנה: ־ס־

היא שפטה את־ישראל בעת ההיא:

4 ודבורה אשה נביאה / אשת לפידות //

5 והיא יושבת תחת־תמר דבורה / בין
הרמה ובין בית־אל בהר אפרים // ויעלו
אליה בני ישראל למשפט:
6 ותשלח / ותקרא לברק בן־אבינעם /
מקדש נפתלי // ותאמר אליו הלא צוה
יהוה אלהי־ישראל / לך
ומשכת בהר תבור / ולקחת עמך / עשרת
אלפים איש / מבני נפתלי ומבני זבלון:
7 ומשכתי אליך אל־נחל קישון /
את־סיסרא שר־צבא יביןlxxii / ואת־רכבו
ואת־המונו // ונתתיהו בידך:
8 ויאמר אליה ברק / אם־תלכי עמי
והלכתי // ואם־לא תלכי עמי לא אלך37:
9 ותאמר הלך אלך עמך / אפס כי לא
תהיה תפארתך / על־הדרך אשר אתה
הולך / כי ביד־אשה / ימכר יהוה
את־סיסרא // ותקם דבורה ותלך עם־ברק
קדשה:

S ◇   N/D/J ◇   C/R

10 ויזעק ברק את־זבולן ואת־נפתלי
קדשה / ויעל[38] ברגליו / עשרת אלפי
איש // ותעל עמו דבורה:
11 וחבר הקיני נפרד מקין / מבני חבב
חתן משה // ויט אהלו / עד־אלון בצענים
אשר את־קדש:
12 ויגדו לסיסרא // כי עלה ברק
בן־אבינעם הר־תבור: ‎-ס-
13 ויזעק סיסרא את־כל־רכבו / תשע
מאות רכב ברזל[lxxiii] / ואת־כל־העם אשר
אתו // מחרשת הגוים[lxxiv] אל־נחל קישון:
14 ותאמר דברה אל־ברק קום / כי זה
היום אשר נתן יהוה את־סיסרא בידך /
הלא יהוה יצא לפניך // וירד ברק מהר
תבור / ועשרת אלפים איש אחריו:
15 ויהם יהוה את־סיסרא ואת־כל־הרכב /
ואת־כל־המחנה לפי־חרב לפני ברק //
וירד סיסרא מעל המרכבה וינס ברגליו:
16 וברק רדף אחרי הרכב ואחרי המחנה /
עד חרשת הגוים // ויפל כל־מחנה סיסרא
לפי־חרב / לא נשאר עד־אחד:
17 וסיסרא נס ברגליו /
אל־אהל יעל / אשת חבר הקיני // כי
שלום / בין יבין מלך־חצור[lxxv] / ובין בית
חבר הקיני:
18 ותצא יעל לקראת סיסרא ותאמר
אליו / סורה אדני סורה אלי אל־תירא //
ויסר אליה האהלה / ותכסהו בשמיכה:
19 ויאמר אליה השקיני־נא מעט־מים כי
צמאתי // ותפתח את־נאוד החלב ותשקהו
ותכסהו:
20 ויאמר אליה / עמד פתח האהל // והיה
אם־איש יבוא ושאלך / ואמר היש־פה
איש ואמרת אין:
21 ותקח יעל אשת־חבר את־יתד האהל
ותשם את־המקבת בידה / ותבוא אליו
בלאט / ותתקע את־היתד ברקתו / ותצנח
בארץ // והוא־נרדם ויעף[39] וימת:
22 והנה ברק רדף את־סיסרא / ותצא יעל
לקראתו / ותאמר לו / לך ואראך /
את־האיש אשר־אתה מבקש // ויבא
אליה / והנה סיסרא נפל מת / והיתד
ברקתו:

23 ויכנע אלהים ביום ההוא / את יבין
מלך־כנען // לפני בני ישראל:

S ◇ N/D/J ◇ C/R

24 ותלך יד בני־ישראל הלוך וקשה / על
יבין מלך־כנען // עד אשר הכריתו / את
יבין מלך־כנען: ‪-פ-‬

5 1 ותשר דבורה / וברק בן־אבינעם //
ביום ההוא לאמר:

2 בפרע פרעות בישראל /
בהתנדב עם // ברכו יהוה:

3 שמעו מלכים / האזינו רזנים //
אנכי ליהוה / אנכי[40] אשירה /
אזמר ליהוה / אלהי ישראל:

4 יהוה בצאתך משעיר /
בצעדך משדה אדום /
ארץ רעשה /
גם־שמים נטפו[41] //
גם־עבים נטפו מים:[42]
5 הרים נזלו[43] /
מפני יהוה // זה סיני[44] /
מפני יהוה אלהי ישראל:

6 בימי שמגר בן־ענת /
בימי יעל[45] /
חדלו ארחות[46] //
והלכי נתיבות /
ילכו ארחות עקלקלות:
7 חדלו פרזון /
בישראל חדלו //

עד שקמתי דבורה /
שקמתי אם בישראל:
8 יבחר אלהים חדשים /
אזל‪ו‬ <חמש‪>‬י <ערים[47] //

מגן אם־יראה ורמח /
בארבעים אלף בישראל:

9 לבי[48] לחוקקי ישראל /
המתנדבים בעם //
ברכו יהוה:

10 רכבי אתנות צחרות /
ישבי על־מדין /
והלכי על־דרך שיחו:

11 מקול מחצצים / בין משאבים /
שם יתנו צדקות יהוה /
צדקת פרזנו בישראל //

S ◇   N/D/J ◇   C/R

אז ירדו לשערים עם־יהוה[49]:

12 עורי עורי דבורה /
עורי עורי דברי־שיר //
קום ברק /
ושבה שביך בן־אבינעם:

13 אז ירד שריד / לאדירים
עם // יהוה ירד־לי בגבורים:

14 מני אפרים / שרשם בעמלק[50] /
אחריך בנימין בעממיך //
מני מכיר / ירדו מחקקים /
ומזבולן / משכים בשבט ספר:
15 ושרי ביששכר[51] עם־דברה /
ויששכר כן ברק /
בעמק שלח ברגליו //

בפלגות ראובן / גדלים חקקי־לב:
16 למה ישבת / בין המשפתים /
לשמע שרקות עדרים //
לפלגות ראובן / גדולים חקרי־לב[52]:
17 גלעד / בעבר הירדן שכן /
ודן / למה יגור אניות //
אשר / ישב לחוף ימים /
ועל מפריו ישכון:

18 זבלון / עם חרף נפשו למות
ונפתלי // על מרומי שדה:

19 באו מלכים נלחמו /
אז נלחמו מלכי כנען /
בתענך על־מי מגדו //
בצע כסף לא לקחו:

20 מן־שמים נלחמו // הכוכבים
ממסלותם / נלחמו עם־סיסרא:
21 נחל קישון גרפם /
נחל קדומים
נחל קישון //
תדרכי נפשי עז:

22 אז הלמו עקבי־סוס<י>ם //
דהרות[53] דהרות אביריו:

23 אורו מרוז אמר מלאך יהוה /
ארו ארור ישביה //
כי לא־באו לעזרת יהוה /
לעזרת יהוה בגבורים:

S ◊　　　　　　N/D/J ◊　　　　　C/R

24 תברך מנשים יעל /
אשת חבר הקיני //
מנשים באהל תברך:
25 מים שאל חלב נתנה //
בספל אדירים הקריבה חמאה:
26 ידה ליתד תשלחנה[54] /
וימינה להלמות עמלים //
והלמה סיסרא
מחקה ראשו /
ומחצה וחלפה רקתו:
27 בין רגליה / כרע נפל שכב //
בין רגליה כרע נפל /
באשר כרע /
שם נפל שדוד:

28 בעד החלון נשקפה /
ותיבב אם סיסרא בעד האשנב //
מדוע בשש רכבו לבוא /
מדוע אחרו / פעמי מרכבותיו:
29 חכמות שרותיה תעניּנה //
אף־היא תשיב אמריה לה:
30 הלא ימצאו יחלקו שלל /
רחם רחמתים לראש גבר /
שלל צבעים לסיסרא /
שלל צבעים רקמה //
צבע רקמתים
לצוארי שלל[55]:

31 כן יאבדו כל־אויביך יהוה /
ואהביו / כצאת השמש בגברתו //

ותשקט הארץ ארבעים שנה: –פ–

JUDGES 6:1–8:32, 33–9:57

S ◊　　　　　　N/D/J ◊　　　　　C/R

6 1 ויעשו בני־ישראל הרע בעיני
יהוה // ויתנם יהוה ביד־מדין שבע
שנים:
2 ותעז יד־מדין על־ישראל //

מפני מדין עשו־להם בני ישראל /
את־המנהרות אשר בהרים / ואת־המערות
ואת־המצדות:
3 והיה אם־זרע ישראל // ועלה מדין
ועמלק ובני־קדם ועלו עליו:
4 ויחנו עליהם / וישחיתו את־יבול
הארץ / עד־בואך עזה // ולא־ישאירו
מחיה בישראל / ושה ושור וחמור:

S ◇	N/D/J ◇	C/R

5 כי הם ומקניהם יעלו ואהליהם / יבאו
כדי־ארבה לרב / ולהם ולגמליהם אין
מספר // ויבאו בארץ לשחתה:
6 וידל ישראל מאד מפני מדין //

ויזעקו בני־ישראל אל־יהוהbxxvi: ‎-פ-‏
7 ויהי כי־זעקו בני־ישראל
אל־יהוהbxxvii //

על אדות מדין:
8 וישלח יהוה איש נביא אל־בני
ישראל // ויאמר להם כה־אמר יהוה
אלהי ישראל /

אנכי העליתי אתכם ממצרים / ואציא
אתכם מבית עבדיםbxxviii:
9 ואצל אתכם מיד מצרים /

ומיד כל־לחציכם //

ואגרש אותם מפניכם / ואתנה לכם
את־ארצםbxxix:
10 ואמרה לכם / אני יהוה אלהיכם /
לא תיראו את־אלהי האמרי / אשר אתם
יושבים בארצםbxxx // ולא שמעתם
בקולי56 bxxxi: ‎-פ-‏

11 ויבא מלאך יהוה / וישב תחת האלה
אשר בעפרה / אשר ליואש אבי העזרי //
וגדעון בנו חבט חטים בגת / להניס מפני
מדין:
12 וירא אליו מלאך יהוה // ויאמר אליו /
יהוה עמך גבור החיל:

13 ויאמר אליו גדעון בי אדני / ויש יהוה
עמנו / ולמה מצאתנו כל־זאת //

ואיה כל־נפלאתיו אשר ספרו־לנו
אבותינו לאמר / הלא ממצרים העלנו
יהוה /

ועתה נטשנו יהוה / ויתננו בכף־מדין:
14 ויפן אליו יהוה / ויאמר / לך בכחך
זה / והושעת את־ישראל מכף מדין //
הלא שלחתיך:

15 ויאמר אליו בי אדני /

במה אושיע את־ישראל //

הנה אלפי הדל במנשה / ואנכי הצעיר
בבית אבי:
16 ויאמר אליו יהוה / כי אהיה עמך //
והכית את־מדין כאיש אחד:
17 ויאמר אליו / אם־נא מצאתי חן
בעיניך // ועשית לי אות / שאתה מדבר
עמי:

S ◇   N/D/J ◇   C/R

18 אל־נא תמש מזה עד־באי אליך /
והצאתי את־מנחתי / והנחתי לפניך //
ויאמר / אנכי אשב עד שובך:
19 וגדעון בא / ויעש גדי־עזים
ואיפת־קמח מצות / הבשר שם בסל /
והמרק שם בפרור // ויוצא אליו אל־תחת
האלה ויגש: ‎–ס‎

20 ויאמר אליו מלאך האלהים / קח
את־הבשר ואת־המצות והנח אל־הסלע
הלז / ואת־המרק שפוך // ויעש כן:
21 וישלח מלאך יהוה / את־קצה
המשענת אשר בידו / ויגע בבשר
ובמצות // ותעל האש מן־הצור / ותאכל
את־הבשר ואת־המצות / ומלאך יהוה /
הלך מעיניו:
22 וירא גדעון / כי־מלאך יהוה
הוא // ‎–ס‎

ויאמר גדעון / אהה אדני יהוה /
כי־על־כן ראיתי מלאך יהוה / פנים
אל־פנים:
23 ויאמר לו יהוה שלום לך אל־תירא //
לא תמות:
24 ויבן שם גדעון מזבח ליהוה /
ויקרא־לו יהוה שלום // עד היום הזה /
עודנו / בעפרת אבי העזרי: ‎–פ‎

25 ויהי בלילה ההוא / ויאמר לו יהוה /
קח את־פר־השור אשר לאביך / ופר השני
שבע שנים // והרסת / את־מזבח הבעל
אשר לאביך / ואת־האשרה אשר־עליו
תכרת:
26 ובנית מזבח ליהוה אלהיך / על ראש
המעוז הזה במערכה // ולקחת את־הפר
השני / והעלית עולה / בעצי האשרה
אשר תכרת:
27 ויקח גדעון עשרה אנשים מעבדיו /
ויעש / כאשר דבר אליו יהוה // ויהי
כאשר ירא את־בית אביו / ואת־אנשי
העיר מעשות יומם ויעש לילה:
28 וישכימו אנשי העיר בבקר / והנה נתץ
מזבח הבעל / והאשרה אשר־עליו
כרתה // ואת הפר השני / העלה
על־המזבח הבנוי:
29 ויאמרו איש אל־רעהו / מי עשה הדבר
הזה // וידרשו ויבקשו / ויאמרו / גדעון
בן־יואש / עשה הדבר הזה:

S ◊　　　　N/D/J ◊　　　　C/R

30 ויאמרו אנשי העיר אל־יואש / הוצא
את־בנך וימת // כי נתץ את־מזבח הבעל /
וכי כרת האשרה אשר־עליו:
31 ויאמר יואש לכל אשר־עמדו עליו
האתם תריבון לבעל / אם־אתם תושיעון
אותו / אשר יריב לו יומת עד־הבקר //
אם־אלהים הוא ירב לו / כי נתץ
את־מזבחו:
32 ויקרא־לו ביום־ההוא ירבעל לאמר //
ירב בו הבעל / כי נתץ את־מזבחו: –פ-

33 וכל־מדין ועמלק ובני־קדם נאספו
יחדו // ויעברו ויחנו בעמק יזרעאל:

34 ורוח יהוה / לבשה את־גדעון //
ויתקע בשופר /

ויזעק אביעזר אחריו:
35 ומלאכים שלח בכל־מנשה[57] / ויזעק
גם־הוא אחריו // ומלאכים שלח / באשר
ובזבלון ובנפתלי / ויעלו לקראתם:
36 ויאמר גדעון אל־האלהים //

אם־ישך מושיע בידי את־ישראל כאשר
דברת:

37 הנה אנכי / מציג את־גזת הצמר
בגרן // אם טל יהיה על־הגזה לבדה /
ועל־כל־הארץ חרב / וידעתי / כי־תושיע
בידי את־ישראל כאשר דברת:
38 ויהי־כן / וישכם ממחרת / ויזר
את־הגזה // וימץ טל מן־הגזה / מלוא
הספל מים:
39 ויאמר גדעון אל־האלהים / אל־יחר
אפך בי / ואדברה אך הפעם // אנסה
נא־רק־הפעם בגזה / יהי־נא חרב
אל־הגזה לבדה / ועל־כל־הארץ
יהיה־טל:
40 ויעש אלהים כן בלילה ההוא //
ויהי־חרב אל־הגזה לבדה / ועל־כל־הארץ
היה טל: –פ-

7 1 וישכם
ירבעל הוא גדעון /
וכל־העם אשר אתו / ויחנו על־עין חרד //
ומחנה מדין היה־לו מצפון / מגבעת
המורה בעמק:
2 ויאמר יהוה אל־גדעון / רב העם אשר
אתך / מתתי את־מדין בידם // פן־יתפאר
עלי ישראל לאמר / ידי הושיעה לי:
3 ועתה / קרא נא באזני העם לאמר /
מי־ירא וחרד / ישב ויצפר מהר הגלעד //

S ◇ N/D/J ◇ C/R

וישב מן־העם / עשרים ושנים אלף /
ועשרת אלפים נשארו: ‎–ס–

4 ויאמר יהוה אל־גדעון / עוד העם רב /
הורד אותם אל־המים / ואצרפנו לך
שם // והיה אשר אמר אליך זה ילך
אתך / הוא ילך אתך / וכל אשר־אמר
אליך / זה לא־ילך עמך / הוא לא ילך:
5 ויורד את־העם אל־המים // ‎–ס–

ויאמר יהוה אל־גדעון / כל אשר־ילק
בלשונו מן־המים כאשר ילק הכלב /
תציג אותו לבד / וכל אשר־יכרע
על־ברכיו לשתות:[58]
6 ויהי / מספר המלקקים ב‹לשונ›ם[59] /
שלש מאות איש // וכל יתר העם / כרעו
על־ברכיהם לשתות מים: ‎–ס–

7 ויאמר יהוה אל־גדעון / בשלש מאות
האיש המלקקים אושיע אתכם / ונתתי
את־מדין בידך // וכל־העם / ילכו איש
למקמו:

8 ויקחו את־צדה העם בידם ואת
שופרתיהם / ואת כל־איש ישראל שלח
איש לאהליו / ובשלש־מאות האיש
החזיק // ומחנה מדין / היה לו מתחת
בעמק: ‎–פ–

9 ויהי בלילה ההוא / ויאמר אליו יהוה /
קום רד במחנה // כי נתתיו בידך:
10 ואם־ירא אתה לרדת // רד אתה ופרה
נערך אל־המחנה:
11 ושמעת מה־ידברו / ואחר תחזקנה
ידיך / וירדת במחנה // וירד הוא ופרה
נערו / אל־קצה החמשים אשר במחנה:
12 ומדין ועמלק וכל־בני קדם נפלים
בעמק / כארבה לרב // ולגמליהם אין
מספר / כחול שעל־שפת הים לרב:
13 ויבא גדעון / והנה־איש / מספר לרעהו
חלום // ויאמר הנה חלום חלמתי / והנה
צל‹י›־ל[60] לחם שערים מתהפך במחנה
מדין / ויבא עד־האהל ויכהו ויפל
ויהפכהו למעלה ונפל האהל:
14 ויען רעהו ויאמר אין זאת / בלתי /
אם־חרב גדעון בן־יואש איש ישראל //
נתן האלהים בידו / את־מדין
ואת־כל־המחנה: ‎–פ–

S   ◇   N/D/J   ◇   C/R

15 ויהי כשמע גדעון את־מספר החלום
ואת־שברו וישתחו // וישב אל־מחנה
ישראל / ויאמר קומו / כי־נתן יהוה
בידכם את־מחנה מדין:
16 ויחץ את־שלש־מאות האיש שלשה
ראשים // ויתן שופרות ביד־כלם וכדים
רקים / ולפדים בתוך הכדים:
17 ויאמר אליהם / ממני תראו וכן
תעשו // והנה אנכי בא בקצה המחנה /
והיה כאשר־אעשה כן תעשון:
18 ותקעתי בשופר / אנכי וכל־אשר
אתי // ותקעתם בשופרות גם־אתם /
סביבות כל־המחנה / ואמרתם ליהוה
ולגדעון: –פ–

19 ויבא גדעון ומאה־איש אשר־אתו
בקצה המחנה / ראש האשמרת התיכונה /
אך הקם הקימו את־השמרים / ויתקעו
בשופרות / ונפוץ הכדים אשר בידם:
20 ויתקעו שלשת הראשים בשופרות
וישברו הכדים / ויחזיקו ביד־שמאולם
בלפדים / וביד־ימינם / השופרות
לתקוע // ויקראו / חרב ליהוה ולגדעון:
21 ויעמדו איש תחתיו / סביב למחנה //
וירץ כל־המחנה ויריעו וינ<ו>סו[61]:
22 ויתקעו שלש־מאות השופרות / וישם
יהוה / את חרב איש ברעהו
ובכל־המחנה // וינס המחנה עד־בית
השטה צררתה / עד שפת־אבל מחולה
על־טבת:
23 ויצעק איש־ישראל מנפתלי ומן־אשר
ומן־כל־מנשה // וירדפו אחרי מדין:
24 ומלאכים שלח גדעון בכל־הר אפרים
לאמר / רדו לקראת מדין ולכדו להם
את־המים / עד בית ברה ואת־הירדן //
ויצעק כל־איש אפרים וילכדו את־המים /
עד בית ברה ואת־הירדן:
25 וילכדו שני־שרי מדין את־ערב
ואת־זאב / ויהרגו את־ערב בצור־ערב
ואת־זאב הרגו ביקב־זאב / וירדפו
את־מדין // וראש־ערב וזאב / הביאו
אל־גדעון / מעבר לירדן:
8 1 ויאמרו אליו איש אפרים מה־הדבר
הזה עשית לנו / לבלתי קראות לנו / כי
הלכת להלחם במדין // ויריבון אתו
בחזקה:

S ◇ N/D/J ◇ C/R

2 ויאמר אליהם / מה־עשיתי עתה ככם //
הלוא / טוב עללות אפרים מבציר
אביעזר:
3 בידכם נתן אלהים את־שרי מדין
את־עתב ואת־זאב / ומה־יכלתי עשות
ככם // אז / רפתה רוחם מעליו / בדברו
הדבר הזה:
4 ויבא גדעון הירדנה // עבר הוא /
ושלש־מאות האיש אשר אתו / עיפים
ורדפים:
5 ויאמר לאנשי סכות / תנו־נא ככרות
לחם / לעם אשר ברגלי // כי־עיפים הם /
ואנכי / רדף אחרי זבח וצלמנע מלכי
מדין:
6 ויאמר שרי סכות / הכף זבח וצלמנע
עתה בידך // כי־נתן לצבאך לחם:
7 ויאמר גדעון / לכן / בתת יהוה את־זבח
ואת־צלמנע בידי // ודשתי את־בשרכם /
את־קוצי המדבר ואת־הברקנים:
8 ויעל משם פנואל / וידבר אליהם
כזאת // ויענו אותו אנשי פנואל / כאשר
ענו אנשי סכות:
9 ויאמר גם־לאנשי פנואל לאמר // בשובי
בשלום / אתץ את־המגדל הזה: ‒פ‒

10 וזבח וצלמנע בקרקר / ומחניהם עמם
כחמשת עשר אלף / כל הנותרים / מכל
מחנה בני־קדם // והנפלים / מאה
ועשרים אלף איש שלף חרב:
11 ויעל גדעון / דרך השכוני באהלים /
מקדם לנבח ויגבהה // ויך את־המחנה /
והמחנה היה בטח:
12 וינוסו / זבח וצלמנע / וירדף
אחריהם // וילכד את־שני מלכי מדין /
את־זבח ואת־צלמנע / וכל־המחנה
החריד:
13 וישב גדעון בן־יואש מן־המלחמה //
מלמעלה החרס:
14 וילכד־נער מאנשי סכות וישאלהו //
ויכתב אליו את־שרי סכות ואת־זקניה /
שבעים ושבעה איש:
15 ויבא אל־אנשי סכות / ויאמר / הנה
זבח וצלמנע // אשר חרפתם אותי לאמר /
הכף זבח וצלמנע עתה בידך / כי נתן
לאנשיך היעפים לחם:
16 ויקח את־זקני העיר / ואת־קוצי
המדבר ואת־הברקנים //

S ◇ N/D/J ◇ C/R

וַיֹּד<שׁ>⁶² בָּהֶם / אֶת אַנְשֵׁי סֻכּוֹת:
17 וְאֶת־מִגְדַּל פְּנוּאֵל נָתַץ // וַיַּהֲרֹג
אֶת־אַנְשֵׁי הָעִיר:
18 וַיֹּאמֶר / אֶע־זֶבַח וְאֶת־צַלְמֻנָּע / אֵיפֹה
הָאֲנָשִׁים / אֲשֶׁר הֲרַגְתֶּם בְּתָבוֹר / וַיֹּאמְרוּ
כָּמוֹךָ כְמוֹהֶם / אֶחָד / כְּתֹאַר בְּנֵי הַמֶּלֶךְ:
19 וַיֹּאמַר / אַחַי בְּנֵי־אִמִּי הֵם // חַי־יְהוָה /
לוּ הַחֲיִתֶם אוֹתָם / לֹא הָרַגְתִּי אֶתְכֶם:
20 וַיֹּאמֶר לְיֶתֶר בְּכוֹרוֹ / קוּם הֲרֹג אוֹתָם //
וְלֹא־שָׁלַף הַנַּעַר חַרְבּוֹ כִּי יָרֵא / כִּי עוֹדֶנּוּ
נָעַר:
21 וַיֹּאמֶר זֶבַח וְצַלְמֻנָּע / קוּם אַתָּה
וּפְגַע־בָּנוּ / כִּי כָאִישׁ גְּבוּרָתוֹ // וַיָּקָם
גִּדְעוֹן / וַיַּהֲרֹג אֶת־זֶבַח וְאֶת־צַלְמֻנָּע / וַיִּקַּח
אֶת־הַשַּׂהֲרֹנִים / אֲשֶׁר בְּצַוְּארֵי גְמַלֵּיהֶם:
22 וַיֹּאמְרוּ אִישׁ־יִשְׂרָאֵל אֶל־גִּדְעוֹן /
מְשָׁל־בָּנוּ גַּם־אַתָּה / גַּם־בִּנְךָ גַּם בֶּן־בְּנֶךָ //
כִּי הוֹשַׁעְתָּנוּ מִיַּד מִדְיָן:
23 וַיֹּאמֶר אֲלֵהֶם גִּדְעוֹן / לֹא־אֶמְשֹׁל אֲנִי
בָּכֶם / וְלֹא־יִמְשֹׁל בְּנִי בָּכֶם // יְהוָה יִמְשֹׁל
בָּכֶם:
24 וַיֹּאמֶר אֲלֵהֶם גִּדְעוֹן / אֶשְׁאֲלָה מִכֶּם
שְׁאֵלָה / וּתְנוּ־לִי / אִישׁ נֶזֶם שְׁלָלוֹ //
כִּי־נִזְמֵי זָהָב לָהֶם / כִּי יִשְׁמְעֵאלִים הֵם:
25 וַיֹּאמְרוּ נָתוֹן נִתֵּן // וַיִּפְרְשׂוּ
אֶת־הַשִּׂמְלָה / וַיַּשְׁלִיכוּ שָׁמָּה / אִישׁ נֶזֶם
שְׁלָלוֹ:
26 וַיְהִי מִשְׁקַל נִזְמֵי הַזָּהָב אֲשֶׁר שָׁאָל /
אֶלֶף וּשְׁבַע־מֵאוֹת זָהָב / לְבַד
מִן־הַשַּׂהֲרֹנִים וְהַנְּטִפוֹת וּבִגְדֵי הָאַרְגָּמָן /
שֶׁעַל מַלְכֵי מִדְיָן / וּלְבַד מִן־הָעֲנָקוֹת /
אֲשֶׁר בְּצַוְּארֵי גְמַלֵּיהֶם:
27 וַיַּעַשׂ אוֹתוֹ גִדְעוֹן לְאֵפוֹד / וַיַּצֵּג אוֹתוֹ
בְעִירוֹ בְעָפְרָה /

וַיִּזְנוּ כָל־יִשְׂרָאֵל אַחֲרָיו שָׁם // וַיְהִי
לְגִדְעוֹן וּלְבֵיתוֹ לְמוֹקֵשׁ:
28 וַיִּכָּנַע מִדְיָן / לִפְנֵי בְּנֵי יִשְׂרָאֵל /

וְלֹא יָסְפוּ לָשֵׂאת רֹאשָׁם //

וַתִּשְׁקֹט הָאָרֶץ אַרְבָּעִים שָׁנָה

בִּימֵי גִדְעוֹן: -פ-
29 וַיֵּלֶךְ יְרֻבַּעַל בֶּן־יוֹאָשׁ וַיֵּשֶׁב בְּבֵיתוֹ:
30 וּלְגִדְעוֹן / הָיוּ שִׁבְעִים בָּנִים / יֹצְאֵי
יְרֵכוֹ // כִּי־נָשִׁים רַבּוֹת הָיוּ לוֹ:
31 וּפִילַגְשׁוֹ אֲשֶׁר בִּשְׁכֶם / יָלְדָה־לּוֹ
גַם־הִיא בֵן // וַיָּשֶׂם אֶת־שְׁמוֹ אֲבִימֶלֶךְ:

S ◇   N/D/J ◇   C/R

32 וימת גדעון בן־יואש בשיבה טובה //
ויקבר / בקבר יואש אביו / בעפרה אבי
העזרי: ‎-פ-

33 ויהי כאשר מת גדעון / וישובו בני
ישראל / ויזנו אחרי הבעלים // וישימו
להם בעל ברית לאלהים:
34 ולא זכרו בני ישראל / את־יהוה
אלהיהם // המציל אותם מיד
כל־איביהם מסביב:
35 ולא־עשׂו חסד / עם־בית ירבעל
גדעון // ככל־הטובה / אשר עשה
עם־ישראל: ‎-פ-

9 1 וילך אבימלך בן־ירבעל שכמה /
אל־אחי אמו // וידבר אליהם /
ואת־כל־משפחת בית־אבי אמו לאמר:
2 דברו־נא באזני כל־בעלי שכם מה־טוב
לכם / המשל בכם שבעים איש / כל בני
ירבעל / אם־משל בכם איש אחד //
וזכרתם / כי־עצמכם ובשׂרכם אני:
3 וידברו אחי־אמו עליו / באזני כל־בעלי
שכם / את כל־הדברים האלה // ויט לבם
אחרי אבימלך / כי אמרו אחינו הוא:
4 ויתנו־לו שבעים כסף / מבית בעל
ברית // וישׂכר בהם אבימלך / אנשים
ריקים ופחזים / וילכו אחריו:
5 ויבא בית־אביו עפרתה / ויהרג
את־אחיו בני־ירבעל שבעים איש על־אבן
אחת // ויותר יותם בן־ירבעל הקטן כי
נחבא: ‎-ס-
6 ויאספו כל־בעלי שכם וכל־בית מלוא /
וילכו / וימליכו את־אבימלך למלך //
עם־אלון מצב אשר בשכם:
7 ויגדו ליותם / וילך ויעמד בראש
הר־גרזים / וישׂא קולו ויקרא //
ויאמר להם /

שמעו אלי בעלי שכם /
וישמע אליכם אלהים:

8 הלוך הלכו העצים /
למשח עליהם מלך //
ויאמרו לזית מלוכה[63] עלינו:
9 ויאמר להם הזית /
החדלתי את־דשני /
אשר־בי יכבדו אלהים ואנשים //
והלכתי / לנוע על־העצים:

S ◇   N/D/J ◇   C/R

10 ויאמרו העצים לתאנה //
לכי־את מלכי עלינו:
11 ותאמר להם התאנה /
החדלתי את־מתקי /
ואת־תנובתי הטובה //
והלכתי / לנוע על־העצים:

12 ויאמרו העצים לגפן //
לכי־את מלוכי[64] עלינו:
13 ותאמר להם הגפן /
החדלתי את־תירושי /
המשמח אלהים ואנשים //
והלכתי לנוע על־העצים:

14 ויאמרו כל־העצים אל־האטד //
לך אתה מלך־עלינו:
15 ויאמר האטד אל־העצים /
אם באמת אתם משחים אתי
למלך עליכם / באו חסו בצלי //
ואם־אין / תצא אש מן־האטד /
ותאכל את־ארזי הלבנון:

16 ועתה / אם־באמת ובתמים עשיתם /
ותמליכו את־אבימלך // ואם־טובה
עשיתם עם־ירבעל ועם־ביתו / ואם־כגמול
ידיו עשיתם לו:

17 אשר־נלחם אבי עליכם // וישלך
את־נפשו מנגד<ו>[65] / ויצל אתכם מיד
מדין:
18 ואתם קמתם על־בית אבי היום /
ותהרגו את־בניו שבעים איש על־אבן
אחת // ותמליכו את־אבימלך בן־אמתו
על־בעלי שכם / כי אחיכם הוא:

19 ואם־באמת ובתמים עשיתם עם־ירבעל
ועם־ביתו היום הזה // שמחו באבימלך /
וישמח גם־הוא בכם:
20 ואם־אין / תצא אש מאבימלך / ותאכל
את־בעלי שכם ואת־בית מלוא // ותצא
אש מבעלי שכם ומבית מלוא / ותאכל
את־אבימלך:
21 וינס יותם / ויברח וילך בארה //
וישב שם / מפני אבימלך אחיו: ‏-פ-

22 וישר אבימלך על־ישראל שלש שנים:
23 וישלח אלהים רוח רעה / בין
אבימלך / ובין בעלי שכם //
ויבגדו בעלי־שכם באבימלך:

S ◊   N/D/J ◊   C/R

24 לבוא / חמס שבעים בני־ירבעל //
ודמם / לשום על־אבימלך אחיהם אשר
הרג אותם / ועל בעלי שכם / אשר־חזקו
את־ידיו להרג את־אחיו:

25 וישימו לו בעלי שכם מארבים / על
ראשי ההרים / ויגזלו / את
כל־אשר־יעבר עליהם בדרך // ויגד
לאבימלך: ‎–פ–

26 ויבא געל בן־עבד ואחיו / ויעברו
בשכם // ויבטחו־בו בעלי שכם:

27 ויצאו השדה ויבצרו את־כרמיהם
וידרכו / ויעשו הלולים // ויבאו בית
אלהיהם / ויאכלו וישתו / ויקללו
את־אבימלך:

28 ויאמר געל בן־עבד / מי־אבימלך
ומי־שכם כי נעבדנו / הלא בן־ירבעל
וזבל פקידו // עבדו / את־אנשי חמור אבי
שכם / ומדוע נעבדנו אנחנו:

29 ומי יתן את־העם הזה בידי / ואסירה
את־אבימלך // ויאמר לאבימלך / רבה
צבאך וצאה:

30 וישמע / זבל שר־העיר / את־דברי געל
בן־עבד // ויחר אפו:

31 וישלח מלאכים אל־אבימלך
ב<א>ר<ו>מה[66] לאמר // הנה געל בן־עבד
ואחיו באים שכמה / והנם צרים את־העיר
עליך:

32 ועתה קום לילה / אתה והעם
אשר־אתך // וארב בשדה:

33 והיה בבקר כזרח השמש / תשכים
ופשטת על־העיר // והנה־הוא והעם
אשר־אתו יצאים אליך / ועשית לו /
כאשר תמצא ידך: ‎–ס–

34 ויקם אבימלך וכל־העם אשר־עמו
לילה // ויארבו על־שכם / ארבעה
ראשים:

35 ויצא געל בן־עבד / ויעמד / פתח שער
העיר // ויקם אבימלך והעם אשר־אתו
מן־המארב:

36 וירא־געל את־העם / ויאמר אל־זבל /
הנה־עם יורד / מראשי ההרים // ויאמר
אליו זבל / את צל ההרים אתה ראה
כאנשים: ‎–ס–

37 ויסף עוד געל לדבר / ויאמר / הנה־עם
יורד <י>ים[67] / מעם טבור הארץ //
וראש־אחד בא / מדרך אלון מעוננים:

S   ◇   N/D/J   ◇   C/R

38 ויאמר אליו זבל / איה אפוא פיך אשר
תאמר / מי אבימלך כי נעבדנו // הלא זה
העם אשר מאסתה בו / צא־נא עתה
והלחם בו: ‪-ס‬

39 ויצא געל / לפני בעלי שכם // וילחם
באבימלך:

40 וירדפהו אבימלך וינס מפניו // ויפלו
חללים רבים עד־פתה השער:

41 וישב אבימלך בארומה // ויגרש זבל
את־געל ואת־אחיו משבת בשכם:

42 ויהי ממחרת / ויצא העם השדה //
ויגדו לאבימלך:

43 ויקח את־העם / ויחצם לשלשה
ראשים / ויארב בשדה // וירא / והנה
העם יצא מן־העיר / ויקם עליהם ויכם:

44 ואבימלך / והראשים אשר עמו /
פשטו / ויעמדו / פתח שער העיר // ושני
הראשים / פשטו על־כל־אשר בשדה
ויכום:

45 ואבימלך נלחם בעיר / כל היום
ההוא / וילכד את־העיר / ואת־העם
אשר־בה הרג / ויתץ את־העיר / ויזרעה
מלח: ‪-פ‬

46 וישמעו / כל־בעלי מגדל־שכם //
ויבאו אל־צריח / בית אל ברית:

47 ויגד לאבימלך / כי התקבצו /
כל־בעלי מגדל־שכם:

48 ויעל אבימלך הר־צלמון / הוא
וכל־העם אשר־אתו / ויקח אבימלך
את־הקרדמות בידו / ויכרת שוכת עצים /
וישאה / וישם על־שכמו // ויאמר
אל־העם אשר־עמו / מה ראיתם עשיתי /
מהרו עשו כמוני:

49 ויכרתו גם־כל־העם איש שוכה / וילכו
אחרי אבימלך וישימו על־הצריח / ויציתו
עליהם את־הצריח באש // וימתו גם
כל־אנשי מגדל־שכם כאלף איש
ואשה: ‪-פ‬

50 וילך אבימלך אל־תבץ // ויחן בתבץ
וילכדה:

51 ומגדל־עז היה בתוך־העיר / וינסו
שמה כל־האנשים והנשים / וכל בעלי
העיר / ויסגרו בעדם // ויעלו על־גג
המגדל:

52 ויבא אבימלך עד־המגדל / וילחם
בו // ויגש עד־פתח המגדל לשרפו באש:

S ◇	N/D/J ◇	C/R

53 ותשלך אשה אחת פלח רכב על־ראש
אבימלך // ותרץ את־גלגלתו:
54 ויקרא מהרה אל־הנער נשא כליו /
ויאמר לו שלף חרבך ומותתני / פן־יאמרו
לי אשה הרגתהו // וידקרהו נערו וימת:
55 ויראו איש־ישראל כי מת אבימלך //
וילכו איש למקמו:

56 וישב אלהים / את רעת אבימלך //
אשר עשה לאביו / להרג את־שבעים
אחיו:
57 ואת / כל־רעת אנשי שכם / השיב
אלהים בראשם // ותבא אליהם / קללת
יותם בן־ירבעל: ־פ־

JUDGES 10:1-5, 6–12:7, 8-15

S ◇	N/D/J ◇	C/R

10 1 ויקם אחרי

אבימלך להושיע את־ישראל /

תולע בן־פואה בן־דודו איש יששכר //
והוא־ישב בשמיר בהר אפרים:
2 וישפט את־ישראל / עשרים ושלש
שנה // וימת ויקבר בשמיר: ־פ־

3 ויקם אחריו /
יאיר הגלעדי //
וישפט את־ישראל / עשרים ושתים שנה:
4 ויהי־לו שלשים בנים / רכבים
על־שלשים עירים / ושלשים עירים
להם //
להם יקראו חות יאיר / עד היום הזה /
אשר בארץ הגלעד:
5 וימת יאיר / ויקבר בקמון: ־פ־

6 ויספו בני ישראל / לעשות הרע בעיני
יהוה / ויעבדו את־הבעלים
ואת־העשתרות ואת־אלהי ארם
ואת־אלהי צידון ואת אלהי מואב / ואת
אלהי בני־עמון / ואת אלהי פלשתים //
ויעזבו את־יהוה ולא עבדוהו:
7 ויחר־אף יהוה בישראל // וימכרם
ביד־פלשתים / וביד בני עמון:
8 וירעצו וירצצו את־בני ישראל / בשנה
ההיא // שמנה עשרה שנה / את־כל־בני
ישראל אשר בעבר הירדן / בארץ
האמרי אשר בגלעד:

S ◊   N/D/J ◊   C/R

9 ויעברו בני־עמון את־הירדן / להלחם
גם־ביהודה ובבנימין ובבית אפרים //
ותצר לישראל מאד:

10 ויזעקו בני ישראל / אל־יהוה[lxxxii]
לאמר //

חטאנו לך / <>כי[68] עזבנו את־אלהינו /
ונעבד את־הבעלים: -פ-

11 ויאמר יהוה אל־בני ישראל // הלא
ממצרים ומן־האמרי[69] / ומן־בני עמון[70]
ומן־פלשתים[71]:

12 וצידונים ועמלק ומ<די>ן[72] / לחצו
אתכם // ותצעקו אלי / ואושיעה אתכם
מידם:

13 ואתם עזבתם אותי / ותעבדו אלהים
אחרים // לכן לא־אוסיף להושיע אתכם:

14 לכו /
וזעקו אל־האלהים[lxxxiii] /
אשר בחרתם בם // המה יושיעו לכם
בעת צרתכם:

15 ויאמרו בני־ישראל אל־יהוה חטאנו /
עשה־אתה לנו / ככל־הטוב
בעיניך[lxxxiv] //

אך הצילנו נא היום הזה:

16 ויסירו את־אלהי הנכר מקרבם /
ויעבדו את־יהוה // ותקצר נפשו בעמל
ישראל: -פ-

17 ויצעקו בני עמון / ויחנו בגלעד //
ויאספו בני ישראל / ויחנו במצפה:
18 ויאמרו העם שרי גלעד איש
אל־רעהו / מי האיש / אשר יחל / להלחם
בבני עמון // יהיה לראש / לכל ישבי
גלעד: -פ-

11 1 ויפתח הגלעדי / היה גבור חיל /
והוא בן־אשה זונה // ויולד גלעד
את־יפתח:
2 ותלד אשת־גלעד לו בנים // ויגדלו
בני־האשה ויגרשו את־יפתח / ויאמרו לו
לא־תנחל בבית־אבינו / כי בן־אשה אחרת
אתה:
3 ויברח יפתח מפני אחיו / וישב בארץ
טוב / ויתלקטו אל־יפתח אנשים ריקים /
ויצאו עמו: -פ-
4 ויהי מימים // וילחמו בני־עמון
עם־ישראל:

S ◇ N/D/J ◇ C/R

5 ויהי / כאשר־נלחמו בני־עמון
עם־ישראל // וילכו זקני גלעד / לקחת
את־יפתח מארץ טוב:
6 ויאמרו ליפתח / לכה / והייתה לנו
לקצין // ונלחמה בבני עמון:
7 ויאמר יפתח לזקני גלעד / הלא אתם
שנאתם אותי / ותגרשוני מבית אבי //
ומדוע באתם אלי עתה / כאשר צר לכם:
8 ויאמרו זעני גלעד אל־יפתח / לכן עתה
שבנו אליך / והלכת עמנו / ונלחמת בבני
עמון // והיית לנו לראש / לכל ישבי
גלעד:
9 ויאמר יפתח אל־זקני גלעד /
אם־משיבים אתם אותי להלחם בבני
עמון / ונתן יהוה אותם לפני // אנכי /
אהיה לכם לראש:
10 ויאמרו זקני־גלעד אל־יפתח // יהוה /
יהיה שמע בינותינו / אם־לא כדברך כן
נעשה:
11 וילך יפתח עם־זקני גלעד / וישימו
העם אותו עליהם לראש ולקצין // וידבר
יפתח את־כל־דבריו לפני יהוה
במצפה: ־פ־
12 וישלח יפתח מלאכים / אל־מלך
בני־עמון לאמר // מה־לי ולך / כי־באת
אלי להלחם בארצי:
13 ויאמר מלך בני־עמון אל־מלאכי
יפתח / כי־לקח ישראל את־ארצי בעלותו
ממצרים /
מארנון ועד־היבק ועד־הירדן[lxxxv] //
ועתה / השיבה אתהן בשלום:
14 ויוסף עוד יפתח // וישלח מלאכים /
אל־מלך בני עמון:
15 ויאמר לו / כה אמר יפתח //
לא־לקח ישראל את־ארץ מואב[lxxxvi] /
ואת־ארץ בני עמון[lxxxvii]:
16 כי בעלותם ממצרים // וילך ישראל
במדבר עד־ים־סוף / ויבא קדשה:
17 וישלח ישראל מלאכים אל־מלך
אדום לאמר אעברה־נא בארצך[lxxxviii] /
ולא שמע מלך אדום[lxxxix] /
וגם אל־מלך מואב שלח ולא אבה // וישב
ישראל בקדש:
18 וילך במדבר / ויסב את־ארץ אדום[xc]
ואת־ארץ מואב[xci] / ויבא ממזרח־שמש
לארץ מואב / ויחנון בעבר ארנון[xcii] //

S ◊	N/D/J ◊	C/R

ולא־באו בגבול מואב /

כי ארנון גבול מואב[xciii]:

19 וישלח ישראל מלאכים / אל־סיחון

מלך־האמרי[xciv] מלך חשבון[xcv] // ויאמר

לו ישראל[xcvi] / נעברה־נא בארצך[xcvii]

עד־מקומי[xcviii]:

20 ו<ימא>ן[73] סיחון את־ישראל עבר

בגבלו[xcix] / ויאסף סיחון את־כל־עמו[c] /

ויחנו ביהצה[ci] // וילחם עם־ישראל[cii]:

21 ויתן יהוה אלהי־ישראל את־סיחון

ואת־כל־עמו ביד ישראל[ciii] ויכום[civ] //

ויירש ישראל / את כל־ארץ האמרי[cv]

יושב הארץ ההיא:

22 ויירשו / את כל־גבול האמרי[cvi] //

מארנון ועד־היבק / ומן־המדבר

ועד־הירדן[cvii]:

23 ועתה יהוה אלהי ישראל / הוריש

את־האמרי / מפני עמו ישראל[cviii] //

ואתה תירשנו:

24 הלא את אשר יורישך[74] כמוש אלהיך

אותו תירש[cix] / ואת כל־אשר הוריש

יהוה אלהינו מפנינו אותו נירש[cx]:

25 ועתה / הטוב טוב אתה /

מבלק בן־צפור מלך מואב[cxi] //

הרוב רב עם־ישראל / אם־נלחם נלחם

בם:

26 בשבת ישראל בחשבון ובבנותיה

ובערעור ובבנותיה / ובכל־הערים אשר

על־ידי ארנון[cxii] /

שלש מאות שנה // ומדוע לא־הצלתם

בעת ההיא:

27 ואנכי לא־חטאתי לך / ואתה עשׂה אתי

רעה להלחם בי // ישפט יהוה השפט

היום / בין בני ישראל / ובין בני עמון:

28 ולא שמע / מלך בני עמון // אל־דברי

יפתח / אשר שלח אליו: -פ-

29 ותהי על־יפתח רוח יהוה / ויעבר

את־הגלעד ואת־מנשה // ויעבר את־מצפה

גלעד / וממצפה גלעד / עבר בני עמון:

30 וידר יפתח נדר ליהוה ויאמר //

אם־נתון תתן את־בני עמון בידי:

31 והיה היוצא / אשר יצא מדלתי ביתי

לקראתי / בשובי בשלום מבני עמון //

והיה ליהוה / והעליתהו עולה: -פ-

32 ויעבר יפתח אל־בני עמון להלחם //

ויתנם יהוה בידו:

S ◇ N/D/J ◇ C/R

33 ויכם מערוער ועד־בואך מנית עשרים
עיר / ועד אבל כרמים / מכה גדולה
מאד // ויכנעו בני עמון / מפני בני
ישראל: ־פ־
34 ויבא יפתח המצפה אל־ביתו / והנה
בתו יצאת לקראתו / בתפים ובמחלות //
ורק היא יחידה / אין־לו ממנו בן או־בת:
35 ויהי כראותו אותה ויקרע את־בגדיו /
ויאמר אהה בתי הכרע הכרעתני / ואת
היית בעכרי // ואנכי / פציתי־פי
אל־יהוה / ולא אוכל לשוב:
36 ותאמר אליו / אבי פציתה את־פיך
אל־יהוה / עשֹה לי / כאשר יצא מפיך //
אחרי אשֹר עשֹה לך יהוה נקמות מאיביך
מבני עמון:
37 ותאמר אל־אביה / יעשֹה לי הדבר
הזה // הרפה ממני שנים חדשים / ואלכה
<>[75] על־ההרים / ואבכה על־בתולי /
אנכי ורע<ו>ת<י>[76]:
38 ויאמר לכי / וישלח אותה שני
חדשים // ותלך היא ורעותיה / ותבך
על־בתוליה על־ההרים:
39 ויהי מקץ שנים חדשים / ותשב
אל־אביה / ויעשֹ לה / את־נדרו אשר
נדר // והיא לא־ידעה איש / ותהי־חק
בישראל:
40 מימים ימימה / תלכנה בנות ישראל /
לתנות / לבת־יפתח הגלעדי // ארבעת
ימים בשנה: ־ס־

12 1 ויצעק איש אפרים /
ויעבר צפונה // ויאמרו ליפתח מדוע
עברת להלחם בבני־עמון / ולנו לא קראת
ללכת עמך / ביתך / נשֹרף עליך באש:
2 ויאמר יפתח אליהם / איש ריב / הייתי
אני ועמי ובני־עמון[77] מאד // ואצעק
אתכם / ולא־הושעתם אותי מידם:
3 ואראה כי־אינך[78] מושיע / ואשֹימה
נפשי בכפי ואעברה אל־בני עמון / ויתנם
יהוה בידי // ולמה עליתם אלי היום הזה
להלחם בי:
4 ויקבץ יפתח את־כל־אנשי גלעד /
וילחם את־אפרים // ויכו אנשי גלעד
את־אפרים / כי אמרו פליטי אפרים
אתם / גלעד / בתוך אפרים <>[79]:
5 וילכד גלעד את־מעברות הירדן
לאפרים // והיה כי יאמרו פליטי אפרים

S ◇	N/D/J ◇	C/R

אעברה / ויאמרו לו אנשי־גלעד האפרתי
אתה ויאמר לא:
6 ויאמרו לו אמר־נא שבלת ויאמר
סבלת / ולא יכין לדבר[80] כן / ויאחזו
אותו / וישחטוהו אל־מעברות הירדן //
ויפל בעת ההיא מאפרים / ארבעים ושנים
אלף:

7 וישפט יפתח את־ישראל שש שנים //
וימת / יפתח הגלעדי / ויקבר
בע‹י›‹ר‹ו› ‹ב[מ]צפה› גלעד[81]: ־פ־

8 וישפט אחריו את־ישראל /
אבצן מבית לחם:
9 ויהי־לו שלשים בנים / ושלשים בנות
שלח החוצה / ושלשים בנות / הביא
לבניו מן־החוץ // וישפט את־ישראל שבע
שנים:
10 וימת אבצן / ויקבר בבית לחם: ־פ־

11 וישפט אחריו את־ישראל /
אילון הזבולני // וישפט את־ישראל עשר
שנים:
12 וימת אלון הזבולני // ויקבר באילון
בארץ זבולן: ־פ־

13 וישפט אחריו את־ישראל //
עבדון בן־הלל הפרעתוני:
14 ויהי־לו ארבעים בנים / ושלשים בני
בנים / רכבים על־שבעים עירם // וישפט
את־ישראל שמנה שנים:
15 וימת עבדון בן־הלל הפרעתוני //
ויקבר בפרעתון בארץ אפרים / בהר
העמלקי: ־פ־

JUDGES 13:1–16:31

S ◇	N/D/J ◇	C/R

13 1 ויספו בני ישראל / לעשות הרע
בעיני יהוה // ויתנם יהוה ביד־פלשתים
ארבעים שנה: ־פ־

2 ויהי איש אחד מצרעה ממשפחת הדני
ושמו מנוח // ואשתו עקרה ולא ילדה:
3 וירא מלאך־יהוה אל־האשה // ויאמר
אליה / הנה־נא את־עקרה ולא ילדת /
והרית וילדת בן:
4 ועתה השמרי נא / ואל־תשתי יין
ושכר // ואל־תאכלי כל־טמא:

S ◇   N/D/J ◇   C/R

5 כי הנך הרה וילדת בן / ומורה
לא־יעלה על־ראשו / כי־נזיר אלהים יהיה
הנער מם־הבטן //
והוא / יחל להושיע את־ישראל מיד
פלשתים:

6 ותבא האשה / ותאמר לאישה לאמר /
איש האלהים בא אלי / ומראהו / כמראה
מלאך האלהים נורא מאד // ולא
שאלתיהו אי־מזה הוא / ואת־שמו
לא־הגיד לי:

7 ויאמר לי / הנך הרה וילדת בן // ועתה
אל־תשתי יין ושכר / ואל־תכלי
כל־טמאה / כי־נזיר אלהים יהיה הנער /
מן־הבטן עד־יום מותו: ־פ־

8 ויעתר מנוח אל־יהוה ויאמר // בי
אדוני / איש האלהים אשר שלחת /
יבוא־נא עוד אלינו / ויורנו / מא־נעשה
לנער היולד:

9 וישמע האלהים בקול מנוח // ויבא
מלאך האלהים עוד אל־האשה / והיא
יושבת בשדה / ומנוח אישה אין עמה:

10 ותמהר האשה / ותרץ ותגד לאישה //
ותאמר אליו / הנה נראה אלי האיש /
אשר־בא ביום אלי:

11 ויקם וילך מנוח אחרי אשתו // ויבא
אל־האיש / ויאמר לו / האתה האיש
אשר־דברת אל־האשה ויאמר אני:

12 ויאמר מנוח / עתה יבא דבר<>ך[82] //
מה־יהיה משפט־הנער ומעשהו:

13 ויאמר מלאך יהוה אל־מנוח // מכל
אשר־אמרתי אל־האשה תשמר:

14 מכל אשר־יצא מגפן היין לא תאכל /
ויין ושכר אל־תשת / וכל־טמאה
אל־תאכל // כל אשר־צויתיה תשמר:

15 ויאמר מנוח אל־מלאך יהוה //
נעצרה־נא אותך / ונעשה לפניך גדי
עצים:

16 ויאמר מלאך יהוה אל־מנוח /
אם־תעצרני לא־אכל בלחמך / ואם־תעשה
עלה / ליהוה תעלנה // כי לא־ידע מנוח /
כי־מלאך יהוה הוא:

17 ויאמר מנוח אל־מלאך יהוה מי שמך //
כי־יבא דבר<>ך[83] וכבדנוך:

18 ויאמר לו מלאך יהוה / למה זה תשאל
לשמי // והוא־פלאי: ־ס־

19 ויקח מנוח את־גדי העזים
ואת־המנחה / ויעל על־הצור ליהוה //

S ◇ N/D/J ◇ C/R

‹ה›מפל‹י›א⁸⁴ לעשות / ומנוח ואשתו
ראים:

20 ויהי בעלות הלהב מעל המזבח
השמימה / ויעל מלאך־יהוה בלהב
המזבח // ומנוח ואשתו ראים / ויפלו
על־פניהם ארצה:

21 ולא־יסף עוד מלאך יהוה / להראה
אל־מנוח ואל־אשתו // אז ידע מנוח /
כי־מלאך יהוה הוא:

22 ויאמר מנוח אל־אשתו מות נמות // כי
אלהים ראינו:

23 ותאמר לו אשתו / לו חפץ יהוה
להמיתנו לא־לקח מידנו עלה ומנחה /
ולא הראנו את־כל־אלה // וכעת / לא
השמיענו כזאת:

24 ותלד האשה בן / ותקרא את־שמו
שמשון // ויגדל הנער / ויברכהו יהוה:

25 ותחל רוח יהוה / לפעמו במחנה־דן //
בין צרעה ובין אשתאל: –פ–

14 1 וירד שמשון תמנתה // וירא אשה
בתמנתה מבנות פלשתים:

2 ויעל ויגד לאביו ולאמו / ויאמר / אשה
ראיתי בתמנתה מבנות פלשתים // ועתה /
קחו־אותו לי לאשה:

3 ויאמר לו אביו ואמו / האין בבנות
אחיך ובכל־עמי אשה / כי־אתה הולך
לקחת אשה / מפלשתים הערלים //
ויאמר שמשון אל־אביו אותה קח־לי /
כי־היא ישרה בעיני:

4 ואביו ואמו לא ידעו / כי מיהוה היא /
כי־תאנה הוא־מבקש מפלשתים // ובעת
ההיא / פלשתים משלים בישראל: –פ–

5 וירד שמשון ‹›⁸⁵ תמנתה // ויבא‹›⁸⁶
עד־כרמי תמנתה / והנה כפיר אריות /
שאג לקראתו:

6 ותצלח עליו רוח יהוה /
וישסעהו כשסע הגדי / ומאומה אין
בידו // ולא הגיד לאביו ולאמו / את־אשר
עשה:

7 וירד וידבר לאשה //
ותישר בעיני שמשון:

8 וישב מימים לקחתה / ויסר לראות / את
מפלת האריה // והנה עדת דבורים בגוית
האריה ודבש:

9 וירדהו אל־כפיו / וילך הלוך ואכל /
וילך אל־אביו ואל־אמו /

S ◇　　　　N/D/J ◇　　　　C/R

ויתן להם ויאכלו // ולא־הגיד להם / כי
מגוית האריה רדה הדבש:
10 וירד אביהו אל־האשה // ויעש שם
שמשון משתה / כי כן יעשו הבחורים:
11 ויהי כראותם אותו // ויקחו שלשים
מרעים / ויהיו אתו:
12 ויאמר להם שמשון / אחודה־נא לכם
חידה // אם־הגד תגידו אותה לי שבעת
ימי המשתה ומצאתם / ונתתי לכם
שלשים סדינים / ושלשים חלפת בגדים:
13 ואם־לא תוכלו להגיד לי / ונתתם אתם
לי שלשים סדינים / ושלשים חליפות
בגדים // ויאמרו לו / חודה חידתך
ונשמענה:
14 ויאמר להם /

מהאכל יצא מאכל /
ומעז יצא מתוק //

ולא יכלו להגיד החידה שלשת ימים:
15 ויהי ביום ה<ר>ביעי[87] / ויאמרו
לאשת־שמשון פתי את־אישך / ויגד־לנו
את־החידה / פן נשרף אותך ואת־בית
אביך באש // הלירשנו / קראתם לנו
הלא:
16 ותבך אשת שמשון עליו / ותאמר
רק־שנאתני ולא אהבתני / החידה חדת
לבני עמי / ולי לא הגדתה // ויאמר לה /
הנה לאבי ולאמי לא הגדתי ולך אגיד:
17 ותבך עליו שבעת הימים / אשר־היה
להם המשתה // ויהי ביום השביעי /
ויגד־לה כי הציקתהו / ותגד החידה לבני
עמה:
18 ויאמרו לו אנשי העיר ביום השביעי /
בטרם יבא החרסה /

מה־מתוק מדבש /
ומה עז מארי //

ויאמר להם /

לולא חרשתם בעגלתי /
לא מצאתם חידתי:

19 ותצלח עליו רוח יהוה /
וירד אשקלון ויך מהם שלשים איש /
ויקח את־חליצותם / ויתן החליפות /
למגידי החידה // ויחר אפו / ויעל בית
אביהו: –פ–

S ◇   N/D/J ◇   C/R

20 ותהי אשר שמשון // למרעהו / אשר
רעה לו:

15 1 ויהי מימין בימי קציר־חטים /
ויפקד שמשון את־אשתו בגדי עזים /
ויאמר / אבאה אל־אשתי החדרה //
ולא־נתנו אביה לבוא:

2 ויאמר אביה / אמר אמרתי כי־שׂנא
שנאתה / ואתננה למרעך // הלא אחתה
הקטנה ממנה / תהי־נא לך תחתיה:

3 ויאמר להם שמשון / נקיתי הפעם
מפלשתים // כי־עשׂה אני עמם רעה:

4 וילך שמשון / וילכד שלש־מאות
שועלים // ויקח לפדים / ויפן זנב
אל־זנב / וישם לפיד אחד בין־שני הזנבות
בתוך:

5 ויבער־אש בלפידים / וישלח בקמות
פלשתים // ויבער מגדיש ועד־קמה
ועד־כרם ‹ו[עד־]›זית[88]:

6 ויאמרו פלשתים מי עשה זאת /
ויאמרו / שמשון חתן התמני / כי לקח
את־אשתו / ויתנה למרעהו // ויעלו
פלשתים / וישרפו אותה
ואת־‹בית ›אביה[89] באש:

7 ויאמר להם שמשון / אם־תעשׂון
כזאת // כי אם־נקמתי בכם ואחר אחדל:

8 ויך אותם שוק על־ירך מכה גדולה //
וירד וישב / בסעיף סלע עיטם: ‑ס‑

9 ויעלו פלשתים / ויחנו ביהודה //
וינטשו בלחי:

10 ויאמרו איש יהודה / למה עליתם
עלינו // ויאמרו / לאסור את־שמשון
עלינו / לעשות לו / כאשר עשה לנו:

11 וירדו שלשת אלפים איש מיהודה /
אל־סעיף סלע עיטם / ויאמרו לשמשון /
הלא ידעת כי־משלים בנו פלשתים /
ומה־זאת עשית לנו / ויאמר להם /
כאשר עשׂו לי / כן עשיתי להם:

12 ויאמרו לו לאסרך ירדנו / לתתך
ביד־פלשתים // ויאמר להם שמשון /
השבעו לי / פן־תפגעון בי אתם:

13 ויאמרו לו לאמר / לא כי־אסר נאסרך
ונתנוך בידם / והמת לא נמיתך //
ויאסרהו / בשנים עבתים חדשים /
ויעלוהו מן־הסלע:

14 הוא־בא עד־לחי / ופלשתים הריעו
לקראתו //

S ◇　　　　N/D/J ◇　　　　C/R

ותצלח עליו רוח יהוה /
ותהיינה העבתים אשר על־זרועותיו /
כפשתים אשר בערו באש / וימסו אסוריו
מעל ידיו:
15 וימצא לחי־חמור טריה // וישלח ידו
ויקחה / ויך־בה אלף איש:
16 ויאמר שמשון /

בלחי החמור / חמור חמרתים //
בלחי החמור / הכיתי אלף איש:

17 ויהי ככלתו לדבר / וישלך הלחי
מידו // ויקרא למקום ההוא רמת לחי:
18 ויצמא מאד / ויקרא אל־יהוה ויאמר /
אתה נתת ביד־עבדך / את־התשועה
הגדלה הזאת / ועתה אמות בצמא /
ונפלתי ביד הערלים:
19 ויבקע אלהים את־המכתש
אשר־בלחי / ויצאו ממנו מים וישת /
ותשב רוחו ויחי // על־כן קרא שמה / עין
הקורא אשר בלחי / עד היום הזה:

　　　　　　　　　　　　　　　　20 וישפט את־ישראל בימי פלשתים
　　　　　　　　　　　　　　　　עשרים שנה: ־פ־

16 1 וילך שמשון עזתה // וירא־שם
אשה זונה / ויבא אליה:
2 <ויגד>[90] לעזתים לאמר / בא שמשון
הנה / ויסבו ויארבו־לו כל־הלילה בשער
העיר // ויתחרשו כל־הלילה לאמר /
עד־אור הבקר והרגנהו:
3 וישכב שמשון עד־חצי הלילה / ויקם
בחצי הלילה / ויאחז בדלתות שער־העיר
ובשתי המזוזות / ויסעם עם־הבריח /
וישם על־כתפיו // ויעלם אל־ראש ההר /
אשר על־פני חברון: ־פ־

4 ויהי אחרי־כן /
ויאהב אשה בנחל שרק / ושמה דלילה:
5 ויעלו אליה סרני פלשתים / ויאמרו לה
פתי אותו / וראי במה כחו גדול / ובמה
נוכל לו / ואסרנחו לענתו // ואנחנו
נתן־לך / איש / אלף ומאה כסף:
6 ותאמר דלילה אל־שמשון / הגידה־נא
לי / במה כחך גדול // ובמה תאסר
לענותך:
7 ויאמר אליה שמשון / אם־יאסרני /
בשבעה יתרים לחים אשר לא־חרבו
וחליתי והייתי כאחד האדם:

S   ◇   N/D/J   ◇   C/R

8 ויעלו־לה סרני פלשתים / שבעה יתרים
לחים אשר לא־חרבו // ותאסרהו בהם:
9 והארב / ישב לה בחדר / ותאמר אליו /
פלשתים עליך שמשון // וינתק
את־היתרים / כאשר ינתק פתיל־ הנערת
בהריחו אש / ולא נודע כחו:
10 ותאמר דלילה אל־שמשון / הנה התלת
בי / ותדבר אלי כזבים // עתה הגידה־נא
לי / במה תאסר:
11 ויאמר אליה / אם־אסור יאסרוני
בעבתים חדשים / אשר לא־נעשה בהם
מלאכה // וחליתי והייתי כאחד האדם:
12 ותקח דלילה עבתים חדשים ותאסרהו
בהם / ותאמר אליו פלשתים עליך
שמשום / והארב ישב בחדר // וינתקם
מעל זרעתיו כחוט:
13 ותאמר דלילה אל־שמשון / עד־הנה
התלת בי ותדבר אלי כזבים / הגידה לי /
במה תאסר // ויאמר אליה / אם־תארגי /
את־שבע מחלפות ראשי עם־המסכת
‹ותקעת ביתד וחליתי והייתי כאחד
האדם:›
14 ‹ותישנהו דלילה ותארג את־שבע
מחלפות ראשו עם־המסכת›[91] ותתקע
ביתד / ותאמר אליו / פלשתים עליך
שמשון // וייקץ משנתו / ויסע את־היתד
הארג ואת־המסכת:
15 ותאמר אליו / איך תאמר אהבתיך /
ולבך אין אתי // זה שלש פעמים התלת
בי / ולא־הגדת לי / במה כחך גדול:
16 ויהי כי־הציקה לו בדבריה כל־הימים
ותאלצהו / ותקצר נפשו למות:
17 ויגד־לה את־כל־לבו / ויאמר לה מורה
לא־עלה על־ראשי / כי־נזיר אלהים אני
מבטן אמי // אם־גלחתי וסר ממני כוי /
וחליתי והייתי ככל־האדם:
18 ותרא דלילה / כי־הגיד לה
את־כל־לבו / ותשלח ותקרא לסרני
פלשתים לאמר עלו הפעם / כי־הגיד
לי‹י›[92] את־כל־לבו // ועלו אליה סרני
פלשתים / ויעלו הכסף בידם:
19 ותישנהו על־ברכיה / ותקרא לאיש /
ותגלח[93] / את־שבע מחלפות ראשו //
ותחל לענותו / ויסר כחו מעליו:
20 ותאמר / פלשתים עליך שמשון //

S   ◇   N/D/J ◇   C/R

ויקץ משנתו / ויאמר אצא כפעם בפעם
ואנער / והוא לא ידע / כי יהוה סר
מעליו:
21 ויאחזוהו פלשתים / וינקרו
את־עיניו // ויורידו אותו עזתה /
ויאסרוהו בנחשתים / ויהי טוחן בבית
האסירים:
22 ויחל שער־ראשו לצמח כאשר
גלח: ‎־פ־

23 וסרני פלשתים / נאספו לזבח
זבח־גדול לדגון אלהיהם ולשמחה //
ויאמרו /

נתן אלהינו בידנו /
את שמשון אויבינו:

24 ויראו אתו העם / ויהללו
את־אלהיהם // כי אמרו /

נתן אלהינו בידנו
את־אויבנו /
ואת מחריב ארצנו /
ואשר הרבה את־חללינו:

25 ויהי כי טוב לבם / ויאמרו / קראו
לשמשון וישחק־לנו // ויקראו לשמשון
מבית האסירים / ויצחק לפניהם /
ויעמידו אותו בין העמודים:
26 ויאמר שמשון אל־הנער המחזיק בידו
הניחה אותי / וה<>משני[94] את־העמדים /
אשר הבית נכון עליהם // ואשען עליהם:
27 והבית / מלא האנשים והנשים /
ושמה / כל סרני פלשתים // ועל־הגג /
כשלשת אלפים איש ואשה / הראים
בשחוק שמשון:
28 ויקרא שמשון אל־יהוה ויאמר //

אדני יהוה זכרני נא
וחזקני נא אך הפעם הזה האלהים[95] /
ואנקמה נקם־אחת
משתי עיני מפלשתים:

29 וילפת שמשון את־שני עמודי התוך /
אשר הבית נכון עליהם / ויסמך עליהם //
אחד בימינו ואחד בשמאלו:
30 ויאמר שמשון / תמות נפשי
עם־פלשתים / ויט בכח / ויפל הבית
על־הסרנים / ועל־כל־העם אשר־בו //
ויהיו

S ◇	N/D/J ◇	C/R

המתים אשר המית במותו /
רבים מאשר המית בחייו:

31 וירדו אחיו וכל־בית אביהו וישאו
אתו / ויעלו ויקברו אותו /
בין צרעה ובין אשתאל /
בקבר מנוח אביו //

והוא שפט את־ישראל עשרים שנה: ‎–פ‎–

JUDGES 17:1–18:31

S ◇	N/D/J ◇	C/R

17 1 ויהי־איש מהר־אפרים ושמו
מיכיהו:
2 ויאמר לאמו אלף ומאה הכסף אשר
לקח־לך / ואת<>[96] אלית וגם אמרת
באזני / הנה־הכסף אתי אני לקחתיו //
ותאמר אמו / ברוך בני ליהוה:
3 וישב את־אלף־ומאה הכסף לאמו //
ותאמר אמו הקדש הקדשתי את־הכסף
ליהוה מידי לבני / לעשות פסל ומסכה /
ועתה אשיבנו לך:
4 וישב את־הכסף לאמו // ותקח אמו
מאתים[97] כסף ותתנהו לצורף / ויעשהו
פסל ומסכה / ויהי בבית מיכיהו:

5 והאיש מיכה לו בית אלהים // ויעש
אפוד ותרפים[98] / וימלא את־יד אחד
מבניו ויהי־לו לכהן:

| | 6 בימים ההם / אין מלך בישראל // | |
| | איש הישר בעיניו יעשה: ‎–פ‎– | |

7 ויהי־נער מבית לחם יהודה /

| | ממשפחת יהודה // והוא לוי והוא | |
| | גר־שם: | |

8 וילך האיש מהעיר /

| | מבית לחם יהודדה / | |

לגור באשר ימצא // ויבא הר־אפרים
עד־בית מיכה לעשות דרכו:
9 ויאמר־לו מיכה מאין תבוא // ויאמר
אליו לוי אנכי מבית לחם יהודה / ואנכי
הלך / לגור באשר אמצא:
10 ויאמר לו מיכה שבה עמדי / והיה־לי
לאב ולכהן / ואנכי אתן־לך עשרת כסף
לימים / וערך בגדים ומחיתך // וילך
הלוי[99]:
11 ויואל <>[100] לשבת את־האיש // ויהי
הנער לו / כאחד מבניו:

S ◇ N/D/J ◇ C/R

12 וימלא מיכה את־יד הלוי / ויהי־לו
הנער לכהן // ויהי בבית מיכה:
13 ויאמר מיכה / עתה ידעתי כי־ייטיב
יהוה לי // כי היה־לי הלוי לכהן:

18 1 בימים ההם / אין מלך בישראל //

ובימים ההם / שבט הדני / מבקש־לו
נחלה לשבת / כי לא־נפלה לו עד־היום
ההוא בתוך־שבטי ישראל בנחלה: ‪‑ס‑

2 וישלחו בני־דן ממשפחתם חמשה
אנשים מקצותם אנשים101 בני־חיל
מצרעה ומאשתאל / לרגל את־הארץ
ולחקרה / ויאמרו אלהם / לכו חקרו
את־הארץ //

ויבאו הר־אפרים עד־בית מיכה / וילינו
שם:
3 המה עם־בית מיכה / והמה הכירו
את־קול הנער הלוי // ויסורו שם /
ויאמרו לו מי־הביאך הלם / ומה־אתה
עשה בזה ומה־לך פה:
4 ויאמר אלהם / כזה וכזה / עשה לי
מיכה // וישכרני / ואהי־לו לכהן:
5 ויאמרו לו שאל־נא באלהים // ונדעה /
התצליח דרכנו אשר אנחנו הלכים עליה:
6 ויאמר להם הכהן לכו לשלום // נכח
יהוה / דרככם אשר תלכו־בה: ‑פ‑

7 וילכו חמשת האנשים / ויבאו לישה //
ויראו את־העם אשר־בקרבה /
יושבת־לבטח כמשפט צדנים שקט
ובטח / ואין־מכלים דבר בארץ יורש
עצר102 / ורחקים המה מצדנים / ודבר
אין־להם עם־אדם:
8 ויבאו אל־אחיהם צרעה ואשתאל //
ויאמרו להם אחיהם מה אתם:
9 וימרו / קומה ונעלה עליהם / כי ראינו
את־הארץ והנה טובה מאד // ואתם
מחשים אל־תעצלו / ללכת לבא לרשת
את־הארץ:
10 כבאכם תבאו אל־עם בטח / והארץ
רחבת ידים / כי־נתנה אלהים בידכם //
מקום אשר אין־שם מחסור / כל־דבר
אשר בארץ:
11 ויסעו משם103 ממשפחת הדני /
מצרעה ומאשתאל // שש־מאות איש /
חגור כלי מלחמה:

S ◇   N/D/J ◇   C/R

12 ויעלו /

ויחנו בקרית יערים ביהודה // על־כן
קראו למקום ההוא מחנה־דן / עד היום
הזה / הנה / אחרי קרית יערים:

13 ויעברו משם הר־אפרים //

ויבאו עד־בית מיכה:
14 ויענו חמשת האנשים לרגל את־הארץ
<>104 / ויאמרו אל־אחיהם / הידעתם / כי
יש בבתים האלה אפוד ותרפים / ופסל
ומסכה // ועתה דעו מה־תעשו:
15 ויסורו שמה / ויבאו אל־בית־הנער
הלוי בית מיכה // וישאלו־לו לשלום:
16 ושש־מאות איש / חגורים כלי
מלחמתם / נצבים פתח השער // אשר
מבני־דן:
17 ויעלו חמשת האנשים / ההלכים לרגל
את־הארץ / באו שמה / לקחו את־הפסל
ואת־האפוד / ואת־התרפים ואת־המסכה //
והכהן נצב פתח השער / ושש־מאות
האיש / החגור כלי המלחמה:
18 ואלה באו בית מיכה / ויקחו את־פסל
האפוד / ואת־התרפים ואת־המסכה //
ויאמר אליהם הכהן / מה אתם עשים:
19 ויאמרו לו החרש שים־ידך על־פיך
ולך עמנו / והיה־לנו לאב ולכהן // הטוב
היותך כהן / לבית איש אחד / או היותך
כהן / לשבט ולמשפחה בישראל:
20 וייטב לב הכהן / ויקח את־האפוד /
ואת־התרפים ואת־הפסל // ויבא בקרב
העם:
21 ויפנו וילכו // וישימו את־הטף
ואת־המקנה / ואת־הכבודה לפניהם:
22 המה הרחיקו מבית מיכה //
והאנשים / אשר בבתים אשר עם־בית
מיכה / נזעקו / וידביקו את־בני־דן:
23 ויקראו אל־בני־דן / ויסבו פניהם //
ויאמרו למיכה / מה־לך כי נזעקת:
24 ויאמר את־אלהי אשר־עשיתי לקחתם
ואת־הכהן ותלכו ומה־לי עוד // ומה־זה
תאמרו אלי מה־לך:
25 ויאמרו אליו בני־דן / אל־תשמע קולך
עמנו // פן־יפגעו בכם / אנשים מרי
נפש / ואספתה נפשך ונפש ביתך:
26 וילכו בני־דן לדרכם // וירא מיכה
כי־חזקים המה ממנו / ויפן וישב
אל־ביתו:

S ◇ N/D/J ◇ C/R

27 והמה לקחו את אשר־עשה מיכה /
ואת־הכהן אשר היה־לו / ויבאו על־ליש
על־עם שקט ובטח / ויכו אותם
לפי־חרב // ואת־העיר שרפו באש:
28 ואין מציל כי רחוקה־היא מצידון /
ודבר אין־להם עם־אדם /

והיא בעמק אשר לבית־רחוב //

ויבנו את־העיר וישבו בה:
29 ויקראו שם־העיר דן / בשם דן
אביהם / אשר יולד לישראל //

ואולם ליש שם־העיר לראשנה:

30 ויקימו להם בני־דן את־הפסל[105] //

ויהונתן בן־גרשם בן־מ<>שה[106] הוא
ובניו / היו כהנים לשבט הדני / עד־יום
גלות האר<ון>[107]:
31 וישימו להם את־פסל מיכה אשר
עשה // כל־ימי היות בית־האלהים
בשלה: -פ-

JUDGES 19:1–21:25

S ◇ N/D/J ◇ C/R

19 1 ויהי בימים ההם / ומלך אין
בישראל //

ויהי איש לוי / גר בירכתי הר־אפרים /
ויקח־לו אשה פילגש /
מבית לחם יהודה:
2 ותזנה עליו פילגשו / ותלך מאתו
אל־בית אביה /
אל־בית לחם יהודה //
ותהי־שם / ימים ארבעה חדשים:

3 ויקם אישה וילך אחריה / לדבר
על־לבה להשיבו / ונערו עמו וצמד
חמרים // ותביאהו בית אביה / ויראהו
אבי הנערה / וישמח לקראתו:
4 ויחזק־בו חתנו אבי הנערה / וישב אתו
שלשת ימים / ויאכלו וישתו / וילינו
שם:

5 ויהי ביום הרביעי / וישכימו בבקר
ויקם ללכת // ויאמר אבי הנערה
אל־חתנו / סעד לבך פת־לחם ואחר
תלכו:
6 וישבו / ויאכלו שניהם יחדו וישתו //
ויאמר אבי הנערה אל־האיש / הואל־נא
ולין ויטב לבך:

S ◇ N/D/J ◇ C/R

7 ויקם האיש ללכת // ויפצר־בו חתנו /
וישב וילן שם:

8 וישכם בבקר ביום החמישי ללכת /
ויאמר אבי הנערה / סעד־נא לבבך /
והתמהמהו עד־נטות היום // ויאכלו
שניהם:

9 ויקם האיש ללכת / הוא ופילגשו
ונערו // ויאמר לו חתנו אבי הנערה הנה
נא רפה היום לערב / לינו־נא הנה חנות
היום לין פה וייטב לבבך / והשכמתם
מחר לדרככם / והלכת לאהלך:

10 ולא־אבה האיש ללון / ויקם וילך /
ויבא עד־נכח יבוס /
היא ירושלם /
ועמו / צמד חמורים חבושים / ופילגשו
עמו:

11 הם עם־יבוס / והיום <י>ר֑ד֡[108] מאד //
ויאמר הנער אל־אדניו / לכה־נא ונסורה
אל־עיר־היבוסי הזאת ונלין בה:

12 ויאמר אליו אדניו / לא נסור אל־עיר
נכרי / אשר לא־מבני ישראל הנה //
ועברנו עד־גבעה:

13 ויאמר לנערו / לך ונקרבה באחד
המקמות / ולנו בגבעה או ברמה:

14 ויעברו וילכו // ותבא להם השמש /
אצל הגבעה
אשר לבנימן:

15 ויסרו שם / לבוא ללון בגבעה //
ויבא / וישב ברחוב העיר / ואין איש
מאסף־אותם הביתה ללון:

16 והנה איש זקן / בא מן־מעשהו
מן־השדה בערב / והאיש מהר אפרים /
והוא־גר בגבעה //
ואנשי המקום בני ימיני:

17 וישא עיניו / וירא את־האיש הארח
ברחב העיר / ויאמר האיש הזקן אנה תלך
ומאין תבוא:

18 ויאמר אליו / עברים אנחנו מבית־לחם
יהודה עד־ירכתי הר־אפרים / משם
אנכי / ואלך / עד־בית לחם יהודה //
וא<ל>־<בית־י>[109] אני הלך / ואין איש
מאסף אותי הביתה:

19 וגם־תבן גם־מספוא יש לחמורינו / וגם
לחם ויין יש־לי ולאמרך / ולנער
עם־עבדיך // אין מחסור כל־דבר:

S ◇　　　　N/D/J ◇　　　　C/R

20 ויאמר האיש הזקן שלום לך / רק
כל־מחסורך עלי // רק ברחוב אל־תלן:
21 ויביאהו לביתו / ויב<>ל[110]
לחמורים // וירחצו רגליהם / ויאכלו
וישתו:
22 המה מיטיבים את־לבם / והנה אנשי
העיר אנשי בני בליעל / נסבו את־הבית /
מתדפקים על־הדלת // ויאמרו אל־האיש
בעל הבית הזקן לאמר / הוצא
את־האיש אשר־בא אל־ביתך ונדענו:
23 ויצא אליהם / האיש בעל הבית /
ויאמר אלהם / אל־אחי אל־תרעו נא //
אחרי אשר־בא האיש הזה אל־ביתי /
אל־תעשו את־הנבלה הזאת:
24 הנה בתי הבתולה ופילגשהו /
אוציאה־נא אותם וענו אותם /
ועשו להם / הטוב בעיניכם //
ולאיש הזה לא תעשו / דבר הנבלה
הזאת:
25 ולא־אבו האנשים לשמע לו / ויחזק
האיש בפילגשו / ויצא אליהם החוץ //
וידעו אותה ויתעללו־בה כל־הלילה
עד־הבקר / וישלחוה בעלות השחר:
26 ותבא האשה לפנות הבקר // ותפל
פתח בית־האיש אשר־אדוניה שם
עד־האור:

27 ויקם אדניה בבקר / ויפתח דלתות
הבית / ויצא ללכת לדרכו // והנה האשה
פילגשו / נפלת פתח הבית / וידיה
על־הסף:
28 ויאמר אליה קומי ונלכה ואין
ענה[111] // ויקחה על־החמור /

ויקם האיש / וילך למקמו:
29 ויבא אל־ביתו / ויקח את־המאכלת
ויחזק בפילגשו / וינתחה לעצמיה /
לשנים עשר נתחים // וישלחה / בכל
גבול ישראל:
30 והיה כל־הראה / ואמר לא־נהיתה
ולא־נראתה כזאת / למיון עלות
בני־ישראל מארץ מצרים / עד היום
הזה // <ויצוה אל־האנשים אשר שלח
לאמר כה תאמרו לכל־איש ישראל
הנהיתה כדבר הזה למיום עלות בני
ישראל מארץ מצרים עד היום הזה>[112]
שימו־לכם עליה עצו ודברו: ־פ־

S ◇   N/D/J ◇   C/R

20 1 ויצאו כל־בני ישראל / ותקהל
העדה כאיש אחד /
למדן ועד־באר שבע / וארץ הגלעד //
אל־יהוה המצפה:
2 ויתיצבו פנות כל־העם / כל שבטי
ישראל /
בקהל עם האלהים //
ארבע מאות אלף איש רגלי שלף
חרב: –פ–

3 וישמעו בני בנימן / כי־עלו בני־ישראל
המצפה // ויאמרו בני ישראל / דברו /
איכה נהיתה הרעה הזאת:
4 ויען האיש הלוי / איש האשה הנרצחה
ויאמר // הגבעתה אשר לבנימן / באתי
אני ופילגשי ללון:
5 ויקמו עלי בעלי הגבעה / ויסבו עלי
את־הבית לילה // אותי דמו להרג /
ואת־פילגשי ענו ותמת:
6 ואחז בפילגשי ואנתחה / ואשלחה /
בכל־שדה נחלת ישראל // כי עשו זמה
ונבלה בישראל:
7 הנה כלכם בני ישראל // הבו לכם דבר
ועצה הלם:

8 ויקם כל־העם / כאיש אחד לאמר // לא
נלך איש לאהלו / ולא נסור איש לביתו:
9 ועתה / זה הדבר / אשר נעשה
לגבעה // ‹נ‹על‹›ה113 עליה בגורל:
10 ולקחנו עשרה אנשים למאה לכל
שבטי ישראל / ומאה לאלף ואלף
לרבבה / לקחת צדה לעם // לעשות
לבואם לגבע‹ת›114 בנימן / ככל־הנבלה /
אשר עשה בישראל:
11 ויאסף כל־איש ישראל אל־העיר /
כאיש אחד חברים: –פ–

12 וישלחו שבטי ישראל אנשים /
בכל־שבטי בנימן לאמר // מה הרעה
הזאת / אשר נהיתה בכם:
13 ועתה תנו את־האנשים בני־בליעל
אשר בגבעה ונמיתם /

ונבערה רעה מישראלcxiii //

ולא אבו ‹בני›115 בנימן / לשמע / בקול
אחיהם בני־ישראל:
14 ויאספו בני־בנימן מן־הערים
הגבעתה // לצאת למלחמה עם־בני
ישראל:

S ◇　　　　　　N/D/J ◇　　　　　　C/R

15 ויתפקדו בני בנימן ביום ההוא
מהערין / עשרים וששה אלף איש שלף
חרב // לבד מישבי הגבעה התפקדו /
שבע מאות איש בחור:
16 מכל העם הזה / שבע מאות איש
בחור /
אטר יד־ימינו //
כל־זה / קלע באבן אל־השערה ולא
יחטא: –פ–

17 ואיש ישראל התפקדו / לבד מבנימן /
ארבע מאות אלף איש שלף חרב // כל־זה
איש מלחמה:

18 ויקמו ויעלו בית־אל וישאלו באלהים /
ויאמרו בני ישראל / מי יעלה־לנו
בתחלה / למלחמה עם־בני בנימן //
ויאמר יהוה יהודה בתחלה:

19 ויקומו בני־ישראל בבקר // ויחנו
על־הגבעה: –פ–

20 ויצא איש ישראל / למלחמה
עם־בנימן // ויערכו אתם איש־ישראל
מלחמה אל־הגבעה:
21 ויצאו בני־בנימן מן־הגבעה // וישחיתו
בישראל ביום הוא / שנים ועשרים אלף
איש ארצה:
22 ויתחזק העם איש ישראל // ויספו
לערך מלחמה / במקום / אשר־ערכו שם
ביום הראשון:
23 ויעלו בני־ישראל / ויבכו לפני־יהוה
עד־הערב / וישאלו ביהוה לאמר /
האוסיף / לגשת למלחמה / עם־בני בנימן
אחי // ויאמר יהוה עלו אליו: –פ–

24 ויקרבו בני־ישראל אל־בני בנימן ביום
השני:
25 ויצא בנימן לקראתן מן־הגבעה ביום
השני / וישחיתו בבני ישראל עוד / שמנת
עשר אלף איש ארצה // כל־אלה שלפי
חרב:
26 ויעלו כל־בני ישראל וכל־העם ויבאו
בית־אל / ויבכו וישבו שם לפני יהוה /
ויצומו ביום־ההוא עד־הערב // ויעלו
עלות ושלמים לפני יהוה:
27 וישאלו בני־ישראל ביהוה //

ושם / ארון ברית האלהים / בימים
ההם:

S ◇   N/D/J ◇   C/R

28 ופינחס בן־אלעזר בן־אהרן עמד
לפניו / בימים ההם

לאמר / האוסף עוד לצאת למלחמה
עם־בני־בנימן אחי אם־אחדל // ויאמר
יהוה עלו / כי מחר אתננו בידך:
29 וישם ישראל ארבים / אל־הגבעה
סביב: –פ–

30 ויעלו בני־ישראל אל־בני בנימן
ביום השלישי // ויערכו אל־הגבעה כפעם
בפעם:
31 ו־יצאו בני־בנימן לקראת העם / הנתקו
מן־העיר // ויחלו להכות מהעם חללים
כפעם בפעם / במסלות אשר אחת עלה
בית־אל / ואחת גבעתה בשדה / כשלשים
איש בישראל:
32 ויאמרו בני בנימן / נגפים הם לפנינו
כבראשנה // ובני ישראל אמרו / ננוסה
ונתקנהו / מן־העיר אל־המסלות:

33 וכל איש ישראל / קמו ממקומו /
ויערכו בבעל תמר // וארב ישראל מגיח
ממקמו ממערה־גבע[116]:
34 ויבאו מנגד לגבעה עשרת אלפים איש
בחור מכל־ישראל / והמלחמה כבדה //
והם לא ידעו / כי־נגעת עליהם
הרעה: –פ–

35 ויגף יהוה את־בנימן לפני ישראל /
וישחיתו בני ישראל בבנימן ביום ההוא /
עשרים וחמשה אלף ומאה איש //
כל־אלה שלף חרב:
36 ויראו בני־בנימן כי נגפו // ויתנו
איש־ישראל מקום לבנימן / כי בטחו
אל־הארב / אשר שמו אל־הגבעה:
37 והארב החישו / ויפשטו אל־הגבעה //
וימשך הארב / ויך את־כל־העיר
לפי־חרב:
38 והמועד / היה לאיש ישראל
עם־הארב // <>[117] / להעלותם משאת
העשן מן־העיר:
39 ויהפך איש־ישראל במלחמה // ובנימן
החל להכות חללים באיש־ישראל
כשלשים איש / כי אמרו / אך נגוף נגף
הוא לפנינו / כמלחמה הראשנה:
40 והמשאת / החלה לעלות מן־העיר
עמוד עשן // ויפן בנימן אחריו / והנה
עלה כליל־העיר השמימה:

S ◇ N/D/J ◇ C/R

41 ואיש ישראל הפך / ויבהל איש
בנימן // כי ראה / כי־נגעה עליו הרעה:
42 ויפנו לפני איש ישראל אל־דרך
המדבר / והמלחמה הדביקתהו // ואשר
מהע>י<ר>[118] / משחיתים אותו בתוכו:
43 <וי>כתרו[119] את־בנימן הרדיפהו /
מנוחה הדריכהו // עד נכח הגבעה
ממזרח־שמש:
44 ויפלו מבנימן / שמנה־עשר אלף
איש // את־כל־אלה אנשי־חיל:
45 ויפנו וינסו המדברה אל־סלע הרמון /
ויעללהו במסלות / חמשת אלפים איש //
וידביקו אחריו עד־גדעם / ויכו ממנו
אלפים איש:
46 ויהי כל־הנפלים מבנימן / עשרים
וחמשה אלף איש שלף חרב ביום ההוא //
את־כל־אלה אנשי־חיל:
47 ויפנו וינסו המדברה אל־סלע הרמון /
שש מאות איש // וישבו בסלע רמון /
ארבעה חדשים:
48 ואיש ישראל שבו אל־בני בנימן ויכום
לפי־חרב / מעיר מתם עד־בהמה / עד
כל־הנמצא // גם כל־הערים הנמצאות
שלחו באש: ־פ־

21 1 ואיש ישראל / נשבע במצפה
לאמר // איש ממנו / לא־יתן בתו לבנימן
לאשה:
2 ויבא העם בית־אל / וישבו שם
עד־הערב / לפני האלהים // וישאו
קולם / ויבכו בכי גדול:
3 ויאמרו / למה / יהוה אלהי ישראל /
היתה זאת בישראל // להפקד היום
מישראל שבט אחד:
4 ויהי ממחרת / וישכימו העם / ויבנו־שם
מזבח // ויעלו עלות ושלמים: ־פ־

5 ויאמרו בני ישראל / מי אשר לא־עלה
בקהל מכל־שבטי ישראל אל־יהוה // כי
השבועה הגדולה היתה / לאשר לא־עלה
אל־יהוה המצפה לאמר מות יומת:
6 וינחמו בני ישראל / אל־מנימן אחיו //
ויאמרו / נגדע היום שבט אחד מישראל:
7 מה־נעשה להם לנותרים לנשים //
ואנחנו נשבענו ביהוה / לבלתי תת־להם
מבנותינו לנשים:
8 ויאמרו / מי / אחד משבטי ישראל /
אשר לא־עלה אל־יהוה המצפה //

S　◇　　　　N/D/J　◇　　　　C/R

והנה לא בא־איש אל־המחנה מיביש
גלעד אל־הקהל:

9 ויתפקד העם / והנה אין־שם איש /
מיושבי יבש גלעד:

10 וישלחו־שם העדה / שנים־עשר אלף
איש מבני החיל // ויצוו אותם לאמר /
לכו והכיתם את־יושבי יבש גלעד
לפי־חרב / והנשים והטף:

11 וזה הדבר אשר תעשו / כל־זכר /
וכל־אשה ידעת משכב־זכר תחרימו:

12 וימצאו מיושבי יביש גלעד / ארבע
מאות נערה בתולה / אשר לא־ידעת איש
למשכב זכר // ויביאו אותם אל־המחנה
שלה /

אשר בארץ כנען: ‑ס‑

13 וישלחו כל־העדה / וידברו אל־בני
בנימן / אשר בסלע רמון // ויקראו להם
שלום:

14 וישב בנימן בעת ההיא / ויתנו להם
הנשים / אשר חיו / מנשי יבש גלעד //
ולא־מצאו להם כן:

15 והעם נחם לבנימן // כי־עשה יהוה
פרץ בשבטי ישראל:

16 ויאמרו זקני העדה / מה־נעשה
לנותרים לנשים // כי־נשמדה מבנימן
אשה:

17 ויאמרו / ירשת פליטה לבנימן //
ולא־ימחה שבט מישראל:

18 ואנחנו / לא נוכל לתת־להן נשים
מבנותינו // כי־נשבעו בני־ישראל
לאמר / ארור / נתן אשה לבנימן: ‑ס‑

19 ויאמרו הנה חג־יהוה בשלו מימים
ימימה /

　　　　　　　　　　　　　אשר מצפונה לבית־אל מזרחה השמש /
　　　　　　　　　　　　　למסלה / העלה מבית־אל שכמה //
　　　　　　　　　　　　　ומנגב ללבונה:

20 ויצו<ו>[120] / את־בני בנימן לאמר //
לכו וארבתם בכרמים:

21 וראיתם / והנה אם־יצאו בנות־שילו
לחול במחלות / ויצאתם מן־הכרמים /
וחטפתם לכם איש אשתו מבנות שילו //
והלכתם ארץ בנימן:

22 והיה כי־יבאו אבותם או אחיהם
לר<י>ב[121] אלינו / ואמרנו אליהם חנונו
אותם / כי לא לקחנו איש אשתו
במלחמה //

S ◇ N/D/J ◇ C/R

כי לא אתם נתתם להם כעת תאשמו: ‪‪-ס-‬

23 ויעשו־כן בני בנימן / וישאו נשים
למספרם / מן־המחללות אשר גזלו //
וילכו / וישובו אל־נחלתם / ויבנו
את־הערים / וישבו בהם:
24 ויתהלכו משם בני־ישראל בעת ההיא /
איש לשבטו ולמשפחתו // ויצאו משם /
איש לנחלתו:

25 בימים ההם / אין מלך בישראל //
איש הישר בעיניו יעשה:

REDACTION-CRITICAL NOTES TO THE APPENDIX

[i] In this appendix the text of Judges is presented in three columns: (1) right (C/R), materials that seem to have been assembled/composed under the rhetorical aims of a compiler/redactor; (2) centre (N/D/J), materials copied/edited from traditions now preserved in the book of Numbers, Deuteronomy or Joshua (an outcrop to the right indicating an editorial insertion/adaptation); (3) left (S), materials apparently copied/edited from an otherwise unknown source (an outcrop to the right indicating a possible editorial insertion/adaptation). To the far right is indicated a proposed identification of what may have been the two final compilational strata in Judges: a penultimate compilation (|) and its redaction (‖). For a discussion of issues relevant to forming a stratigraphy of compilation and/or redaction in Judges, see excursus 1.

[ii] Judg. 1:1aβ-b edits Judg. 20:18a (cf. 20:23aγ-ζ; 20:27a, 28aβ-δ).

[iii] Judg. 1:2a edits Judg. 20:18b (cf. 20:23b; 20:28bα).

[iv] Judg. 1:10aαβ summarizes *Josh. 15:13aα, 14aα.

[v] Judg. 1:10aγ edits Josh. 14:15aα. Cf. Josh. 15:13b. See L. G. Stone, "From Tribal Confederation to Monarchic State: The Editorial Perspective of the Book of Judges" (PhD diss., Yale University, 1988), pp. 196-99.

[vi] Judg. 1:10b = Josh. 15:14bα. See Stone, "Tribal Confederation" (1988), pp. 196-99.

[vii] Judg. 1:11a ויעל משם אל־ישבי דבר [וילך משם אל־יושבי דביר Josh. 15:15a. The orthography of Judges may reflect later scribal conventions. However, with regard to relative dating from orthography, one should exercise caution in such matters as may affect merely scribal, rather than redactional, activity (cf. Judg. 1:21 <יבשי> [ישבי יושבי Josh. 15:63; and Judg. 1:15b תחתית ... [עלית תחתיות ... עליות Josh. 15:19b). See Stone, "Tribal Confederation" (1988), pp. 199-200 n. 15.

[viii] Judg. 1:11b ושם־דביר לפנים קרית־ספר [ושם־דבר לפנים קרית־ספר Josh. 15:15b. See the preceding note.

[ix] Judg. 1:13a ממנו [הקטן □ = Josh. 15:17a. Judg. 1:13a = Judg. 3:9b. The MT and OG of Josh. 15:17, in a book that often preserves the older form of materials that it has in common with Judges, testify to the original absence of הקטן ממנו. Contra M. L. Margolis (ed.), *The Book of Joshua in Greek, according to the Critically Restored Text with an Apparatus Containing the Variants of the Principal Recensions and of the Individual Witnesses* (Paris, 1931), pp. 289-90, the OG of Josh. 15:17 probably did not preserve ὁ νεώτερος, which is present in E(h), S(n, dpt), P(Gbc Syh÷, x), C(ANΘglouyb₂ Arm), M(aikma₂; ej, sz, fv [the last 6 MSS in *Catenae group* = C in Josh. 15:7-17:1]) but which is omitted from his "relatively pure" Egyptian group: E(Bqr Sah Eth OLat). Cf. Stone, "Tribal Confederation" (1988), pp. 127-28, 202-7, 283, 285.

[x] Judg. 1:15a תנה־לי [הבה־לי Josh. 15:19a.

[xi] Judg. 1:12-15 = Josh. 15:16-19.

[xii] Judg. 1:20a conflates Josh. 14:13b[i] and Josh. 14:6b[ii] (cf. Josh. 15:13a). See Stone, "Tribal Confederation" (1988), pp. 196-99.

[xiii] Judg. 1:20b = Josh. 15:14a. Stone, "Tribal Confederation" (1988), pp. 196-99.

[xiv] Judg. 1:21 edits *Josh. 15:63. See Stone, "Tribal Confederation" (1988), pp. 207-9.

ˣᵛ Judg. 1:27a edits *Josh. 17:11a, 12a. See Stone, "Tribal Confederation" (1988), pp. 210-12.

ˣᵛⁱ Judg. 1:27b = Josh. 17:12b. See Stone, "Tribal Confederation" (1988), pp. 210-12.

ˣᵛⁱⁱ Judg. 1:28 edits *Josh. 17:13.

ˣᵛⁱⁱⁱ Judg. 1:29 edits *Josh. 16:10. See Stone, "Tribal Confederation" (1988), pp. 212-13.

ˣⁱˣ Judg. 2:1bα may allude to Josh. 24:5b-6aα, 17aβ or Deut. 4:20a, 37b; 5:6β; 6:12b, 21b; (7:9b?); 8:14bβ; 9:26b.

ˣˣ Judg. 2:1bβ may allude to Deut. 6:10aαβⁱ; 7:1aαβ; 8:7a.

ˣˣⁱ Judg. 2:1bγ may allude to Deut. 6:10aβⁱⁱ, 18bγ; 7:8aβ, 12bγ, 13bδ; 8:1bγ, 18b; 11:21aγ.

ˣˣⁱⁱ Judg. 2:1bδε may allude, albeit reciprocally, to Deut. 31:16bδε, 20bγ.

ˣˣⁱⁱⁱ Judg. 2:2aαβ alludes to Deut. 7:2bβⁱ (cf. Josh. 23:12a).

ˣˣⁱᵛ Judg. 2:2aγ alludes to Deut. 7:5aβ.

ˣˣᵛ Judg. 2:3a may allude to Josh. 23:9aα, 13a; 24:18aα.

ˣˣᵛⁱ Judg. 2:3b may allude to Josh. 23:13bαβ or Deut. 7:16b. The nonoracular divine speech of Judg. 2:1b-3 may be part of a redactor's interpolation in 2:1-5 (cf. Stone, "Tribal Confederation" [1988], pp. 128, 241-47).

ˣˣᵛⁱⁱ Judg. 2:6 edits Josh. 24:28 (לנחלתו: / איש את־העם יהושע וישלח). Cf. Stone, "Tribal Confederation" (1988), 250-51, though on both pages וילכו is mistakenly transliterated *wayyēlek* and the diagram on p. 250 mistakenly omits את־הארץ לרשת from Judg. 2:6. The addition of לרשת את־הארץ ... וילכו בני־ישראל by the Judges compiler/redactor places emphasis upon the responsibility of the tribes to possess the land.

ˣˣᵛⁱⁱⁱ Judg. 2:7a ויעבד ישראל [ויעבדו העם Josh. 24:31a.

ˣˣⁱˣ Judg. 2:7bγ ואשר ידעו [אשר ראו Josh. 24:31bγ.

ˣˣˣ Judg. 2:7bγ [הגדול □ Josh. 24:31bγ.

ˣˣˣⁱ Judg. 2:7 edits Josh. 24:31, changing ידעו to ראו and adding הגדול for emphasis. Cf. Stone, "Tribal Confederation" (1988), pp. 250, 251-52.

ˣˣˣⁱⁱ Judg. 2:8 = Josh. 24:29aβ-b. Josh. 24:29aα (האלה הדברים אחרי ויהי) has been omitted, probably by the compiler/redactor (Stone, "Tribal Confederation" [1988], pp. 250, 251).

ˣˣˣⁱⁱⁱ Judg. 2:9aβ בתמנת־חרס [בתמנת־סרח Josh. 24:30aβ except ḥrs Arab (cf. בתמנת־סרח Josh. 19:50 except Θαμαρχάρης B*, Chamahares OLat). Stone infers that the alteration of חרס to סרח in Joshua is "probably scribal, not editorial" (Stone, "Tribal Confederation" [1988], p. 251 n. 62).

ˣˣˣⁱᵛ Judg. 2:9aβ אשר בהר־אפרים [בהר אפרים Josh. 24:30aβ.

ˣˣˣᵛ Judg. 2:9 = Josh. 24:30. LXX Josh. 24:28-31 has the same verse order as MT/LXX Judg. 2:6-9 (= MT Josh. 24:28, 31, 29-30) except that OG Josh. 24:31 appends: ἐκεῖ ἔθηκαν μετ' αὐτοῦ εἰς τὸ μνῆμα [Bqr c,x ai Cyr. : ἐν τῷ μνήματι, gn,pt Sah], εἰς ὅ [Br c,x ai : ἐν ῷ, AMNΘ rell(except q b) Sah Cyr.] ἔθαψαν αὐτὸν ἐκεῖ, τὰς μαχαίρας τὰς πετρίνας ἐν αἷς περιέτεμεν τοὺς υἱοὺς Ἰσραὴλ ἐν Γαλγάλοις, ὅτε ἐξήγαγεν αὐτοὺς ἐξ [ἐκ γῆς, gnw,pt Arm-edn Sahᵗ] Αἰγύπτου καθά συνέταξεν αὐτοῖς [Br Sah : αὐτῷ, q w i Eth : □ AMNΘ rell Arm OLat Syh] Κύριος· καὶ ἐκεῖ εἰσιν ἕως τῆς σήμερον ἡμέρας. The entire appended reading, Syh(÷).

ˣˣˣᵛⁱ Judg. 2:11a may allude to Deut. 4:25bγⁱ; 9:18bβⁱ; 17:2bβⁱ or 31:29bβ (or, antithetically, 6:18a; 12:25bβ, 28bβγ; 13:19b or 21:9b).

xxxvii Judg. 2:12aα may allude to Josh. 24:16aγ, 20aα or possibly Deut. 31:16bγ (cf., reciprocally, 17aα). Cf. Deut. 31:20bβ.

xxxviii Judg. 2:12aβ may allude to Josh. 24:5b-6aα, 17aβ or Deut. 4:20a, 37b; 5:6β; 6:12b, 21b; 8:14bβ; 9:26b.

xxxix Judg. 2:12aγ edits *Deut. 6:14a but may allude to Josh. 23:16aβγ; 24:16b, 20aβ or Deut. 8:19aγ-εⁱ; 31:18b, 20bα.

xl Judg. 2:12aγδ edits *Deut. 6:14.

xli Judg. 2:12aε may allude to Josh. 23:7bγ, 16aδ or Deut. 5:9a; 8:19aεⁱⁱ; 11:16bγ.

xlii Judg. 2:12b may allude to Deut. 4:25bγⁱⁱ; 31:29bγ.

xliii Judg. 2:13a may allude to Josh. 24:16aγ, 20aα or Deut. 31:16bγ (cf., reciprocally, 17aα). Cf. Deut. 31:20bβ.

xliv Judg. 2:14aα may allude to Josh. 23:16bα or Deut. 7:4bα; 11:17aα; 31:17aα.

xlv Judg. 2:14aβ may allude, antithetically, to Josh. 24:8bα, 11b or Deut. 7:2a.

xlvi Judg. 2:17aβγ may allude to Josh. 24:16b, 20aβ or Deut. 8:19aγ-εⁱ; 31:16bαβ, 18b. Cf. Judg. 8:27aγ, 33aγ.

xlvii Judg. 2:17aδ may allude to Josh. 23:7bγ, 16aδ or Deut. 5:9a; 8:19aεⁱⁱ; 11:16bγ.

xlviii Judg. 2:17b may allude to Deut. 9:12bαβ or 31:29aγ. The whole of 2:17 may be a redactor's interpolation (Stone, "Tribal Confederation" [1988], pp. 125, 128, 253).

xlix Judg. 2:18bβ may allude to Deut. 26:7bβ.

l Judg. 2:19aγ-εⁱ appears to edit *Deut. 8:19aγ-εⁱ but may allude to Josh. 23:7bβ, 16aβγ; 24:16b, 20aβ or Deut. 31:20bα.

li Judg. 2:19aεⁱⁱ appears to edit *Deut. 8:19aεⁱⁱ but may allude to Josh. 23:7bβγ, 16aδ or Deut. 5:9a; 11:16bγ.

lii Judg. 2:20a may allude to Josh. 23:16bα or Deut. 7:4bα; 11:17aα; 31:17aα.

liii Judg. 2:20bβγ may allude to Josh. 23:16aα.

liv Judg. 2:21a may allude to Josh. 23:13a.

lv The phraseology of Judg. 2:22bα is distinctly deuteronomic (cf. Deut. 8:6; 10:12bα; 11:22; 19:9a; 26:17bα; 28:9b; 30:16aβγ [so 2 Sam. 22:22; 1 Kgs 2:3]).

lvi Judg. 2:23b may allude, antithetically, to Josh. 24:8bα, 11b or Deut. 7:2a. The non-oracular divine speech of 2:20-23 may be part of a redactor's interpolation (Stone, "Tribal Confederation" [1988], pp. 128, 246, 254-56).

lvii Judg. 3:3aα חמשת סרני פלשתים העזתי והאשדודי והאשקלוני הגתי [חמשת סרני פלשתים והעקרוני והעוים Josh. 13:3b.

lviii Judg. 3:3aβ מתימן כל־ארץ הכנעני [וכל־הכנעני Josh. 13:4aα.

lix Judg. 3:3aβ ומערה אשר לצידנים עד־אפקה עד גבול האמרי [והצידני Josh. 13:4aβ-b.

lx והחוי of Judg. 3:3aγ refers to a people not cited in Josh. 13:3b-5. Thus, we may infer that the compiler of Judges inserted it to specify the inhabitants of Lebanon as Ahivites (= Achaians). It is not equivalent to והעוים (Avvites) in Josh. 13:3bγ. For a treatment of the etymology and ethnic identity of the Ahivites, see O. Margalith, "The Hivites", ZAW 100 (1988), pp. 60-70.

lxi Judg. 3:3aδ והארץ הגבלי וכל־הלמנון מזרח השמש [והחוי ישׁב הר הלבנון Josh. 13:5aαβ.

lxii Judg. 3:3bα מבעל גד תחת הר־חרמון [מהר בעל חרמון Josh. 13:5aγδ.

lxiii Judg. 3:3bβ = Josh. 13:5b. The whole of Judg. 3:3 may edit *Josh. 13:3b-5. It selectively mentions the same key peoples and localities in virtually the same sequence, i.e., חמשת סרני פלשתים ... כל־ארץ הכנעני ומערה אשר לצידנים ... וכל־הלמנון ... מבעל גד תחת הר־חרמון עד לבוא חמת:

^lxiv Judg. 3:5 may edit *Exod. 3:8b. The same list of six native inhabitants appears in the same order. The first half-verse may form a phraseological connection to Judg. 1:29b, 30bα, 32a, 33aγ (Stone, "Tribal Confederation" [1988], p. 257).

^lxv Judg. 3:6a may allude to Josh. 23:12b or Deut. 7:3 (ולא תתחתן בם בתך לא־תתן לבנו ובתו לא־תקח לבנך).

^lxvi Judg. 3:6b alludes to Deut. 7:16bα (ולא תעבד את־אלהיהם). The whole of 2:20–3:6 may be a redactor's addition (cf. Stone, "Tribal Confederation" [1988], pp. 254-58).

^lxvii Judg. 3:9b = Judg. 1:13a. See the note on Judg. 1:13a.

^lxviii Judg. 4:2aγ edits 4:17bβ.

^lxix Judg. 4:2bα edits 4:7aβ.

^lxx Judg. 4:2bβ edits 4:13aαγb. Cf. B. Lindars, "Deborah's Song: Women in the Old Testament", *BJRL* 65 (1982–1983), p. 163 n. 11.

^lxxi Judg. 4:3bα edits 4:13aβ (*pace* Lindars, "Deborah's Song" [1982–83], pp. 163-64 n. 14).

^lxxii Judg. 4:7aβ is edited in 4:2bα.

^lxxiii Judg. 4:13aβ is edited in 4:3bα.

^lxxiv Judg. 4:13aαγb is edited in 4:2bβ.

^lxxv Judg. 4:17bβ is edited in 4:2aγ.

^lxxvi Judg. 6:6b may allude to Josh. 24:7aα or Deut. 26:7a under the influence of the addition of Judg. 6:7-10. Cf. Judg. 6:7a; 10:10a, 14aβ.

^lxxvii Judg. 6:7a may allude to Josh. 24:7aα or Deut. 26:7a. Cf. Judg. 6:6b; 10:10a, 14aβ.

^lxxviii Judg. 6:8bβγ edits Josh. 24:17a.

^lxxix Judg. 6:9 may allude to Josh. 24:8, 12a.

^lxxx Judg. 6:10aγ^iiδ (את־אלהי האמרי אשר אתם יושבים בארצם) = Josh. 24:15aεʃ.

^lxxxi Judg. 6:10b alludes to Josh. 24:24b (ובקולו נשמע). The collocation of themes and vocabulary between Judg. 6:7a, 8bβγ, 9, 10aγδb and Josh. 24:7a, 8, 12a, 15a, 17a, 24b (or Deut. 26:7-9) would appear to be intentional. The nonoracular divine speech of Judg. 6:8b-10 may be part of a redactor's interpolation in 6:7-10 (Stone, "Tribal Confederation" [1988], pp. 128, 246, 318-19, 359-64).

^lxxxii Judg. 10:10a may allude to Josh. 24:7aα or Deut. 26:7a. Cf. Judg. 6:6b, 7a; 10:14aβ.

^lxxxiii Judg. 10:14aβ may allude to Josh. 24:7aα or Deut. 26:7a. Cf. Judg. 6:6b, 7a; 10:10a. The nonoracular divine speech of Judg. 10:11-14 may be part of a redactor's interpolation in 10:10-14 (Stone, "Tribal Confederation" [1988], pp. 128, 246, 319, 359-64).

^lxxxiv Judg. 10:15aβγ may allude antithetically to Deut. 12:8aα/b.

^lxxxv Judg. 11:13aγ (מארנון ועד־היבק ומן־המדבר ועד־הירדן [מארנון ועד־היבק ועד־הירדן] Judg. 11:22b. Both may edit Num. 21:24bα^iiβ, מארנן עד־יבק עד־בני עמון.

^lxxxvi Judg. 11:15bα alludes to Num. 21:10-20 and/or Deut. 2:9, 13-18.

^lxxxvii Judg. 11:15bβ alludes to Num. 21:24b and/or Deut. 2:19, 37.

^lxxxviii Judg. 11:17aα edits Num. 20:14a, 17aα and may allude to Deut. 2:4-6 (cf. 2:29a).

^lxxxix Judg. 11:17aβ alludes to Num. 20:20-21.

^xc Judg. 11:18aβ^i edits Num. 21:4aβ.

^xci Judg. 11:18aαβ alludes to Num. 21:13aαβ and/or Deut. 2:8b.

xcii Judg. 11:18aγδ edits Num. 21:10b.

xciii Judg. 11:18bβ = Num. 21:13bα. Judg. 11:8 may allude to Deut. 2:8, 13.

xciv Judg. 11:19aαβⁱ = Num. 21:21 (except לאמר).

xcv Judg. 11:19aβⁱⁱ may conflate also Deut. 2:24a or 26a.

xcvi Judg. 11:19bα may edit Num. 21:21 (ישראל ... לאמר).

xcvii Judg. 11:19bβⁱ edits Num. 21:22aα and/or Deut. 2:27aα.

xcviii Judg. 11:19bβⁱⁱ may allude to Num. 21:22bβ and/or Deut. 2:29b.

xcix Judg. 11:20aα edits Num. 21:23aα and may allude to Deut. 2:30a.

c Judg. 11:20aβ = Num. 21:23aβ. Cf. Deut. 2:32.

ci Judg. 11:20aγ edits Num. 21:23aγ. Cf. Deut. 2:32.

cii Judg. 11:20b edits Num. 21:23b. Cf. Deut. 2:32.

ciii Judg. 11:21aⁱ conflates Deut. 2:30b-31, 33.

civ Judg. 11:21aⁱⁱ edits Num. 21:24a.

cv Judg. 11:21bαβ edits Num. 21:24bαⁱ.

cvi Judg. 11:22a alludes to Num. 21:24bαⁱ, וייֹרש את־ארצו.

cvii Judg. 11:22b מארנון ועד־היבק ועד־הירדן [מארנון ועד־היבק ומן־המדבר ועד־הירדן
Judg. 11:13aγ. Both may edit Num. 21:24bαⁱⁱβ, מארנן עד־יבק עד־בני עמון. Cf. Deut.
2:34a, 36.

cviii Judg. 11:23a may allude to Num. 21:30-31. Cf. Judg. 11:24b.

cix Judg. 11:24a may allude to Num. 21:29.

cx Judg. 11:24b may allude to Num. 21:30-31. Cf. Judg. 11:23a.

cxi Judg. 11:25aγ edits Num. 22:4b (cf. 22:2a).

cxii Judg. 11:26aαβ edits Num. 21:25, 26bγ (cf. 21:27, 30-31).

cxiii This expression (Judg. 20:13aβ) is especially prevalent in Deuteronomy where it refers to purging Israel of idolaters (Deut. 13:6b; 17:7b); those in contempt of the rule of priests, Levites or judges (17:12bβ); murderers (19:13b); false witnesses (19:19b); rebellious sons (21:21aβ); the sexually immoral (22:21b, 22b, 24b) and kidnappers (24:7bβ). Cf. 1 Kgs 22:47; 2 Kgs 23:24; 2 Chron. 19:3.

TEXT-CRITICAL NOTES TO THE APPENDIX

[1] The critical text presented in this appendix was prepared with primary interest in the rhetoric of Judges. Text-critical discussions and emendations are selected and are not intended to represent an exhaustive critical edition of the book. For a discussion of issues related to scribal developments in Judges, see excursus 2.

[2] *Judg. 1:10aαβ.* After the OG: καὶ ἐπορεύθη Ἰούδας πρὸς τὸν Χαναναῖον τὸν κατοικοῦντα ἐν Χεβρών, LXX-AI(except A),AIII(except Mb₂,h),B-group(except ef*,j) all insert: καὶ ἐξῆλθεν Χεβρὼν ἐξ ἐναντίας. MS A omits: ἐν Χεβρὼν καὶ ἐξῆλθεν Χεβρών. Since also AII(gn,ptv), AIII(M,h) and the *Vorlage* of OLat omit: καὶ ἐξῆλθεν Χεβρών, we may infer that the inserted clause was absent from the earliest form of the OG (so also B. Lindars, *Judges 1-5: A New Translation and Commentary* [A. D. H. Mayes (ed.), Edinburgh, 1995], p. 82). MS w omits: ἐξ ἐναντίας, and the next words: τὸ δὲ ὄνομα Χεβρὼν ἦν (attested in Aabcx gln MNy,h[Χεβρὼν post ἦν] a₂ OLat). The original form of the OG probably had: καὶ ἐπορεύθη Ἰούδας πρὸς τὸν Χαναναῖον τὸν κατοικοῦντα ἐν Χεβρών. τὸ δὲ ὄνομα Χεβρὼν ἦν ἔμπροσθεν Καριαθαρβοκ (OLat *Cariarthar*; cf. Lindars, *Judges 1-5* [1995], p. 82), which corresponds to the MT. The insertion: καὶ ἐξῆλθεν Χεβρὼν ἐξ ἐναντίας probably preserves a variant doublet that was based upon a misconstrued Hebrew *Vorlage* (i.e., ם<ה>י>, משם־חברון לפני־חברון read for MT: ושם־חברון לפנים; cf. 1:11a). Thus, neither BHS nor J. A. Soggin (*Judges: A Commentary* [J. Bowden (trans.), OTL, London, 2d edn, 1987], p. 22) need have cited this as a plus.

[3] *Judg. 1:11a ‖ Josh. 15:15a.* The MT parallel Josh. 15:15a has יעל, attested also in the OG of Judg. 1:11, so MT Judg. 1:11a may have been secondarily influenced by the verb in 1:10a (so J. Hollenberg ["Zur Textkritik des Buches Josua und des Buches der Richter", *ZAW* 1 (1881), pp. 101-2]; G. F. Moore, *A Critical and Exegetical Commentary on Judges* [ICC, Edinburgh, 1895], p. 26; C. F. Burney, *The Book of Judges with Introduction and Notes* [London, 2d edn, 1920], p. 10; Lindars, *Judges 1-5* [1995], p. 26). OG Judg. 1:11 does not seem to have arisen solely as an inner-Greek variant influenced by OG Josh. 15:15: καὶ ἀνέβη (= ויעל); cf. the pl. form of OG Judg. 1:11: καὶ ἀνέβησαν (= [ויעל]ו*), O´ (via θ´ or α´) AII(ptv) AIII B-group OLat] καὶ ἐπορεύθησαν (= וילך), AI(Aabcx) AII(glnw) z(mg) Eth Syh.

Perhaps, in the proto-MT, the seeming contradiction of 'ascending' from Hebron to the lower altitude of Debir prompted a deliberate alteration from original ויעל. On the other hand, an original וילך better conforms to the overall ascent–descent arrangement of Judg. 1:4-8 and 1:9-17/18 (cf. especially 1:9, ואחר ירדו בני יהודה). Note also the parallel arrangement between Judg. 1:10aα וילך יהודה, 10b ויכו; and 1:17aα וילך יהודה 17aβ ויכ; and observe that both verses rename the conquered city (1:10aγ and 1:17bβ). Although 1:11-15 presents a longer account, the openings follow the same arrangement: 1:11aα וילך; 1:12aβ אשר־יכה; and the conquered city is renamed (1:11b). Cf. L. G. Stone, "From Tribal Confederation to Monarchic State: The Editorial Perspective of the Book of Judges" (PhD diss., Yale University, 1988), pp. 200-202.

[4] *Judg. 1:14aⁱ ‖ Josh. 15:18aⁱ.* The variants of Judg. 1:14a and its MT parallel in Josh. 15:18a align as follows:

Judg. 1:14a: וַתְּסִיתֵהוּ MT Tg / 3 f. sg (□ 3 m. sg suff.) LXX-AII(glw,ptv) Psht //

וַיְסִיתֶהָ* Vg LXX-AI,AII(gw,ptv),B-group

Josh. 15:18a: וַתְּסִיתֵהוּ MT Tg Vg LXX-*E*(Bhoqr),*P1*(Gbc),*P2*(x),*C*(ANΘyb₂),*M*(aikma₂),
M-cat(ej,sz,fv) / 3 f. sg (□ 3 m. sg suff.) Psht //
וַיְסִיתֶהָ* (Vg) LXX-*Sa*(gn),*Sb*(dpt) Sah OLat(vid)

Contra D. Barthélemy (*Critique textuelle de l'Ancien Testament*, vol. 1, *Josué, Juges, Ruth, Samuel, Rois, Chroniques, Esdras, Néhémie, Esther* [OBO 50/1, Fribourg, Switzerland, 1982], p. 36), who understands the Psht form *'trgrgt* in Judges as a passive that corresponds to the second alternative in both passages, the Ethpalpel of *rg* is intensive intransitive reflexive (cf. PS, p. 527b) and should, therefore, be taken as in line with the first. Although Lindars wrongly transcribed the Psht form in Judges as "*'tgrgrt* 'desire earnestly' (root *gr*)", his suggestion that it "must surely be a corruption of *'tgrgt* = 'be stirred up' (root *grg*), which is used in Joshua" remains viable, provided that it be translated not as passive but, again, as intensive intransitive reflexive, 'provoke/stir up oneself, incite/coax oneself' (*Judges 1-5* [1995], p. 84; cf. PS, p. 77b).

The MT, LXX-AII(l) and Psht of Judges attest the f. form of the verb so that Achsah is the subj. However, the nature of her action varies between coaxing her husband (MT), hesitancy (LXX-AII[l]) and self-motivation (Psht). Apart from MS l, the LXX-AII MSS have a doublet that preserves two distinct strata of the LXX tradition. Although the earliest stratum of these Lucianic MSS (attested singly in MS l) preserves a translation that misconstrued the root sense of Hi. סות ('to incite, allure, instigate'), it is probably this stratum that preserves the most ancient form of the Greek Judges, and it attests the f. form of the Hebrew verb (cf. Barthélemy, *Critique textuelle*, vol. 1 [1982], p. 36, and note that, in the OG of Judges, ὑπεστείλατο is immediately preceded by the inf. ἐκπορεύεσθαι plus the 3 f. sg acc. [of respect] αὐτὴν, making Achsah the subj.). The later LXX stratum (joined by OLat, Syh and Vg) more correctly construed the meaning of the Hebrew root but rendered Othniel the initiator of the action.

In Judges, all LXX families except the Lucianic have some form of the text: καὶ συνεβουλεύσατο αὐτῷ λέγουσα αἰτήσομαι τὸν πατέρα μου (with Achsah initiating). However, most Lucianic MSS of Joshua (i.e., g[n],dpt) support a text: καὶ συνεβούλευσεν αὐτῇ [= וַיְסִיתֶהָ] λέγων αἰτῆσαι τὸν πατέρα σου (with Othniel initiating). It would appear that the OG of Josh. 15:18a had: καὶ συνεβουλεύσατο αὐτῷ λέγουσα αἰτήσομαι τὸν πατέρα μου ἀγρόν. Thus, we are left with the impression that the later (Lucianic) level of Joshua (contra Lindars, who describes the Lucianic MSS of Joshua as "the older text/reading" [*Judges 1-5* (1995), pp. 29, 83]) agrees with the later LXX stratum of Judges as to Othniel initiating and, conversely, the oldest (Lucianic) stratum of Judges, though misconstruing the verb, agrees with the earliest stratum of Joshua as to Achsah being the subj. As Moore (*Judges* [1895], p. 29) argued:

> The difficulty occasioned by the gender of the verb is evaded by all the versions [except Targum] in different ways, but a comparison of their variations ... is not favourable to the supposition that they read וַיְסִיתֶהָ [*sic*], *he instigated her* ... ; nor is it explained how this easy and natural reading was supplanted in both Jos[hua] and Jud[ges] by the much more difficult ותסיתהו of [the consonantal Hebrew text].

Those who give priority to the witness of what is here called the later LXX stratum and its daughter versions include: Burney (*Judges* [2d edn, 1920], p. 13), JB, H. W. Hertzberg (*Die Bücher Josua, Richter, Ruth: übersetzt und erklärt* [ATD 9, Göttingen, 1953], p. 145), NEB, R. G. Boling (*Judges: Introduction, Translation and Commentary* [AB 6A, Garden City, N.Y., 1975], pp. 56-57), Soggin (*Judges* [2d edn, 1987], p. 22) and REB. Those who favour the witness of the MT as original include: RSV, JPSV[2], Y. Kaufmann (*The Book of Judges* [Jerusalem, 1961-1962], p. 80 [Hebrew]), W. F. Albright (*Yahweh and the Gods of Canaan* [Jordan Lectures, 1965; London, 1968], p. 42), NAB, NIV, Barthélemy (*Critique textuelle*, vol. 1 [1982], pp. 35-36), NRSV and Lindars (*Judges 1-5*

[1995], pp. 83-84). P. G. Mosca, while regarding the MT as original, rendered וַתְּסִיתֵהוּ לִשְׁאוֹל as "she beguiled him, asking ..." so that לִשְׁאוֹל introduces an adverbial, rather than a purpose, clause and the 3 m. sg suff. on וַתְּסִיתֵהוּ designates "her father" rather than Othniel as the obj. ("Who Seduced Whom? A Note on Joshua 15:18//Judges 1:14", *CBQ* 46 [1984], pp. 18-22). In this view, Othniel would play no role at all in the action of Josh. 15:18-20//Judg. 1:14-15. Mosca does not seem justified, however, in attributing the sense 'beguiled' to the root סות simply because that may have been the effect of the action performed here. It may be agreed that a general *sensus malus* is denotatively inherent in סות (Mosca, "Who Seduced Whom?" (1984), p. 22 n. 19; so Soggin, *Judges* [2d edn, 1987], p. 22), but evidence for its meaning 'beguile' is limited. Its usage in 2 Chron. 18:31 ("thus God allured them away from him") with the privative מִמֶּנּוּ may indeed involve mild deception (cf. Job 36:16 also with privative מִן; BDB, p. 694b 1.b). However, a sense 'entice, beguile' in contexts where סות is used should not necessarily be understood to derive from the meaning of the root. Any such sense for the term would have to be limited to instances where its usage in context demanded it (e.g., perhaps Isa. 36:18 = 2 Chron. 32:15) and not assigned where it could mean simply 'incite, stir up, instigate', a sense clearest when it precedes בְּ 'against' (e.g., 1 Sam. 26:19 [subj. יהוה]). The creative proposal of A. B. Ehrlich that וַתְּסִיתֵהוּ be emended to וַתְּסִירֵהוּ "[und] sie liess ihn bei Seite treten" and that the "Subjekt zu לִשְׁאל [sic] ist die junge Frau" nevertheless lacks the support of any text or version (*Randglossen zur hebräischen Bibel: Text-kritisches, sprachliches und sachliches* [7 vols., Leipzig, 1908-1914], vol. 3, *Josua, Richter, I und II Samuelis* [1910], repr. edn [Hildesheim, 1968], p. 46 [on Josh. 15:18]).

In any case, it seems preferable to follow the text of the MT, understanding that the variants arose from difficulty in understanding the basic sense of סות, 'to coax, entice' (cf. Job 36:18), and its relation to its 3 m. sg suff. The antecedent of the 3 m. sg suff. in this case would be Achsah's newly-wed husband.

⁵ *Judg. 1:14a*ⁱⁱ ‖ *Josh. 15:18a*ⁱⁱ. MT: הַשָּׂדֶה. Apart from the omission of the article ה from הַשָּׂדֶה, Josh. 15:18 is identical to Judg. 1:14a. In Judg. 1:14a, the article may indi-cate previous reference, i.e., the field(s) of Debir. Thus, just as Caleb was granted the field(s) and environs surrounding Hebron (Josh. 21:12), a city that he later captured, Achsah justly desires for Othniel a grant of the field(s) surrounding Debir, the city that he captured. The discrepancy about the article may have arisen either because of a dit-tography of the previous ה in Judg. 1:14a (so Soggin, *Judges* [2d edn, 1987], p. 22; Lindars, *Judges 1–5* [1995], p. 84) or from a haplography in Josh. 15:18a. It has also been suggested that later orthographic convention may account for the difference (Stone, "Tribal Confederation" [1988], p. 199). However, since only the hexaplaric MSS of LXX Judg. 1:14a (i.e., Abx Syh[vid]) insert the article, it is probably secondary in MT Judg. 1:14a. Cf. Hollenberg, "Zur Textkritik" (1881), pp. 101-2; and Moore, *Judges* (1895), p. 29.

⁶ *Judg. 1:15b* ‖ *Josh. 15:19b*. The LXX plus in this verse suggests that the MT tradi-tion may have suffered haplography:

– (כָּלֵב) MT Tg Psht Vg //

*(כָּלֵב) כְּלִבָּה LXX Syh(÷)

W. Rudolph suggested, on the basis of the LXX plus that follows Χαλὲβ: κατὰ τὴν καρδίαν αὐτῆς, that the *Vorlage* of the LXX had כָּלֵב כְּלִבָּה ("Textkritische Anmerkungen zum Richterbuch", in *Festschrift Otto Eissfeldt zum 60. Geburtstage, 1. September 1947, dargebracht von Freunden und Verehren* [J. Fück (ed.), Halle an der Saale, 1947], p. 199; so also *BHS*; Boling, *Judges* [1975], pp. 51, 57). Thus, the omission of the second word from the MT and other versions could be accounted for on the basis of a haplography within the MT tradition. Alternatively, the Hebrew may originally have had כְּלִבָּה alone, which was later revised to כָּלֵב under the influence of the three other uses of this name within this context (Judg. 1:11-15; so Rudolph, "Textkritische Anmerkungen" [1947], p. 199). Lindars suggested that the LXX plus arose "from a corrupt dittography of *klb* in the *Vorlage* of the OG" (Lindars, *Judges 1-5* [1995], p. 32). On the other hand, κατὰ τὴν καρδίαν αὐτῆς may simply preserve an OG mistranslation of original כָּלֵב that was later supplemented in the LXX tradition with the insertion of the proper noun. Some Hebrew MSS of the parallel text (Josh. 15:19b) omit כָּלֵב altogether (e.g., L), but very many preserve כָּלֵב alone. No MS or version of Josh. 15:19b preserves a variant that parallels κατὰ τὴν καρδίαν αὐτῆς of Judg. 1:15b, and, given the fact that it is witnessed only by the LXX of Judges, support for its originality in either Joshua or a common source of Joshua and Judges is weak. However, if the plus in the LXX of Judg. 1:15b reflected accurately its Hebrew *Vorlage*, one would need to ask whether it was newly added only in one textual stream or in original Judges, and one would need to seek rhetorical motivations.

As to the meaning of the variants, if the Hebrew text had originally shown: כָּלֵב כְּלִבָּה, it would have helped to emphasize the conformity of Caleb's will to Achsah's wishes more than does the present MT, which simply lists what Caleb gave her. Thus, the fuller text better characterizes Achsah's as the dominant will in this segment (Judg. 1:11-15). This would not be out of keeping with the segment as a whole, since throughout Achsah shifts from the status of mere chattel, subservient to her father's will (in both places where she is named), to the role of one whose will holds sway over both husband and father. Following the MT of Judg. 1:11-15, Achsah is named twice and referred to eleven times, Caleb named four times and referred to ten times, and Othniel named once and referred to three times. Hence, it is the evolution of the relationship between Caleb and Achsah as father and daughter that it seems most strongly featured here. Ironically, Achsah is characterized as having influence over Caleb precisely because she has submitted to Caleb's will. Nevertheless, the rhetoric of this characterization does not depend upon the inclusion of כְּלִבָּה. In sum, while neither the textual data nor the internal rhetoric is decisive, the majority of considerations seem to point toward the presence of כָּלֵב alone in Judg. 1:15b.

[7] *Judg. 1:16aα.* Before קֵינִי, the LXX-B-group (y[ex corr], Bdefsz,a₂,oq) supplies "Jethro" (Exod. 3:1) while the OG (so LXX-Aabcx,k glnw,pt MNb₂,hᵇ iru,m; also Arm Eth OLat Thdt) supplies "Hobab" (Num. 10:29; Judg. 4:11) to furnish a specific antecedent for חתן משה "the father-in-law of Moses". Lindars recommended that the latter be restored as "having been lost by haplography" (*Judges 1-5* [1995], p. 35). Some LXX MSS (e.g., v; also Eusebius, *Onomasticon*) supply both proper names. Probably neither name is original (hence the conjecture ויקין חתן משה עלה, approved by A. Kuenen, *Historisch-critisch Onderzoek naar het Onstaan en de Verzameling van de Boeken des Ouden Verbonds* [3 vols., Amsterdam, 2d edn, 1885-1892], vol. 1 [1885], p. 367; and K. Budde, *Die Bücher Richter und Samuel: Ihre Quellen und ihr Aufbau* [Giessen, 1890], p. 9, but see p. 86; cf. Moore, *Judges* [1895], p. 32). Moore's suggestion that, in view of the sg verb in 1:16b, "and Hobab the Kenite" was original rather than "and the sons of Hobab the Kenite", is made doubtful by the fact that no BH or LXX MS omits "sons" (*Judges* [1895], pp. 31-32; cf. Budde, *Richter und Samuel* [1890], p. 9 n., 86; Burney, *Judges* [2d edn, 1920], p. 14). It seems more probable that חתן משה had been inserted into 1:16 as a conflation with Judg. 4:11 (possibly when 1:16 was added to Judges) both to identify more precisely the Kenites in question and to furnish a literary anticipation of Judg. 4:11 and that its insertion then prompted a scribe/translator of the LXX tradition to insert the proper name "Hobab" (from Judg. 4:11; cf. Num. 10:29) to serve as an antecedent.

[8] *Judg. 1:16aβ.* The second occurrence of יְהוּדָה in the MT is not supported by the OG:

— (מִדְבַּר)* LXX-AI(Aabcx,k),AII(glnw,ptv) OLat Syh(א) Eth //
(מִדְבַּר) יְהוּדָה MT Tg Psht (Vg) LXX-AIII(MNyb₂,h),B-group Arm

The OG, and presumably its Hebrew *Vorlage*, did not preserve the second occurrence of 'Ιούδα, attested only in LXX-AI(Abc) Arm Eth and Syh(א) where it came into the LXX as a hexaplaric insertion. As for the MT, its reduplication of יְהוּדָה could be accounted for as an intentional scribal clarification (i.e., neither an accidental dittography nor "a corruption of the he-*locale* (if the text originally read *midbara*)" [Lindars, *Judges 1–5* (1995), p. 38]).

Moore, rejecting an identification of the wilderness of Judah with the Negeb of Arad, cited Josh. 15:61-62, where En-gedi is the southernmost city listed in the wilderness of Judah (*Judges* [1895], p. 32 n. †). On the basis of usage, it is doubtful whether the designation מִדְבַּר יְהוּדָה was even appropriate in reference to the Negeb where Arad was located (cf. Num. 21:1; 33:40) (contra Burney, *Judges* [2d edn, 1920], pp. 15-16). Admittedly, the construction מִדְבַּר יְהוּדָה, as such, appears only here and in Ps. 63:1, where it lacks geographical specificity. The construction מִדְבַּר יְהוּדָה would have referred to the rain-shadow east of the water-divide in Judah (cf. Josh. 15:61-62), in distinction from נֶגֶב יְהוּדָה (cf. Josh. 15:21-32). The designation נֶגֶב, later used to refer to populated subdivisions of the region south of Judah's hill-country and Shephelah (1 Sam. 27:10; 30:14; Judg. 1:16), referred more broadly to the vast hilly steppe region south of Hebron as far as Kadesh-barnea (cf. Gen. 20:1; Num. 13:29, of Amalekites; Josh. 15:19 = Judg. 1:15).

[9] *Judg. 1:16aγ.* MT: −. It is possible that OG ἐπὶ καταβάσεως reflects original במורד* (cf. the LXX of Josh. 10:11; 3 Kgdms 7:29; Mic. 1:4), which, because it had the same final letters as the following word עֲרָד, fell out by haplography from the tradition underlying the MT (an explanation endorsed by Budde [*Richter und Samuel* (1890), p. 10]; Albright [*Yahweh* (1968), pp. 35-36 n. 82], who related במורד ערד* here with במורד בית־חורון in Josh. 10:11 and במורד חורנים in Jer. 48:5; and S. Mittmann ["Ri. 1,16f. und das Siedlungsgebiet der Kenitischen Sippe Hobab", *ZDPV* 93 (1977), pp. 212-35], who located this habitat of the Kenites SE of Tell el-milḥ). However, a possibility remains that במורד* in the *Vorlage* of the LXX was a corruption from במדבר* (so Moore, *Judges* [1895], p. 34; followed by W. Nowack, *Richter, Ruth, und Bücher Samuelis* [HKAT I/4, Göttingen, 1902], and R. Kittel, *Das Buch der Richter*, in *HSAT*³ [Tübingen, 1909]). Cf. the summary of Burney, *Judges* (2d edn, 1920), pp. 16-17. Lindars offered a fresh argument in favour of the MT minus, namely, that OG καταβάσεως is

> an exceptional rendering of *negeb* here, correcting the OG νότος ['south']. ... Here [in the OG correction] however ἔρημος ['desert'] could not be used, as it had just been used for *midbar*, and so κατάβασις (used for *midbar* in Josh 8.24 ...) was chosen as an alternative (*Judges 1–5* [1995], p. 38).

[10] *Judg. 1:16bⁱ.* The LXX and Vg attest only one of the two verbs in MT Judg. 1:16b. Perhaps the original insertion of וַיֵּלֶךְ into MT Judg. 1:16b was occasioned by the appending of וַיֵּשֶׁב אֶת־עֲמָלֵק* "and Amalek dwelt with him" at the end of the verse. Thus, וַיֵּלֶךְ in MT Judg. 1:16b would be resumed in some sense by the first word in MT Judg. 1:17a so that the reduplication of וַיֵּלֶךְ in MT Judg. 1:16b and 1:17a that frames this clause might be but another instance of resumptive repetition marking a secondary insertion (cf. H. M. Wiener, *The Composition of Judges ii 11 to I Kings ii 46* [Leipzig, 1929]; S. Talmon, "The Presentation of Synchroneity and Simultaneity in Biblical Narrative", in *Studies in Hebrew Narrative Art through the Ages* [J. Heinemann and S. Werses (eds.),

ScrHier 27, Jerusalem, 1978], pp. 9-26; H. Van Dyke Parunak, "Oral Typesetting: Some Uses of Biblical Structure", *Bib* 62 [1981], pp. 153-68, especially pp. 160-62; J. Trebolle Barrera, "Redaction, Recension, and Midrash in the Books of Kings", *BIOSCS* 15 [1982], pp. 12-35; A. Berlin, *Poetics and Interpretation of Biblical Narrative* [BLS 9, Sheffield, 1983], pp. 126-28; B. O. Long, "Framing Repetitions in Biblical Historiography", in *Proceedings of the Ninth World Congress of Jewish Studies, Jerusalem, August 4-12, 1985: Division A, The Period of the Bible* [Jerusalem, 1986], pp. 69-76; M. Anbar, "La 'reprise'", *VT* 38 [1988], pp. 385-98; J. Trebolle Barrera, "The Story of David and Goliath (1 Sam 17-18): Textual Variants and Literary Composition", *BIOSCS* 23 [1990], pp. 16-30; Lindars, *Judges 1-5* [1995], p. 174). However, perhaps some later scribal offence at the idea of a Judahite subgroup cohabiting with Amalek may have posed the difficulty that occasioned the removal of -קל- after -עֲמָ- and the change in word division to the present form of the MT. It may be significant that Greek ἀμαληκ appears only among LXX-B-group members of the *Kaige* family that likewise attest the duplication of וַיֵּלֶךְ. See the following note.

[11] *Judg. 1:16b*[ii]. The variants disagree as to the ending of the verse:

אִתּוֹ עֲמָלֵק OLat / אֶת־הָעָם עֲמָלֵק LXX-B-group(defsz) Sah //
אֶת־הָעָם MT Tg Psht Vg LXX-AI,AII,AIII,B-group(B,irua₂,mq)

The MT suggests that the Kenites went up (pl.) and went (sg) and dwelt (sg) אֶת־הָעָם "with the people"—presumably, the people of Judah (so the *Mṣdt Dvd*; J. J. Slotki, "Judges: Introduction and Commentary", in H. Freedman and J. J. Slotki, *Joshua and Judges* [A. Cohen (ed.), SBB, London, 1950], p. 161). Lindars, who decided that the MT, "though manifestly unsatisfactory, should be accepted without emendation", nevertheless identified "the people" with the Canaanites (*Judges 1-5* [1995], p. 40, comparing Judg. 1:17 and Num. 21:1, 3). Moore recommended that the MT be emended to read אֶת עַמּוֹ "[with] *his people* [i.e., the main body of the Kenites]" (*Judges* [1895], pp. 32, 34; allowed also by K. Budde, *Das Buch der Richter* [K. Marti (ed.), KHAT 7, Freiburg, i. B., 1897], p. 9). Such an emendation may be excluded, however, on the ground that it erroneously presupposes that Hobab was a Kenite instead of their ancestor (cf. Judg. 1:16; 4:11; with Num. 10:29; contra B. G. Webb, *The Book of the Judges: An Integrated Reading* [JSOTS 46, Sheffield, 1987], pp. 89, 234 n. 38).

It is to be expected that lack of concord in number between the Hebrew verbs עָלוּ and וַיֵּלֶךְ וַיֵּשֶׁב may have given rise in some versions to restoring the numerical concord. Thus, BHS probably mistakenly proposed that the final Hebrew verbs be emended to pl. forms on the basis of pl. concord in certain LXX MSS (mistaken for OG). First, lack of numerical concord reflects common Hebrew narrative style (GKC, §145). Second, while it is true that the LXX-AI family, which evinces the same lack of concord as the MT, shows hexaplaric influence by translating both sg verbs (of which only the latter is attested in the OG witnesses: AII[glnow], B-group[B,q] OLat), it is because the sg form of the LXX-AI verbs concurs with the sg form in the OLat that it would be mistaken to conclude that this sg form was a hexaplaric trait. The OG probably had a sg verb (so W. G. Lambert, "[Review:] I. Soisalon-Soininen, *Die Textformen der Septuaginta-Übersetzung des Richterbuches*", *VT* 2 [1952], p. 188 n. 1). On the other hand, the lack of numerical concord may have given rise to the view that a subj. different from the Kenites was implied. The latter accords with the function of "Amaleq" in OLat *[et habitauit] cum eo Amalec* "[and] Amaleq [dwelt] with him [i.e., with the Kenite(s)]". However, the presence of ἀμαληκ in LXX-B-group(defsz) and Sah, which have pl. concord between their verbs, does not contradict the MT on the point that the Kenites are the subj.: "and they [i.e., the Kenites] dwelt with the people Amalek". Hollenberg regarded τοῦ λαοῦ "the people", which appears in all LXX MS families, as a secondary insertion modelled after MT הָעָם ("Zur

Textkritik" [1881], p. 102). He proposed the emendation: אֶת עֲמָלֵק (cf. Moore, *Judges* [1895], p. 34).

Apart from deliberate harmonization, it is difficult to see how הָעֲמָלֵקִי ,עֲמָלֵק (so Budde, *Richter und Samuel* [1890], pp. 9-10; idem, *Richter* [1897], p. 9; S. R. Driver, *Notes on the Hebrew Text and the Topography of the Books of Samuel, with an Introduction on Hebrew Palaeography and the Ancient Versions, and Facsimiles of Inscriptions and Maps* [Oxford, 1890], p. 93, [2d edn, 1913; repr. edn, Winona Lake, Ind., 1984], p. 122; Moore, *Judges* [1895], p. 34; BDB, p. 766a; Burney, *Judges* [2d edn, 1920], p. 17; Boling, *Judges* [1975], p. 58; Soggin, *Judges* [2d edn, 1987], p. 23) or הָעָם could have arisen secondarily. Webb, favouring הָעָם as original, argued against the variant [הָעֲמָ]לקִי by saying: "the loss of the 'missing' letters in the MT cannot be explained in terms of any familiar type of scribal error. It appears more likely to me that העמלקי was itself an early emendation made under the influence of 1 Sam. 15.6 and/or Num. 24.20-22" (*Judges* [1987], p. 234 n. 36; cf. p. 89). This simultaneous loss and addition of letters both preceding and following -עמ- is a two-step process that, if secondary, could hardly have occurred entirely accidentally.

On the other hand, Lambert's proposal of אִתּוֹ עֲמָלֵק* "with him Amaleq" in the *Vorlage* of OG, on the basis of OLat *[et habitauit] cum eo Amalec* "[and] Amaleq [dwelt] with him", might account for the availability of ה for a transfer to -הָעָם in the MT ("[Review:] Soisalon-Soininen, *Textformen*" [1952], p. 188; followed by Barthélemy, *Critique textuelle*, vol. 1 [1982], pp. 73-74). As for the final letters, there are two possibilities: either (1) original consonantal אתהעמוילך for אֶת־הָעָם וַיֵּלֶךְ was misconstrued as אִתּה עֲמוֹילֵךְ (by a scribe or translator who was careless of medial וי and unapprised of the fact that Amaleq properly ends with ק), which seems unlikely, or (2) the consonantal text אתהעמלקוילך for אִתּה עֲמָלֵק וַיֵּלֵךְ suffered the loss of -לק- and a change in word division. See the preceding note.

G. R. Driver ("Once Again Abbreviations", *Textus* 4 [1964], p. 81) suggested that העם in Judg. 1:16 may have been a scribal abbreviation for הָעֲמָלֵקִי. The proposal is possible, but, because he can offer no proof that this abbreviation was either "very well known or has occurred in the immediate context", it seems unlikely that abbreviation is the best explanation as to how הָעָם arose secondarily.

A resolution is difficult, for, if either הָעֲמָלֵקִי\עֲמָלֵק or הָעָם came about as a result of deliberate 'correction', it is possible to explain its secondary emergence. The former alternatives would constitute a harmonization specifying "the people" with whom the Kenites dwelt (cf. 1 Sam. 15:6-7; 27:8, 10; Num.13:29; 24:20-22), whereas the latter alternative would constitute a spurning of the mention of "Amaleq" in regional Judah, understandable if the scribe were strongly pro-Judahite and unaware of the corroborating evidence (i.e., 1 Sam. 15:6, etc.). Another such usage of הָעָם occurs in Judges' framework (18:20): וַיִּבֹא בְּקֶרֶב הָעָם "and he went along with the people [i.e., the Danite migrants]". Webb reasoned, in support of the originality of הָעָם, that the compiler may have intended 1:16 to show how the Kenites benefitted specifically from Judah's occupation of the Negeb as the fulfillment of Moses' compensatory promise to Hobab for accompanying and guiding Israel (Num. 10:32): "whatever good YHWH does for us, we will do for you" (*Judges* [1987], p. 89). Of course, this rhetorical strategy could as well provide a scribe with motivation for altering an original עֲמָלֵק אִתּה to אֶת־הָעָם. On the other hand, while עֲמָלֵק* is preserved in an early Greek translation, it may reflect a harmonization (with, e.g., 1 Sam. 15:6; 27:8, 10; Num. 24:20-21) motivated either by a desire to specify the referent of הָעָם or the need to emend a textual difficulty after -עמ-. Yet if, as seems most likely, the variant arose through a deliberate scribal emendation, then it is perhaps easier to explain the motivation for simplifying the rarer and potentially more offensive אִתּה

עֲמָלֵק to the more common and less offensive אֶת־הָעָם than the reverse. Thus, אִתּה עֲמָלֵק seems more probably the original form of the Hebrew text.

¹² *Judg. 1:18a.* In the first part of Judg. 1:18, the LXX negates Judah's capture of Gaza, Ashkelon, Ekron and their respective environs and reflects a different Hebrew verb in its *Vorlage*. With the MT agree the Tg, Psht and Vg. The LXX stands alone in negating Judah's capture of the Philistine cities of Gaza, Ashkelon and Ekron and in attesting הוֹרִישׁ*. It is possible that Moore was correct to surmise that the LXX translator was 'harmonizing' here (cf. Judg. 1:19; 3:3; Josh. 13:3), though the harmonization could also have arisen in the scribal tradition of the LXX *Vorlage* (*Judges* [1895], p. 38). Further inclination to harmonize vocabulary may have come from a desire to interpolate to Judah the pattern established by the combination of the next verse (1:19b) with most other tribes in the chapter (1:27aα, 29aα, 30aαβ, 31aαβ, 33aαβ). BHS, following J. D. Michaelis (*Deutsche Übersetzung des Alten Testaments mit Anmerkungen ...* [13 vols., Göttingen, 1773–1785]), H. Graetz (*Geschichte der Juden von den ältesten Zeiten bis auf die Gegenwart* [11 vols., Leipzig, 1860–1906]), *HSAT*⁴ and RL, proposed that the LXX of Judg. 1:18 was based upon וְלֹא הוֹרִישׁ. Others, who accept the LXX variant as original, explain MT וַיִּלְכֹּד as a transcriptional error for וְלֹא לָכַד (cf. Moore, *Judges* [1895], p. 38). However, it should be observed that לָכַד also recurs in the chapter (1:8a, 12a, 13a).

Another account is that of Josh. 15:45–47, where the Philistine cities of Ekron, Ashdod and Gaza are allotted to Judah, which seems at first to support the MT here. However, from comparing Josh. 13:3, which lists the Philistine cities among the large land areas yet to be conquered near the close of Joshua's life, one may discern that Josh. 15:45–47 may have been referring only to cities imputed to Judah. Judg. 3:3, which lists "the five rulers of the Philistines" among the unconquered nations left to test Israel, also agrees with the sense of the LXX here. Thus, all the corroborating passages seem to agree with the sense of the LXX. On the basis of this agreement, many scholars have taken the LXX to be original. Soggin said, "all contemporary commentators with the exception of J. Gray" have sided with the LXX here (*Judges* [2d edn, 1987], p. 23). Lindars also endorsed the LXX here, but his assertion that "Ekron was a Philistine foundation without previous Canaanite existence" was based upon a survey done before excavations of Tel Miqne (Khirbet el-Muqannaᶜ) (*Judges 1–5* [1995], p. 43, citing Y. Aharoni, *The Land of the Bible: A Historical Geography* [A. F. Rainey (trans. and ed.), Philadelphia, 2d edn, 1979], p. 270). Evidence since discovered in strata IX, VIIIB and VIIIA had already proven that there were pre-Philistine, Canaanite occupations at the site during the Late Bronze Age (cf. S. Gitin and T. Dothan, "The Rise and Fall of Ekron of the Philistines: Recent Excavations at an Urban Border Site", *BA* 50 [1987], pp. 198, 200–201, 202; T. Dothan and S. Gitin, "Ekron of the Philistines: How They Lived, Worked and Worshiped for Five Hundred Years", *BAR* 16/1 [1990], pp. 24–25).

However, Barthélemy has suggested that the Greek translator, conscious of the contradiction of his Hebrew text with the aforementioned passages, simply substituted καὶ οὐκ ἐκληρονόμησεν (a translation of וְלֹא־הוֹרִישׁ from Judg. 1:27, etc.) for וַיִּלְכֹּד (*Critique textuelle*, vol. 1 [1982], p. 74; cf. A. G. Auld, "Judges i and History: A Reconsideration", *VT* 25 [1975], p. 272, and Webb, *Judges* [1987], p. 234 n.43, who both regard the LXX as a harmonization). Barthélemy's solution seems all the more attractive in the light of the generally positive portrayal that the author/redactor of Judges' framework sections gives the tribe of Judah. In addition, he has rightly observed that, if the LXX variant were original, then 1:18 should follow 1:19 in the order of narration characteristic of Judg. 1:1–36. Therefore, the more difficult text of the MT (Tg, Vg, Psht) should be taken to explain the emergence of the LXX variant.

The problem remains to explain the apparent contradiction within the MT tradition. Why does the MT of Judg. 1:18a claim that Judah captured Gaza, Ashkelon and Ekron against the prior claim of Josh. 13:3 and the following claim of Judg. 3:3 that these Philistine cities were within unconquered territory? Apart from attributing incompetence to the compiler of Judges (a solution that one should posit only as a last resort), the simplest solution would be to recognize that the compiler so restructured the received materials that the chronological sequence of events no longer appears from a straightforward reading of the text. This is a common phenomenon in biblical literature (cf. the reversed sequence of Isa. 36–37 and 38–39 or Ezra 4:1–5:2 that, if ordered chronologically, would read: 4:1-5; 4:24-5:2; 4:6-23—cf., H. G. M. Williamson, *Ezra, Nehemiah* [WBC 16, Waco, Tex., 1985], pp. 56-60, 65-66). Note also the reversed chronological order of the two final episodes of Judges (17–18; 19–21), whose events appear to have occurred early in the period of the judges (18:30, contemporary with Jonathan, son of Gershom, son of Moses; 20:1, before the period of foreign domination; 20:28, contemporary with Phinehas, son of Eleazar, son of Aaron [cf. Josh. 22:13, 31-32; 1 Chron. 6:3-4]; and 20:18, 26-28, when the ark was at Bethel). Hence, the events of the final episodes of Judges are antecedent to those of several accounts that precede it in literary order. Thus, if Judg. 3:3 (as part of the subsection 2:6–3:6) were referring to a time historically antecedent to that of Judg. 1:18a (which is part of the subsection 1:1–2:5), then the apparent contradiction would be explained. But the immediate contradiction of Judg. 1:18 by 1:19 renders this proposal unlikely. In this instance, therefore, there seems to be better justification for positing a sequence of events in which Judah, having once captured Gaza, Ashkelon and Ekron from the Canaanites (Judg. 1:18a), subsequently lost these cities to those plain dwellers who used iron chariots (Judg. 1:19b).

Possibly the change in military situations implied by Judg. 1:18 and 1:19 reflects a technological change or the incursion of a new population. Cf. Judg. 1:19b אֶת־יֹשְׁבֵי הָעֵמֶק כִּי־רֶכֶב בַּרְזֶל לָהֶם with references to the Canaanites of the Beth-shan and Jezreel plains in Josh. 17:16 אֶת־הַכְּנַעֲנִי כִּי רֶכֶב and Josh. 17:18 וְרֶכֶב בַּרְזֶל בְּכָל־הַכְּנַעֲנִי הַיֹּשֵׁב בְּאֶרֶץ־הָעֵמֶק בַּרְזֶל לוֹ. Perhaps only after the second major incursion of the Sea Peoples (ca. 1190 BCE) did the territories of Gaza, Ashdod, Ashkelon, Gath and Ekron come to be regarded as those of חֲמֵשֶׁת סַרְנֵי פְלִשְׁתִּים—the situation reflected in Josh. 13:2-5 and Judg. 3:3. It is not known whether the Philistines *per se* or the Canaanites who antedated them regained Gaza, Ashkelon and Ekron from Judah. On the distinction between two Sea Peoples' incursions, in ca. 1230 and 1190 BCE, see E. H. Merrill, *Kingdom of Priests: A History of Old Testament Israel* (Grand Rapids, 1987), pp. 157-58.

The possession of these cities by the Philistines would have been the ostensible situation at the time of the compilation of the book of Judges (cf. Judg. 3:3; Josh. 13:2-5). At least such oscillation of territorial possession was thought to have occurred elsewhere in Judah during the period of the Judges. After the end of the conquest led by Joshua, during which Jerusalem was not conquered (cf. the absence of mention of Jerusalem from Josh. 10:28-42), Judah, in collaboration with Simeon, conquered Jerusalem from the Canaanites (Judg. 1:8). It was after this that Judah lost Jerusalem to the Jebusites, whom they were subsequently unable to dislodge—a situation ostensibly still prevailing at the time of the addition of Josh. 15:63 to the book of Joshua. However, since the environs of Jebus/Jerusalem were encompassed properly within the perimeter of Benjaminite territory (Josh. 15:8; 18:16, 28), the blame for the failure to dislodge the Jebusites from Jerusalem was properly laid against Benjamin—a propriety reflected only in the book of Judges (Judg. 1:21; cf. 19:10-11). Thus, from the pro-Judahite vantage point of the book of Judges, Judah is credited with having conquered Jerusalem (1:8) but not much discredited for having lost control of it, since it was a city properly within Benjamin's realm of responsibility (1:21).

[13] *Judg. 1:18b*. LXX: καὶ τὴν Ἄζωτον καὶ τὰ περισπόρια αὐτῆς, Aabc tv MNyb₂ Arm Syh [τὸ ὅριον, h | αὐτῶν, p]] Zotum OLat : καὶ τὴν Ἄζωτον καὶ τὰ ὅρια αὐτῆς,

gnow : οὐδὲ τὴν Ἄζωτον οὐδὲ τὰ περισπόρια αὐτῆς, k Bdez,irua₂,q [τὰ ὅρια, fs*] : □ x 1 m. It is doubtful that the OG would have had the form of city-name τὴν Ἄζωτον, since the OG for אַשְׁדּוֹד would be Ἀσεδωδ or the like (cf. OG Josh. 15:46-47), not the Hellenized Ἄζωτον (OLat: Zotum). Further, it is doubtful that this plus reflects the original Hebrew (contra Boling, Judges [1975], pp. 51, 58, who said it dropped out by haplography), for the plus probably entered OG Judg. 1:18 by a conflation of the mention of Ashdod in Josh. 15:46-47 as a city allotted to Judah with the phraseology, καὶ τὰ περισπόρια αὐτῆς (= BH וְאֶת־מִגְרָשֶׁ[י]הָ), of OG Josh. 21:4-39 (= 1 Chron. 6:40-66) passim. Although it is doubtful that the motivation for the LXX plus was "to make up the number of the Philistine cities" (so Lindars, Judges 1-5 [1995], p. 85), for then one might have expected in the plus a mention of Gath as well, the absence of mention of Gath from Jer. 25:20, Zeph. 2:4 and Zech. 9:5-7 suggests that the Philistine pentapolis may have become a tetrapolis by the end of the seventh century BCE (cf. Dothan–Gitin, "Ekron of the Philistines" [1990], p. 24b).

¹⁴ Judg. 1:19bα. MT: לֹא לְהוֹרִישׁ. LXX: οὐκ ἐδύνατο, Aacx glw,ptv OLat Syh Thdt] οὐκ ἠδυνάσθησαν, AIII(except N) B-group(B,irua₂) : οὐκ ἠδυνήθησαν, B-group(defsz,q). Tg took כי as causal and interpolated: בתר כן דחבו לא יכילו לתרכא "Because they sinned they were not able to drive out …" (trans. D. J. Harrington and A. J. Saldarini, Targum Jonathan of the Former Prophets: Introduction, Translation and Notes, in The Aramaic Bible, vol. 10 [M. McNamara (ed.), Edinburgh, 1987], p. 60)—Judah's sin explaining their inability to expel the inhabitants of the plain. M. Dahood ("Scriptio defectiva in Judges 1,19", Bib 60 [1979], p. 570) restores לָאָה "he was weak, unable" (cf. Gen. 19:11; Exod. 7:18; Akk. la'û, Ug. l'y, "to be weak"). On the basis of one Hebrew MS, a marginal reading, the OG (and OLat), Tg and Vg, BHS, Boling (Judges [1975], p. 58), perhaps Webb (Judges [1987], pp. 89, 234-35 n. 44) and clearly Lindars (Judges 1-5 [1995], p. 45) restore לֹא־יָכוֹל, assuming that haplography gave rise to the 'ungrammatical' MT (cf. Josh. 15:63; 17:12a; M. Fishbane, Biblical Interpretation in Ancient Israel [Oxford, 1985], p. 203 and n. 88). Boling's discussion probably reflects what actually occurred, though this emendation should not necessarily be followed. Inasmuch as there seems to have been a deliberate effort on the part of the compiler or an editor (or scribe) of Judg. 1 to remove יכל from his/her Vorlage (cf. Judg. 1:21, 27a with Josh. 15:63; 17:12a, respectively [cf. Moore, Judges (1895), pp. 38, 39; Burney, Judges (2d edn, 1920), pp. 2, 19, 21; Webb, Judges (1987), pp. 91, 235-36 n. 50]), this repeated phenomenon was probably motivated by rhetorical concerns (pace Lindars, Judges 1-5 [1995], p. 45, cf. p. 50). Therefore, perhaps one could correct the edited form by removing ל from לְהוֹרִישׁ, since it may be an unnecessary vestige of original לֹא יָכוֹל לְהוֹרִישׁ (from which the compiler or an editor removed only יָכוֹל). Soggin, however, reasoned that ל in לְהוֹרִישׁ arose as a dittography from the preceding לֹא (Judges [2d edn, 1987], p. 24). It is possible, however, that לֹא of the MT construction לֹא לְהוֹרִישׁ was intended to have the force of an independent clause (= אֵין + inf. cstr): "for it was not possible to dispossess" (cf. Amos 6:10; 1 Chron. 5:1; 15:2; in Aram. Dan. 6:9; C. F. Keil and Franz Delitzsch, Biblischer Commentar über das Alten Testament, vol. II/1, Josua, Richter und Ruth, by C. F. Keil [Leipzig, 1863], ET: Biblical Commentary on the Old Testament, vol. 4, Joshua, Judges, Ruth [J. Martin (trans.), Edinburgh, 1868]; repr. edn, Commentary on the Old Testament, 10 vols., vol. 2, Joshua, Judges, Ruth, I & II Samuel [Grand Rapids, 1976], p. 257; S. R. Driver, A Treatise on the Use of the Tenses in Hebrew and Some Other Syntactical Questions [Oxford, 3d edn, 1892], §202, 2; GKC, §114l; Stone, "Tribal Confederation" [1988], pp. 218-19), so that Judah is portrayed as being obedient to the point of making conquest even of cities in the valley, though the impossibility of retaining them is stated impersonally.

¹⁵ *Judg. 1:19bβ*. MT: רֶכֶב בַּרְזֶל לָהֶם. OG: 'Ρῆχαβ διεστείλατο αὐτήν ("Rechab [a PN?] divided/separated it [the plain] for himself [aor. mid.]"), Abcx w OLat Syh] 'Ρῆχαβ διεστείλατο αὐτοῖς ("Rechab gave command to/concerning them"), a l,v* B : 'Ρῆχαβ διεστείλατο αὐτοῖς καὶ ἅρματα σίδηρα αὐτοῖς ("Rechab gave command to/concerning them and they [had] iron chariots"), k gn MNy,h efsz,irua₂,mq [αὐτοῖς¹] αὐτούς, d Arm | ἅρματα] pr τὰ, 18.209 | αὐτοῖς²] pr ἦν, o,ptvᵃ b₂ Sah]. OG, perhaps by corruption, read: <>רכב <ה<בדיל לה and translated הבדיל = διαστέλλω 'to separate, divide, command expressly' (LSJ 412b-13a; cf. Moore, *Judges* [1895], p. 39; Lindars, *Judges 1-5* [1995], p. 85).

¹⁶ *Judg. 1:20bβ*. LXX-AII, AIII, and part of B-group preserve a variant doublet in 1:20b, of which the first translates ערי*: καὶ ἐκληρονόμησεν ἐκεῖθεν τὰς τρεῖς πολεῖς τῶν υἱῶν 'Ενάκ καὶ ἐξῆρεν ἐκεῖθεν τοὺς τρεῖς υἱοὺς 'Ενάκ, gw,dptv b₂,h esz,iᵃ⁷ru,m [ἐκληρονόμησαν, 1 | □ ἐκεῖθεν¹ a₂,m | □ τὰς, MNy | pr τὰς, Arm(ℵ mend pro ÷) ἅ pr καὶ², Syh(÷) ἅ ἐξῆραν, 128 Syh ἅ □ τρεῖς², n]. The remaining MSS of LXX-B-group preserve only the former variant: καὶ ἐκληρονόμησεν ἐκεῖθεν τὰς τρεῖς πολεῖς τῶν υἱῶν 'Ενάκ, Bf,i*,o [ἐκληρονόμησαν, q].

A substream of LXX-AI MSS preserves a version of the variant doublet from which τῶν υἱῶν 'Ενάκ is absent: καὶ ἐκληρονόμησεν ἐκεῖθεν τὰς τρεῖς πολεῖς καὶ ἐξῆρεν ἐκεῖθεν τοὺς τρὶς υἱοὺς 'Ενάκ, A Eth [□ ἐκεῖθεν¹, OLat | □ τὰς, c | ἐκεῖθεν²] ἐκεῖ, b | τρὶς] τρεῖς, bc | *Enoc*, OLat]. MSS x,k of AI preserve only that variant of the doublet that accords with the MT: καὶ ἐξῆρεν ἐκεῖθεν τοὺς τρεῖς υἱοὺς 'Ενάκ.

Either MS B and its congeners attest a haplography of ערי*את־שְׁלֹשׁ עָרֵי בְנֵי הָעֲנָק from or the situation that resulted in both τὰς τρεῖς πολεῖς and τοὺς τρεῖς υἱοὺς in AI attests a corruption at the place where the MT now has את־שְׁלֹשָׁה בְנֵי. In either case, there is no warrant for accepting the variant translation of ויורש as original—nor, indeed, for positing an additional verb וַיְגָרֶשׁ (contra Boling, *Judges* [1975], pp. 51, 59), since both κληρονομεῖν and ἐξαίρειν are alternative renderings of ירש in the LXX in general and in Judges (even Judg. 1) in particular (Z. Talshir, "Double Translations in the Septuagint", in *VI Congress of the International Organization for Septuagint and Cognate Studies, Jerusalem 1986* [C. E. Cox (ed.), Atlanta, Ga., 1987], pp. 51-52; cf. also Lindars, *Judges 1-5* [1995], pp. 46-47).

¹⁷ *Judg. 1:21aα*. MT: יָשַׁב] יוֹשְׁבֵי Josh. 15:63a. Several Hebrew MSS evidence that it is possible that final י fell out of L Judg. 1:21a either by haplography or by an attempt to restore numerical concord (cf. 1:27aβ). No prep. ־בְ should be prefixed to the following word, ירושלם (*pace* Lindars, *Judges 1-5* [1995], p. 85). Lindars misquotes Josh. 15:63 as having יושבי בירושלם, whereas it has only יושבי ירושלם.

¹⁸ *Judg. 1:22a*. MT: בֵּית־יוֹסֵף. OG: οἱ υἱοὶ 'Ιωσήφ (= בני יוסף*). Since בני יוסף is by far the more common phrase in the 'Octateuch' and since, after the pl. verb, correction of the *constructio ad sensum* to numerical concord would be natural in a translation, the LXX variant is insignificant (so Moore, *Judges* [1895], p. 41; cf. Burney, *Judges* [2d edn, 1920], p. 21; Lindars, *Judges 1-5* [1995], p. 52).

¹⁹ *Judg. 1:22b*. MT: (עָמָּם) וַיהוָה. OG: καὶ 'Ιούδας μετ' αὐτῶν, AI(Abcx),AII(glnw,tv) OLat Eusebius] καὶ Κύριος ἦν μετ' αὐτῶν, AIII,B-group. The variant in the LXX probably arose as a result of corruption in (or a tacit emendation of) its *Vorlage* from ויהוה to ויהודה (so Moore, *Judges* [1895], pp. 41-42; Webb, *Judges* [1987], p. 236 n. 54; contra Boling, *Judges* [1975], p. 59, who regarded ויהודה as original and inferred that ויהוה was the result of conflation with 1:19). Budde conjectured an original ויהושע (*Richter und Samuel* [1890], pp. 58-59; idem, *Richter* [1897], p. 11; endorsed by Burney, *Judges* [2d edn, 1920], p. 22). Lindars wrongly cites Budde and Burney as supporting an original ויהודה (*Judges 1-5* [1995], p. 53).

²⁰ *Judg. 1:23aⁱ.* MT: וַיְתִירוּ. OG: καὶ παρενέβαλον, Aabcx,k glnw,ptv MNyb₂,h(παρενέβαλεν) z(mg) Arm] *et coeperunt expugnare,* OLat : *apprehenderunt,* Sah : + καὶ κατεσκέψαντο, B,ir,mo [pr οἶκος ιῆλ, q] : καὶ κατεσκάψαντο, e : καὶ κατεσκάψαν, dsz(txt) : καὶ κατεκόψαν, f : καὶ κατεκόψαντο, u. Vg: *cum obsiderent.* The OG (= וַיַּחֲנוּ* [so F. Giesebrecht, according to BDB, p. 1064b]; cf. Exod. 15:27, where LXX: παρενέβαλον δὲ = MT: וַיַּחֲנוּ, and Judg. 9:50b LXX-B-group, though the OG had καὶ περιεκάθισεν) and Vg probably reflect attempts to make sense of the rare verb—the former leading Josephus to surmise a long siege of Bethel (*Ant.* V.ii.6 §§130-31) (cf. Moore, *Judges* [1895], p. 42). Ehrlich conjectured וַיֵּחָרוּ "they tarried" (*Randglossen,* vol. 3 [1910], repr. edn, p. 69; cf. Gen. 32:5 and 2 Sam. 20:5 [Kethib: וייחר; Qere: וָיֵּחָר]; BDB, pp. 29a, 405a). Lindars described a Jewish tradition that read וַיִּוָּתְרוּ* < יתר 'to remain, be left over' (hence περιεσεύθησαν [< περισσεύω 'be left over'] in the LXX MS z[mg] [ascribed to α´ by F. Field (ed.), *Origenis Hexaplorum quae supersunt; sive Veterum Interpretum Graecorum in totum Vetus Testamentum Fragmenta* (2 vols., Oxford, 1875), vol. 1, p. 402 n. 45] and in the Psht: *wpšw* [< *pwš* 'to remain, stay']) (*Judges 1-5* [1995], p. 53).

²¹ *Judg. 1:23aⁱⁱ.* MT: בֵּית־יוֹסֵף. LXX: οἱ υἱοὶ ιῆλ, lw,ptv b₂ : *filii Istrahel,* OLat : οἶκος ιῆλ, A(ιῆλ)abc(pr ὁ)x,k MNy z(mg) Arm : οἱ υἱοὶ Ἰωσηφ, gn : □ B-group (except q). Moore considered the expression of the subj. superfluous and, hence, perhaps not original in Hebrew (*Judges* [1895], p. 42). However, there seems little ground here for emending the MT (so also Lindars, *Judges 1-5* [1995], p. 53). Cf. Judg. 1:22a.

²² *Judg. 1:24bα.* MT: –. OG: καὶ ἔλαβον αὐτόν. Budde suggested that וַיֹּאחֲזוּ בּו* or וַיֹּאחֲזוּהוּ* may have fallen out of the MT before the similar form וַיֹּאמְרוּ (*Richter* [1897], p. 11; so Burney, *Judges* [2d edn, 1920], p. 22). Cf. Judg. 16:21, MT: וַיֹּאחֲזוּהוּ, OG: καὶ ἐπελάβοντο αὐτοῦ; and Judg. 1:6b, MT: וַיֹּאחֲזוּ אֹתוֹ, OG: καὶ ἔλαβον αὐτόν (Abⁱx, glno*[vid]w OLat[*ceperunt*]). Lindars did not endorse the OG plus (*Judges 1-5* [1995], p. 54).

²³ *Judg. 1:26bα.* MT: – וַיִּבֶן. OG: καὶ ᾠκοδόμησεν ἐκεῖ (= שָׁם וַיִּבֶן*). Boling explained the LXX plus as a contamination from שְׁמָה "its name" three words later (*Judges* [1975], p. 60). Lindars likewise called it "a misplaced dittograph" (*Judges 1-5* [1995], p. 86).

²⁴ *Judg. 1:27aγ.* MT: Kethib: יֹשֵׁב; Qere: יֹשְׁבֵי (also MT Josh. 17:11a). Cf. the note on Judg. 1:21a יֹשֵׁב. Lindars, too, supported the Qere (*Judges 1-5* [1995], p. 86).

²⁵ *Judg. 1:36aα.* The primary textual difficulty in this verse is the witness of the LXX-AI and LXX-AII families to the presence of a second gentilic noun not attested in the MT:

– (הָאֱמֹרִי) MT Tg Psht Vg LXX-AIII,B-group //

(הָאֱמֹרִי) הָאֱדֹמִי* LXX-AI,AII Arm Eth(vid) Syh(sub ÷)

Apart from the LXX-AI,AII and its daughter versions, here listed in support of the addition, most versions agree with the MT. Barthélemy agreed with Hollenberg that the OG probably read הָאֱדֹמִי הָאֱמֹרִי and argued, from comparison with Num. 34:4 and Josh. 15:3, that the gentilic "Edomite" is welcome here since it was, in fact, the border of Edom that was being described (Hollenberg, "Zur Textkritik" [1881], p. 104; Barthélemy, *Critique textuelle,* vol. 1 [1982], p. 75). Thus, Barthélemy translated: "et la frontière des Amorites était constituée par les Edomites depuis ...", as had Hollenberg: "und die Grenze der Amoriter bilden die Edomiter vom Aufstieg der Skorpione, von Petra an und weiter nach Süden".

Of course, it could likewise be argued that the LXX-AI,AII families simply preserve a corrupt Hebrew dittograph that appeared in the *Vorlage* of the OG (so Lindars, *Judges 1-5* [1995], p. 88). If not purely accidental, the dittograph may preserve a marginal correction made by a scribe who thought, on the basis of the similarity of the border markers to those of Num. 34:4 and Josh. 15:3, that הָאֱמֹרִי should be restored to an original הָאֲדֹמִי, especially if that scribe thought that the simultaneous confusion of ד and ר with transposition of דמ > מר could have given rise to הָאֱמֹרִי under the force of its prior mention in this context (1:34, 35). This 'correction' to הָאֲדֹמִי may then have come to be preserved with הָאֱמֹרִי in copies of this Hebrew MS. The emendation would have been spurious, of course, but the possibility of the scenario just described lessens the need to see הָאֲדֹמִי as having dropped out of the original Hebrew text by haplography. Indeed, evidence of harmonization in the OG, seen already in 1:18a, should dissuade us from following the OG simply because it represents the most ancient witness to the Hebrew text (cf. Barthélemy, *Critique textuelle*, vol. 1 [1982], p. 75: "Comme l'a proposé Hollenberg, il faut donc suivre ici le *G. C'est la forme textuelle la plus ancienne à laquelle la critique textuelle nous permette de remonter.").

On the interpretative level, if הָאֲדֹמִי alone had originally stood here, as most now conclude, one would need to explain what connection Edom's frontier with Judah was thought to have either to the preceding summary of Dan's confinement by the Amorites (1:34-35) or to the following description of Israelite weeping and sacrifice at Bochim (2:1-5). Those who think that הָאֲדֹמִי was original include: Moore, *Judges* (1895), pp. 54-56; Burney, *Judges* (2d edn, 1920), p. 33; NEB; J. D. Martin, *The Book of Judges* (CBC, Cambridge, 1975), p. 75; J. Gray, *Joshua, Judges, Ruth* (NCBC, Basingstoke, 2d edn, 1986), p. 242; Soggin, *Judges* (2d edn, 1987), p. 25; REB; and tacitly Stone, "Tribal Confederation" (1988), p. 239 and n. 48. That the geographical movement resulting from the description of the tribes in 1:1-33 has a definite northward progression would seem to imply that the mention of Dan in 1:34-35 was made from the vantage point of a writer who was already aware of Dan's migration to the northernmost region of Israel. Viewed in this way, the description of Dan's confinement by the Amorites in 1:34-35 would constitute the historical background and rationale for Dan's migration described in 18:1-31, and it would be only in connection with Dan that the writer took interest in the Amorites at all. If this northward trend was a controlling principle in the arrangement of 1:1-35, then an isolated note on an Edomite border, at the southern extremity of Judah, would disrupt this northward trajectory. This view is supported by Z. Kallai, who also argued, by reference to the fixed south-to-north pattern in pre-exilic arrangements of tribal allotments, that a reading "the Edomite" in Judg. 1:36 misses the main point of the formula, which uses Sela as a representative designation for Edom ("The Southern Border of the Land of Israel—Pattern and Application", *VT* 37 [1987], p. 442, cf. n. 12). Of course, it could be argued that a northward trend in the tribal descriptions (1:1-33), once completed by the description of the early territorial troubles of the now northernmost tribe (1:34-35), was simply rounded off with a return to the southernmost extremity of Israel (1:36). Yet an isolated description of Edom's frontier would not fit into the otherwise consistent concern of 1:1-35 with territorial encroachments on the tribes of Israel. The border described in 1:36 properly constituted the southern boundary of Judah's allotment and, thus, could not be seen as an encroachment on the territory of Judah (cf. Num. 34:4; Josh. 15:3). If seen as describing the proper (Edomite) southern boundary of both Judah and Israel, 1:36 would not fit the concern of 1:1-35 with territorial encroachments upon Israel. Yet again, it could be argued that this was the very aim of the writer, since Judah would thus appear in a more favourable light.

On the other hand, an original הָאֱמֹרִי in 1:36 would suggest either that the Amorites had overtaken the region of the Edomites to the south of Judah's southernmost border or that the Amorites had continued to hold part of Judah's Negeb. The former view suffers from the fact that it, too, fails to share the otherwise consistent concern of 1:1-35 with foreign encroachment upon Israelite lands. Yet it could reasonably be argued that this detail was included as incidental to the connection of the Amorites with the Danites, especially if the compiler had been concerned to explain how the Amorites, who had forced the Danites to migrate, were themselves later forced southward into Edom by the power of the Joseph tribes (cf. 1:35b). The portrayal of the Ephraimite (Joseph) tribes as a powerful military entity is a motif that recurs throughout the episodes of Judg. 3:7–16:31 and the double dénouement of 17–21. This option might also be consistent with the generally negative characterization of Dan in the book of Judges, a tribe too weak to inherit its own territory (leaving that for the Ephraim tribes to finish) yet capable of bullying the Ephraimite Micah and a defenceless village (18:1–29). However, 1:36 need not bear a consequential relationship to 1:35b. It may simply refer to the situation of early Amorite enclaves described by 1:34–35a. Mention in 1:34–35a of Amorite enclaves in the Danite Valley of Aijalon would not be inconsistent with the alleged situation of the early phase of the period of the judges, after Joshua's expulsion of the Amorites from the hill country (Josh. 10:5, 12; cf. 11:3) but before the second incursion of the Sea Peoples ca. 1190 BCE. However, the overall concern of 1:1–33 with 'Canaanites' may accurately reflect the concerns of Israel after the death of Joshua (cf. J. Bright, *A History of Israel* [Philadelphia, 3d edn, 1981], pp. 115-16; Merrill, *Kingdom* [1987], pp. 144-45, nn. 4, 8).

The latter view, that 1:36 explains how the Amorites continued to hold much of Judah's Negeb and Shephelah adjacent to Dan, better fits the context's main concern with Dan. Keil (*Richter* [1863], ET: *Judges* [1868], repr. edn, vol. 2, pp. 261-63) understood 1:36 to refer to the Amorite's southern border extent at the time of the conquest of Canaan by Israel, thus explaining their continued presence in the Aijalon Valley (cf. reference to the inhabitants of this region as Canaanites [Num. 14:45; 21:3] but more specifically as Amorites [Deut. 1:44]). He also argued that מֵהַסֶּלַע refers not to the city Petra east of the Arabah (cf. 2 Kgs 14:7; Isa. 16:1) but to the rock located in the desert of Zin southwest of the Ascent of the Scorpions (Num. 20:8, 10; cf. Num. 34:4; Josh. 15:2-3; so also J. Gray, "Israel in the Song of Deborah", in *Ascribe to the Lord: Biblical and Other Studies in Memory of Peter C. Craigie* [L. Eslinger and G. Taylor (eds.), JSOTS 67, Sheffield, 1988], p. 424 n. 6). Thus, Judg. 1:36 describes the easternmost and westernmost points along the Amorite's southern border and better fits the focus of Judg. 1:36 upon the proximity of this foreign enclave to the region of Dan. Cf. A. E. Cundall (*Judges*, in A. E. Cundall and L. Morris, *Judges and Ruth: An Introduction and Commentary* [TOTC 7, London, 1968], pp. 62-63), who speculated that the detail of 1:36 may have been included, albeit incidentally, because it was part of a fuller border description from which the writer was quoting. The interest in the Amorites that began with concern for the Danites (1:34–35a) may then be seen in 1:36 to note the extent of the Amorite enclave into the Negeb of Judah (though, significantly, Judah is not mentioned). This detail may bear only incidentally upon the previous verses' concern with Amorite restrictions upon Danite expansion, but it would, at least, conform to the controlling interest of 1:1–35 in foreign settlement within Israelite tribal territories. It is doubtful that 1:36 should be understood to take interest primarily in Judah, however, for this would disrupt the northward flow of descriptions of territorial difficulties experienced by the tribes. It would also disrupt the pattern of single groupings of tribal descriptions by returning to an interest in the territory of Judah, remote from Judah's main description in 1:1–20. In either view, an original הָאֱמֹרִי would avert the disruption of the otherwise consistent northward movement of tribal descriptions in 1:1–35 that would be introduced by inserting here a detail of purely Edomite interest. Those who prefer הָאֱמֹרִי as original include: AV; RV; RSV; É. Dhorme, *La Bible: L'Ancien Testament, I* (Bibliotheque de la Pléiade 120, Paris, 1956), pp. 719-20; NIV; Webb, *Judges* (1987), pp. 238-39 n. 77; and NRSV.

An original with both nations' names (הָאֱמֹרִי הָאֲדֹמִי), as in the LXX-AI,AII MSS, would be limited to describing the Amorites as inhabiting the Negeb of Judah to the north of Edom's northern border. As such, it has the same strengths and limitations as הָאֱמֹרִי alone understood to refer to the Amorite occupation of Judah's Negeb.

On the strength of both rhetorical concerns and the geographical structure in 1:1-35, it would appear that an original הָאֱמֹרִי (alone) would have been most consistent with the context. Judg. 1:36 is a parenthetical note that describes the southern extent of the early Amorite enclave whose northern extent had reached the allotment of Dan (1:34-35a). It was probably coincidence with the description of Judah's border with Edom that invited the insertion of הָאֲדֹמִי (in harmony with Num. 34:3-4 or Josh. 15:1, 3).

[26] *Judg. 2:1a.* The main difficulty here consists of the variants listed in the LXX MS families. The variants align thus:

אֶל־הַבֹּכִים MT Tg Psht Vg // –

LXX *אֶל־הַבֹּכִים *[וַ]אֶל בֵּית אֵל *[וַ]אֶל בֵּית יִשְׂרָאֵל

It seems that the LXX tradition does little more than list several variants, each introduced with an editorial καί. Both the Syh and Arm (33 40 112 121) mark their translations of καὶ ἐπὶ βαιθὴλ καὶ ἐπὶ τὸν οἶκον Ἰσραήλ with an obelus (÷) while LXX MS x omits these words entirely. C. E. Cox proposes that the asterisk in the Arm is an error for the obelus (*Hexaplaric Materials Preserved in the Armenian Version* [SBLSCS 21, Atlanta, Ga., 1986], p. 110). Moore's suggestion that καὶ ἐπὶ τὸν οἶκον Ἰσραήλ constitutes a doublet for καὶ ἐπὶ βεθηλ seems tenable, especially in the light of the former's absence from the OLat (*Judges* [1895], p. 60). The presence of this kind of doublet constitutes considerable evidence that these LXX variants were based upon a Hebrew *Vorlage* that included בית (so A. V. Billen, "The Old Latin Version of Judges", *JTS* 43 [1942], p. 147). There may have been two different translations (βεθ-, τὸν οἶκον) for one use of בית or one translation each for two separate uses of בית. Again, the discrepancy between βεθηλ and Ἰσραηλ may have arisen as an inner-Greek corruption, since they share the same ending. However, supposing that the OG had had καὶ ἐπὶ τὸν οἶκον ιηλ (so LXX-AII[ptv]), it is not difficult to see how ιηλ could have been (mis-)construed as either a transliteration of Hebrew אֵל or the abbreviation for יִשְׂרָאֵל. This might account for the rise of καὶ ἐπὶ βεθηλ alongside καὶ ἐπὶ τὸν οἶκον Ἰσραηλ and may even explain how this doublet came to be reinserted into the tradition underlying MSS ptv in front of its own ancestor ἀπὸ Γαλγαλων καὶ ἐπὶ τὸν οἶκον ιηλ. Alternatively, the OG may originally have had *ἀπὸ Γαλγαλων καὶ ἐπὶ βεθηλ from which βεθηλ was misconstrued as βεθ ἠλ and hence οἶκον ιηλ. This is not in itself proof that the LXX *Vorlage* represented the original Hebrew wording, but it may offer a clue as to the discrepancy between the MT and LXX traditions if the Hebrew had originally read בית אל with, or instead of, אל־הבכים. Billen ("Old Latin" [1942], p. 147) argued that, although no MS omits the equivalent of OLat *Klauthmon*, OLat (Lugd) indirectly witnesses that the word came into the Latin version at a different time from the rest of the story, since in 2:1 the Greek word is transliterated whereas in 2:5 it is translated *ploratio*. In any case, both the MT and LXX attest here original consonantal אל, the former as a preposition ('to'), the latter either as a separate noun ('god') or as an afformative in the name 'Israel'.

Unless removal was deliberate, it is not easy to discern why *בֵּית אֵל or *בֵּית יִשְׂרָאֵל, supported by the LXX, should have fallen completely from the Hebrew tradition if either had been original. In support of this, the preservation of a space after אֶל־הַבֹּכִים in the Masoretic tradition may suggest that a scribal convention was here at work. On the divergence of opinion as to the purpose of the space inserted in the middle of the verse, see Moore, *Judges* (1895), pp. 60-61. If we suppose that the LXX witnesses the original phrase among its list of variants, which included in even the best MSS and versions (gn, cf. OLat) a translation for אֶל־הַבֹּכִים, any alleged alteration to the Hebrew text must have taken place early. It is not difficult to imagine how a pro-Judahite scribe, within the period

of the monarchy, may have found repugnant either וַיַּעַל מַלְאַךְ־יהוה מִן־הַגִּלְגָּל אֶל־בֵּית־אֵל,
had he shared in the Judahite aversion toward the idol shrine that still functioned at
Bethel, or אֶל־בֵּית־יִשְׂרָאֵל, had he shared in a Judahite aversion toward the northern tribes
in general. Such a situation may have prompted an omission of original אֶל בֵּית אֵל or אֶל
בֵּית יִשְׂרָאֵל.

Of the two variants presented by the LXX alone, biblical–historical considerations
would favour אֶל בֵּית אֵל over אֶל בֵּית יִשְׂרָאֵל. The latter would be tautological, since, as
part of the territory of Israel, Gilgal would not have been a place from which one could go
to בֵּית יִשְׂרָאֵל. The expression בֵּית יִשְׂרָאֵל was apparently coined after the period of the
united monarchy (cf. early uses in Ruth 4:11; 1 Sam. 7:2-3; 2 Sam. 1:12; 6:5, 15; Exod.
40:38[?]). On the other hand, the fact that the ark was said to have been at בֵּית אֵל on at
least one occasion early in the period of the judges (20:18, 23, 26-28; 21:2, 4) might
accord with Judges' representation here of the angel of YHWH ascending from Gilgal to
Bethel, where the Israelite tribes wept and offered sacrifice (2:1a, 5b). It seems that, at the
time of the Benjaminite war, the ark was taken to Mizpah, to which the Israelites initially
rallied for 'holy war' (20:1). However, it would be difficult to prove, as some have
argued, that Mizpah had become the ark's regular resting site subsequent to its move, during Joshua's day, from Gilgal (Josh. 4:19; 5:9-10; 9:6; 10:7-8, 15, 43) to Shiloh (Josh.
18:1, 8, 10; 22:9, 12); especially since Shiloh was then still active as the centre of annual
worship (21:19a, 20-23) and remained the site of the sanctuary until Samuel's time
(1 Sam. 1:3, 9). The account of Judg. 20–21 avers only that the ark (apart from the
sanctuary) was at Mizpah on one occasion of 'holy war' and that it accompanied Phinehas,
son of Eleazar, to Bethel, where the Israelites prepared for battle (cf. Phinehas, son of
Eleazar, serving in a similar capacity in Josh. 22:11-34; especially vv. 12, 13, 30-33).

The potential ambiguity of בֵּית אֵל, which could mean in Judg. 20:18, 26-28; 21:2
either 'sanctuary of god' or the name of the border city between Ephraim and Benjamin, is
dispelled by two considerations: (1) the fact that where the former is meant, apart from
this context, the form אֱלֹהִים is invariably used rather than אֵל and (2) the proximity of
Bethel both to Mizpah (where the Israelites had initially rallied their forces, cf. 20:1, 3;
21:1, 5, 8) and to Gibeah (from which the Israelites deployed their forces, cf. 20:31).
Those who see here the city name include: RV; RSV; Cundall, *Judges* (1968), p. 202; NEB;
NIV; Soggin, *Judges* (2d edn, 1987), pp. 292-93; NRSV; and REB. Those who take the
view that בֵּית אֵל here means 'sanctuary of god' include: Vg; AV; Boling, *Judges* (1975),
p. 285; and Merrill, *Kingdom* (1987), p. 181, n. 93. Judg. 20:18, 23, 26-28 and 21:2, 4
give the clearest explanation as to why Israelites might have found occasion both to weep
and to sacrifice and, throughout, use Hebrew vocabulary (in the MT) and Greek
vocabulary (in the LXX) similar to that expected to underlie the LXX variants of Judg.
2:1a. Thus, the LXX of 2:1a may preserve a scribe's harmonizing collocation connecting
2:1-5 with chs. 20–21. It remains possible, however, that the LXX variants preserve an
original collocation of vocabulary identifying the incident of 2:1-5 with that of chs. 20–21
at Bethel. C. H. Cornill took the view that LXX 'Bethel' preserves Judges' Hebrew text
that, at a late stage of compilation, introduced into chs. 20–21 (i.e., 20:23, 26 and 21:2)
references to weeping at Bethel that were borrowed from 2:1-5 (*Einleitung in das Alte
Testament* [GTW II/1, Freiburg i. B., 1891], ET: *Introduction to the Canonical Books of
the Old Testament* [TTL, G. H. Box (trans., from the 5th German edn), London, 1907],
p. 173). According to the LXX, the latter passage would have been intended to close the
book of Judges with a development of the incident described only summarily in 2:1-5 of
the prologue. A similar anticipation in Judges' prologue of matters to be developed in its
closing chapters is evident in the case of Dan, whose confinement by the Amorites (1:34-
36) explains their desire to seek an inheritance elsewhere (18:1-31). At least the OG,
reflecting בֵּית אֵל, would seem to point in that direction.

454 APPENDIX

MT הַבֹּכִים, with the article, seems unwarranted, since there has been no prior reference to weepers in the context, but it probably only parallels the arthrous form מִן־הַגִּלְגָּל. Webb (*Judges* [1987], p. 240 n. 83) showed that arthrous הַגִּלְגָּל is the regular form for this toponym (44 of 46 times in the MT). Cf. the regular anarthrous form בֹּכִים in 2:5a, which conforms to a stereotyped naming formula pattern (e.g., Gen. 33:17; 2 Sam. 5:20) to which even anarthrous Gilgal takes no exception (Josh. 5:9). Hence, the variation between הַבֹּכִים (2:1a) and בֹּכִים (2:5a) is so stylistically conditioned as to be rhetorically insignificant. Had this passage been designed as a toponymic aetiology, one may have expected the old name of the site to occur somewhere in 2:1-5 (cf. other toponymic aetiologies in Judges' framework: 1:26, which offers only the name Luz, since it is a newly built city; and 18:12, naming Mahaneh-Dan, which probably had no previous name; however, non-aetiological naming texts in the framework of Judges may also include dual names: Kiriath-Arba, renamed Hebron [1:10]; Kiriath-sepher, renamed Debir [1:11-12]; Luz, renamed Bethel [1:22-23]; and Laish [18:7, 27], renamed Dan [18:29]). On the other hand, the name 'Weepers' may have been merely eponymous (especially if applied to Bethel) and not intended fully to replace the proper name. Wellhausen observed, on the basis of Gen. 35:8 ("she was buried beneath the oak that is below Bethel. And he [Jacob] named it 'Oak of Weeping [אַלּוֹן בָּכוּת]'"), that [הַ]בֹּכִים of Judg. 2:1, 5 was probably to be sought in the vicinity of Bethel (*Die Composition des Hexateuchs und der historischen Bücher des Alten Testaments* [Berlin, 2d edn, 1889], p. 215; cf. Stone, "Tribal Confederation" [1988], pp. 243-44, comparing Gen. 35:6-8). The MT variant is unsettling only to the extent that it leaves the modern reader wondering what connection this description has with a specific event and place in Israel's history (cf. Webb, *Judges* [1987], pp. 105, 241 n. 94; 234 n. 41; Lindars, *Judges 1-5* [1995], pp. 76-77).

[27] *Judg. 2:3bα*. The main difficulty in Judg. 2:3 is to discern whether the MT: (1) came about by haplography and corruption from *לְצִנִינָם בְּצִדֵּיכֶם (cf. Num. 33:55), (2) mistook ר for ד when copying original *לְצָרִים or (3) accurately preserved a word צַד with the lexical meaning of either (a) 'trap, snare' (|| מוֹקֵשׁ), (b) 'side', hence idiomatically 'opponent, adversary' (cf. BA לְצַד lit. 'against the side', hence prepositionally 'against, opposed to' [Dan. 7:25]) or (c) 'opponent, adversary' (cf. Arab. *diddun* 'contrary, opposed, adverse'; *ddd* III 'to be contrary, opposed'):

לְצִדִּים 'sides; opponents, adversaries' MT Tg Vg (Psht) //
*לְצָרִים 'oppressors' LXX(συνοχάς 'oppression') OLat //
*לְצִנִינָם בְּצִדֵּיכֶם Moore conjecture

The Psht translation *lhryqwt'* 'vanity, nothingness' seems to reflect a translator's attempt to define the Hebrew term from its etymology in Syr. *ṣd'* 'wear out, become desolate/void'. Despite the misapprehension, the Psht was probably reading the form of the MT variant.

Moore suggested emending MT צִדִּים to צִדֵּיכֶם and implied that לְצִנִינָם should also be reinserted (comparing Num. 33:55 ... [וְ]לְצִנִינָם בְּצִדֵּיכֶם והיה "will become ... thorns in your sides"; cf. also Josh. 23:13 בְּעֵינֵיכֶם (והיו לכם לפח ולמוקש בצדיכם ולצננים), since the text probably suffered haplography (*Judges* [1895], pp. 59, 61-62; so Qimḥi; BDB, p. 841a; NIV; Webb, *Judges* [1987], p. 240 n. 91; Lindars, *Judges 1-5* [1995], p. 79). This is a viable solution to the difficulty, but the basis for such an emendation is nowhere attested in either the MT tradition or among the variants of Judg. 2:3.

The LXX and OLat translate so as to suggest that they either read or were tacitly restoring לְצָרִים 'adversaries'. The latter form may have been read by the OG translator, who rendered it συνοχάς 'oppression' (< συνοχή), but one cannot be certain which Hebrew term the OG translator was reading. For συνοχή, LSJ cite only Judg. 2:3 with the sense 'trap, gin, snare' (p. 1724a, II. 6), presuming that the LXX was translating צָדִים, which had a sense parallel to that of מוֹקֵשׁ 'snare' (i.e., וְהָיוּ לָכֶם לְצָדִים ‖ וֵאלֹהֵיהֶם יִהְיוּ לָכֶם לְמוֹקֵשׁ). However, both *BHS* and Barthélemy (*Critique textuelle*, vol. 1 [1982], p. 76) cited the LXX as supporting the alleged variant לְצָרִים, which is valid here if συνοχή were being used in the more widely attested sense of 'distress, affliction, oppression' (LSJ, p. 1724a, II. 5). Indeed, this was the sense given συνοχάς in Judg. 2:3 by J. F. Schleusner (ed.), *Novus Thesaurus Philologico-Criticus siue Lexicon in LXX et Reliquos Interpretes Graecos ac Scriptores Apocryphos Veteris Testamenti* (5 vols., Leipzig, 1821), vol. 5, p. 212, though Schleusner proposed that the LXX may have been translating צָדִים from a root צוד* 'to be hostile, opposed' (cf. Arab. *ḍiddun* 'contrary, opposed, adverse'; *ḍdd* III 'to be contrary, opposed').

BHS, following the suggestion of Friedrich Delitzsch (*Prolegomena eines neuen hebräisch-aramäischen Wörterbuches zum Alten Testament* [Leipzig, 1886], p. 75 n. 4), proposed that the MT may have understood צָד in the sense of Akk. *ṣaddu* 'net, snare, trap'. Cf. מְצוּדָה 'net' from צוד 'hunt' (for which BDB [p. 844b] compare Akk. *ṣâdu* 'hunt'—though *CAD* translates *ṣâdu* A, 1. 'to prowl, to make one's rounds, to turn about, to whirl' [16:57-58]). So also KB, II *צָד 'Schlinge' (p. 793a). However, *CAD* (16:56-57) does not attest for *ṣaddu* such a sense, but only the sense 'sign, signal' (so the NEB of Judg. 2:3 "[they will] decoy [you]"; also the REB).

There is a possibility that צָד had a sense 'opponent, adversary' from a root צוד* 'to be hostile, opposed' (cf. Arab. *ḍiddun* 'contrary, opposed, adverse'), though this term is rare in BH (so A. Schultens, *Animadversiones philologicae et criticae ad varia loca Veteris Testamenti* [Leiden, 1769], p. 160; J. A. Dathe, *Libri historici Veteris Testamenti* [Halle, 1784], ad loc.; cf. J. A. Montgomery, *A Critical and Exegetical Commentary on the Book of Daniel* [ICC, Edinburgh, 1927], pp. 315-16). Yet, in view of the solidity of the MT in preserving such a difficult form, it may be prudent to retain it as original (so Barthélemy, *Critique textuelle*, vol. 1 [1982], p. 76).

Thus, in the light of the preservation of לְצָדִים, notwithstanding its rarity, the MT may be taken as sound if צָדִים means 'opponents, adversaries'. In any case, the sense would not much differ from that of לְצָרִים* 'adversaries', which would offer the next best alternative.

[28] *Judg. 2:4aγ*. So the MT. LXX: πάντα ιηλ, A(ιסλ) glw Eth OLat] πάντας υἱοὺς ιηλ, AI(except A) AII(ptv) AIII B-group(except e,jmo) : πάντας τοὺς υἱοὺς ιηλ, B-group(e,jmo). The OG lacked a translation for בני "sons of". This may have been true of its Hebrew *Vorlage*, and perhaps the original Hebrew lacked it, but such would be difficult to prove. Motivation for its secondary insertion into the MT because of a lack of numerical concord between ישׂראל and the following pl. verbs is lessened by the presence of העם.

[29] *Judg. 2:21b*. MT: + וַיָּמֹת. In LXX-AII(glnw) καὶ ἀφῆκεν (□ OLat) immediately follows Ἰησοῦς but commences a new sentence. Moore doubted the originality of either MT וימת or LXX καὶ ἀφῆκεν (= ויניח*) (*Judges* [1895], p. 75). Soggin retained both the MT and LXX readings, apparently understanding ἀφῆκεν to be a euphemism for death: "when he went away" (i.e., pres. < ἀφήκω 'arrive; depart', rather than aor. < ἀφίημι 'discharge, let go') (*Judges* [2d edn, 1987], p. 40). Webb concluded that וימת is awkward and probably not original, though he suggested reading it as equivalent to במותו "when he died" (*Judges* [1987], p. 242 n. 110; so also Lindars, *Judges 1-5* [1995], pp. 93, 110-11). Perhaps the MT and probably the LXX reflect an early conflation with Judg. 2:8a designed to absolve Joshua of blame by clarifying that only death prevented him from completing the conquest.

[30] *Judg. 2:22bα*[i]. MT: אֶת־דֶּרֶךְ (so the Psht, Vg and LXX). However, this is numerically incongruous with succeeding בָּם. Perhaps אֶת־דֶּרֶךְ was originally אֶת־דַּרְכֵי (so Tg) but

suffered the loss of final ׳ because the latter was mistaken for an abbreviation for the succeeding יהוה (so also Lindars, *Judges 1-5* [1995], p. 111). Cf. E. Tov, *Textual Criticism of the Hebrew Bible* (Minneapolis, 1992), pp. 256-57, regarding the MT rendering of יהוה for the final ׳ on ביתי in MT Judg. 19:18 (OG: οἶκόν μου). See the following note.

31 *Judg. 2:22bα*[ii]. MT: בָּם (so Tg: בהון), which lacks numerical concord with its antecedent אֶת־דֶּרֶךְ. A few marginal indications in the MT MSS suggest בָּהּ, which agrees with the renderings of the Psht: *bh*; Vg: *in ea*; and LXX: ἐν αὐτῇ. However, the greater likelihood is that the antecedent אֶת־דֶּרֶךְ was originally אֶת־דַּרְכֵי (so Tg). So also Lindars, *Judges 1-5* [1995], p. 111. See the preceding note.

32 *Judg. 3:2aβ*. The MT has here דַּעַת, which is probably a corruption. Moore had initially proposed that דעת be retained and that דרות, a corrupt doublet, and ללמדם, a gloss on the latter, be removed (*Judges* [1895], pp. 77-78; also Budde, *Richter* [1897], p. 25). As more conservative options, however, either it should be transposed to follow ללמדם or be altogether deleted as a gloss that had been intended to specify an obj. of the inf. ללמדם (so LXX; Moore in *SBOT*, vol. 7 [1900], pp. 3, 29; *BHS*; Lindars, *Judges 1-5* [1995], p. 114). Had it been a marginal gloss intended to specify the obj. of ללמדם, its mistaken insertion here might be explained by its similarity to the following word דרות.

33 *Judg. 3:13bγ*. Whether one reads the pl. וַיִּירְשׁוּ (so the MT, Tg and Psht *passim*; subj.: the named peoples) or the sg וַיִּירַשׁ* (subj.: Moab) of the alleged *Vorlagen* of the Vg and OG (OLat) is of minor consequence, but, in regard to such shifts of number, the MT is probably more to be trusted as preserving this characteristic of Hebrew narrative syntax than the versions, which tend to remove it (*pace BHS*; J. A. Soggin, "׳Ehud und ʿEglon: Bemerkungen zu Richter iii 11b-31", *VT* 39 [1989], p. 96, who favours the sg as "die bessere Lesart"; and Lindars, *Judges 1-5* [1995], p. 138, who says "it is best to read singular *wayyiraš*" yet wrongly cites the Tg as supporting the sg).

34 *Judg. 3:19bβ*. There are two translation traditions for Judg. 3:19b. In the MT this presents an apparent incongruity between command and action. The variants align as follows:

וַיֵּצְאוּ MT Tg Psht (Vg) LXX-AI(except k),AII,AIII Arm Eth OLat Syh //

וַיּוֹצֵא* LXX-AI(k),B-group //

וַיֹּצִאוּ* NEB conjecture

As given by the MT, the relationship between Eglon's command of silence (sg interjection הָס 'Hush') and his attendants' exit (pl. indicative) presents what seems to be a *non sequitur*. The Vg, which seems to follow the MT, attempts to circumvent the difficulties incurred by specifying the addressee of the interjection in a paraphrase: "he commanded silence".

Otherwise, a perception of incongruity between the actions has given rise to two different lines of interpretation/translation that have attempted to resolve it. One line presents Eglon as addressing Ehud with the interjection, הס, then as the subj. of the next verb by emending MT וַיֵּצְאוּ to וַיּוֹצֵא*: "he said, 'Hush!' and sent out his attendants" (so LXX-AI[k],B-group; Soggin, *Judges* [2d edn, 1987], p 51; cf. Qimḥi). Thus, σ´ translated: ὁ δὲ εἶπεν σίγα ἀποπεμψαμένου δὲ αὐτοῦ πάντας τοὺς παρεστηκότας αὐτῷ. *BHS* likewise suggested that ἐξαπέστειλεν ἀφ᾽ ἑαυτοῦ of LXX-B-group (and k) derived from Hebrew וַיֹּצִא*. Hence, the NEB rendered the sentence: "Eglon called for silence *and dismissed* all his attendants", suggesting that the pl. MT form וַיֵּצְאוּ may have derived from וַיֹּצִיא* (cf. Lev. 24:23 "they led/took out"; so L. H. Brockington, *The Hebrew Text of the Old Testament: The Readings Adopted by the Translators of the New English Bible* [Oxford and Cambridge, 1973], p. 35; also the REB). Barthélemy suggested that the translation underlying the B-group and k (i.e., ἐξαπέστειλεν ἀφ᾽ ἑαυτοῦ πάντας) was a harmonization with LXX Gen. 45:1 (ἐξαποστείλατε ἀπ' ἐμοῦ) (*Critique textuelle*, vol. 1 [1982], p. 77).

Another line attempts to harmonize the senses of both command and consequent action by assuming that the command was addressed to the attendants (notwithstanding the sg form of הָס) and that the attendants were the subject of the second verb: "he said, 'Go out!/Hush!', and his attendants went out" (so the Tg; Psht; LXX-AI; Josephus; Rashi; Ralbag; E. Bertheau, *Das Buch der Richter und Ruth* [KEHAT 6, F. Hitzig et al. (eds.), Leipzig, 1845], p. 70; J. Bachmann, *Das Buch der Richter: Mit besonderer Rücksicht auf die Geschichte seiner Auslegung und kirchlichen Verwendung*, vol. 1 [Berlin, 1868-1869], p. 212; Keil, *Richter* [1863], ET: *Judges* [1868], repr. edn, vol. 2, p. 297; Moore, *Judges* [1895], p. 95; Burney, *Judges* [2d edn, 1920], p. 71; Boling, *Judges* [1975], p. 84; Lindars, *Judges 1-5* [1995], pp. 144, 161). The LXX-AII text-type preserves a variant doublet for הָס that, in effect, conflates the two preceding schemes for resolving the narrative incongruity of the verse (cf. Barthélemy, *Critique textuelle*, vol. 1 [1982], p. 77).

Had Ehud been the addressee of the command, one would expect in the verse some explicit command from the king to have initiated the consequent departure of his royal attendants. Indeed, a mistaken assumption that הָס was an impv sg seems to have induced the problematic view that Ehud was its addressee and that it implied that Ehud should keep the matter secret. If, however, הָס is regarded as an interjection, then, assuming that the addressees of the command were the attendants, one would have no difficulty accounting for the lack of numerical concord between its apparently sg form and the plurality of those addressed. In fact, there is precedent for this phenomenon (cf. Amos 8:3; Zeph. 1:7), so the alternative that reckons the attendants to have been the addressees seems least problematic if הָס is understood to connote 'solitude' as a metonymical reflex of its basic sense, 'silence'. It was this customary lack of numerical concord that prompted BDB (p. 245a) to regard הַס (pausal הָס) as an interjection, though it does elsewhere appear in a form analogous to the impv pl. (as though from a root הָסָה*, i.e., הַסּוּ 'Be silent!' in Neh. 8:11) and as a denom. Hi. pret. 3 m. sg (וַיַּהַס) "and [Caleb] silenced [the people]" in Num. 13:30). Although there is no MS evidence to support it, there is a remote possibility that an original הַסּוּ stood here in the text (cf. Neh. 8:11, on analogy with a Qal impv m. pl. < הָסָה*) and that final וֹ- was removed as though it had been a reduplication of the following conj.

In conclusion, it may be an assumed incongruity in the MT between Eglon's command and the courtiers' action that gave rise to the alternative translation traditions. In all probability, the MT preserves the earliest form and vocalization of the text. Here the interjection הָס 'Hush' was probably addressed to the royal attendants, a convention of the royal court that implied that the king wanted privacy. Note, however, that in the post-exilic prophets the idiom הַס מִפְּנֵי יהוה "Hush before YHWH" connotes attentive respect in anticipation of a decree of YHWH from his temple (cf. Hab. 2:20; Zeph. 1:7; Zech. 2:17).

35 *Judg.* 3:28aα. MT: רִדְפוּ. LXX: καταβαίνετε, AI(except b,k),AII(except n),AIII] κατάβητε, B-group. Thus, the OG had καταβαίνετε < רדו*. Soggin considered both the MT and OG variants viable alternatives (*Judges* [2d edn, 1987], p. 52; idem, "'Ehud und 'Eglon" [1989], p. 97). Some earlier commentators rejected the impv construction רדפו אחרי "pursue after me" as unidiomatic, since it is elsewhere unattested in this sense (Moore, *Judges* [1895], pp. 102-3; Burney, *Judges* [2d edn, 1920], pp. 74-75). Lindars, too, emended the impv to רדו, saying that "the objection to MT is that Hebrew *radap* 'aḥăre is a technical expression for pursuit of an enemy (cf. 1.6; 4.16; 7.23, etc.)" (*Judges 1-5* [1995], p. 154). Yet, although the sense 'follow' for רדף is elsewhere unattested, it is not impossible (so AV; RV; RSV; NEB; NIV; NRSV; REB; cf. BDB, p. 922b). If, indeed, רדפו אחרי were unidiomatic, it becomes more difficult to explain how פ came to be inserted secondarily; however, if the MT preserves the original, it may be

argued that the OG translated the verb tacitly as יֵרֵד on the basis of the frequency of this verb in the context (cf. 3:27b, 28b).

[36] *Judg. 3:30c**. The OG plus at the end of the verse attests one of Judge's recurring motifs exactly where one might have expected the MT to place it if it had been following the pattern used elsewhere in Judges. Is the MT deficient or the LXX conflated in relation to the original?

   – (שָׁנָה) MT Tg Psht Vg LXX-AI(x) //

   (שָׁנָה) *וישפט אהוד אתם עד אשר מת LXX-AI(except x),AII,AIII,B-group Arm(ℵ mend pro
   ÷) Sah Eth OLat Syh

The LXX plus offers a translation of idiomatic BH: καὶ ἔκρινεν αὐτοὺς 'Αὼδ ἕως οὗ ἀπέθανεν < וישפט אהוד אתם עד אשר מת *(ἕως οὗ < עד אשר) עד אשר occurs in Deut. 2:14; 9:21; Josh. 3:17 [ἕως οὗ, S, P : □ οὗ, E, C = Margolis' OG]; Judg. 4:24 [LXX-AII(w,dptv),B-group(B,a₂,mq)]; Judg. 5:7 [עַד-שַׁ]; cf. BDB, p. 724b II.1.[a]). It is possible, therefore, that OG Judg. 3:30c* is based upon a Hebrew *Vorlage*.

Some have thought that the LXX plus preserves the original text, which suffered haplography in the course of transmission (e.g., O. Grether, "Die Bezeichnung 'Richter' für die charismatischen Helden der vorstaatlichen Zeit", *ZAW* 57 [1939], p. 113 n. 3; T. Ishida, "The Leaders of the Tribal Leagues: 'Israel' in the Pre-Monarchic Period", *RB* 80 [1973], pp. 521-22). However, there are no external features of the semantic unit represented by Judg. 3:30c*, such as *homoeoteleuton*, that might explain its accidental omission from the text had it been original. Deliberate omission also seems unlikely, since there is nothing in the plus that is inherently offensive or that might contradict other biblical texts.

Others have inferred that the LXX attests an insertion made during the course of transmission (J. Schreiner, *Seputaginta-Massora des Buches der Richter: Eine textkritische Studie* [AnBib 7, Rome, 1957], p. 49). The latter view represents the more probable alternative. Although the OG plus may be based upon a Hebrew *Vorlage*, the precise phraseology of the plus is sufficiently at variance from other recurrences of the two motifs in Judges—elsewhere contiguous in 10:2; 12:7, 9b-10α, 11b-12a, 14b-15a—to raise doubts about its authenticity (so also Lindars, *Judges 1-5* [1995], p. 155). See chapter 1 on the standard form of the F1 motif (שנים N אֶת-יִשְׂרָאֵל PN וישפט) and the G1 motif (וימת PN). This argument may be countered, however, by the view that the very distinctiveness of the phraseology of Judg. 3:30c* attests its authenticity, since, were it a conflation with similar motifs elsewhere in Judges, it would have followed them exactly. The fact that the plus comprises a complete semantic unit increases the likelihood that it was deliberately inserted into the tradition underlying the OG. Deliberate insertion would have been motivated: (1) by the desire to harmonize the account of Ehud with motif elements usually present in the judge accounts but here lacking (see the discussion on motifs F1 and G1 in chapter 1) and (2) by the reference to the death of Ehud in the succeeding account (4:1b), which otherwise lacks an explicit antecedent.

In all probability, the LXX is a conflated version of the original text that, in this instance, is best preserved by the MT. The consensus of opinion as to the spurious nature of the OG plus is such that the AV, RV, RSV, *BHS*, NEB, NIV, NRSV and REB neither acknowledge nor cite it as a variant.

[37] *Judg. 4:8b*. The LXX plus finds corroboration neither in the MT nor among the other versions:

   –, MT Tg Psht Vg //

   LXX *כִּי לֹא יָדַעְתִּי[\וֶאֱדַע] אֶת-הַיּוֹם אֲשֶׁר יַצְלִיחַ יְהוָה מַלְאָכוֹ אִתִּי

For the retroversion of Hebrew צלח (usually Hi.) from Greek εὐοδόω, cf. the LXX of Gen. 24:27; Dan. 8:11; and Judg. 18:5 with the MT of Gen. 24:21, 40, 42, 56; Dan. 8:12, 24, 25; and Judg. 18:5. Burney retroverted: כִּי לֹא יָדַעְתִּי אֶת־יוֹם הַצְלִיחַ מַלְאַךְ יַהֲוֶה אֹתִי "for I know not the day whereon the Angel of Yahweh shall prosper me" (*Judges* [2d edn, 1920], p. 89).

There do not seem to be any other textual difficulties in the immediate context that might have prompted this discrepancy. *BHS* suggested that the LXX plus derived from a Hebrew gloss that compared Judg. 4:14: וַתֹּאמֶר דְּבֹרָה אֶל־בָּרָק קוּם כִּי זֶה הַיּוֹם אֲשֶׁר ... יַהֲוֶה. K. F. Houbigant first suggested that in Judg. 4:14 Deborah was making allusion to the ignorance that Barak confesses according to the LXX and that this mention of ignorance must figure in the original form of the story (*Biblia Hebraica cum notis criticis et versione latina ad notas criticas facta* ... [4 vols., Paris, 1753], vol. 2, p. 97). Others who have accepted the LXX plus as original include: H. Graetz (*Emendationes in Plerosque Sacrae Scripturae Veteris Testamenti Libros* ... [G. Bacher (ed.), 3 vols., Breslau, 1892–1894], vol. 3 [1894], ad loc.); G. L. Studer (*Das Buch der Richter: grammatisch und historisch erklärt* [Bern, 1835], pp. 106-7); W. Frankenberg (*Die Composition des deuteronomischen Richterbuches (Richter ii,6–xvi), nebst einer Kritik von Richter xvii–xxi* [Marburg, 1895], ad loc.); M.-J. Lagrange (*Le livre des Juges* [Ebib 2, Paris, 1903], p. 69); and Soggin (*Judges* [2d edn, 1987], pp. 61, 65, 73); cf. Burney, *Judges* (2d edn, 1920), p. 89.

In regard to the LXX plus, *BHS* confirmed the suggestion of Bachmann that the plus was made up of borrowings from the context (*Richter*, vol. 1 [1868–69], pp. 265-66). Bachmann added that the references to the "angel of YHWH" and to "the assistance of YHWH" were borrowed from Judg. 5:23 (cf. Budde, *Richter* [1897], p. 37; Nowack, *Richter* [1902], p. 35). Barthélemy cautioned that the formulae used in the gloss are more characteristic where the LXX plus finds a perfect response in 4:14, not according to the MT but according to the Tg: ואמרת דבורה לברק קום ארי דין יומא דמסר יוי ית סיסרא בידך הלא מלאכא דיוי נפיק לאצלחא קדמך "And Deborah said to Barak: 'Arise, for this is the day on which the Lord has given Sisera into your hand. Is not *the angel of* the Lord going forth *to ensure success* before you?'" (*Critique textuelle*, vol. 1 [1982], p. 77, following Burney, *Judges* [2d edn, 1920], p. 89; cf. Y. Amit, "Judges 4: Its Content and Form", *JSOT* 39 [1987], p. 107 n. 15). The omission of this plus from LXX MS x reflects no alternative text-type within the LXX, since this cursive (along with k and d) frequently attempts to delete passages that on Origen's assumptions (as indicated by the obelus) ought to be deleted (cf. A. V. Billen, "The Hexaplaric Element in the LXX Version of Judges", *JTS* 43 [1942], p. 17).

Probably the LXX gloss was inserted through a conflation of 4:14 with 5:23 that attempted to justify Barak's reluctance by means of an appeal to Deborah's unique charismatic insight (so H.-D. Neef, "Der Sieg Deboras und Baraks über Sisera: Exegetische Beobachtungen zum Aufbau und Werden von Jdc 4,1-24", *ZAW* 101 [1989], p. 32; cf. Budde, *Richter* [1897], p. 37; Nowack, *Richter* [1902], p. 35; Moore in *SBOT*, vol. 7 [1900], p. 31; Burney, *Judges* [2d edn, 1920], p. 89; Barthélemy, *Critique textuelle*, vol. 1 [1982], p. 78). D. F. Murray proposed that "the LXX text of *vv.* 8 f. represents, not a version of MT glossed ... but a true variant version" so that "the shorter MT could have resulted from the narrator's desire to tighten up the text ... or to heighten the implicit condemnation of Barak's hesitancy" ("Narrative Structure and Technique in the Deborah-Barak Story [Judges iv 4-22]", in *Studies in the Historical Books of the Old Testament* [J. A. Emerton (ed.), SVT 30, Leiden, 1979], p. 168 n. 30). However, if the shorter version of 4:8 (in the MT) had resulted from "the narrator's desire to tighten ... or to heighten", in what sense are we to suppose that the earlier, longer version (in the *Vorlage* of the LXX) is likewise "a true variant version" unless we are meant to infer that the book of Judges had survived in two different editions?

In any case, the MT and the versions other than the LXX offer what seems to be the earliest form of the text (so also Lindars, *Judges 1–5* [1995], p. 189, comparing Exod. 23:20). It is rhetorically valuable, however, that while the LXX plus probably compensates for the OG translator's aversion to allowing Barak to incriminate himself in 4:8b, it also perhaps attests that he understood the Hebrew text without the plus to do just that. In a similar way, the Midrash on Judg. 4:8 interprets Barak's words to mean, "If you go with me to the battlefield, I will then be able to accompany you in Song!" (F. Gottlieb, "Three Mothers", *Judaism* 30 [1981], p. 196). This Midrash takes its interpretation from the mention of Barak singing with Deborah in 5:1 and may reflect the same aversion as that of the OG translator to Barak's self-incrimination in MT Judg. 4:8.

[38] *Judg. 4:10aβ*. Rudolph suggested that after וַיַּעַל the destination לְתָבֹר had fallen out by haplography because of similarity with the preceding ל of וַיַּעַל and the following בר of בְּרַגְלָיו ("Textkritische Anmerkungen" [1947], p. 199; cf. Lindars, *Judges 1–5* [1995], p. 190). It is doubtful, however, that such a geographical reference would have appeared in this form, since this chapter elsewhere uses only the full designation הַר־תָּבוֹר (Judg. 4:6, 12, 14). In the Gideon account, however, תָּבוֹר stands without הַר־, as it does also in Josh. 19:12, 22 (see Judg. 8:18, which Moore [*Judges* (1895), pp. 226-27, 228] contended was originally טַבּוּר [= טַבּוּר הָאָרֶץ "navel/centre of the land" of 9:37] and was emended to comport with the locale mentioned in 6:33).

[39] *Judg. 4:21b*. MT (L): וְהוּא־נִרְדָּם וַיָּעַף (Ni. ptcp m. sg and Qal pret. 3 m. sg < עִיף 'be faint') "and he being fast asleep—he became exhausted [and died]". A weight of textual support authenticates the form וַיָּעַף in conflict with the fact that in normal word order it is the ptcp that is preceded by an independent pron. subj. Several Hebrew MSS attest the syntactically simpler וְהוּא־נִרְדַּם וַיָּעַף (Ni. perf. 3 m. sg and Qal pret. 3 m. sg), though it conveys the unnatural narrative sequence, "and as for him, he had fallen fast asleep and was exhausted". Perhaps to be preferred for rhetorical reasons is the form וְהוּא־נִרְדָּם וְיָעֵף (Ni. ptcp m. sg and adj. 'faint, exhausted' [cf. the Psht]) "and he being overwhelmed by sleep and exhausted" (so Budde, *Richter* [1897], p. 39; Moore, *Judges* [1895], pp. 124, 125-26). Lindars followed G. R. Driver in deriving the form from עוּף\עִיף 'to swoon, spasm, convulse', though Lindars translated 'collapsed' (*Judges 1–5* [1995], pp. 173, 200, 203-4; G. R. Driver, "Problems of Interpretation in the Heptateuch", in *Mélanges bibliques: Rédigés en l'honneur de André Robert* [TICP 4, Paris, 1957], pp. 66-76, especially p. 74).

[40] *Judg. 5:3bβ*. Because of repetitive stylistics in Judg. 5:2-31a such as the prevalence of epanalepsis and climactic parallelism (e.g., 5:3, 23b, 27, 30; cf. Pss. 29:1-2; 96:1-2, 7-8) as well as its triadic pattern of strophic repetitions (see the discussion in chapter 2), it is inadvisable to resort to the claim that dittography is the cause of repetition unless no stylistic ground may be found for such a repetition. This would appear to be the case in several places where textual emendations have been proposed. On epanalepsis and climactic parallelism in Judg. 5, see P. Ruben, "The Song of Deborah", *JQR* 10 (1897–1898), pp. 542, 544, 553, 556; G. Gerleman, "The Song of Deborah in the Light of Stylistics", *VT* 1 (1951), pp. 175-78; J. Blenkinsopp, "Ballad Style and Psalm Style in the Song of Deborah: A Discussion", *Bib* 42 (1961), pp. 67, 73 (cf. n. 1); H.-P. Müller, "Der Aufbau des Deboraliedes", *VT* 16 (1966), pp. 447-49. The proposal of I. W. Slotki ("The Song of Deborah", *JTS* 33 [1932], pp. 341-54) that the lack of synonymous parallelism in Judg. 5 was caused by a failure to preserve the blank spaces customarily left beneath words to be repeated—words that Slotki proposed to restore—is also to be rejected on stylistic grounds (cf. Gerleman, "Song of Deborah" [1951], p. 177 n. 2; A. J. Hauser, "Judges 5: Parataxis in Hebrew Poetry", *JBL* 99 [1980], p. 23 n. 1).

The repetition of אנכי preserved in MT Judg. 5:3bαβ (אנכי ליהוה / אנכי אשירה) is probably epanaleptic, despite scribal efforts to remove the latter occurrence from a few

Hebrew MSS, the Psht and the OG (probably on the grounds of translation technique) (cf. *BHS*). In this instance, both the prevalence of epanaleptic repetition in the poem and the fact that the second אנכי serves well the metrical structure of the verse evidence its authenticity (so Gerleman, "Song of Deborah" [1951], p. 177; Blenkinsopp, "Ballad Style" [1961], pp. 66-67). The fact that parallelism involving repetition of the 1 c. sg personal pronoun is attested also in Ug. (*'ank* || *'ank*; cf. L. R. Fisher [ed.], *Ras Shamra Parallels*, vol. 1 [Rome, 1972], p. 118), Akk. (*Gilgamesh* I.v.1-2) and Arab. (semantic parallelism without independent pronouns in Quran 109:2-5) may lessen doubt about its authenticity here (cf. P. C. Craigie, "Parallel Word Pairs in the Song of Deborah", *JETS* 20 [1977], p. 18 §3; Lindars, *Judges 1-5* [1995], pp. 228, 288).

⁴¹ *Judg. 5:4aδ*. The OG variation from ἐταράχθη 'remained confused' (5:4a) to ἔσταξαν 'stopped' (5:4b), in translating the words now preserved in the MT as a repetition of נטפו 'dripped rain' (5:4a,b; cf. Ps. 68:9), has prompted many text critics to emend the former occurrence of נָטְפוּ, whether to נָמֹטוּ 'were shaken, disturbed' (Ehrlich, *Randglossen*, vol. 3 [1910], repr. edn, p. 81), נָמֹגוּ 'melted away' (Budde, *Richter und Samuel* [1890], p. 104; Moore, *Judges* [1895], p. 141; Ruben, "Song of Deborah" [1897-98], p. 543; Burney, *Judges* [2d edn, 1920], p. 112; *BH³*; *BHS*), נָטֹפוּ (the NEB [cf. Brockington, *Hebrew Text* (1973), p. 36]; and apparently REB [though Lindars cites the REB as reading נָמֹטוּ (*Judges 1-5* [1995], p. 232)]) or נָטִיוּ 'bowed, declined' (Gray, *Judges* [2d edn, 1986], p. 265). However, here is probably just another example of poetic epanalepsis, the LXX translator's elegant variation notwithstanding (cf. Gerleman, "Song of Deborah" [1951], p. 177 n. 1; Hauser, "Judges 5" [1980], p. 30 n. 18).

W. F. Albright argued that נטף itself may mean 'to shake' ("A Catalogue of Early Hebrew Lyric Poems [Psalm lxviii]", *HUCA* 23, Part I [1950-1951], p. 20) and this view is followed by J. M. Myers, "The Book of Judges: Introduction and Exegesis", in *IB*, vol. 2, p. 720; reservedly by P. D. Miller, *The Divine Warrior in Early Israel* (HSM 5, Cambridge, Mass., 1973), pp. 87-90; and M. D. Coogan, "A Structural and Literary Analysis of the Song of Deborah", *CBQ* 40 (1978), p. 146. However, many authorities support the sense 'to drip' (e.g., AV; RV; Moore, *Judges* [1895], p. 141; BDB, p. 642b; JPSV; RSV; Boling, *Judges* [1975], p. 101 [contra Coogan, "Song of Deborah" (1978), p. 146 n. 13]; NIV; NRSV) as does the balanced positioning of the hymn's 'water' motif among the strophes (see the discussion in chapter 2).

⁴² *Judg. 5:4b*. Some have reasoned from the similarity of content between 5:4aδ and 5:4b that the latter is a gloss explaining the anticlimactic verb נטפו in the former (so W. F. Albright, "The Earliest Forms of Hebrew Verse", *JPOS* 2 [1922], p. 75 n. 1; Myers, "Introduction", *IB*, vol. 2, p. 720; É. Lipiński, "Juges 5,4-5 et Psaume 68,8-11", *Bib* 48 [1967], pp. 185, 199). Lindars's excision of 5:4b as a gloss was motivated in part by its absence from the parallel to Judg. 5:4-5 in Ps. 68:8-9 and in part from its disruption of metrical and semantic properties that Lindars found exemplified in Ps. 68:8-9 (Lindars, *Judges 1-5* [1995], pp. 229, 231-32). Again, a recognition of the pervasive epanaleptic style in the hymn should warn against any policy aimed at removing redundancies simply because they are redundancies.

⁴³ *Judg. 5:5aα*. MT: נָזֹלוּ (Qal perf. 3 m. pl. < נזל 'to flow, trickle' [BDB, p. 633b; cf. Num. 24:7 (of water in vessels), Exod. 15:8 (ptcp 'the flows', || מִים)]). The MT is supported by the Vg (*fluxerunt*); AV; RV; Moore, *Judges* (1895), pp. 141-42; Hertzberg, *Richter* (1953), p. 171; JB; A. Globe, "The Text and Literary Structure of Judges 5,4-5", *Bib* 55 (1974), pp. 174-75; and Hauser, "Judges 5" (1980), p. 31, n. 20.

However, the OG has: ἐσαλεύθησαν (= נָזֹלוּ, Ni. perf. 3 m. pl. < זלל 'to shake, quake' [BDB, p. 272b; cf. Isa. 63:19 (of mountains); 64:2?]), AI,AII(except glnw),AIII,B-group] ἐσαλεύθη, AII(glnw). Also supporting נָזֹלוּ are the Psht; Tg; JPSV; Burney, *Judges* (2d edn, 1920), pp. 103, 112; RSV; J. Jeremias, *Theophanie: Die*

Geschichte einer alttestamentlichen Gattung (WMANT 10, Neukirchen–Vluyn, 1965), p. 7 n. 3; *BHS*; NEB; NIV; Miller, *Divine Warrior* (1973), p. 224 n. 75; Boling, *Judges* (1975), p. 108; Coogan, "Song of Deborah" (1978), p. 146, n. 14; NRSV; REB; and Lindars, *Judges 1–5* (1995), pp. 209, 232-33. Further, the semantic parallelism between ארץ רעשה (5:4aγ) and הרים נזלו (5:5aα) supports the sense 'shake, quake' (so Globe, "Judges 5,4-5" [1974], p. 174, though he endorsed the MT here).

Probably 'shake, quake' is the most likely sense, on the strength of the Isaiah parallel. On the possible by-form relationship of זלל and נזל (cf. קוט and נקט), see BDB, p. 876b; GKC, §§30h, 67dd, 72dd.

[44] *Judg. 5:5bα.* On the basis of its omission from LXX-AIII(MNyb₂,h) Syh, many have considered זה סיני of 5:5bα to be a scribal gloss. Ruben imprecisely ascribed the omission to LXX MS A and its congeners ("Song of Deborah" [1897–98], p. 542, n. 2). Others who omit זה סיני as a gloss include Moore, *Judges* (1895), pp. 141-42; Burney, *Judges* (2d edn, 1920), p. 113; Albright, "Earliest Forms" (1922), p. 75 n. 3; C. A. Simpson, *Composition of the Book of Judges* (Oxford, 1957), p. 18; Müller, "Aufbau des Deboraliedes" (1966), p. 454; JB; Fishbane, *Biblical Interpretation* (1985), pp. 54-55, 75 n. 30; and Lindars, *Judges 1–5* (1995), pp. 209, 229, 233-34. Among ancient and early modern versions, when זה סיני has been retained, it has usually been considered a parallel to הרים נזלו\נגזלו (so the LXX, Vg, AV, RV, JPSV, RSV).

Probably זה סיני should be retained, but it should be interpreted as an epithet of יהוה parallel to אלהי ישראל (5:5bβ). On the function of זה as a demonstrative pronoun used in epithets attested at Ugarit, Mari and in Arab. cognates, see Ehrlich, *Randglossen*, vol. 3 (1910), repr. edn, pp. 81-82; W. F. Albright, "The Song of Deborah in the Light of Archaeology", *BASOR* 62 (1936), p. 30; Lipiński, "Juges 5,4-5" (1967), p. 198; Blenkinsopp, "Ballad Style" (1961), p. 67; Globe, "Judges 5,4-5" (1974), pp. 170-71 n. 2; idem, "The Literary Structure and Unity of the Song of Deborah", *JBL* 93 (1974), p. 493, n. 1. This view is further supported by the resulting parallel structure between 5:5 and 5:4aγδb (so Myers, "Introduction", *IB*, vol. 2, p. 720; NEB; NIV; Globe, "Judges 5,4-5" [1974], pp. 169-71, 178; NRSV; REB):

ארץ רעשה / גם־שמים נטפו //
גם־עבים נטפו מים:
הרים נזלו / מפני יהוה // זה סיני /
מפני יהוה אלהי ישראל:

[45] *Judg. 5:6aβ.* Many have proposed an omission or emendation of בימי יעל (5:6aβ) on the ground that Jael would not have been regarded important enough to characterize a period (as were Shamgar [5:6aα] and Deborah) (so Budde, *Richter* [1897], p. 42; Nowack, *Richter* [1902], p. 44; H. Gressmann, *Die Anfänge Israels: Von 2. Mosis bis Richter und Ruth* [SAT I/2, Göttingen, 2d edn, 1922], p. 184; W. Richter, *Die Bearbeitungen des 'Retterbuches' in der deuteronomischen Epoche* [BBB 21, Bonn, 1964], p. 72; Ruben, "Song of Deborah" [1897–98], p. 542; Müller, "Aufbau des Deboraliedes" [1966], p. 452 n. 3). However, this perception runs counter to the rhetoric of both the prose and hymnic versions in which Jael figures as the real heroine (so Gerleman, "Song of Deborah" [1951], p. 176 n. 1; cf. Lindars, *Judges 1–5* [1995], pp. 235-36). Indeed, Jael furnishes an ideal parallel to Shamgar (בימי שמגר בן־ענת, 5:6aα) because of her analogous willingness to act alone and to use an instrument of daily life (a tent peg, as Shamgar's ox goad [cf. 3:31]) to achieve deliverance on behalf of YHWH when no proper instruments of war could be found among the masses of Israel (5:8b).

[46] *Judg. 5:6aγ.* MT: אֳרָחוֹת (nom. m. pl. abs.) 'paths, highways' (AV; RV; BDB, p. 73a 1; JPSV; NIV). Read probably אֹרְחֹ[וֹ]ת 'caravans' (nom. [Qal ptcp f.] pl. abs.; ‖ והלכי נתיבות; cf. Qal ptcp m. sg in Judg. 19:17). So RV(mg); Moore, *Judges* (1895),

p. 143; Burney, *Judges* (2d edn, 1920), p. 114; RSV; *BHS*; NAB; NEB; NRSV; REB; Coogan, "Song of Deborah" (1978), p. 147, n. 16; Lindars, *Judges 1–5* [1995], pp. 209, 236, 288-89.

⁴⁷ *Judg. 5:8aβ*. MT: אָז לָחֶם שְׁעָרִים. After the syntactical question of the subject of יִבְחַר, the main difficulty with this half-verse is in interpreting the present form of MT 5:8aβ.

*אָזל<ו> חמש<י> ערים: Lindars conjecture //
*אָז לחמ<ו> שערים: Coogan conjecture (LXX) //
אָז לחם שערים: MT Tg Psht Vg LXX //
*אָז לחמש ערים: Craigie conjecture

Taking into consideration the translation technique of the various versions, all the ancient versions support some form of the consonantal text preserved in the MT (cf. Billen, "Old Latin" [1942], pp. 140, 142; J. Schreiner, "Textformen und Urtext des Deboraliedes in der Septuaginta", *Bib* 42 [1961], p. 191). The AV, RV and JPSV rendered the half-verse: "They chose new gods; then was war in the gates". Similarly the RSV has: "When new gods were chosen, then war was in the gates" (also NRSV). These translations assume that יִבְחַר represents the indefinite use of the 3 m. sg form (GKC, §144d), imply that this text alone preserves a nominal form לָחֶם 'war' (BDB, p. 535b) and convey the interpretation that the subsequent warring and weaponlessness of Israel were the result of their choosing gods other than YHWH (so K. J. Cathcart, "The 'Demons' in Judges 5:8a", *BZ* NS 21 [1977], pp. 111-12; Coogan, "Song of Deborah" [1978], p. 147).

A different course was taken by the NEB translators, who both viewed אלהים as the subject of 5:8aα and repointed לָחֶם שְׁעָרִים to read *לָחֲם שְׂעָרִים: "They chose new gods; they consorted with demons [mg: satyrs]" (cf. Brockington, *Hebrew Text* [1973], p. 36). Many have followed the NEB in 5:8aα, taking it to indicate the positive result of Deborah's arising (cf. P. C. Craigie, "Some Further Notes on the Song of Deborah", *VT* 22 [1972], pp. 350-51; Soggin, *Judges* [2d edn, 1987], p. 82; B. Lindars, "Deborah's Song: Women in the Old Testament", *BJRL* 65 [1982–1983], p. 168 n. 22; REB), and several new proposals for the emendation of 5:8aβ have come forth. Craigie proposed a different word division from that of the MT: *אָז לחמש ערים "then was there for five cities …?" ("Further Notes" [1972], pp. 350-51; endorsed by Soggin: "In those times there was no defence for five cities" [*Judges* (2d edn, 1987), p. 86]), but the number five seems without warrant. Coogan emended 5:8aβ through the introduction of a *mater lectionis* that may not have been written in the earliest form of the hymn: *אָז לחמ<ו> שערים "then they fought at the gates" (Coogan, "Song of Deborah" [1978], p. 147 n. 24; citing ἐπολέμησαν of the LXX-B-group). Lindars reconstituted 5:8aβ through both new word divisions and the insertion of two *matres lectionis*: *אָזל<ו> חמש<י> ערים "the armed men of the cities came forth" ("Deborah's Song" [1982–83], p. 168 n. 22). On the rare and mostly poetic use of the verb אזל, see BDB, p. 23b. On the military designation חֲמֻשִׁים 'those armed' (Qal pass. ptcp or adj. m. pl. < חמש 'to arm, bear arms [for battle]'?), see BDB, p. 332b. Lindars's most recent modification to this emendation, *אָז אזל<ו> חמש<י> ערים, retains prep. אז on the ground that it "restores the unstressed relation of it to a narrative verb, as in vv. 11, 13, 19, 22, thus preserving the metre" (*Judges 1–5* [1995], p. 240).

In the light of the triadic pattern of repetitions among the five strophes in Judg. 5:2-31a (5:6-8, 11b-13, 14-18, 19-22, 23-30), it seems warranted to view 5:6-7a and 5:8b as matching negative portrayals of the anarchy in Israel that resulted from the tribes' reluctance to bear arms (see the discussion in chapter 2). Between these negative portrayals is 5:7b-8a that, according to pattern, should be expected to give a positive portrayal of Israel taking up arms so as to end the anarchy. Judg. 5:7b presents the arising of Deborah so that what follows in 5:8a should be expected to present the tribes acting positively in response. This expectation is best fulfilled in the emendation of Lindars, even though it has no versional support, because it presents Israel's military not as fighting but as coming forth to fight. This is precisely the theme one should expect if, according to pattern, this bifid form of 5:7b-8a corresponds to the bifid form of 5:12 that analogously presents Deborah being summoned, then Barak being summoned, to take captives. It further stands to reason that an original ‏*אֱזֹל> ‹חֻמֵּשׁ> עָרִים‎, which would have preserved two rare lexemes, may have been 'emended' to a form thought to be in keeping with the hymn's recurrent use of ‏אָז‎ + perf. (cf. 5:11b, 13a, 19a, 22a), use of the root ‏לחם‎ 'to fight, do battle' (though Ni. in 5:19[2x], 20[2x]) and the use of ‏שְׁעָרִים‎ in 5:11b. Indeed, it may have been the supposed similarity of 5:8aβ to 5:11b, where two of the preceding similarities converge, that prompted the word division of the MT.

⁴⁸ *Judg. 5:9aα.* MT: ‏לְבִּי‎. Many modern interpreters repoint the MT to ‏*לִבּוּ‎ (Qal impv m. pl. < ‏לבב‎) 'take heart' and take the following prep. ‏ל‎ as a sign of the vocative (so G. R. Driver, "Problems in Judges Newly Discussed", *ALUOS* 4 [1962–1963], p. 9; followed by the NEB; Craigie, "Further Notes" [1972], pp. 350-51; Globe, "Song of Deborah" [1974], p. 503, n. 26; Soggin, *Judges* [2d edn, 1987], p. 87; and the REB). However, it would be very rare, and is hence rather doubtful, that the form ‏לבִיּוּ‎ should be impv. Moreover, while in Ug. *l* may be (indeed often is) vocative, there are no sure examples of this in BH. The latter fact speaks against other proposed emendations to impv forms, whether to Pi. (denom.) ‏לַבְּבִי‎ (Rudolph, "Textkritische Anmerkungen" [1947], p. 201, comparing Song 4:9 [wrongly cited as 4:1 in Lindars, *Judges 1-5* (1995), p. 242]), to Qal ‏לְכוּ‎ (Burney, *Judges* [2d edn, 1920], pp. 103, 122, following a private suggestion of C. J. Ball; cf. Gray, *Judges* [2d edn, 1986], p. 268) or to Pi. (pausal) ‏לַבָּיוּ‎ (T. F. McDaniel, *Deborah Never Sang: A Philological Study on the Song of Deborah [Judges Chapter V]* [Jerusalem, 1983], ad loc., comparing Arab. *labaya* 'to obey; respond'; cf. C. Rabin, "Judges v, 2 and the 'Ideology' of Deborah's War", *JJS* 6 [1955], pp. 125-34) (see Lindars, *Judges 1-5* [1995], p. 242). The MT as it stands has been interpreted: "My heart is toward the governors ..." by the AV, RV, and JPSV; "My heart goes out to the commanders ..." by the RSV and NRSV; "My heart is with the commanders ..." by Boling (*Judges* [1975], p. 102, cf. p. 110; cf. 5:15b ‖ 5:16b); or "My thoughts turn to the commanders ..." by Lindars (*Judges 1-5* [1995], p. 209).

⁴⁹ *Judg. 5:11b ‖ 5:13.* In Judg. 5, five of its eight strophes (i.e., 5:6-8, 11b-13, 14-18, 19-22, 23-30) are arranged so that a pair of either positive or negative portrayals frame a middle section of (usually) contrasting disposition, whether negative or positive in tone (i.e., 5:6-7a[-], 7b-8a[+], 8b[-]; 5:11b[+], 12[+], 13[+]; 5:14-15a[+], 15b-17[-], 18[+]; 5:19[-], 20-21[+], 22[-]; 5:23[-], 24-27[+], 28-30[-]) (see the discussion in chapter 2). The pervasiveness of this stylistic feature of the hymn raises serious doubt about the judgement that 5:11b represents a scribal gloss based upon 5:13 (contra Budde, *Richter und Samuel* [1890], p. 103; idem, *Richter* [1897], p. 44; Ruben, "Song of Deborah" [1897–98], p. 542; Nowack, *Richter* [1902], p. 48; Burney, *Judges* [2d edn, 1920], p. 130; Gressmann, *Anfänge Israels* [2d edn, 1922], p. 184; O. Grether, *Das Deboralied: Eine metrische Rekonstruktion* [BFCT 43/2, Gütersloh, 1941], ad loc.; Müller, "Aufbau des Deboraliedes" [1966], p. 450 n. 2; Lindars, *Judges 1-5* [1995], pp. 210, 248, 259). Further, corroboration for the authenticity of the strophic parallelism between repetitions of ‏ירד‎ in 5:11b and 5:13 may be found in Ug. (*yrd ‖ yrd*; cf. Fisher, *Ras Shamra Parallels*, vol. 1 [1972], p. 213) and Akk. (*arādu ‖ arādu*; *Ishtar* 86-87) (cf. Craigie, "Parallel Word Pairs" [1977], p. 19 §§11-12).

⁵⁰ *Judg. 5:14aβ.* MT: ‏שָׁרְשָׁם בַּעֲמָלֵק‎ (so the AV, RV, JPSV, and NIV). The OG had: ἐτιμωρήσατο αὐτοὺς ἐν κοιλάδι (< ‏*יְשָׁרְשָׁם בָּעֵמֶק‎), LXX-AI(Aabcx,k),AII(glnw,dptv), AIII(MNyb₂) Arm Sah Eth OLat. Cf. Schreiner, "Textformen" (1961), pp. 190, 191;

E. Tov, "The Textual History of the Song of Deborah in the A Text of the LXX", *VT* 28 (1978), p. 225.

Following the OG, most have understood שרשם to represent a verb: e.g., (1) שָׁם ‹י‹שָׂרוּ "they set out thither" (RSV; Gray, *Judges* [2d edn, 1986], p. 272; NRSV; cf. ‹שָׂרוּ שִׁבְעַם‹ מלכם proposed by M. Rose on comparison with Judg. 1:7; 8:30; 9:2; 12:14 ["'Siebzig Könige' aus Ephraim (Jdc. v 14)", *VT* 26 (1976), pp. 447-52]); (2) מְ‹י‹שָׂרְשׁ‹ס (Po. ptcp m. pl. < שרשׁ 'take root'; fig. 'establish oneself firmly'; cf. Isa. 40:24; Job 5:3) "'si pianta stabilmente' = occupa fortemente la valle, cominciando risolutamente la battaglia vittoriosa" (P. T. Piatti, "Una nuova interpretazione metrica, testuale, esegetica, del Cantico di Dèbora [Giudici 5,2-31]", *Bib* 27 [1946], pp. 180-81); or (3) שָׂרְ‹י‹שׁ‹ס (Qal ptcp. m. pl. < שרשׁ 'take root'; fig. 'establish oneself firmly') "showed a brave front [in the vale]" (NEB; cf. Brockington, *Hebrew Text* [1973], p. 36; "rallied in the vale" REB). If שרשם were verbal, 5:14aαβ would offer a good parallel to מני מכיר ירדו מחקקים in 5:14bαβ. However, the parallelism with 5:14bαβ might support equally well the proposal of Craigie, who, endorsing בָּעֵמֶק שָׂרְשָׁם*, suggested that שרשם might represent (as perhaps also שלשין in Exod. 15:4) Egyptian *srs*: "officers (go down) into the valley" ("Further Notes" [1972], pp. 351-52; so also Lindars, *Judges 1-5* [1995], pp. 252-53).

Following H. Cazelles ("Déborah [Jud. v 14], Amalek et Mâkîr", *VT* 24 [1974], pp. 235-38), J. A. Soggin has taken 'Amalek' to represent the hill country of the Amalekites in Ephraim (Judg. 12:15), an area in which was situated Pirathon (= modern Farata, coordinates 166-177, six miles SW of modern Nablus) ("Amalek und Ephraim, Richter 5,14", *ZDPV* 98 [1982], pp. 58-62; idem, *Judges* [2d edn, 1987], pp. 88-89 [though, because p. 89 erroneously preserves the form of the 1st edn (1981), see the French translation: *Le Livre des Juges* (CAT V b, Geneva, 1987), pp. 82-83]). The presence of Amalekites in central Cisjordan is affirmed in Judg. 6:3, 33; 7:12 (cf. 7:1) as is their presence elsewhere in Judg. 1:16b* (see the note on Judg. 1:16b above) and 3:13. These references may even evidence an attentive interest of the Judges compiler in the dealings and movements of the Amalekites.

With such a prevalence of concern with the Amalekites in Judges possibly giving rise to the MT variant, on the one hand, and the alleged parallelism of מני אפרים שרשם בעמק in 5:14aαβ to מני מכיר ירדו מחקקים in 5:14bαβ and to the use of בעמק in 5:15aγ, on the other, it is difficult to establish with certainty which variant arose secondarily. Indeed, the reasons for rejecting either variant as secondary may have induced E. A. Knauf to want to delete both on the assumption that, whichever came first, it seems to be a conflating gloss the deletion of which would only enhance the metre (cf. 2+2+1 in 5:6b; 2+3 in 5:15b, 27b; "Zum Text von Ri 5,14", *Bib* 64 [1983], pp. 428-29). However, the fact that an emendation to בָּעֵמֶק* is made so attractive by its mention in the immediate context makes it more likely that the OG made the emendation tacitly during translation than that the MT generated here a new reference to Amalek on the basis of the more remote references in Judg. 3:13; 6:3, 33; 7:12 (cf. 7:1); 12:15 and perhaps (if not yet corrupted in the tradition underlying the MT) 1:16b*. Therefore, the MT variant should probably be retained (cf. Coogan, "Song of Deborah" [1978], p. 149, n. 38).

[51] *Judg. 5:15aα.* MT: וְשָׂרַי בְּיִשָּׂשכָר "And my officers in Issachar (were) with Deborah". Most read: וְשָׂרֵי בְּיִשָּׂשכָר "[and] the officers in Issachar" (so LXX-AII[ptv],AIII,B-group, Psht, Tg, Vg; cf. "[and] the princes of Issachar" in the AV; RV; JPSV; RSV; NIV; Boling, *Judges* [1975], p. 112; Coogan, "Song of Deborah" [1978], p. 149, n. 41; NRSV; REB; and Lindars, *Judges 1-5* [1995], pp. 255-56), though a number of alternative emendations have been suggested. Burney proposed: וְשָׂרַיִךְ יִשָּׂשכָר* "And thy princes, Issachar" (cf. *Judges* [2d edn, 1920], p. 136; so the Vg [*principales tui Issachar*]). Schreiner restored the OG of 5:14bδ-15aα as: ἐκεῖθεν ἐν σκήπτρῳ διηγήσεως ἐνισχύοντος Ισσαχαρ ("Textformen" [1961], pp. 192-93), for which the Hebrew *Vorlage*

may be retroverted: ‏*מִשׁ<>ם בשבט ספר <ו><שׂרי <ב><ישׂשׂכר‎. The NEB proposed ‏*וְשָׂרֶב יִשָׂשכָר‎ (‏שׂרב‎ = ‏סרב‎ "to rebel"?) "Issachar joined ... in the uprising" (cf. Brockington, *Hebrew Text* [1973], p. 36). C. Rietzschel reasoned that ‏ושׂרי‎, as ‏וישׁשׂכר‎ and ‏כן ברק‎, was a scribal gloss added to the original form of 5:15a: ‏*בִּיׂשָׂשכָר עַם־דְּבוֹרָה // בָּעֵמֶק שָׁלְחוּ בְּרַגְלָיו‎ ("Zu Jdc 5:14b-15a", *ZAW* 83 [1971], pp. 211-25). The most prudent policy here seems to be to follow the majority of ancient and modern authorities in reading ‏וְשָׂרֵי בְּיִשָׂשכָר‎. On the use of the cstr state before prep. ‏ב‎, cf. 2 Sam. 1:21; Isa. 9:2; GKC, §130a).

[52] *Judg. 5:16b.* Although scholarly doubt about the authenticity of the almost verbatim repetition of 5:15a in 5:16b prompted the NEB to omit the latter half-verse (cf., e.g., Moore, *Judges* [1895], p. 154, n. **; Burney, *Judges* [2d edn, 1920], p. 104; Lindars, *Judges 1-5* [1995], pp. 210, 259), the repetitive style of the poem and the heightened rebuke achieved by the doubled description of Reuben's deliberation over whether to rally with the other tribes tell in favour of retaining 5:16b (so Globe, "Song of Deborah" [1974], p. 504; Boling, *Judges* [1975], pp. 103, 112; Soggin, *Judges* [2d edn, 1987], p. 90).

[53] *Judg. 5:22b.* MT: ‏סוּס מִדַּהֲרוֹת‎. The OG (ἵππων, AI[abc],AII[w,dptv],AIII,B-group[m] Arm Eth OLat Syh) and Vg (*equorum*) suggest that their *Vorlagen* may have had ‏סוּסים<>ם‎, from which the final *mêm* was lost by haplography (cf. the following ‏מדהרות‎ of the MT) (so *BHS*; Gray, *Judges* [2d edn, 1986], pp. 278-79; Lindars, *Judges 1-5* [1995], pp. 211, 271, 292-93). However, many reason that the *mêm* was simply displaced to the following word through mistaken word division (so L. Alonso-Schökel, "Erzählkunst im Buche der Richter", *Bib* 42 [1961], p. 162; G. R. Driver, "Problems in Judges" [1962-63], ad loc.; Boling, *Judges* [1975], p. 113; D. K. Stuart, *Studies in Early Hebrew Meter* [HSM 13, Missoula, Mont., 1976], p. 136 n. 28; Coogan, "Song of Deborah" [1978], p. 150 n. 50; Hauser, "Judges 5" [1980], pp. 32, 34 n. 27).

[54] *Judg. 5:26aα.* MT: ‏תִּשְׁלַחְנָה‎ (Qal pret. 3 f. pl.). More probable is ‏תִּשְׁלְחֶנָה‎ (Qal pret. 3 f. sg + 3 f. sg suff. [resumptive of the *casus pendens* ‏יד‎]) (so Moore, *Judges* [1895], p. 165; BDB, p. 1018a[?]; and reservedly, Burney, *Judges* [2d edn, 1920], p. 153 n. *; Lindars, *Judges 1-5* [1995], p. 278) or, perhaps, ‏*תִּשְׁלַחֶנָּה‎ (Qal emph. 3 f. sg), a preservation of the alleged early Northwest Semitic emphatic form (*pace* GKC, §§ 47k and 58i-l on so-called energic *nûn*; cf. Burney, *Judges* [2d edn, 1920], pp. 152-53 n. *; *BHS* [?]; D. N. Freedman, "Archaic Forms in Early Hebrew Poetry", *ZAW* 72 [1960], p. 102; G. R. Driver, "Problems in Judges" [1962-63], ad loc.; D. A. Robertson, *Linguistic Evidence in Dating Early Hebrew Poetry* [SBLDS 3, Missoula, Mont., 1972], pp. 116-17; F. M. Cross and D. N. Freedman, *Studies in Ancient Yahwistic Poetry* [SBLDS 21, Missoula, Mont., 1975], p. 19 n. r; Boling, *Judges* [1975], p. 114; Coogan, "Song of Deborah" [1978], pp. 150-51, n. 52; Lindars, *Judges 1-5* [1995], pp. 211, 278).

[55] *Judg. 5:30b.* The MT ‏שָׁלָל לְצַוְּארֵי‎ "for the necks of the booty" requires emendation. Three proposals seem tenable. (1) The proposal that final ‏שָׁלָל‎ be emended to ‏שֵׁגָל‎ 'queen, consort' (BDB, p. 993b), which requires that the pl. ‏לְצַוְּארֵי‎ have sg sense (i.e., the pl. of local extension [GKC, §124b]; cf. Gen. 27:16; 45:14), may be justified because: (a) ‏שׁלל‎ may have been mistakenly repeated from its three previous occurrences in the verse; (b) the two previous uses of prep. ‏ל־‎ show persons with whom booty was to be shared so the last could also be expected to do so; (c) not only would it be fitting for Sisera to take spoil for his consort, but, inasmuch as the verse portrays the words of the noble ladies, it also portrays their self-interest (so Bertheau, *Richter und Ruth* [1845], p. 101; Wellhausen, *Composition* [2d edn, 1889], p. 220; *BHS*). (2) Of two alternative proposals, that ‏לְצַוְּארֵי‎ be emended to either ‏לְצַוְּארוֹ‎ ("for his [Sisera's] neck") or ‏לְצַוְּארָיו‎ ("for their necks"), the former finds corroboration from LXX-AI,AII (περὶ τράχηλον αὐτοῦ) and LXX-AIII,B-group (τῷ τραχήλῳ αὐτοῦ)—in which case ‏שָׁלָל‎ would be in apposition to ‏רִקְמָה צֶבַע‎ ‏רִקְמָתָיִם‎: "embroidery, doubly embroidered dyed cloth for his neck as booty" (Keil,

Richter [1863], ET: *Judges* [1868], repr. edn, vol. 2, pp. 323, 325; Lindars, *Judges 1–5* [1995], pp. 212, 284-85, 295-96). (3) The NEB and REB ("to grace the victor's neck") proposed to emend only the vocalization from שָׁלָל to *שֹׁלֵל* "(the) spoiler", which likewise requires that לְצַוְּארֵי be a pl. of local extension (GKC, §124*b*; Brockington, *Hebrew Text* [1973], p. 36; Boling, *Judges* [1975], pp. 105, 115). The latter proposal seems the more attractive, since it requires no emendation to the consonantal text and makes good sense.

⁵⁶ *Judg. 6:7-10.* Judg. 6:7-10 is absent from the fragment 4QJdgᵃ, which otherwise presents the section of Judg. 6:3-13 (see F. M. Cross's written communication cited by Boling, *Judges* [1975], p. 40; J. Trebolle Barrera, "Textual Variants in 4QJudgᵃ and the Textual and Editorial History of the Book of Judges", *RevQ* 14 [1989], pp. 229-45; Tov, *Textual Criticism* [1992], pp. 344-45). This lacuna may be taken to accord with the view of both Moore and Burney, advanced decades before the Qumran discoveries, that these verses comprise a later addition (Moore, *Judges* [1895], pp. 177, 181; Burney, *Judges* [2d edn, 1920], pp. xli-l, 177). For Judg. 6:7-10, Moore inferred a later hand within the E (Elohist) tradition. Thereafter, Burney posited that the addition was from a pre-deuteronomic redactor of the late Ephraimitic school (E², i.e., second Elohist). It is unlikely, however, that the difficulty presented by the omission of 6:7-10 from 4QJdgᵃ reflects more than just a scribal omission, since even the Greek version, with which 4QJdgᵃ otherwise conforms, retains the verses in question except for the omission of the first part of v. 7. Because the omission reflected in the Qumran fragment does not appear to have arisen by *homoeoarcton*, it may attest either a form of Judges that circulated without 6:7-10 or, perhaps, one copyist's discomfort with and deliberate deletion of this editorial stratum of the book.

⁵⁷ *Judg. 6:35aα.* After בְּכָל־, a Cairo geniza MS has the plus הר אפרים ו, probably inserted to rebut Ephraim's accusation in 8:1 that Gideon had failed to summon them—though Gideon offers no such disclaimer. The insertion may have arisen in the Gideon story by analogy from the Jephthah story, where, in 12:1-3, Jephthah rebuts Ephraim's analogous accusation with the disclaimer that he had indeed summoned Ephraim—though his disclaimer remains unsubstantiated in the narrative.

⁵⁸ *Judg. 7:5bδ.* The main difficulty in this verse is the divergence between the ellipsis of the apodosis in MT Judg. 7:5bδ (Tg) and the various ways in which the ancient versions (OG, Psht, Vg) supplied the apodosis. However, it seems clear from the variation among renderings of the OG (μεταστήσεις αὐτὸν καθ' ἑαυτόν "you shall separate him by himself"), Psht ('*qymyhy 'khd*' "have him stand alone") and Vg (*in altera parte erunt* "shall be on the other part") that each was supplying the ellipsis in translation. Therefore, their Hebrew *Vorlagen* probably attested the same ellipsis as that of the MT and Tg (so AV; RV; RSV; NIV; contra *BHS*; NEB [cf. Brockington, *Hebrew Text* (1973), p. 37]; and REB). The NRSV supplies the ellipsis in translation without emending the Hebrew text.

⁵⁹ *Judg. 7:6aβ.* The main problem in this verse is the variance in Judg. 7:6a in describing those who were lapping either בידם אל־פיהם "with their hand to their mouth" (MT; so Tg, Psht, Vg) or *בלשונם* "with their tongue" (OG: ἐν τῇ γλώσσῃ αὐτῶν). A solution to the question of the means by which Gideon's selected few lapped (7:6a) is difficult to substantiate. Boling's "reconstructed text" of 7:5bδ-6a is endorsed by Soggin and Webb (Boling, *Judges* [1975], pp. 143, 145; Soggin, *Judges* [2d edn, 1987], p. 137; Webb, *Judges* [1987], p. 252 n. 89):

7:5bδ*	תציג אותו לבד	בידם אל־פיהם	וכל אשר־יכרע על־ברכיו לשתות מים
7:6a*	שלש מאות איש	בלשונם	ויהי מספר המלקקים

Yet, this reconstruction seems both conflated and improbable. First, for the reasons given in the preceding note, it is doubtful that *תציג אותו לבד* was present in 7:5bδ* in the

Hebrew *Vorlagen* of the OG, Psht and Vg. Second, Boling's citation of מים* in 7:5bδ* is attested only in LXX MS y and is thus hardly original (probably having been conflated from 7:6bβ). Third, his allegation that בידם אל־פיהם originally appeared after 7:5bδ, rather than in 7:6aβ, is neither supported by MS evidence nor is it feasible since its pl. suffixation would not suit the context of 7:5bδ as well as that of 7:6aβ. Thus, while Boling appealed to the potential for "vertical displacement", then "haplography" because of *homoeoteleuton*, it is improbable that the present variance between the MT and OG arose entirely by accident.

Seeking to establish logical congruity in the verse, the NEB has transposed בידם אל־פיהם from 7:6aβ to follow 7:6b. BHS suggested the same but also recommended replacing בידם אל־פיהם in 7:6aβ with בלשונם* from the OG. Both emendations offer a reading that is significantly more coherent than that of the MT, though not more than that of the OG. Both lack MS support for the transposition of בידם אל־פיהם to the end of 7:6.

An appropriate question to pose is: Which versional tradition of 7:6a is most likely to have resulted from deliberate alteration? A scribe in the MT tradition may have deliberately altered an original text, attested by the OG, to minimize a possibly undignified characterization of Gideon's few as lapping "with their tongue"—thus explaining that they did so "with their hand to their mouth", though strangely retaining the seemingly more explicitly negative characterization in 7:5bβ: כל אשר־ילק בלשונו מן־המים כאשר ילק הכלב. Contrariwise, a scribe in the OG tradition may have altered an original form, attested by the MT and its congeners, so as to remove the incompatibility thought to exist in the MT that he who laps "with his tongue from the water as a dog laps" (7:5bβ) cannot refer also to those who lap "with their hand to their mouth" (7:6aβ).

Both versions attest an opposition between the few, who did *not kneel* but who *lapped as a dog laps*, and the many, who *did kneel* in order *to drink* (i.e., not to lap). How do these versions differ in their conception of how Gideon's few were lapping? In the MT, *lapping as a dog laps* refers to the use of the tongue to convey water from the hand to the mouth, and *not kneeling* may imply alternatively standing, lying down or crouching upright on two feet. The MT may thus attest a positive basis for selecting the few as those who would not kneel. The problem with the MT, however, is that it offers no reason as to why those who preferred to convey the water to their mouths with their hands in order to lap like a dog should not also be able to kneel. In the OG, *lapping as a dog laps* refers to the use of the tongue to convey water not from the hand but directly from the spring to the mouth, and *not kneeling* may imply either lying down or being on 'all fours' (as a dog). The OG may thus attest a negative basis for selecting the few (so Boling, *Judges* [1975], p. 146), but not necessarily. The portrayal of the three hundred in the OG could be interpreted positively if they were thus seen not to drink with potentially unclean hands (cf. Deut. 23:10-15; Lev. 15:7, 11) or to release their weapons in order to drink using their hands. In any case, there seems to be no way to reconcile the data with the assertion of L. R. Klein that, "careful reading of the text suggests a two-step process of selection" in which 7:5 distinguishes those who kneel from those who do not kneel but lap directly, whereas 7:6 distinguishes kneelers who lap out of their hands from kneelers who bow to drink directly (*The Triumph of Irony in the Book of Judges* [JSOTS 68, BLS 14, Sheffield, 1988], pp. 56-57).

The MT variant בידם אל־פיהם is probably best viewed as a scribal insertion, perhaps originally a marginal gloss intended to explain how those who knelt were able to drink. Then, a later scribe may have inserted this gloss into the text at its present location. The OG derivation from בלשונם* may attest the original reading, in which case the MT gloss came to replace it, or it may reflect an inner-Greek conflation. If בלשונם* were original, however, it may have been that which motivated a proto-MT glossator to offer a corresponding identification of the body part that the kneelers used to convey water to their mouths.

[60] *Judg. 7:13bβ*. Kethib: צְלוּל. Qere: צְלִיל (so one Cairo Geniza MS and many Hebrew MSS).

[61] *Judg. 7:21b*. Kethib: וַיָּנִיסוּ (Hi. pret. 3 m. pl.). Qere: וַיָּנוּסוּ (Qal pret. 3 m. pl.; so the versions; *BHS*).

[62] *Judg. 8:16bα*. MT: וַיֹּדַע "and he caused to know/taught; disciplined" (so Qimḥi, the AV, RV, RSV, NEB, NIV and REB)] *וַיָּדָשׁ "and he threshed/scourged/flailed" (cf. 8:7b; so the OG; Psht; Vg; *BHS*; Boling, *Judges* [1975], pp. 154, 157; Soggin, *Judges* [2d edn, 1987], pp. 153, 155; and the NRSV). For philological and textual alternatives to ידע in MT Judg. 8:16, see D. W. Thomas, "The Root ידע in Hebrew", *JTS* 35 (1934), pp. 298-306; idem, "Some Rabbinic Evidence for a Hebrew Root yd^c = wd^c", *JQR* NS 37 (1946-1947), pp. 177-78; E. J. Liebreich, "Observations on 'Some Rabbinic Evidence for a Hebrew Root yd^c = wd^c' (*JQR* XXXVII, 177-8)", *JQR* NS 37 (1946-1947), pp. 337-79; J. Reider, "Etymological Studies: ידע or ירע and רעע", *JBL* 66 (1947), pp. 315-17; J. Barr, *Comparative Philology and the Text of the Old Testament* (Oxford, 1968), repr. edn (London, 1983), pp.19-20, 328 no. 151; J. A. Emerton, "A Consideration of Some Alleged Meanings of yd^c in Hebrew", *JSS* 15 (1970), pp. 145-80; W. Johnstone, "yd^c II, 'Be Humbled, Humiliated'?", *VT* 41 (1991), pp. 49-62.

On the text of Judg. 8:16, see J. Kennedy, *An Aid to the Textual Amendment of the Old Testament* (Edinburgh, 1928), p. 109; B. Lindars, "Some Septuagint Readings in Judges", *JTS* NS 22 (1971), pp. 10-14; Barthélemy, *Critique textuelle*, vol. 1 (1982), p. 97; E. Tov, "Did the Septuagint Translators Always Understand Their Hebrew Text?", in *De Septuaginta: Studies in Honour of John William Wevers on His Sixty-fifth Birthday* (A. Pietersma and C. Cox [eds.], Mississauga, Ontario, 1984), p. 55.

[63] *Judg. 9:8b*. Kethib: מְלוּכָה. Qere: מָלְכָה (so many Hebrew MSS; cf. Judg. 9:12b). See Tov, *Textual Criticism* (1992), pp. 259-60.

[64] *Judg. 9:12b*. Kethib: מְלוּכִי. Qere: מָלְכִי (so many Hebrew MSS; cf. Judg. 9:8b).

[65] *Judg. 9:17bα*. MT: מִנֶּגֶד. Emend to מִגִּדֹו (supposing that it suffered haplography of final ו; so *BHS*).

[66] *Judg. 9:31a*. MT: בְּתָרְמָה. Emend to בָּארוּמָה or בָּארְמָה (cf. Judg. 9:41; *BHS*).

[67] *Judg. 9:37aγ*. MT: יוֹרְדִים. LXX: καταβαίνων κατὰ θάλασσαν < *יוֹרֵד יָם. H. Eshel and Z. Erlich argued that טבור הארץ should be identified with Ras e-Tagur on the SW corridor of Jebel Kabir and that the LXX reading is preferable to that of the MT on geographical and contextual grounds ("Abimelech's First Battle with the Lords of Shechem and the Question of the Navel of the Land", *Tarbiz* 58 [1988-1989], pp. 111-16 [Hebrew]; cf. BDB, p. 411a, 9).

[68] *Judg. 10:10bβ*. Codex L: וְכִי] כִּי (so several Hebrew MSS, Psht, Vg, LXX).

[69] *Judg. 10:11bα*. MT: וּמִן־הָאֱמֹרִי. All the versions use the pl.: *וּמִן־הָאֱמֹרִים (so Tg [ומן האמוראי]), *וְהָאֱמֹרִים (so OG [οἱ Ἀμορραῖοι] and Vg) or *וּמוֹאָבִים (so Psht [wmw'by']), probably reflecting only a translator's preference for homogeneity with other pl. forms in the vicinity (e.g., note the pl. renderings of consonantal מצרים in the Tg, Psht, Vg and OG).

[70] *Judg. 10:11bβ^i*. After Ἀμμὼν, the OG addition of καὶ Μωὰβ (LXX-AI[except k],AII[except dptv],AIII,B-group[ira₂] Arm Eth OLat Syh[sub ÷]) probably reflects an accretion to the Hebrew tradition underlying the OG. Cf. Psht (wmw'by' wbny 'mwn), which, substituting 'Moabites' for 'Amorite(s)', preserves the sevenfold enumeration.

[71] *Judg. 10:11bβ^ii*. If the prepositions מִן of the MT (Tg, LXX B-group) are original, the verb has either been suppressed by anacoluthon or fallen out by haplography (cf. GKC, §167b). Those who emend a supposed haplography in the MT insert *הוֹשַׁעְתִּי אֶתְכֶם

(cf. 10:12b) (so *BHS*, following Rudolph, "Textkritische Anmerkungen" [1947], p. 204; and, tacitly, the AV, RV, RSV and NRSV), yet this solution seem dubious since these verbs elsewhere always take מְיַד (cf. Moore, *Judges* [1895], p. 282). Perhaps because of this incongruity, the NEB, NIV, REB and Soggin (*Judges* [2d edn, 1987], p. 202) followed the OG (LXX-AI,AII,AIII), Psht and Vg, which attest in 10:11b neither a verb nor the repeated use of preposition מִן (cf. Billen, "Hexaplaric Element" [1942], p. 13). Yet it is difficult to see why the MT, if secondary, should have inserted מִן without including an appropriate verb. Therefore, perhaps the easiest solution is to regard anacoluthon as accounting also for the diminution of מְיַד to simple מִן in the absence of the verb (so, apparently, Moore, *Judges* [1895], p. 278).

⁷² *Judg. 10:12aα.* MT: וּמָעוֹן (so Moore, *Judges* [1895], pp. 280, 282; the RSV; NIV; and NRSV)] וּמִדְיָן*, OG (καὶ Μιδιαμ) (so *BHS*; NEB; REB; Soggin, *Judges* [2d edn, 1987], p. 202). The emendation וּמוֹאָב* is without warrant (contra J. N. M. Wijngaards, *The Dramatization of Salvific History in the Deuteronomic Schools* [P. A. H. de Boer (ed.), *OTS* XVI, Leiden, 1969], p. 58).

⁷³ *Judg. 11:20aα.* MT: וְלֹא־הֶאֱמִין [וַיְמָאֵן*, so Num. 20:21 (cf. OG: καὶ οὐκ ἠθέλησεν); D. Marcus, *Jephthah and His Vow* (Lubbock, Tex., 1986), p. 61 n. 22; J. Van Seters, "The Conquest of Sihon's Kingdom: A Literary Examination", *JBL* 91 (1972), p. 185 : וְלֹא אָבָה*, OG (καὶ οὐκ ἠθέλησεν), cf. Judg. 11:17aγ : וְלֹא אָבָה וַיְמָאֵן*, *BHS*. Cf. Num. 21:23, וְלֹא־נָתַן.

⁷⁴ *Judg. 11:24a.* Because of a perceived double accusative (of which the 2 m. sg suff. is one dir. obj.), the RV translated here with a different sense from "dispossessed", used for the same verbal form in 11:24b, namely: "giveth thee to possess" (i.e., Moore's first alternative, *Judges* [1895], p. 295; cf. the NEB and NIV: "gives you"). But because of a lack of concord between this sense and that of the same verbal form in 11:24b, *BHS* (R. Meyer) cited the OG: κατεκληρονόμησέν σοι "has bequeathed to you", apparently implying that it may attest יוֹרִישׁ לָךְ* with indir. obj. marked by prep. -לְ. Alternatively, *BHS* restated the proposal of Moore that -ךָ be deleted as a dittography (comparing the same verb in 11:24).

The MT may stand, however, since the OG and the consensus of modern Hebraists agree that the pron. suff. attached directly to the verb may function as an indir. obj., equivalent in sense to prep. -לְ + pron. suff. (e.g., Zech. 7:5; Jer. 31:3; cf. E. König, *Historisch-kritisches Lehrgebäude der hebräischen Sprache* [2 vols., Leipzig, 1881, 1897], II/2, Syntax, §21; GKC, §117x; C. Brockelmann, *Hebräische Syntax* [Neukirchen, 1956], §97a; J. A. Emerton, "Notes on Two Proposed Emendations in the Book of Judges [11:24 and 16:28]", *ZAW* 85 [1973], p. 221).

⁷⁵ *Judg. 11:37bβ.* MT: + וְיָרַדְתִּי. On the ground that MT ירדתי is difficult logically (elsewhere only YHWH goes down upon the mountains; cf. BDB, p. 433a 2.; contra Qimḥi), many emend to וְרַדְתִּי* (< רוד 'to wander, roam'; cf. Jer. 2:31); cf. Tg (ואתנגיד "and wander [lit. and extend myself]"); Psht (*ʾhlk* "walk about"); Vg (*circumeam*); W. R. Smith in J. S. Black, *The Book of Judges* (SCBS, Cambridge, 1892); BDB, pp. 433a 1.g, 923b; Kittel, *Richter* (1909); G. A. Cooke, *Judges and Ruth* (Cambridge Bible, Cambridge, 1913), ad loc.; Burney, *Judges* (2d edn, 1920), p. 323. Boling regards ירדתי as a by-form of the root רוד (*Judges* [1975], p. 209). Cf. P. Trible, "The Daughter of Jephthah: An Inhuman Sacrifice", in *Texts of Terror: Literary and Feminist Readings of Biblical Narratives* (OBT 13, Philadelphia, 1984), pp. 103-4, 114 n. 44. However, on the ground that MT ירדתי is difficult also syntactically (BH would not normally tolerate a cons. perf. [וירדתי] between an impv [הרפה] and coh. [ואלכה], on the one hand, and another coh. [ואבכה], on the other), ירדתי should probably be omitted as a scribal dittography and then corruption from the MT Kethib ורעיתי (so M. L. Margolis, "A Passage in Ecclesiasticus and Judg. 11,37", *ZAW* 21 [1901], pp. 271-72; H. M. Orlinsky,

"Critical Notes on Gen 39:14-17; Jud 11:37: II. The Corrupt Character and Origin of wᵉiāraḍtî in Jud 11:37", *JBL* 61 [1942], pp. 92-97; cf. Marcus, *Jephthah* [1986], p. 30). Nor is the verb repeated in the sequel in 11:38.

[76] *Judg. 11:37bδ.* The Kethib: יְוַרְעִיתִי* is probably a corruption (though cf. Song 1:9). The Qere: וְרֵעוֹתַי is preferable (cf. 11:38b; Orlinsky, "Critical Notes" [1942], p. 96 n. 21).

[77] *Judg. 12:2aγ.* The OG (LXX-AI[except k],AII,AIII,B-group[z(txt)] Arm Sah OLat Syh) translates: καὶ οἱ υἱοὶ Ἀμμὼν ἐταπείνουν με (עִנּוּנִי*) σφόδρα from which some have inferred that the MT lost an original עָנְוִי (or perhaps עֲנוֹנוּ) by haplography after עַמּוֹן (cf. Moore, *Judges* [1895], pp. 306-7, 308; Budde, *Richter* [1897], p. 89; *BHS*). In all probability, however, the OG was simply paraphrasing the Hebrew idiom. Most EVV follow the MT—the AV and RV: "I and my people were at great strife with the children of Ammon"; RSV: "I and my people had a great feud with the Ammonites" (so NEB ["had a feud"], REB ["grave feud"]); NIV: "I and my people were engaged in a great struggle with the Ammonites" (RSV ["were engaged in conflict"]).

[78] *Judg. 12:3aα.* MT: אֶינֶךָ (so Tg: לֵיתָךְ). The OG (LXX-AI,AII,AIII,B-group[except B] Arm Sah[vid] Eth[vid] Syh) translates the obj. clause as: ὅτι οὐκ ἦν ὁ σώζων (כִּי-אֵין*) מוֹשִׁיעַ; so J. F. A. Sawyer, "What Was a mošiaʿ?", *VT* 15 [1965], p. 476 n. 1; *BHS*); the OLat omits 12:3aα. The Psht translates as the OG: dlyt mn dprq ly. The Vg does not translate the obj. clause (*quod cernens posui in manibus meis animam meam*). The latter versions are probably only translators' options for the reading preserved in the MT. Most EVV follow the MT (so the AV, RV, RSV, NEB, NIV, NRSV and REB).

[79] *Judg. 12:4b.* MT: + בתוך מנשה (after אפרים בתוך גלעד אתם אפרים פליטי אמרו כי) (Tg Psht Vg σ′). The text of the OG reflected in the LXX-AII family has suffered from haplography in some of its members, but all its members attest the minus of 12:4bβ-δ (so LXX-AII[glo,ptv],Holm–Pars,108,128 OLat). Other LXX codices omit all of 12:4b (LXX-AI[a,k],AII[n,d],Holm–Pars,64 Arm[sub ẋ] Syh[sub ẋ])—this haplography of 12:4bα from the OG probably resulting from *homoeoteleuton* between the first and second uses of Ἐφράιμ. LXX MS w omits 12:4bδ-5aⁱ—also a haplography from the OG probably resulting from *homoeoteleuton* between the second ἄνδρες Γαλαὰδ of 12:4 and the first ἄνδρες Γαλαὰδ of 12:5.

Had the OG minus been original, a deliberate insertion of the plus was hardly needed to make sense of an otherwise semantically difficult or theologically offensive text. The fact that the polysemic wordplay in the repetition of פליטי אפרים between 12:4b and 12:5b commends the plus as beneficial is not determinative of its originality. Yet, even though כי אמרו פליטי אפרים (12:4bβ) finds a similar clause in 12:5b, the creation of 12:4b as a whole must have been deliberate, if it is not entirely original. If בתוך מנשה had entered the tradition underlying the MT and its congeners as a scribal correction for a seemingly geographically incorrect בתוך אפרים, the OG minus may be explained as a haplography caused by *homoeoteleuton/homoeoarcton* between אפרים ויכו (12:4a/4bα) and אפרים* <> וילכד (12:4bδ*/5a). Burney alluded to a rhetorical motivation for 12:4b even as he dismissed it: "It is not clear how the Gileʿadites could ... be called 'fugitives of Ephraim,' and yet be charged with living 'in the midst of Ephraim'; nor, again, is this latter expression, which seems to suggest that the Ephraimites owned or at any rate claimed territory in Gileʿad east of Jordan, susceptible of any explanation" (*Judges* [2d edn, 1920], p. 327). However, if the statement is regarded not as an accusation (a view which may have motivated the correcting insertion of בתוך מנשה) but as a threat, it would be in character for Ephraim (cf. 12:1bγδ) and might find motivation in F. Willesen's apt assessment:

> The matter of the dispute was no doubt the trade route through Transjordania. The
> Ephraimites would not look on passively while the Gileadites gained complete control of a

considerable part of the route by defeating the Ammonites. ... Were the Ammonites to be debarred the Ephraimites thought it wiser to lend a hand (v. 1) making themselves the successors. Or perhaps the Ephraimites took the opportunity of the Gileadite–Ammonite contest for an attempt to establish a supremacy on the other side of the Jordan like that of their Manassite kinstribe. The ideological justification of such an undertaking might be the import of v. 4b ["The אפרתי of the Shibboleth Incident", *VT* 8 (1958), p. 98 n. 1].

Those who regard the MT form of 12:4b as original include: the AV; RV; RSV; Willesen, "Shibboleth Incident" (1958), p. 98 n. 1; the NIV; Boling, *Judges* (1975), pp. 211, 221; Barthélemy, *Critique textuelle*, vol. 1 (1982), pp. 104-5; and the NRSV. Those who view 12:4bβ-δ as a later addition include: Moore, *Judges* (1895), p. 308; Burney, *Judges* (2d edn, 1920), p. 327; Billen, "Hexaplaric Element" (1942), p. 15; idem, "Old Latin" (1942), p. 144; W. Richter, "Die Überlieferungen um Jephtah, Ri 10,17–12,6", *Bib* 47 (1966), p. 519; Soggin, *Judges* (2d edn, 1987), p. 221; Trebolle Barrera, "Textual Variants" (1989), pp. 240-41; the NEB; and REB. Cf. M. Harel, "Gilead within Ephraim within Manasseh," in *Eretz Shomron: The Thirtieth Archaeological Convention September 1972* (J. Aviram [ed.], Jerusalem, 1973), pp. 47-51 [Hebrew].

[80] *Judg. 12:6aβ.* MT: יָכִין לְדַבֵּר. The finite verb in ולא יכין לדבר כן is vocalized by most MT MSS: יָכִין (Hi. impf 3 m. sg < כון), which, as a transitive verb, seems difficult to explain before an inf. (*pace* BDB, p. 466b 3. '*give attention*'). Several Hebrew MSS attest יָבִין (Qal impf 3 m. sg < בין) 'would understand' (cf. BDB, p. 106b 2.d.). As an alternative to the emendation יִכּוֹל* 'would be able' (cf. Moore, *Judges* [1895], p. 309), which presupposes a confusion of ל and נ (cf. אבל\ן, 1 Sam. 6:18; ויתנ\ול, 2 Sam. 18:9), G. R. Driver proposed יִכּוֹן* (Ni. impf 3 m. sg < כון) 'would be prepared/ready', comparing Syr. m°kānâ 'created, apt' and Syr. m°kayan in *hau mâ m°kayan kyânhôn l°me°bad* "which their nature was not made/fitted to do" ("Mistranslations in the Old Testament", *WO* 1 [1947–1952], p. 31). However, if the MT variant were transitive so that לדבר was revocalized: ולא יָכִין לַדָּבָר כן* "and would not form the word correctly", using –ל to indicate the obj. (GKC, §117n; though elsewhere attested only for בין, cf. Deut. 32:29; Pss. 73:17; 139:2; Job 9:11), then the MT may stand.

[81] *Judg. 12:7bγ.* MT: בְּעָרֵי גִלְעָד "in the cities of Gilead" (so the Tg; contra "in *one of* the cities of Gilead" of the AV, RV and JPSV) is unlikely to have been the original text, unless one accepts the notion that Jephthah was buried in more than one city (so *Bereshit Rabbah* 60:3). The Vg *in civitate sua Galaad* attests בְּעִירוֹ גלעד*, similar though equally unlikely since Gilead (in apposition) was not a city. The OG ἐν τῇ πόλει αὐτοῦ ἐν Σεφε Γαλαάδ (cf. Josephus, *Ant.* V.vii.12 §270: ἐν τῇ αὐτοῦ πατρίδι Σεβεη· τῆς Γαλαδηνῆς δ'ἐστὶν αὕτη) attests a Hebrew *Vorlage* with בְּעִירוֹ בַמ[צפה גלעד* and thus partly preserves the most sensible variant—מ perhaps having fallen out of במצפה* by haplography (caused by confusion of ב and מ) in the Hebrew *Vorlage* of the OG. Moore suggested that the original ended with only בעירו and that conflation with the structure of 12:15b caused גלעד (so the MT, Tg and Vg; cf. הגלעדי in 12:7bβ) or במצפה גלעד (so the Hebrew *Vorlage* of the OG; cf. 11:29) to be imported (*Judges* [1895], p. 310). The RSV "in his city in Gilead" (so the NEB ["his own city"], NRSV ["his town"] and REB ["his own town"]), follows not the OG but a recension that omitted Σεφε (i.e., LXX-AI[k],AII[n],B-group[B,irua₂,m]; whereas LXX-AI[Aabcx],AIII[MNyb₂,h],B-group[sz,jq] omit ἐν Σεφε). However, the attestation of גלעד in all versions, even though its preservation makes for difficulty, and the preservation of גלעד בַמ[צפה* in the OG (LXX-AII[ἐν Σεφε Γαλαάδ, dptv : ἐν Σεφ Γαλαάδ, glw : Σεφε Γαλαάδ, Holm-Pars,84 : εἰς ἐφ'Γαλαάδ, o]) despite its apparent corruption in the Hebrew *Vorlage* of the OG, speaks rather for the originality of בַמ[צפה גלעד*. At least there seems to be no reason to suppose that the alleged conflation of 12:4b with 11:29 was an inner-Greek development,

since מצפה גלעד of 11:29 is rendered τὴν σκοπιὰν Γαλαὰδ in the LXX. Cf. Barthélemy, *Critique textuelle*, vol. 1 (1982), p. 106; Webb, *Judges* (1987), pp. 73, 230 n. 74.

[82] *Judg. 13:12aβ.* L: דְּבָרֶיךָ. Many Hebrew MSS, the Psht, Vg and LXX support the sg דְּבָרְךָ (so Moore, *Judges* [1895], p. 321; *BHS*; Soggin, *Judges* [2d edn, 1987], p. 234). Cf. the note on Judg. 13:17b.

[83] *Judg. 13:17b.* Kethib: דְּבָרֶיךָ; Qere: דְּבָרְךָ (also many oriental Hebrew MSS, the Psht and LXX). Those who support the sg דבר include: Moore, *Judges* [1895], p. 321; *BHS*; Soggin, *Judges* [2d edn, 1987], p. 234. Cf. the note on Judg. 13:12a.

[84] *Judg. 13:19bα.* MT: וּמַפְלִא (לעשׂות) (so the Tg, which here and elsewhere renders BH הפליא by פרשׁ [Pael or Aphel]; LXX-B Sah). Better is the emendation, הַמַּפְלִיא (לעשׂות) "the one who (works) wondrously" (cf. Isa. 28:29), from LXX-AI,AII, Vg (so Moore, *Judges* [1895], pp. 322, 324-25). On a proposed restoration of the alleged haplography of the divine name from the MT and LXX-B-group, cf. Boling, *Judges* (1975), p. 222; Webb, *Judges* (1987), p. 166.

[85] *Judg. 14:5a.* MT: + ואביו ואמו (so the Tg, Psht, Vg and LXX). Because of the difficulty of explaining how Samson's parents could remain unaware that he had killed a lion (14:6) if they had been accompanying him (14:5a), some scholars omit ואביו ואמו as an early scribal interpolation (so Moore, *Judges* [1895], pp. 329-30; Burney, *Judges* [2d edn, 1920], pp. 354, 357; *BHS*; Soggin, *Judges* [2d edn, 1987], pp. 239-40). The insertion may have been prompted by any of three considerations: (1) the preceding request of Samson that his parents (especially his father) contract the marriage (14:1-3; cf. 14:10a); (2) the following statement that Samson did not report his killing of the lion to his parents, who were therefore thought to have been present (14:6b); and (3), among those who assume that אביהו in 14:10a is also an interpolation (so Moore, *Judges* [1895], p. 329; Burney, *Judges* [2d edn, 1920], p. 360; Soggin, *Judges* [2d edn, 1987], p. 241), the difficulty that a later scribe may have had with the notion that Samson contracted his own marriage in disregard of custom and parental authority. It is certainly conceivable that the following contested but graphically similar ויבא could have induced the insertion of ואביו ואמו as a gloss. See the following note.

[86] *Judg. 14:5bα.* MT: ויבא (so the Tg, Psht and Vg). LXX: καὶ ἐξέκλινεν (usually < *ויסר, cf. 14:8; never < *ויבא unless here), OG (A[-λειν]bx,k gln[o]w,dptv h fz[mg],m[o]q Eth OLat Syh)] καὶ ἐξέκλιναν (= *ויסרו), ac MNyb₂ : καὶ ἦλθεν (= *ויבא), Besz[txt],i,j : καὶ ἦλθον (= *ויבאו), rua₂ Sah). Some scholars emend to the sg ויבא (so Moore, *Judges* [1895], pp. 330, 333; Burney, *Judges* [2d edn, 1920], p. 354; *BHS*; Soggin, *Judges* [2d edn, 1987], pp. 239-40). Boling recommended restoring both verbs that underlie the LXX recensions: *ויסר ויבא (*Judges* [1975], p. 230), which restoration would also remove the need to omit as spurious the preceding ואביו ואמו. The same end could not be served by restoring *ויסר alone, however, since this verb is not suitably followed by עד. On the other hand, it may have been the OG translator who tacitly emended *ויבא in translation so as to alleviate the problem of Samson being accompanied by his parents. See the preceding note.

[87] *Judg. 14:15aα.* MT: הַשְּׁבִיעִי (so the Tg, Vg, AV and RV). The OG (τῇ τετάρτῃ) and Psht read הרביעי (RSV, NEB, NIV, NRSV, REB), which better suits the chronological sequence of the narrative (cf. 14:17 and the analogous 3+1 sequence in 16:6-21). The analogy may raise doubts about the validity of Moore's proposal that the original form of the gloss underlying the MT was שׁ<ל>שׁת ימים: ויהי ביום השׁביעי, describing a 6+1 sequence, of which only the last word now remains (*Judges* [1895], p. 337).

[88] *Judg. 15:5b.* MT: זית. Since זית is not necessarily collective, it was thought to be a gen. of attribute modifying כרם ('olive groves'; cf. B. *Berakot* 35a; Qimḥi; Ralbag; Keil, *Richter* [1863], ET: *Judges* [1868], repr. edn, vol. 2, p. 414; 'oliveyards', RV; 'olive

orchards', RSV, TEV). However, since קמה and כרם are generic sg forms, זית should perhaps also be prefaced with וְעֵד־ (so the Tg; Moore, *Judges* [1895], p. 343; and *BHS*) or at least *waw* conj. (so the Vg, OG; alternatively, Moore, *Judges* [1895], p. 343; the NASB; NEB; NIV; NRSV; and REB). Cf. BDB, pp. 268b 1, 501b; and לכרמך <ו>לזיתך, *Exod. 23:11.

[89] *Judg. 15:6bβ*. L: ואת־אביה (so the Tg, Vg, RV, RSV, NASB, NEB, NIV, REB). Many Hebrew MSS, some versions and several scholars read ואת־בית אביה* (cf. 14:15aδ; so the OG; Psht; *BHS*; NAB; TEV; Moore, *Judges* [1895], pp. 342, 343; Simpson, *Composition* [1957], pp. 59, 116; P. R. Ackroyd, "[Review:] C. A. Simpson, *Composition of the Book of Judges*", *JTS* NS 10 [1959], p. 104).

[90] *Judg. 16:2aα*. MT: −. The OG adds καὶ ἀπηγγέλη (< וַיֻּגַּד* [so Moore, *Judges* (1895), pp. 348, 350; Burney, *Judges* (2d edn, 1920), p. 376; *BHS*; the NEB (according to Brockington, *Hebrew Text* [1973], p. 38); Boling, *Judges* (1975), pp. 245, 248; Soggin, *Judges* (2d edn, 1987), p. 253; the NRSV] or וַיִּוָּדַע* [so, alternatively, *BHS*; 'heard', REB]). All the versions (the Tg, Psht, Vg and LXX) attest a verb, which may have been supplied in translation. However, since a deliberate ellipsis seems unnatural here, the haplography should probably be restored.

[91] *Judg. 16:13c-14a**. The haplography of Judg. 16:13c-14a* from the MT (AV, RV) was probably caused by *homoeoteleuton/homoeoarcton*. It is here restored by comparison with a retroversion from the OG: καὶ ἐγκρούσῃς ἐν τῷ πασσάλῳ εἰς τὸν τοῖχον καὶ ἐϕυϕάνῃς ὡς ἐπὶ πῆχυν καὶ ἀσθενήσω καὶ ἔσομαι ὡς εἷς τῶν ἀνθρώπων. καὶ ἐκοίμισεν αὐτὸν Δαλιδα καὶ ἐδιάσατο τοὺς ἑπτὰ βοστρύχους τῆς κεφαλῆς αὐτοῦ μετὰ τῆς ἐκτάσεως (< וּתְקַעַתְּ בַּיָּתֵד <> וְחָלִיתִי וְהָיִיתִי כְּאַחַד הָאָדָם: וַתִּישֵׁנֵהוּ דְלִילָה וַתֶּאֱרֹג אֶת־שֶׁבַע* מַחְלְפוֹת רֹאשׁוֹ עִם־הַמַּסֶּכֶת; cf. the OG καὶ ἐκοίμισεν αὐτὸν < וַתִּישֵׁנֵהוּ* in Judg. 16:19aα; Budde, *Richter* [1897], p. 106; *BHS*; the NEB [so Brockington, *Hebrew Text* (1973), p. 38]; REB; contra Moore, who retroverted from the LXX B-group [*Judges* (1895), pp. 354-55; as also Burney, *Judges* (2d edn, 1920), pp. 380-81; the RSV; NIV; NRSV; and Tov, *Textual Criticism* (1992), p. 240]). That the phrase εἰς τὸν τοῖχον (אֶל־הַקִּיר*) is an insertion from the OG translator, perhaps motivated by a failure to realize that it was an accoutrement of a loom, may be corroborated by its absence from the MT again later in 16:14a. The clause καὶ ἐϕυϕάνῃς ὡς ἐπὶ πῆχυν "and weave [it] as upon a beam" seems also an innovation of the OG translator, since it explains how the hair was to be woven while attached to the wall.

[92] *Judg. 16:18aδ*. Kethib: לה. Qere: לי. The Kethib reflects secondary assimilation to the preceding similar clause in 16:18aβ. Cf. R. Gordis, *The Biblical Text in the Making: A Study of the Kethib-Qere* (New York, 2d edn, 1971), pp. 82, 152.

[93] *Judg. 16:19aγ*. In view of Delilah's preceding summons to the man and the subsequent impersonal use of the 3 f. sg verb in וַתָּחֶל לְעַנּוֹתוֹ ("and it [i.e., the shaving] began to subdue him"), MT וַתְּגַלַּח (*waw* cons. + Pi. pret. 3 f. sg < גלח) "and she shaved" should probably be revocalized to וַתַּגְלַח (*waw* cons. + Hi. pret. 3 f. sg) "and she caused to be shaved", even though the Hi. is not elsewhere attested (G. R. Driver, "Mistranslations" [1947-52], p. 29).

[94] *Judg. 16:26aβ*. Kethib: וְהֵימִשֵׁנִי(י) (Hi. impv m. sg + 1 c. sg suff. [dir. obj.] "cause me to touch [the pillars]" < ימשׁ 'to touch'). Qere: וַהֲמִשֵׁנִי (Hi. impv m. sg + 1 c. sg suff. [dir. obj.] "cause me to feel [the pillars]" < מושׁ 'to feel [through], grope') (so BDB, pp. 413a, 607a; *BHS*).

[95] *Judg. 16:28bα*. MT: הָאֱלֹהִים. LXX: −, Ax glnow,dptv q Eth OLat] θεέ, B-group(except q) : ὁ θς; Gabc. *BHS*, observing the minus of an equivalent for האלהים from the OG and OLat, recommended deleting it from the MT and substituting יהוה for the previous ungrammatical m. הַזֶּה. This emendation followed a suggestion by Budde that

יהוה originally stood in place of הַזֶּה, and that הֱאלהים was a substitute for the former (*Richter* [1897], p. 109). Emerton recommended that MT הַזֶּה, whose m. gender lacks concord with its f. antecedent הפעם, be repointed to הַזֹּה ("Two Proposed Emendations" [1973], p. 222). Indeed, the OG (τὸ ἅπαξ τοῦτο) and OLat (*saemel in hoc* "but this once") do attest the demonstrative pronoun. Original יהוה may have fallen out by *homoeoteleuton* after the demonstrative, but it is also possible that the OG translator simply did not translate הֱאלהים, which he perceived to be tautological, thus missing the chiastic parallelism of 16:28bα:

זכרני נא   אדני יהוה

וחזקני נא אך הפעם הזה האלהים.

⁹⁶ *Judg. 17:2aβ*. Kethib: וְאַתִּי (so L); Qere: וְאַתְּ (so many Hebrew MSS).

⁹⁷ *Judg. 17:4bα*. The primary concern here is with the minus in LXX-AII and the OLat of מָאתַיִם, attested in the MT and all other versions.

מָאתַיִם MT Tg Psht Vg LXX-AI,AIII,B-group //
–, LXX-AII(except l) OLat

The LXX-AII MSS and the OLat, which together frequently represent the text of the OG, agree on the minus of מָאתַיִם*. Yet, although the OG may have lacked a translation for this term, it would not necessarily follow that מָאתַיִם had been lacking from its Hebrew *Vorlage* nor, if it had been lacking, that this *Vorlage* represented the original Hebrew text of Judg. 17:4. On the other hand, the possibility exists that the OG did have διακοσίους τοῦ ἀργυρίου but suffered corruption because of the repetitions in the verse: *καὶ ἔδωκεν τὸ ἀργύριον τῇ μητρὶ αὐτοῦ καὶ ἔλαβεν ἡ μήτηρ αὐτοῦ τὸ ἀργύριον καὶ ἔδωκεν αὐτὸ τῷ χωνευτῇ "And he gave the silver to his mother and his mother took the silver and gave it to the smith". In the foregoing excerpt, note the repetition of καὶ ἔδωκεν both before and after a repetition of τὸ ἀργύριον, which also appears both before and after the similar expressions τῇ μητρὶ αὐτοῦ and ἡ μήτηρ αὐτοῦ (i.e., a palistrophe, a-b-c-cⁱ-bⁱ-aⁱ, matching the Hebrew word order). Given this situation, there is a good chance that original διακοσίους τοῦ ἀργυρίου, which ends similarly to τὸ ἀργύριον (nearly *homoeoteleuton*), was accidentally displaced by the latter through an inner-Greek corruption.

It would be difficult to explain how מָאתַיִם came to be inserted into the MT by scribal accident if it had not been original. If, however, the insertion had been deliberate, one would need to explain: (1) what justification a scribe, rather than the author, would have had for portraying Micah's mother as withholding most of what she had dedicated to YHWH (Judg. 17:3b) if such had not been original and (2) how he settled upon the number two hundred. Rather, the former concern and the latter detail seem to be of an authentic nature and may derive from the original account.

On the rhetorical level, the inclusion of מָאתַיִם does serve the generally negative portrayal of the two Danite cultic objects in Judg. 17–18 by suggesting that both the overlaid carving and cast idol originated from silver that had been doubly embezzled—once from the mother by the son, once by the mother from YHWH (cf. Burney, *Judges* [2d edn, 1920], p. 420; Rudolph, "Textkritische Anmerkungen" [1947], p. 207; Webb, *Judges* [1987], p. 183). Of course, it is possible that two hundred shekels was thought to constitute an appropriate indemnity to avert the curse of Judg. 17:3 (e.g., Lev. 27:15, 19, 27; cf. Moore, *Judges* [1895], p. 376; C. J. Goslinga, *Richteren–Ruth* [KVHS, Kampen, The Netherlands, 3d edn, 1966], ET: *Joshua, Judges, Ruth* [R. Togtman (trans.), BSC, Grand Rapids, 1986], p. 457). Indeed, the account will go on to show the finished objects being stolen once more, namely, by the Danite migrants in Judg. 18.

[98] *Judg. 17:5bα.* MT: וּתְרָפִים. Also Judg. 18:14, 17, 18, 20; cf. C. J. Labuschagne, "Teraphim—A New Proposal for Its Etymology", *VT* 16 (1966), pp. 115-17.

[99] *Judg. 17:10b.* The main concern here is with the authenticity and possible sense of the words וַיֵּלֶךְ הַלֵּוִי in the transition from Judg. 17:10 to 17:11.

וַיֵּלֶךְ הַלֵּוִי   MT Tg Psht LXX-AI,AII(except n),AIII,B-group OLat //
–,   Vg LXX-AII(n)

The MS evidence sides strongly with the MT plus וַיֵּלֶךְ הַלֵּוִי. The Tg and Psht basically follow the MT. The LXX, despite much inner variation, shows καὶ ἐπορεύθη in all MSS but one. The Vg is virtually alone in omitting a translation for the words in question, and there is a good chance that Jerome only tacitly removed וַיֵּלֶךְ הַלֵּוִי from his *Vorlage* out of the same inclination that modern translators have had for regarding these words as spurious (so [after 1950] the RSV, ZB, RL, NAB, NEB, SBJ[3], NIV, TEV, NRSV and REB; contra the AV and RV). Commentators who have regarded וַיֵּלֶךְ הַלֵּוִי as spurious include: Moore, *Judges* (1895), p. 386; Burney, *Judges* (2d edn, 1920), pp. 423-24; Goslinga, *Richteren* (3d edn, 1966), ET: *Judges* (1986), p. 459 n. 11; Boling, *Judges* (1975), p. 257; contra Keil, *Richter* (1863), ET: *Judges* (1868), repr. edn, vol. 2, p. 432.

The OLat (Lyons) has for Judg. 1:10b-11a: *et coegit eum Et abiit Levites et coepit habitare cum viro* "and he urged him. And the Levite departed and began to dwell with the man." Thus, the OLat roughly follows a tradition also preserved in LXX-AII(except n) as to the alleged existence of וַיֹּאֶל [הַלֵּוִי] וַיֵּלֶךְ [הַלֵּוִי] וַיֹּאֶל לָשֶׁבֶת אֶת־הָאִישׁ*. From this it appears that the LXX-AII MSS and the OLat preserve an early Greek conflation of two translation alternatives for וַיֹּאֶל. The first Greek translation alternative, καὶ ηὐδόκησεν, was probably one translation for וַיֹּאֶל, in which it was understood to mean "and he was content, decided, agreed" (cf. וַיֹּאֶל מֹשֶׁה לָשֶׁבֶת Exod. 2:21; BDB, p. 384a 1). This was perhaps mistaken by the OLat (*et coegit [eum]*) for καὶ ηὐδοκίμησεν "and he had influence [with him]" (< εὐδοκιμέω "to be of good repute, gain credit, have influence", LSJ, p. 710a). Kittel's suggestion (*HSAT*[3,4] and *BH*[2,3]), followed by A. Lods (SBC), A. Vincent (SBJ[1,2]) and E. Osty (BO), that the Hebrew basis for the OLat *et coegit eum* had been וַיָּאֶץ בַּלֵּוִי (*waw* cons. + Hi. pret. 3 m. sg < אוץ 'to press, hasten' [BDB, p. 21a]) instead of וַיֵּלֶךְ הַלֵּוִי is unlikely for two reasons: (1) the Hi. of אוץ ('to hasten') is not semantically equivalent to Latin *cogo* (L-Sh, p. 362b, II. B. with acc. 'to urge one to any action, to force, compel, constrain'), and (2) the OLat was following a Greek, not Hebrew, *Vorlage* that, in any case, did attest וַיֵּלֶךְ הַלֵּוִי* (cf. OLat *Et abiit Levites*). Alternatively, *et coegit* may have been an inner-Latin doublet of *et coepit* (so Barthélemy, *Critique textuelle*, vol. 1 [1982], p. 113).

The second Greek translation alternative, καὶ ἤρξατο (so OLat *et coepit*), was probably a loose alternative translation for וַיֹּאֶל, which was understood to mean "and he undertook, ventured", as it may mean when followed by an inf. (Gen. 18:27; cf. Deut. 1:5 without inf.; BDB, p. 384a 2). Of the two conflated translations, *καὶ ἐπορεύθη ὁ λευείτης καὶ ηὐδόκησεν παροικεῖν παρὰ τῷ ἀνδρί* and *καὶ ἐπορεύθη ὁ λευείτης καὶ ἤρξατο παροικεῖν παρὰ τῷ ἀνδρί*, the earliest form of the OG probably had the latter, which coincides with most later LXX MSS and versions (apart from the possible reduplication of הַלֵּוִי*). In any case, the OG attested [הַלֵּוִי] וַיֵּלֶךְ*.

If the original Hebrew had been וַיֵּלֶךְ הַלֵּוִי וַיֹּאֶל <> לָשֶׁבֶת אֶת־הָאִישׁ* (see the following note), then the question remains as to how one should make sense of וַיֵּלֶךְ הַלֵּוִי "and the Levite went" in such a context. If וַיֵּלֶךְ הַלֵּוִי is taken to mean "and the Levite departed", one is left with the difficulty of explaining how he then came to reside with Micah. On the face of it, the MT verse division seems to suggest that the Levite first departed from, then decided to stay with, Micah. Barthélemy, following this latter pattern of interpretation, proposed to understand the implied scenario as: the Levite continued on his tour in search of possible available posts after which he decided in favour of Micah's offer (Barthélemy translates: "... et le lévite s'en alla. Puis le lévite consentit à demeurer avec l'homme ..." [*Critique textuelle*, vol. 1 (1982), p. 113]). Indeed, this interpretation of וַיֵּלֶךְ הַלֵּוִי is imposed upon the reader by the repetition of הַלֵּוִי in the subsequent clause: [וַיּוֹאֶל הַלֵּוִי] לָשֶׁבֶת אֶת־הָאִישׁ, which inclines the reader to interpret: "And [the Levite] consented to stay with the man", making any interpretation of וַיֵּלֶךְ הַלֵּוִי in the sense "and the Levite went along" seem tautological. It is perhaps the impasse of not finding a viable interpretation of וַיֵּלֶךְ that prompted Soggin to adopt the suggestion of G. R. Driver that וילך derived not from הלך but from an otherwise unattested Hebrew root *לכך (cf. Arab. *lkk* 'to hesitate'). Hence, they emended to וַיֵּלֶךְ, which fosters the reading: "and [the Levite] hesitated, [and then the Levite agreed to live with the man]" (G. R. Driver, "Problems in Judges" [1962–63], p. 18; Soggin, *Judges* [2d edn, 1987], p. 266).

In the light of the general context, it is tempting to understand וַיֵּלֶךְ הַלֵּוִי as an example of verbal anacrusis, frequent in Hebrew narrative style (e.g., with הלך: Num. 24:25 וַיָּקָם בִּלְעָם וַיֵּלֶךְ וַיָּשָׁב לִמְקֹמוֹ "Then Balaam arose and *went and returned* to his [home]"; 2 Kgs 3:7 וַיֵּלֶךְ וַיִּשְׁלַח אֶל־יְהוֹשָׁפָט "and he *went and sent* to Jehoshaphat"; 2 Kgs 13:21 וַיֵּלֶךְ וַיִּגַּע הָאִישׁ בְּעַצְמוֹת אֱלִישָׁע "when the [corpse] *went and touched* Elisha's bones"; with קוּם: Gen. 24:10 וַיָּקָם וַיֵּלֶךְ אֶל־אֲרַם נַהֲרַיִם "and he *arose and went* toward Aram-naharaim"; 2 Sam. 14:23; 15:9; 17:23; 1 Kgs 1:50). However, the situation in Judg. 17:10b-11a is unlike these examples of verbal anacrusis in that no actual movement is involved in the accompanying verb. Thus, in view of the fact that one finds a different verse division in the Psht and LXX(OLat), which place the plus at the head of the sentence, and in view of the fact that they likewise omit the MT (and Tg) repetition of הַלֵּוִי, it is possible that these versions (Psht and LXX[OLat]) preserve a text that presented וַיֵּלֶךְ הַלֵּוִי as marking the Levite's immediate departure to take up residence with Micah, after which the following clause, וַיּוֹאֶל <> לָשֶׁבֶת אֶת־הָאִישׁ, meant "and he decided/resolved to stay with the man".

[100] *Judg. 17:11a.* MT: + חלוי; OG: −. The MT may have taken on a reduplication of הַלֵּוִי after וַיּוֹאֶל on analogy with the same expression used twice in the prologue: וַיּוֹאֶל הָאֱמֹרִי לָשֶׁבֶת (Judg. 1:27) and וַיּוֹאֶל הָאֱמֹרִי לָשֶׁבֶת (Judg. 1:35), where וַיּוֹאֶל means "and (he) was determined" (BDB, p. 384a 3). However, it does not seem that the repetition of הַלֵּוִי was here in the *Vorlage* of the OG, since one would then expect the OG to have mimicked the Hebrew word order, as it did in both places in the prologue. In Judg. 1:27, 30, the OG and all later LXX MSS render the idiom: καὶ ἤρξατο ... N ... [τοῦ] κατοικεῖν, mimicking the Hebrew word order: finite verb + subj. + inf. In Judg. 17:10, however, no LXX MS interposes ὁ λευείτης between καὶ ἤρξατο and παροικεῖν. See the preceding note.

[101] *Judg. 18:2aα.* Some versions omit מקצותם אנשים, a haplography probably caused by *homoeoteleuton* (so LXX-AII[glnow,dptv],AIII,B-group[except z(mg),a₂,m] Psht Syh[ℵ]), but cf. ἀπὸ μέρους αὐτῶν, LXX-AI,AII[K] [Arm] Eth OLat. The MT syntactically links מקצותם אנשים בני־חיל, but this rendering disrupts the prosodic parallelism. Moore inferred, "The redundancies of the verse are due to the union of two closely parallel accounts" (*Judges* [1895], p. 388). However, both the repetitions (especially prefixed prep. מִן and אֲנָשִׁים) and the metre in 18:2aαβ establish prosodic parallelism. The repetition of אֲנָשִׁים is syntactically resumptive (cf. resumption of the cstr אַנְשֵׁי in 19:22aβ [וְהִנֵּה אַנְשֵׁי הָעִיר אַנְשֵׁי בְנֵי־בְלִיַּעַל]). As to the appositional relation of אֲנָשִׁים[2] with בְּנֵי־חַיִל, see Judg. 20:13aα (אֶת־כָּל־אֵלֶּה אַנְשֵׁי־חַיִל); cf. 20:44b, 46b תְּנוּ אֶת־הָאֲנָשִׁים בְּנֵי־בְלִיַּעַל.

[102] *Judg. 18:7bγ.* The meaning and relationship of the Hebrew clauses וְאֵין־מַכְלִים דָּבָר and יוֹרֵשׁ עֶצֶר בָּאָרֶץ are uncertain. The ancient versions reflect difficulty in interpreting them.

וְאֵין־מַכְלִים דָּבָר בָּאָרֶץ MT (Tg) LXX-B-group (διατρέπων ἢ καταισχύνων being a doublet for מַכְלִים) //

*וְאֵין־מַכְלִים בָּאָרֶץ Psht //

*וְאֵין־מַכְלִים דָּבָר Vg //

וְאֵין־מְכַלֵּ(י)ם [-] מְכַלְמִים] דָּבָר LXX-AI(+ בָּאָרֶץ [G(ℵ)]),AII,AIII Arm Eth OLat Syh(+ בָּאָרֶץ* sub ℵ) unless = MT

יוֹרֵשׁ עֶצֶר MT (Tg) //

*נוֹגֵשׂ עֶצֶר Psht //

*יוֹרֵשׁ אֹצָר Vg LXX-AI(bcx) B-group //

−, LXX-AI(AG[ℵ]a,k),AII,AIII OLat Syh(ℵ)

Rudolph (followed by *BHS*) argued that יוֹשֶׁבֶת־לָבֶטַח כְּמִשְׁפַּט צִדֹנִים should be transposed immediately after לְיִשָׁה ("Textkritische Anmerkungen" [1947], p. 207). Thus, the part of the emended text up to צִדֹנִים would concern the city's situation and the rest, its occupants. However, neither the Hebrew MSS nor the versions support his suggested transposition, though the antecedent of the f. ptcp יוֹשֶׁבֶת must be the city לְיִשָׁה (antecedent of the suff. of בְּקִרְבָּה) rather than of m. הָעָם. Moore said that the f. ptcp agrees with the gender of the *city*, though this antecedent is unexpressed (*Judges* [1895], p. 391; so BDB, p. 766a).

As for MT וְאֵין־מַכְלִים דָּבָר בָּאָרֶץ, BDB cite מַכְלִים in Judg. 18:7 as a Hi. ptcp but say that the text is corrupt (BDB, p. 484a 1). LXX-B-group and α΄ (καὶ οὐκ ἐνῆν καταισχύνων οὐδὲ διατρέπων) offer the same two-word translation for MT מַכְלִים (albeit in reversed order), referring to the absence of those causing harm and humiliation. Qimḥi commented similarly that "they had no neighbours to harm and humiliate them" (trans. A. A. Macintosh, "The Meaning of *mklym* in Judges xviii 7", *VT* 35 [1985], pp. 68-69). Schreiner has suggested that the B-group here follows α΄ (*Septuaginta-Massora* [1957], p. 103). W. R. Bodine, who does not cite this instance of similarity between the B-text and α΄ (*The Greek Text of Judges: Recentional Developments* [HSM 23, Chico, Calif., 1980], p. 178 n. 181), would perhaps argue that it arose from the common revision underlying both the B-text and θ΄—the latter serving as the base text of α΄ (cf. pp. 152-53). The Tg, Psht, Vg and σ΄ (μηδενὸς ἐνοχλοῦντος ἐν μηδενὶ ἐν τῇ γῇ "no one troubling in anything in the land") translate the MT מַכְלִים with a single word and interpret the clause as referring to the absence of those causing harm. The OG (LXX-AI,AII,AIII) omits anything corresponding to the MT בָּאָרֶץ and takes the clause as referring to the absence of those able to speak. H. Junker ("Konsonantenumstellung als Fehlerquelle und textkritisches Hifsmittel im MT", in *Werden und Wesen des Alten Testaments* [BZAW 66, Berlin, 1936], p. 171) proposed that δυναμένους λαλῆσαι ῥῆμα came from *מוכלים דָּבָר (Ho. ptcp < יכל), but G. R. Driver ("Suggestions and Objections", *ZAW* 55 [1937], p. 71), observing that ῥῆμα stands for דָּבָר, suggested that δυναμένους λαλῆσαι is a paraphrase for the force of the ptcp מכלם read as 'מְכַלְמ* = *מְכַלְמִים after Arab. *kllm* 'spoke'.

Modern scholarly emendations of the Hebrew text include: (1) מַחְסוֹר כָּל־דָּבָר "[there was no] lack of anything" (Rashi; Bertheau, *Richter und Ruth* [1845], p. 207; Soggin, *Judges* [2d edn, 1987], p. 272), comparing Judg. 18:10 (מָקוֹם אֲשֶׁר אֵין־שָׁם מַהְסוֹר כָּל־דָּבָר); (2) אֲשֶׁר בָּאָרֶץ ואין מְכַלֵּא מִדָּבָר בארץ "there is no one to restrain (us) from anything in the land" (so Moore, *Judges* [1895], p. 392); (3) ואין מֶלֶךְ מַדְבִּרן\מְדַבֵּר] בארץ "and there was no king ruling over the land" (Qimḥi and Junker ["Konsonantenumstellung" (1936), p. 171]: מַדְבִּר; G. R. Driver ["Suggestions and Objections" (1937), p. 71] and the NEB: מְדַבֵּר). Qimḥi, commenting on the context of יוֹרֵשׁ עֶצֶר, said: "They had no king over them and no one to take control of the kingship" (trans. Macintosh, "Meaning of *mklym*" [1985], p. 73). Junker was the first to emend to ואין מֶלֶךְ מַדְבִּר בארץ, which he translated: "es war kein König da, der über das Land herrschte", comparing Esth. 1:22, which he emended to וּמַדְבִּר כָּל־נָשָׁיו עִמּוֹ "and keeping in subjection all his women [who were] with him" ("Konsonantenumstellung" [1936], pp. 172-73). However, G. R. Driver ("Suggestions and Objections" [1937], p. 71) argued that הדביר ("throw down [an enemy] on his back"; cf. Pss. 18:48; 47:4) is too strong here and recommended מְדַבֵּר "governing" (cf. Syr. *daber* 'he ruled, governed, administrated'; Arab. *dbbr* 'he managed, ruled'). The first suggestion above, while derived from a parallel verse in the context, lacks support among the Hebrew MSS and versions. The second and third suggestions, with the same limitation as the first, have the advantage of conforming more closely to the existing MT consonantal text.

Macintosh, comparing Arab. *klm* meaning either 'to wound' or 'to speak (authoritatively)', attempted to resolve the difficulty without emendation ("Meaning of *mklym*" [1985], pp. 73-76; cf. J. Reider ["Etymological Studies in Biblical Hebrew", *VT* 4 (1954), p. 280], who was the first to cite Arab. *klm* 'to speak' as a cognate for the Hebrew term in Judg. 18:7a; Barr [*Comparative Philology* (1968), repr. edn, pp. 14-15, 329 no. 176; Tov, *Textual Criticism* (1992), p. 367], who cites Reider with approval). It is true that G. R. Driver ("Suggestions and Objections" [1937], p. 71) had already cited Arab. *klm* 'to speak' as the sense underlying the LXX-A-group translation but apparently without endorsing it as the intended sense of the Hebrew. Macintosh translated: "There was no one speaking with any authority in the land, no one possessing control (i.e. power to rule)" ("Meaning of *mklym*" [1985], p. 73). His translation basically accords with that of the OG and most LXX daughter versions (i.e., if the two words δυναμένους λαλῆσαι "able to speak" may serve for "speak authoritatively").

However, since the root כלם is used frequently in connection with humiliation caused by military defeat (Ni.: Isa. 45:17; 50:7; 54:4; Hi.: Prov. 25:8; Ps. 44:10) and since the primary motivation for the migration of this group of Danites was to find a place free from the military constraints of oppressors (cf. 18:1b with the reference to the Amorites in 1:34-36), it would come as no surprise that this feature of Laish might figure prominently in the interest of the spies (Barthélemy, citing Cassel, argues "qu'il est normal que les espions danites aient noté l'absence d'un monarque capable d'entretenir une armée et d'organiser instantanément une résistance" [*Critique textuelle*, vol. 1 (1982), p. 114]). Thus, the MT וְאֵין־מַכְלִים דָּבָר בָּאָרֶץ may mean simply "and, there being no one humiliating (i.e., metonymy of effect-for-cause signifying military harassment that causes humiliation) anything in the land". Dhorme translated: "personne ne blâmant, dans le pays, le détenteur du pouvoir" (*Bible* [1956], p. 791); Barthélemy (*Critique textuelle*, vol. 1 [1982], p. 114): "causant de la honte sous quelque aspect dans le pays". The NIV, without explanation, translated: "And since their land lacked nothing", suggesting that they may have understood the MT to refer to an impersonal cause of humiliation (i.e., metonymy of effect-for-cause signifying lack/poverty that causes shame) and allegedly supporting this by translating the following clause: "they were prosperous" (see below). This view has the advantages that it requires no emendation and offers a sense roughly equivalent to the parallel report in Judg. 18:10.

BDB suggested that the following idiom, יוֹרֵשׁ עֶצֶר, means "possessor of restraint" (i.e., ruler) (BDB, p. 783b). Junker's translation: "die Herrschaft erblich besitzend" derives the sense 'rulership' from comparison with the verb עצר 'to rule' in 1 Sam. 9:17 (and perhaps 2 Chron. 14:10) ("Konsonantenumstellung" [1936], pp. 171-72). Barthélemy said that יוֹרֵשׁ עֶצֶר, understood as "détenant le pouvoir exécutif", has an epexegetical role with regard to מַכְלִים דָּבָר בָּאָרֶץ (*Critique textuelle*, vol. 1 [1982], p. 114). The Tg זעירין interprets MT עצר as though from the root צער. Barthélemy thought that both the Psht and Vg were merely groping for an interpretation of these words (Barthélemy, *Critique textuelle*, vol. 1 [1982], p. 113). Yet Rudolph, following L. Koehler, preferred the more negative connotation of LXX-B (ἐκπιέζων) and the Psht, emending יוֹרֵשׁ עֶצֶר to נוֹגֵשׂ עֹצֶר

"als drückender Fronvogt" (Rudolph, "Textkritische Anmerkungen" [1947], p. 207; whereas Koehler, following the Psht, had translated: "und auch [war keiner da,] der bedrückte und bedrängte" [< וְיָאֵין יוֹרֵשׁ וְעֶצֶר *[ˀ] ["Hebräische Vokabeln III", ZAW 58 (1940-1941), p. 230]).

The OG has nothing corresponding to the MT עֶצֶר יוֹרֵשׁ. Only the LXX-B-group and the Vg give the latter term the sense 'wealth', for which Budde conjectured that עֶצֶר combines the readings אָצָר (usually אוֹצָר) 'treasure' and עֹשֶׁר 'riches' (cf. BDB, p. 783b; NIV: "they were prosperous"). G. R. Driver argued that B-text θησαυρός rests not on original אוֹצָר but on a sense equivalent to Arab. ʿṣarun 'wealth' ("Suggestions and Objections" [1937], p. 71). In fact, the B-group preserves a doublet ἐκπιέζων θησαυροῦ that gives two different translations for MT עצר, pointed alternatively either עֶצֶר or עֹצֶר (cf. Barthélemy, Critique textuelle, vol. 1 [1982], p 113). Alternatively, M. Dahood has suggested that BH עצר here and in Prov. 30:16 may mean 'be fertile, ample' (cf. Ug. ġṣr; Arab. ġaḍira) (Dahood, "Northwest Semitic Philology and Job", in The Bible in Current Catholic Thought [J. L. McKenzie (ed.), New York, 1962], p. 73; cf. Barr, Comparative Philology [1968], repr. edn, p. 333 no. 252).

In all probability, MT עֶצֶר יוֹרֵשׁ needs no emendation and here means "possessing control". Note the sense 'control/rule' of the verbal form in 1 Sam. 9:17 (cf. W. Richter, Die sogenannten vorprophetischen Berufungsberichte: Eine literaturewissenschaftliche Studie zu 1 Sam 9,1-10,16, Ex 3f. und Ri 6,11b-17 [FRLANT 101, Göttingen, 1970], pp. 35-36; E. Kutsch, "Die Wurzel עצר im Hebräischen", VT 2 [1952], p. 57). Since יוֹרֵשׁ is a m. ptcp, it probably has the same antecedent as the m. ptcps שֹׁקֵט וּבֹטֵחַ (i.e., הָעָם), and the sense "possessing control" better agrees with the semantic fields of שֹׁקֵט וּבֹטֵחַ than does a meaning associated with prosperity. Hence, the preceding clause, וְא[י]ן־מַכְלִים דָּבָר בָּאָרֶץ, should perhaps be read as a parenthetical subordinate clause: "[and,] there being no one causing humiliation (i.e., metonymy for oppressing) in anything" (Macintosh likewise takes דָּבָר as an accusative of respect ["Meaning of mklym" (1985), p. 76; cf. Jer. 38:5]). Indeed, the narrator's concern in Judg. 18:7bβ for military defenselessness, over against concern for agricultural prosperity, better suits the framing descriptions in the verse of the people's tranquility and security (18:7bα) and their remoteness and autonomy (18:7bγ-δ).

[103] Judg. 18:11aα. Rudolph suggested that מֹשֶׁם is a dittography based upon a confusion of the letters ממש– that follow ("Textkritische Anmerkungen" [1947], p. 208). However, since there is no MS support for removing מִשָּׁם, since it is similarly employed after a verb of motion also in Judg. 18:13 and since מִמְּשְׁפַּחַת plus a tribal name occurs elsewhere in a construction where it follows מִן plus a location reference (cf. מִבֵּית לֶחֶם יְהוּדָה מִמְּשְׁפַּחַת יְהוּדָה in 17:7), the appearance of מִשָּׁם here seems stylistically consistent.

[104] Judg. 18:14aα. MT: + לַיִשׁ. LXX: −, AI(G[ẋ]) AII AIII(MNybₐ) B-group(ua₂,m) OLat Syh(ẋ)] Λάισα, AI(except k) B-group(except s,ua₂,mq). It is clear that the OG omitted a translation for MT לַיִשׁ, which may have been absent from its Hebrew Vorlage. The MT plus may be a gloss, since, under the influence of the previous context (18:7), it artificially limits the region of their spying to the city upon which they finally decided. Cf. similar expressions in Judg. 18:2, 17.

[105] Judg. 18:30a. After τὸ γλυπτόν (= הפסל) the OG adds Μειχα (= מיכה)—so AI(Abcx,k) AII(Zglnow,dptv) Arm(ẋ for ÷ in 33mg 40mg 112mg 121[□ γλυπτον] 218) Sah Eth OLat Syh(÷). Perhaps the OG added this specification during translation.

[106] Judg. 18:30bα. Many Hebrew MSS (e.g., L) have suspended נ: מֹנֵשׁה; many other MSS and editions do not suspend the נ. Read with the few MSS, OG (LXX-AI[a] AII B-group[ez,j] Eth[Dillman's codex C] OLat Syh Thdt) and Vg: מֹשֶׁה. So BHS; B. Lindars, "The Israelite Tribes in Judges", in Studies in the Historical Books of the Old Testament (J. A. Emerton [ed.], SVT 30, Leiden, 1979), p. 111 n. 33; Tov, Textual Criticism

(1992), p. 57 and n. 37. It is not difficult to see why a scribe may have found it preferable to avoid associating idolatry with the name of Moses.

[107] *Judg. 18:30bγ*. MT: הארץ. The MT has the support of the Tg, Psht, Vg, OG and almost all EVV (the AV, RV, JPSV, RSV, JB [translating הארץ "the inhabitants of the country"], NAB, NEB [translating הארץ "the people"], NIV, TEV and NRSV). However, a number of other considerations indicate that the Hebrew text may have suffered corruption from original הארון*. At the end of Judg. 18:30b, the MT (with all versions) has the unusual expression גְּלוֹת הָאָרֶץ "exile of the land", which some scholars emend to גְּלוֹת הָאָרוֹן* "exile of the ark."

> גְּלוֹת הָאָרוֹן* no ancient versions //
> גְּלוֹת הָאָרֶץ MT Tg Psht Vg LXX

It is rarely advisable to opt for an emendation without at least some MS support, especially when there is unanimity among the witnesses. However, a number of scholars have expressed dissent from the testimony of the textual witnesses for various reasons. Favouring הָאָרוֹן* instead of MT הָאָרֶץ are: Qimḥi; Houbigant, *Biblia Hebraica* (1753), ad loc.; Burney, *Judges* (2d edn, 1920), pp. 415, 435; A. Schulz, *Das Buch der Richter*, in *HSAT* (Catholic edn), II/4 (Bonn, 1926), p. 95; J. Blenkinsopp, *Gibeon and Israel: The Role of Gibeon and the Gibeonites in the Political and Religious History of Early Israel* (SOTSMS 2, Cambridge, 1972), p. 77; R. van der Hart, "The Camp of Dan and the Camp of Yahweh", *VT* 25 (1975), p. 722, n. 7. Cf. the remarks of Goslinga, *Richteren* (3d edn, 1966), ET: *Judges* (1986), p. 473 n. 42. The REB translated simply "until the exile", thus avoiding reference to either the land or the ark.

Against the MT and its congeners stand the following considerations. First, if an alleged corruption had come about accidentally, it is worth notice that, in some hands of early Judean script, original ון- (of הארון) may have been mistakenly read as ץ- (of הארץ). Such a confusion would require the use of ו as an inner *mater lectionis*, but Judean scribal use of both the Aramaic 'square' script and an orthography with internal *matres lectionis* may have begun as early as the period following the return from exile in 538 BCE. Thus, if such a confusion of letters in Judg. 18:30b took place after the innovation of these scribal practices but before the geographical divergence of the main textual families, the proto-MT and the *Vorlagen* underlying the ancient versions could not be expected to differ. However, the choice between accidental graphic confusion and deliberate change need not be so absolute—a copyist may simply have encountered a form of ן- that caused sufficient hesitation to allow historical–theological traditions to take over.

Second, there are both historical and rhetorical problems with the use of הארץ in Judg. 18:30bγ. (a) The expression גְּלוֹת הָאָרֶץ is not elsewhere attested in BH (Blenkinsopp, *Gibeon and Israel* [1972], pp. 77, 131 n. 55). Other passages speak of Israel, Judah, Jerusalem or Gilgal (all metonymies for their inhabitants) being exiled, but never of the land (without further specification) being exiled (cf. 2 Kgs 17:23; 25:21; Jer. 1:3; 52:27; Amos 5:5). (b) The use of הארץ (a metonymy for its inhabitants; so Tg) leaves undefined the territory that was subjected to exile. Indeed, הארץ does elsewhere function as a subject that is metonymical of inhabitants, but the context is usually sufficiently clear for a reader to discern to what land and what inhabitants it refers (e.g., 2 Sam. 15:23, where context requires that "the whole land" refer only to those of "the tribes of Israel" who had not transferred loyalty from David to Absalom [cf. 2 Sam. 15:2, 6, 10, 13]; or 1 Sam. 14:25, where context requires that "the whole land" refer to Saul's "troops" [i.e., העם in 1 Sam. 14:24, 26]). Thus, in Judg. 18:30bγ, unless "the exile of the land" (without further qualification) has special reference to the exile of the northern tribes in 734/722 BCE or to the exile of the southern tribes in 605/597/586 BCE, context implies that the expression refers to the exile of the land that includes the city of Laish/Dan just discussed. Most scholars take the reference to be to the captivity of the northern tribes (i.e., *the* land being the land that includes the city of Laish/Dan just discussed) in either 734 or 722 BCE, though, from a rhetorical standpoint, this interpretation finds no support from the context of Judg. 17–18 or from the book of Judges. It is a scholarly identification based upon a knowledge of Israel's history after David—a knowledge that no other verse in Judges explicitly attests. Some have taken הארץ to refer to the region occupied by the Philistines—a military conquest more in keeping with the time frame of Judges as a whole—but this view runs into the difficulty that there is elsewhere in the Hebrew Scriptures no claim that the Philistines exiled inhabitants from the territories they occupied.

Third, there are several rhetorical advantages of הארון in Judg. 18:30bγ. (a) The mention of הארון in this Mosaic genealogy (Judg. 18:30b) would parallel mention of הארון in the Aaronic genealogy of Phinehas in Judg. 20:27b-28aαβ. Both Judg. 18:30b and 20:27b-28aαβ are parenthetical insertions that reflect concern with a third-generation cultic officiant (Jonathan, son of Gershom, son of Moses; Phinehas, son of Eleazar, son of Aaron), so it would not be surprising if both should mention the ark. Another clear case of parenthetical insertion, the note on the location of Shiloh in Judg. 21:19aβγb, reflects a concern with the locus of the old cult. (b) In the correspondence between Judg. 18:30b and 30a, הארון furnishes an appropriate antithesis to הפסל as a cult object. The ark represents an appropriate region of responsibility for a Levite (Deut. 9:8-9)—particularly this Levite (Num. 3-4 assigns the ark to the Kohathites, the clan of Moses [cf. 1 Chron. 6:1-3])—whereas the cast image does not. (c) In the parallelism between Judg. 18:30 and 18:31, 18:30a corresponds to 18:31a in representing the Danite establishment of the illegitimate cultic image. This suggests that 18:30b might likewise correspond to 18:31b in referring to a legitimate but contrasting cultic concern. Reference to the period during which the "shrine of God was at Shiloh" (18:31b) would correspond to the mention of the period terminated by the "exile of the ark" (18:30bγ), but intervening is the Levite's genealogy (18:30bαβ). This leads to the conclusion that the object of cultic concern in 18:30 is not so much the establishment of the illegitimate cultic image (18:30a) as the illegitimacy of the attendance of such an image by a Levitical priesthood. In this case, the alternative points of concern could be: (i) the illegitimacy of a Levite's functioning as a priest (cf. Num. 4:20) or (ii) a Levite's attending to an illegitimate cultic image (cf. 18:30abαβ). If the former, we would expect the period to be marked by a contrasting reference to the duration of a legitimate priesthood—not the case in either reading of הארץ or הארון in 18:30bγ. If the latter, we would expect the period to be marked by a contrasting reference to the duration of a legitimate cult object—the case only if הארון were originally in 18:30bγ instead of הארץ. (d) The expression גְּלוֹת הָאָרוֹן has precedent in the parallelism of 1 Sam. 4:21-22 (גלה כבוד ... גלה הלקח ארון האלהים // אל־הלקח ארון האלהים // כבוד מישראל) and finds historical corroboration in Ps. 78:61a (ויתן לשבי עזו) (cf. Burney, *Judges* [2d edn, 1920], p. 415; Blenkinsopp, *Gibeon and Israel* [1972], p. 77; van der Hart, "Camp of Dan" [1975], p. 722 n. 7).

In conclusion, despite an absence of supporting MS evidence, most of the preceding historical and rhetorical considerations support the view that גְּלֹ(וֹ)ת הָאָרֹ(וֹ)ן originally stood in Judg. 18:30b (not גָּלוֹת הָאָרֶץ) and the history of Judges' scribal transmission (with regard to script and orthography) furnishes the conditions that would allow for this alleged accidental confusion to occur prior to the emergence of the ancient versions. Further, although it is not always a valid criterion for textual emendation, the emendation has the advantage of suiting a major doctrine of poetics: one should choose the interpretation that gives maximal significance to all the particulars of a context. Since the rhetoric of Judg. 17–18 ostensibly reflects concern with the legitimacy of cult site and cult objects prior to the monarchy, the proposed reading, if from the hand of the Judges compiler, would better suit the prevailing concern of Judges with the aftermath of incidents contemporary with Israel's judges but antecedent to Israel's united monarchy. Of course, such a scheme might not easily square with the view of P. R. Davies that the very idea of a captivity of the ark is a later tradition, but such a view is, indeed, a matter of interpretation (cf. P. R. Davies, "Ark or Ephod in I Sam. xiv. 18?", *JTS* NS 26 [1975], pp. 82-87; idem, "The History of the Ark in the Books of Samuel", *JNSL* 5 [1977], pp. 9-18; G. W. Ahlström, "The Travels of the Ark: A Religio–Political Composition", *JNES* 43 [1984], pp. 141-49).

[108] *Judg. 19:11aβ*. MT: רַד. GKC (§19*i*) regards the MT as an old textual error for יָרַד (so BDB, p. 432b; and *BHS*, on the basis of OG κεκλικυῖα [LXX-AI,AII,AIII Arm Eth Syh]). The OLat has *erat iam declinatus*. If an unusual form יָרַד (twice in Judg. 5:13; cf. 3 m. pl. יָרְדוּ in 5:11b, 14bα) had undergone aphaeresis (GKC, §19*h*), the MT may correctly preserve this form. The word order, with subject (הַיּוֹם) first, mimics the pattern of the previous colon and signals a second subordinate clause: "Them [being] near Jebus and the day well gone …".

[109] *Judg. 19:18bα*. MT: וְאֶת־בֵּית יְהוָה (so the Tg, Psht and Vg). OG: καὶ εἰς τὸν οἶκόν μου (< וְאֶל־בֵּיתִי*). Abbreviation of the tetragrammaton as י'/ו' may have been practised in early Hebrew MSS and may account for this discrepancy. Thus, either the OG translation reflects a failure to have discerned an intended בֵּית יהוה*, or the MT and its congeners mistook final י on original בֵּיתִי as an abbreviation for יהוה. An original בֵּית יהוה seems reasonable here, since the Levite's itinerary, while journeying from Bethlehem to the hill country of Ephraim, may have entailed a visit to the sanctuary of YHWH at Shiloh. However, this sanctuary is elsewhere in Judges referred to only as בֵּית האלהים (18:31)— which forms an inclusio with the reference to the shrine of Micah as בֵּית־אלהים (17:5)— the name בֵּית־אל (20:18, 26, 31; 21:2, 19) refers only to the city Bethel and nowhere else in Judges is a sanctuary called בֵּית יהוה. Moreover, if Judg. 19:18aα-γ were intended to offer a parallel to the description of 19:18aδ-bα, then just as the place of origin is repeated (בֵּית[־]לֶחֶם יהודה) so should be the destination (i.e., עַד־יִרְכְּתֵי הַר־אֶפְרַיִם = וְאֶת בֵּיתִי*; cf. וַיָּבֹא אֶל־בֵּיתוֹ in 19:29). Most modern authorities side with the witness of the OG (so Moore, *Judges* [1895], pp. 415, 416; Burney, *Judges* [2d edn, 1920], pp. 466-67; the RSV; NASB; JB; *BHS*; NAB; NEB; TEV; Soggin, *Judges* [2d edn, 1987], p. 287; the NRSV; REB; and Tov, *Textual Criticism* [1992], pp. 256-57; contra the AV, RV and NIV).

[110] *Judg. 19:21aβ*. Kethib: וַיִּבּוֹל or וַיָּבוֹל (both Qal pret. 3 m. sg pausal; cf. GKC, §67*f*, *g*). Qere: וַיָּבֶל (Qal pret. 3 m. sg; so many Hebrew MSS).

[111] *Judg. 19:28a*. MT: וְאֵין עֹנֶה "but no one answered" is ambiguous as to the condition of the concubine. The OG mistranslated paraphrastically καὶ οὐκ ἀπεκρίθη αὐτῷ (LXX-AI,AII,AIII, Arm Sah Eth Syh [OLat: *audiuit eum* "she heard him"]; taking עֹנֶה as Qal perf. 3 f. sg, which would be syntactically irregular after וְאֵין) and further explained ἀλλ᾽ ἐτεθνήκει (LXX-AII[except nw(ἐτεθνήσκει)]). Cf. Moore, *Judges* (1895), p. 420; Burney, *Judges* (2d edn, 1920), p. 470; S. Lasine, "Guest and Host in Judges 19: Lot's Hospitality in an Inverted World", *JSOT* 29 (1984), pp. 45, 56 n. 28.

[112] *Judg. 19:30bα**. This Hebrew retroversion is based upon an OG plus that was positioned between translations of MT Judg. 19:30a and 19:30b, the latter of which are presented in the same order as in the MT. Thus, there is no MS evidence to support the NEB transposition of 19:30a to follow both this OG plus and 19:30b. Nevertheless, the NEB translators were justifiably concerned with the incompatibility of the position of the OG plus with the apparent text-form of its *Vorlage*.

The OG begins: καὶ ἐνετείλατο [aor. mid.] τοῖς ἀνδράσιν, which implies a Hebrew text: וַיְצַו הָאֲנָשִׁים (so *BHS*). However, since the position of the OG plus would require that the plus in the alleged Hebrew *Vorlage* commence with a pluperf. (since it describes action anterior to that described in 19:30a), a Hebrew plus in the present position could not have begun: וַיְצַו הָאֲנָשִׁים, for *waw* cons. + the pret. does not elsewhere (and possibly cannot) introduce the pluperf. (cf. S. R. Driver, *Tenses* [3d edn, 1892], §76 Obs.; GKC, §106*f*; *pace* B. K. Waltke and M. O'Connor, *An Introduction to Biblical Hebrew Syntax* [Winona Lake, Ind., 1990], §§33.2.3 [pp. 552-53]). Indeed, had the normal method of expressing the pluperf. in Hebrew occurred, it would have appeared as *waw* disj. + subj. followed by the perf.: וְהָאֲנָשִׁים אֲשֶׁר צִוָּה שָׁלַח לֵאמֹר‎*, which would probably have been rendered into Greek as: *καὶ τοῖς ἀνδράσιν οἷς ἐξαπέστειλεν ἐνετείλατο* (cf. the correspondence in word order between the MT and OG in expressing the pluperf. in 1 Sam. 9:15; 25:21; 28:3; 2 Sam. 18:18; cf. Waltke–O'Connor, *Biblical Hebrew Syntax* [1993], §30.5.2b [p. 490]). For this reason the NEB translators transposed the OG plus and 19:30b (which is logically contiguous with the plus) to precede 19:30a, thereby 'restoring' a form of the text that was thought to be compatible with normal Hebrew syntax for *waw* cons. + the pret. (cf. Brockington, *Hebrew Text* [1973], p. 39).

However, in order for the plus attested by the OG to have fallen out of the MT tradition by a haplography caused by *homoeoteleuton*—both 19:30a and the alleged plus ending with עַד הַיּוֹם הַזֶּה‎—the position of the plus must have originally intervened between 19:30a and 19:30b (i.e., the order that the OG now witnesses). Otherwise, in addition to the haplography, one would need to explain how, after the haplography took place, 19:30b came to be transposed so that it now follows 19:30a not just in the MT but also in the OG, where the plus is retained.

A simpler solution is to retain the position of 19:30a and 19:30b, attested by the MT and OG, and to retrovert from the OG plus a form of Hebrew text that would allow an anterior-to-past-time sense. It should be noticed that in the MT, 19:30a commences with *waw* cons. + the perf. expressing a frequentive sense equivalent to the customary impf: וְהָיָה ... וְאָמַר‎ "And it would happen ... and he would say ..." (GKC, §112 *e-o*; cf. §107*g*). If the following plus had commenced וְצִוָּה אֶל־הָאֲנָשִׁים‎ (*waw* cons. + Pi. perf. 3 m. sg), the consecution with the preceding frequentive verbs may have been explicative—"for he would command the men ..." (suggesting that he commissioned each messenger in succession)—yet may still have expressed action anterior to that of the perfs. in 19:30a. Here the OG's aor. (mid.) *καὶ ἐνετείλατο* simply follows its own precedent of translating the first perf. of 19:30a by using the (second) aor.: *καὶ ἐγένετο* [πᾶς ὁ ὁρῶν ἔλεγεν (pres. act. impf 3 sg)] "And it happened [(that) everyone who saw would say]".

[113] *Judg. 20:9b*. MT: עָלֶיהָ‎. OG: *ἀναβησόμεθα* (< נַעֲלֶה‎*; so *BHS*).

[114] *Judg. 20:10bβ*. MT: לְגֶבַע‎. One Hebrew MS: לְגִבְעָה‎. Emend to לְגִבְעַת‎* (cf. *BHS*).

[115] *Judg. 20:13bα*. Kethib: –. Qere: בְּנֵי‎ (so many Hebrew MSS, the Tg, Psht and LXX; so *BHS*). See Tov, *Textual Criticism* (1992), p. 60, though he mistakenly cites the Vg instead of the Tg as supporting the Qere.

[116] *Judg. 20:33b*. For the difficult MT: מִמַּעֲרֵה־גָבַע‎, the Tg has ממישר גבעתא‎ "from the plain of Gibeah" (= BH מַעֲרֶה‎ "bare [open] space", BDB, p. 789a; so "out of the meadows of Gibeah", AV—hardly a suitable setting for concealing an ambush), and Psht has *mn m‘rt’ dgb‘* "from the cave of Geba" (= BH מְעָרֶה‎ "cave"—though the BH cstr form would be מְעָרַת‎, and 20:29 implies that the ambush took surrounding positions). The OG has *ἀπὸ δυσμῶν τῆς Γαβαα* (AI[k(mg)],AII,AIII Arm Sah Eth Syh) "from the west of Gibeah" (cf. Vg *ab occidentali urbis parte*), which would support the emendation מִמַּעֲרָב־גֶּבַע‎* "on the west of Geba" (Bertheau, *Richter und Ruth* [1845], p. 224; Moore, *Judges* [1895], pp. 437-38; BDB, p. 788a; so *BHS*, the RSV, NIV and NRSV). The LXX B-group attests a transliteration *ἀπὸ μααρα Γαβαα* or the like (*ἀπὸ Μαρααγάβε*, B [so "out of Maareh-geba", RV]; *ἀπὸ μααρα τῆς Γαβαα*, k[txt]) that is dependent on the MT tradition. While the OG or its *Vorlage* could be explained as emending (OG, tacitly) an original ממערה‎, it is difficult to explain why a simpler, original ממערב‎ should be changed, accidentally or deliberately, to ממערה‎. The east-to-west then west-to-east lines of pursuit implied by the context (20:30-32, 39b-40 vs. 34a, 41-43; especially 20:43 עד נכח הגבעה‎

ממזרח־שמש "as far as the eastern vicinity of Gibeah") may have increased preference for ממערב in 20:33, but the westward movement of the main groups subsequent to the ambush seems to reduce the likelihood that the ambush also approached Gibeah from the west. G. R. Driver proposed that MT מִמַּעֲרֵה (from Proto-semitic ʿrw/y) may attest a BH cognate of Arab. ʿarâ I 'repaired to', V 'repaired to a vicinage', whence ʿirw(un) 'edge' and ʿurwat(un) 'vicinage, region, district' ("Mistranslations" [1947–52], p. 30; so "in the neighbourhood of Gibeah", NEB, REB). Thus, a BH lexeme מַעֲרֶה 'approaches, vicinity' may be postulated.

117 *Judg. 20:38bα.* MT: + הֶרֶב, which may represent thé Hi. impv m. sg < רבה (apocopated form with anaptyctic seghol, Ps. 51:4 [Qere]; GKC, §75gg; BDB, p. 915a; Tg Judg. 20:38 דיסגון "that they should increase") but probably preserves an early dittography of the preceding הָאֹרֵב (so Bertheau, *Richter und Ruth* [1845], pp. 225-26; Moore, *Judges* [1895], pp. 441-42; Budde, *Richter* [1897], p. 137; BDB, p. 915b; *BHS*). A 'corrected' form of this dittography, חֶרֶב, is attested in a few Hebrew MSS and in the OG (τῆς μάχης [< חרב] AI[k],AII[Zglnow,dptv],AIII[N],B-group[except z] Arm Sah[vid]), though it has been omitted (probably in translation) from the Psht and Vg.

118 *Judg. 20:42bα.* MT: מֵהֶעָרִים. Probably a dittography of מ from the following word, and secondarily the latter's pl. form, gave rise to the pl. form מהערים. The context requires that Israelites are the ones destroying Benjaminites, and the only Israelites from any city are those who ambushed Gibeah (20:33b, 37, 40). The city of previous reference is therefore probably Gibeah, which is sg in the Vg and OG (OG: ἐν τῇ πόλει, AII[Zglow] Sah; contra ἀπὸ τῆς πόλεως, AII[ptv] Ethᶜ; or ἀπὸ τῶν πόλεων, rell). So *BHS*, the NEB, NRSV and REB; contra the AV, RV, RSV and NIV.

119 *Judg. 20:43aα.* MT: כִּתְּרוּ. OG: καὶ ἔκοψαν (< וַיִּכְרְתוּ or וַיְכַתְּתוּ). Emend to וַיְכַתְּרוּ (so *BHS*).

120 *Judg. 21:20aα.* Kethib: וַיְצַו. Qere: וַיְצַוּוּ (many Hebrew MSS and the versions; so *BHS*).

121 *Judg. 21:22aα.* Kethib: לְרוֹב. Qere: לָרִיב (several Hebrew MSS; so *BHS*).

BIBLIOGRAPHY

Ackroyd, P. R., "[Review:] C. A. Simpson, *Composition of the Book of Judges*", *JTS* NS 10 (1959), pp. 103-6.
——, *The First Book of Samuel*, CBC, Cambridge, 1971.
Aharoni, Y., "The Ten Thousands of Ephraim and the Thousands of Manasseh", in *Eretz Shomron: The Thirtieth Archaeological Convention, September 1972*, J. Aviram (ed.), Jerusalem, 1973, pp. 38-46 [Hebrew].
——, *The Land of the Bible: A Historical Geography*, A. F. Rainey (trans. and ed.), Philadelphia, 2d edn, 1979.
Aharoni, Y.; Avi-Yonah, M., *The Macmillan Bible Atlas*, New York, 1968; rev. edn, 1977.
Aharoni, Y.; Fritz, V.; Kempinski, A., "Excavations at Tel Masos (Khirbet el-Meshâsh): Preliminary Report on the Second Season, 1974", *TA* 2 (1975), pp. 97-124.
Ahlström, G. W., "The Travels of the Ark: A Religio–Political Composition", *JNES* 43 (1984), pp. 141-49.
Albright, W. F., "The Earliest Forms of Hebrew Verse", *JPOS* 2 (1922), pp. 69-86, 284-85.
——, "New Israelite and Pre-Israelite Sites: The Spring Trip of 1929", *BASOR* 35 (1929), pp. 1-14.
——, "The Song of Deborah in the Light of Archaeology", *BASOR* 62 (1936), pp. 26-31.
——, "A Catalogue of Early Hebrew Lyric Poems (Psalm lxviii)", *HUCA* 23, Part I (1950–1951), pp. 1-39.
——, *Yahweh and the Gods of Canaan*, Jordan Lectures 1965, London, 1968.
Alonso-Schökel, L., "Erzählkunst im Buche der Richter", *Bib* 42 (1961), pp. 143-72.
——, "Dos obras recientes sobre el libro de los Jueces", *Bib* 45 (1964), pp. 543-50.
Alter, R., *The Art of Biblical Narrative*, New York, 1981.
Amiran, R., *Ancient Pottery of the Holy Land*, Jerusalem, 1969.
Amit, Y., "Judges 4: Its Contents and Form", *JSOT* 39 (1987), pp. 89-111.
——, "The Story of Ehud (Judges 3:12-30): The Form and the Message", in *Signs and Wonders: Biblical Texts in Literary Focus*, J. C. Exum (ed.), Decatur, Georgia, 1989, pp. 97-123.
——, "Hidden Polemic in the Conquest of Dan: Judges xvii–xviii", *VT* 40 (1990), pp. 4-20.
Anbar, M., "La 'reprise'", *VT* 38 (1988), pp. 385-98.
Andersen, F. I., *The Sentence in Biblical Hebrew*, The Hague, 1974.
Ap-Thomas, D. R., "The Ephah of Meal in Judges vi 19", *JTS* 41 (1940), pp. 175-77.
Auld, A. G., "Judges i and History: A Reconsideration", *VT* 25 (1975), pp. 261-85.
——, "Gideon: Hacking at the Heart of the Old Testament", *VT* 39 (1989), pp. 257-67.
Babcock-Abrahams, B., "'A Tolerated Margin of Mess': The Trickster and His Tales Reconsidered", *JFI* 11 (1975), pp. 147-86.
Bächli, O., "'Was habe ich mit Dir zu schaffen?' Eine formelhafte Frage im Alten Testament und Neuen Testament", *TZ* 33 (1977), pp. 69-80.
——, *Amphiktyonie im Alten Testament: Forschungsgeschichtliche Studie zur Hypothese von Martin Noth*, Basel, 1977.
Bachmann, J., *Das Buch der Richter: Mit besonderer Rücksicht auf die Geschichte seiner Auslegung und kirchlichen Verwendung*, vol. 1, Berlin, 1868-1869.
Ball, C. J., "Cushan-Rishathaim (Judg. iii.7-11)", *ExpTim* 21 (1909–1910), p. 192.

Barr, J., "[Review:] F. I. Andersen, *The Sentence in Biblical Hebrew*. The Hague, 1974", *JTS* NS 27 (1976), pp. 152-53.

—, *Comparative Philology and the Text of the Old Testament*, Oxford, 1968; repr. edn, London, 1983.

Barré, M. L., "The Meaning of *pršdn* in Judges iii 22", *VT* 41 (1991), pp. 1-11.

Bartelmus, R., "Die sogenannte Jothamfabel—Eine politisch-religiöse Parabeldichtung: Anmerkungen zu einem Teilaspeckt der vordeuteronomistischen israelitischen Literaturgeschichte", *TZ* 41 (1985), pp. 97-120.

Barthélemy, D., *Critique textuelle de l'Ancien Testament*, vol. 1, *Josué, Juges, Ruth, Samuel, Rois, Chroniques, Esdras, Néhémie, Esther*, OBO 50/1, Fribourg, Switzerland, 1982.

Barthélemy, D.; Milik, J. T. (eds.), *Qumran Cave I*, DJD I, Oxford, 1955.

Bartlett, J. R., "The Conquest of Sihon's Kingdom: A Literary Re-examination", *JBL* 97 (1978), pp. 347-51.

Barton, J., *Reading the Old Testament: Method in Biblical Study*, Philadelphia, 1984.

Bauer, H., "Zu Simsons Rätsel in Richter Kapitel 14", *ZDMG* 66 (1912), pp. 473-74.

Becker, U., *Richterzeit und Königtum: Redaktionsgeschichtliche Studien zum Richterbuch*, BZAW 192, Berlin, 1990.

Beeston, A. F. L., "Hebrew *šibbolet* and *šobel*", *JSS* 24 (1979), pp. 175-77.

—, "*Šibbōlet*: A Further Comment", *JSS* 33 (1986), pp. 259-61.

Bentzen, A., *Introduction to the Old Testament*, 2 vols., Copenhagen, 1948-1949.

Berlin, A., *Poetics and Interpretation of Biblical Narrative*, BLS 9, Sheffield, 1983.

Bertheau, E., *Das Buch der Richter und Ruth*, KEHAT 6, F. Hitzig et al. (eds.), Leipzig, 1845; 2d edn, 1883.

Biblia Sacra iuxta latinam vulgatam versionem ad codicum fidem iussu Pii PP. XI, cura et studio monachorum Abbatiae Pontificiae Sancti Hieronymi in urbe ordinis Sancti Benedicti edita, vol. 4, *Iosue, Iudicum, Ruth*, Rome, 1939.

Billen, A. V., "The Hexaplaric Element in the LXX Version of Judges", *JTS* 43 (1942), pp. 12-19.

—, "The Old Latin Version of Judges", *JTS* 43 (1942), pp. 140-49.

Bleek, F., *Einleitung in das Alte Testament*, J. F. Bleek and A. Kamphausen (eds.), J. Wellhausen (rev.), Berlin, 4th edn, 1878.

Blenkinsopp, J., "Ballad Style and Psalm Style in the Song of Deborah: A Discussion", *Bib* 42 (1961), pp. 61-76.

—, "Structure and Style in Judges 13-16", *JBL* 82 (1963), pp. 65-76.

—, *Gibeon and Israel: The Role of Gibeon and the Gibeonites in the Political and Religious History of Early Israel*, SOTSMS 2, Cambridge, 1972.

Bodine, W. R., *The Greek Text of Judges: Recentional Developments*, HSM 23, Chico, California, 1980.

—, "*Kaige* and Other Recensional Developments in the Greek Text of Judges", *BIOSCS* 13 (1980), pp. 45-57.

Boecker, H. J., *Redeformen des Rechtslebens im Alten Testament*, WMANT 14, Neukirchen-Vluyn, 1964; 2d edn, 1970.

Böhme, W., "Die älteste Darstellung in Richt. 6,11-24 und 13,2-24 und ihre Verwandtschaft mit der Jahveurkunde des Pentateuch", *ZAW* 5 (1885), pp. 251-74.

Boling, R. G., *Judges: Introduction, Translation and Commentary*, AB 6A, Garden City, New York, 1975.

Boogaart, T. A., "Stone for Stone: Retribution in the Story of Abimelech and Shechem", *JSOT* 32 (1985), pp. 45-56.

Boorer, S., "The Importance of a Diachronic Approach: The Case of Genesis-Kings", *CBQ* 51 (1989), pp. 195-208.

Bos, J. W. H., "Out of the Shadows: Genesis 38; Judges 4:17-22; Ruth 3", *Semeia* 42 (1988), pp. 37-67.

Breasted, J. H., *Ancient Records of Egypt*, 5 vols., Chicago, 1906-1907.

Brekelmans, C. H. W., *De Herem in het Oude Testament*, Nijmegen, 1959.

Brenner, A., "A Triangle and a Rhombus in Narrative Structure: A Proposed Integrative Reading of Judges iv and v", *VT* 40 (1990), pp. 129-38.

Brettler, M., "The Book of Judges: Literature as Politics", *JBL* 108 (1989), pp. 395-418.

Bright, J., *A History of Israel*, Philadelphia, 3d edn, 1981.

Brockelmann, C., *Hebräische Syntax*, Neukirchen, 1956.

Brockington, L. H., *The Hebrew Text of the Old Testament: The Readings Adopted by the Translators of the New English Bible*, Oxford and Cambridge, 1973.

Brooke, A. E.; McLean, N., *The Old Testament in Greek according to the Text of Codex Vaticanus*, Cambridge, 1906-1940.

Brown, F.; Driver, S. R.; Briggs, C. A. (eds.), *A Hebrew and English Lexicon of the Old Testament*, Oxford, 1906; repr. edn, Lafayette, Indiana, 1978.

Buber, M., *Königtum Gottes*, Berlin, 1932; 2d edn, 1936; Heidelberg, 3d edn, 1956; reprinted in *Werke*, vol. 2, *Schriften zur Bibel*, Munich, 1964, pp. 489-723; ET: *The Kingship of God*, R. Scheimann (trans.), London, 3d edn, 1967.

Budde, K., *Die Bücher Richter und Samuel: Ihre Quellen und ihr Aufbau*, Giessen, 1890.

——, *Das Buch der Richter*, K. Marti (ed.), KHAT 7, Freiburg, im Breisgau, 1897.

Buhl, F., *Geographie des alten Palästina*, Leipzig, 1896.

—— (ed.), *Wilhelm Gesenius' Handwörterbuch über das Alte Testament*, Leipzig, 17th edn, 1915.

Buhl, M.-L.; Holm-Nielsen, S., *Shiloh: The Danish Excavations at Tall Sailun, Palestine, in 1926, 1929, 1932 & 1963*, Copenhagen, 1969.

Bullinger, E. W., *Figures of Speech Used in the Bible*, London, 1898; repr. edn, Grand Rapids, 1968.

Burney, C. F., *The Book of Judges with Introduction and Notes*, London, 1903; 2d edn, 1920.

Buttrick, G. A., et al. (eds.), *The Interpreter's Bible*, 12 vols., Nashville, 1953.

Cathcart, K. J., "The 'Demons' in Judges 5:8a", *BZ* NS 21 (1977), pp. 111-12.

Cazelles, H., "Déborah (Jud. v 14), Amalek et Mâkîr", *VT* 24 (1974), pp. 235-38.

Chalcraft, D. J., "Deviance and Legitimate Action in the Book of Judges", in *The Bible in Three Dimensions: Essays in Celebration of Forty Years of Biblical Studies in the University of Sheffield*, D. J. A. Clines, S. E. Fowl and S. E. Porter (eds.), JSOTS 87, Sheffield, 1990, pp. 177-201.

Churgin, P., *Targum Jonathan to the Prophets*, YOSRes 14, New Haven, 1927; reprinted in L. Smolar and M. Aberbach, *Studies in Targum Jonathan to the Prophets* and P. Churgin, *Targum Jonathan to the Prophets*, LBS, New York, 1983.

Cohen, G. G., "Samson and Hercules: A Comparison between the Feats of Samson and the Labours of Hercules", *EvQ* 42 (1970), pp. 131-41.

Coogan, M. D., "A Structural and Literary Analysis of the Song of Deborah", *CBQ* 40 (1978), pp. 143-66.

Cook, S. A., "The Theophanies of Gideon and Manoah", *JTS* 28 (1927), pp. 368-83.

Cooke, G. A., *The History and Song of Deborah*, Oxford, 1892.

——, *Judges and Ruth*, Cambridge Bible, Cambridge, 1913.

Cornill, C. H., *Einleitung in das Alte Testament*, GTW II/1, Freiburg, im Breisgau, 1891; 2d edn, 1892; ET: *Introduction to the Canonical Books of the Old Testament*, G. H. Box (trans.) (from 5th German edn), TTL, London, 1907.

Cox, C. E., *Hexaplaric Materials Preserved in the Armenian Version*, SBLSCS 21, Atlanta, Georgia, 1986.

Craigie, P. C., "Ancient Semitic War Poetry", PhD diss., University of Aberdeen, 1968.
——, "Some Further Notes on the Song of Deborah", *VT* 22 (1972), pp. 349-53.
——, "Parallel Word Pairs in the Song of Deborah", *JETS* 20 (1977), pp. 15-22.
——, *The Problem of War in the Old Testament*, Grand Rapids, 1978.
Crenshaw, J. L., "The Samson Saga: Filial Devotion or Erotic Attachment?", *ZAW* 86 (1974), pp. 470-504.
Cross, F. M., "The Structure of the Deuteronomic History", *Perspectives in Jewish Learning* 3 (1968), pp. 9-24; reprinted as chapter 10: "The Themes of the Book of Kings and the Structure of the Deuteronomistic History", in F. M. Cross, *Canaanite Myth and Hebrew Epic: Essays in the History of the Religion of Israel*, Cambridge, Massachusetts, 1973, pp. 274-89.
——, *Canaanite Myth and Hebrew Epic: Essays in the History of the Religion of Israel*, Cambridge, Massachusetts, 1973.
Cross, F. M., Jr; Freedman, D. N., *Early Hebrew Orthography*, AOS 36, New Haven, Connecticut, 1952.
——, *Studies in Ancient Yahwistic Poetry*, SBLDS 21, Missoula, Montana, 1975.
Crown, A. D., "A Reinterpretation of Judges ix in the Light of Its Humour", *AbrN* 3 (1961-1962), pp. 90-98.
Culley, R. C., "Structural Analysis: Is It Done with Mirrors?" *Int* 28 (1974), pp. 165-81.
——, "Themes and Variations in Three Groups of OT Narratives", *Semeia* 3 (1975), pp. 3-13.
——, *Studies in the Structure of Hebrew Narrative*, Philadelphia, 1976.
Cundall, A. E., "Judges—An Apology for the Monarchy?", *ExpTim* 81 (1969-1970), pp. 178-81.
Cundall, A. E., *Judges*, in A. E. Cundall and L. Morris, *Judges and Ruth: An Introduction and Commentary*, TOTC 7, London, 1968.
Curtis, J. (ed.), *Fifty Years of Mesopotamian Discovery: The Work of the British School of Archaeology in Iraq 1932-1982*, London, 1982.
Dahood, M., "Northwest Semitic Philology and Job", in *The Bible in Current Catholic Thought*, J. L. McKenzie (ed.), New York, 1962, pp. 55-74.
——, "Scriptio defectiva in Judges 1,19", *Bib* 60 (1979), p. 570.
Daniels, D. R., "Is There a 'Prophetic Lawsuit' Genre?", *ZAW* 99 (1987), pp. 339-60.
Dathe, J. A., *Libri historici Veteris Testamenti*, Halle, 1784.
David, Y., "Simsons Rätsel nach der Auffassung des Moses Hayyim Luzzato", *Semitics* 5 (1977), pp. 32-35.
Davies, G. H., "Judges viii 22-23", *VT* 13 (1963), pp. 151-57.
Davies, P. R., "Ark or Ephod in I Sam. xiv. 18?" *JTS* NS 26 (1975), pp. 82-87.
——, "The History of the Ark in the Books of Samuel", *JNSL* 5 (1977), pp. 9-18.
Day, J., "The Destruction of the Shiloh Sanctuary and Jeremiah vii 12, 14", in *Studies in the Historical Books of the Old Testament*, J. A. Emerton (ed.), SVT 30, Leiden, 1979, pp. 87-94.
——, "Bedan, Abdon or Barak in 1 Samuel xii 11?", *VT* 43 (1993), pp. 461-64.
Delcor, M., "Les attaches littéraires, l'origine et la signification de l'expression biblique 'prendre à témoin le ciel et la terre'", *VT* 16 (1966), pp. 8-25.
Delitzsch, Friedrich, *Prolegomena eines neuen hebräisch-aramäischen Wörterbuches zum Alten Testament*, Leipzig, 1886.
——, *Assyrisches Handwörterbuch*, Leipzig, 1896.
Dexinger, F., "Ein Plädoyer für die Linkshänder im Richterbuch", *ZAW* 89 (1977), pp. 268-69.
Dhorme, É., *La Bible: L'Ancien Testament, I*, Bibliotheque de la Pléiade 120, Paris, 1956.

Dietrich, W., *Prophetie und Geschichte: Eine redaktionsgeschichtliche Untersuchung zum deuteronomistischen Geschichtswerk*, FRLANT 108, Göttingen, 1977.

Dion, P.-E., "The 'Fear Not' Formula and Holy War", *CBQ* 32 (1970), pp. 565-70.

Dirksen, P. B., *The Transmission of the Text in the Peshiṭta Manuscripts of the Book of Judges*, MPIL 1, Leiden, 1972.

——, *Judges*, in *The Old Testament in Syriac according to the Peshiṭta Version*, vol. II/2, Leiden, 1978.

——, "Peshiṭta Institute Communication xix: East and West, Old and Young, in the Text Tradition of the Old Testament Peshiṭta", *VT* 35 (1985), pp. 468-84.

——, "The Relation between the Ancient and the Younger Peshiṭta MSS in Judges", in *Tradition and Re-Interpretation in Jewish and Early Christian Literature: Essays in Honour of Jürgen C. H. Lebram*, J. W. van Henten et al (eds.), Leiden, 1986, pp. 163-71.

——, "The Ancient Peshiṭta MSS of Judges and Their Variant Readings", in *The Peshiṭta: Its Early Text and History: Papers Read at the Peshiṭta Symposium Held at Leiden, 30-31 August 1985*, P. B. Dirksen and M. J. Mulder (eds.), MPIL 4, Leiden, 1988, pp. 127-46.

——, "10c4–Judges and I/II Samuel (II,2)", in *The Peshiṭta: Its Early Text and History: Papers Read at the Peshiṭta Symposium Held at Leiden, 30-31 August 1985*, P. B. Dirksen and M. J. Mulder (eds.), MPIL 4, Leiden, 1988, pp. 270-278.

Donner, H.; Röllig, W., *Kanaanäische und aramäische Inschriften*, 3 vols., Wiesbaden, 1963.

Dothan, T.; Gitin, S., "Ekron of the Philistines: How They Lived, Worked and Worshiped for Five Hundred Years", *BAR* 16/1 (1990), pp. 20-25.

Dragga, S., "In the Shadow of the Judges: The Failure of Saul", *JSOT* 38 (1987), pp. 39-46.

Driver, G. R., "Suggestions and Objections", *ZAW* 55 (1937), pp. 68-71.

——, "Mistranslations in the Old Testament", *WO* 1 (1947–1952), pp. 29-31.

——, "Problems of Interpretation in the Heptateuch", in *Mélanges bibliques: Rédigés en l'honneur de André Robert*, TICP 4, Paris, 1957, pp. 66-76.

——, "Problems in Judges Newly Discussed", *ALUOS* 4 (1962–1963), pp. 6-25.

——, "Once Again Abbreviations", *Textus* 4 (1964), pp. 76-94.

Driver, S. R., *A Treatise on the Use of the Tenses in Hebrew and Some Other Syntactical Questions*, Oxford, 1874; 3d edn, 1892.

——, *Notes on the Hebrew Text and the Topography of the Books of Samuel, with an Introduction on Hebrew Palaeography and the Ancient Versions, and Facsimiles of Inscriptions and Maps*, Oxford, 1890; 2d edn, 1913; repr. edn, Winona Lake, Indiana, 1984.

——, *An Introduction to the Literature of the Old Testament*, ITL 1, Edinburgh, 1891; 9th edn, 1913.

Dumbrell, W. J., "'In Those Days There Was No King in Israel; Every Man Did What Was Right in His Own Eyes': The Purpose of the Book of Judges Reconsidered", *JSOT* 25 (1983), pp. 23-33.

Ehrlich, A. B., *Randglossen zur hebräischen Bibel: Textkritisches, sprachliches und sachliches*, 7 vols., Leipzig, 1908–1914; vol. 3, *Josua, Richter, I und II Samuelis*, 1910; repr. edn, Hildesheim, 1968.

Eissfeldt, O., *Die Quellen des Richterbuches: In synoptischer Anordnung ins Deutsche übersetzt samt einer in Einleitung und Noten gegebenen Begründung*, Leipzig, 1925.

——, *Einleitung in das Alte Testament unter Einschluss der Apokryphen und Pseudepigraphen*, Tübingen, 1934; 3d edn, 1964; ET of the 3d edn: *The Old*

Testament: An Introduction including the Apocrypha and Pseudepigrapha, and also the Works of Similar Type from Qumran, P. R. Ackroyd (trans.), Oxford, 1965.

——, "Silo und Jerusalem", in *Volume du Congrès, Strasbourg 1956*, SVT 4, Leiden, 1957, pp. 138-47.

Elliger, K.; Rudolph, W. (eds.), *Biblia hebraica stuttgartensia*, Stuttgart, 1967-1977.

Emerton, J. A., "A Consideration of Some Alleged Meanings of *ydʿ* in Hebrew", *JSS* 15 (1970), pp. 145-80.

——, "Notes on Two Proposed Emendations in the Book of Judges (11:24 and 16:28)", *ZAW* 85 (1973), pp. 220-23.

——, "Gideon and Jerubbaal", *JTS* NS 27 (1976), pp. 289-312.

——, "Some Comments on the Shibboleth Incident (Judges xii 6)", in *Mélanges bibliques et orientaux en l'honneur de M. Mathias Delcor*, A. Caquot, S. Légasse and M. Tardieu (eds.), AOAT 215, Neukirchen-Vluyn, 1985, pp. 149-57.

Erichsen, W., *Papyrus Harris I*, Bibliotheca Aegyptiaca V, Brussels, 1933.

Erman, A.; Grapow, H., *Wörterbuch der ägyptischen Sprache*, 5 vols., Leipzig, 1926-1931.

Eshel, H.; Erlich, Z., "Abimelech's First Battle with the Lords of Shechem and the Question of the Navel of the Land", *Tarbiz* 58 (1988-1989), pp. 111-16 [Hebrew].

Eskhult, M., *Studies in Verbal Aspect and Narrative Technique in Biblical Hebrew Prose*, AUUSSU 12, Uppsala, 1990.

Exum, J. C., "Promise and Fulfillment: Narrative Art in Judges 13", *JBL* 99 (1980), pp. 43-59.

——, "Aspects of Symmetry and Balance in the Samson Saga", *JSOT* 19 (1981), pp. 3-29.

——, "The Theological Dimension of the Samson Saga", *VT* 33 (1983), pp. 30-45.

——, "The Tragic Vision and Biblical Narrative: The Case of Jephthah", in *Signs and Wonders: Biblical Texts in Literary Focus*, J. C. Exum (ed.), Decatur, Georgia, 1989, pp. 59-83.

——, "The Centre Cannot Hold: Thematic and Textual Instabilities in Judges", *CBQ* 52 (1990), pp. 410-31.

Falkner, R. O., "Egypt: From the Inception of the Nineteenth Dynasty to the Death of Ramses III", in *The Cambridge Ancient History*, vol. II/2, Cambridge, 3d edn, 1975, pp. 217-51.

Fensham, F. C., "Did a Treaty between the Israelites and the Kenites Exist?", *BASOR* 175 (1964), pp. 51-54.

Field, F. (ed.), *Origenis Hexaplorum quae supersunt; sive Veterum Interpretum Graecorum in totum Vetus Testamentum Fragmenta*, 2 vols., Oxford, 1875.

Finkelstein, I.; Bunimovitz, S.; Lederman, Z. in Finkelstein, I. (ed.), "Excavations at Shiloh 1981-1984: Preliminary Report", *TA* 12 (1985), pp. 123-80.

Finkelstein, J. J., *The Ox that Gored*, TAPS 71/2, Philadelphia, 1981.

Fish, T., "War and Religion in Egypt and Mesopotamia", *BJRL* (1939), pp. 387-402.

Fishbane, M., *Biblical Interpretation in Ancient Israel*, Oxford, 1985.

Fisher, L. R. (ed.), *Ras Shamra Parallels*, vol. 1, Rome, 1972.

Fohrer, G., *Einleitung in das Alte Testament*, Heidelburg, 1965; ET: *Introduction to the Old Testament*, D. Green [trans.], Nashville, 1968.

Fokkelman, J. P., *Narrative Art in Genesis: Specimens of Stylistic and Structural Analysis*, SSN 17, Assen, The Netherlands, 1975; Biblical Seminar 12, Sheffield, 2d edn, 1991.

Frankenberg, W., *Die Composition des deuteronomischen Richterbuches (Richter ii,6-xvi), nebst einer Kritik von Richter xvii-xxi*, Marburg, 1895.

Freedman, D. N., "Archaic Forms in Early Hebrew Poetry", *ZAW* 72 (1960), pp. 101-7.

Galling, K., "Erwägungen zum Stelenheiligtum von Hazor", *ZDPV* 75 (1959), pp. 1-13.

Gardiner, A. H., "A Pharonic Encomium (II)", *JEA* 42 (1956), pp. 8-20.

Garr, W. R. *Dialect Geography of Syria-Palestine, 1000-586 B.C.E.*, Philadelphia, 1985.

Garsiel, M., *The First Book of Samuel: A Literary Study of Comparative Structures, Analogies and Parallels*, P. Hackett (trans.), Ramat-Gan, 1985.

Gebrandt, G. E., *Kingship according to the Deuteronomistic History*, SBLDS 87, Atlanta, Georgia, 1986.

Gemser, B., "The *Rîb*- or Controversy-Pattern in Hebrew Mentality", in *Wisdom in Israel and in the Ancient Near East: Presented to H. H. Rowley* (M. Noth and D. W. Thomas [eds.], Festschrift H. H. Rowley, SVT 3, Leiden, 1955), pp. 120-37.

Gerleman, G., "The Song of Deborah in the Light of Stylistics", *VT* 1 (1951), pp. 168-80.

Gesenius, W., *Gesenius' Hebrew Grammar*, E. Kautzsch (ed.), A. E. Cowley (trans. and ed.), Oxford, 2d edn, 1910.

——, *Hebräisches und aramäisches Handwörterbuch über das Alte Testament*, R. Meyer, H. Donner and U. Rüterswörden (eds.), Berlin, 18th edn, 1987-.

Geus, C. H. J. de, *The Tribes of Israel: An Investigation into Some of the Presuppositions of Martin Noth's Amphictyony Hypothesis*, SSN 18, Assen, 1976.

Gitin, S.; Dothan, T., "The Rise and Fall of Ekron of the Philistines: Recent Excavations at an Urban Border Site", *BA* 50 (1987), pp. 197-222.

Glaser, O., "Zur Erzälung von Ehud und Eglon (Ri. 3,14-26)", *ZDPV* 55 (1932), pp. 81-82.

Globe, A., "The Literary Structure and Unity of the Song of Deborah", *JBL* 93 (1974), pp. 493-512.

——, "The Text and Literary Structure of Judges 5,4-5", *Bib* 55 (1974), pp. 168-78.

——, "The Muster of the Tribes in Judges 5,11e-18", *ZAW* 87 (1975), pp. 169-84.

——, "'Enemies Round About': Disintegrative Structure in the Book of Judges", in *Mappings of the Biblical Terrain: The Bible as Text*, V. L. Tollers and J. Maier (eds.), Bucknell Review 33/2, Lewisburg, Pennsylvania, 1990, pp. 233-51.

Glock, A., "Warfare in Mari and Early Israel", PhD diss., University of Michigan, 1968.

Good, E. M., *Irony in the Old Testament*, London, 1965; repr. edn, BLS 3, Sheffield, 1981.

Gooding, D. W., "The Composition of the Book of Judges", in *Eretz-Israel: Archaeological, Historical and Geographical Studies*, vol. 16, *Harry M. Orlinsky Volume*, Jerusalem, 1982, pp. 70*-79*.

Gordis, R., *The Biblical Text in the Making: A Study of the Kethib-Qere*, New York, 2d edn, 1971.

Gordon, R. P., "David's Rise and Saul's Demise: Narrative Analogy in 1 Samuel 24-26", *TynBul* 31 (1980), pp. 37-64.

——, "Simplicity of the Highest Cunning: Narrative Art in the Old Testament", *SBET* 6 (1988), pp. 69-80.

Goslinga, C. J., *Richteren-Ruth*, KVHS, Kampen, The Netherlands, 3d edn, 1966; ET in *Joshua, Judges, Ruth*, R. Togtman (trans.), BSC, Grand Rapids, 1986.

Gottlieb, F., "Three Mothers", *Judaism* 30 (1981), pp. 194-203.

Graetz, H., *Geschichte der Juden von den ältesten Zeiten bis auf die Gegenwart*, 11 vols., Leipzig, 1860-1906.

——, *Emendationes in Plerosque Sacrae Scripturae Veteris Testamenti Libros ...*, G. Bacher (ed.), 3 vols., Breslau, 1892-1894.

Gray, J., *Joshua, Judges, Ruth*, NCBC, New York, 1967; Basingstoke, 2d edn, 1986.

——, "Israel in the Song of Deborah", in *Ascribe to the Lord: Biblical and Other Studies in Memory of Peter C. Craigie*, L. Eslinger and G. Taylor (eds.), JSOTS 67, Sheffield, 1988, pp. 421-55.

Greenspahn, F. E., "An Egyptian Parallel to Judg 17:6 and 21:25", *JBL* 101 (1982), pp. 129-30.
———, "The Theology of the Framework of Judges", *VT* 36 (1986), pp. 385-96.
Greenstein, E. L., "The Riddle of Samson", *Prooftexts* 1 (1981), pp. 237-60.
Gressmann, H., *Die Anfänge Israels: Von 2. Mosis bis Richter und Ruth*, SAT I/2, Göttingen, 1914; 2d ed., 1922.
Grether, O., "Die Bezeichnung 'Richter' für die charismatischen Helden der vorstaatlichen Zeit", *ZAW* 57 (1939), pp. 110-21.
———, *Das Deboralied: Eine metrische Rekonstruktion*, BFCT 43/2, Gütersloh, 1941.
Güdemann, M., "Tendenz und Abfassungszeit der letzten Kapitel des Buches der Richter", *MGWJ* 18 (1869), pp. 357-68.
Gunkel, H.; Begrich, J., *Einleitung in die Psalmen: Die Gattungen der religiösen Lyrik Israels*, Göttingen, 1933.
Gunn, D. M., "Narrative Patterns and Oral Tradition in Judges and Samuel", *VT* 24 (1974), pp. 286-317.
———, "The 'Battle Report': Oral or Scribal Convention?", *JBL* 93 (1974), pp. 513-18.
———, "Joshua and Judges", in *The Literary Guide to the Bible*, R. Alter and F. Kermode (eds.), Cambridge, Massachusetts, 1987, pp. 102-21.
Habel, N., "The Form and Significance of the Call Narratives", *ZAW* 77 (1965), pp. 297-323.
Halpern, B., *The Emergence of Israel in Canaan*, SBLMS 29, Chico, California, 1983.
———, "The Assassination of Eglon: The First Locked-Room Murder Mystery", *BibRev* 4/6 (1988), pp. 32-41, 44b-c.
———, "A Message for Eglon: The Case of Ehud Ben-Gera", in *The First Historians: The Hebrew Bible and History*, San Francisco, 1988, pp. 40-69.
Hänsler, H., "Der historische Hintergrund von Richter 3,8-10", *Bib* 11 (1930), pp. 391-418; 12 (1931), pp. 3-26, 271-96, 395-410.
Haran, M., "The Bas-Reliefs on the Sarcophagus of Ahiram King of Byblos in the Light of Archaeological and Literary Parallels from the Ancient Near East", *IEJ* 8 (1958), pp. 15-25, pls. 10B-11.
Harel, M., "Gilead within Ephraim within Manasseh," in *Eretz Shomron: The Thirtieth Archaeological Convention September 1972*, J. Aviram (ed.), Jerusalem, 1973, pp. 47-51 [Hebrew].
Harrington, D. J., "The Prophecy of Deborah: Interpretive Homiletics in Targum Jonathan of Judges 5", *CBQ* 48 (1986), pp. 432-42.
Harrington, D. J.; Saldarini, A. J., *Targum Jonathan of the Former Prophets: Introduction, Translation and Notes*, in *The Aramaic Bible*, vol. 10, M. McNamara (ed.), Edinburgh, 1987.
Hart, R. van der, "The Camp of Dan and the Camp of Yahweh", *VT* 25 (1975), pp. 720-28.
Hartmann, R., "Simsons Füchse", *ZAW* 31 (1911), pp. 69-72.
Harvey, J., "Le 'Rîb-Pattern', réquisitoire prophétique sur la rupture de l'alliance", *Bib* 43 (1962), pp. 172-96.
———, *Le plaidoyer prophétique contre Israël après la rupture de l'alliance: Étude d'une formule littéraire de l'Ancien Testament*, Studia 22, Paris, 1967.
Haupt, P. (ed.), *The Sacred Books of the Old Testament: A Critical Edition of the Hebrew Text Printed in Colours*, 16 vols., Leipzig, 1894-1904.
Hauser, A. J., "The 'Minor Judges'—A Re-evaluation", *JBL* 94 (1975), pp. 190-200.
———, "Judges 5: Parataxis in Hebrew Poetry", *JBL* 99 (1980), pp. 23-41.
———, "Two Songs of Victory: A Comparison of Exodus 15 and Judges 5", in *Directions in Biblical Hebrew Poetry*, E. R. Follis (ed.), JSOTS 40, Sheffield, 1987, pp. 265-84.

Hauser, A. J.; Gregory, R., *From Carmel to Horeb: Elijah in Crisis*, JSOTS 85, BLS 19, Sheffield, 1990.

Hävernick, H. A. C., *Handbuch der historische-kritischen Einleitung in das Alte Testament*, 3 vols., Erlangen, 1839-1856.

Heintz, J.-G., "Oracles prophétiques et 'guerre saint' selon les Archives Royales de Mari et l'AT", in *Congress Volume, Rome 1968*, SVT 17, Leiden, 1969, pp. 112-38, 4 figs.

Hengstenberg, E. W., *Beiträge zur Einleitung in das Alte Testament*, 3 vols., Berlin, 1831-1839.

Herdner, A., *Corpus des tablettes en cunéiformes alphabétiques découvertes à Ras Shamra-Ugarit de 1929 à 1939*, Paris, 1963.

Hertzberg, H. W., *Die Bücher Josua, Richter, Ruth: übersetzt und erklärt*, ATD 9, Göttingen, 1953.

Hesse, F., "Wurzelt die prophetische Gerichtsrede im israelitischen Kult?", *ZAW* 65 (1953), pp. 45-53.

Holmes, R.; Parsons, J. (eds.), *Vetus Testamentum Græcum cum variis lectionibus*, Oxford, 1798-1827.

Hollenberg, J., "Zur Textkritik des Buches Josua und des Buches der Richter", *ZAW* 1 (1881), pp. 97-105.

Houbigant, K. F., *Biblia Hebraica cum notis criticis et versione latina ad notas criticas facta ...*, 4 vols., Paris, 1753.

Hübner, U., "Mord auf dem Abort? Überlegungen zu Humor, Gewaltdarstellung und Realienkunde in Ri 3,12-30", *BN* 40 (1987), pp. 130-40; 1 fig.

Huffmon, H. B., "The Covenant Lawsuit in the Prophets", *JBL* 78 (1959), pp. 285-95.

Humphreys, W. L., "The Story of Jephthah and the Tragic Vision: A Response to J. Cheryl Exum", in *Signs and Wonders: Biblical Texts in Literary Focus*, J. C. Exum (ed.), Decatur, Georgia, 1989, pp. 85-96.

Ishida, T., "The Leaders of the Tribal Leagues: 'Israel' in the Pre-Monarchic Period", *RB* 80 (1973), pp. 514-30.

Jack, J. W., "Cushan-Rishathaim (כּוּשַׁן רִשְׁעָתַיִם)", *ExpTim* 35 (1923-1924), pp. 426-28.

Janzen, J. G., "A Certain Woman in the Rhetoric of Judges 9", *JSOT* 38 (1987), pp. 33-37.

Jeremias, J., *Theophanie: Die Geschichte einer alttestamentlichen Gattung*, WMANT 10, Neukirchen-Vluyn, 1965.

Johnstone, W., "*yd* II, 'Be Humbled, Humiliated'?", *VT* 41 (1991), pp. 49-62.

Jones, G. H., "'Holy War' or 'Yahweh War'?", *VT* 25 (1975), pp. 642-58.

——, "The Concept of Holy War", in *The World of Ancient Israel: Sociological, Anthropological and Political Perspectives*, R. E. Clements (ed.), Cambridge, 1989, pp. 299-321.

Junker, H., "Konsonantenumstellung als Fehlerquelle und textkritisches Hifsmittel im MT", in *Werden und Wesen des Alten Testaments*, BZAW 66, Berlin, 1936, pp. 162-74.

Kallai, Z., "The Southern Border of the Land of Israel—Pattern and Application", *VT* 37 (1987), pp. 438-45.

Kaufmann, Y., *The Book of Judges*, Jerusalem, 1961-1962 [Hebrew].

Kedar-Kopfstein, B., "The Vulgate as a Translation: Some Semantic and Syntactical Aspects of Jerome's Version of the Hebrew Bible", PhD diss., Hebrew University, Jerusalem, 1968.

Keil, C. F.; Delitzsch, Franz, *Biblischer Commentar über das Alten Testament*, vol. II/1, *Josua, Richter und Ruth*, by C. F. Keil, Leipzig, 1863; 2d edn, 1874; ET (from the 1st German edn): *Biblical Commentary on the Old Testament*, vol. 4, *Joshua, Judges,*

Ruth, J. Martin (trans.), CFTL 4/VIII, Edinburgh, 1868; repr. edn, *Commentary on the Old Testament*, 10 vols., vol. 2, *Joshua, Judges, Ruth, I & II Samuel*, Grand Rapids, 1976.

Kennedy, J., *An Aid to the Textual Amendment of the Old Testament*, Edinburgh, 1928.

Keukens, K. H., "Richter 11,37f: Rite de passage und Übersetzungsprobleme", *BN* 19 (1982), pp. 41-42.

Kittel, R., "Die pentateuchischen Urkunden in den Büchern Richter und Samuel", *TSK* 65 (1892), pp. 44-71.

——, *Geschichte der Hebräer*, 2 vols., Gotha, 1888-1893.

——, *Das Buch der Richter*, in *HSAT*, Tübingen, 3d edn, 1909.

—— (ed.), *Biblia hebraica*, Stuttgart, 2d edn, 1913; 3d edn, 1929-1937.

Kjaer, H., "The Excavation of Shiloh", *JPOS* 10 (1930), pp. 87-174.

Klein, L. R., *The Triumph of Irony in the Book of Judges*, JSOTS 68, BLS 14, Sheffield, 1988.

Knauf, E. A., "Zum Text von Ri 5,14", *Bib* 64 (1983), pp. 428-29.

Knight, D. N., *Rediscovering the Traditions of Israel*, SBLDS 9, Missoula, Montana, rev. edn, 1975.

Koehler, L., "Hebräische Vokabeln III", *ZAW* 58 (1940-1941), pp. 228-34.

Koehler, L.; Baumgartner, W., *Lexicon in Veteris Testamenti libros*, Leiden, 2d edn, 1953.

Koehler, L.; Baumgartner, W.; Stamm, J. J., *Hebräisches und aramäisches Lexikon zum Alten Testament*, 4 vols., Leiden, 3d edn, 1967-1990.

Kogut, S., "On the Meaning and Syntactical Status of הִנֵּה in Biblical Hebrew", in *Studies in Bible, 1986*, S. Japhet (ed.), ScrHier 31, Jerusalem, 1986, pp. 133-54.

König, E., *Historisch-kritisches Lehrgebäude der hebräischen Sprache*, 2 vols., Leipzig, 1881, 1897.

Kornfeld, W., "Onomastica aramaica und das Alte Testament", *ZAW* 88 (1976), pp. 105-12.

Kraeling, E. G. H., "Difficulties in the Story of Ehud", *JBL* 54 (1935), pp. 205-10.

Kübel, P., "Epiphanie und Altarbau", *ZAW* 83 (1971), pp. 225-31.

Kuenen, A., *Historisch-critisch Onderzoek naar het Onstaan en de Verzameling van de Boeken des Ouden Verbonds*, 3 vols., Leiden, 1861-1865; Amsterdam, 2d edn, 1885-1892; GT: *Historisch-kritische Einleitung in die Bücher des Alten Testaments*, T. Weber (trans.), 3 vols., Leipzig, 1887-1892.

Kutsch, E., "Die Wurzel עצר im Hebräischen", *VT* 2 (1952), pp. 57-69.

Labat, R., *Le caractère religieux de la royauté Assyro-Babylonienne*, Études d'Assyriologie, Paris, 1939.

Labuschagne, C. J., "*Teraphim*—A New Proposal for Its Etymology", *VT* 16 (1966), pp. 115-17.

Lagrange, M.-J., *Le livre des Juges*, Ebib 2, Paris, 1903.

Lambert, W. G., "[Review:] I. Soisalon-Soininen, *Die Textformen der Septuaginta-Übersetzung des Richterbuches*", *VT* 2 (1952), pp. 184-89.

Landy, F., "Gilead and the Fatal Word", in *Proceedings of the Ninth World Congress of Jewish Studies, Jerusalem, August 4-12, 1985: Division A, The Period of the Bible*, Jerusalem, 1986, pp. 39-44.

Lasine, S., "Guest and Host in Judges 19: Lot's Hospitality in an Inverted World", *JSOT* 29 (1984), pp. 37-59.

Leach, E., *Genesis as Myth and Other Essays*, London, 1969.

Lemaire, A., "L'incident de *sibbolet* (Jg 12,6): Perspective historique", in *Mélanges bibliques et orientaux en l'honneur de M. Mathias Delcor*, A. Caquot, S. Légasse and M. Tardieu (eds.), AOAT 215, Neukirchen-Vluyn, 1985, pp. 275-81.

Lemche, N. P., *Israel i dommertiden: En oversigt over diskussionen om M. Noths "Das System der zwölf Stämme Israels"*, TT 4, Copenhagen, 1972 [Danish].
——, "The Greek 'Amphictyony'—Could It Be a Prototype for the Israelite Society in the Period of the Judges?", *JSOT* 4 (1977), pp. 48-59.
——, *Early Israel: Anthropological and Historical Studies on the Israelite Society before the Monarchy*, SVT 37, Leiden, 1986.
Lewis, C. T.; Short, C., *A Latin Dictionary*, Oxford, 1879.
Licht, J., *Storytelling in the Bible*, Jerusalem, 1978.
Liddell, H. G.; Scott, R., *Greek-English Lexicon*, H. S. Jones (rev.), Oxford, 9th edn, 1925-1940.
Liebreich, E. J., "Observations on 'Some Rabbinic Evidence for a Hebrew Root yd^c = $wd^{c_{'}}$ (*JQR* XXXVII, 177-8)", *JQR* NS 37 (1946-1947), pp. 337-79.
Limburg, J., "The Root ריב and the Prophetic Lawsuit Speeches", *JBL* 88 (1969), pp. 291-304.
Lind, M. C., *Yahweh is a Warrior: The Theology of Warfare in Ancient Israel*, Scottdale, Pennsylvania, 1980.
Lindars, B., "Some Septuagint Readings in Judges", *JTS* NS 22 (1971), pp. 1-14.
——, "Jotham's Fable: A New Form-Critical Analysis", *JTS* NS 24 (1973), pp. 355-66.
——, "The Israelite Tribes in Judges", in *Studies in the Historical Books of the Old Testament*, J. A. Emerton (ed.), SVT 30, Leiden, 1979, pp. 95-112.
——, "Deborah's Song: Women in the Old Testament", *BJRL* 65 (1982-1983), pp. 158-75.
——, "A Commentary on the Greek Judges?", in *VI Congress of the International Organization for Septuagint and Cognate Studies, Jerusalem 1986*, C. E. Cox (ed.), Atlanta, Georgia, 1987, pp. 167-200.
——, *Judges 1-5: A New Translation and Commentary*, A. D. H. Mayes (ed.), Edinburgh, 1995.
Lipiński, É., "Juges 5,4-5 et Psaume 68,8-11", *Bib* 48 (1967), pp. 185-206.
Long, B. O., "Framing Repetitions in Biblical Historiography", in *Proceedings of the Ninth World Congress of Jewish Studies, Jerusalem, August 4-12, 1985: Division A, The Period of the Bible*, Jerusalem, 1986, pp. 69-76.
Luckenbill, D. D., *Ancient Records of Assyria and Babylonia*, 2 vols., Chicago, 1926, 1927.
Luria, B.-Z., "The Account of the Outrage at Gibeah", in *Studies in the Book of Judges*, PIBS 10, Jerusalem, 1966, pp. 463-94 [Hebrew].
Machinist, P. B., "The Epic of Tikulti-Ninurta I: A Study in Middle Assyrian Literature", PhD diss., Yale University, 1978.
Macintosh, A. A., "The Meaning of *mklym* in Judges xviii 7", *VT* 35 (1985), pp. 68-77.
Malamat, A., "Cushan Rishathaim and the Decline of the Near East around 1200 B.C.", *JNES* 13 (1954), pp. 231-42.
——, "The Battle of Gideon against Midian", in *The Military History of the Land of Israel in Bible Times*, J. Levor (ed.), Tel Aviv, 1964, pp. 110-23 [Hebrew].
——, "The Danite Migration and the Pan-Israelite Exodus-Conquest: A Biblical Narrative Pattern", *Bib* 51 (1970), pp. 1-16.
——, "Charismatic Leadership in the Book of Judges", in *Études Sémitiques*, Paris, 1975, pp. 30-35; reprinted in *Magnalia Dei: The Mighty Acts of God: Essays on the Bible and Archaeology in Memory of G. Ernest Wright*, F. M. Cross, W. E. Lemke and P. D. Miller, Jr (eds.), Garden City, New York, 1976, pp. 152-68.
Maly, E. H., "The Jotham Fable—Anti-Monarchial?", *CBQ* 22 (1960), pp. 299-305.
Marcus, D., *Jephthah and His Vow*, Lubbock, Texas, 1986.
Marcus, R., "The Word Šibboleth Again", *BASOR* 87 (1942), p. 39.

Margalith, O., "Samson's Riddle and Samson's Magic Locks", *VT* 36 (1986), pp. 225-34.
——, "The Hivites", *ZAW* 100 (1988), pp. 60-70.
Margolis, M. L., "A Passage in Ecclesiasticus and Judg. 11,37", *ZAW* 21 (1901), pp. 271-72.
—— (ed.), *The Book of Joshua in Greek, according to the Critically Restored Text with an Apparatus Containing the Variants of the Principal Recensions and of the Individual Witnesses*, Paris, 1931.
Marquart, J., "שִׁבֹּלֶת = ephraimitisch סִבֹּלֶת = שִׁבֹּלֶת?", *ZAW* 8 (1888), pp. 151-55.
Martin, J. D., *The Book of Judges*, CBC, Cambridge, 1975.
Matthews, V., "Hospitality and Hostility in Genesis 19 and Judges 19", *BTB* 22 (1992), pp. 3-11.
Mayes, A. D. H., *Israel in the Period of the Judges*, SBT II/29, London, 1974.
——, *The Story of Israel between Settlement and Exile: A Redactional Study of the Deuteronomistic History*, London, 1983.
——, *Judges*, OTG 3, Sheffield, 1985.
McCarter, P. K., *I Samuel: A New Translation with Introduction, Notes and Commentary*, AB 8, Garden City, New York, 1980.
McCarthy, D. J., "II Samuel 7 and the Structure of the Deuteronomic History", *JBL* 84 (1965), pp. 131-38.
——, *Old Testament Covenant: A Survey of Current Opinions* Richmond, Virginia, 1972.
——, "The Uses of *wĕhinnēh* in Biblical Hebrew", *Bib* 61 (1980), pp. 330-42.
McDaniel, T. F., *Deborah Never Sang: A Philological Study on the Song of Deborah (Judges Chapter V)*, Jerusalem, 1983.
McKane, W., *Proverbs: A New Approach*, OTL, London, 1970.
Mendelsohn, I., "The Disinheritance of Jephthah in the Light of Paragraph 27 of the Lipit-Ishtar Code", *IEJ* 4 (1954), pp. 116-19.
Merrill, E. H., *Kingdom of Priests: A History of Old Testament Israel*, Grand Rapids, 1987.
——, "The 'Accession Year' and Davidic Chronology", *JANES* 19 (1989), pp. 101-12.
Michaelis, J. D., *Deutsche Übersetzung des Alten Testaments mit Anmerkungen ...*, 13 vols., Göttingen, 1773-1785.
Miller, P. D., Jr, *The Divine Warrior in Early Israel*, HSM 5, Cambridge, Massachusetts, 1973.
Miscall, P. D., "The Jacob and Joseph Stories as Analogies", *JSOT* 6 (1978), pp. 28-40.
——, *The Workings of Old Testament Narrative*, Philadelphia, 1983.
Mitchell, T. C., *The Bible in the British Museum: Interpreting the Evidence*, London, 1988.
Mittmann, S., "Aroer, Minnith und Abel Keramim (Jdc 11,33)", *ZDPV* 85 (1969), pp. 63-75.
——, "Ri. 1,16f. und das Siedlungsgebiet der Kenitischen Sippe Hobab", *ZDPV* 93 (1977), pp. 212-35.
Montgomery, J. A., *A Critical and Exegetical Commentary on the Book of Daniel*, ICC, Edinburgh, 1927.
Moore, G. F., *A Critical and Exegetical Commentary on Judges*, ICC, Edinburgh, 1895.
——, vol. 7, *The Book of Judges: Critical Edition of the Hebrew Text* (1900), in *The Sacred Books of the Old Testament: A Critical Edition of the Hebrew Text Printed in Colours*, 16 vols., P. Haupt (ed.), Leipzig, 1894-1904.
Moran, W. J., "A Study of the Deuteronomic History", *Bib* 46 (1965), pp. 223-28.
Mosca, P. G., "Who Seduced Whom? A Note on Joshua 15:18//Judges 1:14", *CBQ* 46 (1984), pp. 18-22.

Mullen, E. T., Jr, "The 'Minor Judges': Some Literary and Historical Considerations", *CBQ* 44 (1982), pp. 185-201.

Müller, H.-P., "Der Aufbau des Deboraliedes", *VT* 16 (1966), pp. 446-59.

——, "Der Begriff 'Rätsel' im Alten Testament", *VT* 20 (1970), pp. 465-89.

Murray, D. F., "Narrative Structure and Technique in the Deborah–Barak Story (Judges iv 4-22)", in *Studies in the Historical Books of the Old Testament*, J. A. Emerton (ed.), SVT 30, Leiden, 1979, pp. 155-89.

Musil, A., *Arabaia Petraea III*, Vienna, 1908.

——, *The Manners and Customs of the Rwala Bedouins*, New York, 1928.

Myers, J. M., "The Book of Judges: Introduction and Exegesis", in *IB*, vol. 2, pp. 675-826.

Neef, H.-D., "Der Sieg Deboras und Baraks über Sisera: Exegetische Beobachtungen zum Aufbau und Werden von Jdc 4,1-24", *ZAW* 101 (1989), pp. 28-49.

Nel, P., "The Riddle of Samson (Judg 14,14.18)", *Bib* 66 (1985), pp. 534-45.

Nelson, R. D., "The Redactional Duality of the Deuteronomistic History", PhD diss., Union Theological Seminary, Virginia, 1974.

——, *The Double Redaction of the Deuteronomistic History*, JSOTS 18, Sheffield, 1981.

Neteler, B., *Das Buch der Richter der Vulgata und des hebräischen Textes übersetst und erklärt*, Munster, in Westfalen, 1900.

Niditch, S., "The 'Sodomite' Theme in Judges 19-20: Family, Community, and Social Disintegration", *CBQ* 44 (1982), pp. 365-78.

——, "Samson as Culture Hero, Trickster, and Bandit: The Empowerment of the Weak", *CBQ* 52 (1990), pp. 608-24.

Nielsen, K., *Yahweh as Prosecutor and Judge: An Investigation of the Prophetic Lawsuit (Rîb Pattern)*, F. Cryer (trans.), JSOTS 9, Sheffield, 1978.

——, "Das Bild des Gerichts (RIB-Pattern) in Jes. i-xii: Eine Analyse der Beziehungen zwischen Bildsprache und dem Anliegen der Verkündigung", *VT* 29 (1979), pp. 309-24.

Nöldeke, T., *Untersuchungen zur Kritik des Alten Testaments*, Kiel, 1869.

North, C. R., *The Old Testament Interpretation of History*, London, 1946.

Noth, M., *Die israelitischen Personennamen in Rahmen der gemeinsemitischen Namengebung*, BWANT III/10, Stuttgart, 1928.

——, *Das System der zwölf Stämme Israels*, BWANT IV/1, Stuttgart, 1930; 2d edn, 1966.

——, *Überlieferungsgeschichtliche Studien, I. Die sammelnden und bearbeitenden Geschichtswerke im Alten Testament*, Schriften der Königsberger Gelehrten Gesellschaft, 18. Jahr., Geisteswissenschaftliche Klasse, Heft 2, Halle, 1943, pp. 43-266; Tübingen, 2d edn, 1957; ET of 2d edn, pp. 1-110: *The Deuteronomistic History*, JSOTS 15, Sheffield, 1981.

——, *Geschichte Israels*, Göttingen, 2d edn, 1954; ET: *The History of Israel*, London, 2d edn, 1960.

——, "Der Hintergrund von Richter 17-18" (1962); reprinted in vol. 1, *Archäologische, exegetische und topographische Untersuchungen zur Geschichte Israels*, in *Aufsätze zur biblischen Landes- und Altertumskunde*, 2 vols., H. W. Wolff (ed.), Neukirchen-Vluyn, 1971, pp. 133-47; ET: "The Background of Judges 17-18", in *Israel's Prophetic Heritage: Essays in Honor of James Muilenburg*, B. W. Anderson and W. Harrelson (eds.), The Preachers' Library, London, 1962, pp. 68-85.

Nötscher, F., *Das Buch der Richter*, EB 12, Würzburg, 2d edn, 1953.

Nowack, W., *Richter, Ruth, und Bücher Samuelis*, HKAT I/4, Göttingen, 1902.

Obermann, J., "An Early Phoenician Political Document: With a Parallel to Judges 11:24", *JBL* 58 (1939), pp. 229-42.

O'Connell, R. H., "Proverbs vii 16-17: A Case of Fatal Deception in a 'Woman and the Window' Type-Scene", *VT* 41 (1991), pp. 235-41.

——, "Deuteronomy vii 1-26: Asymmetrical Concentricity and the Rhetoric of Conquest", *VT* 42 (1992), pp. 248-65.

——, "[Review:] U. Becker, *Richterzeit und Königtum: Redaktionsgeschichtliche Studien zum Richterbuch*", *VT* 43 (1993), pp. 133-34.

——, *Concentricity and Continuity: The Literary Structure of Isaiah*, JSOTS 188, Sheffield, 1994.

Oppenheim, A. L. "Cyrus (557-529)", in *The Ancient Near East*, vol. 1, *An Anthology of Texts and Pictures*, J. B. Pritchard (ed.), Princeton, 1958, pp. 206-8.

Orlinsky, H. M., "Critical Notes on Gen 39:14-17; Jud 11:37: II. The Corrupt Character and Origin of *wᵉiāraḏtī* in Jud 11:37", *JBL* 61 (1942), pp. [87-97] 92-97.

Payne Smith, J. (ed.), *A Compendious Syriac Dictionary*, Oxford, 1903.

Pearce, R. A., "Shiloh and Jer. vii 12, 14 & 15", *VT* 23 (1973), pp. 105-8.

Peckham, B., *The Composition of the Deuteronomistic History*, F. M. Cross (ed.), HSM 35, Atlanta, Georgia, 1985.

Piatti, P. T., "Una nuova interpretazione metrica, testuale, esegetica, del Cantico di Dèbora (Giudici 5,2-31)", *Bib* 27 (1946), pp. 180-81.

Polzin, R. M., *Moses and the Deuteronomist: A Literary Study of the Deuteronomic History*, part 1, *Deuteronomy, Joshua, Judges*, New York, 1980.

Porter, J. R., "Samson's Riddle: Judges xiv. 14, 18", *JTS* NS 13 (1962), pp. 106-9.

——, "[Review:] I. Soisalon-Soininen, *Die Textformen der Septuaginta-Übersetzung des Richterbuches*", *JTS* NS 4 (1953), pp. 57-59.

Pretzl, O., "Septuaginta-Probleme im Buch der Richter: Die griecheschen Handschriftengruppen im Buch der Richter untersucht nach ihrem Verhältnis zueinander", *Bib* 7 (1926), pp. 233-69, 353-83.

Pritchard, J. B. (ed.), *The Ancient Near East*, vol. 1, *An Anthology of Texts and Pictures*, Princeton, 1958.

—— (ed.), *Ancient Near Eastern Texts Relating to the Old Testament*, Princeton, 3d edn, 1969.

—— (ed.), *The Ancient Near East in Pictures Relating to the Old Testament*, Princeton, 2d edn, 1969.

—— (ed.), *The Ancient Near East*, vol. 2, *A New Anthology of Texts and Pictures*, Princeton, 1975.

Rabin, C., "Judges v, 2 and the 'Ideology' of Deborah's War", *JJS* 6 (1955), pp. 125-34.

Rad, G. von, *Deuteronomium-Studien*, FRLANT 58, Göttingen, 1947; 2d edn, 1948; ET: *Studies in Deuteronomy*, D. M. G. Stalker (trans.), SBT 9, London, 1953.

——, *Theologie des Alten Testaments*, vol. 1: *Die Theologie der geschichtlichen Überlieferungen Israels*, Munich, 1957; ET: *Old Testament Theology*, vol. 1: *The Theology of Israel's Historical Traditions*, D. M. G. Stalker (trans.), London, 1962.

——, *Der Heilige Krieg im alten Israel*, Zurich, 1951; 2d edn, 1952; 3d edn, 1958; 4th edn, Göttingen, 1965; 5th edn, 1969; ET of 3d edn: *Holy War in Ancient Israel*, M. J. Dawn (trans. and ed.), Grand Rapids, 1991.

——, *Gottes Wirken in Israel*, Neukirchen-Vluyn, 1974; ET: *God at Work in Israel*, J. H. Marks (trans.), Nashville, 1980.

Reade, J., *Assyrian Sculpture*, London, 1983.

Reider, J., "Etymological Studies: יָדַע or יָרַע and רָעַע", *JBL* 66 (1947), pp. 315-17.

——, "Etymological Studies in Biblical Hebrew", *VT* 4 (1954), pp. 276-95.

Rendsburg, G. A., "More on Hebrew *Šibbōlet*", *JSS* 33 (1986), pp. 255-58.

Revell, E. J., "The Battle with Benjamin (Judges xx 29-48) and Hebrew Narrative Techniques", *VT* 35 (1985), pp. 417-33.

Richter, W., *Traditionsgeschichtliche Untersuchungen zum Richterbuch*, BBB 18, Bonn, 1963; 2d edn, 1966.

——, *Die Bearbeitungen des 'Retterbuches' in der deuteronomischen Epoche*, BBB 21, Bonn, 1964.

——, "Die Überlieferungen um Jephtah, Ri 10,17–12,6", *Bib* 47 (1966), pp. 485-556.

——, *Die sogenannten vorprophetischen Berufungsberichte: Eine literaturewissenschaftliche Studie zu 1 Sam 9,1–10,16, Ex 3f. und Ri 6,11b–17*, FRLANT 101, Göttingen, 1970.

Riehm, E., *Einleitung in das Alte Testament*, A. Brandt (rev. and ed.), 2 vols., Halle, 1889–1890.

Rietzschel, C., "Zu Jdc 5:14b-15a", *ZAW* 83 (1971), pp. 211-25.

Robertson, D. A., *Linguistic Evidence in Dating Early Hebrew Poetry*, SBLDS 3, Missoula, Montana, 1972.

Roche, M. de, "Yahweh's *Rîb* against Israel: A Reassessment of the So-Called 'Prophetic Lawsuit' in the Preexilic Prophets", *JBL* 102 (1983), pp. 563-74.

Rose, M., "'Siebzig Könige' aus Ephraim (Jdc. v 14)", *VT* 26 (1976), pp. 447-52.

Rösel, H. N., "Zur Ehud-Erzählung", *ZAW* 89 (1977), pp. 270-72.

——, "The Literary and Geographical Facets of the Shibboleth Story in Judges 12:1-6", in *Studies in the History of the Jewish People and the Land of Israel* 5 (1980), pp. 33-41 [Hebrew].

Rozenberg, M. S., "The *šōfᵉṭîm* in the Bible", in *Eretz-Israel: Archaeological, Historical and Geographical Studies*, vol. 12, *Nelson Glueck Memorial Volume*, Jerusalem, 1975, pp. 77*-86*.

Ruben, P., "The Song of Deborah", *JQR* 10 (1897–1898), pp. 541-58.

Rudolph, W., *Der 'Elohist' von Exodus bis Josua*, BZAW 68, Giessen, 1938.

——, "Textkritische Anmerkungen zum Richterbuch", in *Festschrift Otto Eissfeldt zum 60. Geburtstage, 1. September 1947, dargebracht von Freunden und Verehren*, J. Fück (ed.), Halle an der Saale, 1947, pp. 199-212.

Ryken, L., *The Literature of the Bible*, Grand Rapids, 1974.

Sáenz-Badillos, A.; Targarona, J., "Some Contributions to the Text-History of the Greek Judges", *BIOSCS* 8 (1975), pp. 14-15 [abstract].

Saggs, H. W. F. "Assyrian Warfare in the Sargonid Period", *Iraq* 25 (1963), pp. 145-48.

Satterthwaite, P. E., "Narrative Artistry and the Composition of Judges 17–21", PhD diss., University of Manchester, 1989.

——, "Narrative Artistry in the Composition of Judges xx 29ff.", *VT* 42 (1992), pp. 80-89.

Sawyer, J. F. A., "What Was a *mošiaʿ*?", *VT* 15 (1965), pp. 475-86.

Schlauri, I., "W. Richters Beitrag zur Redaktionsgeschichte des Richterbuches", *Bib* 54 (1973), pp. 367-403.

Schleusner, J. F. (ed.), *Novus Thesaurus Philologico-Criticus siue Lexicon in LXX et Reliquos Interpretes Graecos ac Scriptores Apocryphos Veteris Testamenti*, 5 vols., Leipzig, 1821.

Schmidt, H., "Miscellen: 4. Zu Jdc 14", *ZAW* 39 (1921), p. 316.

Schofield, J. N., "Judges", in *Peake's Commentary on the Bible*, H. H. Rowley and M. Black (eds.), London, 1962.

Schreiner, J., *Septuaginta-Massora des Buches der Richter: Eine textkritische Studie*, AnBib 7, Rome, 1957.

——, "Textformen und Urtext des Deboraliedes in der Septuaginta", *Bib* 42 (1961), pp. 173-200.

Schultens, A., *Animadversiones philologicae et criticae ad varia loca Veteris Testamenti*, Leiden, 1769.

Schulz, A., *Erzählungskunst in den Samuel-Büchern*, Biblische Zeitfragen XI/6-7, Munster, in Westfalen, 1923.

——, *Das Buch der Richter*, in *HSAT* (Catholic edn) II/4, Bonn, 1926.

Seebass, H., "League of Tribes or Amphictyony? A Review of O. Bächli, *Amphiktyonie im Alten Testament: Forschungsgeschichtliche Studie zur Hypothese von Martin Noth*. Basel, 1977", *JSOT* 16 (1980), pp. 61-66.

Segert, S., "Paronomasia in the Samson Narrative in Judges xiii-xvi", *VT* 34 (1984), pp. 454-61.

Sellin, E., *Einleitung in das Alte Testament*, Evangelisch-theologische Bibliothek, Leipzig, 1910; 3d edn, 1920; ET of 3d edn: *Introduction to the Old Testament*, W. Montgomery (trans.), London, 1923.

Shiloh, Y., "[Review:] Marie-Louise Buhl and S. Holm-Nielsen, *Shiloh: The Danish Excavations at Tall Sailun, Palestine, in 1926, 1929, 1932 & 1963*. Copenhagen, 1969", *IEJ* 21 (1971), pp. 67-69.

——, "The Camp at Shiloh", in *Eretz Shomron: The Thirtieth Archaeological Convention September 1972*, J. Aviram (ed.), Jerusalem, 1973, pp. 10-18 [Hebrew].

Simpson, C. A., *Composition of the Book of Judges*, Oxford, 1957.

Slotki, I. W., "The Song of Deborah", *JTS* 33 (1932), pp. 341-54.

Slotki, J. J., "Judges: Introduction and Commentary", in H. Freedman and J. J. Slotki, *Joshua and Judges*, A. Cohen (ed.), SBB, London, 1950, pp. 152-318.

Smend, R., Jr, *Jahwekrieg und Stämmebund: Erwägungen zur ältesten Geschichte Israels*, FRLANT 84, Göttingen, 1963; 2d edn, 1966; ET: *Yahweh War and Tribal Confederation*, Nashville, 1970.

——, "Das Gesetz und die Völker: Ein Beitrag zur deuteronomistischen Redaktionsgeschichte", in *Probleme biblischer Theologie: Gerhard von Rad zum 70. Geburtstag*, H. W. Wolff (ed.), Munich, 1971, pp. 494-509.

——, *Die Entstehung des Alten Testaments*, Theologische Wissenschaft 1, Stuttgart, 1978.

Smith, W. R., in J. S. Black, *The Book of Judges*, SCBS, Cambridge, 1892.

Soden, W. von, "Zum akkadischen Wörterbuch, 61-66", *Or* NS 24 (1955), pp. 144-45.

——, "Die Assyrier und der Krieg", *Iraq* 25 (1963), pp. 131-144.

—— (ed.), *Akkadisches Handwörterbuch*, 3 vols., Wiesbaden, 1965-1981.

Soggin, J. A., "[Review:] W. Richter, *Die Bearbeitungen des 'Retterbuches' in der deuteronomischen Epoche*", *AION* 25 (1965), pp. 299-302.

——, *Judges: A Commentary*, J. Bowden (trans.), OTL, London, 1981; 2d edn, 1987; French translation: *Le Livre des Juges*, C. Lanoir (trans.), CAT V b, Geneva, 1987.

——, "Amalek und Ephraim, Richter 5,14", *ZDPV* 98 (1982), pp. 58-62.

——, "'Ehud und 'Eglon: Bemerkungen zu Richter iii 11b-31", *VT* 39 (1989), pp. 95-100.

Soisalon-Soininen, I., *Die Textformen der Septuaginta-Übersetzung des Richterbuches*, AASF, B72, I, Helsinki, 1951.

Speiser, E. A., "The Shibboleth Incident (Judges 12:6)", *BASOR* 85 (1942), pp. 10-13; reprinted in *Oriental and Biblical Studies: Collected Writings of E. A. Speiser*, J. J. Finkelstein and M. Greenberg (eds.), Philadelphia, 1967, pp. 143-50.

Sperber, A., *The Bible in Aramaic*, vol. 2, *The Former Prophets according to Targum Jonathan*, Leiden, 1959.

Sternberg, M., "Language, World and Perspective in Biblical Narrative Art: Free Indirect Discourse and Modes of Covert Penetration", *Hasifrut* 32 (1983), pp. 88-131 [Hebrew].

——, *The Poetics of Biblical Narrative: Ideological Literature and the Drama of Reading*, ISBL, Bloomington, 1985.

Stolz, F., *Jahwes und Israels Kriege: Kriegstheorien und Kriegserfahrungen im Glauben des alten Israel*, ATANT 60, Zurich, 1972.

Stone, K., "Gender and Homosexuality in Judges 19: Subject–Honour, Object–Shame?", *JSOT* 67 (1995), pp. 87-107.

Stone, L. G., "From Tribal Confederation to Monarchic State: The Editorial Perspective of the Book of Judges", PhD diss., Yale University, 1988.

Stuart, D. K., *Studies in Early Hebrew Meter*, HSM 13, Missoula, Montana, 1976.

Studer, G. L., *Das Buch der Richter grammatisch und historisch erklärt*, Bern, 1835; 2d edn, 1842.

Sukenik, E. L., "Note on a Fragment of an Israelite Stele Found at Samaria", *PEFQS* (1936), p. 156, pl. 3.

Swiggers, P., "The Word *šibbōleṭ* in Jud. xii.6", *JSS* 26 (1981), pp. 205-7.

Talmon, S., "In Those Days There Was No King in Israel", in *Proceedings of the Fifth World Congress of Jewish Studies, Jerusalem 1969*, 5 vols., P. Peli et al. (eds.), Jerusalem, 1971, vol. 1, pp. 135-44 [Hebrew; English summary: vol. 1, pp. 242-43].

——, "The Presentation of Synchroneity and Simultaneity in Biblical Narrative", in *Studies in Hebrew Narrative Art through the Ages*, J. Heinemann and S. Werses (eds.), ScrHier 27, Jerusalem, 1978, pp. 9-26.

Talshir, Z., "Double Translations in the Septuagint", in *VI Congress of the International Organization for Septuagint and Cognate Studies, Jerusalem 1986*, C. E. Cox (ed.), Atlanta, Georgia, 1987, pp. 21-63.

Täubler, E. I., "Cushan-Rishathaim", *HUCA* 20 (1947), pp. 137-42.

——, *Biblische Studien I: Die Epoche der Richter*, H.-J. Zobel (ed.), Tübingen, 1958.

Thomas, D. W., "The Root ידע in Hebrew", *JTS* 35 (1934), pp. 298-306.

——, "Some Rabbinic Evidence for a Hebrew Root *ydʿ* = *wdʿ*", *JQR* NS 37 (1946–1947), pp. 177-78.

Tov, E., "The Textual History of the Song of Deborah in the A Text of the LXX", *VT* 28 (1978), pp. 224-32.

——, "Did the Septuagint Translators Always Understand Their Hebrew Text?", in *De Septuaginta: Studies in Honour of John William Wevers on His Sixty-fifth Birthday*, A. Pietersma and C. Cox (eds.), Mississauga, Ontario, 1984, pp. 53-70.

——, *Textual Criticism of the Hebrew Bible*, Minneapolis, 1992.

Trebolle Barrera, J., "Redaction, Recension, and Midrash in the Books of Kings", *BIOSCS* 15 (1982), pp. 12-35.

——, "Textual Variants in 4QJudgᵃ and the Textual and Editorial History of the Book of Judges", *RevQ* 14 (1989), pp. 229-45.

——, "The Story of David and Goliath (1 Sam 17-18): Textual Variants and Literary Composition", *BIOSCS* 23 (1990), pp. 16-30.

Trible, P., *Texts of Terror: Literary and Feminist Readings of Biblical Narratives*, OBT 13, Philadelphia, 1984.

Trompf, G. W., "Notions of Historical Recurrence in Classic Hebrew Historiography", in *Studies in the Historical Books of the Old Testament*, J. A. Emerton (ed.), SVT 30, Leiden, 1979, pp. 213-29.

Tsumura, D. T., "Bedan, a Copyist's Error?", *VT* 45 (1995), pp. 122-23.

Ulrich, E. (ed.), *Qumran Cave 4: IX: Deuteronomy, Joshua, Judges, Kings*, DJD XIV, Oxford, 1996.

Unterman, J., "The Literary Influence of 'the Binding of Isaac' (Genesis 22) on 'the Outrage at Gibeah' (Judges 19)", *HAR* 4 (1980), pp. 161-66.

Van Dyke Parunak, H. , "Oral Typesetting: Some Uses of Biblical Structure", *Bib* 62 (1981), pp. 153-68.

Van Seters, J., "The Conquest of Sihon's Kingdom: A Literary Examination", *JBL* 91 (1972), pp. 182-97.

——, "Once Again—The Conquest of Sihon's Kingdom", *JBL* 99 (1980), pp. 117-19.

Vaux, R. de, *Les Institutions de l'Ancien Testament*, 2 vols., Paris, 1958, 1960; ET: *Ancient Israel: Its Life and Institutions*, J. McHugh (trans.), 2 vols., London, 1961; 2d edn, 1965.

Veijola, T., *Die ewige Dynastie: David und die Entstehung seiner Dynastie nach der deuteronomistischen Darstellung*, AASF B/193, Helsinki, 1975.

——, *Das Königtum in der Beurteilung der deuteronomistischen Historiographie: Eine redaktionsgeschichtliche Untersuchung*, AASF B/198, Helsinki, 1977.

Vickery, J. B., "In Strange Ways: The Story of Samson", in *Images of Man and God: Old Testament Short Stories in Literary Focus*, B. O. Long (ed.), BLS 1, Sheffield, 1981, pp. 58-73, 119.

Vincent, A., *Le livre des Juges, Le livre de Ruth*, La Bible de Jérusalem, Paris, 2d edn, 1958.

Waldman, N. M., "The Imagery of Clothing, Covering, and Overpowering", *JANES* 19 (1989), pp. 161-70.

Waldow, H. E. von, *Der traditionsgeschichtliche Hintergrund der prophetischen Gerichtsreden*, BZAW 85, Berlin, 1963.

Walters [Katz], P., "[Review:] I. Soisalon-Soininen, *Die Textformen der Septuaginta-Übersetzung des Richterbuches*", *TLZ* 77 (1952), cols. 154-58.

——, "[Review:] J. Schreiner, *Seputaginta-Massora des Buches der Richter: Eine textkritische Studie*", *TLZ* 86 (1961), cols. 829-32.

Waltke, B. K.; O'Connor, M., *An Introduction to Biblical Hebrew Syntax*, Winona Lake, Indiana, 1990.

Webb, B. G., "The Theme of the Jephthah Story (Judges 10:6–12:7)", *RTR* 45 (1986), pp. 34-43.

——, *The Book of the Judges: An Integrated Reading*, JSOTS 46, Sheffield, 1987.

Weimar, P., "Die Jahwekriegserzählungen in Exodus 14, Josua 10, Richter 4 und 1 Samuel 7", *Bib* 57 (1976), pp. 38-73.

Weinfeld, M., *Deuteronomy and the Deuteronomic School*, Oxford, 1972.

Weippert, M., "'Heiliger Krieg' in Israel und Assyrien: Kritische Anmerkungen zu Gerhard von Rads Konzept des 'Heiligen Krieges im alten Israel'", *ZAW* 84 (1972), pp. 460-93.

Wellhausen, J., *Geschichte Israels*, vol 1, Berlin, 1878; republished as *Prolegomena zur Geschichte Israels*, Berlin, 2d edn, 1883.

——, *Die Composition des Hexateuchs und der historischen Bücher des Alten Testaments*, Berlin, 2d edn, 1889.

Wharton, J. A., "The Secret of Yahweh: Story and Affirmation in Judges 13-16", *Int* 27 (1973), pp. 48-66.

Whitelam, K. W., *The Just King: Monarchical Judicial Authority in Ancient Israel*, JSOTS 12, Sheffield, 1979.

Wiener, H. M., *The Composition of Judges ii 11 to I Kings ii 46*, Leipzig, 1929.

Wiese, K., *Zur Literarkritik des Buches der Richter*, BWANT 40/2, Stuttgart, 1926.

Wijngaards, J. N. M., *The Dramatization of Salvific History in the Deuteronomic Schools*, P. A. H. de Boer (ed.), *OTS* XVI, Leiden, 1969.

Willesen, F., "The אפרתי of the Shibboleth Incident", *VT* 8 (1958), pp. 97-98.

Williamson, H. G. M., *Ezra, Nehemiah*, WBC 16, Waco, Texas, 1985.

Wolff, H. W., *Bibel—Das Alte Testament: Eine Einführung in seine Schriften und in die Methoden ihrer Erforschung*, Stuttgart, 1970; ET: *The Old Testament: A Guide to Its Writings*, K. R. Crim (trans.), London, 1974.

Wood, L., *Distressing Days of the Judges*, Grand Rapids, 1975.

Wood, R. A., "The Major Judges and the Judgment of the Deuteronomist", unpublished paper presented at the SBL Annual Meeting, Anaheim, California, November 19, 1989.

Wright, G. E., "The Lawsuit of God: A Form-Critical Study of Deuteronomy 32", in *Israel's Prophetic Heritage: Essays in Honor of James Muilenburg*, B. W. Anderson and W. Harrelson (eds.), New York, 1962, pp. 26-67.

Würthwein, E., "Der Ursprung der prophetischen Gerichtsrede", *ZTK* 49 (1952), pp. 1-16; reprinted in *Wort und Existenz: Studien zum Alten Testament*, Göttingen, 1970, pp. 111-26.

Wüst, M., "Die Einschaltung in die Jiftachgeschichte. Ri 11,13-26", *Bib* 56 (1975), pp. 464-79.

Zakovitch, Y., "The Sacrifice of Gideon (Jud 6,11-24) and the Sacrifice of Manoaḥ (Jud 13)", *Shnaton* 1 (1975), pp. 151-54, XXV [Hebrew; English summary].

Zapletal, V., *Das Buch der Richter: übersetzt und erklärt*, EHAT VII/1, Munster, in Westfalen, 1923.

Zimmern, H., *Akkadische Fremdwörter als Beweis für babylonischen Kultureinfluss*, Leipzig, 2d edn, 1917.

Zobel, H.-J., *Stammesspruch und Geschichte: Die Angaben der Stammessprüche von Gen 49, Dtn 33 und Jdc 5 über die politischen und kultischen Zustände im damaligen 'Israel'*, BZAW 95, Berlin, 1965.

INDEX OF BIBLICAL REFERENCES

INDEX OF AUTHORS

SUPPLEMENTS TO VETUS TESTAMENTUM

2. POPE, M.H. *El in the Ugaritic texts.* 1955. ISBN 90 04 04000 5
3. *Wisdom in Israel and in the Ancient Near East.* Presented to Harold Henry Rowley by the Editorial Board of Vetus Testamentum in celebration of his 65th birthday, 24 March 1955. Edited by M. NOTH and D. WINTON THOMAS. 2nd reprint of the first (1955) ed. 1969. ISBN 90 04 02326 7
4. *Volume du Congrès* [International pour l'étude de l'Ancien Testament]. Strasbourg 1956. 1957. ISBN 90 04 02327 5
8. BERNHARDT, K.-H. *Das Problem der alt-orientalischen Königsideologie im Alten Testament.* Unter besonderer Berücksichtigung der Geschichte der Psalmenexegese dargestellt und kritisch gewürdigt. 1961. ISBN 90 04 02331 3
9. *Congress Volume,* Bonn 1962. 1963. ISBN 90 04 02332 1
11. DONNER, H. *Israel unter den Völkern.* Die Stellung der klassischen Propheten des 8. Jahrhunderts v. Chr. zur Aussenpolitik der Könige von Israel und Juda. 1964. ISBN 90 04 02334 8
12. REIDER, J. *An Index to Aquila.* Completed and revised by N. Turner. 1966. ISBN 90 04 02335 6
13. ROTH, W.M.W. *Numerical sayings in the Old Testament.* A form-critical study. 1965. ISBN 90 04 02336 4
14. ORLINSKY, H.M. *Studies on the second part of the Book of Isaiah.* — The so-called 'Servant of the Lord' and 'Suffering Servant' in Second Isaiah. — Snaith, N.H. Isaiah 40-66. A study of the teaching of the Second Isaiah and its consequences. Repr. with additions and corrections. 1977. ISBN 90 04 05437 5
15. *Volume du Congrès* [International pour l'étude de l'Ancien Testament]. Genève 1965. 1966. ISBN 90 04 02337 2
17. *Congress Volume,* Rome 1968. 1969. ISBN 90 04 02339 9
19. THOMPSON, R.J. *Moses and the Law in a century of criticism since Graf.* 1970. ISBN 90 04 02341 0
20. REDFORD, D.B. *A study of the biblical story of Joseph.* 1970. ISBN 90 04 02342 9
21. AHLSTRÖM, G.W. *Joel and the temple cult of Jerusalem.* 1971. ISBN 90 04 02620 7
22. *Congress Volume,* Uppsala 1971. 1972. ISBN 90 04 03521 4
23. *Studies in the religion of ancient Israel.* 1972. ISBN 90 04 03525 7
24. SCHOORS, A. *I am God your Saviour.* A form-critical study of the main genres in Is. xl-lv. 1973. ISBN 90 04 03792 2
25. ALLEN, L.C. *The Greek Chronicles.* The relation of the Septuagint I and II Chronicles to the Massoretic text. Part 1. The translator's craft. 1974. ISBN 90 04 03913 9
26. *Studies on prophecy.* A collection of twelve papers. 1974. ISBN 90 04 03877 9
27. ALLEN, L.C. *The Greek Chronicles.* Part 2. Textual criticism. 1974. ISBN 90 04 03933 3
28. *Congress Volume,* Edinburgh 1974. 1975. ISBN 90 04 04321 7
29. *Congress Volume,* Göttingen 1977. 1978. ISBN 90 04 05835 4
30. EMERTON, J.A. (ed.). *Studies in the historical books of the Old Testament.* 1979. ISBN 90 04 06017 0
31. MEREDINO, R.P. *Der Erste und der Letzte.* Eine Untersuchung von Jes 40-48. 1981. ISBN 90 04 06199 1
32. EMERTON, J.A. (ed.). *Congress Vienna* 1980. 1981. ISBN 90 04 06514 8
33. KOENIG, J. *L'herméneutique analogique du Judaïsme antique d'après les témoins textuels d'Isaïe.* 1982. ISBN 90 04 06762 0

34. BARSTAD, H.M. *The religious polemics of Amos*. Studies in the preachings of Amos ii 7B-8, iv 1-13, v 1-27, vi 4-7, viii 14. 1984. ISBN 90 04 07017 6
35. KRAŠOVEC, J. *Antithetic structure in Biblical Hebrew poetry*. 1984. ISBN 90 04 07244 6
36. EMERTON, J.A. (ed.). *Congress Volume*, Salamanca 1983. 1985. ISBN 90 04 07281 0
37. LEMCHE, N.P. *Early Israel*. Anthropological and historical studies on the Israelite society before the monarchy. 1985. ISBN 90 04 07853 3
38. NIELSEN, K. *Incense in Ancient Israel*. 1986. ISBN 90 04 07702 2
39. PARDEE, D. *Ugaritic and Hebrew poetic parallelism*. A trial cut. 1988. ISBN 90 04 08368 5
40. EMERTON, J.A. (ed.). *Congress Volume*, Jerusalem 1986. 1988. ISBN 90 04 08499 1
41. EMERTON, J.A. (ed.). *Studies in the Pentateuch*. 1990. ISBN 90 04 09195 5
42. McKENZIE, S.L. *The trouble with Kings*. The composition of the Book of Kings in the Deuteronomistic History. 1991. ISBN 90 04 09402 4
43. EMERTON, J.A. (ed.). *Congress Volume*, Leuven 1989. 1991. ISBN 90 04 09398 2
44. HAAK, R.D. *Habakkuk*. 1992. ISBN 90 04 09506 3
45. BEYERLIN, W. *Im Licht der Traditionen*. Psalm LXVII und CXV. Ein Entwicklungs-zusammenhang. 1992. ISBN 90 04 09635 3
46. MEIER, S.A. *Speaking of Speaking*. Marking direct discourse in the Hebrew Bible. 1992. ISBN 90 04 09602 7
47. KESSLER, R. *Staat und Gesellschaft im vorexilischen Juda*. Vom 8. Jahrhundert bis zum Exil. 1992. ISBN 90 04 09646 9
48. AUFFRET, P. *Voyez de vos yeux*. Étude structurelle de vingt psaumes, dont le psaume 119. 1993. ISBN 90 04 09707 4
49. GARCÍA MARTÍNEZ, F., A. HILHORST AND C.J. LABUSCHAGNE (eds.). *The Scriptures and the Scrolls*. Studies in honour of A.S. van der Woude on the occasion of his 65th birthday. 1992. ISBN 90 04 09746 5
50. LEMAIRE, A. AND B. OTZEN (eds.). *History and Traditions of Early Israel*. Studies presented to Eduard Nielsen, May 8th, 1993. 1993. ISBN 90 04 09851 8
51. GORDON, R.P. *Studies in the Targum to the Twelve Prophets*. From Nahum to Malachi. 1994. ISBN 90 04 09987 5
52. HUGENBERGER, G.P. *Marriage as a Covenant*. A Study of Biblical Law and Ethics Governing Marriage Developed from the Perspective of Malachi. 1994. ISBN 90 04 09977 8
53. GARCÍA MARTÍNEZ, F., A. HILHORST, J.T.A.G.M. VAN RUITEN, A.S. VAN DER WOUDE. *Studies in Deuteronomy*. In Honour of C.J. Labuschagne on the Occasion of His 65th Birthday. 1994. ISBN 90 04 10052 0
54. FERNANDÉZ MARCOS, N. *Septuagint and Old Latin in the Book of Kings*. 1994. ISBN 90 04 10043 1
55. SMITH, M.S. *The Ugaritic Baal Cycle. Volume 1*. Introduction with text, translation and commentary of KTU 1.1-1.2. 1994. ISBN 90 04 09995 6
56. DUGUID, I.M. *Ezekiel and the Leaders of Israel*. 1994. ISBN 90 04 10074 1
57. MARX, A. *Les offrandes végétales dans l'Ancien Testament*. Du tribut d'hommage au repas eschatologique. 1994. ISBN 90 04 10136 5
58. SCHÄFER-LICHTENBERGER, C. *Josua und Salomo*. Eine Studie zu Autorität und Legitimität des Nachfolgers im Alten Testament. 1995. ISBN 90 04 10064 4
59. LASSERRE, G. *Synopse des lois du Pentateuque*. 1994. ISBN 90 04 10202 7
60. DOGNIEZ, C. *Bibliography of the Septuagint – Bibliographie de la Septante (1970-1993)*. Avec une préface de Pierre-Maurice Bogaert. 1995. ISBN 90 04 10192 6
61. EMERTON, J.A. (ed.). *Congress Volume*, Paris 1992. 1995. ISBN 90 04 10259 0

62. SMITH, P.A. *Rhetoric and Redaction in Trito-Isaiah*. The Structure, Growth and Authorship of Isaiah 56-66. 1995. ISBN 90 04 10306 6
63. O'CONNEL, R.H. *The Rhetoric of the Book of Judges*. 1996. ISBN 90 04 10104 7